Lost and Found in Early Irish Law

Medieval Law and Its Practice

Edited by

John Hudson (*University of St Andrews*)

VOLUME 036

The titles published in this series are listed at *brill.com/mlip*

Lost and Found in Early Irish Law

Aidbred, *Heptad 64, and* Muirbretha

By

Charlene M. Eska

BRILL

LEIDEN | BOSTON

Cover illustration: Detail of Trinity College, Dublin MS 1387, *olim* H.5.15, p. 16b21, § 1 *Aidbred* (CIH 2163.33). The image is reproduced by permission of The Board of Trinity College Dublin.

The Library of Congress Cataloging-in-Publication Data is available online at http://catalog.loc.gov
LC record available at http://lccn.loc.gov/2022024672

Typeface for the Latin, Greek, and Cyrillic scripts: "Brill". See and download: brill.com/brill-typeface.

ISSN 1873-8176
ISBN 978-90-04-51284-9 (hardback)
ISBN 978-90-04-52072-1 (e-book)

This book is printed on acid-free paper and produced in a sustainable manner.

For Nick, again

Contents

Acknowledgements

The list of those individuals and institutions who deserve thanks for their support of this book project is very similar to those acknowledged for the previous book (a critical edition and translation of *Anfuigell*, published in *A Raven's Battle-Cry*) as a result of the fact that I was simultaneaously working on both *Anfuigell* and *Aidbred* before I realized that I was dealing with two different texts rather than one.

First and foremost, I should like to thank the anonymous reader at Brill for their helpful suggestions for improvements. This project has benefitted greatly from their expertise. Any errors are, of course, my own. Particular thanks are owed to Joseph F. Eska and Paul Russell who have both offered assistance at various points in the process of editing and translating the texts.

I should like to thank Virginia Polytechnic Institute & State University, College of Liberal Arts and Human Sciences, for Niles Research Grants during the summers of 2014 and 2018 which enabled me to view many of the manuscripts and finish some of the crucial stages of writing for this project. I also gratefully acknowledge the assistance of an American Philosophical Society Franklin Research Grant during the summer of 2015, which enabled me to conduct research in the United Kingdom and view more of the relevant manuscripts. Particular thanks is owed to the Department of English at Virginia Polytechnic Institute & State University for a research leave during Fall 2017. During my research leave, I was fortunate to be granted status as an Honorary Research Associate in the Department of Anglo-Saxon, Norse, and Celtic at the University of Cambridge during Easter and Michaelmas terms in 2017. I am also grateful to Magdalen College, University of Oxford, for a Visiting Fellowship, October 1–December 31, 2017. Both institutions provided me with time, space, resources, and the opportunity to be part of warm and welcoming intellectual communities.

Parts of this book are based on papers given at: the thirty-seventh, thirty-eighth, and thirty-ninth annual Harvard Celtic Colloquium, the forty-first and forty-second annual meetings of the Celtic Studies Association of North America, and the sixteenth International Congress of Celtic Studies. The feedback and comments received from members of those audiences have been very helpful.

During the course of writing this book, I have had the pleasure of working in many libraries and should like to acknowledge the assistance I have received from the librarians at: Trinity College, Dublin; The British Library; the Royal Irish Academy; University Library, University of Cambridge; English Faculty Library, University of Cambridge; Weston Library, University of Oxford; Oxford Law Library, University of Oxford; Longwall Library, Magdalen College, Oxford (with special thanks to Daryl Green); and the Celtic Library, Jesus College, Oxford. In particular, I should like to thank the College Librarian at Jesus College, Owen McKnight, for his assistance and for making the Celtic Library such a comfortable space to work.

Debts of gratitude are owed to Dorothy Africa, Sharon Paice MacLeod, Jeff Mann, Sarah McKibben, Suzanne Morse; Alice Taylor-Griffiths, Jim Tibbs, Giovanni Varelli, Ralph Walker, and Malcolm Wallis (for sharing his knowledge of maritime law, especially as it pertains to shipwrecks). I should also like to thank the Porters Lodges at both Jesus College and Magdalen College, Oxford.

I should also like to thank Marcella Mulder and John Hudson for their guidance and support, and Noortje Maranus for typesetting expertise.

My mother and her husband have offered encouragement throughout. My brother has been my emotional rock; Tallulah has reminded me to laugh. To my son, Nicholas Shipman, I owe a debt of gratitude which can never be repaid, and to him this book is dedicated.

C.M.E.
Blacksburg, VA

Tables

Abbreviations

AL	*Ancient Laws and Institutes of Ireland*, 6 vols., eds. W.N. Hancock et al. (Dublin, 1865–1901).
BL	British Library
CCIH	Liam Breatnach, *A Companion to the Corpus Iuris Hibernici* (Dublin, 2005).
CIH	*Corpus Iuris Hibernici*, 6 vols. paginated consecutively, ed. D.A. Binchy (Dublin, 1978).
CLH	*Clavis Litterarum Hibernensium*, 3 vols., ed. Donnchadh Ó Corráin (Turnhout, 2017).
Comm.	Commentary
eDIL	*eDIL 2019: An Electronic Dictionary of the Irish Language*, based on the Contributions to a Dictionary of the Irish Language (Dublin, 1913–1976).
EIF	Fergus Kelly, *Early Irish Farming* (Dublin, 1997).
EIWK	T.M. Charles-Edwards, *Early Irish and Welsh Kinship* (Oxford, 1993).
GEIL	Fergus Kelly, *A Guide to Early Irish Law* (Dublin, 1988) (2009 reprint with updated bibliography).
GOI	Rudolf Thurneysen, *A Grammar of Old Irish*, eds. and trans. D.A. Binchy and Osborn Bergin (Dublin, 1946).
Ior	*Llyfr Iorwerth*, ed. Aled Rhys Wiliam (Cardiff, 1960).
MI	Middle Irish (*c.* 900–1200)
O'Dav	*O'Davoren's Glossary*, ed. Whitley Stokes, *Archiv für celtische Lexikographie* 2 (London, 1904), pp. 197–504.
OED	*Oxford English Dictionary*
OI	Old Irish (*c.* 600–900)
NKS	Den nye kongelige samling
PIE	Proto-Indo-European
RIA	Royal Irish Academy
SM	*Senchas Már*
TCD	Trinity College, Dublin
ZCP	*Zeitschrift für celtische Philologie*

Grammatical Abbreviations

acc.	accusative
act.	active
adj.	adjective
adv.	adverb
art.	article
comp.	comparative
cond.	conditional
conj.	conjunction
cons.	consuetudinal
cop.	copula
dat.	dative
def.	definite
demon.	demonstrative
du.	dual
f.	feminine
fut.	future
gen.	genitive
impv.	imperative
ind.	indicative
indeclin.	indeclinable
indef.	indefinite
m.	masculine
n.	neuter
neg.	negative
nom.	nominative
num.	numeral
part.	participle
pass.	passive
perf.	perfect
pl.	plural
poss.	possessive
pres.	present
pret.	preterite
pron.	pronoun
pronom.	pronominal
rel.	relative
sg.	singular
subj.	subjunctive
subst.	substantive
superl.	superlative
vb.	verb
vn.	verbal noun

PLATE 1 Trinity College, Dublin MS 1387, *olim* H.5.15, p. 16b21, §1 *Aidbred* (CIH 2163.33)

PLATE 2 Trinity College, Dublin MS 1387, *olim* H.5.15, p. 8a1, §1 *Anfuigell* (CIH 2146.16)

Irish Legal Texts Cited in This Volume

For those not familiar with the medieval Irish legal corpus, what follows is a list of the Irish law texts referenced herein, both in the introductory material and in the Irish legal material itself. Not all of the texts below have been critically edited. For those that have, the full reference for each text can be found in the Printed and Digital Sources section of the Bibliography. Both *GEIL* 264–286, and *CCIH* 160–321, contain more detailed descriptions and bibliographic information for these and other early Irish legal texts. Both of these sources have been used to provide the translations of the titles below.

Old Irish title	English meaning	Main content
Aidbred	'Claiming'	A tract concerning the recovery of lost or stolen property, primarily livestock.
Anfuigell	'Wrong Judgment'	A tract concerning a range of legal scenarios difficult to judge or where judgment is hindered by a lack of evidence.
Ántéchtae (Breth)	'Splendid Propriety (of Judgments)'	A tract concerning a wide range of topics, including satire, procedure, and arson.
Bechbretha	'Bee-Judgments'	A tract concerning bee-keeping.
Bretha Crólige	'Judgments on Blood-Lyings'	A tract concerning sick-maintenance.
Bretha Comaithchesa	'Judgments of Neighborhood'	A tract concerning neighborhood responsibilities, mainly in respect to land management and livestock offenses.
Bretha Déin Chécht	'The Judgments of Dían Cécht'	A tract concerning personal injury and the payments due to physicians.
Bretha Éitgid	'Judgments of Inadvertence'	A tract concerning accidental injury and death.
Bretha im Ḟuillemu Gell	'Judgments Regarding Pledge-Interests'	A tract concerning the items which can be pledged by specific members of society.
Bretha im Gatta	'Judgments Concerning Thefts'	A tract on theft.
Bretha Nemed Dédenach	'The Last *Bretha Nemed*'[1]	A tract on the privileges of poets.

1 The phrase *bretha nemed* means 'judgments of privileged persons'.

(*cont.*)

Old Irish title	English meaning	Main content
Cáin Aicillne	'The Law of Base Clientship'	A tract concerning base clientship.
Cáin Ónae	'The Law of Lending'	A tract concerning two types of loans.
Cáin Ṡóerraith	'The Law of Noble Fief'	A tract concerning free clientship.
Cethairṡlicht Athgabálae	'The Four Paths of Distraint'	A tract concerning distraint.
Coibnes Uisci Thairidne	'Kinship of Conducted Water'	A tract concerning the regulations for conducting water over private property to power a mill.
Cóic Conara Fugill	'The Five Paths of Judgment'	A tract concerning legal procedure.
Córus Aithni	'The Regulation of Depositing'	A fragmentary text on deposits.
Córus Bésgnai	'The Regulation of Discipline'	A tract concerning the obligations of the church and the laity to each other.
Córus Fine	'The Regulation of Kindred'	A tract concerning the kin-group.
Córus Íubaile	'Regulation of Limitation Periods'	A fragmentary tract concerning a range of topics including contracts, advocates, honor-price, poets, and damage to a house.
Frithfolaid Ríg Caisil fri Túatha Muman	'Counter-obligations of the king of Cashel towards the peoples of Munster'	A short tract on the reciprocal obligations between the king of Cashel and the people of Munster.
Di Astud Chirt ⁊ Dligid	'On the Establishing of Right and Entitlement'	A tract concerning a wide variety of topics, including the establishment of lawful ownership, inheritance, kingship, ordeals, and legal entry.
Di Astud Chor	'On the Securing of Contracts'	A tract concerning contract law.
Di Ércib Fola	'On *Éric*-fines for Bloodshed'	A tract concerning injuries inflicted without a weapon and their associated fines.
Díre-tract	'A Tract on *Díre*'	A tract concerning honor-price and other fines.

(*cont.*)

Old Irish title	English meaning	Main content
Findṡruth Fíthail	'The Fair Stream of Fíthal'	A wisdom text.
Fot Féinechais[2]	'Extent of Irish Law'	The fragments of text concern penalties for sheltering an outlaw and the obligations of clients when their lord dies.
Immathchor nAilella 7 Airt	'Mutual Restitution between Ailill and Art'	A short text on the paternity of twins.
Lebor na Cert	'Book of Rights'	An idealized hierachical record of the tributes owed by territorial kings to provincial kings and the king of Ireland.
The MacEgan Legal Treatise by Giolla na Naomh Mac Aodhagáin	The text is not given a specific title in the manuscripts.	A summary of Irish law from the point of view of a thirteenth-century Irish lawyer.[3]
Muirbretha	'Sea-Judgments'	A fragmentary tract on maritime law.
Róda, cis lir-side?	'Roads, How Many are There?'	A tract on the different categories of roads.
Sechtae	'Heptads'	A text containing legal material on a wide range of topics arranged in groups of seven.
Tecosca Cormaic	'The Instructions of Cormac'	A wisdom text on the duties and characteristics of a good king.
Tír Cumaile	'Land Worth a *Cumal*'	A text on the value of different types of land.
Uraicecht Cóel	'Slender Primer'	The fragments of text and commentary concern such topics as theft, arson, and liability.

2 See *CCIH* 258–259; Breatnach does not provide a translation of the title of the text.

3 This text is particularly valuable for the information it provides regarding some of the ways Irish law changed after the Norman invasion in 1169 CE.

Measures of Value

The legal texts use various terms to indicate relative amounts of value. Although the equivalences can differ across texts, Kelly provides the following general guidelines: '1 milch cow = 1 ounce of silver = 2 *sét*s = 1/3 *cumal*'.[1] *Sét* is the general term for any item of value, be it livestock or other form of property. It is also used as a unit of currency where it is usually equivalent to twelve scruples (there are 24 scruples in an ounce) or half a milch cow.[2] Although *cumal* means 'female slave', in the legal texts it is normally used as a unit of value rather than in its literal meaning.[3] Throughout the editions presented herein, these terms are normally left untranslated; where appropriate, *sét* is translated as 'property' when the texts are referring to property in general rather than to an item's value.

1 *GEIL* 116.

2 See *GEIL* 114–116; and *EIF* 589–591 for a full discussion of these and other measures of value in Irish laws.

3 *GEIL* 112–113; *EIF* 591–593; and Charlene M. Eska, "Women and Slavery in the Early Irish Laws," *Studia Celtica Fennica* 8 (2011): 29–39.

Introduction

The texts in this volume, *Aidbred* 'Claiming', Heptad 64, and *Muirbretha* 'Sea-Judgments', all concern missing property, whether the property has been lost by accident or by theft. Generally speaking, *Aidbred* concerns stolen livestock or other items lost on land; *Muirbretha* concerns items lost at sea, shipwrecks, and general principles regulating harbors and profits from the seashore; and Heptad 64 combines concepts found in both texts and presents a complex system of compensation for the finder based on where the lost item was found. Thus, it makes sense to edit all three texts together because by combining all three of them, one is able to get a picture of the complete medieval Irish legal procedure not only for the rightful owner being able to reclaim lost or stolen property, but also for the compensation owed to the finder for retrieving and keeping the property safe until the owner is found.

None of these texts has a modern edition or translation; in fact, *Aidbred* was only rediscovered in 2017.[1] Before discussing this newly discovered text, it is worth situating Heptad 64 and *Muirbretha* within the wider context of the early Irish legal corpus. The contents of each text will be discussed in greater detail below in the sections devoted to the individual texts.

To start with Heptad 64, it should be noted that the edition of the heptads found in the *Ancient Laws and Institutes of Ireland* is problematic, as are those of most of the other texts in these volumes.[2] *AL* is a six-volume (the sixth volume is a glossary) edition and translation of many of the early Irish legal texts. The work was undertaken as part of the Brehon Laws Commission, the volumes being published between 1865 and 1901 by multiple editors. While the importance of such a monumental task and its achievements should be adequately acknowledged and appreciated, the generally poor quality of the editorial methods and translations has rendered the work as a whole rather a disappointment and quite often misleading in places. That being said, *AL* still contains the only editions and translations of many of the Irish legal texts.

1 Part of the following material has been reworked from Appendix 5 in Charlene M. Eska, ed. and trans., *A Raven's Battle-Cry: The Limits of Judgment in the Medieval Irish Legal Tract Anfuigell*. Medieval Law and Its Practice 27 (Leiden: Brill, 2019), pp. 304–306.

2 *AL* 5: 118–351; *CIH* 1.1–64.5; and *CCIH* 291–292. See T.M. Charles-Edwards, "Review Article: The *Corpus Iuris Hibernici*," *Studia Hibernica* 20 (1980): 141–162, at 141–143. For further discussion of *AL*'s shortcomings and the intellectual and political climate in which the work was undertaken, see idem, "Whitley Stokes and Early Irish Law," in *The Tripartite Life of Whitley Stokes (1830–1909)*, eds. Elizabeth Boyle and Paul Russell (Dublin: Four Courts Press, 2011), pp. 161–174.

 | DOI:10.1163/9789004520721_002

The Irish legal heptads comprise 65 distinct texts covering a wide range of legal topics; the 65 heptads are assumed to comprise the entire collection. The heptads are the ninth text within the *Senchas Már* 'Great Tradition' collection of legal texts.[3] By contrast, both *Muirbretha* and *Aidbred* are only fragmentarily attested, but the fragments of text are accompanied by glosses and commentaries which help to fill in the legal picture. While *Muirbretha*, the 38th text in the *Senchas Már*, has been discussed in the secondary literature[4] and fragments of it are found in AL,[5] there has yet to be a systematic study of all the fragments, including the fragments found in O'Davoren's Glossary.[6] *Aidbred* is not discussed in the secondary literature at all because it is a new legal text only recently rediscovered.

Previous scholarship considered *Aidbred* to have been lost, when it was actually mistaken for the second half of the legal text *Anfuigell*. Transcriptions and translations of both *Aidbred* and *Anfuigell* exist and were completed by John O'Donovan as part of the work he was doing with Eugene O'Curry for the Brehon Laws Commission. In both the transcription and translation, both texts are run together without a break. O'Donovan's unpublished translation has serious flaws, which are mainly the result of his own transcription choices and the fact the he was working at a time when there were few—and no reliable—editions of the legal texts and almost no secondary scholarship on the subject. Furthermore, he was also working without the lexicographical resources available to scholars now, such as *eDIL*, the lack of which would have made his task as a translator very difficult.

Although the transcripts of John O'Donovan and Eugene O'Curry are frequently cited in *eDIL*, they are rarely translated. While there are numerous citations from *Anfuigell* (and, thus, also *Aidbred*, but not under that title) in *eDIL*, they are not labeled as such; the citations simply cite the O'Donovan or O'Curry transcription and the relevant MS citation. In fact, the citations are rarely translated even when one has been provided by O'Donovan or O'Curry. For some of the more problematic citations, however, *eDIL* refers to the unpublished dictionary slips (housed in the RIA) compiled by Charles Plummer.[7] One

3 *CCIH* 291–292.

4 For example, *GEIL* 107–108 and 276–277; and *CCIH* 304–305. For specific discussion, see Jonathan Wooding, *Communication and Commerce along the Western Sealanes AD400–800* (Oxford: Tempus Reparatum, 1996), pp. iv, 19–20, 33, 51, 68–71, and 95.

5 *AL* 3: 422.1–433.17.

6 All of the citations in O'Davoren's Glossary which might be from *Muirbretha* are edited and translated following the fragments of *Muirbretha*.

7 These are cited as 'Plummer MS notes' in *eDIL*. The earlier fascicles did not make use of Plummer's notes, but they were included in the later fascicles.

cannot fault the early editors of *eDIL* as it was begun when very few of the Irish legal texts were edited, and it is still the case today that many important texts are lacking a modern edition and translation; these editorial practices, however, have obscured the textual origins of many of the citations in *eDIL*.

During the course of editing the text which had been traditionally identified as *Anfuigell*,[8] it became apparent that a new and different text began at p. 16b21. Following the end of § 58 in the main MS source, TCD 1387, [*olim* H.5.15], there is a large decorated initial letter of the size and ornamentation only used in this MS for the start of new texts (see Plate 1 and cf. Plate 2). The decorated initial is the start of a fragment of OI text beginning *Aidbriud ardnemed fola di maigin* (*CIH* 2163.33). *Anfuigell* covers a wide range of subject matter and rarely spends more than one section on a single topic, but starting with the word *aidbriud* and continuing in TCD MS 1387 up to p. 22a5 (*CIH* 2173.37), the subject matter is consistently about the legal process of regaining lost or stolen property. Not only is the subject matter different from *Anfuigell*, but the MS source attestation pattern changes dramatically from that of *Anfuigell*.[9] What we have starting here is the separate legal text, *Aidbred* 'Claiming'.[10]

A list of the main sources for *Anfuigell* 'Wrong Judgment' according to *CCIH* 164 follows; the numbers refer to pages in *CIH*.

A 2146.15–2173.41, TCD MS 1387 [H.5.15]
B 979.23–980.17, TCD MS 1337 [H.3.18]
C 167.19–170.6, Oxford University, Bodleian Library MS Rawl. B. 506
D 984.16–985.23, TCD MS 1337 [H.3.18]
E 1017.1–1018.25, TCD MS 1337 [H.3.18]
F 1269.21–1276.17, BL MS Egerton 88
G 2069.43–2076.20, TCD MS 1336 [H.3.17]

The list above requires modification (see below) to account for the separation of *Anfuigell* from *Aidbred*.

Anfuigell 'Wrong-Judgment'
A 2146.15–2163.32, TCD MS 1387 [H.5.15]
B 979.23–980.17, TCD MS 1337 [H.3.18]
C 167.19–170.6, Oxford University, Bodleian Library MS Rawl. B. 506

8 *Anfuigell*, ed. and trans. Eska, in *A Raven's Battle-Cry*.
9 See the concordance of both texts, pp. 70–73.
10 The text as it survives in all of the MS sources consists only of fragments of the OI text, but it is accompanied by copious legal commentaries, much like *Anfuigell*.

D 984.16–985.23, TCD MS 1337 [H.3.18]
E 1017.1–1018.25, TCD MS 1337 [H.3.18]

Aidbred 'Claiming'[11]
A 2163.33–2173.41, TCD MS 1387 [H.5.15]
F 1269.21–1276.17, BL MS Egerton 88
G 2069.43–2076.20, TCD MS 1336 [H.3.17]

In order to make it easier to reference these texts as they appear in the published literature, the manuscript *sigla* for *Anfuigell* and *Aidbred* have been kept distinct from each other except where they overlap, and the same *sigla* used in *CCIH* for the main versions has been kept here.[12]

The title of a legal text known as *Aidbred* is given in John Lynch's 1662 *Cambrensis Eversus* in the form *Aidbreatha*. In chapter 20 Lynch responds to charges made by Gerald of Wales that '*Hibernos "gentem exlegem"*'[13] "the Irish were a nation without laws,"[14] and to prove Gerald wrong, Lynch helpfully provides the names and descriptions of several Irish legal texts. One of the titles he lists is *Aidbreatha*, and he tells us that the text is about theft.[15] *Aidbred* is the verbal noun of *ad-fíri* 'claims, sues', but it is also a legal term for the process by which one's stolen property can be regained if found in someone else's possession. Matthew Kelly's translation of Lynch from 1850 is noteworthy for the fact that some of the footnotes in chapter 20 were written by John O'Donovan, who produced a transcription of TCD MS 1387. The footnotes written by O'Donovan have his initials after them. O'Donovan has a footnote on *Aidbreatha* which simply says "copy in H.3.17 and H.3. 18,"[16] which refers, of course, to two of the composite legal manuscripts owned by Trinity College, Dublin. He does not tell us where in these two manuscripts the text can be found.

11 Just as there are many more MS sources for *Anfuigell* than are listed here, there are a number of additional sources for material related to *Aidbred*. These sources are listed in the Manuscript Sources section, pp. 60–66.

12 A concordance to both texts and their overlapping manuscript sources can be found in the Concordances section, pp. 70–73.

13 John Lynch, *Cambrensis Eversus* (Saint Malo, 1662), quoted in Matthew Kelly, trans., *Cambrensis Eversus*, 3 vols. (Dublin: The Celtic Society, 1848–1854), 2: 362. Lynch does not tell us his source for this quotation from Gerald of Wales, but it appers as though he is paraphrasing Book 3, ch. 25 of his *Topographia Hibernica*, which concerns the inauguration of the king of Tír Chonaill; Gerald of Wales, *Topographia Hibernica*, ed. James F. Dimok in *Giraldi Cambrensis Opera*, vol. 5 (London: Longman, Green, Reader, and Dyer, 1867), p. 169.

14 Kelly, *Cambrensis Eversus*, 2: 363.

15 Kelly, *Cambrensis Eversus*, 2: 369.

16 Kelly, *Cambrensis Eversus*, 2: 369, n. k.

Aidbred remained undiscussed until 2005 in *CCIH*, where Breatnach addresses the attested titles of the early Irish legal texts; in reference to Lynch's list of legal texts (of which all but two have a separate discussion in his chapter) he comments: "the remaining two appear to be corrupt, and since it is unclear what they might be corruptions of they may be noted here."[17] He then quotes Lynch and Kelly on *Aidbred* and says that "the only suggestion I can make is that *Aidbhreatha* might be a corruption of *Gaitbretha*, an otherwise unattested variant of *Bretha im Gatta*, tract 24 of *Senchas Már*."[18] The other title refers to a text on maritime law, which has not been identified or may not even be extant.

To sum up so far, there is the title of a legal text mentioned by Lynch in 1662; O'Donovan in 1850 refers to two MSS which contain the text; and Breatnach in 2005 says that the title in Lynch is corrupt. It is worth taking a closer look at Lynch's list of legal texts. It contains the following titles found in this order: *Meillbreatha, Fiondsuth, Ainteachtbreatha, Anfuighilbreatha, Fotha mór, Fotha beag, Aidbreatha, Corus fine, Eidgheadh, Dula, Cain Fuithribhe, Cui drubhartaigh bearro, Cain lanamna mór, Cain lanamna beag, Fuidfeinchais*, and *Cain borachtu*. Lynch appends the word *breatha*, nom. pl. of *breth* 'judgment, legal decision', to most of the titles in his list.[19] The spellings of the titles are those given in Lynch. He mentions other texts in passing, but this is the main list. As Breatnach notes, we can identify more or less all of these.[20] The question then is: What is Lynch's source for these texts? Where did he get his information? He tells us, in fact, that his source was the antiquary Dubhaltach Mac Fhirbhisigh:[21]

> Vidi ego plura è pergameno spissa legume Hibernicarum volumina, et in illis textum charactere grandiori conscriptum lineis modice disjunctis faciliori vocum interpretatione minutioribus literis inserta. Uberiora commentaria per paginam diffusa textum obibant eadem omninò ratione qua textum et glossam in libris utriusque juris aspicimus. Ex his superiores titulos ante aliquot annos decerpsit Duvaldus Virbisius.[22]

---

17 *CCIH* 161.

18 *CCIH* 161–162.

19 It is unclear whether Lynch himself added *breatha* to the titles, or whether that is how his source presented them.

20 *CCIH* 161.

21 For Dubhaltach's life and career, see Nollaig Ó Muraíle, *The Celebrated Antiquary: Dubhaltach Mac Fhirbhisigh (c. 1600–1671), his Lineage, Life and Learning*. Maynooth Monograph 6 (Maynooth: An Sagart, 1996).

22 Kelly, *Cambrensis Eversus*, 2: 374.

> I saw a great number of thick volumes of Irish laws, with the text written in large characters, and a large space between the lines, to admit more conveniently in smaller letters a glossary on the meaning of the words. The page was covered over with copious commentaries, inserted between the text, as are usually seen in compilations of canon or civil law. Some years ago, Duvald Mac Firbis transcribed from these books the titles which I have given.[23]

Lynch could not have had a better source for his information because Dubhaltach at one point owned all (or parts of) the main manuscripts (other than Egerton 88) where *Aidbred* is found,[24] and O'Donovan is correct that parts of the text are found in H.3.17 and H.3.18.[25]

Despite the fragmentary nature of the texts in this volume, they are important for a number of reasons. The largest corpus of pre-twelfth-century European vernacular literary, historical, and institutional texts, other than Latin and Greek, is in medieval Irish.[26] Because Ireland was never absorbed into the Roman Empire, the Irish legal system possesses a wealth of tradition and custom found nowhere else in Europe, although influence from canon law and patristic sources is evident in some of the legal texts. The early Irish legal texts seem to have been redacted within a fairly narrow window of time, c. 650–800. The glosses and commentary that accompany the texts, however, can range from the Old Irish period (600–900 CE) to the Middle Irish (900–1200 CE) and Early Modern Irish (1200–1600 CE) periods. Most of the surviving Irish legal manuscripts date from the fourteenth through sixteenth centuries. Thus, it is not unusual for very old texts to be found in later manuscripts accompanied by glosses and commentary, which can range over several hundred years. When the legal texts were being copied over the years, the tradition was for the scribes, not-uncommonly members of learned or legal families,

---

23 Kelly, *Cambrensis Eversus*, 2: 375.

24 William O'Sullivan, "The Book of Domhnall Ó Duibhdábhoireann, Provenance and Codicology," *Celtica* 23 (1999): 276–299, at 277; and idem, "The Manuscript Collection of Dubhaltach Mac Fhirbhisigh," in *Seanchas: Studies in Early and Medieval Irish Archaeology, History and Literature in Honour of Francis J. Byrne*, ed. Alfred P. Smyth (Dublin: Four Courts Press, 2000), pp. 439–447.

25 For example, TCD MS 1336 [H.3.17] = *CIH* 2069.43–2076.20 and TCD MS 1337 [H.3.18] = *CIH* 713.4–9.

26 Robin Chapman Stacey, "Law and Order in the *Very* Old West: England and Ireland in the Early Middles Ages," in *Crossed Paths: Methodological Approaches to the Celtic Aspect of the European Middles Ages*, eds. Benjamin T. Hudson and Vickie Zieglar (Lanham, MD: University Press of America, 1991), pp. 39–60, at 45.

to keep the old text without really altering much of the text itself except for matters of orthography, or sometimes they update the language, but not always in a consistent fashion.[27] Over time, whatever material accompanied the text, such as glosses and commentary, was in turn copied along with the text, which explains how there can be a ninth-century text in a sixteenth-century manuscript, and it explains the linguistic range of the accompanying commentaries.

While there was significant criticism of the value of the legal glosses and commentaries in earlier scholarship,[28] it is now accepted that the glosses and commentaries are not necessarily examples of lawyers playing clever linguistic games in the style of Isidore of Seville's *Etymologiae*[29] or building unrealistic legal systems in the commentaries, but rather reflect actual intellectual and legal concerns.[30] As an example, when Giolla na Naomh Mac Aodhagáin set out to compile his legal treatise as a means for instructing young lawyers, he used not only the legal texts themselves, but also the commentaries. For example, he frequently paraphrases some of the commentaries from *Aidbred* in § 5

27 *GEIL* 225–238.

28 See, for example, D.A. Binchy, "The Linguistic and Historical Value of the Irish Law Tracts," *Proceedings of the British Academy* 29 (1943): 195–227 (and separately paginated 3–35), at 211–212; also published in *Celtic Law Papers: Introductory to Welsh Medieval Law and Government*, ed. Dafydd Jenkins (Bruxelles: Les Editions de la Librairie Encyclopédique, 1973), pp. 71–107, at 90–91; and T.M. Charles-Edwards, "The Manuscript Transmission of *Bretha Comaithchesa*," in *Authorities and Adaptations: The Reworking and Transmission of Textual Sources in Medieval Ireland*, eds. Elizabeth Boyle and Deborah Hayden (Dublin: Dublin Institute for Advanced Studies, 2014), pp. 95–120, at 100–101.

29 Paul Russell, "Laws, Glossaries and Legal Glossaries," *ZCP* 51 (1998): 85–115; idem, *'Read it in a glossary': Glossaries and Learned Discourse in Medieval Ireland*. Kathleen Hughes Memorial Lectures 6 (Cambridge: Department of Anglo-Saxon, Norse, and Celtic, 2008), pp. 2–8; and Alice Rebecca Taylor-Griffiths, *Studies in Medieval Irish Legal Ancillary Material* (unpublished Ph.D. dissertation: Department of Anglo-Saxon, Norse, and Celtic, University of Cambridge, 2020), pp. 18–23.

30 Riona Doolan, "Marginalia, Incorporated Commentaries or Reference Commentaries: The Terminology of Later Legal Sources," in *Fír Fesso: A Festschrift for Neil McLeod*, eds. Anders Ahlqvist and Pamela O'Neill. Sydney Series in Celtic Studies 17 (Sydney: The University of Sydney, 2018), pp. 87–96; Charlene M. Eska, "Varieties of Early Irish Legal Literature and the *Cáin Lánamna* Fragments," *Viator* 40 (2009): 1–16; Rowena Finnane, *Late Medieval Irish Law Manuscripts: A Reappraisal of Methodology and Context*. Sydney Series in Celtic Studies 13 (Sydney: The University of Sydney, 2013); Katharine Simms, "The Brehons of Later Medieval Ireland," in *Brehons, Serjeants and Attorneys: Studies in the History of the Irish Legal Profession*, eds. Daire Hogan and W.N. Osborough (Blackrock, Co. Dublin: Irish Academic Press, 1990), pp. 51–76; eadem, "The Contents of Later Commentaries on the Brehon Law Tracts," *Ériu* 49 (1998): 23–40; and *CCIH* 353.

of his treatise, and he also refers to material from Heptad 64 in the same order in which it is presented in the text, as noted by Kelly.[31] In addition to illustrating some of the texts that he had access to, it also shows how much of the law presented in the commentaries represents current thirteenth-century legal principles in action.[32]

A summary of each of the three texts under discussion follows. The principle of ordering the texts as *Aidbred* followed by Heptad 64 and *Muirbretha* concerns the general location of the disputed property: *Aidbred* deals mainly with livestock; Heptad 64 is concerned not so much with what was found, but as to where the item was found; and *Muirbretha* deals with shipwrecks and property which was found either in the water or on the shore.

Aidbred

The editing of fragmentary texts is fraught with many problems, the most obvious being determining how much of the actual tract is extant and distinguishing it from the ancillary glosses and commentaries. Despite the tendency for legal scribes to write excerpts from the tracts in larger sized letters than the glosses and commentary, this is not always the case. Thus, script size alone cannot be the determining factor. In the case with *Aidbred*, there are some sections (e.g., §§ 1a, 2, 7) where fragments of the tract are quoted in the commentaries. In fact, some fragments (or versions thereof) are recoverable only from the commentaries (e.g., § 2, 10, 11). As such, it is not always easy to determine where these fragments should be grouped in relation to the others, and, indeed, how many distinct sections are reflected in the edited section groupings. The commentaries also contain quotations which may or may not be part of the text,

31 Giolla na Naomh Mac Aodhagáin, *The MacEgan Legal Treatise*, ed. and trans. Fergus Kelly in *The MacEgan Legal Treatise: An Early Modern Irish Law-Text by Giolla na Naomh Mac Aodhagáin (†1309)* Early Irish Law Series 8 (Dublin: Dublin Institute for Advanced Studies, 2020), p. 161. Most of the references to *Anfuigell* in the volume are actually to *Aidbred.*

32 For the mix of Irish and English Common Law in Ireland at the time, see, for example, Gearóid Mac Niocaill, "Irish Law and the Armagh Constitution of 1297," *The Irish Jurist* 6 (1971): 339–344; idem, "Aspects of Irish Law in the Late Thirteenth Century," in *Historical Studies 10: Papers Read before the Eleventh Irish Conference of Historians, 1973*, ed. G.A. Hayes-McCoy (Indreabhán, Co. na Gaillimhe: Cló Chois Fharraige, 1976), pp. 25–42; and idem, "The Interaction of Laws," in *The English in Medieval Ireland: Proceedings of the First Joint Meeting of the Royal Irish Academy and the British Academy, Dublin, 1982*, ed. J. Lydon (Dublin: Royal Irish Academy, 1984), pp. 105–117.

such as that found in source A, § 1a. Sometimes the connection between surviving tract and accompanying gloss and commentary can be less than obvious. This is particularly true of fragmentarily attested texts and will also be an issue with regard to *Muirbretha*. Bearing all of this in mind, what follows is a summary of the twelve sections of the edited text.

The overarching concern of the text is how to retrieve one's lost or stolen property. The text focuses on livestock, especially cattle, which could be stolen or wander away of their own accord. It is not simply enough to spot one's lost cow in someone else's field and take it back without giving notice; that would be considered a form of theft. There is a formal legal process for claiming the property. The details of the process vary depending on the status of the individuals involved, whether the individuals are local or non-local, and whether the property was stolen.

Section 1: *Concerning the oath the plaintiff swears.* The extracts from the first section are interspersed with glosses and commentaries and are spread across several MS sources.[33] In the main MS source, source A, the extracts can be strung together to form a string of continuous text:

> *Aidbriud ardnemed fola[d] di maigin, ⁊ iss e luighi dober: nad n-arlui uad i rath, na cundrad, na h-oin, na h-aithne, na h-airliugud, na h-aititiu, ⁊rl-. ⁊ imtongar and sin o gradaib ecalsa for gradaib tuaithe ar dilaat secht ngraid eclasa for secht ngradaib túaithe.*
>
> Let a high noble claim [his] property immediately, and this is [the] oath that he swears: that it did not part from him as a fief or contract or private loan or deposit or commercial loan or acknowledgement, etc. And it is sworn like that by [the] ecclesiastical grades against [the] lay grades because [the] seven ecclesiastical grades prevail over [the] seven lay grades.

This is not the case with the majority of the sections. The text has been edited to reflect the ordering of the tract and commentary in source A, which necessitated dividing the tract and commentaries into subsections. Each subsection is discussed further below.

---

33 The format of having an excerpts of tract interspersed by commentary from a variety of sources is commonly seen not only in fragmantaruly attested texts, such as *Anfuigell* and *Aidbred*, but also in the texts referred to a 'Digests'; *CCIH* 325–326. See also *CCIH* 350–353 for a discussion of the layering and accumulation of glosses and commentary into later texts.

The text begins by stating that someone of high noble status can claim their property immediately upon seeing it, provided that he[34] swears an oath that the property being sued for did not leave him as part of what he would give to a client as a fief, or as a private or commercial loan, or as a deposit, or as part of another type of agreement. These are all common situations where one's property could legally be in someone else's possession. The text goes on to state that the same oath is to be sworn by those in the seven ecclesiastical grades, and adds that the ecclesiastical grades can over-swear the seven lay grades. This last statement has the feel of being added in at a later point in time to take into account how a pre-existing legal procedure would work were ecclesiastics involved; ecclesiastics appear nowhere else in the text.

In the medieval Welsh laws, we find similar provisions where the laws not only describe the procedure for claiming one's stolen property when it has been found in someone else possession,[35] but the laws also distinguish between property which has been given into another's possession as a loan, whether for private or commercial use, deposit, gift, or as part of some other agreement.[36] A passage in the *Cyfnerth* version of the laws lists the six ways a person can be parted from their property:

> O whe fford yg6ahan dyn ae da: o goll ac aghyfarch a lledrat; benficc a lloc ac adneu. Or teir kyntaf, y dylyir dala a damd6g. Or teir ereill, ny dylyir onyt eturyt megys yroder.

---

34 Although the masculine pronoun is used here and throughout as the grammatical default, this is not to say that women might not have been allowed to follow the same (or a similar) legal procedure. Generally speaking, women had limited independent legal agency under early Irish law; *GEIL* 75–78. Despite this, the versions of some legal procedures when deployed by women were on a smaller scale than those deployed by their male counterparts. For example, the procedure prescribed for women regarding legal entry was shorter in duration, involved sheep instead of horses, and female witnesses; *GEIL* 186–188.

35 Like the early Irish laws, the Welsh laws describe the procedure for claiming one's lost or stolen property, beginning with identifying the property as one's own and the proper swearing of oaths in front of witnesses by both the plaintiff and defendant necessary for either to have a legal claim on the disputed property; Dafydd Jenkins, ed. and trans., *The Law of Hywel Dda: Law Texts from Medieval Wales* (Llandysul, Dyfed: Gomer Press, 1986), pp. 156–169; *Ior* §§ 111–115. For a discussion of the Welsh laws relating to theft, see Thomas Charles-Edwards, "The Welsh Laws of Theft: Iorwerth *v* the Rest," in *Tair Colofn Cyraith. The Three Columns of Law in Medieval Wales: Homicide, Theft, and Fire*, eds. T.M. Charles-Edwards and Paul Russell (Bangor: The Welsh Legal History Society, 2007), pp. 108–130.

36 Thomas Glyn Watkin, *The Legal History of Wales* (Cardiff: University of Wales Press, 2012, 2nd ed.), pp. 64 and 67–69; Jenkins, *The Law of Hywel Dda*, 161–162 and 173–174; *Ior* §§ 113 and 124.

> In six ways does a person lose his chattels: by loss and surreption and theft; by loan and hire and deposit. In the first three cases, he is to discover and to swear to them. In the three others, he is not to do so unless they are restored as they are given.[37]

In the *Iorwerth* texts, the oath that the plaintiff needs to swear regarding his property found in another's possession is strikingly similar to what we find in the Irish laws:

> Ac euelly tyget er haulur nat oed perchennauc ydau a uedhey na'e werthu na'e prynu namen euo, ac ygyt a henne nat aeth y ganthau nac o rod nac ouenfyc nac en adneu na'y werthu na'e rody, namen y duyn e ganthau en lledrat neu o agkyuarch, neu o'e golly; ac enwy e dyd neu e nos e collet en er uythnos ac enwy yr uythnos en e mys ac enwy e mys en e tymhaur ac enwy e tymhaur en e wluyden.
>
> And so let the claimant swear that there was no owner of it who had power either to sell it or buy it save himself, and in addition to that, that it did not leave him either by gift or by loan, or on deposit, nor was it sold or given, but taken from him by theft or surreption, or lost. And let him name the day or night of the week when it was lost, and name the week of the month, and name the month of the season, and name the season of the year.[38]

Subsection 1a: *Making a claim*. The commentaries accompanying the Irish text provide further details about how the general process described above worked. Firstly, it is established which groups of people were allowed to take the claimed property on the strength of their oath alone without compurgators; they are allowed to take the property with them wherever they find it until it is conclusively proven to be theirs or not.[39] These people include a bishop, a

---

37 Text: *Welsh Medieval Law Being a Text of the Laws of Howel the Good*, ed. and trans. Arthur W. Wade-Evans (Oxford: Clarendon Press, 1909), p. 118, ll. 4–8. Translation: *Welsh Medieval Law*, 259.

38 Text: *Ior* § 113.20. Translation: Jenkins, *The Law of Hywel Dda*, 161–162.

39 Like other medieval legal systems, such as those in Wales and England, the early Irish laws required a certain number of compurgators to validate one's oath; see, for example, Watkin, *The Legal History of Wales*, 73; John Baker, *An Introduction to English Legal History* (Oxford: Oxford University Press, 2019, 5th ed.), pp. 6–8; and O.F. Robinson, T.D. Fergus, and W.M. Gordon, *European Legal History: Sources and Institutions* (Oxford: Oxford University Press, 2000, 3rd ed.), pp. 12–13 and 27–28.

lord, and a poet; due to the high status of each of these figures, the strength of their oath alone is enough to establish legal right to the property being claimed. Aside from these people, the commentary also adds that the oath of a single person proves a case when the oath is sworn by a king in battle, a woman in labor, a bishop during mass when he is between the host and the chalice, and a righteous man right before his death.[40] The assumption is that the fear of imminent death or endangering one's soul would be serious enough situations such that the person swearing the oath would not lie.

The standard procedure for those belonging to the ranks of secular society is that each person who claims their property from someone of lower social rank needs to have at least one compurgator who will support their oath. Those of high noble status are exempted from this rule at the beginning of the legal process. Otherwise, the claimant needs to swear his oath with compurgators supporting him. It should be noted that this is not the same as providing evidence that the property is his. Each person can swear up to the value of their honor-price, which is based generally on gender and social rank.[41] The number of necessary compurgators depends on the status of the individuals involved. Furthermore, with regard to stolen livestock, the number of compurgators varies depending on the value of the livestock in question, e.g., four compurgators are necessary for "a sheep, pig, goat or anything of lesser value" and seven are required for "livestock ranging from a hen to a cow."[42] The unworthy plaintiff needs twice as many compurgators to prove his case against a worthy defendant.[43] It should also be borne in mind that certain classes of people (except

40 Cf. the Welsh tractate *Y Naw Tafodiog* 'The Nine Tongued-Ones', which concerns those whose sole testimony is believed without the aid of compurgators. The list includes a lord between two of his men, a priest between two of his monks, and a woman regarding her virginity; Jenkins, *The Law of Hywel Dda*, 61–62; and Paul Russell, "Arrangement and Development of the Three Columns Tractate," in *Tair Colofn Cyfraith*, pp. 60–91, especially 61–64.

41 *GEIL* 7–12, 201, and 203; on those considered semi-free and unfree, see also Alice Rio, "'Half-Free' Categories in the Early Middle Ages: Fine Status Distinctions before Professional Lawyers," in *Legalism: Rules and Categories*, eds. Paul Dresch and Judith Scheele (Oxford: Oxford University Press, 2015), pp. 145–150. Not everyone in early Irish society had an honor-price, such as those considered unfree, and one could lose one's honor-price (or a portion thereof) for a variety of reasons, such as committing a crime or not having enough property to maintain a particular social rank. The value of a person's honor-price determined not only the amount up to which they could swear, but also the amount they could guarantee as a surety. For a variety of serious crimes committed against someone, such as theft or violating their protection, a person's honor-price (or a fraction of it) could be assessed as a fine to be paid to the wronged party by those liable.

42 *The MacEgan Legal Treatise* § 2.2–11 and discussion 135–138.

43 The terms *indraic* 'worthy, honorable' and *eisinnraic* 'unworthy, dishonorable' (the nega-

in exceptional circumstances)[44] were not legally able to act as compurgators, give evidence, or act as a plaintiff or defendant on their own behalf. Those considered legally unqualified to provide legal evidence include: slaves, castaways, foreigners, the semi-free, the senile, the mentally incapacitated, those without land, thieves, prostitutes, and clerics who have "fallen from holy orders."[45] In this section, the text is concerned with someone of a higher social status claiming their property from someone of a lower social status; the commentaries in section 3 continue this topic and also discuss claims between people of equal social ranks.[46]

The commentaries then provide a list of four (and later six) stages in the legal process which precede the final legal claiming of the disputed property. These stages do not apply in their entirety to the high noble who takes his property with him when he sees it. The commentaries describe each of the four stages as follows. The preliminary oath, *remad*, is the oath that he swears that the property did not part from him in sale, contract, etc. The next step is seizing, *lámugad*, which is defined as stretching out his hand onto his head of cattle; in other words, laying his hands on his property. The third step is 'possession', *cron*, which refers to the process of putting the disputed property into the custody of a neutral third party for safeguarding until the legal judgment, *breth*, is given.[47] The final stage is the legal judgment given by the judge hearing the case. The commentaries make a point of stating that the stages of the process must be followed in their correct order. If the plaintiff were to seize the property before giving the preliminary oath, the plaintiff would be assessed half the fine of theft as if he had stolen the property. The six stages listed in the second part of the commentary are looking, intention, preliminary oath, seizing, possession, and

---

tive of *indraic*) are used to refer to those who are in good legal standing and those who are not, respectively, regarding the performance of certain legal actions.

44 *GEIL* 202–203.

45 *GEIL* 68, 204–213, especially 206; and Fergus Kelly, "Whodunnit? Indirect Evidence in Early Irish Law," *Proceedings of the Harvard Celtic Colloquium* 35 (2015): 1–17. The topic of ordeal will be discussed more fully below with regard to § 3. Early Irish law is not unique in limiting the legal ability of aliens; for similarities with medieval English laws, see Keechang Kim, *Aliens in Medieval Law: The Origins of Modern Citizenship* (Cambridge: Cambridge University Press, 2000), pp. 1–9, and for the medieval Welsh laws, see Jenkins, *The Law of Hywel Dda*, 114–119.

46 One of the commentaries in source A briefly mentions that when a claim is made between two people of the same social rank, the person from whom the property is claimed provides the evidence if the plaintiff claims the disputed livestock was born in his possession. The commentaries in section 3 provides greater detail about this process.

47 In the case of stolen livestock, this is effectively impounding them until a judgment is given.

judgement. In the list of four stages, looking and intention are left out. 'Looking', *silliud*, is defined as seeing one's property, and 'intention', *imrádud*, is having the property on his mind.

In terms of how all of this works, let's say that John's beloved cow, Maisy, has gone missing and has been gone for a week. Once John notices that she is gone, he notifies everyone in the local community that Maisy has vanished and that he is looking for her (see § 6). It is possible that Maisy was stolen or had wandered off (maybe John had not kept his fences in good repair), or perhaps something frightened her and she ran. John really wants Maisy back and does the responsible thing, which is to go to the seven standard locations in the neighboring communities where people tend to gather and exchange news, e.g., the local mill, the blacksmith's, the lord's residence, etc. Along the way, he sees Maisy (or at least he thinks that it is Maisy), so he locates the owner of the grazing enclosure where he found her, formally makes a claim that one of the cows is actually his, and makes the preliminary oath in front of witnesses, we assume. The owner of the grazing enclosure denies John's claim, and, in fact, John is not entirely certain that the cow that he saw is Maisy. Either way, John puts his hand on the cow's head and claims her as his. At this point, the cow is then taken into the custody of a neutral third party in John's territory.[48] If John thinks that Maisy had been stolen, then the presumed thief has to travel to John's territory for the legal proceedings, and the cow must also be impounded there (see § 10).[49] Meanwhile, John continues to wonder whether he has really claimed the correct cow or made a mistake. He is given time to find a former milker, who left John's employ after Maisy went missing and now works a few territories away, so that she can come and verify the cow's identity (see § 2). When she arrives, she is convinced that the cow in question is Maisy (and Maisy recognizes her, as cows will recognize those who regularly milk them), yet the milker is of lower social rank than John; both John and the defendant are of the same social rank and considered to be legally capable members of their com-

---

48 The Irish term *túath* has a range of meanings and is frequently used in the texts edited here to refer to the laity (as opposed to members of the clergy) and to both a physical territory and the community of people associated with the territory; *eDIL* s.v. 1 *túath*. The term is left untranslated in the edition when it refers to a territory or the members of a specific territory.

49 On settling disputes across territorial boundaries, see Jacqueline Bemmer, "The Early Irish Hostage Surety and Inter-Territorial Alliances," *Historical Review* 89 (May 2016): 191–207; and Andrew Ó Donnghaile, "An Overview of Inter-Territorial Law in Early Medieval Ireland," *Peritia* 30 (2019): 197–214. For the role of poets in dispute settlement and retrieving stolen cattle, see Liam Breatnach, "Addenda and Corrigenda to 'The Cauldron of Poesy' (*Ériu* 32, 45–93)," *Ériu* 35 (1984): 189–191.

munities. Because of this, it will take a total of fourteen compurgators to swear oaths in front of a judge that the cow in question is Maisy and belongs to John.[50] The defendant can still deny all this, and he can do it with only seven compurgators, but those compurgators would need to swear that the defendant had the cow all along or that he had legitimately (he thought) bought it from someone else. If it turns out that the defendant had thought he had legitimately bought Maisy from someone legally able to sell her, the judge will decide in John's favor, and he gets Maisy back. That then leaves the defendant to pursue the thief who sold him the stolen cow, i.e., Maisy, so that he can get his money back from the thief and bring him to justice. The thief would not only have to pay back the defendant the price paid for Maisy, but also pay fines to John for stealing Maisy in the first place and to the defendant for selling him stolen goods (see § 4).

It should be noted that the commentary from source AA brings up the possibility that the person claiming stolen property does not necessarily need to be the owner of the stolen property. The claimant might recognize the property as being stolen, and, thus, start the legal process of suing for it. According to the commentary, the plaintiff in this situation is allowed to take the stolen property from the defendant and guard it until the rightful owner is found to take the property away.

Subsection 1b: *Concerning clientship, specifically the regulations concerning the goods that a lord gives to a client as a fief.*[51] Early Irish law distinguished between two broad classes of clientship: base clientship and free clientship. In base clientship arrangements, the lord provides the client with livestock, land, or other goods, the value of which depends on the social rank of the client. These goods are referred to in the texts by the term *taurchrecc* 'fore-purchase'. In addition, the lord also provides the client with goods worth the amount of the client's honor-price, which the texts refer to by the term *séoit taurchluideo* '*séts* of subjection'.[52] In this clientship arrangement, the lord also plays a role in

---

50 Women are normally only allowed to give evidence in a limited number of circumstances, such as those involving other women, including legal entry, or sexual matters; *GEIL* 202 and 207–208. That being said, it would be unusual for the female milker's evidence to be discounted in cases such as this, especially if the female milker's evidence is crucial for the stolen livestock to be returned to their rightful owner. There is evidence to suggest that the professional milker could be male or female, so it is uncertain whether the legal commentaries here invisioned only male milkers being able to provide evidence with regard to missing or stolen livestock; *EIF* 450–451.

51 The best explanation of the intricacies of the various clientship relationships is found in *GEIL* 29–33.

52 The legal texts use various terms to indicate relative amounts of value. For a list of equivalent values, see the Measures of Value, p. XIX.

some of the client's legal affairs, such as acting as a surety. In return, the client is obligated to pay his lord an annual food rent, which is proportional to the value of the fief, host a winter feast for his lord (to the best of the client's ability), provide a determined amount of annual manual labor and perform duties such as accompanying his lord to assemblies and on military campaigns, and other tasks associated with the security of the territory, such as patrolling the borders of the territory to watch for raiders, whether by land or sea. If the client pays the food render for seven years and fulfills his other obligations, the fief becomes his. Both the client and the lord can decide to end the clientship agreement, but there are penalties (depending on the circumstances) for each to do so. In a free clientship arrangement, the lord provides the client a fief, but he does not pay him '*sét*s of subjection'. The annual food rent is much higher in this arrangement. Furthermore, the client is not obligated to pay the food rent in the seventh year, but he must provide the lord with the equivalent livestock or goods that he was originally given by the lord as a fief. The free client, like the base client, must also accompany his lord to assemblies, provide manual labor, etc. Unlike a base clientship arrangement, the lord or client can end the arrangement at any time without incurring penalties, and, if the lord should die during the course of the arrangement, the client is obligated to return the fief to the lord's heirs.

The commentaries for this subsection of §1 are mainly concerned with the details surrounding the fate of the fief. The commentary begins with the proportion of the fief the lord forfeits to his client relative to the number of annual food rents the client has paid until the lord's death. The commentary then shifts to what proportion of the fief is due to the lord's heirs and/or the client's heirs in the event that either the lord or the client dies or both of them die. Throughout the material from source A, the commentaries provide a number of direct quotations from both the tracts and commentaries of other legal texts. Not all of the quotations have been identified; those which have are from *Fot Féinechais*, *Cáin Aicillne*, *Cáin Ṡóerraith*, and *Bretha Nemed Toísech*.

Subsection 1c: *Contracts*. Generally speaking, a contract made in good faith between two adults (who are considered legally capable of making contracts) witnessed by sureties is considered binding from 24 hours onwards, and it is unlawful for one of the contracting parties to try to get his property back afterwards. If, however, it turns out that the contract was made without a surety and/or that the contracted goods contained a hidden defect, the purchaser of the defective property can recover a proportion of its value even after the 24 hours have passed provided that the complaint is made within ten days. If the defect is known at the time of the contract and sureties have been appointed, the plaintiff is not able to recover anything. If the defect is not known at the time of the contract and sureties have been appointed, the plaintiff can recover half the value of the defective goods. If the defect is known at the time of the contract and no sureties have been appointed, the plaintiff can recover two-thirds of the value of the defective goods. If defect is not known at the time of the contract and sureties have not been appointed, the plaintiff can recover the entire value of the defective goods. The same legal principles are found in other texts, such as in the commentaries to §§1 and 5 from *Córus Bésgnai* and *Di Astud Chor* §§2 and 26.[53]

Subsection 1d: *Private loans.*[54] The commentary lists three circumstances where the lender can forfeit all or part of the value of the property lent to another person. All of these circumstances arise when the loaned property was damaged while in the borrower's possession. The commentaries also add that the degree of financial responsibility by the borrower is determined by whether the borrower is a kinsman, someone from the local community, or a non-local person and whether there was a surety appointed to guarantee the loaned property's return.

Subsection 1e: *Items deposited with another person for safe keeping.*[55] The commentaries divide the information regarding deposits into two broad categories. The first deals with the owner's responsibilities towards his deposited property; the second deals with the responsibilities of the person safe-guarding the property. The owner of the property is not to abandon the deposited property. If he fails to come check on the property, even though he has sworn to do so, the entirety of the deposited property is forfeit after ten years. The exception to this is if necessity kept the owner away. The protector is also able to put a time limit on how long he will guard the property in his care; if the owner does not redeem the property at the appointed time, it is forfeit to the protector. It is also possible that the owner may pledge to give the protector compensation, whether of something else or by granting use of the property, while it is in the other's care.

The person entrusted with the property has the option to take a surety to guarantee that he would be free from any liability if the deposited property

---

53 Neil McLeod, *Early Irish Contract Law*. Sydney Series in Celtic Studies 1 (Sydney: University of Sydney, 1992), pp. 39–43, discusses each of these permutations and includes a chart listing the percentages recoverable relative to knowledge (or not) of the defect and the presence (or not) of sureties.

54 For the different types of loans recognized in early Irish law, see Neil McLeod, "*Ón* and *airliciud*: Loans in Medieval Irish Law," in *Celts and their Cultures at Home and Abroad: A Festschrift for Malcolm Broun*. Sydney Series in Celtic Studies 15. Eds. Anders Ahlqvist and Pamela O'Neill (Sydney: University of Sydney, 2013), pp. 169–196.

55 For the regulations governing deposits, see *GEIL* 120.

should be damaged while in his care. The protector is not liable as long as he takes care of the deposited property as well as he takes care of his own. This operates under the assumption that he takes good care of his own property. If he does not, compensation is determined according to whether the owner of the property knew he was entrusting his own property to someone who did not properly take care of their own chattels. Deposits are also the subject of § 8.32–34 of *The MacEgan Legal Treatise* and of some of the commentary in § 1 of *Anfuigell* where the same legal principles apply regarding the responsibilities of the person safe-guarding the deposited property.[56]

Subsection 1f: *Commercial loans.*[57] Commercial loans are assumed to be given for the borrower to be able to hire out to a third party or use otherwise. The commentaries present situations where all or part of a commercial loan can become forfeit to the borrower. They assume that both the lender and borrower have given commercial loans to each other and that both have lost their respective loaned property due to neglectful safe-guarding. As both parties have lost the property that they loaned, the value of the items is offset against each other. If they are equivalent, no one receives any compensation. If one item was worth more than the other, the value that they had in common is forfeit, and the owner of the more valuable item is compensated until he receives the full value of the loaned item, less the amount forfeited.

Subsection 1g: *Acknowledgment of transfer of property by sale.* The commentary states that if 24 hours have passed since a sale was conducted with the owner's full acknowledgement, the original owner cannot claim his property back. The commentary quotes a section of tract from *Bretha im Ḟuillemu Gell* where it is stated that penalties apply to anyone who tries to get their property back after the requisite time has passed. An exception to this is where one of the contracting parties was not operating with their full mental capacity; in those cases, the 24-hour window starts from the time the person has regained their full mental faculties.[58]

Subsections 1h and 1i: *Oaths sworn by ecclesiastics.* The commentaries present a parallel system between the ecclesiastical and lay grades regarding over-swearing various members of their respective communities. The text itself states that the ecclesiastical grades will always be able to over-swear the (equivalent?) lay grades. As seen above in **1a**, the oaths of bishops and kings are

56 See the discussions in Kelly, *The MacEgan Legal Treatise*, 230–231; and Eska, *A Raven's Battle-Cry*, 12.

57 See McLeod, "*Ón* and *airliciud*: Loans in Medieval Irish Law;" and cf. § 1d above.

58 See McLeod, *Early Irish Contract Law*, 24–25; and *GEIL* 158–163.

sufficient alone, whereas lower members of the ecclesiastical and lay grades need compurgators to prove their oaths.

Section 2: *Periods of delay*. This section deals with the periods of delay given to the plaintiff in order to bring his cowherd or milker to the disputed livestock so as to verify whether the disputed property is his.[59] The testimony of the cowherd or milker is crucial because the plaintiff is uncertain whether the livestock in question is actually his; not only would the cowherd and milker have a better chance of being able to identify the livestock in question definitively, but the animals themselves would recognize them. The periods of delay account for whether the plaintiff is far from home and/or whether his cowherd or milker is at a distant location from where the plaintiff finds his livestock.[60] If the plaintiff consults with his cowherd or milker and they feel confident that the livestock in question is his, he proves it according to his own status. If there is doubt, the proof is according to the status of the cowherd or milker. In both cases, it is the plaintiff who swears the preliminary oath. The second half of source G shifts to situations where the defendant may or may not have used the disputed property while it was in his possession (and may or may not even have the disputed property in his possession any longer). The fines imposed on the defendant in these situations depend on when the disputed property was used relative to the time of the claim being made, and whether the disputed property is in his possession when the claim was made. These scenarios are revisited in § 4, which concerns the handling of stolen goods.

Section 3: *Maintaining possession of the disputed property*. The tract for this section at first glance bears little relation to the topics covered in the commentaries. The tract states that everyone against whom a claim is made is able to keep the disputed property in his possession until judgment is given about the true ownership of the disputed property. It is difficult to determine whether the second half of the tract, which is preserved in F, is actually part of the tract itself or a quotation from another text. It is further complicated by the fact that the text may be corrupt. Thus, the translation of that part of the text is very tentative; the textual notes provide further discussion. The commentary cross-references itself in two ways; the first part of the commentary states that claims between members of society who are of unequal social status are dealt with in

---

59 In the society depicted by the legal evidence, professional herders were usually male, and professional milkers could be male or female; *EIF* 443 and 450–451.

60 As suggested by Kelly, *The MacEgan Legal Treatise*, 166, the delays might take into account the cowherd or milker being in someone else's employment at the time that the plaintiff finds his livestock.

a previous section, and that in that section a noble has his property in his possession until a legal decision is given, and, secondly, that the material which follows in the commentary is concerned primarily with claims between members of the same social status.

With regard to claims between people of the same social status, the disputed property remains with the defendant until a judgment is given, and the defendant has to prove that the disputed property belongs to him. The commentary then refers to equal and unequal claims, which means that the plaintiff and defendant claim their right to the disputed property by the same or different types of ownership, respectively. The commentary then discusses three types of ownership. The first is a claim of purchase with prior right, which is defined as a situation where the defendant had purchased the property in question before it went missing from the plaintiff. For example, the defendant purchased the property on April 1, and the plaintiff states the property went missing on April 15. The second is a claim of purchase without prior right, where the defendant acquired the property after it went missing from the plaintiff. For example, the defendant purchased the property on April 15, and the plaintiff states the property was stolen on April 1. The third is a claim of growth. It refers to the claim that the livestock was born in the defendant's possession and has never left his possession since it was born.[61]

With regard to social status and equal and unequal claims, when someone of higher status claims from someone of lower status, both parties must prove each claim that they make and each refute each claim made by the other party.

---

61 The explanation given here of these three types of ownerhip is clearer than that in Eska, *A Raven's Battle-Cry*, 173, n. 476. The third type of ownership is also found in Welsh law, i.e., *geni a meithrin* 'birth and rearing'; *Llyfr Colan* § 383, ed. Dafydd Jenkins (Caerdydd: Gwasg Prifysgol Cymru, 1963); *Ior.* § 114.1–9; and Jenkins, *The Law of Hywel Dda*, 162. The procedure in Welsh law for reclaiming one's lost or stolen livestock is similar to that found in Irish law. The claimant sees his livestock in someone else's possession, claims his property, and, if no one objects, takes the property with him and then takes it to a judge who confirms his right to it. If there is an objection to the claimant's right to the property, he and the defendant establish their respective claim to the disputed property. The claimant makes a plea that the property left him by theft or some other loss, i.e., the property had no right to be in the defendant's possession. The defendant then enters his plea while having one hand on the disputed livestock and the other on a relic. The prescribed pleas he can make are: *geni a meithrin* 'birth and rearing', *cadw cyn coll* 'keeping without losing', and *arwaesaf* 'voucher to warranty'. The process is discussed in detail by Dafydd Jenkins, "Crime and Tort and the Three Columns of Law," in *Tair Colofn Cyfraith*: *The Three Columns of Law in Medieval Wales*: *Homicide, Theft and Fire*, eds. T.M. Charles-Edwards and Paul Russell. The Welsh Legal History Society v (Bangor: The Welsh Legal History Society, 2007), pp. 1–25, at 5–9.

Two scenarios are exempted from this procedure: when someone not considered to be fully legally worthy has a claim of purchase with prior right or a claim of growth; and in the second, the other party is considered legally worthy and has a claim of purchase without prior right. In both of these scenarios, the defendant and plaintiff each only have to prove the type of ownership upon which they are basing their claim.

Unequal social status also comes into play as part of the claiming process when the defendant is not considered legally worthy and the plaintiff is. In the commentaries discussed so far, the litigants are of the same or unequal social status, but both parties are considered to be worthy. This is not the case here.

When the defendant is not considered to be legally worthy, the disputed property is given to a neutral third party for safe-guarding until the final legal judgment is given, regardless of whether the defendant submits to the law of claiming. Another version of the commentary says that the disputed property is handed over to the plaintiff if the defendant does not 'submit to law'. Submitting to law refers to acknowledging the legal process and agreeing to abide by it. If the plaintiff is considered to be legally worthy and submits to judgment, the disputed property remains in his possession; if he does not submit to judgment, the property is given to a neutral third party for safe-guarding. Furthermore, if the plaintiff is legally worthy and the defendant legally unworthy and they each claim the disputed livestock was born in their possession, the plaintiff proves his case if he has compurgators supporting his claim. The only way for the unworthy person to prove his case against the plaintiff is if he undergoes a successful ordeal. As discussed by Robert Bartlett, ordeals were a feature of some medieval European legal systems, and it was not uncommon for foreigners or those not considered trustworthy to have to undergo a judicial ordeal.[62] Similar to the early Irish laws, early English law also uses the

---

62 Robert Bartlett, *Trial by Fire and Water: The Medieval Judicial Ordeal* (Oxford: Oxford University Press, 1986), pp. 5–9, 29, 32, and 43–48; Robinson, *European Legal History*, 129; Baker, *English Legal History*, 7–8; GEIL 209–211; Christophe Archan, "Ordeal by Fire in Medieval Ireland," *Peritia* 24–25 (2013–2014): 197–212; Kelly, "Whodunnit? Indirect Evidence in Early Irish Law," 7–8; Robin Chapman Stacey, *The Road to Judgment: From Custom to Court in Medieval Ireland and Wales* (Philadelphia: University of Pennsylvania Press, 1994), pp. 118–119; Niamh Wycherley, *The Cult of Relics in Early Medieval Ireland* (Turnhout: Brepols, 2015), p. 132; Whitley Stokes, ed. and trans., "The Irish Ordeals, Cormac's Adventure in the Land of Promise, and the Decision as to Cormac's Sword," in *Irische Texte mit Wörterbuch*, eds. Ernst Windisch and Whitley Stokes, 4 vols. (Leipzig: S. Hirzel, 1891) vol. 3:1, pp. 183–229 and 283; Vernam Hull, "Miscellanea Hibernica," ZCP 30 (1967): 7–11; Liam Breatnach, ed. and trans., "A Fragmentary Old Irish Text on Oaths," in *Fír Fesso: A Festschrift for Neil McLeod*, eds. Anders Ahlqvist and Pamela O'Neill. Sydney Series in Celtic Studies 17 (Sydney: The University of Sydney, 2018), pp. 53–64; and cf. the passage on ordeals in *Di*

notion of 'trustworthy' and 'untrustworthy' in relation to who must undergo an ordeal as a means of providing proof.[63]

22. ⁊ sy ælc getrywa man, þe tihtbysig nære, ⁊ naðor ne burste ne að ne ordal, innan hundrede anfealdre lade wyrðe.
22.1. And ungetrywan men ceose man anfealdne að on þrim hundredum, ⁊ þryfealdne að, swa wide swa hit to ðære byrig hyre; oððon ga to þam ordale.
22.1.a. And ofgá man anfealde lade mid anfealdan foraðe ⁊ þryfealde lade mid þryfealdan foraðe.
22.2. And gyf þegen hæbbe getrywne man to foraðe for hine, *þæt* swa sig; gyf he næbbe, ofga sylf his spæce.
22.3. ⁊ ne beo æfre ænig forað forgyfen.[64]

22. And every trustworthy man, who has not been frequently accused, and has failed neither at oath nor at ordeal, is to be entitled to the simple process of exculpation within his hundred.
22.1. And for an untrustworthy man one is to select a simple oath within three hundreds, and a three-fold oath from the area which belongs to the borough, or he is to go to the ordeal.
22.1.a. And a simple process of exculpation is to be set on foot by a simple preliminary oath, and a three-fold process of exculpation by a three-fold preliminary oath.
22.2. And if the thegn has a trustworthy man to give the preliminary oath in his stead, that may be so done; if he has not, he is himself to set on foot his suit.
22.3. And no preliminary oath is ever to be remitted.[65]

The commentaries in sources F, P, and AA mention the issue of thieves and claiming prior right. The commentaries make it clear that prior right cannot be claimed amongst thieves even when they make contracts amongst themselves

Astud Chirt ⁊ Dligid, CIH 237.35–238.25 (I should like to thank Paul Russell for this reference). Ordeals as a form of proof are absent from Welsh law, cf. Huw Pryce, *Native Law and the Church in Medieval Wales* (Oxford: Clarendon Press, 1993), pp. 37–39 and 236.

63 Discussed in Bartlett, *Trial by Fire and Water*, 32.

64 II Cnut § 22; Felix Liebermann, ed., *Die Gesetze der Angelsachsen* 3 vols. (Halle: M. Niemeyer, 1903–1916), 1: 324–326.

65 Dorothy Whitelock, trans., *English Historical Documents*: *Vol. 1, c. 500–1042*, 2nd ed. (London: Eyre & Spottiswoode, 1979), p. 457.

because each knows for a fact that they are making a contract with someone who has a known track record as a thief.

Section 4: *Concerning the person who receives stolen goods.*[66] The commentaries divide the penalties into three broad categories which depend on the culpability of the middle man. The man who receives stolen goods is not necessarily a criminal in all situations, and the commentaries explore the various permutations of his liability. In the first category, the receiver of the stolen goods is said to be fully lawful in that he does not know the good were stolen, nor that the seller was a thief. He is free from any legal liabilities provided that he names the person who sold him the stolen goods and the person to whom he himself in turn sold the stolen goods (if he did so). As literally a 'man of middle theft', *fer medongaite*, he stands between the thief and the person to whom he himself sold the stolen goods. Crucially here, he does not know that he was dealing with a thief or handling stolen goods, and he cooperates with the legal process. He is also given a period of time to search for the thief in order to bring him to justice and get his own property back, i.e., the property he exchanged with the thief to buy the stolen goods in the first place.

The situation becomes more complicated if he sold the goods on to a third party. If he did so, the receiver of stolen goods gives the third party his original property back (or property worth the same amount as the stolen goods, including the value of any young the stolen livestock might have produced in the meantime), and the plaintiff gets his original stolen property back. At the end of the process, the thief is left with nothing, the other parties are left with the property (or the equivalent value) with which they started out. Furthermore, the thief owes fines to both the plaintiff and the receiver of stolen goods.

These fines increase significantly for the thief (once he or she is found) if either the plaintiff or receiver of stolen goods received restitution of the value of the property in question first as a result of casting lots.[67] The fullest account

66 See the general discussion on theft in *GEIL* 147–149; and for broader discussion on moving stolen goods, see W. Mitchell, *An Essay on the Early History of the Law Merchant* (Cambridge: Cambridge University Press, 1904), pp. 93–124. The main early Irish text on theft, *Bretha im Gatta*, does not overlap with the material discussed in any of the texts in this volume. On the whole, the focus of *Bretha im Gatta* is much more ecclesiastical than the texts edited herein; "*Bretha im Gatta*," ed. and trans. Vernam Hull, *ZCP* 25 (1956): 211–225; and *CCIH* 297. The receiver of stolen goods is also dealt with in medieval Welsh law; Jenkins, *The Law of Hywel Dda*, 156–157; *Ior.* § 111.1–9; for discussion, see Paul Russell, "*Y Naw Affaith*: Aiding and Abetting in Welsh Law," in *Tair Colofn Cyfraith*: *The Three Columns of Law in Medieval Wales*: *Homicide, Theft and Fire*, The Welsh Legal History Society v, eds. T.M. Charles-Edwards and Paul Russell (Bangor: The Welsh Legal History Society, 2007), pp. 146–170.

67 *GEIL* 208–209; and Richard Sharpe, "Dispute Settlement in Medieval Ireland: A Prelimi-

of this is given in the commentary to source CC. In a situation where the receiver of stolen goods bought the stolen property in good faith from someone unknown or from someone outside the territory, and that person cannot be found,[68] the plaintiff and receiver of stolen goods can divide the value of the stolen property in half. For each of them to receive the missing half that they are due, they each need to hire a surety to pursue the thief and bring the thief to justice. They can decide to cast lots[69] to see which of them would receive the full amount of the restitution, i.e., their respective missing half, first. The other party would still receive their missing half once the surety acquired the full amount from the thief. If this is the case, the thief not only has to pay the full value of the stolen property, but he owes proportions of the increase in any livestock and honor-price to each of them.

The half-liable receiver of stolen goods knows that he has purchased something from a thief, but he does not know that the property itself is stolen. The receiver of stolen goods must hand over the stolen property immediately if it is in his possession. If he sold the stolen property to a third party, the goods that he received as part of that exchange are handed over to the plaintiff. In other words, he is not given a period of time to seek either the thief or the third party. Furthermore, he owes the plaintiff the full fine of a thief and half the plaintiff's honor-price. When the thief is brought to justice, he owes the receiver of stolen goods fines and the amount of half his honor-price; his full honor-price has been reduced as a result of having made a contract with a known thief.

The fully liable receiver of stolen goods either knows both the thief and the fact that the goods are stolen, or he only knows that the goods in question are stolen. Regardless of whether he has the stolen property or not, he returns the stolen property or pays the equivalent to the plaintiff. He is not given a chance to find the thief or the third party to whom he might have sold the property. When the thief is brought to justice, he does not pay the receiver of stolen goods anything, unless they made a prior agreement.

The commentary in source A then moves on to the nature of the stolen property; the commentaries in all the sources focus on cases of stolen livestock, but

---

nary Inquiry," in *The Settlement of Disputes in Early Medieval Europe*, eds. Wendy Davies and Paul Fouracre (Cambridge: Cambridge University Press, 1986), pp. 169–189, especially 176–177 and 184–185.

68 This topic is dealt with again in the commentaries in § 6.

69 They are not obligated to cast lots; if they decide to do so, both must agree to it. One scenario where casting lots would be an attractive solution for both parties would be when the stolen property is not physically divisible, e.g., a single cow.

inanimate items are mentioned in passing.[70] Inanimate chattels are straightforward; they are returned.[71] With livestock the situation is more complicated as the commentaries take into account the fact that the livestock may or may not have performed various tasks of labor, such as pulling a plough or bulling, the livestock could have produced young or milk, or the livestock might even have died in the interval. In particular, young born to the livestock after they have been stolen are to be returned along with the original livestock. It is right that the owner should have the young as the young would likely have been born had they remained in the owner's possession. Fines are also to be paid to the plaintiff as a result of the livestock losing value as they age past a certain point as they will not be as productive, and, thus, not as valuable as they were when stolen.

The commentaries also take into account the legal status of the plaintiff when calculating the full amount of the fines owed to the plaintiff for the theft. A distinction is made between those who are considered to be legally worthy and those who are not, and within each category a distinction is made between those who make good use of their property and those who do not. The fine owed to each category of person is higher if they make good use of their property. Although one may have enough property to maintain a certain social rank and honor-price, one's honor-price can be reduced if the property is not put to good use.[72]

Furthermore, the commentaries also calculate fines owed by both the thief and the receiver of stolen goods based on the circumstances under which the thief stole the property. Table 1 (p. 26) is based on the commentary in source A. Whether the thief stole from the owner's exact or excess property is what determines the amount of honor-price owed by the receiver of stolen goods. 'Exact' property refers to the amount of property someone needs to maintain their honor-price at a certain level; 'excess' is any amount over that.[73] Fines for the thief depend on where he stole the property, and whether there was a cowherd. If there was a cowherd present in any of these situations, the thief

---

70 The default scenario, generally speaking, in medieval laws concerning theft is that the stolen property is livestock; cf. the Welsh *Three Columns of Law* where the section on theft concerns theft of livestock; *Ior.* § 111–115; and Jenkins, *The Law of Hywel Dda*, 156–169.

71 Although the commentaries do not provide details, one assumes that if the stolen item is not returned in the same state it was when stolen, then the thief would need to pay further compensation to make up for the loss in value of the original item.

72 For a full discussion, see McLeod, "Property and Honour-Price in the Brehon Law Glosses and Commentaries," *The Irish Jurist* 31 (1996): 280–295.

73 For a full discussion of this legal principle, see McLeod, "Property and Honour-Price in the Brehon Law Glosses and Commentaries," 280–295.

TABLE 1 Table of fines owed by the thief and receiver of stolen goods. The table lists the conditions by which the fines owed by the thief and receiver of stolen goods are calculated. The conditions follow the order in which they are presented in the commentary. An × in a cell indicates that the condition is mentioned as part of the calculation in a given scenario. If the cell is empty, that condition is not factored in. For example, the first line of the table reads that the thief pays the owner his full honor-price if he steals the property from inside the precinct, there is not a cowherd present, and the stolen goods form part of the property necessary for the owner to maintain his full honor-price.

	Precinct	Outside precinct	Cowherd	Exact property	Excess property	Full honor-price	Half honor-price
Thief	×			×		×	
	×				×	×	
		×		×			×
		×			×		×
		×	×	×		×	
		×	×		×	×	
	×		×	×		×	
	×		×		×	×	
Fully liable receiver of					×	×	
stolen goods				×			×
Half-liable receiver of					×	×	
stolen goods				×			×

automatically owes the owner full honor-price. Otherwise, the thief owes the owner full honor-price for property (exact or excess) taken from inside the precinct and half-honor-price for property (exact or excess) taken from outside the precinct. The commentaries state that the reason half honor-price is owed by the receiver of stolen goods when the thief steals from the owner's exact property is that the theft of the property has thereby reduced the owner's honor-price, which was dependent on maintaining a certain amount of property to keep his social status and the value of his honor-price. Stealing from the owner's excess property does not reduce the amount of property he needs to maintain his social status and honor-price, which means that he has his full honor-price at the time that the thief made a bargain with the receiver of stolen goods, and, thus, is owed his full honor-price by the receiver of stolen goods.

Commentary from sources F and G provide information regarding the surety who guaranteed stolen goods.[74] If the surety guaranteed goods which were stolen for the receiver of the stolen goods and the surety was unaware that the goods were stolen, there is no legal recourse for the receiver of stolen goods because sureties can never legally bind stolen property. Furthermore, the surety is owed a fine of misrepresentation. If, however, the surety knew that the goods were stolen, he is liable for a variety of fines which depend on what, exactly, he went surety for.

Some of the commentaries from sources F, CC, and DD concern the penalties associated with taking the disputed property from a neutral third party; the property had been deposited with him for safe-keeping until a judgment could be made regarding ownership. The fullest account of the fines associated with this activity are to be found in the commentary in § 10 from source A (*CIH* 2172.15–2173.26). The material presented in these commentaries also relates to topics dealt with in the commentaries in § 3 regarding disputed property being given into the hands of a neutral third party. To understand what is going on with these commentaries, they must be put into the larger context of the claiming process. The larger context is provided by the commentary in § 10, source A.

As is known from the tract and commentaries in § 2, if the plaintiff thinks that he has found his stolen livestock in someone else's possession, but he is not completely certain that the livestock in question is his, he is allowed a period of time to seek his milker or cowherd to help identify the livestock. The amount of time the plaintiff is given to seek these people depends on how far away they are. In the commentaries in § 4 under discussion here, we also find mention of either party invoking a surtety at this stage of the process for the disputed property. It is possible that the plaintiff (or even the defendant) could be assessed fines for taking livestock from the neutral third party before it has been identified by a milker or cowherd and before it has been judged to be his own property or not.

If the person who takes the disputed property knows it is not rightfully his, he owes the owner full honor-price, penalties, and complete restitution of the disputed property. He also owes the owner of the green where the disputed property was being kept full honor-price. If he is uncertain that he is the owner of the property and he carries it off, he also owes fines.

Section 5: *The person who receives stolen goods* (*continued*). The interpretation of § 5 is rather more tentative than that of the previous sections, but it

74 See also *GEIL* 148.

seems to continue the subject of § 4 concerning the person who receives stolen goods. The tract says that a thief is not paid restitution unless it is the thief who makes a claim, presumably from the receiver of stolen goods according to the commentary. The two extracts of tract are only found in source G and may or may not be continuous. The first commentary mentions that the thief does not receive a reward for either helping to track down the stolen livestock or providing information as to their whereabouts.[75]

Section 6: *Searching for the stolen property*. This section continues with the topic of searching for one's stolen property. The tract shifts from focusing on the receiver of stolen goods to focusing on the legal obligations of the owner of the stolen property. The second extract from the tract is only found in source F and shifts back to the person who receives stolen goods. This extract, thus, may be misplaced here. The majority of the material in the commentaries concerns the procedure for when someone unwittingly buys stolen property from someone outside the territory. Some of the material in these commentaries is touched upon in several of the commentaries associated with § 4.[76]

The tract begins with the statement that it is considered neglect for a noble not to look for his stolen property. The commentaries all state that everyone in

---

75 See also Heptad 64, source J below. The subject of tracking comes up in §§ 2 and 4 of *The MacEgan Legal Treatise*; see the discussion by Kelly, op. cit., 141 and 158–161; and Mac Niocaill, "Aspects of Irish Law in the Late Thirteenth Century," 36–37; although much later than the period of the tract or commentaries, see also *Calendar of the State Papers, Relating to Ireland, of the Reign of James I, 1615–1625, Preserved in Her Majesty's Public Record Office, and Elsewhere*, ed. Charles W. Russell and John P. Prendergast (London: Longman & Co., 1880), March 26, 1617, no. 348 'Tracks in the County of Down', pp. 153–154. In § 4 of *The MacEgan Legal Treatise*, the author presents us with a situation where stolen livestock have been tracked to a particular location. If the inhabitants of that location cannot prove that the track of the livestock continues out of the area, they are considered to be liable for the fines associated with theft. If, however, the livestock were tracked along a hard-packed road or other path regularly used by cattle, they are not considered financially liable for the theft. In cases where the track is difficult to follow, witnesses may be called upon to provide evidence. Tracking livestock across territorial boundaries is also dealt with in the tenth-century 'Agreement of the Dunsæte', which provides provisions for tracking stolen livestock across the English and Welsh border; for discussion with translation, see Thomas Charles-Edwards, "The Three Columns: A Comparative Perspective," in *Tair Colofn Cyfraith: The Three Columns of Law in Medieval Wales: Homicide, Theft and Fire*, eds. T.M. Charles-Edwards and Paul Russell. The Welsh Legal History Society v (Bangor: The Welsh Legal History Society, 2007), pp. 26–59, at 53–59. For the linguistic and legal implications of the agreement, see Paul Russell, "Bilingualisms and Multilingualisms in Medieval Wales: Evidence and Inference," *Transactions of the Honourable Society of Cymmrodorion* (2019): 7–22, at 11–12 and further bibliography therein.

76 See sources A, G, N, CC, and DD.

the community should be aware that his property was stolen. If he does not let it be known, someone else in the community could accidently buy his stolen property. In early Irish law, the concept of 'negligence', *anfot*, applies to situations where injury has resulted not as a result of bad intentions, but rather as a result of irresponsibility. Normally fines are due from the one guilty of neglect to the injured party.[77] None of the commentaries mention the noble being responsible financially for not declaring that his property was stolen. The commentaries do, however, note that anyone who knowingly buys stolen property pays a fine and is not allowed to keep any of the increase which the stolen livestock may have produced while in his possession.

The majority of the commentaries concern the liability of the receiver of stolen goods when the stolen property is purchased from someone considered to be an outsider, which is defined as anyone not from the same territory or province (regardless of whether the territories had a protocol between them at the time of purchase or not), but does not include any non-locals who are currently in the hire of or under any contract with someone from the community. In this last instance, purchasing anything from those people would be considered the same as a sale from a local.

If the stolen goods were purchased from an outsider (who may or may not be the actual thief), the receiver of stolen goods has the choice of either a period of time to find the seller (this applies when the two territories still have a treaty), or the restitution[78] is divided in half between himself and the original owner (this is the standard procedure when the seller is unknown or there is no longer a treaty between the territories). If the receiver of stolen goods chooses to seek out the seller/thief, he does not receive half of the restitution, even if his search for the seller is unsuccessful; the original owner receives all of it. The receiver of stolen goods would only receive the full restitution of his property if he found the seller and was able to get back his property, or the value thereof. If he and the owner decide to divide the restitution in half, each of them takes a surety to seek the seller. They also cast lots to see which of them first receives the remainder of the restitution owed to them. The way this works is that if one of the sureties successfully tracks down the thief and obtains the restitution, the receiver of stolen goods and the original owner each get half of this amount.

77 For a discussion of this topic, see Neil McLeod, *Bloodshed and Compensation in Ancient Ireland* (Perth: Centre for Irish Studies, Murdoch University, 1999), pp. 7–15.

78 'Restitution', *aithgein*, in this case refers to the stolen property itself or, in cases where there has been a chain of sales, the property that he received for selling the stolen property to another party. The commentary in source F provides details regarding the threefold-division of the restitution when multiple parties are involved.

Thus, at the end of the process, each ends up with the same value of property they started out with before the original theft. The lots decide which of them receives their missing half first.

Section 7: *The division of profits from the stolen livestock*. The commentaries in section seven concern the division of profits that the receiver of stolen goods and owner take from the work and increase produced by the stolen livestock, e.g., dairy products and offspring. These provisions take into account the fact that there could be a considerable length of time between when the property went missing and when the final judgment on the property is given. The commentaries from all three sources refer back to the excerpt of tract which states that cattle-trespass incurs half the value associated with the labor for pasturing, caring for, and breeding the stolen livestock; these activities take place while the stolen livestock is in the possession of the fully lawful receiver of stolen goods. 'Cattle-trespass' refers to cattle trespassing on someone else's land to graze, lie down, etc. Because someone else's livestock has used the land without permission, the owner of the land receives compensation.[79] The tract and commentary interpret the stolen livestock being on the receiver of stolen goods' land as a form of trespass because the stolen livestock do not rightfully belong to him, even though he purchased the livestock in good faith. The profits are divided into three parts: the receiver of stolen goods receives a third for providing the land; the original owner receives a third for providing the livestock; the remaining third is divided in half so that each of them receives half of the profits of the remaining third associated with labor.

Section 8: *Concerning young cattle*. The excerpt of tract is difficult to interpret as the translation is tentative, but it seems to concern young cattle. The commentary provides the procedure which needs to be followed by anyone who finds lost property on land or in the sea. For the finder to receive a full share of what was found on land, he needs to make a proclamation that he has found the livestock (or lost item) at seven specific locations in the territory. These locations are places where people in the territory would regularly frequent, such as the mill. If he finds something in the sea, he needs to proclaim the find in the same seven places (or whichever places are designated as the equivalent) throughout the three nearest territories. The sea is considered the fourth territory, and that refers to proclaiming the find to nearby sailors.[80] If

---

79 In some circumstances, such as if the cattle were being pursued, the owner of the land does not receive compensation; *EIF* 137.

80 For items found in the sea, the number of territories to notify increases as it is possible that the item could have been carried by the tide or washed downstream from some distance

the property remains unused in his possession for ten days after doing so, he has a full share of it. If he does not proclaim the find and it does not remain unused in his possession for ten days, he owes the full fine of theft.

If the finder only proclaimed the find to people in the same proximity as he found it, and it remains safe and unused with him until the end of ten days, he is entitled to a share worth half the value of what he found. If he used the property before ten days had passed, he owes half the fine for theft. He owes half the fine for using it because he publicized the find at only two locations instead of the seven mentioned above.

If he does not proclaim the find at all, but it remains unused in his possession for ten days, (or he proclaims at the seven locations, but uses it), he does not get a share of the fine and he does not owe a fine for theft, although he does owe restitution of the property or its value. The reason there is not a fine for theft in the first of these two provisions is that the finder, one assumes, did not conceal the property when the rightful owner found it in his possession.[81] In the second instance, the finder does not owe a fine for theft because he proclaimed the find at presumably all seven of the designated locations and did not in any way try to conceal the fact that he had found someone else's property.

The percentage of the reward or fine owed by the finder depends on the degree to which he proclaims the find and whether he takes proper care of it

---

away. See further Baker, *English Legal History*, 413–414; and Robinson, *European Legal History*, 104–105. On a side note, in medieval England the finder of a dead body was obligated to notify the four neighbors closest to the find; once ordeals were abolished, juries were commonly drawn from the four neighboring townships; R.F. Hunnisett, *The Medieval Coroner* (Cambridge: Cambridge University Press, 1961), pp. 9–17. Although not directly related to medieval Ireland, it is interesting to note that, in early medieval Brittany, the geographical range that non-aristocratic lay-people traveled to conduct public business, i.e., acting as a witness, surety, or compurgator, was within or between neighboring communities, normally not more than three or four village communities away from their own community; Wendy Davies, *Small Worlds: The Village Community in Early Medieval Brittany* (London: Duckworth, 1988): pp. 109–126. A similar concept to the four neighboring territories appears in the law of neighborhood where each farmer gives a fore-pledge to the four neighbors on each of the four sides of his property; *Bechbretha* § 2 and discussion on 92–93; *Bechbretha*, eds. and trans. Thomas Charles-Edwards and Fergus Kelly. Early Irish Law Series 1 (Dublin: Dublin Institute for Advanced Studies, 1983). *Bretha Comaithchesa* (*CIH* 577.33–34 and *AL* 4: 106.2–3) lists the four locations in a territory where a landowner is supposed to announce that he has found horses he does not recognize trespassing on his land; see also *The MacEgan Legal Treatise* § 5.1–4 (which is based on the commentary to Heptad 64) and the discussion by Kelly, op cit., 161–162 which also discusses the example from *Bretha Comaithchesa*.

81 This reason is not given in the commentary, but see Heptad 64, sources B, C, and J for a fuller version of these conditions, pp. 280–281, 282–285, 296–299, respectively.

or uses it before ten days have passed. The point of the system is to reward the finder for trying to publicize the find so that the rightful owner can retrieve it.

Section 9: *Witnesses*. This section concerns worthy individuals acting as witnesses as part of the claiming process. The commentaries concern the number of compurgators trustworthy and untrustworthy individuals need regarding property that was seen with them or not. The general legal principle is that the untrustworthy person, who himself cannot act as a witness or compurgator, needs twice the number of compurgators as those considered trustworthy.

Section 10: *Where a case should be heard*. This section concerns both the location where the case is heard and the location to which the cattle are moved when a formal claim has been made. According to the tract, the disputed livestock are taken to the cattle enclosure which is closest to the plaintiff.[82] Furthermore, the case itself is heard in the territory where the plaintiff formally makes his case, which is assumed to be his own territory or one where he feels that he has enough legal standing to get justice. The quotations of tract from §11 found in the commentary from source J (and material in the §10 commentary) explicitly state that it is the one who commits an offense who travels to the plaintiff's territory for judgment.

The commentary from source A provides the fullest version of material which is also found in §4, sources F, CC, and DD, concerning the fines associated with taking the disputed property from the neutral third party before or after the time the plaintiff was given to seek his milker or cowherd, but before the time that the judgment was given. The fines depend on whether the property was taken before or after the period of seeking the milker or cowherd was over, and whether the disputed property turns out to belong to the person who took it from the neutral third party. It is possible that the plaintiff or the defendant could have taken the property. Fines are owed to the neutral third party and to the rightful owner of the property (if it was not the owner who took the property from the neutral third party).

Source J returns to scenarios involving the receiver of stolen goods; the general content of some of this material is repeated in the commentaries in §11. In those situations, the receiver of stolen goods goes to the plaintiff's territory for judgment. When he buys goods from a thief, the case is heard in the territory in which he made the sale. If the plaintiff claims his property from someone considered to be a fully or half unlawful receiver of stolen goods, the plaintiff

---

82 Impounding livestock is also found as part of the process of distraint where cattle are taken to a holding pen until the case is resolved; *GEIL* 178. The fullest account of the process of impounding cattle is given in *Di Chetharślicht Athgabála* (*CIH* 422.15–35 and *AL* 1: 268.19–22).

can decide in which territory he wants the case to be heard. The commentary also touches on situations where the defendant commits a crime or makes a contract or bargain in his own territory, but then leaves the territory without a compelling reason to do so; judgment is given in the territory where he committed the offense, even though it is his own territory. In cases where the defendant left the territory for a compelling reason and distraint of the disputed property is taken in his absence, he is allowed to make a claim against the distraint in the external territory. In this situation, he must not cede to the law of his own territory and he must take back his distrained property and bring it into the external territory to make the claim there.

Section 11: *The defendant travels to the plaintiff's territory for judgment.* This section largely repeats material already covered in § 10 in both the tract and commentaries. Most of the sources for both sections overlap with each other, and sources A and J quote parts of the tract within their respective commentaries. The tract states that the person who commits an offense is the one who travels to the plaintiff's territory for judgement. The commentaries reiterate this and add in scenarios involving the guilty party leaving the territory to avoid prosecution.

Section 12: *Someone who has a claim.* The final section of the tract is only preserved in source A. The commentary concerns claims which are made by those of the same or different legal standing. Versions of the commentary are also found in the commentaries in § 3. It is hard to tell whether sections 11 and 12 belong together or even as part of section 10 due to the amount of overlap between them in content.

Heptad 64

While the procedure for claiming lost or stolen livestock is the main concern of *Aidbred*, Heptad 64 is concerned with the location where an item is found and the finder's share of the found property.

The *Sechtae* 'Heptads' as a collection are listed as the ninth tract within the *Senchas Már* 'Great Tradition' legal collection, following *Córus Bésgnai* and preceding *Bretha Comaithchesa*. The composition of the *Senchas Már* has traditionally been dated to the second half of the seventh or early eighth century.[83]

83 Rudolf Thurneysen, "Aus dem irischen Recht IV," *ZCP* 16 (1927): 167–230, at 186–187; idem, "Das keltische Recht," *Zeitschrift der Savigny-Stiftung für Rechtsgeschichte. Germanisch Abteilung* 55 (1934): 81–104, at 88 [translated into English in "Celtic Law," in *Celtic Law Papers: Introductory to Welsh Medieval Law and Government.* Studies Presented to the

It consists of approximately 48 distinct legal tracts, which the literature traditionally divides into thirds.[84] The heptads belong at the beginning of the middle third of these divisions. The modern numbering of the individual heptads follows that printed in *AL*, where the collection has an additional seventeen heptads;[85] in reality, the collection consists of 65 heptads. As Breatnach has noted, the seventeen additional heptads, which are labeled as such and which directly follow the main heptad collection in *AL*, do not actually come from this collection, but are taken from a variety of other sources. There is one complete version of the heptads, which is found in Oxford, Bodleian Library MS Rawl. B. 487; this is the fullest collection and it consists of all 65 heptads. Fragments of the collection are found scattered across several other sources, not all of which are directly part of this collection.[86]

Heptads are lists of seven items grouped by a legal theme. For example, seven places where battles are not fought, seven things not considered as stock, seven types of women not entitled to honor-price, etc. Having legal themes grouped together in this way functions as a mnemonic device, especially as each heptad more or less begins the same way with 'there are seven X according to Irish law which Y'.[87]

Heptad 64 is concerned with the seven categories of found objects. The categories are grouped by general location and further subdivided into 'frequented' and 'unfrequented' places within each category of location. The locations are given as follows: a dwelling, an enclosure, a green, rough ground, a wood or mountain, the shore, and the sea. Within these categories, the system as laid out in the commentaries is formulaic, and the categories of items found on land have more in common with each other procedurally than items found on the shore or in the water. It should be noted that all of the versions of the heptad list the wood and mountain together as one category. The term used for an enclosure, *cathair*, can refer to any form of an enclosed dwelling place, be it a

International Commission for the History of Representation and Parliamentary Institutions 42. Ed. Dafydd Jenkins (Bruxelles: Les Editions de la Librairie Encyclopédique, 1973), pp. 51–70, at 56]; *GEIL* 245; but see also Liam Breatnach, *The Early Irish Law Text Senchas Már and the Question of its Date*. E.C. Quiggin Memorial Lecture 13. (Cambridge: Department of Anglo-Saxon, Norse and Celtic, 2011), p. 42.

84 Liam Breatnach, "On the Original Extent of the *Senchas Már*," *Ériu*, 47 (1996): 1–43; *CCIH* 268–286; and Neil McLeod, "Review Article: A True Companion to the *Corpus Iuris Hibernici*," *Peritia* 19 (2005): 136–163.

85 *AL* 5: 118–373.

86 *CCIH* 291–292; and Thurneysen, "Das keltische Recht," 89–90 ["Celtic Law," 57–58].

87 Cf. the Welsh legal triads; for overview and discussion, see *The Legal Triads of Medieval Wales*, ed. and trans. Sara Elin Roberts (Cardiff: University of Wales Press, 2007).

fortress, or monastic settlement, or settlement generally.[88] In the heptad, the precise meaning is not always unambiguous.

A word should be said here about the main MS source for Heptad 64, the Oxford, MS Rawl. B. 487 version of the heptad, source A, because the heptad and accompanying material is edited in this volume in a manner quite different than it is in *AL* or *CIH*. In the MS, the scribe has arranged the material as a series of excerpts of the heptad interspersed with glosses and commentary. Although the scribe follows the common practice of writing the text of the heptad in larger letters than the surrounding glosses and commentary (a practice which he follows for the other heptads in this section of the MS), here (and in Heptad 65) he breaks from his usual pattern. The heptad itself is written in larger letters as we would expect, but after copying the heptad, the scribe has written excerpts of the heptad again followed by some of the commentary in larger letters as well. This seems to result from the fact that parts of the commentary were probably glossed in the exemplar, and, over time, the total amount of glosses and commentary for the heptad grew to be quite substantial. Copy to copy, one can see how it would be possible for all the glossed material to be reinterpreted potentially as tract. It is also possible that multiple glosses on the heptad itself were later reinterpreted as glossed commentary. Furthermore, by writing the excerpts of the heptad and commentary in larger letters, it is easier to accommodate all of the glossed commentaries while imposing a system of organization on the page. The larger letters make it easier to find commentaries based on topic within the heptad.[89] This layout has been interpreted by the editors of *AL* as the heptad consisting of the original list of seven items along with everything written in larger letters. Although it appears as though the heptad is quite large, it is really only a list of seven items, just as in the other heptads. If one were to rearrange all the material written in larger letters as continuous text, it would look like the following:

> [A]tait *secht* frith*e* la *Féniu*: frithe treibe, frithe cathrach, frith*e* faiche, frithe raiti, frith*e* rofida [nó] frithe sleibe, frithe tra*cht*a, frith*e* fairge.
>
> Frithe treibe: dilis a cuigad do fir fodagaib. Frithe treibe: ma iar teora aid*h*cib tiasar do, mad eccoimded. Mad coim*ded*, a ceathraime do fir fodngaib.

88 *eDIL* s.v. 1 *cathair*.

89 A detailed discussion can be found in Charlene M. Eska, "The Transmission of Glosses: Script Size and Irish Legal Commentary," *North American Journal of Celtic Studies* 6 (2022): 78–101.

Frith*e* cathrach: dilis a cethruime do fir fodngaib, munub i cuaird lis sluaig. Mad [e]ad on, is trian do fir fodngaib.

Frithe faich*e*: a trian do fir fodngaib, mad eccoimdig*h*. Mad coimdigh, is leath.

Frithe raiti: a l*eth* do fir fodagaib, ma eccoimdi[g]. Ma coimdig*h*, is da trian.

Frith*e* rofeda no sleib*e*: dilis a da trian do fir fodngaib, ma eccoim*deg*. Ma coimde[g], is teora ce[t]h(t)ramna do fir fodngaib. Frithe raoda no sleibe: da trian do fir fodngaib ⁊ aentrian do fir isi ae, no do neoch foceirr amach. No confodla eturru i nde a imairiltnig a taisig, muniu broga ne*cht*ar n-aei.

Frithe tra*cht*a: dilis do fir fodngaib a*cht cóic*id a loige do fir [bunaid] (odngaib), ma eccoimdi[g]. Mad coimdi[g], is dilis a*cht cóic*ed*h seiss*ed a loige do neoch besa ae riam.

[Fr]ithi fairge: dil*es* do neoch fotagaib *acht cóic*ed*h seiss*ed*h* a loid*he* do neoch bes ai riam.

There are seven [categories of] finds according to Irish law: something found in a dwelling, something found in an enclosure, something found on a green, something found on rough land, something found in a wood or something found on a mountain, something found on the shore, something found in the sea.

Something found in a dwelling: a fifth of it is forfeit [sc., a fifth of its value] to [the] person who finds it. Something found in a dwelling: if it is found after three nights, if [it is found in] an unfrequented place. If [it is found in] a frequented place, a fourth of it for [the] person who finds it.

Something found in an enclosure: a fourth of it is forfeit to [the] person who finds it, unless it may be within a host's enclosure. If it be so, it is a third [of its value] for [the] person who finds it.

Something found on a green: a third of it for [the] person who finds it, if [it is found in] an unfrequented place. If [it is found in] a frequented place, [the finder receives] half of it.

Something found on rough land: half of it for [the] person who finds it, if [it is found in] an unfrequented place. If [it is found in] a frequented place, it is two thirds.

Something found in a wood or on a mountain: two thirds of it is forfeit to [the] person who finds it, if [it is found in] an unfrequented place. If [it is found in] a frequented place, it is three fourths for [the] person who finds it. Something found in a wood or on a mountain: two thirds for [the] person who finds it and one third for the owner, or for someone who may

TABLE 2 Percentage of item's value awarded to the finder

Find type	Unfrequented	Frequented
dwelling	1/5	1/4
enclosure	1/4	1/3
green	1/3	1/2
rough land	1/2	2/3
wood or mountain	2/3	3/4
shore	4/5	29/30
sea	29/30	29/30

lose [it]. Or it is equally divided between them in two, the restitution of which [each] mutually deserves, if neither of them establishes [his right to it].

Something found on the shore: [it is] forfeit to [the] person who finds it, except a fifth of its value for the original owner, if [it is found in] an unfrequented place. If [it is found in] a frequented place, it is forfeit except a fifth of a sixth [sc., 1/30] of its value for [the] previous owner.

Something found in the sea: [it is] forfeit to [the] person who finds it, except a fifth of a sixth [sc., 1/30] of its value for [the] previous owner.

In the edition of the heptad, only the list of seven items is edited as the primary text.

The commentaries provide an elaborate, yet in principle fairly simple, system for calculating the reward someone receives for finding a lost item (whether an inanimate object or livestock), publicizing the find,[90] and then safeguarding the property for a period of time in order for the rightful owner to retrieve the property. The reward system is illustrated in Table 2.

The finder receives a higher percentage of the value of the found item for finding something in a frequented place, and Kelly has suggested that the reasoning seems to be that the amount is higher for a likely place due to the fact that the chance of it being found by a thief or other unscrupulous person is higher, therefore the finder gets a larger reward for doing the right thing and trying to locate the owner.[91] In terms of how this works, it can be seen that the

90 For publicizing the finding of lost property, see also the commentary in § 8 of *Aidbred* and the discussion of that material in the Introduction, pp. 214–217 and 30–32, respectively.

91 *GEIL* 123–124.

TABLE 3 Definitions of unfrequented and frequented places

Find type	Unfrequented	Frequented
dwelling	storeroom, containers, recesses, sleeping compartments, animal stalls, dark places	floor, furniture, bright places, places where people frequent, interior walls, level surfaces, peaceful places
enclosure	recesses, gardens, secluded places	square, churchyard, main streets, places where people frequent
green	borders, recesses, secluded places, places not frequented by people	hillocks, places of assembly, paths, level places, places where people frequent
rough land	glens, ditches, secluded places, places not frequented by people	paths, level places
wood	any place not mentioned as frequented[a]	glades, little gardens,[b] places where people frequent
mountain		paths, level places
shore	places where only boats frequent	places where people and boats frequent
sea	no distinction made	no distinction made

a For both a wood and a mountain, unfrequented places are stated to be any place not specifically listed as frequented. The commentaries provide different examples of frequented places for a wood versus a mountain even though both of these locations are generally grouped together.

b EIF 389 interprets *clúainti* and *guirtíni* as 'damp pastures' and 'tilled fields', respectively.

reward for a find in a likely place in a dwelling is given as a fourth, while the reward for a find in an unlikely place is given as a fifth. Table 3 has examples of frequented and unfrequented places in each location category. The items on the chart are compiled from information across all the versions of the heptad's commentaries; not every version provides the same amount of information.

The commentaries are particularly valuable for this heptad as we are provided with a lot of information about the architecture and general description of each location type. For example, likely places in a dwelling are said to be the floor, furniture, bright places, places where people frequent, interior walls, level surfaces, and peaceful places. Unlikely places are storerooms, containers, recesses, sleeping compartments, animal stalls, and dark places. While every dwelling might not have every one of these items, it does give us a good sense of the types of items that the lawyers pictured as being fairly standard for a dwelling. This general pattern holds, with the amount of the reward increasing, all the way up to the last item, that is, a find of the sea, where the distinction between likely and unlikely is not made. The reason for this is that a slightly different system comes into play for items found in the water. The system presented in the commentaries is the same system found in the commentaries to *Muirbretha* and will be discussed below.[92]

The commentaries in sources A, B, and C also make a distinction between the *dliged fríthi* 'law of finding' and the *dliged tabarta* 'law of taking'. The law of finding involves the process already discussed of finding the item, announcing it, and safeguarding it, and is associated with the reward percentages for the finder detailed in Table 2 above, except for the amount listed for finding something in a frequented place on the shore or finding anything in the sea. The commentary states that in those cases, the law of taking operates instead, and that is the reason that the reward fractions increase to 29/30 for the finder. In these cases, the finder does not need to follow the procedure described for the law of finding. Furthermore, as will be discussed in more detail with regard to *Muirbretha*, there is a different system of rewards involved with salvaging property found in the water between the shore and the ninth wave of the sea, which is reckoned as the distance beyond which there is no guarantee that items floating on the sea will be washed to shore.

The commentaries in sources A, B, and C also mention situations where property has been found, but it was not able to be retrieved. The person who makes such a find declares that he has done so; this person who gives notice is different from the person who finds the property and is able to retrieve it. The person who gives notice as to the property's location (and rightful owner) receives a percentage of the value of the property when it has been retrieved. It is also possible to find livestock and move them to a safer location, even if that location is not the finder or owner's land. If the livestock were moved to a worse location than where they were found, the finder owes a fine for theft. For livestock which has been found dead in the woods or on a mountain, the finder can skin the animal, divide the carcass, and bring that back as proof for finding the property due to the difficulty of moving a whole dead animal from a remote location.

With regard to the proclamation of found property, the commentaries in sources A, B, and C provide a system which largely corresponds to that found in the commentary from source A of *Aidbred* § 8. Table 4 below (based on source

92 See pp. 47–48.

TABLE 4 Rewards and fines for proclaiming found property (source B). The table presents the conditioning factors in the order in which they appear in the commentary. Y indicates that the finder did something as specified in the commentary, N indicates that the finder did not do something as specified in the commentary, and the cell is empty if the commentary makes no mention of a particular activity. For example, the second row indicates that the finder did not proclaim the find at the prescribed locations, that he used it before ten days had passed, and, thus, that he owes the owner the full fine for theft.

Proclaimed	**Remains in his possession for ten days or uses it after ten days**	**Uses it before ten days**	**Concealment**	**What the finder owes**	**What the finder receives**
Y	Y				His share and use of the property
N		Y		The full fine of theft	
N	Y			Restitution	
Y		Y		Restitution	
Y (but only to people in the same dwelling and settlement)	Y				A half share of the find
N (to people in the same dwelling and settlement)	Y			Half the fine of theft	
Y (when someone comes looking for it)			N		His share
N (when someone comes looking for it)		Y		Half penalty	

B) lists whether the finder receives a reward for finding the lost property, or whether he receives a reduced award or owes a fine for either not proclaiming that the property has been found or using it before ten days have passed.

Source J provides two versions of the system. The first version centers around whether the finder proclaimed the find within ten days of finding the property.

TABLE 5 Rewards and fines for proclaiming found property (source J), first version. The table presents the conditioning factors in the order in which they appear in the commentary. Y indicates that the finder did something as specified in the commentary, N indicates that the finder did not do something as specified in the commentary, and the cell is empty if the commentary makes no mention of a particular activity. For example, the third row indicates that the finder did not declare the find at the prescribed locations within ten days of finding the item, but that he neither used the item nor concealed it when someone came looking for it, thus the property is simply taken away from him and he does not owe any fines.

Proclaimed before ten days	**Uses it after ten days**	**Uses it before ten days**	**Concealment**	**What the finder owes**	**What the finder receives**
Y		N			His full share
Y		N		Full fine of theft if charges are brought against him[a]	
N	N		N	Property taken from him and he does not get a share	
Y		Y	N	Double	
Y (but only to people in the same dwelling and settlement)		Y		Half the fine of theft and he does not get a share	

a Although the text does not specifiy the conditions under which the 'finder' is charged with theft, one possible interpretation of the commentary is that the thief says he found the property when, in fact, he stole it.

The second version aligns with the version of the system presented in sources A, B, and C, but it differs for some of the specific conditions. The details are given in Tables 5 and 6.

Source J also has material concerning items which have been carried by the currents of fresh or saltwater streams. Unfortunately, this part of the commentary seems to be missing parts of the text and the reward percentages do not always match up with the fullest version of the material, which is found in the commentary from source C of *Muirbretha* and now discussed.

TABLE 6 Rewards and fines for proclaiming found property (source J), second version. The table presents the conditioning factors in the order in which they appear in the commentary. Y indicates that the finder did something as specified in the commentary, N indicates that the finder did not do something as specified in the commentary, and the cell is empty if the commentary makes no mention of a particular activity. For example, the second row indicates that the finder did not declare the find at the prescribed locations, that he used the property after ten days, and that he owes one and a half times the value of the item, e.g., if the item is worth 4 scruples, he would owe a total of 6 scruples.

Proclaimed	Remains in his possession for ten days or uses it after ten days	Uses it before ten days	Concealment	What the finder owes	What the finder receives
Y	Y			The original owner's share	His share and use of the property
N	Y			Half doubling of the value of the property[a]	
N	N (in this case he does not use it)			The property is taken from him and he does not get a share.	If it was stolen from him, he gets the full fine of theft for it.
Y	Y				His share and use of the property[b]
N		Y		The full fine when information is brought against him.[c]	
Y (proclaimed when someone came looking for it)			N		His share
N		Y	N	A half fine	

a In the commentaries, 'half doubling' is used to refer to an amount one and a half times the item's value (the situation presented here), or the amount due from someone as a fine.
b The conditioning factors are the same as the first set given in the sequence.
c Cf. the same conditions given in the version in source C.

Muirbretha

Unfortunately, there are very few fragments of tract and commentary relating to the broad topics of shipwrecks and commerce on the seas surviving from early medieval Ireland. Furthermore, those fragments are not strictly maritime law *per se*, but rather regulate what happens when ships and other valuable items (including some varieties of marine life) are either taken from the water fairly close to land or have washed up on the shore. Technically, these situations fall within the category of land law as they do not regulate what happens between captains and crew on board ship, or between merchants and shippers, and the legal right to these items depends on who has rights over the foreshore.[93] It should also be noted that the legal rights to goods which wash up on the shore varied greatly in the middle ages. The surviving legal systems can be divided into two general categories, depending on whether the original owner of the goods retains all (or nearly all) rights to his goods at all times, or whether the owner of the land where they wash up has all (or nearly all) the rights to those goods.[94]

The main source for legal material relating to the sea, shipwrecks, and items which wash up on the shore is *Muirbretha*.[95] The text itself is the 38th tract within the *Senchas Már* collection of legal texts. Unfortunately, the surviving excerpts of the tract are very fragmentary, and most of the information that we have about sea laws is found in the commentaries. Furthermore, there is some debate about how much of it there really is, i.e., whether the excerpts of tract found in *Bretha Éitgid* are original to *Bretha Éitgid* or derived from *Muirbretha*, and whether the relevant commentaries belong originally to either text.[96]

---

93 Gearoid Mac Niocaill, "Jetsam, Treasure Trove and the Lord's Share in Medieval Ireland," *The Irish Jurist* 6 (1971): 103–110; Edda Frankot, *'Of Laws of Ships and Shipman': Medieval Maritime Law and its Practice in Urban Northern Europe* (Edinburgh: Edinburgh University Press, 2012), p. 3; for broader discussions, see Benjamin Hudson, *Irish Sea Studies 900–1200* (Dublin: Four Courts Press, 2006); Robinson, *European Legal History*, 93–96, 104–105; Baker, *English Legal History*, 413–414; Hunnisett, *The Medieval Coroner*, 6–7; Stuart A. Moore, *A History of the Foreshore and the Law Relating thereto. With a hitherto Unpublished Treatise by Lord Hale, Lord Hale's "De jure maris," and Hall's Essay on the Rights of the Crown in the Sea-shore*, 3rd ed. (London: Stevens & Haynes, 1888); W. Mitchell, *An Essay on the Early History of the Law Merchant*; Susan Rose, *The Medieval Sea* (London: Continuum, 2007); Robin Ward, *The World of the Medieval Shipmaster: Law, Business and the Sea, c. 1350–1450* (Woodbridge, Suffolk: The Boydell Press, 2009); and Michael McCormick, *Origins of the European Economy: Communications and Commerce AD 300–900* (Cambridge: Cambridge University Press, 2001).

94 This topic will be discussed further below.

95 Discussions of the text itself and its contents can be found in *GEIL* 276–277; and Wooding, *Communication and Commerce*, iv, 19–20, 33, 51, 68–71, and 95.

96 *CCIH* 304–305.

The sea and foreshore were a major source of revenue for both the local king and the owner of the shore. All of the commentaries, in one way or another, are concerned with who has what right to items which wash up on the shore. This same concern with revenue is reflected in other medieval laws as well. For example, in medieval Wales, the sea was considered to be one of the king's three 'packhorses,' where a 'packhorse' is reckoned as a source of income. In the excerpts below from the Welsh laws, we find not only the prerogative of the king to have any items which wash up on the shore and rights to any shipwrecks (unless he has granted those rights to someone else), but we also find mention of harbor fees.[97]

> Vyth pynuarch brenhyn: mor a dyffeyth ac achanauc gulat arall, lleyder, maru en surth anuab, maru e kaffo ebedyyu, camgyluus e caffo dyrue neu kamluru e ganthau.
>
> The eight packhorses of the King: the sea, and waste, and a needy person from another country, and a thief; a man suddenly dead leaving no son, a dead man for whom he gets *ebediw*, an offender from whom he gets *dirwy* or *camlwrw*.[98]
>
> Puybynnac byeyffo tyr eg glan traeth, ef byeuuyd keulet a'r tir o'r traeth, a gunaet koret arnau os men; eythyr o buru e mor peth e'r tyrneu e'r traeth, e brenhyn byeuuyd hunnu, canys pynuarch brenhyn yu emor.
>
> Whoever owns land alongside the shore, he owns the same breadth of shore as of the land, and let him make a weir on it if he wants to. But if the sea casts something onto the land or onto the shore, it will belong to the King, for the sea is the King's packhorse.[99]

97 Watkin, *The Legal History of Wales*, 5–6 and 63–64; Llinos Beverly Smith, "The *Gravamina* of the Community of Gwynedd Against Llywelyn ap Gruffudd," *Bulletin of the Board of Celtic Studies* 31 (1984): 158–176, especially 162, 164, and 168–169; and see also Huw Pryce and Gwilym Owen, "Medieval Welsh Law and the Mid-Victorian Foreshore," *The Journal of Legal History* 35:2 (2014): 172–199.

98 Text: *Ior* § 43.1–3. Versions of this are also in *Llyfr Blegywryd*, ed. Melville Richards in *Cyfreithiau Hywel Dda yn ôl llawysgrif Coleg yr Iesu LVII Rhydychen*. 2nd ed. (Caerdydd: Gwasg Prifysgol Cymru, 1990), p. 51.30–34; Stephen J. Williams & J. Enoch Powell, eds. *Llyfr Blegywryd*, 2nd ed. (Caerdydd: Gwasg Prifysgol Cymru, 1961), p. 47.1–6; Latin A, ed. Hywel D. Emanuel in *The Latin Texts of the Welsh Laws* (Cardiff: University of Wales Press, 1967), p. 135.10–15; Latin B, ed. Emanuel, *The Latin Texts of the Welsh Laws*, 205.26–31 and; Latin D, ed. Emanuel, *The Latin Texts of the Welsh Laws*, 377.4–11. Translation: Jenkins, *The Law of Hywel Dda*, 40.35–39.

99 Text: *Ior* § 88.1–4. Translation: Jenkins, *The Law of Hywel Dda*, 112.16–20.

> O tyr llog ar tir y teyrn bieu. Ac or tyr llog ar tir escob deu hanner uyd rɞg y brenhin ar escob.
>
> If a ship be wrecked on the land of a lord, the lord has it; and if the ship be wrecked on the land of a bishop, it is divided between the king and the bishop.[100]
>
> O deruyd torry llong can talu e tholl ohoney, y brenyn byeu e da; ac ny dyly hytheu both hep talu toll namyn try llanu a thri threy, a cen torro hytheu guedy talo y toll ny dyleyr udunt dym oc eu da, canys breynt alldudyon brenyn a uyd arnadunt o hynny allan; a kyn trycco hytheu urth y aghor uyth ena, ny dyleyr e gerru ac ny dyleyr duyn gwystyl arney namyn er hyn a ddoes en agheureythyaul en tyr e pryodaur, sef uy ynny er aghor eguystyl e toll.
>
> If it happens that a ship breaks up before she has paid her toll, her goods belong to the King, and it is not right for her to be without paying toll except for three flows and three ebbs; and though she should break up after paying her toll, there is no right to any of her goods from them, for they will have the status of king's aliens from then on; and though she should remain there at anchor for ever, it is not right to drive her away and it is not right to take any gage from her save what she has unlawfully put into the proprietor's land, and that the anchor as gage for the toll.[101]

Source A for *Muirbretha* is concerned with the watchman's duty to immediately report any shipwrecks that he might spot. Acting as a watchman for raiders, pirates, and wrecks were part of the normal tasks of *fuba* 'attack' and *ruba* 'defense' which clients were expected to carry out for their lord.[102] For reporting the wreck, he is entitled to a reward, the amount of which depends

---

100 Text: *Llyfr Cyfnerth*, ed. Wade-Evans, in *Welsh Medieval Law*, 114.11–13. Translation: *Llyfr Cyfnerth*, Wade-Evans, in *Welsh Medieval Law*, 257.17–20. Cf. also *Damweiniau Colan*, ed. Dafydd Jenkins in *Damweiniau Colan: Llyfr y Damweiniau yn ôl llawysgrif Peniarth 30* (Aberystwyth: Cymdeithas Lyfrau Ceredigion: 1973), § 242; and Latin D, ed. Emanuel, *The Latin Texts of the Welsh Laws*, 389.32–35.

101 Text: *Damweiniau Colan*, § 357. Translation: Jenkins, *The Law of Hywel Dda*, 112.25–37.

102 *GEIL* 31. One assumes that, once a wreck has been spotted, the lord's clients were also obligated to guard the wreck until it could be divided up in accordance with local practice. The obligation of reporting and guarding wrecks is also found in Wales; see *The Black Book of St. David's*, ed. and trans. J.W. Willis-Bund (London: The Honourable Society of Cymmrodorion, 1902), pp. 81, 89, 91, 93, and 115.

on the value of the ship's cargo. If he fails in his duties, he owes fines, which depend on the likelihood of the ship being seized and the value of the ship's cargo, if known. Part of the large fine that he owes involves paying a portion of the honor-price of each person who was entitled to a share in the wreck and restitution of part of the value of his reward; the maximum amount that he would owe would be seven *cumal*s and complete restitution of his share in the wreck. It should be noted that, in situations where it is doubtful that the ship could have been seized, regardless of whether the cargo was known, the king is responsible for paying half of the seven *cumals*; he is responsible for the entire amount if it is certain that the ship could not be seized. While it may seem odd, at first glance, that the local king should be responsible for a portion of the fine, it must be borne in mind that the king receives the most valuable item from any wreck. Furthermore, if the local king takes some responsibility for wrecks which may or may not be salvaged, it might possibly discourage wrecks going unreported or intentional wrecking by the local community members in an attempt to increase their own personal wealth; source B provides further examples of the local king taking financial responsibility for the failure (or wrongdoing) of some of his subjects when that failure has a negative financial impact on the community at large.[103] Those entitled to a share in the wreck are the local lord, the owner of the shore where the ship wrecked, the watchman, and the members of the local community who are capable of attack and defense.[104]

Source B continues the topic of the king's revenue, which includes details not only of various sources of profit for the king who has coastal territory, but also how much of that revenue he was expected to give to the church. According to the commentary, every year he owed his own original church 28 *cumal*s, which is subdivided into four categories: grain, milk, mast, and harbor profits. The assumption is that the king will deliver actual grain, mast, etc. to the church. Nothing is due to the church from any items cast ashore unless the mast or grain crops fail or boats are turned away from the harbor. If the king cannot deliver the milk or grain itself, he is obligated to make up the difference with revenue he received from goods cast ashore (or something of the equivalent

---

103 On the problem of wrecking, see Maryanne Kowaleski, *The Havener's Accounts of the Earldom and Duchy of Cornwall, 1287–1356* (Exeter: Devon and Cornwall Record Society, 2001), pp. 14, 18–19, 24, 26, and 61–62. It should also be noted that in medieval Cornwall salvagers were also entitled to a portion of the value of the goods that they found. This reward was to help counteract the pillaging of (un)reported wrecks; eadem, 27. The society depicted in the early Irish laws does not seem to have the equivalent of the medieval English havener or coroner.

104 This information is provided in the commentaries in sources B and C.

value). The seven *cumal*s (or fourteen if both the milk and grain fail) are then distributed evenly to the members of his *túath*. The assumption is that most members of the community would be the lord's clients and, as such, probably farmers who would all suffer if the grain or milk failed. If the mast fails, the seven *cumal*s are distributed only to those whose livelihood depends on the mast crop. What is unclear in the commentary is whether the king himself makes these distributions, or whether he makes the payment to the church, which then delivers the economic relief to the community.

The distribution of the seven *cumal*s[105] for ships being turned away from the harbor is different. If the landing place was known to the community, half of the amount is due to the king; if it was unknown, half the amount is for the people who owned the landing places, and the other half is for the rest of the community. The commentary does not state any specific reasons for the ships being turned away from the harbor, although one suspects that bad weather does not figure as a conditioning factor. One assumes that one potential reason the ships did not come to shore was sea raiders. It would be the king's responsibility to keep the waters surrounding his territory free from pirates, and, thus, safe for ships to land and conduct business.

Much like royal fish in England to this day, the king was entitled to a percentage of some of the marine life caught off his territory.[106] If the sea creatures were driven away by people, the king is responsible for paying the owner of the shore half of the seven *cumal*s and the other half goes to the rest of the community. The final paragraph of the commentary repeats information provided by the commentaries in sources A, C, and J for Heptad 64 and will be discussed in further detail below.

Source C is problematic as the excerpts of tract and commentary are found within the fragmentary text *Bretha Éitgid*. Thus, it is uncertain how much, or even any, of the material from this source is from *Muirbretha*. That being said, the topics covered in the excerpts and commentaries are directly relevant to the Irish regulations on salvage and finding lost property. Each of the three excerpts and commentaries deals with a discrete topic.

The first is concerned with salvaging items from the sea. The commentaries here and in Heptad 64 make a distinction between items retrieved closer to shore and those retrieved from 'beyond the ninth wave', which, based on material given in the third commentary for this source, is reckoned to be approx-

105 Source A assigns the king seven *cumals* to pay to those eligible in his *túath* when a wrecked ship cannot be seized.

106 The commentary mentions the marine life that the king was entitled to as salmon, seals, and porpoises; see also *EIF* 408.

imately 300 ft.[107] Whatever the precise distance, it is beyond the distance at which it would be certain that the items would wash up on the shore. Items which someone intentionally goes into the water to retrieve from this distance are entirely forfeited to the salvager due to the inherent danger associated with retrieving the property. Items salvaged between the shore and the ninth wave are calculated as forfeit to the salvager based on whether the owner is a local or non-local, and whether permission has been granted by the owner. The fullest version of this system is given in source E and will be discussed in greater detail below.

The second commentary concerns material touched upon in previous commentaries: the division of goods and any wrecked ships which wash up on shore. The owner of the shore receives everything up to the value of five *séts*. If anything worth more than that washes up, the property is divided as if it were a ship: the king gets the most valuable item and anything else so that he receives a total of a third of the ship's value; one third is divided amongst the members of the local community, and the other third goes to the owner of the shore. If the owner of the shore is in a clientship relationship, his lord or church receives a percentage of his share. The commentary also mentions that, if a ship is blown off course and lands in a territory different from its destination, the division of the ship is according to the territory in which she landed. The commentary does not specify whether this is necessarily a case of shipwreck.

This commentary also mentions situations where ships come to harbor to conduct trade and refers to the dues which are to be paid by the shipmaster for being allowed to conduct trade with the community. The commentary also mentions the scenario where a ship lands in a domain close to their destination. In this case, they are obligated to pay the owner of the shore for firewood and fresh water; the amount paid is determined by the value of the ship's cargo. It should be noted that not all harbors were necessarily as welcome to foreign ships as others.[108]

Of note in this regard is the passage from the c. 1245 Icelandic *Laxdæla Saga* where Olaf the Peacock journies to Ireland to find his maternal grandfather.[109] The ship is blown off course by a storm, and the captain, Orn, is worried as they are far from any market town or harbor where foreigners are supposed to have legal protection. Orn says:

107 *EIF* 569–570.
108 See the citations from *Cethairṡlicht Athgabálae* in Appendix 10.
109 I should like to thank Mary Valante for drawing this passage to my attention.

> "Þat hygg ek, at vér hafim ekki góða atkvámu, þvi at þetta er fjarri hǫfnum þeim eða kaupstǫðum, er útlendir menn skulu hafa frið, því at vér erum nú fjaraðir uppi svá sem hornsíl; ok nær ætla ek þat lǫgum Íra, þótt þeir kalli fé þetta, er vér hǫfum með at fara, með sínum fǫngum, því at heita láta þeir þat vágrek, er minnr er fjarat frá skutstafni."

> "I don't think we have landed at a good place, for this is far from the harbours and market-towns where foreigners are supposed to have safe-conduct; and here we are, left high and dry like stickle-backs on a beach. I think I'm right in saying that under Irish law they can confiscate all our goods, for they claim everything as flotsam, even when the sea has ebbed less from a ship than it has from here."[110]

In the text, the crew are worried not only about their goods being confiscated, but also about themselves. As Mary Valante remarks in her discussion of this passage, "Even though the saga is a literary construct written after the Viking Age, it demonstrates that it was well-known that only the Norse market towns offered safe refuge for merchants in Viking-Age Ireland."[111] It should be noted that the Vikings living in Ireland generated income by taxing those living and working in Viking towns such as Dublin. While some of the commentaries from *Muirbretha* support this statement, other commentaries suggest otherwise, although what we see could be a difference between landing in a harbor (even if it is not the one intended) and landing in a more remote area and the dangers associated with that.

Being blown off course or shipwrecked posed a number of obvious problems for sailors. With regard to medieval England, Bracton notes that, for a ship to truly be considered a wreck, there must be no survivors.[112] While Bracton is cer-

---

110 Text: *Laxdœla Saga: Halldórs Þættir Snorrasonar Stúfs Þáttr*, ed. Einar Ól. Sveinsson. Íslenzk Fornrit 5 (Reykjavík: Hið Íslenzka Fornritafélag, 1934), p. 54. Translation: *Laxdœla Saga*, trans. Magnus Magnusson and Hermann Pálsson (New York: Penguin Classics, 1969), pp. 90–91.

111 Mary A. Valante, "Taxation, Tolls and Tribute: The Language of Economics and Trade in Viking-Age Ireland," *Proceedings of the Harvard Celtic Colloquium* 18 (1998): 242–258, at 251.

112 Henry de Bracton, *De Legibus et Consuetudinibus Angliæ*, 4 vols., ed. George Woodbine, trans. Samuel E. Thorne (London: Publications of the Selden Society, 1968–1977), vol. 2, p. 339. http://amesfoundation.law.harvard.edu/Bracton/Common/index.htm Accessed September 28, 2019. Survivorship was a twelfth-century innovation of the English laws on wreck; Rose Melikan, "Shippers, Salvors, and Sovereigns: Competing Interests in the Medieval Law of Shipwreck," *The Journal of Legal History* 163 (1990): 163–182, at 172.

tainly not always a true reflection of English Common Law, what he presents on wrecks and royal fish matches what is found in other sources, and it highlights the dangers sailors faced whether wrecked in England or Ireland.[113]

Castaways can be difficult to spot on the legal landscape. The task is made more difficult in that the medieval Irish word *muirchuirthe*, which is a compound of the noun *muir* 'sea' and the participle of *cuirithir* 'puts, places' and thus literally means 'that which is sent or thrown up by the sea', has two primary definitions: a) one come overseas, a foreigner, and b) property cast up by sea.[114] Furthermore, there are a number of reasons one can be in a foreign territory, including trade, as a result of being set adrift as a punishment,[115] for religious reasons,[116] or shipwrecked. Appendix 10 contains a representative selection of the term as it is found in the Irish legal material. Its precise meaning is not clear cut in all of the examples, i.e., 'foreigner', 'castaway', 'property', but it is clear that the term more often than not refers to a foreigner. The *muirchuirthe* does not have an independent social status within the community and must be under the legal protection of someone else; his honor-price is usually calculated as a third of the person's who is legally responsible for him.[117]

Before returning to the legal commentaries under discussion, it is worth noting in passing that in the final prose section, dated to the twelfth century, of the Irish literary text *Aided Echach maic Maireda*, we find the dispute between Comgall of Bangor, Beoán of Tech Dabeóc, and the fisherman Fergus from Mulleague over who has possession of the mermaid (or part salmon, part woman), Lí Bán. Comgall claims her because she had been caught in his territory, Fergus claims her because she has been caught in his net, and Beoán claims her

113 Bracton also notes that the king has the right to all goods which wash up on the shore or are found in the water close enough to shore to guarantee that they would wash up on shore (unless the king has granted those rights to someone else); this does not take into account any payments for salvagers. If items are found out at sea, they become the property of the finder; de Bracton, *De Legibus et Consuetudinibus Angliæ*, vol. 2, p. 339. http://amesfoundation.law.harvard.edu/Bracton/Common/index.htm Accessed September 28, 2019; and Kowaleski, *The Havener's Accounts of the Earldom and Duchy of Cornwall*, 24. See also *Anfuigell* § 5 where a *deorad Dé* 'exile of God' has landed in an unfamiliar territory and must prove his identify by performing miracles. If he fails to perform three miracles, all or part of his possessions are forfeit to the locals.

114 *eDIL* s.v. *muirchuirthe*.

115 Mary E. Byrne, "On the Punishment of Sending Adrift," *Ériu* 11 (1932): 97–102; Pamela O'Neill, "Old Irish *Muirchrech* 'Sea Boundary'," *Ériu* 67 (2018): 1–10; and *GEIL* 5 and 219–221.

116 T.M. Charles-Edwards, "The Social Background of Irish *Peregrinatio*," *Celtica* 11 (1976): 43–59.

117 *GEIL* 6; and see the examples in Appendix 10.

because she had agreed to meet him of her own free will. After fasting against God to decide the case, an angel instructs them to yoke two stags to a chariot, and wherever they take her is where she belongs. The decision is in Beoán's favor as the stags take her to Tech Dabeóc, where she dies upon receiving baptism.[118]

The third commentary from source C concerns material similar to that mentioned in the commentary to Heptad 64, source J, i.e., the percentage of an item's value that the finder receives for either finding it on the bank of a stream or fetching it from the stream itself. The commentary divides the streams into three categories: freshwater, salt and freshwater, and streams that are an inlet of the sea. The percentage that the finder receives is laid out in Table 7 below; percentages are higher the farther the object travels and whether the finder had to go into the water to retrieve the item versus finding the property on the shore. Overall the percentages increase as the risk of injury retrieving the item increases. For example, one presumes that a stream which is an inlet of the sea is tidal and likely deeper than a stream which is a mix of salt and freshwater or a stream which is freshwater only, thus the finder receives higher percentages for retrieving anything from this type of stream as opposed to a freshwater stream. The distance the item needs to travel in a stream which is an inlet of the sea also decreases significantly for the finder to receive the same relative percentage of an item which travels the same distance in a freshwater stream.

Source D continues the topic of items carried a distance by the currents of streams, but the commentary does not provide as much detail as source C. The commentary in source D also provides information on the reward a salvager receives for retrieving items between the shore and the ninth wave; more details are given in the commentary in Source E discussed below. All of the reward percentages are consistent with what is found elsewhere.

Source E concerns the salvage of goods between the shore and the ninth wave of the sea. The percentage of the item's value that the salvager receives depends on whether the owner is a local and whether the salvager has the owner's permission to help rescue the goods from the water. Three conditioning factors are involved with regard to permission; the commentary refers to them as *fémed* 'refusal', *airíasacht* 'permission', and *áine* 'amusement'. As defined by the commentaries, 'refusal' is when the owner refuses to go into the water to

118 *Aided Echach maic Maireda*, ed and trans. Ranke de Vries, in *Two Texts on Loch nEchach*. Irish Texts Society 65 (London: The Irish Texts Society, 2012), §§ 11–18, pp. 214–219; and 128 for a discussion on the term *murchuirthe* in *De causis torchi Corc' Óche*.

TABLE 7 Reward for finding items cast ashore or fetched from a stream. The table below is divided into categories based on the type of stream mentioned, the distance the item traveled, whether the item was cast ashore or fetched from the water, and the percentage of the item's value that the finder receives as a reward. A + indicates that the commentary mentions a specific condition. For example, the second row indicates that the finder receives 1/3 of the item's total value for finding an item cast ashore by a freshwater stream which has traveled a distance of twelve territories from where it was lost. The assumption is that the distance the item traveled is established when the rightful owner comes to look for it.

Type of water	Distance traveled				Reward
Freshwater stream					
Cast ashore	Across 9 territories	Across 12 territories	Beyond 12 territories	At land closest to the sea	
	+				1/4
		+			1/3
			+		1/2
				+	2/3 (of its total value)
Cast ashore after the item has been carried by the stream to the sea[a]	50 cubits	100 cubits	150 cubits	200 cubits[b]	
	+				¼ (of the remaining 1/3 of the item's value)
		+			½ of the remaining 1/3

a This category applies to items which have been carried by the stream down to the sea. The percentage that the finder receives is for items which have been cast ashore after they have been carried down to the sea. The distance that the item travels back to land from the sea determines the finder's percentage. The assumption is that anything beyond 200 cubits (i.e., beyond the ninth wave of the sea) will not be carried back to shore by the waves or tide. If the item is found floating between the ninth wave and the shore, the final third of the item's value is distributed according to refusal, permission, and the kindred. See Table 8 below in the discussion of source E for the reward percentages for salvaging goods at this distance.

b This is the standard distance reckoned to be beyond the ninth wave when taking items from the sea.

TABLE 7 Reward for finding items cast ashore or fetched from a stream. (*cont.*)

Type of water	Distance traveled				Reward
			+		¾ of the remaining 1/3
				+	All of the remaining 1/3
Taken from the stream[c]	Across 3 territories	Across 6 territories	Across 9 territories		
	+				1/3
		+			2/3
			+		All of it[d]
Salt and freshwater stream					
Cast ashore	Across 3 territories	Across 6 territories	Across 9 territories	Across 12 territories	
	+				1/4
		+			1/2
			+		3/4
				+	All of it
Taken from the stream	Across 2 territories	Across 3 territories	Across 4 territories	Across 6 territories	
	+				1/3
		+			1/2
			+		2/3
				+	All of it
Stream that is an inlet of the sea					
Cast ashore[e]	Across 3 territories	Across 6 territories	Across 9 territories		
	+				1/3
		+			2/3
			+		All of it

c This is for an item taken from the freshwater stream itself before the item is washed into the sea.

d For all of the following cells where the reward is given as the item's entire value, it is uncertain whether the commentaries mean the item's entire value or a percentage of the item's value up to half or two-thirds of it.

e The reward percentages are the same as for an item taken from a freshwater stream.

TABLE 7 Reward for finding items cast ashore or fetched from a stream. (*cont.*)

Type of water	Distance traveled			Reward
Taken from the stream	Across 2 territories	Across 3 territories	Across 4 territories[f]	
	+			1/2
		+		2/3
			+	All of it up to half its total value

f The distances and percentages given here do not always agree with those presented in the similar commentary found in Heptad 64, source J, but that section of the commentary is missing parts of the text and is corrupt in other ways.

retrieve his own goods; 'permission' is when the salvager has the owner's permission to retrieve the property; and 'amusement' is when the salvager does it of his own accord for amusement; these last two definitions are supplied by the corresponding commentary in source C. The commentary in source E then provides the percentages that the salvager receives for retrieving items in standing water, such as a pond. The structure is based on that for taking items between the shore and the ninth wave. The tables below illustrate both systems. Finally, the commentaries to both sources C and E touch upon situations where the rescuer has risked his own life to retrieve the property. In these situations, the salvager is entitled to the entire value of the item.

At this point, it is worth pausing to put the Irish material within its broader context; the system presented in the Irish material is not unique to Ireland.[119] It should be borne in mind, however, that similarities across legal systems do not necessarily mean that there was direct influence or borrowing between systems; it could well be the case that what is seen in the surviving records are common solutions to common problems.[120]

119 There is a large body of scholarship on medieval maritime law and shipwrecks. The subject can only be treated in a cursory way here. For a brief overview of the different medieval maritime codes, see Robinson, *European Legal History*, 91–106.

120 Frankot, *'Of Laws of Ships and Shipmen'*, 27; and eadem, "Medieval Maritime Law from Oléron to Wisby: Jurisdictions of the Law of the Sea," in *Communities in European History: Representations, Jurisdictions, Conflicts*, eds. Juan Pan-Montojo and Frederik Pedersen (Pisa: Pisa University Press, 2007), pp. 151–172.

TABLE 8 Reward for salvaging items from between the shore and the ninth wave of the sea. The table is based on *Muirbretha*, source E. The order of conditioning factors follows the order in which they appear in the commentary. Y indicates that a condition is present, N indicates that a condition is absent. For example, the fourth row indicates that the salvager helped rescue a local's goods for his own amusement, and, thus, receives as a reward a third of the property's value.

Local	Stranger	Refusal	Permission	Amusement	Reward for the salvager
Y	N	Y	Y	N	All of it
Y	N	Y	N	N	2/3
Y	N	N	Y	N	2/3[a]
Y	N	N	N	Y	1/3
N	Y	Y	Y	N	2/3
N	Y	Y	N	N	1/3
N	Y	N	Y	N	1/3
N	Y	N	N	Y	2/3 of the 1/3 (i.e., 2/9), or 1/2 of the 1/3 (i.e., 1/6), or nothing

a If there is great danger to the salvager's life, the entire value of the property is forfeited to him; this information is supplied by the commentary in source C.

TABLE 9 Reward for salvaging items from a pool or pond. The table is based on *Muirbretha*, source E. The order of conditioning factors follows the order in which they appear in the commentary. Y indicates that a condition is present, N indicates that a condition is absent. For example, the first row indicates that the salvager helped rescue a non-local's goods when the non-local refused to go after them himself, and, thus, the salvager receives as a reward a two-thirds of the property's value.

Local	Stranger	Refusal	Permission	Amusement	Reward for the salvager
N	Y	Y	Y	N	All of it
N	Y	Y	N	N	2/3
N	Y	N	Y	N	1/3[a]
Y	N	Y	N	N	All of it
Y	N	N	Y	N	2/3
Y	N	N	N	Y	1/3

a The text does not provide the conditions for when the stranger gives permission for the salvager to retrieve the items for his own amusement. One assumes that the salvager would receive little or nothing for the effort, if the reward structure follows the same general pattern given here and above.

Many European maritime laws have their ultimate origin in the Rhodian Sea Laws, which date to the seventh century to eighth century CE, and are themselves based on earlier written sources and local maritime customs.[121] It has long been noted that heavily commercialized areas, such as the eastern Mediterranean and Baltic Sea, give more rights to any lost cargo to the original owner than the finder; these areas were generally more influenced by Roman law and often were not feudal societies.[122] Geographic areas which are not as heavily commercialized in these ways give more rights to the finder than the original owner. Within the context of shipwrecks, the differences between Roman law and the customs in medieval England were remarked upon by Gerald of Wales:

> In antiquis eciam Anglorum legibus ab aliquo sanctorum, ut credimus, regum, de quibus infra dicetur, constitutis, maior equitas, cum tamen illa maxima fuerit, reperitur. Statutum enim fuerat quod, si unus de naufragio euaserit, eciam pauperrimus, et nauem et totum quod ad terram uenerit et quod saluari poterit solus obtinebit, item si nullus euaserit, heredibus naufragorum, si comparuerat, totum restituetur. Nostris tamen diebus, tam Anglie quam Vallie nec non et Hibernie maritimis finibus, longe aliter fieri uidimus, non solum in terries principum at laycorum, uerum, quod est exemplo perniciosius, episcoporum et ordinis ecclesiastici prelatorum; ubi naue scilicet ui tempestatis ad saxa collisa uel eciam sabulo infixa, quanquam integra fere tota saluisque plerumque personis cunctisque et possessionibus, quia non ad portum ueniens desideratum, uel quia non adeo prospere at uolebant, statim ab accolis predonibusque crudelissimis, tanquam ad predam undique concurrentibus, omnia rapi, distrahi et dissipari.

> In the old laws of the English, which were established, we believe, by one of the holy kings, of whom we shall speak later, greater justice is found, although that [in Roman Law] was great. For it was ordained that, if one person escaped from a shipwreck, even a very poor person, he alone would obtain the ship and all that had come to land and could be salvaged; again, if no one escaped, everything that turned up would be restored to the heirs of those who had been shipwrecked. But in our own days, on

121 Melikan, "Shippers, Salvors, and Sovereigns," 165–166; and Walter Ashburner, ed., *Nomos Rhodon Nautikos: The Rhodian Sea-Law* (Oxford: The Clarendon Press, 1909), pp. lxxxv–lxxxvii.

122 Melikan, "Shippers, Salvors, and Sovereigns," 178.

> the shores of England, Wales and Ireland too, we see that things are done quite differently, not only in the lands of rulers and laymen but, which is a much more harmful example, in the lands of bishops and prelates of the ecclesiastical order; namely, that when a ship has been dashed against rocks by the force of a storm or even just stranded on the sand, although it may be almost intact and all the people on board and the goods are for the most part unharmed, because it has not come to its intended harbour, or because it has not fared as well as they wished, immediately everything is seized, dragged off, and scattered by the inhabitants and by the cruelest plunderers, running up from all sides to their prey.[123]

In this way, the legal material from medieval Ireland is very similar to what survives from medieval England and Wales.

Furthermore, the same system whereby the king has the right to a percentage of the harbor dues,[124] some types of marine life (leaving aside taxing fisherman for their catch), and rights to wreck[125] are also found in the Irish legal commentaries. Although there definitely are administrative differences, the broad legal principles are the same; the seashore was a great revenue generator.

It is also known from these accounts that the custom whereby the finder receives (or argues it is his right to receive) any item found floating out to sea was in operation. Additionally, we also find that the fact that anyone helping in

123 Text: Gerald of Wales, *Instruction for a Ruler (De Principis Instructione)*, ed. and trans. Robert Bartlett (Oxford: Clarendon Press, 2018), p. 350: translation, p. 351. The larger discussion is found on pages 346–353; and see the editor's note concerning the veracity of all of Gerald's statement on the English rights to wreck, 350, n. 946; with regard to the changing definitions of shipwreck in the English laws, see Frankot, *'Of Laws of Ships and Shipman'*, 28, n. 4. On the rights to shipwrecks being given to various religious houses, see Melikan, "Shippers, Salvors, and Sovereigns," 176–177.

124 This is a transferable right; see Melikan, "Shippers, Salvors, and Sovereigns," 176–177. For medieval Connaught, see Mac Niocaill, "Jetsam, Treasure Trove, and the Lord's Share in Medieval Ireland," especially 105–109. In medieval Wales, Gruffudd ap Cynan bequeathed the harbor dues of Abermenai to his wife, Angharad, on his death in 1137; *Vita Griffini filii Conani: The Medieval Latin Life of Gruffudd ap Cynan*, ed. and trans. Paul Russell (Cardiff: University of Wales Press, 2005), § 35.3.

125 See the discussions of these topics in Tom Johnson, "Medieval Law and Materiality: Shipwrecks, Finders, and Property on the Suffolk Coast, ca. 1380–1410," *American Historical Review* 120 (2015): 407–432, at 411–415, 418–422, and 426–427; and Kowaleski, *The Havener's Accounts of the Earldom and Duchy of Cornwall*, 23–27. It should be noted, however, that modern English maritime law is largely based on the thirteenth-century *Rules of Oléron*; Lionel H. Laing, "Origins of the Admiralty Jurisdiction in England," *Michigan Law Review* 45 (1946): 163–182, at 168.

a salvage operation was also entitled to a fee for doing so. The British Isles are not alone in assigning a reward to the salvager. It should be noted that in areas where there is a significant difference between the water line at high tide and low tide, the percentage that the finder receives depends on the distance that the item is from the shore;[126] generally in areas where the difference in water level between high and low tide, e.g., the Mediterranean, is not very great, the salvager gets a higher percentage the farther down in the water the item is.[127]

In conclusion, when one pieces together the scattered legal material concerning early Irish maritime law, one finds a system which is remarkably similar in many ways to what is attested for medieval Cornwall, Wales, and England. For example, the rights of local lords and/or the king to wrecks, certain marine life, and the foreshore generally, and the laws regarding salvage are also similar. While one may argue that what we find from Cornwall is English law and that what we find from Wales is the result of English influence,[128] one could also argue that the Irish legal commentaries are late enough to have been influenced by English law, and such an argument would account for the striking similarities between the legal systems. Although one can argue that there are historical and political reasons for the laws in England, Wales, and Cornwall to be so similar, it is harder to argue a similar legal influence for the earliest layers of the Irish laws. But one could argue, alternatively, that what we see in reality are common solutions to common problems and also ways of generating income from and by coastal communities.[129] Thus, similarities in the legal systems are

---

126 See the Irish commentaries discussed above; and cf. the laws discussed in Melikan, "Shippers, Salvors, and Sovereigns," 168–169. In the fifteenth-century Wisby Sea Law cited by Melikan, the finder receives the largest share of the value of the item if it is found out to sea and not within sight of land, a smaller percentage when the item is in sight of land, and an even smaller percentage when the item is found on the shore; this three-fold division is found in other medieval legal systems as well (some of which add a fourth distance, as it were, salvaging items from the bottom of the sea).

127 Ibid; and *Nomos Rhodon Nautikos: The Rhodian Sea-Law*, III.47.

128 The situation in Scotland is a bit different due to its geographical position closer to the more commercialized communities of the North Sea and Baltic; see Frankot, *'Of Laws of Ships and Shipmen'*, where the port of Aberdeen is taken as being representative.

129 This is not to suggest that the Irish did not engage in long-distance trade during the medieval period; see Christopher Loveluck and Aidan O'Sullivan, "Travel, Transport and Communication to and from Ireland, *c.* 400–1100: An Archaeological Perspective," in *The Irish in Early Medieval Europe: Identity, Culture and Religion*, eds. Roy Flechner and Sven Meeder (London: Palgrave, 2016), pp. 19–37; and Timothy O'Neill, *Merchants and Mariners in Medieval Ireland* (Dublin: Irish Academic Press, 1987). It should also be stressed that there was a tremendous amount of local variation in the attested laws and customs surrounding shipping and salvage; see Melkin, "Shippers, Salvors, and Sovereigns."

probably more the result of similar status-based societies finding similar solutions to common legal issues, such as who has the right to what washes up on shore. The sea and seashore have always been a source of revenue for kings and property owners, and the surviving legal material certainly reflects that.

Manuscript Sources

There is a considerable amount of overlap between the manuscript sources for *Anfuigell* and *Aidbred*. As such, several of the descriptions printed below are identical to those printed in the edition of *Anfuigell*, 48–54. The manuscript sigla for the first six sources of both texts are the same as those given in *CCIH* 164–165 for ease of reference. The Concordance of sources for both texts (in the table which follows this section) shows the sources for each text so that the degree of overlap and divergence between them can be easily seen. The manuscript sigla used for *Aidbred* are not the same as those used for *Anfuigell* unless they share the same manuscript source, which explains some of the gaps in the sigla used here. Because so many of the surviving legal manuscripts are composite manuscripts, there are many independent witnesses to the texts even when those witnesses are preserved in the same manuscript. Due to the fragmentary nature of the surviving material, it is not possible to determine the textual relationship of the various sources to each other. That being said, source A preserves the largest amount of the tract itself. The fact that so many of the commentaries contain slightly different, yet overlapping, versions of the same material further adds to the difficulty of trying to tease out the relationship of the commentaries to specific texts. The very nature of the early Irish legal material is compilatory. Thus, it is not always possible to determine which text borrowed a commentary from another if both texts touch upon the same subject matter. What can be said here in principle also holds true for Heptad 64 and *Muirbretha* below, and is especially true for *Muirbretha* as so little of the text itself survives. All of the manuscript sources as printed in *CIH* have either been checked against the manuscripts themselves or against available online images.

Aidbred

A TCD MS 1387, *olim* H.5.15,[1] pp. 16b20–22a5; *CIH* 2163.33–2173.41; *CLH* no. 685. No date appears in the MS itself, but the catalog suggests the possibility of the fifteenth-century.[2] In the MS, *Anfuigell* is the text immediately before *Aidbred*,

1 T.K. Abbott and E.J. Gwynn, *Catalogue of Irish Manuscripts in the Library of Trinity College, Dublin* (Dublin: Hodges, Figgis, & Co., 1921), pp. 249–252.

2 Abbott and Gwynn, *Catalogue of Irish Manuscripts*, 249.

 | DOI:10.1163/9789004520721_003

and *Ántéchtae* is after it.[3] The MS as it survives is not complete, but the contents are entirely legal and in the hand of one scribe.[4] The scribe identifies himself in a note on p. 7a42 at the very end of *Findṡruth Fíthail* which reads 'Seaa*n* discribsit do m*ac* Ædagai*n*' 'Seán wrote (this) for Mac Aedagáin'. The MS catalog prints the colophon as 'Seán doscrib do mac aedagáin',[5] but the text clearly has a later Latin form, *discripsit*, not the preterite/perfect of Irish *scribaid*.[6] The scribe is also responsible for writing TCD MS 1337, *olim* H.3.18, pp. 871–874.[7] Both TCD MS 1337 and 1387 formed part of Edward Lhuyd's Irish manuscript collection, and both were also once owned by Dubhaltach Mac Fhirbhisigh.[8]

Throughout the MS, the scribe generally distinguishes the OI legal tract itself from the occasional glosses and commentary by using larger-sized letter forms for the tract and smaller-sized letters forms for the glosses and commentary. The individual texts start with a very large decorated initial (see plates 1 and 2 for the beginning of *Aidbred* and *Anfuigell*, respectively), and subsections within texts frequently have a large-to-medium-sized ornamented initial. The decorated letters are executed with black ink and a reddish/orange pigment. Subsections within commentaries are not uncommonly indicated by letters which have been written slightly larger than the surrounding commentary and decorated in the same colored pigment used for the larger letters. The writing in the MS is in two columns in iron-gall ink. While the MS does contain the occasional illegible marginal note, such as that at the bottom of p. 7, no other hands were involved with the copying of the legal material. The scribe makes corrections to his work throughout the MS. These corrections tend to be in a lighter colored ink and written with a wider-cut pen than he generally employs for copying the main text, e.g., p. 11 between the columns of text. Most of these corrections seem to have been done at a later stage than the copying of the text itself. His usual method of cancellation is erasure. The scribe's hand varies between neat and tidy, e.g., 8a3–6, and rather sprawling, e.g., the bottom of p. 24b.

3 *CCIH* 88.

4 Excluding the section on injury written on the back of p. 27 written in a different hand. Page 27 is a triangular wedge of vellum out of keeping with the rest of the MS.

5 Abbott and Gwynn, *Catalogue of Irish Manuscripts*, 249. The scribal colophon is not at the foot of p. 7a as the catalog states, but rather two thirds of the way down column a.

6 I should like to thank Paul Russell for identification of this Latin form.

7 O'Sullivan, "The Book of Domhnall Ó Duibhdábhoireann," 277.

8 O'Sullivan, "The Book of Domhnall Ó Duibhdábhoireann," 277; and idem, "The Manuscript Collection of Dubhaltach Mac Fhirbhisigh," 439.

F BL MS Egerton 88,[9] f. 4ra14–5vb end;[10] *CIH* 1269.21–1276.17; *CLH* no. 689; *CCIH* 52. The MS was written over a number of years in the 1560s and early 1570s in a number of hands. This is a composite MS consisting mostly of legal material and glossaries.[11]

G TCD MS 1336, *olim* H.3.17,[12] cols. 604–617; *CIH* 2069.43–2076.20; *CLH* no. 682; *CCIH* 83 and 165. The material starts a new section in this composite MS. The MS has been dated to the fifteenth and sixteenth centuries.[13] The section comprising cols. 431–680 was mostly written by Aodhagán Mac Aodhagáin "between 1574 and 1577."[14] At the bottom of col. 615, he writes his name: 'Misi Aod*hagain*'.

J TCD MS 1336, *olim* H.3.17;[15] *CLH* no. 682; *CCIH* 78, 79, and 326–337. The material from this source is from Digest D; the numbering follows that given in *CCIH*.[16] For ease of reference, the citations from the digest are listed by the section of *Aidbred* followed by the section of Digest D: § 3 (12) *CIH* 1961.20–23, cols. 463–464; § 10 (17) *CIH* 1973.11–40, cols. 482–483; § 11 (17) *CIH* 1973.1–10, 1973.17–18, col. 482. Cols. 431–680 were written between 1574 and 1577 mainly by Aodhagán Mac Aodhagáin.[17]

M TCD MS 1387, *olim* H.5.15,[18] p. 6a; *CIH* 2141.27–30; *CLH* no. 685; *CCIH* 88 and 253–257. The citation is from a collection of extracts from *Findṡruth Fíthal* with commentary. The scribe is the same as source A.

P TCD MS 1337, *olim* H.3.18,[19] p. 185a–188a; *CIH* 711.24–713.26; *CLH* no. 683; *CCIH* 31. This material is from a series of citations from various texts. The scribe is

9 Standish Hayes O'Grady, *Catalogue of the Irish Manuscripts in the British Museum*, vol. 1 (London: The British Museum, 1926), 85–141, at 87.

10 *CIH* uses an older foliation system for this MS. Sometimes the foliation system used in *CIH* matches the current system; sometimes it does not.

11 For the disposition of the hands, see O'Sullivan, "The Book of Domhnall Ó Duibhdábhoireann," 291.

12 Abbott and Gwynn, *Catalogue of Irish Manuscripts*, 129.

13 Abbott and Gwynn, *Catalogue of Irish Manuscripts*, 125.

14 O'Sullivan, "The Manuscript Collection of Dubhaltach Mac Fhirbhisigh," 442.

15 Abbott and Gwynn, *Catalogue of Irish Manuscripts*, 127.

16 For a discussion of the Irish legal digests and their relationship to each other, see *CCIH* 322–337.

17 O'Sullivan, "The Manuscript Collection of Dubhaltach Mac Fhirbhisigh," 442.

18 Abbott and Gwynn, *Catalogue of Irish Manuscripts*, 250. A possible date of the fifteenth century is given in the *Catalogue*, 249.

19 Abbott and Gwynn, *Catalogue of Irish Manuscripts*, 146.

unidentified. This is a composite manuscript; the editors of the *Catalogue* suggest that most of the material up to p. 668 was probably written in the sixteenth century.[20] Source P is given in its entirety in Appendix 4.

Q RIA 23 Q 6 [1243], p. 4a–b; *CIH* 1144.36–1145.11; *CLH* no. 677; *CCIH* 48. The material is from Digest A (8). This is a composite manuscript consisting of five sections, four of which contain legal material. The text here is from the first section, which is acephalous and dates to 1575.[21]

U TCD MS 1336, *olim* H.3.17,[22] col. 659b *marg. inf.* and *dext.*; *CIH* 2110.10–19; *CLH* no. 682; *CCIH* 85 and 308. This source consists of a marginal commentary associated with *Córus Aithni*. Cols. 431–680 were written between 1574 and 1577 mainly by Aodhagán Mac Aodhagáin.[23] This material is edited in Appendix 6.

V TCD MS 1363, *olim* H.4.22,[24] p. 73b; *CIH* 1575.1–4; *CLH* no. 684; *CCIH* 69. This is a composite legal manuscript. The citation is from a collection of citations with commentary on various topics.

W TCD MS 1337, *olim* H.3.18, p. 151 (x);[25] *CIH* 684.17–21; *CLH* no. 683; *CCIH* 30. The material is from a collection of citations on various topics with commentary. This material is edited in Appendix 7.

X University of Oxford, Bodleian Library, MS Rawl. B. 506,[26] f. 17c; *CIH* 85.10–17; *CLH* no. 695; *CCIH* 14. This is a composite manuscript; the section where the citation is found dates to the fourteenth century.[27] The citation is from a commentary on separating from a lord, which is associated with *Cáin Ṡóerraith*.

20 Abbott and Gwynn, *Catalogue of Irish Manuscripts*, 358.

21 See the catalog description on the Irish Script on Screen website for the disposition of hands: https://www.isos.dias.ie/. Accessed January 27, 2021. See also O'Sullivan, "The Book of Domhnall Ó Duibhdábhoireann," 283.

22 Abbott and Gwynn, *Catalogue of Irish Manuscripts*, 130.

23 O'Sullivan, "The Manuscript Collection of Dubhaltach Mac Fhirbhisigh,"442.

24 Abbott and Gwynn, *Catalogue of Irish Manuscripts*, 204 and 212. The reading in *CIH* has not been checked against the MS due to COVID travel restrictions.

25 Abbott and Gwynn, *Catalogue of Irish Manuscripts*, 145; and O'Sullivan, "The Manuscript Collection of Dubhaltach Mac Fhirbhisigh," 441.

26 Brian Ó Cuív, *Catalogue of Irish Language Manuscripts in the Bodleian Library at Oxford and Oxford College Libraries* (Dublin: Dublin Institute for Advanced Studies, 2001), p. 222.

27 Ó Cuív, *Catalogue of Irish Language Manuscripts in the Bodleian Library*, 217.

Y TCD MS 1337, *olim* H.3.18,[28] p. 330c; *CIH* 847.37–848.10; *CLH* no. 683; *CCIH* 38. The citation is from a collection of citations from various sources on a range of topics.

Z TCD MS 1337, *olim* H.3.18,[29] pp. 144–145a; *CIH* 673.35–674.25; *CLH* no. 683; *CCIH* 29. The citation is from a collection of citations on various topics with commentary. This material is edited in Appendix 8.

AA TCD MS 1336, *olim* H.3.17;[30] *CLH* no. 682. The material forms part of Digest C; the numbering follows that given in *CCIH*.[31] For ease of reference, the citations from the digest are listed by the section of *Aidbred* followed by the section of Digest C: § 1 (19) *CIH* 1929.39–1930.1, col. 438, *CCIH* 75; § 2 (19) *CIH* 1930.5–10, col. 438, *CCIH* 75; § 3 (38) *CIH* 1940.39–1941.4, col. 444, *CCIH* 76; and § 10 (19) *CIH* 1930.1–5, col. 438, *CCIH* 75. Cols. 431–680 were written between 1574 and 1577 mainly by Aodhagán Mac Aodhagáin.[32]

BB TCD MS 1336, *olim* H.3.17,[33] col. 649a;[34] *CIH* 2096.25–33; *CLH* no. 682; *CCIH* 84. The citation is from a collection of citations from various texts. Cols. 431–680 were written between 1574 and 1577 mainly by Aodhagán Mac Aodhagáin.[35]

CC University of Oxford, Bodleian Library, MS Rawl. B. 506,[36] ff. 54b–55b; *CIH* 171.21–174.6; *CLH* no. 695; *CCIH* 22. This material is part of a series of commentaries on various topics. This section of the MS dates to the fourteenth century.[37]

DD TCD MS 1337, *olim* H.3.18,[38] p. 268a–b; *CIH* 800.16–802.5; *CLH* no. 683; *CCIH* 35. This commentary on the receiver of stolen goods takes up the entire page.[39]

28 Abbott and Gwynn, *Catalogue of Irish Manuscripts*, 148; O'Sullivan, "The Manuscript Collection of Dubhaltach Mac Fhirbhisigh," 442.
29 Abbott and Gwynn, *Catalogue of Irish Manuscripts*, 145.
30 Abbott and Gwynn, *Catalogue of Irish Manuscripts*, 127.
31 For a discussion of the Irish legal digests and their relationship to each other, see *CCIH* 322–337.
32 O'Sullivan, "The Manuscript Collection of Dubhaltach Mac Fhirbhisigh," 442.
33 Abbott and Gwynn, *Catalogue of Irish Manuscripts*, 129.
34 Although the entire page is labeled as col. 649, it consists of text written in two columns.
35 O'Sullivan, "The Manuscript Collection of Dubhaltach Mac Fhirbhisigh," 442.
36 Ó Cuív, *Catalogue of Irish Language Manuscripts in the Bodleian Library*, 222.
37 Ó Cuív, *Catalogue of Irish Language Manuscripts in the Bodleian Library*, 217.
38 Abbott and Gwynn, *Catalogue of Irish Manuscripts*, 147.
39 O'Sullivan, "The Manuscript Collection of Dubhaltach Mac Fhirbhisigh," 442; he iden-

EE TCD MS 1337, *olim*, H.3.18,[40] pp. 323–324; *CIH* 842.34–843.2; *CLH* no. 683; *CCIH* 37. The citations are from a collection of citations on a range of texts and topics.

FF TCD MS 1337, *olim* H.3.18,[41] pp. 341–343; *CIH* 859.34–861.14; *CLH* no. 683; *CCIH* 39. The citations largely repeat those from source P and are from a collection of citations from various texts. Variants from source FF are provided in Appendix 4.

GG TCD MS 1337, *olim* H.3.18,[42] p. 348; *CIH* 865.30–37; *CLH* no. 683; *CCIH* 39. The material is from a collection of citations on various topics.

JJ BL MS Egerton 88;[43] *CLH* no. 689. The material forms part of Digest B; the numbering follows that given in *CCIH*.[44] Digest B (27) is given in its entirety in Appendix 3. For ease of reference, the citations from the digest are listed by the section of *Aidbred* followed by the section of Digest B: § 1 (27) *CIH* 1314.7–10, f. 22d;[45] § 2 (27) *CIH* 1314.15–20, f. 22d; and § 10 (27) *CIH* 1314.10–14, f. 22d.

O'Dav O'Davoren's Glossary, BL Egerton 88;[46] *CLH* no. 689 for the manuscript and no. 889 for the text itself. There is a concordance of O'Davoren's Glossary entries to specific texts in *CCIH* 109–156. O'Davoren's Glossary is extant in two versions independent of each other: BL MS Egerton 88, ff. 80ra–93rc[47] (*CIH* 1466.11–1531.24) and TCD MS 1317, *olim* H.2.15B, pp. 45–60 (120–135 in the older pagination). The TCD version was written in 1569 and lacks the letters *A* and *B*, most of *C*, and the section containing *S*, *T*, and *U* is badly damaged.[48] The TCD version is not printed in *CIH*. The two versions are referred to as E and F, respec-

tifies the hand on p. 268 as belonging to Hand X, but it lacks some of the distinguishing features of his hand as seen on p. 267, e.g., the rightward slant of the bow on the ⟨g⟩.

40 Abbott and Gwynn, *Catalogue of Irish Manuscripts*, 148.

41 Abbott and Gwynn, *Catalogue of Irish Manuscripts*, 148; and O'Sullivan, "The Manuscript Collection of Dubhaltach Mac Fhirbhisigh,"442. Hand X appears to be the scribe for these citations.

42 Abbott and Gwynn, *Catalogue of Irish Manuscripts*, 148; and O'Sullivan, "The Manuscript Collection of Dubhaltach Mac Fhirbhisigh,"442.

43 O'Grady, *Catalogue of the Irish Manuscripts in the British Museum*, 96.

44 For a discussion of the Irish legal digests and their relationship to each other, see *CCIH* 322–337; for this entry, see 57.

45 F. 21d in the older foliation system used in *CIH*.

46 O'Grady, *Catalogue of the Irish Manuscripts in the British Museum*, 108–109.

47 The older pagination is listed in Eska, *A Raven's Battle-Cry*, 54.

48 Abbott and Gwynn, *Catalogue of Irish Manuscripts*, 93; and *CCIH* 100–108.

tively, by their editor, Whitley Stokes. Stokes edited the text twice. He edited the text first in *Three Irish Glossaries*, which does not consider the TCD version.[49] The BL version was edited in vol. 2 of *Archiv für celtische Lexikographie* with emended readings from the TCD version.[50] The list of relevant glossary entries is as follows: § 1, entry no. 1385, *CIH* 1522.1–2; and § 10, no. 1140, *CIH* 1511.28–29.

Heptad 64[51]

A University of Oxford, Bodleian Library, MS Rawlinson B. 487, ff. 62d–63c; *CIH* 55.18–61.7; *CLH* no. 693; *CCIH* 13. This is the fullest version of the heptad. It is written in one hand. This is a composite MS with the heptad collection in the third section.[52]

B RIA MS 23 Q 6 [1243], pp. 40b–41b; *CIH* 1209.16–1212.2; *CLH* no. 677; *CCIH* 51. The material is found in the fourth of five sections in this composite MS. This section dates to *c.* 1565/1566 and contains citations from a variety of legal texts.[53] The heptad is written in Domhnall's hand.[54]

C TCD MS 1336, *olim* H.3.17,[55] cols. 298–302; *CIH* 1851.25–1854.13; *CLH* no. 682; *CCIH* 72. The heptad is found as part of a large section of the MS which contains citations, glosses, and commentary from texts in the first and middle thirds of the *Senchas Már* legal collection.[56]

D TCD MS 1337, *olim* H.3.18,[57] p. 383b; *CIH* 906.30–35; *CLH* no. 683; *CCIH* 41. The heptad is found as part of a large section of the MS which contains cita-

---

49 *Three Irish Glossaries*, ed. Whitley Stokes (London: Williams & Norgate, 1862), pp. 47–124.

50 "O'Davoren's Glossary," ed. and trans. Whitley Stokes in *Archiv für celtische Lexikographie* 2, eds. Whitley Stokes and Kuno Meyer (Halle: Niemeyer, 1904), pp. 197–504.

51 Each of the sources for Heptad 64 is edited independently within the main text. See also *CCIH* 291–292.

52 Ó Cuív, *Catalogue of Irish Language Manuscripts in the Bodleian Library*, 134–141; see 136–137 for the disposition of the hands.

53 See the catalog description for the dates, contents, and the scribes involved with this section of the MS: https://www.isos.dias.ie/. Accessed January 27, 2021.

54 O'Sullivan, "The Book of Domhnall Ó Duibhdábhoireann," 292.

55 Abbott and Gwynn, *Catalogue of Irish Manuscripts*, 125.

56 *CCIH* 71.

57 Abbott and Gwynn, *Catalogue of Irish Manuscripts*, 148; and O'Sullivan, "The Manuscript Collection of Dubhaltach Mac Fhirbhisigh,"442.

tions, glosses, and commentary from texts in the first and parts of the middle thirds of the *Senchas Már* legal collection.[58]

J TCD MS 1336, *olim* H.3.17, cols. 595–602; *CIH* 2062.27–2067.26; *CLH* no. 682; *CCIH* 83. Source J for Heptad 64 is the same as source J for *Aidbred*. Here the citation is from Digest D (46).

O'Dav Entry no. 488, *CIH* 1484.10–11, is appended to the end of source J. For a discussion of O'Dav, see pp. 65–66.

Muirbretha[59]

A Oxford, Bodleian Library MS Rawlinson B. 506,[60] ff. 40d–41a; *CIH* 139.32–140.8;[61] *CLH* no. 695; *CCIH* 18. The material is found within a section containing citations from a variety of legal texts.

B Oxford, Bodleian Library MS Rawl. B. 506,[62] ff. 56d–57a; *CIH* 177.34–178.26;[63] *CLH* no. 695; *CCIH* 22. The material is found within a section containing citations from a variety of legal texts.

C TCD MS 1433, *olim* E.3.5,[64] pp. 49b–50b; *CIH* 314.17–316.36; *CLH* no. 687; *CCIH* 24. This section of the MS dates to the sixteenth century,[65] and contains a version of *Bretha Éitgid*.[66] The scribe is Torna Ó Maoil Chonaire.[67] Although the

58 *CCIH* 40. There is also a set of glosses on Heptad 64 found on p. 9 of TCD MS 1401. The source is Dubhaltach Mac Fhirbhisigh's legal glossary; the glosses in this text do not correspond exactly to any of the material edited herein. A critical edition and translation of Dubhaltach's legal glossary is currently in preparation.

59 Each of the sources is edited independently within the main text. See also *CCIH* 304–305.

60 Ó Cuív, *Catalogue of Irish Language Manuscripts in the Bodleian Library*, 222; for the fourteenth-century date and scribal information, see 217.

61 The scribe of this commentary is the same scribe who copied the *Muirbretha* commentary later in the same MS (source B).

62 Ó Cuív, *Catalogue of Irish Language Manuscripts in the Bodleian Library*, 222; for the fourteenth-century date and scribal information, see 217.

63 The scribe of this commentary is the same scribe who copied the *Muirbretha* commentary earlier in the same MS (source A).

64 Abbott and Gwynn, *Catalogue of Irish Manuscripts*, 308.

65 Abbott and Gwynn, *Catalogue of Irish Manuscripts*, xx.

66 *CCIH* 176–182.

67 *CCIH* 4; and R. Mark Scowcroft, "*Leabhar Gabhála*, Part I: The Growth of the Text," *Ériu* 38 (1987): 81–142, at 86.

citations and commentary are found within *Bretha Éitgid*, it is possible that the citations and/or commentaries might originate from *Muirbretha*. If nothing else, the subject matter of all three commentaries is relevant.[68]

D TCD MS 1337, *olim* H.3.18, p. 425a; *CIH* 959.7–16; *CLH* no. 683; *CCIH* 42. The material is from a collection of citations from a variety of texts.

E RIA MS 23 Q 6 [1243], p. 42a; *CIH* 1212.3–34; *CLH* no. 677; *CCIH* 51. The material follows directly from the citation from Heptad 64, source B. The material is also written in Domhnall's hand.[69]

O'Dav There are a number of entries from O'Davoren's Glossary which probably (or possibly) come from or relate to some of the topics related to the law of the sea and seashore. These entries are grouped together following source E as a separate section. For a discussion of O'Dav, see pp. 65–66.

68 See also *GEIL* 276–277.
69 O'Sullivan, "The Book of Domhnall Ó Duibhdábhoireann," 292.

Concordances of MS Sources with *CIH*

Concordance of Sources and Sections of Text

	A	B	C	D	E	F	G	H	I	J	K	L	M	N	O	P	Q	R	S
Anfuigell																			
Heading	×	×																	
§1	×																	×	
§2	×	×							×									×	
§3	×		×		×														
§4	×	×								×								×	
§5	×	×																	
§6	×	×	×																
§7	×									×	×								
§8	×	×							×			×							
§9	×																		
§10	×									×									
§11	×		×																
§12	×		×							×									
§13	×																		
§14	×																		
§15	×												×						
§16	×																		
§17	×		×																
§18	×																		
§19	×													×					
§20	×									×									
§21	×																		
§22	×														×				
§23	×					×													
§24	×																		
§25	×																		
§26	×															×			
§27	×																		
§28	×																		
§29	×																		
§30	×																×		
§31	×																	×	
§32	×														×				×
§33	×																		
§34	×														×				
§35	×																		
§36	×									×									
§37	×																		

 | DOI:10.1163/9789004520721_004

U	V	W	X	Y	Z	AA	BB	CC	DD	EE	FF	GG	HH	II	JJ	KK	LL	O'Dav
																		×
													×					
						×									×			
														×				
														×				
																×		
															×			
																	×	
																	×	

(*cont.*)

	A	B	C	D	E	F	G	H	I	J	K	L	M	N	O	P	Q	R	S
§ 38	×								×										
§ 39	×																		
§ 40	×																		
§ 41	×																		
§ 42	×																		
§ 43	×																		
§ 44	×																		
§ 45	×		×																
§ 46	×																		
§ 47	×																		
§ 48	×		×		×														
§ 49	×												×						
§ 50	×																		
§ 51	×		×	×	×														
§ 52	×			×															
§ 53	×			×	×														
§ 54	×			×	×														
§ 55	×				×														
§ 56	×			×															
§ 57	×		×	×	×			×											
§ 58	×		×	×												×			
Aidbred																			
§ 1	×					×	×										×		
§ 2	×					×	×										×		
§ 3	×					×	×			×			×			×			
§ 4	×					×	×									×			
§ 5							×												
§ 6	×					×	×												
§ 7	×					×	×												
§ 8	×																		
§ 9	×						×												
§ 10	×									×						×	×		
§ 11	×									×									
§ 12	×																		

J	V	W	X	Y	Z	AA	BB	CC	DD	EE	FF	GG	HH	II	JJ	KK	LL	O'Dav
																		×
																		×
×			×	×		×									×			×
	×					×									×			
						×	×				×							
		×			×			×	×		×							
										×								
										×								
						×					×				×			×
												×						

Concordance of Sections of *Aidbred* and MS Sources with *CIH*

§1: A 2163.33–2168.17; F 1269.21–1270.15; G 2069.43–2070.6; Q 1144.38–1145.1 (Appendix 3); U 2110.10–19 (Appendix 6); X 85.10–17; Y 847.37–848.10; AA 1929.39–1930.1; JJ 1314.7–10 (Appendix 3); O'Dav 1522.1–2

§2: A 2168.18–27; F 1275.41–1276.17; G 2070.7–34; Q 1145.6–11 (Appendix 3); V 1575.1–4; AA 1930.5–10; JJ 1314.15–20 (Appendix 3);

§3: A 2168.28–2169.7; F 1270.16–1271.33; G 2073.10–33; J 1961.20–23; M 2141.27–30; P 711.24–25, 712.1–3, 713.10–22 (see also Appendix 4); AA 1940.39–1941.4; BB 2096.25–33; FF 859.34, 860.40–861.11 (see Appendix 4)

§4: A 2169.8–2171.20; F 1271.34–1274.35; G 2070.35–2073.9, 2073.34–2075.11; P 713.4–9 (see also Appendix 4); W 684.17–21 (Appendix 7); Z 673.35–674.25 (Appendix 8;) CC 171.21–174.6; DD 800.16–802.5; FF 860.34–39 (see Appendix 4)

§5: G 2075.12–18

§6: A 2171.21–31; F 1274.36–1275.40; G 2075.19–34; EE 842.34–37

§7: A 2171.32–36; F 1275.1; G 2075.35–2076.11; EE 842.38–843.2

§8: A 2171.37–2172.10

§9: A 2172.11–14; G 2076.12–20

§10: A 2172.15–2173.26, 2173.34–35; J 1973.11–40; P 711.25–29 (see also Appendix 4); Q 1145.1–5 (Appendix 2); AA 1930.1–5; FF (see Appendix 4); JJ 1314.10–14 (Appendix 3); O'Dav 1511.28–29

§11: A 2173.27–37; J 1973.1–10, 1973.17–18; GG 865.30–37

§12: A 2173.38–41

Heptad 64 MS Sources with *CIH*

Source A, *CIH* 55.18–61.7
Source B, *CIH* 1209.16–1212.2
Source C, *CIH* 1851.25–1854.13
Source D, *CIH* 906.30–35
Source J, *CIH* 2062.27–2067.26

Muirbretha MS Sources with *CIH*

Source A, *CIH* 139.32–140.8

Source B, *CIH* 177.34–178.26

Source C, *CIH* 314.17–316.36[1]

Source D, *CIH* 959.7–16

Source E, *CIH* 1212.3–34

1 *GEIL* 276–277, suggests that source C ends at *CIH* 316.8, but the commentary associated with the text continues to *CIH* 316.36.

Notes on the Dates of the Texts

Dating fragmentary texts such as *Aidbred* and *Muirbretha* poses a series of challenges to the editor, not least of which is trying to determine whether the fragments of the tract belong with the texts under consideration. An additional consideration is that not every fragment will preserve features which are diagnostic for closely dating a text. As discussed in the Introduction at p. 33 the general consensus is that most of the early Irish legal texts were redacted in the seventh and eighth centuries, and the *Senchas Már* was likely redacted *c.* 650–700. This puts the date for Heptad 64 and *Muirbretha* at approximately the same time as or a little earlier than *Aidbred*. There is no linguistic evidence to suggest a date for *Aidbred* (as it survives) any earlier than 750 CE. Heptad 64 and *Muirbretha* (as they survive) contain no linguistic features that would contradict the dates given for the *Senchas Már*, but neither text contains features that are associated with the earliest (or latest) language of the OI period. Some of the glossing associated with sources A and D of Heptad 64 are noteworthy for containing object agreement markers, (conventionally termed 'infixed pronouns'), some of which (the class C 'infixed pronouns') found in relative clauses suggest a date to the OI period;[1] source D is from the *Old Irish Glosses on the Senchas Már*, which has been dated to the "middle of the eighth century."[2] That being said, all three texts were redacted within the OI period, although the accompanying glosses and commentaries range from the OI to the Early Modern Irish periods. Many of these features are discussed in the linguistic notes accompaning each text.

The commentaries are notoriously difficult to date as many of them have been taken from other texts, possibly reworked, and collected into the MSS as blocks of commentary originating from different sources and different time periods. For example, almost all of the commentary from source A, § 1b is a mixture of quotations from the tract and commentary preserved in versions of *Cáin Aicillne*, *Cáin Ṡóerraith*, and *Bretha Nemed Toísech*; and part of the commentary from *Cáin Aicillne* quotes another text, *Fot Féinechais*, which is only fragmentarily attested. The last paragraph of the commentary from source F, § 2 is from *The MacEgan Legal Treatise* § 5.13–20; this text dates to the Early

1 Joseph F. Eska, "Where Have All the Object Pronouns Gone? The Growth of Object Agreement in Earlier Celtic," *ZCP* 57 (2009–2010): 25–47; and Aaron Griffith, "Old Irish Pronouns: Agreement Affixes vs. Clitic Arguments," in *Formal Approaches to Celtic Linguistics*, ed. Andrew Carnie (Cambridge: Cambridge Scholars Publishing, 2011), pp. 65–93.

2 *CCIH* 344.

 | DOI:10.1163/9789004520721_005

Modern Irish period.[3] The commentary in source A, § 8 is identical in content to commentary associated with Heptad 64, sources A, B, and C. Commentary in source J, Heptad 64, has content identical to that found in commentaries in sources C and E from *Muirbretha*.

The majority of the commentaries are MI in all three texts. Fergus Kelly has provided a linguistic roadmap for the dating of MI legal commentaries. Many of the commentaries display some of the features he discusses, such as independent pronouns where one would expect an OI object agreement marker, the 3 sg, pres. act. ind. conjunct ending *-ann*/*-enn*, and the confusion of *ro*, *do*, and *no*.[4]

3 *The MacEgan Legal Treatise*, 15–16; source F for *Aidbred* is Kelly's source C.

4 Fergus Kelly, *Marriage Disputes: A Fragmentary Old Irish Law-Text*. Early Irish Law Series 6 (Dublin: Dublin Institute for Advanced Studies, 2014), pp. 18–21.

Editorial Method

Aidbred has been divided into twelve sections, which generally follow the divisions in the main MS source for the text, source A, aside from § 5, which is only preserved in source G. The scribe of source A normally begins each new section of text with a larger initial letter, which is frequently decorated with an orange pigment. Neither Heptad 64 nor *Muirbretha* have the same attestation pattern as *Aidbred*, so every source for each of these texts is edited individually and not divided into numbered sections.

When the sources quote material directly from the OI tract itself, that material is printed in **bold** letters, e.g., § 1a **Aidbriud**. When the sources quote material from other texts, particularly excerpts of tract rather than commentary, that material is printed within "quotation marks" to distinguish it as a textual quotation within the commentary, e.g., § 1b where source A is quoting *Fot Féinechais*. *Italics* are used to indicate expansions of scribal abbreviations, e.g., § 1a b*eth*, and they are also used when translating Latin, e.g., § 4 *as we said above*; text in Latin is edited with the same principles as the Irish. [Square] brackets are used to indicate editorial insertions, e.g., § 1a fola[d]. (Round) brackets are used to indicate editorial deletions, e.g., § 4 ga(a)bait. Italic *h* is used to indicate that the scribe has used a *punctum* or *spritus asper* instead of writing the actual letter form. The convention of leaving the *punctum* over lenited ⟨f⟩ and ⟨s⟩ (when used in the MS) has been retained, e.g., § 4 ṡeoit and § 4 d'ḟir. The *punctum* has been added to these letters when they are restored, e.g., § 4 [ḟ]uil. Punctuation and capitalization have been silently added. As far as possible, the punctuation of the edited text and translation match. Paragraph breaks have been silently added in some places where they do not occur in the MSS; this is intended to make it easier to follow the contents of the commentaries. Whenever a different version of the material is signaled in a source by the phrase *gné aile* 'a different version' (or a similar phrase of the same general meaning), a paragraph break has been inserted.

Variant readings for the OI text of *Aidbred*, however minor, are provided in the critical apparatus. The readings in source A are usually given preference, except when a fragment of the tract is not preserved in A or when other sources provide a superior reading. For example, in § 3 sources A and G only preserve the first three words of the tract for this section; the rest is supplied by the other sources. No attempt has been made to normalize the OI text as doing so would only create a cumbersome apparatus and obscure the actual MS readings. For the sake of editorial transparency, all of the unedited fragments of the canonical tract (or what is likely to be the canonical tract) of *Aidbred* are listed by

 | DOI:10.1163/9789004520721_006

source and section number in Appendix 1 (pp. 353–355). The commentaries are printed in alphabetical order according to their respective source *sigla*. Each commentary begins with its source *siglum* in bold followed by its location in *CIH*. Where commentaries overlap significantly and/or differ from the others only in matters of orthography, the duplicates are given in one of the appendices (e.g., Appendix 2). While many of the commentaries repeat aspects of the same material, some of the sources differ not only in matters of orthography, but also with regard to the arrangement, emphasis, and general content of the material. Despite any overlap with source A, these commentaries are given alongside the commentaries from source A.

Notes which are palaeographical or linguistic in nature are generally confined to the pages containing the Irish text. Notes relating to content or translation issues are generally found under the English translation and/or discussed in the Introduction. Where words have been left untranslated, e.g., *sét* 'item of value, property', an explanation is given in the textual notes or section summary the first time that the word appears. These words are all listed in the Glossary. The titles of other cited Irish legal texts have not been translated in the main body of the text, but they are listed in the section Irish Law Tracts Cited in this Volume, pp. XVI–XVIII.

When the edited text differs from that printed in *CIH* in matters of editorial practice for expanding scribal abbreviations, e.g., § 1 *CIH* 2163.37 'beth' for 'b*eth*', no note is made. It should be noted that the editorial conventions across all six volumes of *CIH* are not consistent. The editorial convention adopted here has been to expand every MS suspension, abbreviation, etc. and print the expanded text in *italics*, even in situations where the expansion is unambiguous. All of the text in *CIH* has been checked against the relevant MS source. When, however, there is a reading different from that in *CIH* which is not the result of differing editorial conventions, it has been noted in the concordance of variant readings to *CIH* in Appendix 12.

The MS abbreviation *im̄* has been expanded throughout as MI 'im*murro*' instead of OI 'im*murgu*' because it appears only in the MI commentaries. MS *dō* has been expanded as 'd*ano*'. Lenited ⟨d⟩ and ⟨g⟩ are frequently used interchangeably in the legal commentaries. These forms have not been emended except in cases where there is the potential for confusion, e.g., source P, Appendix 4 'se(d)[g]a*r*'.

Aidbred

Text, Variants, Commentary, and Translation

§1

[1a] Aidbriud[1] ardnemed fola[d] di maigin[2]

A [*CIH* 2163.33–2164.37] .i. ad*ha*-be*ir*ind[3] co h-ada, co dligth*ech*. In [n]em*ed* ard,[4] a fol*ad* do br*eith* leis di maigin ina tart*hend*[5] (tar) uasul oc um*h*ul, a imde*n*[a]m(a)[6] o bias luc*h*t a fira re cois, ł doalla naill i*na* luga. ⁊ is an*n* ata lu*cht* a fira re cois: in i*nbaid* is g*r*ad *secht*a[7] ac aidbriud a s*ét*(a)[8] ac dui*ne* is isli inas. Ar esceptu*s* do*n* g*r*ad *secht*a,[9] a s*éoit* do b*eth* i*na* toiglenmai*n* sechno*n*

---

1 Aidbriud] id*h*br*iud* **Q** (a space has been left in the MS for an initial ⟨a⟩; see also Binchy, *CIH* 1144, n. j), aidhbriudh **AA**, aid*h*bri **JJ**. In **F**, a large decorated initial ⟨a⟩ starts the text. This part of the tract is only preserved in sources **A**, **F**, **Q**, **AA**, and **JJ**. ‖ ardnemed] ardneimid **F**, ardnei*me*[d] **Q**, ardneim*id* **AA**, airdnei*me*[d] **JJ**. ‖ fola[d]] fola **A**, folu **F**, fol*ad* **Q**, **AA**, **JJ**. ‖ di] do **F**, **Q**, **AA**, **JJ**. ‖ maigin] maigen **A**, mag*in* **Q**, maig*in* **AA**, **JJ**. The last three words in F are separated by commentary from the rest of the tract and are found at *CIH* 1270.8.

---

1 In source A, the ⟨a⟩ is decorated in orange and black paint and is much larger, relatively speaking, than the other decorated initials that start most sections of the text. The form *aidbriud* is problematic. The syntax of the clause, despite its fragmentary nature, requires the word to be a finite verb, however, the form as it appears is more often associated with the nom. of the vn. of *ad-fíri*, i.e., *aidbred*, which is frequently attested in the form *aidbriud*; *eDIL* s.v. *aidbred*. What seems likely here is that the 3 sg. impv. *aidbred* from *aidbrid* (a simplex derived from *ad-fíri*) and the vn. *aidbred* with its variant *aidbriud* (cf. *léicid* and its vn. *léiciud*) have become confused.

2 This portion of the text consists of excerpts of the tract embedded within long runs of commentary in source A. Due to the large volume of material and the number of sources involved, the excerpts of tract and their relevant commentaries are given in the order in which they appear in source A. The continuous line of tract (as edited above) is: Aidbriud ardnemed fola[d] di maigin, ⁊ iss e luig*hi* dober: nad n-arlui uad i rath, na cundrad, na h-oin, na h-aithne, na h-airliugud, na h-aititiu, ⁊rl-. ⁊ imtongar and sin o g*r*adaib ecalsa f*or* g*r*adaib tuait*he* ar dilaat *secht* ngraid ecl*asa* f*or secht* ng*r*adaib t*úaithe* 'Let a high noble claim [his] property immediately, and this is [the] oath that he swears: that it did not part from him as a fief or contract or private loan or deposit or commercial loan or acknowledgement, etc. And it is sworn like that by [the] ecclesiastical grades against [the] lay grades because [the] seven ecclesiastical grades prevail over [the] seven lay grades'.

3 This is an etymological gloss on *aidbred*.

4 One letter is erased before this word in the MS.

5 *tarthend* is a later 3 sg. pres. ind. form of *do-airret*; *eDIL* s.v. *do-airret*, *do-áirret* 'overtakes, seizes, finds'.

6 The text has been emended to the nom. sg. of *imdénam* 'proving'; the gen. sg. form in the MS does not make syntactic sense in the clause.

7 The ⟨a⟩ is written subscript.

8 See also Binchy, *CIH* 2163, n. k.

9 The ⟨a⟩ is written above the numeral.

§1

[1a] Let a high noble claim [his] property immediately[10]

A i.e., *adha-beirind* 'lawfully he sues'[11] lawfully, legally. The high noble, he takes his property with him immediately wherever a noble finds it in the possession of someone of lower [rank],[12] proving it when he has his compurgators beside him, or there is enough oath in his swearing.[13] And it is in the following case[14] that his compurgators are beside him: when it is one of the seven grades who claims his *séts* from a person who is lower [in social rank] than he is. As an exception for the seven grades [i.e., the high noble is given

10 For a discussion of this section, see the Introduction, pp. 9–19. The phrase *di maigin* usually means 'on the spot, immediately', but it can also have the more literal meaning 'from a place'. The law as presented in the tract and commentary can encompass both meanings; the noble takes his property immediately from the place where he finds it; *eDIL* s.v. *maigen*.

11 The first element of this etymological gloss on *aidbred* is likely *eda* 'lawful, legal', or *edda* 'lawful', the latter used in etymological glosses on the preverbal element *ath-*; see *eDIL* s.vv. *eda* and *edda*. Despite the separate headwords, both appear to be the same word; Fergus Kelly, "An Old-Irish Text on Court Procedure," *Peritia* 5 (1986): 74–106, at 92. See also the discussion of *ada* in etymological glosses in Taylor-Griffiths, *Studies in Medieval Irish Legal Ancillary Material*, 35, 37–38, and 88. The form of *beirid* is 3 sg. pres. act. with a MI conj. ending which is unusual in an etymological gloss.

12 The phrase *tar uasul oc umhul* as it stands in the MS is problematic. O'Donovan does not emend the text, and his translation of this passage, p. 1917, suggests that the higher status noble can simply take the property that he claims (with compurgators or an oath) despite it being in the possession of another noble, provided it is a noble of lower rank. If *tar* is a copying mistake resulting from the scribe having just written *tarthend*, it eliminates the problem of finding a meaning for *tar* in this clause. As this phrase does not occur anywhere else in the text, it is difficult to determine whether there is another (or a different) copying mistake here. The substantive form of *umal* refers to someone who is humble or obedient; *eDIL* s.v. *umal*.

13 In other words, he is of sufficient rank to take the property by virtue of his oath alone; see *eDIL* s.v. 2 *do-alla* and cf. the three examples of such people given below. There are specific circumstances when the oath of one person is considered to be sufficient evidence in legal matters. Some of the circumstances presented here fall within that category. Normally compurgators would be necessary to prove a case, especially for someone of lower social status; see *GEIL* 203; and Appendix 2.

14 The phrase *is ann* 'it is in this case'/'it is here' is used frequently in the legal texts to draw attention to a following legal example. While it is clear in the Irish that the material which follows the phrase is the legal example, it is not always immediately apparent in the English translation whether the legal example comes before or after the phrase. For the sake of clarity, the phrase has been translated here and throughout all three texts as 'it is in the following case' to highlight the fact that the legal example follows.

na c*r*ichi ł co mb*erthar* uad iat do reir dlig*id*. Is a*n*d doalla[15] naill i*na* luga: i*nn* i*nbaid* is fiadnaisi rig f*r*i cath, ł mna f*r*i h-uaitne, ł esp*oic* it*er* a p[h]ars ⁊ a c[h]ail*ech*, no fireoi*n* f*r*i bass. No aidb*r*iud, .i. ed [.i.] dlig*ed*, ⁊ b*r*i [.i.] b*r*iath*ar*, ⁊ od*h* [.i.] suad. Is [s]i b*r*iath[ar][16] dligth*ech* in suad*h*: a fola[d] do b*reith* leis do maigi*n* ina tairten*n* o bias[17] lu*cht* a fira re cois, no doalla naill i*na* luga. ł aidb*r*iud, .i. a da bri suad, a da b*r*a do sod, a da mailaig do tu*r*gab*ail* do ac sill*iud* fora *séotu*.

Cet*har*da remuteit[18] in aidb*r*iud, .i. in imdenam,[19] .i. remud ⁊ lamug*ud*, c*r*on ⁊ b*r*et*h*. Remud*h*, æth ria n-æt*h*: dia *m*be in fer oca n-aidbrith*er* ar aird, .i. dias dia luga i ndiaid a*n*dt*esta* ⁊ æ*n*fer dia luga i *n*diaid t*est*a *con*id gat rogat*ad*: cirt ca*ch* techta. Lamug*ud* iar suide, am*ail* isb*eir*: "rigid lam dia mil i*n*dili."[20] Cr*on* iar si*n*: a thab*air*t a c[h]*r*on nosai*n*igen*n* a lai*m* coitci*n*d mad ac esi*n*raic aidb*r*ith*er*, no cid inr*aic* mai*n*e da*m*a dlig*ed*. Dia ndama im*murro* dlig*ed*, is a tab*air*t fiad fiadnaib i*na* laim budein. B*r*et*h* im*murro* iar suide uili.

---

15 The second ⟨a⟩ is written subscript, and it is followed by an ⟨a⟩ that has been erased; see also Binchy, *CIH* 2164, n. a.

16 I follow the emendation suggested by Binchy, *CIH* 2164, n. c.

17 The ⟨a⟩ is written subscript.

18 This word appears to be a form of *remi-tét* 'goes before, precedes'; *eDIL* s.v. *remi-tét*.

19 The phrase *.i. in imdenam* was written interlinearly by the scribe glossing the previous clause; see also Binchy, *CIH* 2164, n. d.

20 It is not possible to determine whether this quotation is from *Aidbred*, although it does not seem to appear in other legal texts. A similar phrase is found in *O'Davoren's Glossary*, nos. 1347 and 1384. Breatnach, *CCIH* 148 and 149, identifies the source for these entries as *Bretha Nemed Dédenach*, *CIH* 1120.27, and *Cáin Ṡóerraith*, *CIH* 1775.27, respectively. The versions from BL Egerton 88 are given here, but see also the editorial notes in Stokes' edition. The translations below are based on those of Stokes; he does not translate either headword. O'Dav no. 1347: Rigid, .i. sine*dh*, *ut est* "rorigid-sa*m* a lam dia cruid." *'Rigid* 'stretches', i.e., stretching out, i.e., *ut est* "he extends his hand to his wealth."' O'Dav no. 1384: Rogad*h* (*ut est*) .i. síned*h*, (.i.) [*ut est*] "is [s]ær do flait*h* cib cui*n* ronc*ar* rogad*h* a lam*h* dia sétaib," .i. is sær don flait*h* cib cuin b*us* c*ar*t*h*anac leis sined a la*m* t*ar* cean*n* a seoit. *'Rogadh* 'extends', i.e., stretching out, *ut est* "it is free for the lord, whenever he desires, to stretch out his hands to his property," i.e., is is free for the lord, whenever he may desire, to stretch out his hands towards his property'.

the following privilege because of his rank], his *séts* are in his possession throughout the territory or until they are taken away from him according to law. It is in the following case that there is enough oath in his swearing:[21] when it is the testimony of a king during a battle, or a woman in labor, or a bishop between his host and his chalice, or a righteous man before death.[22] Or *aidbred* 'claiming', i.e., *ed* i.e., 'law', and *brí* i.e., 'word', and *odh* i.e., 'of a sage'.[23] The lawful testimony of the sage is: he takes his property with him immediately wherever he finds it when he has his compurgators with him, or there is enough oath in his swearing. Or *aidbred* 'claiming', i.e., *a dá brí súad*[24] 'two words of a sage', *a dá brá do sód* 'two eyebrows turning', two eyebrows for the transgression by him of looking at his *séts*.

Four [stages] precede the claiming, i.e., the proving, i.e., preliminary oath and seizing, possession, and judgment. Preliminary oath, an oath before an oath: if the man from whom it is claimed is present, i.e., two men swear for him supporting[25] an untrustworthy witness and one person swears for him supporting a trustworthy witness[26] that it was by theft that it was stolen: each possession [claimed] is lawful. Seizing afterwards, as it says: "he stretches a hand to his head of cattle."[27] Possession after that: he gives his possessions which he specifies into the hand of a neutral third party if it is claimed from an unworthy person, or even though a worthy person, if he does not submit to judgment. If he submits to judgment, however, they are given before witnesses into his own hand.[28] Judgment, however, [follows] after all of these.

---

21 In these situations, the oath alone is sufficient without the need for compurgators.

22 See the discussion in *GEIL* 203; and *CIH* 1570.1–8.

23 The preceding is another etymological gloss on *aidbred*. In this gloss, each of the syllables is broken down and assigned a meaning.

24 This is another series of etymological glosses on *aidbred* where, again, the word is broken down into syllables where each is assigned a meaning.

25 For this use of *i ndiaid* 'supporting' in swearing oaths, see also *The MacEgan Legal Treatise* § 2.2, and the discussion by Kelly, op. cit., 135.

26 On legally capable/trustworthy and incapable/untrustworthy witnesses, see *GEIL* 203; and Introduction, pp. 12–13 and 20–21.

27 Here and elsewhere throughout the text, livestock is given as the standard example of lost or stolen property. Naturally, the legal procedures given in the text can, with modificiations (see Heptad 64 later in this volume), apply to inanimate items as well. Livestock in Irish law, as in medieval Welsh law, is used frequently as an example; cf. *Ior.* §§ 111–115; and Jenkins, *The Law of Hywel Dda*, 156–169.

28 Presumably in this scenario the disputed livestock is given to the plaintiff until a judgment is given.

T*r*i nemid uaisli b*er*ait a fot*h*[a][29] di maigi*n* ina comit*echt* fei*n*, .i. esp*oc* ⁊ fl*aith* ⁊ fil*i*, uair gebid *gre*i*m* fira t*est*a briath*ar* cach æi. Dogni int esp*oc* for-tac*h* | p. 17a *for*a manc*h*u ⁊ fora esmanc*h*u *acht* ma esp*oc* aili nama, ł ni[30] dena*n*d *acht* fora manc*h*u fein nama.[31] Fl*aith*(a)[32] da*no* fora mem*r*a fei*n* nama. Fil*i* da*no* fora cach *acht* fil*i aile*, ł da*no* is *for*a finecin*el* fei*n* dogni. ⁊ fot*h*[33] n-i*n*ais dogni cac*h* æ dib-so.

Cach i*n*draic aidbres ac i*n*dr*aic*, ⁊ cac*h* esi*n*raic oc esinraic: is laisinti 'ga n-aidbrith*er* a imden*am* mad foth n-i*n*ais (n-i*n*ais)[34] dob*er*ait. Oc*us* is aire dlegar a imden*am* do*n*ti aca n-aidbrith*er* ar is de*m*in leo *con*id aice roge*n*air, ar dia*m*at do fir in aidb*r*eda nolecfithea a imdena*m*,[35] roba lai*n*d la cach aid-bread a *sét* gi*n*gub leis.

Seda n-aidb*r*ea, ł a se do n-aidbr*ed*:[36] sill*iud* ⁊ imradug*ud*,[37] reamud[38] ⁊ lamug*ud*, cron ⁊ br*eth*. Sill*iud*, .i. sill*iud* do f*or*a *sét*. Imradug*ud*, .i. f*or*a me*n*-main. Remud, .i. in od remi, resi*n* lanfir ł resi*n* l*eth*fir, in fer ł in dias, na t*u*c i creic no i cu*n*drad he. Lamug*ud*, .i. lam do tab*air*t ina c[h]en*n*. Cron, .i. a chur a c*r*on nosai*n*igen*n* i n-u*r*lai*m* coitci*n*d. Br*eth* do bre*ith*emai*n* air asa h-aithli. & is *cét*faid damad taisce[39] in lamug*ud* ina '*n* remud, co mb*eth* l*eth*fia*ch* gaiti uad a*n*d, ⁊ comad air dob*eth* in l*eth*fia*ch* ar nech rofit*ir* comad taisce rodles de a remud i*n*a in lamug*ud*. ⁊ comad iat g*r*ada in re*m*aid aire desa no da boaire[40]

---

29 Binchy, *CIH* 2164, n. e, suggests emending MS 'fot' to 'foluth', but cf. source F 'fota' below.

30 One letter has been erased after the ⟨n⟩.

31 *nama* was written above the line with reference marks by the scribe.

32 See also Binchy, *CIH* 2164, n. f. The final ⟨a⟩ has been inserted below the line by the scribe.

33 *acht … foth* was written in *marg. sup.* with reference marks by the scribe; see also Binchy, *CIH* 2164, n. g. Throughout the MS, the scribe has made a number of interlinear and marginal corrections. Some of these are in a much lighter colored ink than the surrounding text and written with a bluntly cut pen. The result is that some of the corrections and additions look as though they were written by someone else, but the distinguishing features of ⟨ł, f, and g⟩, for example, are the same.

34 See also Binchy, *CIH* 2164, n. h.

35 The suspension mark for ⟨m⟩ was mistakenly placed over the ⟨n⟩; see also Binchy, *CIH* 2164, n. i.

36 The scribe wrote *ł a se do n-aidbred* in *marg. sin.*, which could be either a gloss or a correction to *seda n-aidbrea* 'six things that pertain to claiming'; see also Binchy, *CIH* 2164, n. j, where he queries whether the phrase is a correction. Binchy states that there are reference marks, but they are not visible in the text itself.

37 The scribe originally wrote 'imragug̅', but corrected the first ⟨g⟩ to a ⟨d⟩ by writing ⟨ł d⟩ over the ⟨g⟩; see also Binchy, *CIH* 2164, n. k.

38 The ⟨a⟩ is written subscript.

39 *Taisce* is a later comparative form of *toísech*; *eDIL* s.v. *toísech* 'first, prior'.

40 The ⟨o⟩ was inserted below the line by the scribe; see also Binchy, *CIH* 2164, n. m.

Three honorable nobles take their property immediately accompanying themselves [i.e., they take their property with them], i.e., a bishop and a lord and poet because the the word of each of them will have the force of [oaths sworn by] compurgators. The bishop over-swears | his monks and members of the monastic community, except only another bishop, or he does not [over-swear] except his own monks only. A lord then [over-swears] the members of his own community only. A poet [over-swears] everyone except another poet, or else it is his own kindred that he over-swears. And each one of them makes a claim of growth.[41] p. 17a

Each worthy person who claims from a worthy person, each unworthy person who claims from an unworthy person: it is up to the one from whom it is claimed to provide the evidence, if they bring a claim of growth.[42] And [the] reason that the one from whom it is claimed ought to provide the evidence is because they[43] are certain that it was born in his possession, because if the plaintiff were allowed to provide the evidence, each would desire to claim *séts* though they might not be his.

Six things that pertain to claiming, or six [stages] pertaining to claiming: looking and intention, preliminary oath and seizing, possession and judgment. Looking, i.e., he looks at his *séts*. Intention, i.e., on his mind. Preliminary oath, i.e., the oath before it, before the full proof or before the half proof, the one man or the two men, that he did not give it in sale or in contract. Seizing, i.e., to put a hand on its [sc., the livestock's] head. Possession, i.e., putting his possessions which he specifies into the custody of a neutral third party. Judgment on it by a judge afterwards. And it is the opinion [of lawyers] that if the seizing were [to happen] before the preliminary oath, there is a half fine of theft due from him for it, and that the half fine would be [imposed] on him because [it is] someone who knows that his preliminary oath would be required of him before the seizing. And the grades of the preliminary oath

41 In other words, they each swear that the disputed livestock was born in their possession.

42 The defendant can refute the plaintiff's claim by stating that the disputed property is his by virtue of being born on his property. This refutation is also found in medieval Welsh law regarding the same legal situation; cf. *Ior.* § 114.1–9; and Jenkins, *The Law of Hywel Dda*, 162. See the discussion on this topic in the Introduction, p. 20, n. 61.

43 The change in number here is puzzling.

medo*n*acha uair fir gaiti fir in remaid, uair da*m*ad fir log enech, robu fir loigi en*ech* fa seotu. Uair ad*eir* dlig*ed*: "naill da*no* oet*h* fo seotu."[44] A n-aeda,[45] [.i.] a t*r*i, risi*n* se romai*n*d, ł is a*mlaid* is (n)æda he ⁊ in *seisidha*[46] romai*n*d ina ell*ach*, .i. a n-æda cu*r*ub nem*ed* f*r*i h-acc*r*a, .i. cu*r*ab g*r*ad *sechta*[47] ac aidb*r*ed a *sét* ac dui*ne* is isli inas, ⁊ cu*r*ab ne[i]ch[48] ni adagara,[49] .i. cu*r*ub lesi*n* nechsi*n* i*n*ni ac*r*as ⁊ nirob c*r*od nech *aile*, ⁊ curub tual*aing* slan ⁊ fretech, .i. sl*an* dara cen*n* budein ⁊ freitech tar cen*n* a fi*ne*.

F [*CIH* 1269.21–1270.15] .i. a[d]-firu[d],[50] .i. ad-fir-fod,[51] .i. in fod*h* dobe*rar* uime i*ar* fir,[52] .i. fiu, .i. imdenum,[53] .i. cen*n* co menma*r*, .i. ad*h*b*ire* bei*r*idh co h-ad*ha* (co h-adha),[54] go dlig*thech*, in [n]eim*ed ard*, .i. in ecl*ais* ł in rig*h*. **A fol*ad* di maig*h*in, ⁊rl.**[55] ⁊ is cutrum*a* ata int imdenan-si*n* uaith*e* f*or* manchu ⁊ esmanch*u* *iar* n-aidb*r*e*d* a set; ⁊ is leo imdenam do g*r*es, cid isel cid*h* uasal.

---

44 It is uncertain whether this is a direct quotation from a legal text or a gloss on a legal text. It should be noted, however, that OI *óeth* 'oath', which derives from PIE *$*h_1oi̯$-to-* was borrowed back in from Germanic at a later point in time (it is historically a loan word into Germanic from Celtic); *OED* s.v. *oath*. In this clause, it is also likely that *óeth* is glossing *noíll* 'oath'.

45 Both the edition and translation of the following three clauses is tentative due to the uncertain meaning of ⟨anaeda⟩. The situation is further complicated by the fact that there are reference marks between ⟨anaeda⟩ and ⟨at*r*i⟩ in the MS, but there is no corresponding text. Thus, it looks as though the scribe made a copying mistake, meant to fix it, but ultimately never did. The word spacing above implies that *aeda* is the nom. pl. of *óeth* 'oath', which is a m. *o*-stem; a nom. pl. form such as *aeda* would be unexpected in OI, but possible in MI due to the spread of the acc. pl. forms. The def. art. form *a n-* would also be unexpected for use with a m. nom. pl. noun. The emendation of ⟨næda⟩ to ⟨æda⟩ in the next clause suggests that the word is a 3 sg. pres. prototonic form of *aeded* 'act of swearing to', but this verb is poorly attested; *eDIL* s.v. *aeded*.

46 An ⟨i⟩ has been erased after the .ui.; see also Binchy, *CIH* 2164, n. n.

47 The ⟨a⟩ is written subscript.

48 I follow the emendation suggested by Binchy, *CIH* 2164, n. o.

49 The second ⟨a⟩ is written subscript; see also Binchy, *CIH* 2164, n. p.

50 I follow the emendation suggested by Binchy, *CIH* 1269, n. d. The gloss mirrors the tense, person, and number of the first word of the text, *aidbriud*; cf. the beginning of source A. The verb is probably a 3 sg, impv. of *ad-fíri* 'sues, claims'.

51 The ⟨od⟩ are written suprascript; see also Binchy, *CIH* 1269, n. e. This is an etymological gloss on *aidbriud*. The final element, *foth* 'claim, property, right', is picked up again in the following explanatory clause.

52 This gloss is written below the line.

53 These two glosses are written above the first two etymological glosses.

54 The scribe mistakenly wrote the phrase twice.

55 Although not written in larger letters, this phrase repeats part of the tract; see below.

are the lord of vassalry and the two *bóaire*s of intermediate rank[56] because the proof of the preliminary oath is the proof of theft, because if it were proof of honor-price, it would be proof of honor-price regarding his *sét*s. Because the law says: "a *noíll* 'oath' then is an oath regarding *séts*." The oaths,[57] i.e., three [are made], before the six [stages mentioned] previously, or it is thus that he swears it and the six [stages] above for his taking possession, i.e., the oaths that he is a noble suing, i.e., he is of the seven grades claiming his *sét*s from a person who is lower than he is, and [each] thing he sues for is his [possession], i.e., anything that he sues for belongs to him and is not the property of someone else, and he is exempt from liability and repudiation, i.e., exempt from liability on his own behalf and repudiation on behalf of his kindred.

F i.e., let him claim, i.e., to prove property, i.e., the property that is given to him after proof, i.e., worthy, i.e., proof, i.e., head to members, i.e., claiming that he conducts lawfully, legally, the high noble,[58] i.e., the church or the king. **His property from the place, etc.**[59] And it is equivalent to that proof from it [sc., the church] on monks and members of the monastic community regarding claiming its *sét*s; and proving by them always, whether low or high [social status].

56 Here the commentary refers to the rank of those who must swear along with the plaintiff with regard to the preliminary oath. The sense is that the compurgators must be of sufficient social status in order for their oath to carry legal weight. A *bóaire* was one of the classifications of free, non-noble farmers in medieval Ireland; *GEIL* 10.

57 The translation of the next three clauses is tentative, but the sense of the passage requires a meaning similar to 'oath'; see also the Brehon law transcripts, O'Donovan, 1920.

58 Cf. the series of etymological glosses at the beginning of source A.

59 This is an excerpt of the tract which has been repeated in the commentary.

Mad fora[60] memr*u* b*u*dein, geib*id* greim fira t*es*ta b*r*iat*har* in uasail oc imdenam fora memru, .i. luig*he* in e*pscuip*[61] ł in rig*h* fo soscel*a*, cid*h* ag aidb*hred* a set ł a ndlig*ed* a mancui*ne*. G*raidh* ecl*ais*i olcena ⁊ graid*h* tuait*hi*, fír t*es*ta leo ag imdenam a set f*or*a memr*u*; ⁊ dogab*ar* as-sin cona fír fo aic*ned* testa ł an*ntes*ta fír in aid*h*bre*da*. ⁊ is an*n* doall*a* nœill ina luige: in inb*aid* is fiad*hnais*i rig*h* f*r*i cath—⁊ *noch*o ris d'[ó]entoisc doc*h*uaid*h* re tab*air*t in cath*a* do denam na fiadhn*aise*, ⁊ dam*ad* riss, *con*a gaban*n* g*r*eim fíra—ł mna f*r*i h-uait*h*ne, .i. in tan is cetfe*cht*ach, .i. luig*he* fo t*r*i uait*he* ite*r* breit*h* in leinib ⁊ a lanassait, ł in tan bís ⁊ uaithne cin*n* in l*einib*[62] uait*he*; ł luig*he* in esp*uic* it*er* a p[h]*ars* ⁊ a c[h]ail*ech* geib*id* g*r*eim fira, ⁊ ni ris d'œntoisc doc*h*uaidh.

Remod*h* riasan lam*ugud* on fir [f]uil acin ag*r*a, .i. mod*h* roime riasan lanfír ł riasan l*eth*fír, .i. riasan lanfir im *secht*[63] cum*a*la ł riasan l*eth*fír im l*eth* *secht*[64] cum*ala*, ł fo aic*ned* fir meod*ongaite* lai*n* ł leth*e*, .i. in fer ł in dias, .i. fer
f. 4rb i ndiaig*h* t*es*ta ima set na fac*us* aicce, |[65] ⁊ œnfer uman set adces aice; fer i

60 The ⟨a⟩ is written subscript.

61 See also Binchy, *CIH* 1269, n. g.

62 See also Binchy, *CIH* 1269, n. h.

63 The scribe has written the Arabic numeral for 'seven' instead of the more usual Roman numeral.

64 The scribe has written the Arabic numeral for 'seven'.

65 This is the folio under the current foliation system; *CIH* 1269 uses the older system where this folio is labeled as f. 3b.

If it is on his own members,[66] the word of the noble will have the force of a compurgator [swearing an oath] for the members of his community, i.e., the oath of a bishop or the king on the Gospels [i.e., a king swearing on the Gospels], though it may be claiming his *sét*s or for the law of its monks. Ecclesiastical grades moreover and lay grades, a compurgator with them to prove their *sét*s for the members of their communities; and it is taken from that with the proof according to the nature of a trustworthy or untrustworthy witness proving the claim. And it is in the following case that there is enough oath in his swearing: when it is the testimony of a king during battle—he did not go purposely into battle to act as a witness,[67] and if he did, it does not have the force of proof—or a woman during labor, i.e., when it is [at] the first course [i.e., at the beginning of labor],[68] i.e., an oath three times from her between the birth of the child and its full birth,[69] or when it is [in the aforementioned stage of labor] and delivery of the child's head from her;[70] or the oath of a bishop between his host and his chalice will have the force of proof, and it was not purposefully that he went [between his host and his chalice].[71]

Preliminary oath before the seizing from the man who is sued, i.e., if it is earlier before the full proof or before the half proof, i.e., before the full proof regarding seven *cumal*s or before the half proof regarding half seven *cumal*s, or the same as the man who handles stolen goods fully or half [guilty], i.e., the one man or the two men, i.e., one man supporting a trustworthy witness regarding his *sét* that was not seen in his possession, | and one man regarding f. 4rb

66 Cf. source A above; this refers to over-swearing.

67 In other words, he did not give battle with the sole intention of making himself a witness.

68 Here *cétfechtach* 'of or belonging to the first time' is understood to refer to the beginning of labor rather than the first time a woman is in labor. The sense of the passage is that when the woman is in labor and potentially in danger of death, her sole testimony is accepted as proof.

69 The sense seems to refer to the later stages of childbirth when the child is in the process of being delivered.

70 I should like to thank the anonymous reader for helpful comments on this passage.

71 In a citation from a text on testimony, there is a list of ten situations where the testimony of a single person is considered to be sufficient evidence. These include a king in battle, a bishop between the host and his chalice, a sick man on the verge of death, a man who has waited at the altar, i.e., undergone an ordeal, and a woman in childbirth in danger of death; see the discussion in *GEIL* 203; *CIH* 1570.1–8; and *CCIH* 69.

ndiag*h* an*n*[t]*est*a uman sed adceas aice, ⁊ dias uman *sét* na fac*us* aice. ⁊ iss e luig*h*i dober: **na n-arl*a*[72] uag*h*a i rat*h*, ⁊rl-.**[73] ⁊ cuma iat grad*h* an ramad*h*, .i. aire deasa[74] no da boir*ig* m*edona*cha,[75] uair fior gaid*e* fior an ramadh, uair dama fior loig*h* en*ech*, robo fior l*oige*[76] en*ech* fo s*éot*u, uair ad*e*r dl*iged*: "nœill d*ano* oet*h* fo s*éot*u." ⁊ is cetf*aid* damad tusca an lamug*h*[ud][77] na in ramug*h*,go mb*et*dis *cóic* seoit ł l*eth*fiach gaid*e* fuir ind. Na nech fuatuig*h* set na bi[d] lais a comrach nar(?) iall(?)ad[78] bre*th*, ⁊ cumu air dobetis na fechsin, ar nech eoluch dfitir cuma tusc*a in* remad*h* na in lamug*h*[ud].

.i.[79] fo cetoir, .i. ní tet (dia no) og[80] esin*n*raic aid*h*bris, .i. in *sét* no in luig*h*i ł ina l*uige*,[81] .i. a fola[d] do maig*h*in las, *in* neme[d] mad*h* og memuir tig*h* co rug*a* a fol*ad* iarna imd*h*enam. Amail adber breat*h*um: "a fola[d] i coi*m*ita*cht* in ardnem*id* don maig*h*in a mbi g*o* ruct*har* adh a br*eth* ime." Trí nem*id* uaisli beruit a fot*h*a do maig*in* ina coimita*cht* fen, .i. easbog[82] ⁊ flait*h* ⁊ fil*i*, uair geb*id* greim fiuru t*est*a bria*th*ar cach ǽ. Dogni int espog fortach fora manc*ha* ⁊ for esmancha a*cht* ma easb*og aile* nama, no ní denan*n* a*cht* f*or*a ma*n*ch*u* fe*n* nama. Fl*aith* d*ano* f*or*a memr*u* fe*n* nama. Fil*i* d*ano* f*or* cac*h* a*cht* for fil*id aile*, no d*ano* is f*or*a cinel fe*n* doní. ⁊ is fot*h* n-inais dogní g*ach* ǽ dib*h*.

---

72 I understand this to be a 3 sg. pret. prototonic form of *as-luí*; see *eDIL* s.v. *as-luí* 'escapes, absconds, evades'.

73 Although not written in larger letters, the phrase *na n-arla uagha i rath* is part of the tract. It is taken into account below in the next part of this section. The commentary which accompanies it, however, belongs here thematically; cf. the similar commentary in source A above.

74 The second ⟨a⟩ is written subscript; see also Binchy, *CIH* 1269, n. i.

75 In the MS, this is written as 'm.i.ach̄'; cf. 'm.i.g.' for 'medongaite'.

76 See also Binchy, *CIH* 1270, n. a.

77 From *CIH* 1270.3–10, there are large gaps in the printed text. The reason is a large brown stain that runs left to right diagonally across the top portion of col. b. The Brehon Law transcripts of the same material (O'Curry, 2148) also have large gaps. In what follows, I have filled in the missing text without comment, except where my reading differs from *CIH*. I should like to thank the staff at the British Library for providing me with access to an ultraviolet light to view this section of the MS.

78 The reading of the last two words is tentative. The stain is particularly thick on this part of the MS and it looks like some of the ink might have run.

79 The commentary at *CIH* 1270.6–7 belongs with this section of the text. There is a *cenn fo eitte* symbol under the stain in the MS which was not visible to O'Curry or Binchy. Thus, these two lines of commentary belong with the fragment of tract *folu do maigin*.

80 I follow the emendation suggested by Binchy, *CIH* 1270, n. g.

81 Binchy, *CIH* 1270, n. i, queries whether this last word is a correction. It is difficult to determine whether the last phrase is a correction.

82 The ⟨a⟩ is written subscript.

the *sét* that was seen in his possession; one man supporting an untrustworthy witness regarding the *sét* that was seen in his possession, and two people regarding the *sét* that was not seen in his possession. And this is the oath that he swears: **that it did not part from him as a fief, etc.**[83] And the grades of the preliminary oath are, i.e., the lord of vassalry or the two *bóaire*s of intermediate rank, because the proof of the preliminary oath is proof of theft, because if it were proof of honor-price, it would be proof of honor-price regarding *sét*s, because [the] law says: "*noíll* 'oath' then is an oath regarding *séts*."[84] And it is the opinion [of lawyers] that if the seizing happened before the preliminary oath, there would be five *sét*s or the half penalty of theft imposed on him in that case. The one seizing *sét*s let him not have his binding that which the judgment does not bind(?),[85] and that fine is imposed on him, because every knowledgable person knows that the preliminary oath is before the seizing.

i.e.,[86] immediately, i.e., he does not go who claims from an unworthy person, i.e., the *sét* or of the oath or for his oath, i.e., he immediately possesses his property, the noble if it is with a member of the household so that he took his property after the proof. As a judge says: "his property accompanying the high noble immediately from [the place in] which it may be until law is given in judgement regarding it." Three high nobles who take their property immediately along with themselves, i.e., a bishop and a lord and a poet, because the word of each one will have the force of [an oath sworn by] compurgators. The bishop over-swears his monks and the members of the monastic community except only another bishop, or he does not [over-swear] except his own monks only. A lord then [over-swears] the members of his own community only. A poet then [over-swears] everyone except another poet, or else it is his own kindred that he over-swears. And each one of them makes a claim of growth.

83 This is another fragment of tract which has crept into the commentary. See the next section of edited tract below.
84 The same fragment of law is quoted in source A above.
85 The reading, and thus the translation, of this clause is uncertain.
86 The following section of commentary is preceded by the tract *folu do maigin*, CIH 1270.8.

AA[87] [*CIH* 1929.39–1930.1] .i. ma t*uc* fer ai[d]b*h*reda a ream*od*,[88] luig*h*e[d] inti oc*ar* ai[d]b*h*re[d] na fit*ir* gu*r*ab gat. ⁊ m*an*a luig*he*, berig*h* in fer [aidbreda][89] amac*h* i*ar*na imden*am* *con*a fiac*h* gaite, fo aic*ned* sell*aig* lainfeic*h* ł l*eth*feic*h*. ⁊ gingurab leis, *nos*be*ire* dia taisce co fest*ar* fer bun*aid*.

[1b] ⁊ iss e luig*hi* dober: nad n-arlui[90] uad i rath

A [*CIH* 2164.38–2166.26] .i. is e luigi dob*eir* fer in remaid: nac*h*as erluaidest*ar*[91] i rrath do celib he, ni rodilsig*ed* uad uili, nac*h* a l*eth*, nac*h* a t*r*ian.

"Dilsi in rat*ha* uili ar *secht* mbiadaib *co* ngab*ail* treb*air*e co taba*ir*t sét turclaide co tecmaisi*n* eca na fl*ath*a.[92]

Dilsi a l*eth*i ar t*r*i biadaib, co let*h* mbid. Dilsi a da t*r*ia*n* ar cet*r*i biadaib co (t)[d]a[93] *trian* mbid. Dilsi a t*r*in ar da[94] mbiadaib co t*r*iu*n* mbid. A dilsi uili

---

5 ⁊ ... dober] *om.* A. The fragments of tract in source F are embedded in the previous commentary and not written in the characteristically larger letters normally used for the tract; *CIH* 1269.40–41. ‖ nad] na n- F. ‖ arlui] arl*a* F. ‖ uad] uag*ha* F. ‖ i] *om.* A. ‖ rath] Followed by ⁊rl- F. Only A and F preserve this part of the tract.

---

87 Digests A (8) (source Q, Appendix 2), B (27) (source JJ, Appendix 3), and C (19) (source AA) repeat some of the same material, but with orthographic differences; *CCIH* 324. Digest B (27) is given in its entirety in Appendix 3, although it is likely that the last half of the digest entry does not belong with *Aidbred*. The relevant material from Digest C is given with the text and translation because material from *Aidbred* is found in multiple sections of Digest C. This same commentary is also found in sources Q and JJ.

88 The ⟨a⟩ is written subscript.

89 For this emendation, see source BB, *Aidbred* § 3.

90 *-arlui* is a 3 sg. pret. prototonic form of *as-luí*; see *eDIL* s.v. *as-luí*. The ⟨nar⟩ were inserted below the line by the scribe; see also Binchy, *CIH* 2164, n. q.

91 See *eDIL* s.v. *airlúaidid*, however, *eDIL* never gives the meaning; cf. *eDIL* s.v. *ar-lúaidi*. The verb glosses *arluí*.

92 This and the following ten paragraphs are quotations from a mix of commentary and tract from *Cáin Aicillne*, not all of which is found in the printed editions exactly as it is quoted here. The text is edited in *AL* 2: 222–340; and Rudolf Thurneysen, "Aus dem irischen Recht I," *ZCP* 14 (1923): 335–394. See also Rudolf Thurneysen, "Aus dem irischen Recht II," *ZCP* 15 (1925): 238–276, at 238 n. 1 and 259–260; idem, "Aus dem irischen Recht III," *ZCP* 15 (1925): 302–376, at 370–376; and idem, "Aus dem irischen Recht IV," *ZCP* 16 (1927): 167–230, at 205–210. See also *CCIH* 289. For this quotation, see also *CIH* 1786.26–29 and 1788.10–25 found in Appendix 5; *AL* 2: 270.6–26; and Thurneysen, "Aus dem irischen Recht I," 364–365.

93 I follow the emendation suggested by Binchy, *CIH* 2165, n. a.

94 The ⟨a⟩ is written subscript.

AA i.e., if the man claiming swore his preliminary oath, the one from whom it was claimed swears that he did not know it was stolen. And unless he swears [thus], the man claiming takes away [the property] after proving it along with the fine of theft, the same as that of a culpable onlooker [guilty to the extent of] full fine or half fine. And though it is not his, he takes it to guard it until [the] original owner is known.

[1b] and this is [the] oath that he swears: that it did not part from him as a fief

A i.e., this is the oath the man of the preliminary oath swears: that he did not give it as a fief for clients, [that] it was not all forfeited by him, nor half or it, nor a third of it.[95]

"The entire fief is forfeit after [paying] seven food rents[96] with taking a surety, with giving *sét*s of submission, until the lord's death occurs.

Half of it is forfeit after [paying] three and a half food rents. Two thirds of it is forfeit after [paying] four and two thirds food rents. A third of it after

95 For what follows, see *GEIL* 29–33.

96 The fief becomes the property of the client after the lord has died, if the client has paid the full rent for a minimum of seven years; *GEIL* 29.

ar *secht* mbiadaib. Dilsi t*r*in i*n* ratha ar scath enig na t*r*eb*aire* ⁊ ar ne*m*tab*air*t *sét* tu*r*claide. Dilsi a l*eth*i ar æ*n*biad*h*.[97]

Dilsi a da t*r*in ar da mbia(b)[d]*aib*.[98] Dilsi a t*r*in cen biad it*ir*, *seiss*id[99] cechtarde i*n* *cét*.[100] da biad ⁊ t*r*ian ari*n* mbiad tan*ai*se ⁊ a t*r*ian ce*n* biad it*ir*; co tecmaisi*n* eca na fl*ath*a si*n*.

Caide deit*h*b*ir* at*ar*ru-si*n* ⁊ in bail ata i Fut Fe*n*ec*h*uis:[101] 'na*ch* dile*s* dagrath destenaib fl*ath*a fo chletha [i] ci[u]l[102] ce*n* teora fe*cht*a fletigi, uair is rat*h* ce*n* seotu tu*r*claide ce*cht*ar de?' Cid fo*dera* co fuil dilsi t*r*in in rat*h*a ce*n* biad it*ir* su*n*d, ⁊ ce dobe*rtha* æ*n*biad ł da biad, mai*n*e t*h*o*racht* in biad uile, *con*ach am*al* tarba? Is e in fa*th* fo*dera*: comroga leo mar*æn* in fogn*am* a*n*d
p. 17b so, .i. re[103] co*m*arbaib | in fl*ath*a ⁊ re comarbaib in celi, ⁊ is e roga co*m*arba na fl*ath*a t*h*all in fogn*am*, ⁊ ni h-ail re comarbaib in celi he. ⁊ ce dobe*r*a æ*n*biad ł da biad, mai*n*e t*h*o*racht* in biad uili, is egen in rat*h* d'aisiuc.

Ma ta in fla*ith* ina beath*aid*, cid marb i*n* cele, is egi*n* in fogn*am* do den*am* no in rat*h* d'aisiuc. ⁊ cid fata bes ac fogn*am* in cele, mu*n*ar gab t*r*eb*air*i re[104] dilsi in rat*h*a, cid iar n-ecaib na flatha[105] is ecen in rath d'aisiuc no i*n* fogn*am* do denu*m*."[106]

---

97 The ⟨biad*h*⟩ were added at the end of the line by the scribe in a lighter colored ink. The ⟨a⟩ is written subscript; see also Binchy, *CIH* 2165, n. b.

98 I follow the emendation suggested by Binchy, *CIH* 2165, n. c.

99 The ⟨id⟩ were written above the line by the scribe.

100 The ⟨c⟩ is inserted below the line; see also Binchy, *CIH* 2165, n. d.

101 The phrase *i fut fenechius* is written *marg. sin.* in a hand which might not be the scribe's, but it is the same hand which has made other corrections to the text; see also Binchy, *CIH* 2165, n. e.

102 I follow the emendation suggested by Breatnach, *CCIH* 259.

103 The prep. *ré* here and below is unexpected; one would expect the prep. *la* as it would continue *leo* used in the previous clause and it is the usual prep. following *áil*.

104 The ⟨e⟩ was inserted below the line by the scribe; see also Binchy, *CIH* 2165, n. g.

105 The phrase *na flatha* is added above the line with a reference mark by the same hand which made the other corrections; see also Binchy, *CIH* 2165, n. h.

106 *denum* is written under *do* at the end of the line.

[paying] two and a third food rents. All of it is forfeit after seven food rents. A third of the fief is forfeit in exchange for the honor-price of the surety and for not giving *sét*s of submission. Half of it is forfeit after [paying] one food rent.

Two thirds of it is forfeit after [paying] two food rents. A third of it is forfeit without [paying] food rent at all, a sixth for each of the first two food rents and a third for the second food rent and a third without [paying] food rent at all; that is until the lord's death occurs.

What is the difference between these and where [it says] in *Fot Féinechais*:[107] 'nor is a good fief forfeit to the remnants of a lord concealed in death without three banqueting occasions, because each of them is a fief without *sét*s of submission?'[108] What is the reason that a third of the fief is forfeit without food rent at all here, and though one food rent or two food rents might be given, unless the entire food rent is forthcoming, that is not as a profit? This is the reason that brings it about: they themselves agree on the service in this case, i.e., with the heirs of the lord | and with the heirs p. 17b
of the clients, and the heirs of the lord yonder choose the service, and it is not the wish of the heirs of the client. And though he gives one or two food rents, unless the entire food rent is forthcoming, it is necessary to give back the fief.

If the lord is alive, though the client is dead, it is necessary to do the service or to give back the fief. And though the client may have been serving a long time, unless he takes a surety against forfeiture of the fief, even after the lord dies it is necessary to give back the fief or to do the service."

107 See *CCIH* 258–259, for a discussion of this fragmentary legal text.

108 The interpretation of this passage relies on the edition and translation in *CCIH* 259. The 'remnants' are understood by Breatnach to refer to the dead lord's clients.

& is as gabur si*n*: "mana rofera fla*ith*[109] *séot*u tu*r*claide, is[110] dil*es* trian[111] a *sét* iar n-ecaib na fl*ath*a do*n* c*h*eli (*for*sin celi)[112] ce*n*ni robiath*a* itir. Ma robiath*a* fa æn, is dil*es* l*eth* na *sét*. Ma robiath*a* fa di, is dil*es* a da t*r*ian. Ma robiath*a* fa t*r*i, is dil*es* uile mai*n*e rome*th*a fair."[113]

⁊ da la dec caemt*echt*a cac*h*a bliadna, .i. noc*h*a daerrath si*n* ⁊ noc*h*a saerrath *acht* cin*neth* airithe arin mbiath*ad* ⁊ arin mancuine. Armot*h*a is biathad o*cht*air cac*h*a bliadna co cend o*cht* mbliadan, .i. daerrat*h* eiside an*n*-seic, ⁊ isi*n* o*cht*mad bliad*nai* is díl*es* é ar *secht* mbíadaib co ngabail trebaire.[114]

& is ass gabur: "a dilsi *ar secht* mbiad*aib co* ngab*ail* t*r*eba*i*ri, co tab*air*t sét tu*r*claide, co tecmaisi*n* eca na fl*atha*."[115]

"Dil*es* cac*h* tu*r*creic i*ar* fogn*am* tec*h*ta ce*n* met*h*, ce*n* foll*ugud*, ce*n* elgui*n*, ce*n* ecell co cen*n secht* mbliad*nae* ma fl*aith* bes m*ar*b."[116]

---

109 *flaith* is added above the line in the same hand which made the other corrections; see also Binchy, *CIH* 2165, n. h.

110 Across from this word in *marg. dext.*, written in the same hand as the other corrections, is the word 'se*n*ch[as]'; see also Binchy, *CIH* 2165, h. i.

111 The ⟨r⟩ is inserted below the line by the scribe; see also Binchy, *CIH* 2165, h. j.

112 I follow the emendation suggested by Binchy, *CIH* 2165, n. k.

113 The commentary here is quoting a portion of tract from *Cáin Aicillne*; cf. *CIH* 486.9–12: Mani roera flaith seotu turcluide, is dilis | [p. 42b] trian na set iar n-ecaib na fl*ath*a don ceili, mani rometha fair forsin cele, ceni robiatha eitir. Ma robiatha fa æn, is dilis a leth na set. Ma robiat*h*a fa di, is dilis a da trian na set. Ma robiatha fa tri, is dilis uili mana rometha fair. 'Unless a lord bestowed *sét*s of submission, a third of the *sét*s are forfeit | [p. 42b] after the lord's death to the client, unless the client failed him in any duty, though he did not provide refection at all. If he provided refection once, half of the *sét*s are forfeit. If he provided refection twice, two thirds of the *sét*s are forfeit. If he provided refection thrice, the entirety is forfeit, unless he [i.e., the client] failed him in any duty.'; *AL* 2: 262.14–19; and Thurneysen, "Aus dem irischen Recht I," 363–364.

114 This paragraph is written in *marg. sup.* by the scribe with reference marks; see also Binchy, *CIH* 2165, n. l. In *marg. sup. inter. col.*, the phrase ⟨.i. gne .ii.⟩, *.i. gne aile*, 'i.e., different version' was partially cut off as a result of trimming the top of the page. It is not possible to determine whether the phrase was written by the scribe. It is possible that the material comes from another version of *Cáin Aicillne*.

115 Cf. the quotation from commentary to *Cáin Aicillne* above at *CIH* 2164.40–41 and see Appendix 5, *CIH* 1788.13–14.

116 The commentary is quoting a portion of tract from *Cáin Aicillne*; cf. *CIH* 486.24–25; *AL* 2: 268.11–13; Thurneysen, "Aus dem irischen Recht I," 364–365; idem, "Aus dem irischen Recht II," 260.

And that is taken from: “unless a lord provides *sét*s of submission, a third of the *sét*s are forfeit to the client after the death of the lord though refection was not provided at all. If refection had been provided once, half of the *sét*s are forfeit. If refection had been provided twice, a third of it is forfeit. If refection had been provided three times, the entirety is forfeit unless there had been a failure [in providing refection] for him [sc., the lord].”

And twelve days of accompanying of every year, i.e., that is neither base fief nor free fief but a certain agreement for the refection and for the service due. Afterwards it is providing refection for eight people every year until the end of eight years, i.e., this is base fief here, and in the eighth year it is forfeit for seven food rents with taking a surety.

And it is taken from: “it is forfeit after seven years with taking a surety, with giving *sét*s of submission, until the lord’s death occurs.”

“Every fore-pledge is forfeit after proper service without failure, without neglect, without malice, without carelessness until the end of seven years if the lord is dead.”

"Nimt*ha* mad e in celi bes m*ar*b. Dlig*id* in fl*aith*[117] cel*e* do co*m*arbaib in celi ar de mis fri fuir*ired* fri gell fri dail fri dlig*ed* fri ruba fri fuba."[118] & cid fech dleg*ar* do*n* cheli, noc*ha* dligen*n* inni dogeb isi*n* rath do cu*r* indtib. ⁊ gid athgab*ail* gab*ar* de, nocha dleg*ar* na *séotu* dogeib i rrat*h* do gab*ail* *in*dtu ł go rofogna[119] in rat*h* am*ail* adubart*mar*[120] romai*nd*. ⁊ is as gabar sin: "a u*r*coilltib athg*abal*a."[121]

No bo in raith, .i. cid særrat*h*,[122] cid dærrat*h*, *no*cha dleg*ar* a ngab*ail* a cinaid nechtair dib, ł curub diles do*n* c*h*eli;[123] dærrat*h* sin.

Mad iar særath*aib* im*murro*, ci ar[r]uibdith*er*[124] in fl*aith* *fichet* bli*adna* ł *cethracha* bliad*na*, doaiscebat[125] collna s*ét* do comarbaib. & adeir: "sær do*n* fl*aith* cib cui*n* roc*ar*a rogad a lai*m*i dia s*ét*aib. Is mesi mai*n*e astaith*er* fri somai*n*e,"[126] .i. is cui*m*gech fl*aith* særrath aisiuc na s*ét* *tu*c isi*n* rat*h* mine sire in cele fuill*ed* re særrath co raib dærrat*h* a*n*d, ⁊rl-. Is aire adbeir-sin: "is mesech in cele mad sgid[127] lais gin astu cel*sine* fair, ⁊ is mesech a athcu*r* cib cui*n* rocara, *acht* forogglana seotu na fl*ath*a *co*na somai*n*e do neoch foruillet a mamaib na fl*ath*a."[128]

117 A letter has been erased between the ⟨f⟩ and the ⟨l⟩; see also Binchy, CIH 2165, n. m.

118 The commentary quotes another portion of the tract from *Cáin Aicillne*; cf. CIH 486.31–33 and 1788.1–3; AL 2: 268.14–18; and Thurneysen, "Aus dem irischen Recht I," 364–365.

119 The ⟨a⟩ is written subscript although it is difficult to determine whether it a later correction by the scribe; see also Binchy, CIH 2165, n. n.

120 The ⟨u⟩ is written above the ⟨d⟩.

121 The origin of this quotation is unknown.

122 The ⟨rat*h*⟩ was inserted below the line by the scribe; see also Binchy, CIH 2165, n. o.

123 *curub … cheli* is added above the line with reference marks by the scribe; see also Binchy, CIH 2165, n. p.

124 I follow the emendation suggested by Bergin, who interprets the form as the perfective pres. subj. pass. of *ar-biatha*; Osborn Bergin, "On the Syntax of the Verb in Old Irish," *Ériu* 12 (1938): 197–214, at 206, n. 3. See also *eDIL* s.v. *ar-biatha* 'feeds, supplies food rent'; and Thurneysen, "Aus dem irischen Recht II," 249, n. 2.

125 The verb appears to be a 3 pl. pres. subj. of *do-aisicc* 'makes restitution, restores'.

126 The commentary quotes part of the tract from *Cáin Ṡóerraith*; cf. CIH 1775.27–28: Saoer do flaith cip cun rocara rogad laime dia setuib. Is misech maine astaith*er* fri sommuine n-aircendch*a*. 'The lord is free to stretch out his hand to his *sét*s whenever he likes. He is entitled [to do so] unless it is bound by a fixed [agreement regarding] revenue [or service].'; AL 2: 210.14–16; and Thurseysen, "Aus dem irischen Recht II," 248–251. The text is edited in AL 2: 194–220; and Thurneysen, "Aus dem irischen Recht II," 238–259; see idem, "Aus dem irischen Recht IV," 211–213, for addenda and corrigenda. See also CCIH 288–289.

127 For *sgith*; see also Binchy, CIH 2166, n. b.

128 The commentary quotes another part of the tract from *Cáin Ṡóerraith*; cf. CIH 1774.16: ⁊ is meisech athcur cidp cuin rocara 'And he is entitled to give [it] back whenever he

"It is not the case if it is the client who is dead. The lord is entitled to a client from the heirs of the client for two months for refection, for pledge, for assembly, for law, for defense, for attack." And though debts are owed by the client, he [sc., the lord] is not entitled to that which he will receive as fief to pay for them. And though distraint is taken from him, he [sc., the lord] is not entitled to seize the *sét*s that he will receive as fief, or until the fief serves as we have said previously. And that is taken from: "from legal decisions regarding distraint."

Or cows of the fief, i.e., whether free fief or base fief, he [sc., the lord] is not entitled to seize them for the liability of either of them, or until it is [sc., they are] forfeit to the client; that is base fief.

If it is according to free fiefs, however, though the lord may have received food rent[129] for 20 years or 40 years, the original *sét*s must be returned to his heirs. And it says: "the lord is free to stretch out his hand to his *sét*s whenever he likes. He is entitled [to do so] unless it is bound by profit," i.e., a lord of free fiefs is able to take back the *sét*s he gave for the fief unless the client asks for an addition to the free fief so that it would be a base fief then, etc. The reason that it says that: "the client is entitled not to bind the clientship on him if he does not want to do so. And he is entitled to give it back whenever he likes, but he discharges [the debt of] the lord's *sét*s with the profit that adds to it [while he is] subject to the lord's obligations."

---

likes.'; *AL* 2: 206.7–8; Thurneysen, "Aus dem irischen Recht II," 246–248; and idem, "Aus dem irischen Recht IV," 211–212.

129 See Bergin, "On the Syntax of the Verb in Old Irish," 206, n. 3.

⁊ ce der si*n*, adb*eir* a n-i*n*ad *aile*: "o beit maræ*n* ina mbeth*aid*, in fl*aith* ⁊ in cele, ł nec*ht*ar de, *noch*a cu*m*aing imscar do g*r*es i ssærrat*h*aib ce*n* achur saire co[130] *séot*u."[131]

Ona biad maraen[132] ina mbeath*aid* no na biad nec*ht*ar de, gunic com*arba* f*or* comarba gi*n* *séot*u a athcur, no ua f*or* ua, ł iarmo f*or* iarmo, ł i*n*dua f*or* i*n*dua. Is a*n*d conic com*arba* for araili a athcu*r* in tan is o*n* g*r*ad is nesa rogab rath. ⁊ ma ta g*r*ad et*ar*ru, is ua [for ua].[133] Mas da g*r*ad [ḟ]uil et*ar*ru, is iarmo[134] for i*ar*mo. Mas t*r*i g*r*aid, is i*n*dua f[o]r(i)[135] h-i*n*dua. Is as gabur si*n*:[136] "rat*h* ernes *aire*[137] tuisi do boaire ni h-at*h*cuirth*er*[138] co n-athcu*r*ith*er* ua for ua," uair in lin g*r*ad bes it*er* inti dob*eir* in rath ⁊ inti dia tab*arr*[139] is e lin coibdelach[140] aicheras[141] in rath gi*n* *séot*u; ⁊ særrath si*n*. Is e in fa*th* na cu*m*ai*n*g com*arba* f*or* araili a at*h*cu*r* ara i*n*dligt*h*ig[142] do rath do gab*ail* ac*h*t on g*r*ad is nesa.

& atb*eir* a n-inad *aile*: "conic duine imsgar gid re' grad fl*ath*a budein gid
p. 18a re grad fl*ath*a ec*ht*rand *ar* acobair | saire co *séot*u ł gan seotu i særrathaib, ⁊rl-."[143]

---

130 The word *co* is inserted above the line by the scribe; see also Binchy, *CIH* 2166, n. c.

131 This might be another quotation from part of the tract from *Cáin Ṡóerraith*, but, if so, it is not attested elsewhere.

132 The second ⟨a⟩ is written subscript.

133 I follow the emendation suggested by Binchy, *CIH* 2166, n. d.

134 The ⟨iar⟩ is inserted above the line with a reference mark by the scribe; see also Binchy, *CIH* 2166, n. e.

135 I follow the emendation suggested by Binchy, *CIH* 2166, n. f.

136 At the end of this line in the MS, the words 'bre*th*a ne*m*i in*n* so' are written in *marg. dext.* by the scribe. The text which follows *Is as gabur sin* is commentary from *Bretha Nemed Toísech*; cf. *CIH* 2230.24–24: Rath eirnes aire tuise (ł ard) do bouire ni atcuirter *co n*-aithcuirter ua for ua, co taisbenud bid tanaisi eca o chomorbu do comorbodh. 'A fief that a lord of precedence bestows to a *bóaire* is not returned until it is returned by a grandson to a grandson, until proof that there may be an heir following death from heir to heir.' It should noted that the scribe corrected 'tuise' to 'ard', but this might be a mistake; see Binchy, *CIH* 2230, n. k. See also *CCIH* 89 and 188–191.

137 *aire* is inserted below the line by the scribe.

138 The ⟨r⟩ is written over a minim as a correction.

139 The ⟨a⟩ is written subscript; cf. Binchy, *CIH* 2166, n. h.

140 Two letters have been erased after this word; see also Binchy, *CIH* 2166, n. i.

141 The scribe corrected 'aigeras' to 'aicheras' by writing 'ł ch' above the ⟨g⟩. Binchy, *CIH* 2166, n. j, suggests reading this word as *aithchuires*.

142 Binchy, *CIH* 2166, n. k, queries whether this word should be read as *dliged*.

143 This is another quotation from commentary associated with *Cáin Ṡóerraith*; *CIH* 1774.29–30; *AL* 2: 206.24–25; and Thurneysen, "Aus dem irischen Recht II," 246–248.

And though it says that, it says in another place: "when they are both alive, the lord and the client, or one of them, there is not the ability to separate ever in free fiefs without returning freedom [sc., freedom from the bond of clientship] with the *séts*."

When they are both not alive, or either of them is, heir can [separate] from heir without returning the *séts*, or grandson from grandson, or great-grandson from great-grandson, or great-great-grandson from great-great-grandson. It is then that an heir can [separate] from another by returning them [sc., the *séts*] when it is from the nearest grade that he accepted the fief. And if there is a grade between them, it is grandson from grandson. If it is two grades that are between them, it is great-grandson from great-grandson. If it is three grades, it is great-great-grandson from great-great-grandson. And that is taken from: "a fief that a lord of precedence bestows to a *bóaire* is not returned until it is returned by a grandson to a grandson," because the number of grades that are between the one who gives the fief and the one to whom it is given is the [same] number of kinsmen who return the fief without *séts*; and that is free fief. The reason an heir is not able to separate from another by returning [the *séts*] is on account of the illegality for him to take a fief except from the grade that is closest.

And it says in another place: "a person can separate either from [the] grade of his own lord or from the grade of an external lord because it binds | p. 18a
freedom with *séts* or without *séts* for free fiefs, etc."

Is a*n*d is a[th]chur saire co seotu ł gi*n* sé*ot*u in tan is e i*n* g*r*ad fl*ath*a is nesa dorat i*n*t rath dia celi; at*h*cu*r*id-seic co seotu ⁊ athcu*r*id com*arba* for com*arba* ge*n* seoto.

Co*n*scarat ci*n* imdiub*airt*, .i. is e co*m*rai*n*d ait*h*fegth*ar* ite*r* fl*aith* særrait*h* ⁊ a celi: as ⁊ los ⁊ g*ert* ⁊ in [ḟ]orb*airt* i*n* rat*h* do dul i n-ag*aid* in cutr*uma* biata ⁊ manc*h*ui*ne* t*ucustar* in celi do*n* fl*aith*. ⁊ ma[144] mairid i*n* rat*h*, nochan [ḟ]uil fuill*ed* do les, u*air* cia dosroi*m*li æs. ⁊ mai*ne* m*aire*nd, aith*gin* feib rorat*h* & da rer-si*n* cid a cor ł a cun*n*rad c*uire*s in celi iat, nocha[145] dil*es* on fl*aith* iat. Gid a ngait, ł a n-anfis, ł ar eci*n* b*e*r*ar* o*n* celi iat, noc*ha* dil*es* o*n* fl*aith* iat.

X [*CIH* 85.10–17][146] Is and ata int at*h*cur s*aire* gu seotu i*n* inbaid*h* marit aræn in flait*h* ⁊ in ceile, no marid*h* neac*htar* de: nucu cæ*mh*nac*air* an*n* sein i*n*t *aire* d'at*h*cur gen seotu. Is an*n* ata int at*h*cur saire ce*n* seotu i*n* i*n*baid*h* na m*air*-end neac*htar* de: cui*n*nig comarbo f*or* co*mhar*ba[147] in dæire d'athc*h*ur ce*n* seotu, ⁊ is o*n* g*r*ad is neso ragabad*h* i*n* rath an*n*. ⁊ damad *ar* da g*r*ad nucubad cui*mh*cec*h* a at*h*cur ł cu ndernad ua f*or* ua. ⁊ damad dar tri g*r*ad, nugubad*h* cui*mh*gech a at*h*cur ł gu nde*r*nad*h* *iar*mo f*or* *iar*mo. ł gumad*h* bit*h* ac*h* in fognu*m* fa comlin do grad*h*aib d*arar* gabad*h* i*n* rat*h*, nac*h* bad*h*[148] cuimgec*h* a atc*h*ur.

O'Dav [*CIH* 1522.1–2][149] Ruibdith*er*, .i. biath*ad*, *ut est* "sær do co*m*arbaib na fl*ath*a, cid*h* ruibdith*er* in flait*h* *fichet* bl*iadan*," .i. ce biat*ar*.

[1c] na cundrad

A [*CIH* 2166.26–38] .i. noc*ha* d*e*rnaig cu*n*dr*ad* de, ni rodilseoch*ad* e uili, nac*h* a leth, nac*h* a tri*an*. U*air* ma roc*huir* i cor ł a cu*n*drad, ⁊ cu*r*a dil*es* a*n*d iat, is indligth*ech* do a n-aidbred, ⁊ is a*n*d ata a landilsi.

---

21 na cundrad] Only source A preserves this part of the tract.

---

144 After this form a '⁊' has been erased; see also Binchy, *CIH* 2166, n. m.

145 The ⟨a⟩ is written subscript.

146 The commentary from source X is associated with *Cáin Ṡóerraith* and corresponds in part to material in source A beginning at *CIH* 2166.4.

147 The phrase *for comharba* is added in *marg. sin.* with reference marks by the scribe; see also Binchy, *CIH* 85, n. a.

148 The word 'bad*h*' was inserted above the line by the scribe; see also Binchy, *CIH* 85, n. b.

149 O'Dav no. 1385.

It is there that freedom is returned with *sét*s or without *sét*s when it is the nearest grade of a lord who had given the fief to his client; he returns [it] with *sét*s and an heir returns [it] to an heir without *sét*s.

They separate without mutual defrauding, i.e., the joint-division that is reckoned between a lord of free fief and his client: milk and young cattle and manure and increase of the fief is set against the amount of food and of labor the client had given to the lord. And if the fief remains [alive],[150] he does not get an addition with it, even though age may have wasted them. And if they are not alive, restitution of the possession that he bestowed and according to that though in contract or in terms the client changes them, they are not forfeit from the lord. Though they are taken from the client by theft, or in ignorance, or by force, they are not forfeit from the lord.

X It is here that there is returning of freedom with *sét*s whenever both the lord and the client are alive, or one of them is alive: the lord in that case was not able to return [it] without *sét*s. It is here the freedom is returned without *sét*s whenever neither of them is alive: the heir demands the heir of the base client to return [it] without *sét*s, and it is from the closest grade who gave the fief then. And if there are two grades, he does not have the ability to return it until it had been done by a grandson to a grandson. And if there are three grades, he does not have the ability to return it until it had been done by a great-grandson to a great-grandson. Or until it is permanent except for the service in equal number to the grades beyond which he takes the fief, he would not be able to return it.

O'Dav *Ruibdither* 'he is supplied food rent,' i.e., feeding, *ut est* "[it is] free for the lord's heirs, though the lord *ruibdither* 'is supplied food rent' for 20 years," i.e., though he is fed.[151]

[1c] or contract

A i.e., that he has not made a contract with it, all of it was not forfeited, nor half of it, not a third of it. Because if he had changed [them] in bargain or contract, and they are forfeit by bargains then, it is unlawful for him to claim them, and it is then that there is their full forfeiture.

---

150 The phrase refers to livestock.

151 See Stokes, "O'Davoren's Glossary," 442, no. 1385.

Cor da so*chund* co fis co treb*aire*: is fast*aid*e it*er* diub*airt* ⁊ bu*n*ad cu*n*dar*tha* ar cet*ri* h-uarib *fich*it.[152]

Cor da s*ochonn*[153] co treb*ai*ri, ce*n* fis: is[154] fast*aid*i bun*ad* cu*n*dart*ha* ⁊ l*eth* a diub*ar*ta ar *ceth*ra[155] h-u*airi*b *fich*it,[156] ⁊ dob*eir* l*eth* a diub*ar*ta[157] amuig no co raib *dech*mad ina ait[it]i*n*.[158]

Cor da so*chund* co fis, ce*n* treb*ai*ri: is fastait*h*i bu*n*ad cu*n*d*artha*[159] ⁊ *tria*n a diub*ar*t ar *ceth*ra h-uairib *fich*it,[160] ⁊ dob*eir* da t*ria*n a diub*ar*ta amuig no co raib *dech*maid *in*a aititi*n*.

Cor da so*chund*, ci*n* fis ci*n* treb*airi*:[161] is fastait*h*i[162] a bu*n*ad cu*n*dart*ha* uad ar *ceth*ra[163] h-u*air*ib *fich*it,[164] ⁊ dob*eir* a diub*air*t amuig ł co raib *dech*mad[165] ina aititi*n*, .i. b*erair* a co*m*airli comait*hech*.[166]

Is dil*e*s uait*h*ib fe*n* erna redib-si*n*, ⁊ *con*necat a ci*n*d ⁊ a coibdel*aig* arna redib arna dir doib.

[1d] na h-oin

A [*CIH* 2166.38–2167.6] .i. noc*ha* t*uc* ar ias*acht*, ni dodilsech*ad* e uili, na*ch* a le*th*, na*ch* a t*ria*n. ł in oi*n* atbaill ac neoch: ma 'trubull a oi*n*-sium aci*n* fir-si*n*, masa cutr*um*a, bid agaid i n-ag*aid*. Masa l*eth* ł trian fuil er*ar*ru,[167] dil-sit[h]ar[168] fon in*nus*-si*n*.

---

14 na h-oin] Only source A preserves this part of the tract.

---

152 The ⟨it⟩ are written above the line of text.
153 I follow the expansion suggested by Binchy, *CIH* 2166, n. n.
154 The ⟨s⟩ was added below the line by the scribe.
155 The ⟨ra⟩ are written above the line of text.
156 The ⟨it⟩ are written above the line of text.
157 The ⟨a⟩ is written subscript.
158 I follow the emendation suggested by Binchy, *CIH* 2166, n. o.
159 The ⟨a⟩ is written subscript.
160 The ⟨it⟩ are written above the line of text.
161 The ⟨e⟩ was added below the line by the scribe; see also Binchy, *CIH* 2166, n. p.
162 Binchy, *CIH* 2166, n. q., notes the erroneous suspension mark over the first ⟨t⟩.
163 The ⟨ra⟩ are written above the line of text.
164 The ⟨it⟩ are written above the line of text.
165 The ⟨mad⟩ are written above the line of text.
166 *berair* … *comaithech* are written in *marg. sin.* with reference marks by the scribe; see also Binchy, *CIH* 2166, n. r.
167 The ⟨ru⟩ was added below the line by the scribe; see also Binchy, *CIH* 2167, n. a.
168 This word was added above the line by the scribe; see also Binchy, *CIH* 2167, n. b. The verb *dílsid* 'hands over, abandons' is sometimes used for *dílsigid* 'makes forfeit', which is used in the first line of the commentary; *eDIL* s.v. *dílsid*.

A bargain [between] two legally competent people with knowledge, with a surety: both defrauding and original contract are bound from 24 hours.[169]

A contract [between] two legally competent people with a surety, without knowledge: original contract and half for defrauding are bound from 24 hours, and he recovers half for defrauding until ten days [have passed] from acknowledging it.

A contract [between] two legally competent people with knowledge, without a surety: original contract and a third for defrauding are bound after 24 hours, and he recovers two thirds for defrauding until ten days [have passed] from acknowledging it.

A contract [between] two legally competent people without knowledge, without a surety: the original contract is binding by him after 24 hours, and he recovers for defrauding until ten days [have passed] from acknowledging it, i.e., a neighbor's assessment is given.

It is forfeit from them themselves after these time periods, and their chiefs or their relatives are able [to annul the contracts] after the time periods because it is their right [to do so].

[1d] or private loan[170]

A i.e., that he did not give [it] as a loan, all of it was not forfeited, nor half of it, nor a third of it. Or the loan is forfeit to someone: if his loan has fallen forfeit to that man [sc., to another man], if it is equivalent, it will be set off against each other. If it is a half or a third [difference] that is between them, it is forfeited in that manner.

169 For the laws regarding damages recoverable for purchasing defective property, see McLeod, *Early Irish Contract Law*, 39–41. This and the following three paragraphs are related to some of the commentaries in §§1 and 5 (sources A and B) of *Córus Bésgnai*. The commentaries are not copies of each other, and the ordering of material is different in both. Breatnach has collected a series of citations with similar wording in Appendix 3 of his edition of *Córus Bésgnai*, 319–321; the commentary here is not included in his discussion.

170 For the different types of loans recognized in early Irish law, see McLeod, "*Ón* and *airliciud*: Loans in Medieval Irish Law;" and *Cáin Ónae*.

Is a*n*d ata landilsi na h-o*n*a: i*n* ta*n* is oi*n* d'fir fi*n*e ce*n* fonaid*m* a taisic, ci*n* fis difoicheda, is [s]l*an*. Dia *m*be fonaid*m* a taisiuc, is l*eth*ai*th*g*in*.

Is a*n*d ata a l*eth*dilsi: in ta*n* is oi*n* d'fir anfi*n*e ce*n* fonaid*m* a taisic, ce*n* fis difoithe*da*,[171] is l*eth*ai*th*g*in*. Dia *m*be fonaid*m* taisic, is ai*th*g*in*.

Is a*n*d ata[172] *tri*a*n* dilsi: i*n* ta*n* is deor*ad*, da *tri*a*n* dorigne faill uimpi.

[1e] na h-aithne

A [*CIH* 2167.7–33] Dilsi n h-ait*h*ne uili ar *déc* bliadnaib. Dilsi a l*eth*e ar *cóic* bliadnaib. Dilsi a *tr*in ar *tr*i bliad*naib* co *tr*iu*n* mbliadna gan roc*ht*ain dia fis, cia tangas[173] dia fis.[174] Do *sét*aib *aile* rogell*ad* in log a*n*d si*n* ara coi*m*et,[175] u*air* da*m*ad di fei*n*, nochbud dil*es* di do gres *acht dech*mad na rai*n*de [ḟ]acb*us*[176] tall cach n-u*air* e ara taisce.[177] Masa deit*h*birius fo*dera* gan tor*acht*ain da fis, is i*n*a*n*d ⁊ rotista[178] ⁊ rogellta do c*h*urp na h-ait*h*ne. Masa i*n*det*h*biri*us* fo*dera*, is i*n*and ⁊ rogellta do *sét*aib *aile*. Dilsi a l*acht*a ⁊ a ng[n]i*m*raid do*n*ti i fuil*et* lai*m*, *acht* mu*n*ar *acht*aiged*h* a ne*m*caithi*um*.

p. 18b Ma docuaid fer bun*aid* da fis ca*ch*a bliad*na*, a roga do i*n* fuaslaicfe hi ł na fuaslaicfi.

Mai*n*e dech*aid* it*ir*, is a roga do*n* fir tall i*n* tib*r*e re fuaslucad i, ł inn i fei*n* bias aigi. Ma docuaid co h-anmi*n*ic ⁊ no*ch*a dech*aid* ca*ch*a bliad*na*, cuid na mbliad*na* na rai*n*ic fo*n* mud *cét*na; log dlig*thech*[179] rogell*ad* a*n*d si*n*, ⁊ da*m*ad

---

6 na h-aithne] Only source A preserves this part of the tract.

---

171 Binchy, *CIH* 2167, n. d, notes that this form should be read as *difoicheda*.

172 *ata* was added below the line by the scribe; see also Binchy, *CIH* 2167, n. e.

173 One would expect the first vowel to be ⟨o⟩ for the 3 sg. pres. ind. rel. of *tongaid* 'swears'.

174 *gan ... fis* was written in *marg. sin.* with reference marks by the scribe; see also Binchy, *CIH* 2167, n. f.

175 The phrase *ł ara coimet* was added above the line by the scribe; see also Binchy, *CIH* 2167, n. g.

176 'b*us*' was added above the line by the scribe with a reference mark.

177 *ara taisce* was added above the line of text by the scribe with reference marks; see also Binchy, *CIH* 2167, n. h.

178 This verb form is a 3 sg. past. subj. pass of *do-icc* 'comes, approaches'.

179 See Binchy, *CIH* 2167, n. j.

It is in the following case that there is full forfeiture of the loan [by the lender]: when the loan is to a kinsman without guarantee to return it, without knowledge of accidental damage, he [sc., the borrower] is free from liability. If there is a guarantee to return it, it is half restitution [which the borrower owes the lender].

It is in the following case that there is half forfeiture of it [by the lender]: when it is a loan to a non-kinsman without guarantee to return it, without knowledge of accidental damage, it is half restitution. If there is a guarantee of return, it is restitution.

It is in the following case that there is forfeiture of a third [of it by the lender]: when it is [a loan to] a stranger [sc., not someone from the local community], two thirds [if] he [sc., the stranger] has committed negligence regarding it.

[1e] or deposit[180]

A The entire deposit is forfeit after ten years. Half of it is forfeit after five years. A third of it after three and a third years without coming to visit it,[181] though he swears to visit it. For other *sét*s the price for keeping them has been pledged in that case, because if it may be [the item] itself, there would never be a forfeiture of it except the tenth part that he leaves behind every time for its return. If necessity caused [him] not to visit it, it is the same as if he would have come and [the price] had been pledged for the body[182] of the deposit. If non-necessity caused [him not to visit them], it is the same as though [the price] was pledged for other *sét*s. Forfeiture of their milk and their labor to the one in [whose] hand [i.e., possession] they are, except if not using them was stipulated.

If the owner went to visit it every year, it is his choice whether he would redeem it or not. p. 18b

If he did not go at all, it is the choice of the defendant whether he will give a time for redeeming it, or he will have it himself. If he went infrequently and he did not go every year, [the price of] the portion of the year that he did not come is in the same manner; a lawful price had been pledged in that case,

180 For the regulations governing deposits, see *GEIL* 120.

181 The sense is that the person who deposits his property with someone else will come to check on the deposited property and not abandon it. If the owner fails to show up, the property he deposited is forfeit to the one in whose possession it was left.

182 *Corp* is used here to refer to the main part of the deposit itself.

log *acht*aigt*h*i, is a bit*h* air. Man ro*ch*u*in*dig log i*n* *cé*tla, ⁊ rocui*nn*ig i*n* la fa deoig,[183] is a den*am* do *con*id *ar* log doroi*ne*, ⁊ log dlig*thech* do. ⁊ cia nogab*a* fer i*n* seoit a set d'feichem[184] a n-ascaid*h* do isi*n* c*r*i*ch*, no*ch*a becaigen*n* a log ui*m*e-seo*m*.

Cia torad dosli do aurnaid*m*?[185] A ne*m*eireic[186] ci atbala la h-i*n*dili, *acht* dorata naillig, u*air* *n*i iada[187] cuir bel adbeola i*n*ti[188] adro*n*a.

Dia[189] ngab*a* *tr*eb*air*i i*n* fer dia n-ait*h*nit*h*e*r* in ait*h*ne i[s](m)[190] sl*an* do cidbed don*airet*, ma*n*a be faill taisceda f*air* *acht* am*al* a c*r*od fei*n*, ⁊ ge*n* faill f*air*.

Sl*an* do, cia gab*a* treb*air*i gi*n*co gaba, dia fest*ar* fer na h-aithne faill taisceda f*or* c*r*ud i*n*ti dia n-ait*h*nit*er*. Sl*an* do da*no* dia ngab*a* *tr*eb*air*i, cia be*th* faill taisc*e*d*a* uada, ma det*h*b*ir* do i*n* faill.

Ait*h*g*in* fair im*murro*, mai*ne* gab*a* *tr*eb*air*i dia *m*be faill taisc*e*d*a* uad. ⁊ ait*h*g*in* f*air* da*no* cia be*th* *tr*eb*air*i dia *m*be faill taisc*e*d*a* co fis do*n* fir 'ca facab*ar* ⁊ co n-a*n*fis d'fir na h-ait*h*ne. L*et*haith*gin* f*air* dia ngab*a* *tr*eb*aire* im sl*an* do dia *m*be faill taisc*e*d*a*, ⁊ ni do gres *acht* tecmaisi*n* æ*nuair*e. L*et*h*aithgin* f*air* da*no* dia *m*be co*m*et cotec*h*ta ⁊ ni gaib *tr*eb*air*i im sl*an* do.[191]

---

183 The ⟨e⟩ is written suprascript.

184 Binchy, *CIH* 2167, n. k, states that ⟨ḟeich⟩ are written in *rasura* by a different scribe. Although the writing is much more compressed than that of the surrounding commentary, the correction is in the scribe's hand.

185 The ⟨d⟩ is written suprascript.

186 The second ⟨i⟩ was added below the line by the scribe; see also Binchy, *CIH* 2167, n. l.

187 The resolution of *i̅i̅ada* is questioned by Binchy, *CIH* 2167, n. m. He suggests the reading '*n*i iada', but cf. source Y. *CIH* 847.38 prints as 'ini ada' although the abbreviation for the phrase is the same in both MS sources. The form *iada* is interpreted here as the 3 sg. pres. ind. prototonic of *íadaid* 'closes, binds, encompasses'.

188 This form is followed by a space where four or five letters have been erased; see also Binchy, *CIH* 2167, n. n.

189 The commentary from here to the end in sources A and Y is also found in the fragmentary text on deposits, *Córus Aithni* (see Appendix 6).

190 Cf. source U (Appendix 6), *CIH* 2110.10.

191 The last three words were written below the line by the scribe.

and if a price is stipulated, it remains with him. If he did not ask the price on the first day, and he asked [the price] on the last day, he has to prove that it was for a price that he had done [it], and he gets a lawful price. And though the owner of the *sét* can take his *sét* to a law-agent to secure it in the territory, the price for it is not lessened.

What payment does he deserve for [acting as a] security?[192] No compensation though his [sc., the owner's] property may become forfeit, except that which he had given in oath, because an oral contract does not bind what the one who may deposit will forfeit.[193]

If the man to whom the deposit is entrusted takes a surety, he is free from liability, whatever befalls it,[194] unless there may be neglect guarding it except as [he guards] his own cattle, and it [sc., his own property] is not neglected.[195]

He is free from liability, whether he takes a surety or not, if the owner of the deposit knows of neglect of guarding the cattle of the one to whom it is entrusted. He is free from liability then if he takes a surety, though there may be neglect of guarding by him, if he has a reason for the neglect.[196]

Restitution for it,[197] however, unless he takes a surety, if there is neglect of guarding by him. And restitution for it then, though there may be a surety, if there is neglect of guarding with knowledge [of it] by the man with whom it has been left and with ignorance of the owner of the deposit. Half restitution for it if he takes a surety regarding being free from liability if there is neglect of guarding, and never continually, but occurring once. Half restitution for it then if there is proper guarding and he does not take a surety regarding being free from liability.[198]

---

192 In other words, what is the price to be paid for someone to hold one's property in deposit.

193 While *adrona* (and *atrona* in source Y) look like 3 sg. pres. subj. forms of *ad-noí* 'entrusts, commends to, deposits', the meaning is unclear. It is also uncertain whether these forms belong to *ad-noí*; it is possible that they are also gen. sg. forms. The translation of this paragraph and the corresponding one in source Y are tentative.

194 The sense is that as long as he takes a surety and guards the deposited property as carefully as his own, he is not liable if the deposited property should be injured or stolen.

195 In other words, as long as he guards it as well as he guards his own property, which he does not neglect.

196 The sense is that some other necessity caused him to neglect the deposited property.

197 It is difficult to determine whether *fair* in the Irish refers to the deposited property itself or the owner of the deposited property, i.e., 'restitution for it' or 'restitution for him', respectively.

198 For neglecting to care properly for deposited property, see source Y below and *The MacEgan Legal Treatise*, § 8.33 and p. 230.

p. 330c Y [*CIH* 847.37–848.10] | Cia tor*ad* dosli do urnaid*m*? A nei*meiric* ci atbalat lat in*n*ile, *acht* dorata naillig, u*air n*i iada[199] ch*uir* bel atbel*a* anti adro*na*, .i. amaill*e* frit in*n*ile bis i*n* tan *tét* i muda, ⁊ ni icfa-so i*n* aith*gin* atro*na* ci*n*co tesfat t'in*n*ile fei*n*, u*air* tall*a* sl*an* d'ait*hnead* duit.

Dia ngab*a* treb*air*i an fer dia n-aith*ned* in aithne i[s](*m*)[200] sl*an* do cidbe don*airet*, mana be faill taiscead*ha* f*air acht* am*al* a cr*od* fei*n*, ⁊ gi*n* faill f*air*.

Slan dó d*ano*, (d)[c]ia[201] ngab*a* treb*air*i cinco gab*a*, dia fest*ar* fer na aith*ne* faill taisc*eda* for cr*o*d anti dia n-aith*ned*. Sl*an* do d*ano* dia ngab*a* treb*air*i, cia b*eth* faill taisc*eda* uad*ha*, ma d*eth*bir do i*n* faill.

Aithg*in* f*air* im*murro*, mane gab*a* treb*air*i, dia *m*be faill taisc*eda* uad*ha*.[202] ⁊ ait*hgin* f*air* d*ano*, ciad b*eth* treb*airi*,[203] dia *m*be faill taisc*eda* co fis do*n* fir 'ca facab ⁊ co n-ai*n*fis d'fir na ait*hne*. Leat*haithgin* f*air* dia ngab*a* treb*airi im* sl*an* do dia mbe f*aill* taisc*eda*, ⁊ ni do gres *acht* tecmaisi*n* æ*nuaire*. Leat*haithgin* f*air* d*ano* dia mbe a co*m*et coitec*h*ta ⁊ ni gaib *trebairi im* sl*an* do ⁊cc̄.

[1f] na h-airliugud

A [*CIH* 2167.34–41] .i. *ar* cut*r*uma. Is and ata a landilsi ⁊ *t*rian dilsi i*n* airlict*h*i: in tan t*uc* in f*er* amuig, ⁊ is airliug*ud* rob fiu e, uili, ł a let*h*, no a t*r*ian, is dil*es*. Int airliuc*ud*, mas e *t*ria*n* in *séoit* is lais, ⁊[204] ro*airliced*, is dil*es* uad. Mas e a let*h* no[205] uili roairli[c](t),[206] is dil*es* uad. ⁊ faill imcometa r*uc* iat aræn, ⁊rl-

Is and ata landilse i*n* airlice: i*n* tan tuc dui*ne* airlicud amach ar dus, ⁊ tuc i*n* fer amuig airlici*ud* a c*h*omait*h* do-sa*m*, ⁊ a mbit*h* aig*h*id*h* i *n*-aig*h*id*h*, uair is faill co*m*eta ata i cechtar de.

15 na h-airliugud] Only source A preserves this portion of the tract.

199 See the note on this phrase in source A above.
200 Cf. source A above and source U (Appendix 6), *CIH* 2110.10.
201 I follow the emendation suggested by Binchy, *CIH* 848, n. a; cf. source A, *CIH* 2167.26.
202 The word is followed by ⟨mad⁊hb-⟩, which has been erased; see also Binchy, *CIH* 848, n. b.
203 I follow the expansion suggested by Binchy, *CIH* 848, n. c.
204 Binchy, *CIH* 2167, n. o, queries whether the Tironian note should be omitted.
205 A ⟨u⟩ follows this word, but it was erased; see also Binchy, *CIH* 2167, n. p.
206 See also Binchy, *CIH* 2167, n. q.

Y | What payment does he deserve for [acting as a] security? No compensation though they are forfeit with your property, except that which he had given in oath, because an oral contract does not bind what the one who may deposit will forfeit,[207] i.e., as you were with your property when it perishes, and I will not pay the restitution of depositing (?) though your own property will perish, because it was delivered safely to you.[208] p. 330c

If the man to whom the deposit was entrusted takes a surety, he is free from liability, whatever befalls it, unless there is neglect guarding it except as [he guards] his own cattle, and it is not neglected.

He is free from liability then, whether he takes a surety or not, if the owner of the deposit knows of neglect of guarding the cattle of the one to whom it is entrusted. He is free from liability then if he takes a surety, though there may be neglect of guarding by him, if he has a reason for the neglect.

Restitution for it, however, unless he takes a surety, if there is neglect of guarding by him. And restitution for it then, though there may be a surety, if there is neglect of guarding with knowledge [of it] by the man with whom it is left and with ignorance of the owner of the deposit. Half restitution for it if he takes a surety regarding being free from liability if there is neglect of guarding, and never continually, but occurring once. Half restitution for it then if there is its proper guarding, and he does not take a surety regarding being free from liability, etc.

[1f] or commercial loan

A i.e., for an equivalent. Is it in the following case that there is full forfeiture of it and a third of the forfeiture of the loan: when the plaintiff gave [a loan], and it is a loan that is fitting, all, or half of it, or a third of it is forfeit. The loan, if it is a third of the *sét* that he has, and he lent [it], it is forfeited by him. If it is half of it or all [of it] that he lent, it is forfeited by him. And neglect of guarding took them both, etc.

It is in the following case that there is full forfeiture of the loan: when a person gave out a loan in the first place, and the plaintiff gave a loan equal [in value] to it to him, and when there is an equivalent exchange, because it is neglect of guarding that is for each of them.

207 See the note on *adrona* in source A above.

208 The translation of this paragraph is tentative.

⁊ is and ata[209] a l*eth*dilsi ł a t*r*ian dilsi i*n air*lici: in tan dorat in fe*ar* deid*h*enac*h air*lic*iud* is fiu a leth ł a t*r*ia*n* do*n* cetfir.[210]

[1g] na h-aititiu,[211] ⁊rl-.

A [*CIH* 2168.1–10] .i. in aititiu ona cen*n*aib. In re arna[212] dil*es* on mema*r* i*n* cor, is e re iarna[213] dil*es* on ci*nd*, *acht* a feg*ad* cia[214] cor, ⁊rl-

Ma robui nech i n-aititiu a seoit fei*n* 'ca rec i*na* fiad*naise* ci*n* a fuaitr*ed*, noc*ha* roich dia aidbriug.[215] ⁊ is as gaba*r* sin: "nach dui*ne* dob*era* a gell ⁊ focoisli i*arum*, (na bi)[216] a cain ł a cairde diren am*ail* bid *sét* na b*eth* cuit do."[217] ⁊ ce der si*n*, mai*n*ib dil*es* uad iat do rer[218] cuir no cu*n*dart*ha*, conic a tait*h*m*eth*[219] *on* trath co 'raili do*n* codnach, ⁊ ni roith[220] iar*um*; ⁊ fis ⁊ *tre*b*ai*ri.

Uair mad econ*n*, ce dob*eth*-side[221] i n-aititin a set 'ca rec, noc*ha* dil*es* uad iat no co raib re re *cethra* n-u*air fich*it[222] iar tia*cht*ain celli codnaig do.

3 na h-aititiu ⁊rl-] Only source A preserves this part of the tract.

209 *ata* was added above the line by the scribe; see also Binchy, *CIH* 2167, n. b.

210 This paragraph was written in *marg. sup.* with reference marks by the scribe; see also Binchy, *CIH* 2167, n. r.

211 The expected acc. sg. form is *aititin*. The MS clearly has ⟨u⟩ as the final letter, but it could be that the scribe misread an ⟨n⟩ in his exemplar as ⟨u⟩.

212 Binchy, *CIH* 2168, n. a., states that the second ⟨a⟩ is written subscript; it is written on the line.

213 The second ⟨a⟩ is written subscript; see also Binchy, *CIH* 2168, n. a.

214 *cia* was added below the line by the scribe; see also Binchy, *CIH* 2168, n. b.

215 The ⟨u⟩ was added below the line by the scribe; see also Binchy, *CIH* 2168, n. d. *cin … aid* was added above the line with reference marks by the scribe; see also Binchy, *CIH* 2168, n. c. A letter is erased after the ⟨a⟩ in *aidbriug*.

216 I follow the emendation suggested by Binchy, *CIH* 2168, n. e. Cf. also *CIH* 477.14.

217 Here the commentary quotes part of the tract from *Bretha im Ḟuillemu Gell*, *CIH* 477.14–15: Nach dune dorata a gell ⁊ focoissle iarum, i cain no chairdde direnar am*ail* bith set inna beth cuit do. 'Any person who may give his pledge and takes it away afterwards, it is paid according to law or treaty like a *sét* in which he has a share.'

218 The second ⟨r⟩ was added below the line by the scribe.

219 For *taithmech*; see also Binchy, *CIH* 2168, n. f.

220 This is another example of ⟨th⟩ for ⟨ch⟩; see also Binchy, *CIH* 2168, n. f.

221 The ⟨do⟩ was added below the line by the scribe; see also Binchy, *CIH* 2168, n. g.

222 The ⟨it⟩ are written suprascript.

And it is in the following case that there is forfeiture of half of it or forfeiture of a third of the loan: when the second man gave a loan that is worth half of it or a third of it to the first man.

[1g] or acknowledgement, etc.

A i.e., the acknowledgement by the chiefs. The time after which it is forfeited by the member of the community in contract, it is the time after which it is forfeited by the chief, save in regard to which contract, etc.

If anyone acknowledges his own *sét* which is being sold in his presence without opposing it, he cannot claim [it]. And that is taken from: "any person who may give his pledge and takes it away afterwards, let him pay according to law and according to treaty like a *sét* that he has a share in." And though it says that, unless they are forfeited by him according to contract or covenant, it is able to be impugned until the same time the next day by a [legally] responsible person, and he cannot afterwards [make a claim]; and [he has] knowledge and a surety.

When it is someone who is not [in a] legally competent [state of mind], though he might be in acknowledgement of his *sét*s which are being sold, they are not forfeited by him until 24 hours after his senses have returned to him.[223]

223 This covers cases where someone has made a contract when not in possession of his full mental faculties due to drunkenness, illness, or some other form of physical or emotional distress.

[1h] ⁊ imtongar and sin o g*r*adaib ecalsa f*or* g*r*adaib tuait*h*e

p. 19a A [*CIH* 2168.11–14] | Imden*am* a *sét* f*or*a memru, ⁊ geb*id* grem fira t*es*ta b*r*iat*h*a*r* an uasail oc i*m*den*am* a *sét* f*or*a memru. G*r*ad ecl*as*a olcena ⁊ g*r*ad tuait*h*e, fir t*es*ta leo d'imden*am* a *sét*.

G [*CIH* 2069.43–2070.2] .i. is leo imdenam a *sét* f*or*a memr*aib*, ⁊ geib*h*e[224] g*r*eim fíra t*es*ta b*r*iat*har* an uasail oc imdenum a *sét* f*or*a me*m*ra. G*r*aid*h* ecl*ais*i olcena ⁊ g*r*aid*h* t*h*uait*h*e, fír t*es*ta leo d'imdenum a set.

[1i] ar dilaat *secht* ngraid ecl*asa* f*or* *secht* ng*r*adaib *túaithe*

A [*CIH* 2168.15–17] .i. oc aidb*r*iud ruidlis, ⁊ gaib*id* gri*m* fira t*es*ta luigi an esp*oic* no in rig; ⁊ na graid olcena, fir t*es*ta 'na ndiaid d'i*m*den*am* a *sét*.

G [*CIH* 2070.3–6] .i. *ar*na rag*h*b*a* comtis na h-uaisle namá dog*h*nidis i*n* n-imdenum. Is *aire* im*murro* tuc in '*ar*' in*n*, .i. oc aidb*h*riu ruid*h*lis, ⁊ gaib*h*id g*r*eim fír*a* *testa* luig*h*e i*n* espoig ł in rig*h*; ⁊ na graid*h* olcena, fír t*es*ta d'i*m*denu*m* a *sét* ana diaig*h*.

---

1 ⁊] & G; the tracts starts col. 604. ‖ and sin] *om.* G. ‖ g*r*adaib] g*r*ad*h*aib*h* G. ‖ ecalsa] ecal*sa* A. The remainder of the tract is not preserved in G. 8 dilaat] dilat A; the verb *do-lá* is from **di-la-*; *eDIL* s.v. 1 *do-lá*. ‖ *secht*] .uii. A and G. ‖ ngraid] g. G. ‖ ecl*asa*] e. G. ‖ *secht*] uii. A and G. ‖ ng*r*adaib] g. G.

224 The ⟨i⟩ is written subscript.

[1h] And it is sworn like that by [the] ecclesiastical grades against [the] lay grades

A | They prove their *sét*s against the members of their community, and the word of a noble will have the force of [an oath sworn by] a compurgator to prove his *sét*s for the members of his community [e.g., his household and his clients, etc.]. Ecclesiastical grades as well as lay grades, a compurgator with them to prove their *sét*s. p. 19a

G i.e., they prove their *sét*s for the members of their community, and the word of a noble will have the force of [an oath sworn by] a compurgator to prove his *sét*s for the members of his community. Ecclesiastical grades as well as lay grades, a compurgator with them to prove their *sét*s.

1i] because [the] seven ecclesiastical grades prevail[225] over [the] seven lay grades

A i.e., claiming property, and the oath of the bishop or the king has the force of [oaths sworn by] compurgators; and the grades otherwise, a compurgator supporting them to prove their *sét*s.

G i.e., because he may not take that which might be more, only those which he proved.[226] It is because of that, however, that is [i.e., the text] gave the *ar* there,[227] i.e., claiming property, and the oath of the bishop or the king has the force of [oaths sworn by] compurgators; and the grades otherwise, a compurgator supporting them to prove their *sét*s.

225 The verb *do-lá* usually means to 'repel, put away, expel, reject, take away'; the translation here is tentative; see *eDIL* s.v. 1 *do-lá*.

226 In other words, no matter how much the plaintiff claimed, he can only take that which he has proved to be his.

227 The *ar* refers to the *ar* at the beginning of the excerpt of the tract.

§ 2

Doberar[228] dal t*r*eisi no *cóic*the no *dech*m*aid*i no mis co tuca cach a saidbre

A [*CIH* 2168.18–27] .i. mai*ne* fagba i*nd*r*acus* a imden*am* f*r*i sin, is do*n* fir oca *m*bi lecth*ir* a imden*am*. Dui*ne* si*n* ⁊ roba l[e]is[229] i*m*den*am* a seoit[230] do r*eir* in fuid roimir[231] air, ⁊ noc*h*arb ait*h*nid do fei*n* he, ⁊ re n-i*n*dsaigt*h*i dob*er*a[r] do ra h-i[a]rraid a blig[ri](ne)[232] n[o][233] a buachalla, .i. *cóict*hi isi*n* *cét*c*r*ich, ł *dech*mad isi*n* c*r*ich is nesa, ⁊ mi sechno*n* er*enn*. & atb*eir* i mbaili *aile*: "for*ta* f*orus*: ni f*or*toi*n*g fer selba, ⁊rl-."[234] Masa ci*n*dti les t*r*ia acallai*m* a blig[ri](ne) no a buachalla ł 'aireaman[235] *con*id he a *sét* fei*n* e, is fo[a] aicn*ed* fen ata i*n* fir. Mainib ci*n*dti les im*murro*, is fo aicned in buachalla fen[236] no i*n* bligri ata in fir. Iss e in buachaill ł in blig*r*i dob*er*a in fir, ⁊ iss e-sium dob*er*a in remud in cach i*n*ad dib. Tosach besgna, .i. cach remud.

F [*CIH* 1275.41–1276.17] Duine sin ⁊ robad*h* leis imdenam a tseoit do r*e*r in f*huit*h roimir air, & noc*h*arb ait*h*nit do fein é, ⁊ ré n-indsaig*h*e dober*ar* do re h-iarr*aidh* a blig*r*i no a buac*h*all*a*, .i. *cóict*hi isin *cét*c*rich*, ł *dech*m*ad* isin c*rich* is nesa, ⁊ mí secnoin era*nn*. ⁊ atber(t)[237] a n-inad*h* *aile*: "for*ta* i f*orus*: ní f*or*toing fer sealba." Masa cin*n*ti leis t*r*ia agallaim*h* a blig*h*ri no a buac*h*all*a* no airemu*n* *con*id é a *th*set fe*n* e, is fo[a] aicn*ed* fei*n* ata in fior. Munab cin*n*ti

1 doberar ... mis] *om.* G. Q and AA begin with ⁊. In V the phrase 'gne .ii.' is written in *marg. dext.* Dob*erar* Q, AA, JJ. ‖ dal] dail F, Q, V, *om* JJ. ‖ t*r*eisi] *trí* A, V, treisid .⁊rl.- F, t*r*esi Q. F does not preserve any more of this section of the tract, nor does this source follow the order of the material as preserved in A. In the MS, this section of the tract appears immediately after the commentary in § 6. ‖ no] ł A, AA. ‖ *cóic*the] *cóic* A, *cóic*the Q, *cóic*te AA, *cóic*thi JJ. V does not preserve any more of the tract. ‖ no] ł A, AA. ‖ *dech*m*aid*i] *deich* A, *dech*m*aide* JJ. ‖ no] ł Q, AA. no ... saidbre *om* A. ‖ mis] miss Q, mios JJ. Q, AA, and JJ do not preserve any more of the tract.

228 The second ⟨e⟩ in source F is added below the line; see also Binchy, *CIH* 1275, n. m.
229 I follow the emendation suggested by Binchy, *CIH* 2168, n. i.
230 The ⟨i⟩ is added below the line by the scribe.
231 The verb form here and in sources F and G appears to be the 3 sg. pret. of *imm-beir* 'puts, places'.
232 I follow the emendation suggested by Binchy, *CIH* 2168, n. j.
233 I follow the emendation suggested by Binchy, *CIH* 2168, n. k.
234 It is uncertain whether this quotation is from a lost part of the tract to *Aidbred.*
235 The second ⟨a⟩ is written subscript.
236 *fen* was added above the line by the scribe.
237 See also Binchy, *CIH* 1276, n. a.

§2

A delay[238] of three days or five days or ten days or a month is given so that each may find his property[239]

A i.e., unless a worthy person may find proof against that, the person who has it is allowed to prove it. That person [sc., the plaintiff], and he [wished] to prove his *sét* according to the claim that he put on it, and he himself did not recognize it, and a period of seeking is given to him to seek his milker or his cowherd, i.e., five days in the same territory, or ten days in the next territory, and a month throughout Ireland. And it says in another place: "law ordains: the owner of the property does not over-swear, etc." If he is certain through conversing with his milker or his cowherd or his ploughman that it is his own *sét*, the proof is according to his own nature [sc., according to the plaintiff's own social status, character, etc.]. If he is uncertain, however, the proof is according to the nature of the cowherd himself or the milker. It is the cowherd or the milker who may give the proof, and it is he [sc., the plaintiff] who may swear the preliminary oath in each case for them. Beginning of regulation, i.e., each preliminary oath.

F That person [sc., the plaintiff], and he [wished] to prove his *sét* according to the claim that he put on it, and he himself did not recognize it, and a period of seeking is given to him to seek his milker or his cowherd, i.e., five days in the same territory, or ten days in the next territory, and a month throughout Ireland. And it says in another place: "there ensues according to law: the owner of the property does not over-swear." If he is certain by con-

238 For a discussion of this section, see the Introduction, p. 19. Although *eDIL* s.v. 3 *dál* does not list any definitions for the word, the print version of the dictionary provides the definition 'delay, respite'. *eDIL* does state that 3 *dál* belongs with 2 *dál*, although 'delay, respite' is not given as a definition under this headword.

239 For periods of delay for a surety to seek the defendant, see *The MacEgan Legal Treatise* §5.12 and the discussion by Kelly, op. cit., 166–167. The system presented in that text is five days for a defendant in the same territory, ten days in the next, fourteen days in the same province, and a month for searching the whole of Ireland. The system presented in *Aidbred* is three days for the same territory, five days for the next, ten days for the one beyond that, and a month for searching throughout Ireland. One wonders whether the ten days ought to refer to searching within one's own province instead. The crucial difference between the periods of delay presented in both texts is that in *The MacEgan Legal Treatise* the delay is for the plaintiff to seek the defendant; in *Aidbred* the delay is for the plaintiff to seek his cowherd or milker.

leis[240] im*murro*, is fo aicn*ed* in buac*h*all*a* no an blig*h*ri ata in fior. ⁊ is e in buac*h*aill no an blig*r*i dob*eir* in luig*h*i, & is e-sim*h* dob*eir* in remad*h* i ng*a*c inad*h*.

Fri h-imcianug*ud* a crich at*a* an*n*, no d*an*o cenad*h* is fri cui*n*gid imdenma ⁊ fri turra*cht* a muindtere, & do demniug*ud* cona derna go; no go tiosa a fe*r* cumt*h*a a cein, mad*h* é adgnet*h*, cid*h* a tuait*h* a meod*h*an an*n* so.

O togb*us* urr*ad* [.i.] baranta ænf*echt*, ni fuil sealb dona t*r*í selb*aib* do denam 'na deg*h*a, ⁊ dobiad*h* roim*e*. Int urr*ad* togb*us*, is *ed* dlega*r* a in*n*isi*n* ind*us* na raib a cu*mus* aigi urr*ad aile* sis a*cht* a[n]t[241] urr*ad* togb*us*. Iss iat-so na t*r*i selb, .i. s*elb* mach*a* ⁊ ga*n* delug*h* res ó t*h*s*in* anuas; rem*selb* .i. a cen*nach* no a fagb*ail* cena ní is tu*usga* na ad*er* fe*r* na h-agg*r*a a gaid uad*h*a; s*elb* luingi, .i. a cennac*h* a luing, ⁊ is cin*n*ti gu*r*ab dil*us* do lu*cht* na l*uinge* é ⁊ na fuig*h*b*ed* fe*r* an ell*aig* é gi*ngo* gcen*n*ch*ad* siu é. ⁊ masa set aga mbiad*h* la*cht* no gnimr*ad* e, is íoc ó ló an c*r*onaith*e* amach.[242]

---

240 The ⟨i⟩ is written subscript.

241 I follow the emendation suggested by Binchy, *CIH* 1276, n. c.

242 This section of the MS ends here.

versing with his milker or his cowherd or his ploughman that it is his *sét*, the proof is according to his own nature. If he is not certain, however, the proof is according to the nature of the cowherd or the milker. And it is the cowherd or the milker who swears the oath, and it is he who swears the preliminary oath in each case.

In that case there is a great distance from his territory, or, on the other hand, it is to seek proof and the support[243] of his household, and to prove that he may not make a falsehood; or so that he may go a long distance with a companion, if he might recognize it, although it is his [own] *túath* [that adjudges the case] here.

If[244] he [sc., the plaintiff] takes a surety,[245] i.e., a guarantor,[246] at once, he does not make [a declaration] of ownership from the three ownerships afterwards, as there would have been previously. The surety whom he takes, he is obligated to say who [his surety is] so that he does not have the ability [to take] another surety except the surety whom he takes.[247] These are the three types of ownership, i.e., ownership of a cattle-enclosure and without it parting from him from afterwards; prior-possession, i.e., purchasing it or obtaining it previously before the plaintiff says that it was stolen from him; possession of a boat, i.e., purchasing it from a boat, and it is certain that it belongs legally to the boatmen, and that the owner of the property [from the boat] had not obtained it without buying it previously.[248] And if it is a *sét* that has milk or labor, payment [for it] from the day of the legal claim onwards.

---

243 The translation of *turracht* is tentative; see *eDIL* s.v. ? *turracht*.

244 This paragraph is also found in *The MacEgan Legal Treatise* § 5.13–20. Kelly, op. cit., 15–16, and 167–170, suggests that the threefold division of ownership may have been composed by Giolla himself. As Kelly discusses in his edition, it is diffiuclt to say whether Giolla quotes from a legal source which no longer survives or has composed the material himself. The commentary from source F is Kelly's source C; see also Kelly's source B, CIH 1108.28–1109.2. The translation relies on Kelly's, although the order of the first few clauses here is different from that in *The MacEgan Legal Treatise*.

245 For *aurrae* (later *urrad*) in the meaning 'surety', see Kelly, *The MacEgan Legal Treatise*, 165.

246 As noted by Kelly, *The MacEgan Legal Treatise*, 165, *baránta* is a loanword from Anglo-Norman *warantie*.

247 As discussed by Kelly, *The MacEgan Legal Tretaise*, 168, the first part of the commentary concerns the plaintiff taking a surety and announcing it. The second part shifts to defining the three types of ownership and providing examples of how the defendant can argue against the plaintiff's accusations.

248 On the obligation of the merchant to ensure that he was not selling stolen goods, see also Mitchell, *An Essay on the Early History of the Law Merchant*, 94–95.

G [*CIH* 2070.7–34] .i. duine sin ⁊ rob ail leis[249] imdenam a ṡeoit do r*er* in fuit*h* roimir *air*, ⁊ noc*har*b ait*h*nit do é, ⁊ ré n-indsaig*h*e dob*erar* do blig*h*re no do buac*h*aill: *cóic*ti isi*n* *cét*crich, ⁊ *dech*m*ad* isi*n* cric*h* is nesa, ⁊ mí sec*h*noin er*enn*.

Set sin t*est*a o dui*n*e, ⁊ *noch*on ait*h*nit dó fein é, ⁊ is ait*h*nit da blig*h*re no da buac*h*aill. ⁊ is ed*h* dleg*har* ré n-in*n*saig*h* d*h*o re i*arr*aig*h* blig*h*re ł buac*h*alla. ⁊ remud*h* fo' aign*ed* fei*n*, ⁊ fír fo aign*ed* blig*h*re ł b*uachalla*. ⁊ cemad ed*h* bud ail dó imdenum do roc*h*tain dó a dualg*us* a ait*h*ne do b*heth* aga blig*h*re ł aga buac*h*aill, manab ait*h*nit do bude*in* é, noc*h*o roic*h*, no d*an*o cena co roisid, u*air* fo aic*ned* bligre no b*uachalla* ata luc*ht* fíra.

col. 605 Masa cin*n*te lais t*r*e acallaim a b*ligre* no b*uachalla* no *air*em*h*an *con*ad é a *sét* fein é, is fo' aicne fein ata an fír.

Manab cin*n*te lais im*murro*, is fo aic*ned* b*ligre* no b*uachalla* at*a* an fir. Is iat dob*erat*, ⁊ is eisi*m* fein dob*eir* an ram*h*ud*h* in cach inad dib*h*-si*n*. Cid*h* riasan re-si*n*, cid*h* i*ar*san re, cid*h* isi*n* re rocait*h*ist*er* an duine an *sét* aidbr*edu*, ⁊ cin*n*te leis n*ar*ub leis fei*n*, cerbo leis ce*n*cor leis i*ar* tain, landire ⁊ laneneclann ⁊ ait*h*gin uad*h* *con*a h-in*n*ud*h*. Mas isi*n* re rocait*h*ist*er* é a ric*ht* a *sét* fei*n*, ⁊ noc*har* leis i*ar* tain, l*eth*dire ⁊ l*eth*enecl*ann* ⁊ ait*h*gin *con*a h-in*n*ud*h* uad*h*.

M*a* *r*ob leis i*ar* tai*n*, særaig*h* *ar* dire ⁊ *ar* ait*h*gin é, ⁊ l*eth*enecl*ann* uad*h*. Fogaba*r* an *sét* re aidb*hred* an*n* sin, ⁊ munu fag*h*uba*r*, is l*eth*enecl*ann* uad*h* ⁊ cet*h*raime dire la ait*h*gin no l*eth*ait*h*gin.

Mas i*ar*san re rocait*hust*a*r* é a ric*ht* a *sét* fein, ⁊ noc*h*or leis i*ar* tai*n*, is ait*h*gin uad*h*. M*a* *r*obud*h* leis, is [s]la*n* dó. Fogaba*r* an *sét* re aidbr*ed* an*n* sin, ⁊ man fagaba*r*, is l*eth*ait*h*gin ł as a beit*h* ca*n* ní. Can asa ngaba*r* an l*eth*ait*h*gi*n*? Is e an fat*h*: cundtab*air*t coid*h*ce cia *n*ogab*h*ta é. Can asa ngaba*r* b*eth* cen ní? Is as gab*ar*: "am*al* fer meod*h*ongaite landlig*h*t*hech* é, ⁊ ní t*arrus* colon*n* aige re aidb*hred*;" ⁊ ag indr*ud* roaidbr*ed* an *sét* sun*n*, ⁊ damaid*h* dlig*ed* n-aidbr*eda*, ⁊ 'na laim*h* fei*n* leg*ar* é.

249 The ⟨i⟩ is written subscript. In source G, the scribe commonly writes a subscript ⟨i⟩ when it follows an ⟨e⟩ or ⟨s⟩. No further comment will be made of this practice for source G.

G i.e., that person, and he wished to prove his *sét* according to the claim that he put on it, and he did not recognize it, and a time for seeking is given for his milker or for his cowherd: five days in the same territory, and ten days in the next territory, and a month throughout Ireland.

That property is missing from someone, and he himself does not recognize it, and it is recognized by his milker or by his cowherd. A time of seeking is owed to him to seek [his] milker or cowherd. And preliminary oath according to his own nature, and proof according to the nature of the milker or cowherd. And though he may desire proof to obtain it on account of recognizing it by his milker or by his cowherd, if he himself does not recognize it, he does not obtain [it], or on the other hand, in order that he may obtain [it], because it is according to the nature [sc., social status] of [his] milker or cowherd who are compurgators.

If he is certain by conversing with his milker or cowherd or ploughman col. 605
that it is his own *sét*, the proof is according to his own nature.

If he is not certain, however, the proof is according to the nature of [his] milker or cowherd. It is they who swear, and it is he himself who swears the preliminary oath in each case. Whether before that time, or after that time, or in the time that the person had used the *sét* being claimed, and he is certain it was not in his own possession, whether it is in his possession or not afterwards, full penalty-fine and full honor-price and restitution is owed by him with its increase. If it is in the time that he had used it instead of his own *sét*, and it is not in his possession afterwards, half penalty-fine and half honor-price and restitution with its increase [is] owed by him.

If it is in his possession afterwards, he is exempt from penalty-fine and from restitution, and half honor-price from him. The *sét* is obtained at the time of claiming in that case, and if it is not obtained, half honor-price is [due] from him and a fourth of [the] penalty-fine with restitution or half restitution.

If it is after the time that he has used it instead of his own *sét*, and it is not in his possession afterwards, restitution is [due] from him. If it is in his possession, he is free from liability. The *sét* is obtained at the time of claiming in that case, and if it is not obtained, it is half restitution or there may be nothing from it [i.e., he gets nothing from it]. Whence is taken the half restitution? The reason is: doubt on the part that it was taken. Whence is taken that he may be without anything? It is taken from: "he is as the fully unlawful receiver of stolen goods, and the item was not declared by him at the time of claiming;" and by wrong [e.g., by mistake or intentionally] that the *sét* was claimed here, and if it is lawful claiming, and it is left in his own hand.

V [*CIH* 1575.1–4] .i. is é fa*th* ara tabair in ré-sseo: muna fagba in*n*racus a imden*am* frisi*n* re-si*n*, is don fir 'ga mbi leict*er* a imde*n*am .i. t*r*eissi i tuaith i meodón, cuicti i sechtarc*r*ich i*n* coicid, mí sechnoi*n* h-Er*enn* uili.

AA[250] [*CIH* 1930.6–10] ⁊ is *air*e isb*erar* na ree-so, *ar* m*an* fagb*a* f*e*r ai[d]b*hreda* in*n*ruc*us* imdenma *f*risi*n* re-sin, is don f*e*r oca mbe leict*ir*[251] imden*am*. ⁊ ma*r* ad*er*: "no ma trum*a* t*arrus*t*ar* tanus[t]e do tiug*hlaith*i taidb*h*si teora ton*n*,"[252] .i. doni t*ríar* la in*n*raic a fuil f*or* in*n*raic ł la eisin*nraic* f*or* eisin*nraic*. ⁊ dia t*air*ge in ci*n*tac*h* dul d'fir Dé, is dó leict*ir*, *ar* ni fuil fir is t*air*e d'*imdenam*[253] 'nas i*n* fir t*airges*.[254]

250 See also the same commentary found in sources Q (Digest A (8), *CIH* 1145.6–11, Appendix 2) and JJ (Digest B (27), *CIH* 1314.14–20, Appendix 3).

251 The first ⟨i⟩ is written subscript. In this section of the MS, whenever an ⟨i⟩ follows an ⟨e⟩, it is normally written subscript.

252 It is uncertain whether this quotation is from *Aidbred.*

253 See also Binchy, *CIH* 1930, n. a.

254 See also Binchy, *CIH* 1930, n. b.

V i.e., this is [the] reason that he is given this time: unless a worthy person may find proof against that matter, the person who has it is allowed to prove it, i.e., three days within the *túath*, five days in an external territory in the province, a month throughout all Ireland.

AA And it is from that that those times are mentioned, because unless a worthy person claiming may find proof against that matter, the person who has it is allowed to prove [it]. And as it says: "or if conclusive evidence is obtained by the tanist at the last day of life shown by three waves,"[255] i.e., three people prove with a worthy person who is against a worthy person, or with an unworthy person against an unworthy person. And if the first undergoes a successful ordeal, it is permitted for him, because there is not a truth which is more wretched[256] to prove than the truth which he offers.[257]

---

255 The translation of this clause is tentative.

256 *Taire*, the superl. of *táir* 'mean, base, valueless', is difficult to interpret since the sense of the passage (which occurs not only here, but also in several other sources where versions of this passage are found) is that the proof that the ordeal produces is taken as reliable as it is technically the proof that God offers. If the form does come from *táir*, the meaning might be along the lines of 'more wretched' or 'more sorrowful', in that undergoing an ordeal could be a terrible experience, depending on the type of ordeal. It is possible that the word is a mistake for the comp. of *tairise* 'trusthworthy, worthy of confidence', but it would require an emendation in all the sources.

257 If the religious proof involves a physical ordeal, such as the ordeal of the cauldron, rather than swearing on relics, it is possible that the verb *tairges* should be translated as 'than it produces', referring to the physical evidence of the person's truth produced by the ordeal; *GEIL* 209–211; Archan, "Ordeal by Fire in Medieval Ireland," 197–212; and Bartlett, *Trial by Fire and Water*, especially 5–9, 29, and 43–48. See also the material from the Digest C in § 10, source AA, and sources Q (Appendix 2) and JJ (Appendix 3).

§3

Cach aidbriud docuisin, cach laisi n-aidbrith*er*, is lais a tuinide co tartur a fol*ud* fris amail rogab: "cia fothu disli fo suidi tarrai[n]g?[258] Foreith dilis (n)indlis."[259]

A [*CIH* 2168.28–2169.7] Is ed fuil anuasanai uasal for (uasal) isil[260] ac aidb*r*ed a *séoit*, no cen*n* f*or* meamar, ɫ i*n*draic f*or* esi*n*draic. & iss *ed* fil a*n*d in *sét* do b*eth* a comit*echt* an uasail[261] co tair dlig*ed* ui*m*e. ⁊ it*er* da comp*er*sai*n* ata i*n* *sét* sisinai, ⁊ iss *ed* is coir in *sét* do beth a lai*m* i*n*ti acar h-aidb*r*ed e co tair dlig*ed* ui*m*e.

Ob*us* comp*er*sana co' celi, ecl*as*dacda co ecl*as*dacda,[262] no tuata co tuata, ɫ i*n*draic co indraic, no esi*nraic* co esi*n*draic,[263] is lesi*n*ti aca n-aidbrith*er* in *sét* imden*am* a fothaib comardaib ⁊ l*eth*ardaib. ⁊ mad he an fer[264] aile imres[265] in foth l*eth*ard, is do lecar.

---

1 Cach] Source **J** begins with oc*us*. Only **F** preserves the majority of the tract. ‖ aidbriud] aidb*r*iud*h* **P**, aib*h*re **J**, aidb*r*iud **FF**. ‖ docuisin] docuisi*n* **P**, **FF**, dochuisi*n* **J**. Sources **A** and **G** end at this point. ‖ cach] cac*h* **P**, cac*h* **J**. ‖ laisi] laisia **P**. The second ⟨i⟩ is written subscript; see also Binchy, *CIH* 711, n. i. The gloss .i. oca 'i.e., from whom' is an interlinear gloss on *cach laisia* written by the scribe in source **P**. laisa **FF**. ‖ n-aidbrither] aid*h*britht*er* **P**, aib*h*right*er* **J**, aid*h*brith*er* **FF**. ‖ lais] la **F**. ‖ a] *om.* **F**. ‖ tuinide] tuin*ide* **J**. Source **BB** only preserves *is lais a tuinide*. Sources **P**, **J**, and **FF** end here. In **P**, .i. a airiseam 'i.e., its remaining' is an interlinear gloss on *a tuinide* written by the scribe.

---

258 It is likely that a suspension mark was omitted during copying.

259 The nasalization is likely a result of a misplaced suspension mark.

260 The correction *ɫ isil* was added above the line by the scribe; see also Binchy, *CIH* 2168, n. l.

261 The first ⟨a⟩ was added below in a later hand; see also Binchy, *CIH* 2168, n. m.

262 'co ecl*as*' was added above the line with a reference mark by the scribe; see also Binchy, *CIH* 2168, n. n.

263 The ⟨a⟩ is written subscript.

264 The ⟨r⟩ was added above the line by the scribe; see also Binchy, *CIH* 2168, n. o.

265 The verb is a MI 3 sg. pres. ind. rel. form of *imm-beir* 'puts, places, applies, practices'. In MI, *imm-beir* has a simplex form *imrid*; *eDIL* s.v. *imm-beir*.

§3

Every claiming that there is, everyone from whom it is claimed, it is in his possession until the property is decided against him, as [the law] said: "what is the reason that he is entitled to take [it] away according to this? *Díles* 'possession' is equivalent to *indles* 'non-possession'."[266]

A What is above [concerns] a noble claiming his *sét* against a plebeian, or a chief against a subject, or a worthy person against an unworthy person. And what is there is the *sét* is to accompany the noble [sc., in his possession] until law decides regarding it. And the *sét* [referred to] below is between two people of equal rank, and what is proper is for the *sét* to be in the hand of the one from whom it was claimed until law decides regarding it.

When it is two people of equal rank [claiming against] each other, an ecclesiastic against an ecclesiastic, or a layman against a layman, or a worthy person against a worthy person, or an unworthy person against an unworthy person, it is up to the one from whom the *sét* is claimed to prove [it] by equal or unequal claims. And if it is the other man who brings the unequal claim, it is permitted to him [to bring the proof].

---

266 For a discussion of this section, see the Introduction, pp. 19–23. The first two clauses of the tract are tentatively translated in Kelly, *The MacEgan Legal Treatise*, 163: "each suing which exists, everyone by whom one is sued (?)." It is uncertain whether source F is quoting another part of *Aidbred* or another legal text, assuming that the material is a quotation. If it is a quotation, the source has not been identified. The translation is tentative. The first part requires understanding *disli* as a form of *do-slí* with possible confusion with a metathesized form of *díles*. The second part seems to be a legal maxim although its precise meaning in this context is unclear. It could refer to the fact that having physical possession of an item does not constitute ownership of the item.

Masa ecl*as*dacda co tuata, no i*n*draic co esi*n*dr*aic*, no ce*n*d co mema*r*, is leo-side imden*am* in cac*h* foth a mbia eliugud doib ⁊ in cach fot*h* uili, cid iat aidbres cid aca aidbrith*er*, cenmot*h*at da fot*h*: fot*h* creca co remdilsi ł fot*h* n-i*n*ais ocin esi*n*raic, ⁊ fod c*r*eca nama 'con i*n*draic. In tan is foth creca co re*m*dilsi no fot*h* n-inais 'con esinraic ⁊ fot*h* creca nama 'con i*n*draic, a denum don esi*n*draic *con*id fot*h* c*r*eca co re*m*dilsi ł[267] *con*id fot*h* n-i*n*ais di he, ⁊ a den*am* don i*n*raic *con*id fot*h* creca ce*n* remdilsi di.

⁊ ait*h*fega*r* in cen*n*ach d'urr*ad* no in cen*n*ach d'anurr*ad* di he. Mad cen*n*ach d'urr*ad*, be*r*a[r] aithg*in* *con*a h-i*n*dad[268] uad, ⁊ mad cen*n*ach d'anurr*ad* is roi*n*d ar do.

Is iat na fuit*h* comarda .i. foth n-inais aca mar*æn* ł f*oth* c*r*eca co remdilsi no ci*n* remdilsi. Is iat na fuit*h* le*th*arda: foth n-inais '*con* dara de ⁊ f*oth* c*reca* co re*m*dilsi no ce*n* remd*ilsi* '*con*ti *aile*, ł f*oth* c*reca* co remd*ilsi* [ocin dara de][269] ⁊ f*oth* c*r*e*ca* nama '*con*ti *aile*.

F [*CIH* 1270.16–1271.33] Mas esin*n*raic intí ogar h-aid*h*br*ed* in set, ce damun*n* dlig*ed* n-aid*h*bre*da* cinco *n*daman*n*, is urlaim coitcend. No d*an*o mana dama, is a br*eth* don indraic le fo *cét*oi[r].

---

267 The ⟨ł⟩ was added above the line by the scribe; see also Binchy, *CIH* 2168, n. n.
268 The second ⟨d⟩ was added above the line by the scribe; see also Binchy, *CIH* 2169, n. a.
269 I follow the emendation suggested by Binchy, *CIH* 2169, n. d.

If it is an ecclesiastic against a layman, or a worthy person against an unworthy person, or a chief against a subject, it is up to them to prove each claim regarding which they are sued and the entirety of every claim, whether it is they who claim or are claimed from, except for two claims: the unworthy person has a claim of purchase with prior right or a claim of growth,[270] and the worthy person only has a claim of purchase. When it is an unworthy person who has a claim of purchase with prior right or a claim of growth, and the worthy person has a claim of purchase only, the unworthy person proves that it is a claim of purchase with prior right or that it is a claim of growth that he had for it, and the worthy person proves that it is a claim of purchase without prior right that he had for it.

And it is to be considered [whether] the purchase of it was from a local freeman or an outsider.[271] If it is a purchase from a local freeman, restitution with its increase is taken from him, and if it is a purchase from an outsider, it is divided in two.[272]

The equal claims are, i.e., they both have a claim of growth or a claim of purchase with prior right or without prior right. The unequal claims are: one of them has a claim of growth and the other one has a claim of purchase with prior right or without prior right, or one of them has a claim of purchase with prior right and the other has a claim of purchase only.

F If[273] the one from whom the *sét* was claimed is an unqualified person, whether he submits to the law of claiming or not, it [sc., the property] is [handed over to] a neutral third party. On the other hand, if he does not submit [to judgment], it is brought by him to the worthy person immediately.

---

270 The sense of the second claim is that the livestock was born in the possession of the one from whom it is claimed; see *eDIL* s.v. *inás*.

271 The terms *aurrad* and *anurrad* refer, respectively, to someone who is a freeman originally from the community in question, and one who does not have the status of an *aurrad*. The latter term is sometimes used of outlaws or wanderers, but the sense in the legal texts herein is that it refers to anyone who is not a local; *eDIL* s.vv. *aurrae* and *anurrad*.

272 In the last situation given, presumably the property was purchased from someone outside the community who is no longer around and incapable of being tracked down by either party, and, thus, the division in two so that each party has half the value to mitigate their respective financial loss. This type of division appears again in § 4 and other material concerning the purchase of stolen goods from someone outside the community.

273 The commentary from F is discussed in Kelly, *The MacEgan Legal Treatise*, 163, in relation to § 5.5–8 of Giolla's treatise.

Mas in*n*raic in duine agar h-aid*h*bre*d* in s*ét*, ⁊ dama dlige*d* n-aid*h*bre*da*, in s*ét* do b*eth* ana laim bude*n*. ⁊ muna dam*a*, is urlaim coitcend. Ma*r* ade*r*: **inti na daim a rer fo*r*is, ⁊rl-, ⁊ intí d*haimus*, ⁊rl-.**[274]

Cidh fo*dera* urlaim coitcen*n* do damt*hain* don esinraic su*nn*, ⁊ é da rad*h*: **ni suite*r* fri remdilsi cia b*eth* ite*r* taitib?**[275] Iss é an fath fo*dera*: eisin*n*rac*us* remt*echt*ach im ernailib *aile* dorin*n*e sund, ⁊ is coir cia rod*ham*t*h*a urlaim coitcend do. ⁊ an bail*e* a n-abair tu[a]s:[276] **ní suitir fri remdilsi, ⁊rl-**, uman s*é*-sin fe*n*, rofes esin*nracus* in duine tuas, ⁊ am*al* fer m*edongaite*[277] in*n*dl*ig*-*thech* u*min* s*ét*-si*n* é, ⁊ coir ci*ngo* da*mth*a u*r*lai*m* coitcenn do.

f. 4va Cach in*n*raic aid*h*b*h*res a set ag indr*aic* ⁊ g*ach* eisin*n*rai*c* og esin*n*rai*c*, is laisantí aga ndaid*h*bri*ter* a imdenam mad*h* fot*h*a n-inais doberait. Oc*us* is aire dleg*ar* a imdenum dontí aga n-aid*h*bri*ter*: ar is demin leo conad ac*o* rogenar; ar diama d'fer in aid*h*bre*da* nolecf*ide* a imdenam, robo lain*n* la cach aid*h*bri*ud* tṡeoit gi*n*gorab lais.

Cach in*nraic* im*murro* aid*h*bred*us* a s*ét* ag esin*nraic*, ⁊ is fot*h* n-i*n*ais imrit[278] i ndis, is laisin in*nraic* a imdenam go fior t*esta* ina diag*h*, mane tairg*e*[279] in an*ntest* fior Dé; dia dtairg*e* im*murro*, ni fil fior is tair*e* d'imdenam fair inas in fior t*h*airg*us*.

274 These two citations may or may not belong with *Aidbred*. Based on the fact that the citations also are found in sources P and FF, where they are glossed, it stands to reason that it is probable that these citations are part of *Aidbred* embedded within the commentary; see Appendix 4 for the full context of sources P and FF. It should be noted that source F here provides the negative conditional citation, whereas sources P and FF only provide the positive condition.

275 The citation here and below is also found in sources P, FF, and AA Digest C (38). As with the citations above in the previous paragraph, the citation here has not been identified as belonging to a known legal text. Based on the fact that the citation is repeated across a cluster of texts quoting material known to come from *Aidbred*, it is probable that the citation is part of the tract of *Aidbred*. For sources P and FF, see below and Appendix 4; for source AA, see below.

276 I follow the emendation suggested by Binchy, *CIH* 1270, n. m.

277 The word is abbreviated as 'm.i.g.' in the MS; see also Binchy, *CIH* 1270, n. n.

278 The verb is a MI 3 pl. pres. ind. form of *imm-beir* 'puts, places, applies, practices'.

279 The verb is a 3 sg. pres. ind. of *do-fairget*; *eDIL* s.v. *do-fairget* 'offers, attempts, ventures'.

If the person from whom the *sét* was claimed is a worthy person, and he submits to the law of claiming, the *sét* is to be in his own hand. And if he does not submit [to judgment], it is [handed over to] a neutral third party. As it says: **the one who does not submit according to law, etc.**, and **the one who submits, etc.**

What causes its submission to a neutral third party by the unworthy one here, and where it says: **it is not established by prior right though it may be amongst thieves**? This is the reason that causes it: previous unworthiness regarding other things that he did here, and [it is] proper that it was submitted to a neutral third party by him. And the place above where it is said that **it is not establisheded by prior right, etc.**, regarding that *sét* itself, the unworthiness of the person above was known, and he [is] like an unlawful receiver of stolen goods regarding that *sét*, and it is proper though that it is not submitted to a neutral third party by him.

Each worthy person who claims his *sét* from a worthy person and each unworthy person [who claims his *sét*] from an unworthy person, it is up to the one from whom it is claimed to prove it [i.e., must provide proof] if they bring claims of growth. And a freeman is entitled to its proof by the one from whom it is claimed: because they are certain that it belongs to the one with whom it was born; because if the plaintiff would be permitted to prove it, it would be that he would desire the disputed *sét* which might not be his. f. 4va

Each worthy person, however, who claims his *sét* from an unworthy person, and it is a claim of growth that they both bring, it is up to the worthy one to prove it with compurgators supporting him,[280] unless the untrustworthy witness[281] undergoes an ordeal. If he undergoes [the ordeal], however, there is not a truth which is more wretched[282] to prove for it than the truth which he offers.[283]

280 The translation of *ina diagh* follows that in *The MacEgan Legal Treatise*, § 2.2; see also the discussion by Kelly, op. cit., 135.

281 The word *ainteist* is used of anyone not legally capable of acting as a witness or who would be considered an untrustworthy witness; see *eDIL* s.v. *ainteist*; and *Di Ércib Fola*, § 10.2. In some circumstances it seems to be used as a term for a suspect; see *The MacEgan Legal Treatise* § 2.22; and Kelly, op. cit., 142.

282 The precise meaning of *táire*, the comp. of *táir* 'mean, base, valueless', is obscure to me; see *eDIL* s.v. 1 *táir*; and see the discussion on this word in the note to source AA § 2.

283 See the note on ordeals in the note to source AA § 2.

Mad*h* fot*h* n-inais imris[284] in esin*nraic* ⁊ fot*h* creca imris in in*nraic*, is laisin esin*nraic* a imdenam. Ma t*h*ug fer aid*h*br*eda* a remad*h*, luig*h*i[d][285] intí ogar h-aid*h*br*ed* na fit*ir con*ad gad. ⁊ mana t*h*ard in luig*h*i-sin, b*eir*id*h* an fer [aidbreda] am*uich* in *sét* iarna *im*denam gona fiac*h* gaide fo aigni seall*aig* lanfe[i](*t*)[c]*h* no l*eth*fe[i](*t*)[c]*h*. ⁊ gingu*r*ab lais, nomb*erann* dia t*h*aisci g*o* f*est*ar fer bunad*h*, mas in*nraic*. ⁊ mu*n*ab in*nraic*, tabr*ad* a laim indraca fri h-urnaid*h* fir bunaid*h*.

Mas indr*aic* ⁊ esin*nraic* doral*a* iman *sét*, cid*h* í in inraic aid*h*b*h*res cidh aic*e* aid*h*br*iter*, is lé a sena no a imdenam, cid*h*b*eth* [foth] bus ail do d*he*. ⁊ is *cét*f*aid* gach uair do b*eth* fot*h* n-*in*ais no fot*h* creca co remdilsi agin esin*nraic*, ⁊ fot*h* creca gan remdilsi agin in*nraic*, coma hí in esin*nraic* dod*en*a imdenam. ⁊ iss é fa*th* a imdenum dí: nach tairisi laisin i*nraic* turt*acht* ant seoit, ⁊ diama tairisi, is sí dod*hen*a.

Mas *da* in*n*raic no *da* esin*nraic* doral*a* uman *sét*, is laisintí oga tar*rus* e a imdenam, cid*h*bé fot*h* b*us* ail les d'i*mairt air*.

Cid*h* in*n*raic cid*h* esin*nraic*, is lais tuin*ide* int seoit a*cht* rodama dlig*ed* ⁊ g*o* dtard*a* treb*air*i.

284 The verb is a MI 3 sg. pres. ind. rel. form of *imm-beir* 'puts, places, applies, practices'.

285 See also Binchy, *CIH* 1271, n. a.

If it is a claim of growth that the unworthy person brings and a claim of purchase that the worthy person brings, it is up to the unworthy person to prove it. If the plaintiff swore his preliminary oath, the one from whom it was claimed swears that he did not know that it was stolen. And if he did not swear that oath, the plaintiff takes away the *sét* after proving it along with the fine of theft equivalent to [that of] a culpable onlooker[286] [charged with the] full fine or half fine. And though it may not be his, he takes it to be guarded [by a neutral third party] until the owner is known, if he is a worthy person. And if he is not a worthy person, let it be given into the hand of a worthy person to hold for the owner.

If it is a worthy person and an unworthy person who happened [to quarrel] regarding the *sét*, whether it is the worthy person who claims it or from whom it is claimed, he denies it or proves it, whatever claim he wishes regarding it.[287] And it is the opinion [of lawyers] that each time an unworthy person might have a claim of growth or a claim of purchase with prior right, and a worthy person has a claim of purchase without prior right, it is the unworthy person who will prove it. And this is the reason it is proved by him: it is not fitting for the worthy person to describe[288] the *sét*, and if it may be fitting, it is he who will prove it.[289]

If it is two worthy people or two unworthy people who happened [to quarrel] regarding the *sét*, the one with whom it was found proves it, whatever claim he wishes to bring regarding it.

Whether a worthy person or an unworthy person, the *sét* remains in his possession provided that he submitted to judgment and that he gives a surety.[290]

---

286 The *sellach* 'culpable onlooker' was a person who was witness to a crime in progress and did nothing to hinder it. As such, the *sellach* was liable for a range of fines depending on his degree of culpability, e.g., instigating a crime carried greater penalties than watching a crime in progress; *GEIL* 154–157. Medieval Welsh law also considered onlookers to illegal activities as having a degree of legal culpability; Jenkins, *The Law of Hywel Dda*, 143; *Ior.* §104.6.

287 See also §12 and source P, *CIH* 711.28–29 (and FF, Appendix 4).

288 The translation of *turtacht* is tentative; see *eDIL* s.v. ? *turtacht*.

289 The reason the worthy person does not have the first chance to prove ownership is because it is a case of a claim by growth or a claim of purchase with prior right.

290 The commentary here contradicts the procedure given in the first paragraph of the commentary above.

Masa cend co mem*h*ur, no eslaisdacda co tuat*a*, no innr*aic* co h-esin*n*r*aic*, is leo-sid*h*e imdenum i ng*a*c fot*h* da dtig eliug*h*[ud] [dóib ⁊ in cach foth][291] uile ⁊ i fot*h*a comarda ⁊ l*eth*arda, cid*h* iat aid*h*br*edus* cid*h* aca aid*h*br*iter*, a*cht* cenmot*h*a *dá* fot*h*a, .i. fot*h* creca g*o* remdilsi no fot*h* n-inais 'con esin*n*r*aic* ⁊ fot*h* crec*a* nama ogan in*n*r*aic*. Is a d*h*enam don esin*n*raic conad*h* f*oth* creca g*o* rem*dilsi*, no gonad f*oth* n-i*nais* dí e. ⁊ a d*henam* don in*n*r*aic* conad f*oth creca* ci*n* rem*dilsi* dí e.

⁊ a feg*ad* an cen*nach* d'urr*ad* no i*n* cen*nach* d'a*n*urr*ad* é. ⁊ masa cen*nach* d'urr*ad* é, b*erar* ai*thgin* gona h-i*nna* uait*h*i. ⁊ masa[292] cen*nach* d'a*n*urr*ad*, is roi*nn ar* d*h*o eaturr*u*.

f. 4vb Is iat na foth*a* comard*a* .i. foth crec*a* co re*m*dilsi no gi*n* re*m*d*ilsi*, no fot*h* n-i*n*ais ac*a* maræ*n*. ⁊ is iat na fot*h*a l*eth*ard*a* .i. fot*h* crec*a* g*o* re*m*dilse no fot*h* n-i*n*ais agan dara de ⁊ fot*h* crec*a* nama 'c *ar*ele. No iss iat na[293] foth*a* l*eth*arda, .i. fot*h* n-i*n*ais '*con* dara de, ⁊ fot*h creca* g*o* remdilsi no ci*n* re*m*d*ilsi* '*con*tí ele, no f*oth creca* g*o* remdilsi [ocin dara de],[294] ⁊ fot*h creca* nama '*con*tí eile.

Is *ed* is fot*h creca* go remd*ilsi* an*n*: in tan is tasg*a* rocenuig*h* intí ogar h-aid*h*br*ed* é na tall*ad* in *sét* ontí fuil oga n-aid*h*bri*ud*. Is *ed* is f*oth creca* gi*n* remdilsi an*n*: in tan is taisc*e* tall*ad* in *sét* óntí fuil aga n-aid*h*bri*ud* na rocen*n*-ad*h* antí ógar h-aid*h*br*ed* é. Is *ed* is fot*h* n-inais an*n*: a br*eth* aig*e* buden.[295]

G [*CIH* 2073.10–33] .i. cach remad. Is *ed* ḟuil[296] anuasana uas*al* f*or* isil ac aid-br*ed* a seoit, ł cen*n* f*or* memu*r*, no in*n*r*aic* f*or* eisin*n*r*aic*. ⁊ is ed*h* fuil an*n* an *sét* do b*eth* a coi*m*it*echt* in uas*ail* co t*air* dlig*ed* ime. ⁊ it*er dá* compersai*n* ata an *sét* sisanaig*h*, ⁊ is *ed* is coir in *sét* do beit*h*[297] a laim*h* inti agar aidbr*ed* é co t*air* dlig*ed* uime.

291 Cf. the same phrase in sources A above [*CIH* 2168.37–38] and G below [*CIH* 2073.20].
292 The ⟨s⟩ was written above the first ⟨a⟩ by the scribe.
293 Between the ⟨n⟩ and the ⟨a⟩, one letter has been erased.
294 I follow the emendation suggested by Binchy, *CIH* 1271, n. e.
295 Cf. *Anfuigell* § 23, which concerns a similar topic.
296 The scribe placed a *punctum* over the ⟨u⟩ to indicate a lenited ⟨f⟩.
297 The ⟨i⟩ is written subscript.

If it is a chief against a subject, or an ecclesiastic against a layman, or a worthy person against an unworthy person, it is up to them to prove each claim if they are sued and the entirety of every claim and for equal and unequal claims, whether it is they who claim or are claimed from, except for two claims, i.e., the unworthy person has a claim of purchase with prior right or a claim of growth, and the worthy person has a claim of purchase only. It is proved by the unworthy person that it is a claim of purchase with prior right or that it is a claim of growth that he had for it, and it is proved by the worthy person that it is a claim of purchase without prior right that he had for it.

And the purchase from a local freeman or an outsider is taken into account. And if it is a purchase from a local freeman, restitution is given along with the increase in cattle from it. And if it is a purchase from an outsider, it is divided in two between them.

The equal claims are, i.e., they both have a claim of purchase with prior f. 4vb
right or without prior right or a claim of growth. And the unequal claims are, i.e., one of them has a claim of purchase with prior right or a claim of growth, and the other has a claim of purchase only. Or the unequal claims are, i.e., one of them has a claim of growth, and the other one has a claim of purchase with prior right or without prior right, or one of them has a claim of purchase with prior right, and the other has a claim of purchase only.

This[298] is a claim of purchase with prior right then:[299] when the one from whom it was claimed had bought it before the *sét* was stolen from the one who is claiming it. This is a claim of purchase without prior right then: when the *sét* was stolen from the one who is claiming it before the one from whom it was claimed had bought it. This is claim of growth then: it being born in his own possession.

G i.e., each preliminary oath. What is above is [regarding] a noble claiming his *sét* against a plebeian, or a chief against a subject, or a worthy person against an unworthy person. And what is there is the *sét* to be accompanying the noble until law decides about it. And the *sét* [referred to] below is between two people of equal rank, and what is proper is for the *sét* to be in the hand of the one from whom it was claimed until law decides about it.

298 For the remainder of the commentary, cf. *Anfuigell* § 23, source A, *CIH* 2154.1, and p. 25 therein.

299 For discussion on this commentary, see *eDIL* s.v. *remdílse* 'pre-ownership, a prior right'.

Obus comp*er*san*n*a co c*h*ele, ecl*as*daca co h-ecl*as*daca, no tuata co tuata, no in*nraic* co in*n*raic, no h-eisin*n*raic co eisin*nraic*, is leisinti oca n-aidbrit*er* é imde*n*am a fot*h*aib co*marda* ł l*ethar*da. ⁊ ma é in fer aile imres in fot*h* l*ethar*d, is do lecur.

Mas eclaisdaca co tuata, ł in*n*raic co h-eisin*nraic*, ł cen*n* co mema*r*, is leo imdenum in cac*h* fot*h* i mbia eiliug*h*[ud] doib ⁊ cac*h* fot*h* uile, cid iat aidbres cid acu aidbrit*er*, cenmot*ha dá* fot*h* .i. fot*h* creca co reimdilsi no fot*h* n-inais oci*n* eisi*nnraic*, ⁊ fot*h* creca namá oc in*nraic*. A denam don eisin*nraic con*id fot*h* creca co reimdilsi no *con*a fot*h* n-inais di é, ⁊ a denum do*n* in*nraic con*ad fot*h* c*r*eca gin reimdilsi di.

col. 612 ⁊ at*h*fegth*ar* in cen*n*ac*h* d'urr*ad* no d'anurr*ad* di é. Mad | cen*n*ach d'urr*ad* di, b*erar* ait*hgin cona* h-in*n*ud*h* uad*h*. Ma cenn*ac* d'anurr*ad*, is roin*n ar* do.

Iss iat na fuit*h* com*ar*da .i. fot*h* n-inais acu m*ar*aon, no fot*h* creca co re*m*-dilsi ł cin reimdilsi. Is iat na fuit*h* l*ethar*da: fot*h* n-inais 'con d*ar*ade dib ⁊ f*oth* c*r*eca co reimdilsi no ce*n reimdilsi* 'co*n*ti ele, no fot*h* c*reca* co reimd*ilsi* [ocin dara de][300] ⁊ fot*h* n-inais nama 'conti eile. Is ed*h* is f*oth* c*reca* co re*m*d*ilsi* do r*er* in denma-sa: in tan atb*eir* an fer aid*h*bres a gait uad*h*, ⁊ robui aice-sium roi*m*e sin é, ⁊ ni fír doib*h* m*ar*ꝏn do reir na *cét*fada-sa, *acht* cena noc*h*an ait*h*geoin leis-[s]im[301] é, u*air* ní h-inan*n* fot*h* acu m*ar*ꝏn.

J [*CIH* 1961.21–23] .i. cid *sét* cid fera*n*n, .i. indraic roa[d]bhrest*ar* a *sét* ag in*n*-raic sund, no eisin*n*raic ac eisin*n*raic. ⁊ is [s]l*an* di fomailt na *séoit* no in ferain*n* cidbe daró.

M [*CIH* 2141.27–30] Ob*us* comp*er*san*n*a ca celi, ecl*as*dacda co ecl*as*dacda, ł tuata co tuata (co tuata),[302] ł *in*dra*ic* co h-in*nraic*, ł esi*n*dr*aic* co esi*n*dr*aic*, is lesin fer tall a se*n*a na rang*us* cuice, no ce rang*us* nachar cui*n*dced gill na airgi air.

---

300 I follow the emendation suggested by Binchy, *CIH* 2073, n. g.

301 See also Binchy, *CIH* 2073, n. h.

302 See also Binchy, *CIH* 2141, n. m. The phrase has been underlined in the MS.

When it is two people of equal rank [claiming against] each other, an ecclesiastic against an ecclesiastic, or a layman against a layman, or a worthy person against a worthy person, or an unworthy person against an unworthy person, it is up to the one from whom the *sét* is claimed to prove [it] by equal or unequal claims. And if it is the other man who brings the unequal title, it is permitted to him [to bring the proof].

If it is an ecclesiastic against a layman, or a worthy person against an unworthy, or a chief against a subject, it is up to them to prove each claim regarding which they are sued and the entirety of every claim, whether it is they who claim or are claimed from, except for two claims: the unworthy person has a claim of purchase with prior right or a claim of growth, and the worthy person has a claim of purchase only. It is proved by the unworthy person that it is a claim of purchase with prior right or that it is a claim of growth that he had for it, and it is proved by the worthy person that it is a claim of purchase without prior right to it.

And it is to be considered [whether] the purchase of it was from a local freeman or an outsider. If | it is a purchase from a local freeman, restitution col. 612
is given along with the increase in cattle from him. If it is a purchase from an outsider, it is divided in two.

The equal claims are, i.e., they both have a claim of growth or a claim of purchase with prior right or without prior right. The unequal claims are: one of them has a claim of growth, and the other one has a claim of purchase with prior right or without prior right, or one of them has a claim of purchase with prior right, and the other has a claim of purchase only. This is what is claim of purchase with prior ownership according to the proof: when the man who claims says it was stolen from him, and he had it before that, and it is not right for them both according to the opinion [of lawyers], moreover he does not have restitution, because they do not both have the same claim.

J i.e., whether *sét* or land, i.e., a worthy person had claimed his *sét* from a worthy person here, or an unworthy person from an unworthy person. And he is free to use the *sét* or the land, whichever of the two it be.

M When it is two people of equal rank [claiming against] each other, an ecclesiastic against an ecclesiastic, or a layman against a layman, or a worthy person against a worthy person, or an unworthy person against an unworthy person, the defendant denies that he received it, or though he received [it], that neither pledge nor surety was asked of him.

P [*CIH* 712.1–3][303] **Inti da*m*as a reir forais,**[c] **as oca bis tuinide,**[304] .i. cid indr*ai*(d)[c][305] cid eisin*rai*(d)[c] da*m*us dlig*ed*, is coir tui*n*id*h*e i*nth* seoit oca *acht* co roda*m*a dlig*ed* ⁊ co tarda *tre*b*air*e aire.

[c] .i. dlig*ed*

[*CIH* 713.10–22] **Ni**[306] **suit*er* fri reimdilsi cia b*eth* itir t*h*aitib.**[i][307] **Ni tabair re na**[308] **tuinig*h*e fri cura na reimd*h*ilsi,**[j][309] **cia focertat tat(a)ha[i]t**[310] **ilar cor fair eturru imanetar, is di t*h*aitib diren[ar].**[k][311]

p. 187b [i] .i. nochan astaid*h*th*er* 'na laim he ge rob*eth* dilsi rei*mi* it*er* n|a gataig*h*ib re fer i*n* aid*h*b*r*iug*h*a[312]

[j] .i. fri h-indsaig*id* na cor tucud dó re dilsi rei*mh*e

[k] .i. is dona gatai[gi]b[313] eirnith*er* ima b*hreth* uaithib*h*; no is uait*h*ib icth*ar* sm*acht*

303 The second part of the relevant material from source P is below. All of source P is given in Appendix 4. The letters assigned to the glosses here follow the order in which they appear in Appendix 4.

304 The citation is clearly from a legal text, and likely from *Aidbred*; see also sources F, *CIH* 1270.24, and FF (Appendix 4).

305 The emendation here and two words later follows Binchy, *CIH* 712, n. b. The scribe has written what could be read as a ⟨d⟩ above the ⟨r⟩, but I am not entirely convinced that the letter is a ⟨d⟩.

306 There is a small paragraph symbol in *marg. sin.*

307 See also source AA, Digest C (38), *CIH* 1940.39–1941.4, below and *CCIH* 77. Part of the material is also found in Digest B (16), beginning at *CIH* 1306.34.

308 The ⟨a⟩ is written subscript.

309 Along with source P, *CIH* 713.11–12, this fragment of tract is also found in Digest B (32), *CIH* 1318.23–24, *CCIH* 58, and *AL* 4: 268.26 under the erroneously named textual heading *Téd an Fearann a Cintaib*.

310 The scribe of P originally wrote ⟨teatahat⟩ but expunged the ⟨e⟩ by placing a *punctum* under it.

311 *AL* 4: 268.27–28.

312 Binchy, *CIH* 713, n. b, notes that the gloss is interlinear; half of the gloss is interlinear, the other half is written at the top of p. 187b.

313 I follow the emendation suggested by Binchy, *CIH* 861, n. a. Both of the ⟨a⟩s are written subscript.

P **The one who submits according to law,**[c] **is he who has possession**, i.e., whether it is a worthy on an unworthy person who submits to judgment, it is proper that he has possession of the *sét* provided that he submitted to judgment and that he gives a surety for it.

[c] i.e., law

It is not established by prior right though it may be amongst thieves.[i] **Neither time nor possession is given against contracts or prior right,**[j] **though thieves place an abundance of contracts on it amongst themselves in turn, it is by thieves that it is paid.**[k]

[i] i.e., it is not seized in his hand though there should be previous possession amongst the | thieves before the person claiming.[314] p. 187b
[j] i.e., against suing or contract that it was given to him before previous possession.
[k] i.e., it is by the thieves that it is paid regarding its judgment by them, or it is from them that [the] fine is paid.

314 In other words, the fact that the thieves had the item in their possession before the claim was made against it by the owner does not entitle the thieves to a claim of prior right.

Cid fo*dera* urlai*m* c*h*oitc*hind* do damail don eisi*nn*raic isi*n*n inad*h* eile ⁊ se 'ga rad*ha*: **ni suit*er* fri rei*m*d*h*ilsi cia b*eth* it*er* t*h*aitib, ⁊rl-**? Is e in fat*h* fo*dera*: eisindrucus rei*m*t*h*e*cht*ach i*n* n-ernailib rei*m*t*h*e*cht*acha eile dorinde in dui*n*e 'san i*n*nad ele, [⁊][315] am*al* fer medongaite landlig*h*the*ch* i*m*on s*ét*-si*n* he, ⁊ coir cia rod*h*amtha urlai*m* c*h*oitc*henn* do. ⁊[316] in baile ata sund im*morro*:
p. 188a **ni suit*er* fri re*m*dilse ⁊rl-**, i*m*un s*ét*-sa | fein rofes essindruc*us* in duine-se, ⁊ fer medongaite indlig*h*the*ch* imon s*ét*-so hé, ⁊ coir ci*n*co damtha urlai*m* c*h*oit*h*chend dó.

AA[317] [*CIH* 1940.39–1941.4] **Ni suit*er* fri reimdilsi cia b*eth* it*er* taitib, .⁊rl-.**

Cid*h* fo*dera* urlam*h* coitc*henn* *ar*in s*ét* do dam*h*tain don eisindr*aic* isin inat *aile*, ⁊ é aga rada: **ni suit*er* fri reimdilsi**? Is e in fa*th* fo*dera*: eisindruc*us* reim[t]*hecht*ach[a] im ernail (i) *aile* dorin*n*e in duine isin inat *aile*, ⁊ am*al* fer meod*on*gaite laindligtec iman s*ét*-sin é, ⁊ coir ce rodamt*ar* urlam*h* coitc*henn* do. Sun*n* im*murro* iman s*ét*-si*n* fein rofes eisin*nracus*, ⁊ am*al* fer m*e*do*n*gait*e* lanindlig*thech* é, ⁊ coir cinco da*mh*ta urlam*h* coitc*henn* do.

BB [*CIH* 2096.25–33] Uasal roaidbrest*ar* a ṡet ac isiul inuasana, ⁊ comp*er*sand ac araili sisana.

Riad*aid* ca*ch* n-aidbr*iud*: tria cendairde ł t*r*ia cendisli donithe*r*[318] int aidb*r*iud anuasan. Tria torand[ch]lesaige[319] ł tria cascacraige[320] donither sisan.

315 I follow the emendation suggested by Binchy, *CIH* 713, n. i; see also source AA, Digest C (38), *CIH* 1941.1.

316 From here to the end of the paragraph, see also source F above, *CIH* 1270.28–30.

317 This material is from Digest C (38) and partly overlaps with Digest B (16), *CIH* 1306.34–40. The digest heading reads: Doni nach mill*enn* ni um nech iman caing*in* frecnairc a eisin*n*ruc*us* im ernail (i) reim*h*te*cht*a*ch*. 'That unworthy conduct in previous circumstances does not have any deleterious effect on anyone with regard to the present matter'. The translation is from *CCIH* 77.

318 This word is followed by ⟨donith⟩, which has been underlined to indicate that it is a mistake; see also Binchy, *CIH* 2096, n. k.

319 This is probably a form of *torannchless*; see *eDIL* s.v. *torannchless* 'loud noise, explosion, thunder-feat'.

320 Perhaps this is a form of *coscraige*; see *eDIL* s.v. *coscraige* 'victoriousness'.

What causes submission to a neutral third party by the unworthy person in the other place, and its saying: **it is not established by prior right though it may be amongst thieves, etc.**? This is the reason that causes it: previous unworthiness regarding other previous things that the man had done [is what it says] in the other place, and he is as a fully-lawful receiver of stolen goods regarding that *sét*, and [it is] proper that it was submitted to a neutral third party by him. And the place here, however, there is: **it is not established by prior right, etc.**, regarding that *sét* | itself, the unworthiness of that man was known, and he [is as] an unlawful receiver of stolen goods regarding that *sét*, and proper that it was not submitted to a neutral third party by him. p. 188a

AA It is not established by prior right though it may be amongst thieves, etc.

What causes submission of the *sét* to a neutral third party by the unworthy one in the other place, and its saying: **it is not established by prior right**? This is the reason that causes it: previous unworthiness regarding other things that the person did [is what it says] in the other place, and he [is] as a fully-lawful receiver of stolen goods regarding that *sét*, and it is proper though it had been submitted to a neutral third party by him. Here, however, regarding that *sét* itself, the unworthiness [of that man] was known, and he [is] as a fully unlawful receiver of stolen goods, and it is proper though it is not submitted to a neutral third party by him.

BB [Regarding] a noble who has claimed his *sét* from a plebeian above, and people of equal rank [claiming] from another [of the same social status] below.

Authority of each claiming: by purchasing it or by its prior right the claiming is done above. By its loud noise or by its victoriousness [the claiming] is done below.[321]

321 The precise legal meaning of this clause is unclear.

Ma thuc f*er* aidb*r*iuda a remud, luigid inti oca *n*-aidb*r*ed*h* n*ar* fit*ir* *con*id gait. Mani [tard in luige-sin],[322] b*eir*id in fer [aidbreda] i*m*mach i*ar*na imdenu*m* *con*a fia*ch* g*aite* fo aicn*ed* sell*aig* lanfia*ch*aig ł l*ethfiachaig*. ⁊ gingup lais, nomb*eirenn* dia toiscid co fest*ar* fer buna, masa i*n*raic. Mainip i*n*raic im*murro*, tab*r*ad i lai*m* inraice isin c*r*ich re urnaide fir bunaid.[323]

322 Several letters have been erased after *mane*. I follow the emendation suggested by Binchy, *CIH* 2096, n. m.

323 The last paragraph of the commentary was written in *marg. sup.* without reference marks by the scribe; see also Binchy, *CIH* 2096, n. l.

If the plaintiff swore his preliminary oath, the one from whom it was claimed swears that he did not know that it was stolen. If he did not swear that oath, the plaintiff takes away [the *sét*] after proving it along with the fine of theft equivalent to [that of] a culpable onlooker [charged with the] full fine or half fine. And though it is not his, he takes it to be guarded [by a neutral third party] until the owner is known, if he is a worthy person. If he is not a worthy person, however, let it be given into the land of a worthy person in the territory to hold for the owner.[324]

324 The material from this paragraph is also found in sources Q (Appendix 2), AA, and JJ (Appendix 3), *Aidbred* § 1.

§4

Nach fer medongaite docuisin, ⁊rl-

p. 19b A [*CIH* 2169.8–2171.20] In fer medongaite landligth*ech*, is si a ait*h*ne-side: | cen fis gaite no gat*aig*i aice, ⁊ is [s]*lan* do *acht* cu rai*n*desea cia or cen*n*aig ⁊ cia[325] f*r*isa racust*ar*. ⁊ doaisic a i*n*dili do cu*n*dr*adach* uad, .i. d'fir bun*aid*, ⁊ dob*er*ar re n-i*n*dsaigt*hi* do fr*i*[326] iarraid gat*aig*i, ⁊ dob*er*ar tui*n*ide in s*éoit* i*n*a lai*m*. ⁊ mane i*n*disi i*n*ti or cen*n*aig, is fiach cub*us*brait*h* ci*n*dti no cu*n*dtab*ar*tac*h* uad. Mane i*n*disi inti risa rac, is fia*ch* airitin ł diti*n* uad.

Det*h*b*ir* it*er* in fia*ch* airiti*n* ⁊ in fia*ch* ditin, .i. in airitiu, doni do fei*n* hi, ⁊ doni do neoch *aile*. In ditiu *immurro*, do neoch *aile* doni hi. In airitiu *immurro*, ca*ch* uair is do fe*n* doni hi, is fia*ch* gaite cu n-aithg*in* i*n*dti, ⁊ cach uair is do neoch *aile* is fia*ch* gaite ce*n* aithg*in*. In ditiu im*murro*, cid do fei*n* cid do neoch *aile*, is fia*ch* g*aite*[327] *co n*-aithg*in*.

1 Nach] nac*h* FF. ‖ fer] fear F. ‖ medongaite] m.i.g. F, meodong*h*aite *CIH* 2070.35, meodongaite *CIH* 2073.34 G; parts of the tract appear twice in G: *CIH* 2070.35 and 2073.34. ‖ docuisin] docuisi*n* F and P, *om*. *CIH* 2070.35, dochuisin *CIH* 2073.34 G. ‖ ⁊rl-] Sources P and FF add ⁊rl-. Sources CC, DD, W, and Z do not preserve any of the tract.

325 This word was added above the line by the scribe; see also Binchy, *CIH* 2169, n. g.

326 Binchy, *CIH* 2169.11 prints 'f*or*' for ⟨f̄⟩ and queries whether this is a mistake for 'f*ri*'. The suspension mark is ambiguous.

327 *.g.* was added below the line by the scribe.

§ 4

Any receiver of stolen goods who there is, etc.[328]

A The fully lawful receiver of stolen goods, he is characterized thus: | he does not have knowledge of the theft or the thief, and he is free from liability provided that he names[329] the one from whom he bought [the goods] and the one to whom he sold [them]. And he restores his property to the party of the contract, i.e., to the owner, and a period of time for searching is given to him to search for the thief, and possession of the *sét* is given into his hand. And if he does not name the one from whom he bought [the goods], he owes a fine of certain or uncertain complicity. If he does not name the one to whom he sold [the goods], he owes a fine for receiving [stolen goods] or sheltering.[330] p. 19b

The difference between the fine for receiving and the fine for sheltering, i.e., the receiving, he does it for himself, and he does [it] for someone else. The sheltering, however, he does it for someone else. The receiving, however, every time it is for himself that he does it, the aforementioned owes a fine for theft with restitution, and every time it is for someone else, [he owes] a fine for theft without restitution. The sheltering, however, whether for himself or for someone else, [he owes] a fine for theft with restitution.

---

328 For a discussion of this section, see the Introduction, pp. 23–27. The person who receives stolen goods is also found in *The MacEgan Legal Treatise* § 5.29–37; see also the discussion in Kelly, op. cit., 172–176; *GEIL* 148; and Mac Niocaill, "Aspects of Irish Law in the Late Thirteenth Century," 37–38.

329 The verb *indisid* is used here for the receiver of stolen goods letting it be known by name or description the person who sold him the stolen goods (sc., the thief) and the person to whom he inadvertently sold the stolen goods.

330 The term *airitiu* 'receiving' refers to receiving stolen goods, whereas *dítiu* 'sheltering' refers to sheltering someone else, but not naming them. Both activities involve a fine from the receiver of stolen goods.

Masa aithg*in* tarr*us* aice, noc*ha* berar uad hi *no* co t*u*car re n-i*n*dsaigt*hi* do. Mas [s]i in [ḟ]rit*hcr*eic[331] tarr*us* aige, noc*ha* b*er*ar uad hi do gres no co tarth*ar* in ait*h*g*in* amuig. ⁊ am*ail* tarr*ustar* in aithg*in* amuig, cid *co n*-i*n*dud cid cen i*n*dud, is aml*aid* aisices in [f]rit*hcr*eic uad. ł da*no* chena, mu*n*ub aicn*ed* i*n*dud it*ir* do beth aci*n* [ḟ]rit*hcr*eic, cia rob*eth* i*n*dud acan aithg*in*, *con*a h-aisicea i*n*dud lasi*n* frit*h*crec. ⁊ *in* tan tic gat*ai*gi re dlig*ed*, ic*aid* aithg*in* [f]ris-[s]*ium*[332] co los ⁊ as, ⁊ ma ta aice,[333] dilaid aithg*in* ⁊ enecl*ainn*.

Fer medong*aite* landligth*ech*, ce*n* fis g*aite* na gat*ai*gi si*n*, ⁊ frit*h*cerc [*read* frithcreic] tarr*us* i*na* lai*m*, ⁊ i*n*disid i*n*ti or cen*n*aig ⁊ inti f*r*isa rac, ⁊ dob*eir* a mbi 'na laim dara chen*n* amach do*n* fir risa rac se in s*ét* gaite. ⁊ aithfeg*ar* in cen*n*ach d'urr*ad* no in cen*n*ach d'anurr*ad* do he. Ma*n*a fagab*ar* in s*ét* re aidb*r*iud, ni b*er*ar in frit*hcr*eic uad-su*m*.

---

331 The second ⟨i⟩ was written subscript by the scribe.

332 See also Binchy, *CIH* 2169, n. l.

333 This word was added above the line by the scribe; see also Binchy, *CIH* 2169, n. g.

If it is restitution[334] that was found in his possession, it is not taken from him until a period of time for searching is given to him.[335] If it is the counter-purchase that was found in his possession, it is never taken from him until the restitution is found outside [his property].[336] And as the restitution may be found outside [his property], whether with increase or without increase, it is thus that he restores the counter-purchase. Or on the other hand, if it is not known [whether] the counter-purchase has an increase at all, though the restitution might have an increase, he does not restore the increase with the counter-purchase. And when the thief submits to judgment, he [sc., the thief] pays restitution to him with increase and growth, and if [the restitution] has [increase and growth], he pays restitution and honor-price.[337]

The fully lawful receiver of stolen goods, [he is] without knowledge of the theft or the thief, and the counter-purchase was found in his hand, and he names the one from whom he bought [the goods] and the one to whom he sold [the goods], and he gives away that which may be in his hand for it to the man to whom he sold the stolen *sét*. And it is to be considered [whether] the purchase of it was from a local freeman or from an outsider.[338] If the *sét* is not found to be claimed, the counter-purchase is not taken from him.

---

334 The legal term *aithgein* 'restitution, compensation' is used in the commentaries to refer to the disputed goods, here, the stolen property, or the equivalent value of the stolen goods. The term *frithchrec* 'counter-purchase, goods acquired in exchange' refers to the goods that the receiver of stolen goods acquired when he sold the stolen goods to someone else. The assumption of the commentaries is that the counter-purchase (presumably livestock) would be of the equivalent value of the stolen goods. Thus, if the *aithgein* 'restitution' cannot be found (whether the actual property or something of the equivalent value), then in some circumstances the counter-purchase (if there is one) can be given to the owner of the stolen goods in compensation for his original property.

335 In other words, although the receiver of stolen goods possesses property worth the same as the stolen goods, he is given time to seek the thief.

336 In this situation, the receiver of stolen goods has sold the stolen property to someone else. He is given an opportunity to try to get the stolen property back from the person to whom he sold it. He must restore the counter-purchase to its original owner with the same amount of produce which the stolen goods have produced after they were sold to the third party. The adv. *amuig* 'outside, away, afar' is used here to refer to the fact that the stolen property is not on the defendant's property and must be found elsewhere, whether the stolen property is at the next farm or another province.

337 The text does not specify whether the thief pays these fines to the original owner of the goods or the receiver of stolen goods. The version in source F states that the thief pays double restitution along with honor-price.

338 The term *aurrae, aurrad* 'person who is native within the bounds of a community, local freeman' is used in contrast to *anurrad* 'one who does not have the status of an *aurrae*, outlaw, outsider'; *eDIL* s.vv. *aurrae* and *anurrad*. While *anurrad* is frequently found

Mas d'fir medo*ngaite* landligth*ech* rainig in *sét* i n-aithgi*n* do r*eir* dlig*id* c*r*andcair, diabl*ad* d'ic ris ca*ch* nech[339] im*ar* digb*ad*[340] a lam ⁊ *e*necl*ann.* No cu*m*ud l*eth*in*n*ud ⁊ enecl*ann* beos ⁊ diabl*ad* aithg*en*a d'ic ris o gat*ai*gi, ⁊ l*eth*aithg*in* ⁊ l*eth*diabl*ad* ⁊ l*eth*indud ⁊ l*eth*ceth*ar*da d'ic re fer mbun*aid* ⁊ *e*necl*ann.* ł comad ceth*ar*da comlan do. Mas d'fir bun*aid* rai*n*ic an aithg*in* do r*eir* dlig*id* c*r*ancair, diabl*ad* ⁊ enecl*ann* d'ic re ce*cht*ar de. ł comad l*eth*aithg*in* ⁊ l*eth*diablad ⁊ l*eth*i*n*dud d'ic re f*er* medong*aite* ⁊ *e*necl*ann.*

In fer medong*aite* l*eth*indligth*ech,* is [s]i a aithni-side: fis gat*ai*gi aige ⁊ ce*n* fis gaite. ⁊ cid aithg*in* cid frit*h*c*r*eic tarr*us* aige, nocha[341] tabair re n-i*n*dsaigt*hi* do, *acht* a bre*th* uad fo *cét*oir: in aithg*in* co los ⁊ as ⁊ *in* [ḟ]orb*airt,* ⁊ landire ⁊ l*eth*enecl*ann.* & in tan tic gat*ai*gi re dlig*ed,* icaid aithg*in* [f]ris-[s]i*m* co los ⁊ in [ḟ]orb*air*t ⁊ diabl*ad* ⁊ l*eth*enecl*ann.* Is [s]i-side a lanenecl*ann*-su*m,* uair (iside) is esbadach[342] a l*eth*enecl*ann* uad im cu*n*drad do den*am* risi*n* gataide do*na* *sét*aib gaiti. ⁊ is a*n*d is esbadach uad i*n* tan is a cor ł a cu*n*dr*ad* tucad do iat, ⁊ ni h-i*n*draic rofoc*ail* air. Mas a n-er*aic* fog*l*a t*u*cad do iat, ce*n*cob i*n*draic rofoc*ail* air, no cid i cor ł i cu*n*drad, masa[343] i*n*draic rofoc*ail* air, noc*h*a dena*n*d esi*n*dr*aic* de.

---

translated as 'outlaw', the meaning in the commentaries is more generally someone from outside the community. While it is possible that an outlaw could have sold stolen goods in his own or another territory, the term 'outsider' encompasses both the meaning 'outlaw' and 'outsider' more generally; *GEIL* 5–6. It should be borne in mind that the receiver of stolen goods in the commentaries might not be the first person to have received and/or sold the stolen goods in question, and it is also possible that the 'local freeman' referred to in the commentaries could also be the thief. The notion lying behind all this is that the owner has the right to track his property as far as he can, despite how many times his property might have changed hands since the time it was stolen. In Welsh law, there is a similar provision where the owner has the right to trace his property as far as he is able. Furthermore, the receiver of the stolen goods is liable to pay fines no matter how many times the property has changed hands up to the 'hundredth hand'; the legal term used is *cyhyryn canastr* 'sinew of a hundred journeys'; Jenkins, *The Law of Hywel Dda*, 160; *Ior*. § 113.7–11; and see the discussion regarding triad X51 in Roberts, *The Legal Triads of Medieval Wales*, 267.

339 For the MI construction *cach nech* meaning 'person', see *eDIL* s.v. *nech* II.

340 The form *digbad* is interpreted here as the 3 sg. pret. pass. of *do-gaib* 'takes away, lessens'; *eDIL* s.v. *do-gaib* 'takes away, lessens, diminishes'.

341 The ⟨a⟩ was added below the line by the scribe.

342 The correction *ł is esbadach* was added above the line by the scribe; see also Binchy, *CIH* 2170, n. a.

343 The ⟨sa⟩ was added above the line by the scribe; see also Binchy, *CIH*, 2170, n. b.

If it is to a fully lawful receiver of stolen goods that the *sét* came as restitution according to the law of casting lots,[344] double is to be paid to him [by] the person on whose account his hand was emptied[345] and honor-price. Or that it should be half increase and honor-price still and double restitution to be paid to him by the thief, and half restitution and half doubling and half increase and half fourfold to be paid to the owner and honor-price. Or that it should be a complete fourfold [that is paid] to him. If it is to the owner that the restitution came according to the law of casting lots, doubling and honor-price are to be paid to each of them. Or that it should be half restitution and half doubling and half increase to be paid to the receiver of stolen goods and honor-price.

The half unlawful receiver of stolen goods, he is characterized thus: he has knowledge of the thief and he does not have knowledge of the theft. And whether restitution or counter-purchase was found in his possession, a period of time for searching is not given to him, but it is taken from him immediately: the restitution with increase and growth and the produce, and full penalty-fine and half honor-price. And when the thief submits to judgment, he [sc., the thief] pays restitution to him with increase and the produce and doubling and half honor-price. This is his full honor-price, because half of his honor-price is lacking from him for making a bargain with the thief for the stolen *sét*s. And it is then that it is lacking from him when it is in contract or bargain that they were given to him, and it was not a worthy person[346] who gave [his] word about it. If it is as a fine for injury that they were given to him, though it was not a worthy person who gave [his] word about it, or whether [it is] in contract or bargain, if it is a worthy person who gave his word about it, it does not make him an unworthy person.[347]

344 For discussion of the laws regarding casting lots to settle disputes, see *GEIL* 208–209. See also *The MacEgan Legal Treatise* § 5.16; Kelly, op. cit. 169; *Di Ércib Fola*, 148; and Archan, "Ordeal by Fire in Medieval Ireland," 200.

345 The idiom *dígbál láime* 'lessening a hand' (and its variant *do-gaibther lám*) is used in the legal commentaries to refer to someone paying a fine or some other financial liability on behalf of someone else; *eDIL* s.v. *do-gaib*.

346 The commentaries make a distinction between those who are considered *indraic* 'a person who is trustworthy, in good legal standing, qualified to perform certain legal functions' and *eisinnraic* 'unworthy, untrustworthy, person not in good legal standing, unqualified to perform certain legal functions'; *eDIL* s.vv. *indraic* and *eisinnraic*. It should be noted that many people in medieval Irish society would fall into the category of those considered *eisinnraic* in certain legal situations, for example, women, children, those of unsound mind, the unfree, outlaws, etc.; *GEIL* 202–208.

347 The sense of the last sentence is that if a worthy person vouched for the goods, or if they were given to someone as payment for a fine (even though the goods were stolen),

In f*er* medo*n*gaite la*n*indligthe*ch*, is [s]i a aithni-side: co fis gaite ⁊ gat*aig*i
p. 20a aice, ł co fis | gaiti nama. Gid aithg*in* gid f*r*ithc*r*eic tarr*us* aice, nochan [f]uil re n-i*n*dsaigt*h*i do, *acht* a br*eth* uad fo c*ét*oir: in aithg*in* co los ⁊ as ⁊ in [ḟ]orb*air*t, ⁊ landire ⁊ lanenecl*ann*. In tan tic gat*aig*i re dlig*ed*, noc*h*an ica*n*d ni ris *acht* mu*n*ar *acht*aige. ⁊ mas e *acht* ro*acht*aig digbail a lam d'ic ris, is a ic. Masa treb*air*i rogab re dilsi, noc*h*an[348] icth*ar* ni ris, nochan astan*n* treb*air*i na s*éotu* gaite do g*r*es.

Masa marbdili rogat*ad* a*n*d, no beodili acna fuil i*n* [ḟ]orb*air*t, in fuillea*m* dobiad leo f*or* treb*air*i echtra*n*d co ce*n*d mbliad*na* cu*r*ab ed bes leo.

Masa beodili 'canad aice*n*ta i*n*dud do beth, *acht* ma r*u*csat i*n*dud amuig, ma mairid accu he, is aisiuc leo. Mana maire*n*d, is i*nn*ud a m*a*csamla d'aisiuc. Mu*n*a rucsat i*n*dud amuig[349] it*ir*, is c*ét*faid co mbeth a roga i*n*daid .i. serraig firenda lesna ec*h*aib ⁊ laig boinen*n*a lesna buaib[350] d'fir bun*aid*.

---

it does not have a negative effect on the social and legal status of the unwitting receiver of stolen goods.

348 The ⟨a⟩ was added below the line by the scribe; see also Binchy, *CIH*, 2170, n. e.

349 The ⟨a⟩ was added below the line by the scribe. The scribe wrote *amuig* a second time and partially erased it.

350 *.i. ... buaib* starts out as a gloss, but the scribe continues it *inter col.*; see also Binchy, *CIH* 2170, n. g.

The fully unlawful receiver of stolen goods, he is characterized thus: he has knowledge of the theft and the thief, or he only has knowledge | of the theft. Whether restitution or counter-purchase was found in his possession, he does not have a period of time for searching, but it is taken from him immediately: the restitution with increase and growth and the produce, and full penalty-fine and full honor-price. When the thief submits to judgment, he [sc., the thief] does not pay anything to him except if he made a stipulation. And if he made a stipulation to pay him for the emptying of his hand, he pays him.[351] If it is a surety that he took against forfeiture, nothing is paid to him; a surety never binds the stolen *séts*.[352] p. 20a

If it is inanimate chattels that were stolen then, or livestock that have growth, the addition [e.g., increase, earnings] will be with them [sc., with the livestock] in the custody of an external surety until the end of a year so that this is what may be with them.

If it is livestock with whom it is not known [whether] there is young, except if they bore the young [while] away, if it remains[353] with them, it is restored along with them.[354] If it [sc., the young livestock] does not remain [alive], the equivalent young are restored. If they did not bear young at all [while] away, it is the opinion [of lawyers] that the owner should have his choice of young, i.e., male colts with the horses, female calves with the cows.[355]

351 The sense here is that if the thief and receiver of stolen goods had made a prior agreement that the thief was to pay back the receiver of stolen goods for anything he paid out of his own property, then the thief is bound by this prior agreement to pay him back.

352 On the invalidity of contracts for stolen goods, see McLeod, *Early Irish Contract Law*, 25–26; and the commentaries to §48 of *Di Astud Chor*, edited and translated in McLeod, *Early Irish Contract Law*, 283–285, which also concern the receiver of stolen goods and any potential fines owed to or by the surety who is involved in the contracting of stolen goods. If the surety knows the goods are stolen, he is liable for fines.

353 In other words, the young livestock is either alive or with its parent.

354 Although the commentaries make a distinction between *forbart* 'growth, increase, maturity', *fuillem* 'addition, increase, interest, earnings', and *indad* 'young animals, calves, increase, produce', the precise nature of the distinctions is not always clear as their meanings overlap; see also Index 1 in *EIF* for definitions which expand those given in *eDIL*.

355 The significance of the livestock in this clause is unclear, although it could be a sense of restoring like with like.

Masa tarb rogat*ad* a*n*d ⁊ doni dair ⁊ (doni)[356] *ar*th*ar* les ⁊ gnimrad daim, mani de*nann* *acht* *nechtar* de, in*n*i na*ch* de*nann*, ni fuil ni do *ar*a scat*h*.[357] Masa ina colp*thach*aib rogat*ad* iat [ł][358] ina sam*a*scaib,[359] ⁊ *in*a mbuib mora rohaidb*r*ed iat, gabait g*re*im n-aithg*en*a iat budein, ⁊ dire sam*aisc*i no colp*thach* leo.

Mas ina[360] mbuib mora[361] rogat*ad* iat, *acht* ma maire*n*d fei*n*, ga(a)bait g*re*im n[362]-aithg*en*a; cid crin cid cæch cid lethcolp*ach* iat, ⁊ dire inich leo fon ais i tall[ad].[363] ⁊ is a*n*d sin ata in dire i*n*ich ⁊ in aith*gin* esbudach. Is a*n*d ata in n-aithg*in* inich ⁊ in dire esbud*ach*: in inb*aid* rob esbud*ach* ni don aithg*in* in tan rogat*ad* hi, ⁊ an aithg*in* i*n*ich[364] i*n*dti fon ais i tall*ad* hi, ⁊ ni maire*n*d fen a*n*d si*n*, ⁊ dire esbud*ach* i*n*dti fo aicn*ed* na h-esbuda robui aran[365] ai*thgin*.

Aithg*in* co los ⁊ as ⁊ in [ḟ]orb*air*t, ⁊ landire ⁊ lan*e*necl*ann* don i*n*draic doni maith da t*othchus*. Aithg*in* co los ⁊ as ⁊ in [ḟ]orb*air*t, ⁊ landire ⁊ l*eth*enecl*ann* don esi*n*raic doni maith da to[th]ch*us*. Aithg*in* co los ⁊ as ⁊ in [ḟ]orb*air*t na colla,[366] ⁊ nochan [ḟ]uil dire na h-enecl*ann* don in*n*raic na den maith da to[th]ch*us*. No co *m*bet*h* lanenecland, uair ata to[th]ch*us* aice, ⁊ nochan

356 Cf. source F below.

357 *mani … scath* was written in *marg. sup.* with reference marks by the scribe; see also Binchy, *CIH* 2170, n. i.

358 I follow the emendation suggested by Binchy, *CIH* 2170, n. j.

359 The first ⟨a⟩ was added below the line by the scribe; see also Binchy, *CIH* 2170, n. k.

360 The ⟨a⟩ is written subscript.

361 *mora* was added below the line by the scribe; see also Binchy, *CIH* 2170, n. l.

362 The scribe appears to have written (or started) another ⟨n⟩ before this one, but it is partially obscure.

363 See also Binchy, *CIH* 2170, n. n, and the further attestations of this phrase in the commentaries below.

364 *inich* was added below the line by the scribe; see also Binchy, *CIH* 2170, n. l.

365 The second ⟨a⟩ was added below the line by the scribe.

366 The ⟨a⟩ was added below the line by the scribe.

If it is a bull that was stolen then and it bulls and ploughing [is done] by it and [it does] the work of an ox, if it only does one of these, that which it does not do, there is nothing for him in compensation for it [sc., the task the bull did not do]. If they [sc., the livestock] were stolen when they were two-year-old heifers or three-year-old heifers,[367] and they were claimed as large cows, they themselves are the equivalent of restitution, and penalty-fine of a three-year-old heifer or a two-year-old heifer [will be given along] with them.

If they were stolen when they were large cows, provided that they themselves are alive, they are the equivalent of restitution, whether they are withered or blind in one eye or half-shanked,[368] and full penalty-fine along with them according to the age when they were stolen. And it is in this [previous] case that there is full penalty-fine and the restitution is lacking. It is here that there is full restitution and the penalty-fine is lacking: whenever anything from the restitution was lacking when it was stolen, and the full restitution for it according to the age when it was stolen, and it itself is not alive in that case, and penalty-fine is lacking for it according to the defect [sc., what was lacking] that was for the restitution.

Restitution with increase and growth and the produce, and full penalty-fine and full honor-price for the worthy person who makes good [use] of his property.[369] Restitution with increase and growth and the produce, and full penalty-fine and half honor-price for the unworthy person who makes good [use] of his property. Restitution with increase and growth and the produce of the stolen property, and there is neither penalty-fine nor honor-price for the worthy person who does not make good [use] of his property. Or that there should be honor-price, because he has property, and there is

---

367 The commentaries refer to the *colpthach* 'two-year-old heifer' and the *samaisc* 'three-year-old heifer'. The definitions of these terms adopted here and throughout are those from *EIF* 62–64. The definitions in *EIF* differ from those given in *eDIL*, which are 'yearling heifer' and 'heifer', respectively.

368 For defects in cattle, see *EIF* 192–205, especially 204, and the text edited and translated by Kelly, op. cit., Appendix 1, §§1–6, 506–520; and *Di Astud Chor*, the commentaries to §§58 and 60, and discussion by McLeod, op. cit., Appendix 1, 313–326.

369 As thoroughly discussed by McLeod, it is not enough for a person to simply have the requisite amount of property necessary to maintain a certain level of social status. If the person does not make good use of the property that he/she has, the person's honor-price can be lowered. In the case of those who are worthy, but who do not make good use of their property, they are given the token amount of a scruple as their honor-price; McLeod, "Property and Honour-Price," 280–295.

[ḟ]uil dire. Aithg*in* ce*n* los ce*n* as cen in [ḟ]orb*air*t don es*indraic* na dein mai*th* da to[th]ch*us*, ł d'*in*draic in sc*r*ep*ail*.

Nochan [ḟ]uil dethb*ir* maigne na *secht*armaigne a lleth re fer medongaite do g*r*es, ⁊ ata re gat*aig*i. & is e in[370] fa*th*-s*in*: am*al* buachaill d'fir bun*aid* gat*aig*i re cois a *sét*, ⁊ o bias buachaill agna *sét*aib do g*r*es, nochan [ḟ]uil det*hbir* maigne na *secht*arm*aigne* friu. ⁊ is as gabar sin: "dia *m*be muicid[371] mb*r*oga dire dib, cid f*o* ræd*ha* raith, rofes is erithi do collna denta."

370 This word was added below the line by the scribe; see also Binchy, *CIH* 2170, n. l.

371 The first ⟨i⟩ was added below the line by the scribe.

not penalty-fine. Restitution without increase, without growth, without the produce for the unworthy person who does not make good [use] of his property, or the value of a scruple[372] for the worthy person.

There[373] is never a difference between precinct or outside the precinct[374] as regards a receiver of stolen goods, but there is for a thief. And this is the reason: a thief beside his *séts* [is] as a cowherd to the owner, and when the *séts* always have a cowherd, there is not a difference between precinct or outside the precinct for them. And that is taken from: "if there be a swineherd, penalty-fine is awarded for them even though [they go] under a great wood of bracken, it is known that [the fine] must be paid by he who made [the illegal structure which holds] the stolen property."[375]

---

372 For a comparison of the units of value in the Irish legal texts, see *EIF* 587–599.

373 For a discussion of the penalties listed in the commentaries below, see the Introduction, pp. 25–26 and Table 1, which lists the fines owed for the various types of theft found here and in the other versions of the commentary for this section.

374 The legal terms *maigen* 'precinct' and *sechtarmaigen* 'outside a precinct' are used to contrast the geographical area around a residence and the area beyond that, respectively. It is possible that the terms are to be equated with *faithche* 'green, infield' and *sechtar faithchi* 'beyond the green', respectively; see the discussion in *EIF* 370. Fines for offenses committed within the *maigen* are generally higher than for those committed outside the *maigen*. The phrase *maigen dígona* refers to the area around an owner's residence within the precinct, which varies according to social status, in which the owner has additional legal rights, such as the right to provide sanctuary to individuals of the same or lower social status.

375 The legal principle (possibly a direct quotation from another legal text) is difficult. It appears in various forms in several of the sources in this section of the text. The translation here is tentative. The sense seems to be that the swineherd, even one used by multiple households, will know the owner of each of the pigs in his charge, even if they are feeding in the woods and the pigs from the various households have mingled together; for the responsibilities of swineherds, see *EIF* 81–82. See also the fuller explanation of the passage given in source F below, *CIH* 1274.8–12. The interpretation of *déntae* 'manufactured article, structure, building; that which is trained, made' in this clause is based on the explanation given in the version in source F. Based on source F, it would appear that the stolen swine have been confined to an illegally constructed pen.

Mas a maigin tall gat*aig*i na sé*ot*u, cid do *cer*ttoch*us* cid d'f*or*craid to[th]ch*us*a, is laneneecl*ann*. Ma *secht*arm*aigin* tall na sé*ot*u, is l*eth*enecl*ann*. ⁊ ni fuil buachaill and, ⁊ ma ta, is lane*n*ecl*ann* a*n*d cid a maigin cid i *secht*armaig*in*.

Mas d'forc*r*aid to[th]ch*us*a tall in gataige[376] na sé*ot*u, is lane*n*eclann o fir

p. 20b medo*n*gaiti l*eth*e. Mas do ce*ar*toch*us* | tall*ad* gataige na sé*ot*u, l*eth*enecl*ann* o fir medo*n*gaiti leithe. Is a*n*d is cutr*um*a ar fer medo*n*gaite l*eth*e ⁊ ar gataige i*n* inbaid is d'forcraid[377] to[th]ch*us*a tall gataigi na sé*otu* a *secht*armaigin, ⁊ ni fuil buachaill acco: l*eth*enecl*ann* o gataigi a*n*d, ⁊ lane*n*ecland o fir medongat(aig)i[378] lain, ⁊ l*eth*enecl*ann* o fir m*edo*ngaite leithe.

Cid fotera in tan is do *cer*ttoc*hus* tall gataige na seotu [a][379] maigi*n* co fuil lane*n*ecl*ann* o gataigi a*n*d, ⁊ *con*ach fuil ach l*eth*enecl*ann* o fir medo*n*gaite lanindligth*ech*, [⁊][380] in tan is d'forc*r*aid to[th]ch*us*a tall gataige na sé*otu* a *secht*armaigin *con*a fuil *acht* l*eth*eneclaind o gataige a*n*d ⁊ co fuil lanenecla*n*d o fir medong*aite* lain? Is e in fa*th* fo*dera*: in tan is[381] do *cer*ttoch*us* tall gataige na sé*otu* a maigi*n*, robi to[th]ch*us* comlan ac fir bu*n*aid ar ci*n*d gataige, ⁊ coir ce robeith lanenecla*n*d uad i n-airb*er*nad in to[th]ch*us*a.[382] Nocha raib a to[th]ch*us* com(s)l*an*[383] in tan dori*n*de g*ataige* cu*n*drad re f*er* medong*aite* lan[i](e)ndligth*ech*,[384] ⁊ coir ce*n*co beit*h acht* leithenecla*n*d uad.

376 The second ⟨a⟩ is written subscript. It is difficult to determine whether the scribe added it later as a correction, as Binchy, *CIH* 2171, n. a, suggests.

377 The ⟨f⟩ was added below the line by the scribe; see also Binchy, *CIH* 2171, n. b.

378 See also Binchy, *CIH* 2171, n. c.

379 I follow the emendation suggested by Binchy, *CIH* 2171, n. d.

380 I follow the emendation suggested by Binchy, *CIH* 2171, n. e.

381 This word was added below the line by the scribe; see also Binchy, *CIH* 2171, n. f.

382 One letter has been erased after the ⟨c⟩.

383 See also Binchy, *CIH* 2171, n. c.

384 See also Binchy, *CIH* 2171, n. h.

If it is from a precinct that the thief stole the *sét*s, whether from exact property[385] or excess property, [he owes] full honor-price. If it is [from] outside the precinct that he stole the *séts*, [he owes] half honor-price. And there is not a cowherd there, and if there is, [he owes] full honor-price then whether from a precinct or from outside a precinct.

If it is from excess property that the thief stole the *sét*s, full honor-price is owed from the half-liable receiver of stolen goods. If it is from exact property | that the thief had stolen the *séts*, half honor-price is owed from the half-liable receiver of stolen goods. It is here that it is equivalent for the half-liable receiver of stolen goods and for the thief when it is from excess property that the thief stole the *sét*s from outside the precinct, and they do not have a cowherd: half honor-price from a thief then, and full honor-price from the fully liable receiver of stolen goods, and half honor-price from the half-liable receiver of stolen goods. p. 20b

What is the reason that when it is from exact property that the thief stole the *sét*s from a precinct that there is full honor-price owed by the thief then, and there is nothing but half honor-price from the fully unlawful receiver of stolen goods, and when it is from excess property that the thief stole the *sét*s from outside a precinct that there is nothing but half honor-price owed by the thief then and there is full honor-price owed by the fully liable receiver of stolen goods? This is the reason that causes it: when it is from exact property that the thief stole the *sét*s from a precinct, and the owner had complete property before the thief [had taken the property], and it is just that there should be full honor-price owed by him as a result of diminishing the property; his property was not complete when the thief made the bargain with the fully unlawful receiver of stolen goods, and it is just though there should not be anything but half honor-price owed by him [sc., the receiver of stolen goods].

385 The difference between *certtochus* 'exact property' and *forcraid tochusa* 'excess property' is that of property necessary to maintain one's status and honor-price, and property that is owned in excess of the minimum required to maintain one's status and honor-price, respectively. The terms used in the commentaries here are not quite the equivalent of *tochus etarscarthach* 'separable property' and *tochus nemetarscarthach* 'non-separable property' found in other legal commentaries. There the difference is between having property necessary to maintain an independent social status and honor-price, and having property that is not sufficient to maintain an independent social status; see the discussion in McLeod, "Property and Honour-Price".

In tan is d'forc*r*aid to[th]ch*us*a tall*a*[386] gataige na *séotu* a *sechtar*maigin, is amlaid fuair iat ⁊ nocha raib buachaill acco, ⁊ coir cenco b*eth acht* leth*e*necla*nd* uad.[387] ⁊ robi buachaill[388] i lleth re f*e*r medo*ngaite*, uair am*al* buach*aill* d'fir bu*n*aid[389] do reir dlig*id* in g*ataige* do b*eth* re cois a *sét*, ⁊ coir ce rob*eth* lanenecla*nd* uad. ł da*no* cena rolin*ustair* fer bun*aid* a to[th]ch*us* resiu dorigne g*ataige* cu*n*drad re f*er* medong*aite*.

F [*CIH* 1271.34–1274.35] .i. l*eth*indad*h* uaid*he* ⁊ in ait*hgin*, is *ed* a etr*o*caire. L*eth*in*n*dad*h* ⁊ l*eth*ait*hgin*, is *ed* a tr*o*caire. Mana tarr*ustar* lais ne*chtar* d*he*, ni ioca ní itir.[390]

Fear meod*h*angaid*he* lan ndlig*h*tec so sios: cin fis gaiti no gad*aigi* aigi. ⁊ cid*h* ait*hgin* cid*h* frit*h*crec t*harr*t*hus* aice, is [s]lan do a*cht* co roin*n*isi inti ris roreac[391] ⁊ antí dia rocen*naigh*; ⁊ dob*eir* a mbí 'na laim t*ar*a cen*n* amach.

In fer *medongh*aite landligt*hech*, is sí a ait*h*ni-sid*he*: ga*n* fis gait*e* na gad*aigi* aig*e*. ⁊ is [s]lan do a*cht* go roin*n*isi cia dia rocendaig*h* ⁊ na rosena intí risi rec. ⁊ da sena intí ór cendaig*h*, is fiach cub*us*brait*h* cin*n*ti no cont*h*ab*artaigh* uad*h*, no is fiach ditin. ⁊ munar in*n*isi intí resia rec, is fiach cub*us*b*raith* no fiach ditin no fiach airitin.

D*eth*ber it*er* in fiach airiti*n* ⁊ in fiach ditin: in airitiu, doní do fen ⁊ do neoch aile hí, ⁊ do neoch *aile* doní in ditiu. ⁊ g*a*c uair is do bud*ein* doní in airitiu, is fiach gait*e* co n-aithgi*n*. In tan is do neoch aile, is fiach gait*e* cin ait*hgin*. In ditiu im*murro*, cidh do bude*n* cidh do neo*c*h aile dogní, is fiach gait*e* co n-aithgi*n*.

⁊ mas [s]í an aithgi*n* t*harrus* aice, .i. ag fir m*edon*gaite landlightec, noc*ha* mb*er*ar uadha hí do g*re*s no g*o* tuct*ar* ré n-in*n*saighi do ré h-iarr*aid* ga

386 The decision to expand the final syllable as *-a* or *-ais* depends on whether the verb in the commentary is still *do-alla* or its later simplex *tallaid*. Across all the sources for § 4, both the compound verb and the simplex are found in the same sections of the commentaries.

387 A letter has been erased before *uad*.

388 The second ⟨a⟩ is written subscript; see also Binchy, *CIH* 2171, n. j.

389 ⁊ *robi* … *bunaid* was added *inter col.* and between the lines by the scribe; see also Binchy, *CIH* 2171, n. i.

390 This short paragraph is a gloss on the tract.

391 The ⟨a⟩ was written subscript by the scribe; see also Binchy, *CIH* 1271, n. h.

When it is from excess property that the thief steals the *sét*s from outside the precinct, it is as though he had found them, and they did not have a cowherd, and it is just though there should not be anything but half honor-price owed by him. And there is wont to be a cowherd as regards the receiver of stolen goods, because the thief beside his *sét*s is as a cowherd for the owner according to law, and it is just that there should be full honor-price owed by him. Or, on the other hand, the owner had replenished his property before the thief had made a bargain with the receiver of stolen goods.

F i.e., half the increase [is owed] by him and the restitution, this is its strictness [referring to the strictest legal decision]. Half increase and half restitution, this is its leniency. If neither of them is found in his possession, he does not pay anything at all.

This below is the fully lawful receiver of stolen goods: he does not have knowledge of the theft or thief. And whether restitution or counter-purchase was found in his possession, he is free from liability, provided that he named the one to whom he sold [it] and the one from whom he bought [it]; and he gives away that which may be in his hand on its behalf.

The fully lawful receiver of stolen goods, he is characterized thus: he does not have knowledge of the theft or thief. And he is free from liability provided that he named the one from whom he bought [it], and he did not deny the one to whom he sold [it].[392] And if he denies the one from whom he bought [it], he owes a fine of certain or uncertain complicity, or it is a fine for sheltering. And if he does not name the one to whom he sold [it], [he owes] a fine for complicity, or a fine for sheltering, or a fine for receiving [stolen goods].

The difference between the fine for receiving and the fine for sheltering: the receiving, he does it for himself or for someone else, and it is for someone else that he does the sheltering. And every time it is for himself that he does the receiving, he owes a fine of theft with restitution. When it is for someone else, he owes a fine of theft without restitution. The sheltering, however, whether he does [it] for himself or for someone else, he owes a fine of theft with restitution.

And if it is the restitution that was found in his possession, i.e., in the possession of the fully lawful receiver of stolen goods, it is never taken from him until a period of time for searching is given to him to search for the thief.

392 The sense of the verb *sénaid* 'denies' in the passage is that the receiver of stolen goods either denies knowing the person from whom he bought or to whom he sold the stolen goods, or that he refuses to name the same.

taigh.[393] ⁊ berar uadha hí iar ré n-*inn*saigh. & mas sí an f*r*icrec tharrus aice, nocha mb*er*ar uadha hí do *gre*s no go faghbur in aithgin amuigh re h-aidhbr*iud*. ⁊ am*ail* dighb*ai*t*er* lam in f*ir* amuigh uman aithgin cidh g*o* n-in*n*udh cidh gan in*n*ugh, is aml*aid* dighb*aiter* a lam-sum iman f*r*icrec go n-in*n*udh no gan indudh. No d*an*o cena manab aicint*a*[394] in*n*adh it*ir* do b*eth* agan f*r*icrec cia nob*eth* in*n*udh agan aithgi*n*, *con*a h-aisicedh indadh lesin f*r*icr*eic*. ⁊ in tan tic cint*ac* ré dlig*ed*, icaidh aithg*in* co los ⁊ as, ma ta aice, ⁊ diabl*ad* n-ai*thgen*a ⁊ enecl*ainn*.

In fer m*edongait*e laninn*d*ligt*ec*h, is sí a ait*h*ne-sid*h*e: fis gaid*e* ⁊ gadaig*h*, no fis gaide nama.

In fer m*edongaite* l*eth*inn*d*ligtec,[395] fis gadaigh aicidh-sidhe ⁊ noch*an* fuil fis gaid*e*. ⁊ cidh aithg*in* cidh f*r*icr*ec* tharrtus aic*e*, noch*an* tabhart*ar* ré n-in*n*saigh do re h-iarr*aid* gad*aigi*. ⁊ b*er*ar uadha hí fo *cét*oir, .i. go lan ndire f. 5ra ⁊ go lanenecland ó fer meodhongaide laninn*d*lightach,[396] ⁊ (g*o* | landire) co l*eth*dire[397] ⁊ go l*etheneclainn* o fer m*edon*gaide l*eth*inn*d*ligtec.[398] ⁊ a rogha innugh d'f*er* bunadh .i. serraig firinda[399] laisna h-ech*aib* no lœigh boinenna laisna buaibh.

& masa t*h*arb*h* rogad*ad* and, ⁊ doní dair ⁊ b*eir*idh arathar, in*n*udh bo laisan dtarb ⁊ gnimr*ad* daim. ⁊ muna b*er*an*n* arathat, is indugh bo nama.

& an tan tic gad*aige* re dlig*ed*, cidh ioc*us* riu-sium? Ioc*aid* diabl*ad* ⁊ lanenecl*ainn* re fer m*edongait*e landlight*e*ch, et ioc*aid* diabl*ad* ⁊ *leth*enecl*ainn* re fer m*edongaite* l*ethi*nn*d*lig*h*t*ech*. ⁊ is si-si*n* a laneneecl*ann*-som, uair is esb*ad*ach a l*etheneclann* uadha um cunnr*ad* do dhenam resin gad*aige* dona *sét*uibh gaid*e*. & is an*n* is easb*adac*h uadha, in tan is a gcor no a gcun*nrad* tug*ad* do é ⁊ ni h-in*nraic* rofoc*ail* air, doní esin*nraic* dhé. Mas a cor no a cun*n*r*ad* tug*ad* do é, ⁊ in in*nraic* rofocail *air*, no mas a n-erc*a* fog*la immurro* tug*ad* do iat, cidh in*nraic* cing*or*ab in*n*raic rofoc*ail* air, no cidh a cor no a cundr*ad*, mas in*nraic* rofoc*ail* air, noch*a*n denan*n* esin*nraic* dhe.

393 The scribe originally wrote 'gaitaigh' but expunged the first ⟨i⟩ by placing a *punctum* underneath it.

394 This is a later form of *aithne*; *eDIL* s.v. 2 *aithne* 'recognizing, knowing, recognition'.

395 The scribe has written ⟨g̅⟩, but the suspension mark is an error; see also Binchy, *CIH* 1272, n. d.

396 A letter has been erased after the first ⟨n⟩; see also Binchy, *CIH* 1272, n. e.

397 The scribe has added the correction *no co lethdire*; see also Binchy, *CIH* 1272, n. f.

398 The scribe has written ⟨g̅⟩, but the suspension mark is an error; see also Binchy, *CIH* 1272, n. d.

399 This word was added in later above the line; see also Binchy, *CIH* 1272, n. g.

And it is taken from him after the period of time for searching. And if it is the counter-purchase that was found in his possession, it is never taken from him until the restitution is found outside [his property] to be claimed. And as the hand of the plaintiff is emptied regarding the restitution, whether with increase or without increase, it is thus his hand is emptied regarding the counter-purchase with increase or without increase. Or, on the other hand, if it is not known [whether] the counter-purchase has any increase at all though the restitution might have increase, he does not restore the increase with the counter-purchase. And when the guilty party submits to judgment, he pays restitution with increase and growth, if [the restitution] has it [sc., increase and growth], and doubling of restitution and of honor-price.

The full unlawful receiver of stolen goods, he is characterized thus: [he has] knowledge of the theft and thief, or knowledge of the theft only.

The half unlawful receiver of stolen goods, he has knowledge of the thief and he has no knowledge of the theft. And whether restitution or counter-purchase was found in his possession, a period of time for searching is not given to him for searching for the thief. And it is taken from him immediately, i.e., with full penalty-fine and with full honor-price owed by the fully unlawful receiver of stolen goods, and with | half penalty-fine and with half f. 5ra
honor-price owed by the half unlawful receiver of stolen goods. And the owner has his choice of young, i.e., male colts with the horses or female calves with the cows.

And if a bull was stolen then, and it bulls and it pulls a plough, [he gets the] calves with the bull and the labor of an ox. And if it does not pull a plough, [he gets the] calves only.

And when the thief submits to judgment, what does he pay for them? He pays double and full honor-price to the fully lawful receiver of stolen goods, and he pays double and half honor-price to the half unlawful receiver of stolen goods. And that is his full honor-price, because half his honor-price is lacking from him on account of making a bargain with the thief for the stolen *séts*. And it is here that it is lacking from him, when it is in contract or bargain that it was given to him, and it was not a worthy person who gave [his] word about it, it makes him an unworthy person. If it was in contract or bargain that it was given to him, and it is a worthy person who gave [his] word about it, or if it is for paying a fine for injury, however, that they were given to him, whether or not it is a worthy person who gave [his] word about it, or whether in contract or in bargain, if it is a worthy person who gave [his] word about it, it does not make him an unworthy person.

& cia tí gadaigh re dlig*ed*, noch*a*n ican*n* ní re fer m*edongait*e lanindlightec, *acht* manar gab treb*air*i re dighb*ail* a laime. ⁊ ma rogabh, g*a*c ní resar gab, is íoc res, cidh uman athg*ein* cidh uma*n* n-uiliat*aid*.

In fer m*edongait*e lanin*n*dli*g*tec: cidh aithgin cidh fricrec tharrus aig*e*, noch*a*n fuil ré n-in*n*saigh do *acht*, a br*eth* uadha fo *cét*oir: in aithgi*n* g*o* los ⁊ as ⁊ in [f]orb*air*t, ⁊rl-. & in fer m*edongait*e l*eth*in*n*dlig*h*tec, l*eth*dire ⁊ l*eth*ene*clann* ⁊ ai*thgin* cona h-inda uadha.

Masa treb*air*i rogab re dilsi, nochan ict*ar* ní ris, u*air* noch*a*n fastan*n* treb*air*i na *séotu* gaide do g*r*es. & mas re dilsi in*n*udh ant ṡeoit docuaidh-siu*m*, muna bhfuil in*n*adh agint set, damadh *sét* 'gamadh h-aicenta in*n*adh do b*eth* é, *da* mb*eth* in*n*adh bu ferr na ceil*e* isin tigh, gorab edh dob*er*ar les. & in treb*air*e docuaidh and, ma rofit*ir*-side, is fiach airitin uadha. Mas re dilsi in *séoit* g*aide* docuaidh so an*n*, ioc*aid* ai*thgin* cona h-in*n*adh. & mas re dighb*ail* a laime docuaidh, ioc*aid* an uiliat*aid*. ⁊ mana fit*ir*-sec, is slan, ⁊ ioct*air* fiach anfoc*ail* ria. & in fiadha dobaí ina fiad*nais*e, ma rofit*ir*-sec é, is fiach seall*aig* no cub*hus*brait*h* uaidhe. ⁊ man fit*ir*-sec, is [s]lan é-seig an*n*.

In treb*air*e docuaidh in*n*: ma rofit*ir*-seg, is l*eth*fiach airitin uaithi. & mas ré dilsi ant seoit docuaidh, ioc*aid* ai*thgin con*a h-in*n*adh. ⁊ mas re dighb*ail* a laime docuaidh, ioc*aid* an uiliat*aid*. ⁊ man fit*ir*, is slan e-ség an*n*, ⁊ ioct*air* l*eth*fiac*h* anfoc*ail* ria. & an treab*air*i dochuaidh ré laim f*ir* m*edongait*e landli*g*thi an*n*: ma rofit*ir*-sec é, ioc*aid* ai*thgin con*a h-in*n*adh. ⁊ man fit*ir*-sec, is slan.

And though a thief may submit to judgment, he does not pay anything to the fully unlawful receiver of stolen goods unless he takes a surety against diminishing his hand. And if he takes [a surety], each thing for which he took [a surety], it is he who pays for it, whether regarding the restitution or regarding the total amount due.

The fully unlawful receiver of stolen goods: whether restitution or counter-purchase was found in his possession, there is not a period of time for searching [given] to him, but it is taken from him immediately: the restitution with increase and growth and the produce, etc. And the half unlawful receiver of stolen goods, he owes half penalty-fine and half honor-price and restitution with the increase.

If he took a surety against forfeiture, nothing is paid to him because a surety never binds the stolen *sét*s. And if it is against forfeiture of the increase of the *sét* that he went [as surety], if the *sét* does not have any increase, if it is a *sét* that is natural to have an increase [e.g., young] with it, if the increase is better than the one inside,[400] this is what is is given along with it. And the surety who went [surety] then, if he knew [the property was stolen], he owes a fine for receiving [stolen goods]. If it is against forfeiture of the stolen *sét* that he went [surety] then, he pays restitution with the increase; and if it is against emptying his hand that he went [surety], he pays the total amount. And if he did not know, he is free from liability, and a fine of misrepresentation is paid to him. And the witness who witnessed it, if he knew [the property was stolen], he owes a fine [of the same amount as] a culpable onlooker or of complicity. And if he did not know, he is free from liability then.

The surety who went [surety] then: if he knew [the property was stolen], he owes a half fine for receiving [stolen goods]. And if it is against forfeiture of the *sét* that he went [into suretyship], he pays restitution with the increase. And if it is against emptying his hand that he went [into suretyship], he pays the full amount. And if he does not know, he is free from liability then, and a fine for misrepresentation is paid to him. And the surety who went [into suretyship] against [emptying the] hand of the fully lawful receiver of stolen goods then: if he knew, he pays restitution with the increase. And if he did not know, he is free from liability.[401]

400 In other words, the increase is better than the one present, i.e., not part of the livestock taken away in theft.

401 For this and the preceeding paragraph, see the similar commentaries in *Di Astud Chor* § 48 in McLeod, *Early Irish Contract Law*, 283–285.

Mas ina gcolp*a*ca no masa ina sam*aisc*e rogad*ad* iat, ⁊ ina mbuaib mo*r*a rohaibr*ed* iat, gabait fein g*r*eim ar son ai*thgen*a, ⁊ d*ir*e sam*aisc*e no colp[aig]e[402] leo. Mas ina mbuaib mo*r*a rogab*ad* iat, *acht* ma mairit fein, gabait g*r*eim ar son ai*thgen*a, cidh c*r*in cidh cæch cidh l*eth*colp*ach* iat .i. i*m*a tuill*em*,[403] ⁊ d*ir*e inich leo fon æis a tall*tha* iat. ⁊ is an*n* sin ata in d*ir*e ini[c](t)h[404] ⁊ in ai*thgin* espadach. Is and at*a* in ai*thgin* ini[c](t)h ⁊ in d*ir*e esp*adac*: an inb*aid* rob esp*adac* ni don ai*thgin* in tan rogat*ad* hí, ⁊ ni mairind budein an*n*

f. 5rb sin; ai*thgin* ini[c](t)h fon æis a tall*ad* hí, ⁊ dire easbadach | fo aicne na h-esp*ada* robui aran aithgi*n*.

Cuin is mo, ⁊ cuin is lugha, ⁊ cuin is coibes f*or* fer m*edongait*e na f*or* gadaigh? Is and is mo fair: in ta*n* rogad*ustar* in g*adaige* in *sét* d'forc*raid* tothcusa a *secht*armaighin cin æghaire; land*ire* ⁊ lanen*eclann* o fer *medon*gaide, ⁊ l*eth*d*ire* ⁊ *leth*en*eclann* ó gad*aige*, uair geb*id* grem n-a[o](i)gh[a]iri[405] gad*aige* da mbr*eith* go fer m*edongaite*. Is ann as lughu fair, .i. in tan tallust*ar*[406] in *sét* do c*ert*to*th*c*us* f*ir* bun*aid* a maighi*n* gin æghaire; land*ire* ⁊ lanen*eclann* ó gad*aige* an*n*, ⁊ l*eth*d*ire* ⁊ *leth*en*eclann* ó fir m*edongait*e, uair roairbern*ad* an tothcus ar cin*n* f*ir* m*edongait*e. Is and is coibes orr*o*: in tan tallust*ar* in gad*aige* in *sét* d'forc*raid* to*th*c*us* a maig*in co n*-æ*gaire*: landire ⁊ l[a](e)nen*eclann* ó fer m*edongaite*, ⁊ land*ire* ⁊ lanen*eclann* ó gad*aige*.

Gidh riasan ré, cidh iarsan re, cidh isin re buden rofuataig*hustar* in *sét* amach, ⁊ in cin*n*te *con*abu lais bud*ein* hé, land*ire* ⁊ lanen*eclann* ⁊ ai*thgin* *con*a h-in*n*ugh uadh.

402 I follow the emendation suggested by Binchy, *CIH* 1273, n. d.

403 *.i. im tuillem* is written as an interlinear gloss; see also Binchy, *CIH* 1273, n. e.

404 See also Binchy, *CIH* 1273, n. f.

405 I follow the emendation suggested by Binchy, *CIH* 1273, n. h.

406 This is a MI 3 sg. pret. form of *do-alla* 'steals'; see Kim McCone, *A First Old Irish Grammar and Reader Including an Introduction to Middle Irish* (Maynooth: Department of Old and Middle Irish, National University of Ireland, Maynooth, 2005), p. 201.

If they were stolen as two-year-old heifers or three-year-old heifers, and they were claimed as large cows, they themselves are equivalent to restitution, and a penalty-fine of a three-year-old heifer or a two-year-old heifer along with them. If they were stolen as large cows, provided that they themselves remain [alive], they are equivalent to restitution, whether they are withered or blind in one eye or half-shanked, i.e., regarding their merit, and full penalty-fine [is paid] along with them according to the age in which they were stolen. And it is in that [previous] case that there is full penalty-fine and the restitution is lacking. It is in the following case that there is full restitution and the penalty is lacking: whenever anything is lacking from the restitution when it was stolen, and it itself does not survive in that case; full restitution according to the age in which it was stolen, and penalty-fine is lacking | according to the nature of that which was lacking from the restitu- f. 5rb
tion.

When is [the penalty] greater, and when is it less, and when is it the same for the receiver of stolen goods as it is for the thief? It is here that it is greater for him: when the thief had stolen the *sét* from excess property from outside the precinct without a shepherd; full penalty-fine and full honor-price is owed by the [fully unlawful] receiver of stolen goods, and half penalty-fine and half honor-price is owed by the thief, because a thief taking them to the receiver of stolen goods will be equivalent to a shepherd. It is here that it is less for him, i.e., when he stole the *sét* from the owner's exact property from a precinct without a shepherd: full penalty-fine and full honor-price is owed by the thief then, and half penalty-fine and half honor-price is owed by the [fully unlawful] receiver of stolen goods, because the property was diminished on account of the receiver of stolen goods. It is here that it is equivalent for them: when the thief stole the *sét* from excess property from a precinct with a shepherd: full penalty-fine and full honor-price is owed by the [fully unlawful] receiver of stolen goods, and full penalty-fine and full honor-price is owed by the thief.

Whether[407] before the time, or after the time, or during the time that the *sét* had been carried off, and it is certain that it was not his own possession, he owes full penalty-fine and full honor-price and restitution with the increase.

407 For this paragraph, compare sources CC and DD below, where there is similar commentary in reference to the disputed property being carried off from a neutral third party.

Ma 'sin ré rofuataig*hustar* e a ri*cht* a tśeoit [féin],[408] ⁊ nach*ar* lais iar dai*n*, l*eth*d*ire* ⁊ l*etheneclann* ⁊ ai*thgin con*a h-in*n*ad uadh. & ma rob*o* lais, sær ar d*ire* ⁊ ar ai*thgin* e ⁊ l*etheneclann* uadh. Fogabur in *sét* re aidhbr*iud* an*n* sin, ⁊ mana faghb*aiter,* is l*etheneclann* uadh ⁊ cethraim*the* d*ire* ⁊ ai*thgin* no l*ethaithgin.* Mas iarsa*n* re rofuat*aigustar* é a ri*cht* a *séoit* fen, ⁊ nochar̄[409] lais iar d*ain,* is ai*thgin* uadh. ⁊ madh rob*o* lais iar d*ain,* is sl*an* do. Fogabhur in *sét* re aidhbr*iud* an*n* si*n*, ⁊ mana faghb*aither,* is l*ethaithgin* no is b*eth* gi*n* ni.

Can asa ngabhth*ar* an l*ethaithgin*? Is as gabt*air*: "con*n*tabairt cuich é cia nogabhtha." Can asa ngabht*ar* a b*eth* ci*n* ni? Is as gabht*air*: "am*al* fer m*edon*-g*aite* dligtech é, ⁊ noch*an* tarr*ustar* colund aice, ⁊ noch*an* (tarr*aiter*) aidhbr*i*-*ter*[410] fri[th]cr*ec* ag fer m*edongaite* dligtech do g*res*."[411]

Is res ata *deith*b*ir*[412] maig*ne* ⁊ *secht*arm*aigne*, re fer teall*aig* faith[ch]i do g*res*. & is res ata *deith*b*ir* cer*t*tothchusa ⁊ forcr*aid* tothchusa, re fer m*edon*-g*aite*. Noch*an* [ḟ]uil *deith*b*ir* maig*ne* na *secht*armaig*ne* a l*eth* re fer m*edon*-g*aite* do g*res*, ⁊ ata re gad*aige*. ⁊ iss é an fa*th* si*n*: am*al* buachaill d'fir bunadh g*adaige* re cois a *sét,* ⁊ am*al* gad*aige* an tan na bí buachaill. ⁊ ó bias buachaill agna *séot*u do g*res*, noch*an* [ḟ]uil *deith*b*ir* maighni na *secht*arm*aigne* friu. ⁊ is as gabt*air* si*n*: "dia mbe mucaidh, mbrothar dibh d*ire* cidh fo refedha raith" .i. madha raib*e* muc*aid acu,* raite*r* lane*neclann* do in*n*tibh. Cidh fo rofidh no cidh fo roraithnigh dech siat, rofes as n-erraithi de collna denta, .i. rofes *con*ad é icus, intí doroine denta indlig*thech* frisi*n* col*ainn.*

408 I follow the emendation suggested by Binchy, *CIH* 1273, n. i.

409 Binchy, *CIH* 1273, n. j, notes that the suspension mark over the ⟨a⟩ is an error.

410 The scribe added the correction *no nochan aidhbriter*; see also Binchy, *CIH* 1274, n. a.

411 The source of these quotations has not been identified.

412 The scribe has written '.x.b̄'.

If it is during the time that it was carried off in mistake for his own *sét*, and it is not in his possession afterwards, he owes half penalty-fine and half honor-price and restitution with the increase. And if it was his possession, he is free from penalty-fine and from restitution, and he owes half honor-price. The *sét* is found to be claimed in that case, and if it is not found, he owes half honor-price and a quarter penalty-fine and restitution or half restitution. If it is after the time that it was carried off in mistake for his own *sét*, and it is not his possession afterwards, he owes restitution. And if it was his possession afterwards, he is free from liability. The *sét* is found to be claimed in that case, and if it is not found, [he owes] half restitution, or he is without anything.

Whence is the half restitution taken? It is taken from: "uncertainty of each of them though it is stolen." Whence is taken his being without anything? It is taken from: "as he is a fully lawful receiver of stolen goods, and the stolen item is not found in his possession, and the lawful receiver of stolen goods' counter-purchase is never claimed."

Regarding for whom there is a distinction [between] precinct and outside the precinct: always for the owner of the household green.[413] And regarding for whom there is a distinction between exact property and excess property: for the receiver of stolen goods. And there is never a distinction between precinct and outside the precinct regarding the receiver of stolen goods, but there is for the thief. And that reason is: a thief beside his *sét*s is as a cowherd for the owner, and he is as a thief when there is not a cowherd. And when the *sét*s always have a cowherd, there is not a distinction [between] precinct or outside the precinct for them. And that is taken from: "if there be a swineherd, penalty-fine is awarded for them even though [they go] under a great wood of bracken," i.e., if they had a swineherd, full honor-price is awarded for them, whether they may go under a great wood or great bracken; it is known that [the fine] must be paid by he who made [the illegal stucture for the confined] stolen property, i.e., it is known who pays it, the one who made the illegal structure for the stolen property.[414]

413 The word *faithche* can refer to "the whole area which surrounds a dwelling," any green or open space by an enclosure or dwelling, a playingfield, or pastureland used for cattle; *EIF* 370; *eDIL* s.v. *faithche, faidche*. See also Heptad 64 at p. 251.

414 See also the shorter version of this explanation in source A at p. 155, *CIH* 2170.38–39.

Mas do c*erttothchus* tallust*ar* g*adaige* na *séot*u, [cid][415] a maigin cidh a *secht*armaig*in*, ⁊ ata buachuill ac*aib*, lanene*clann* ó gad*aige* an*n*, ⁊ l*eth*ene*clann* o fer m*edongaite* lanindlightec, ⁊ a l*eth*-sec ó fer m*edongaite* l*eth*inn*d*l*ig*tec.

Ma rofuataigh in *sét* on urlaim coit*chinn* cin deonugh dí, cidh raisin ré cidh iarsi*n* ré, ⁊ masa cin*n*ti lais *con*ach lais, land*ire* ⁊ lanene*clann* ⁊ ai*thgin* coml*an* an*n* d'fer an *séoit*, ⁊ an *cutrum*a d'ene*clainn* ata an*n* g*a*c inadh sun*n*. Iss é an *cu*(tu)trum*a*-si*n th*ormaig*hus* cain do sm*acht* an*n* re tæbh int seoit, ⁊ la*nene*cla*nn* d'fer na fai[th]ch*e*. & marob í a tuicsi gorob les, ⁊ ni les iar d*ain*, l*eth*ene*clann* d'fer na f*aithche* ann, ⁊ l*eth*ene*clann* ⁊ l*eth*d*ire* ⁊ ai*thgin* com*lan* d'fer an s*éoit*.

f. 5va Masa les iar dain hé, l*eth*ene*clann* d'fer ant s*éoit* ann, ⁊ l*eth*ene*clann* d'fer na fai[th]ch*e*, uair noch*a*n ican*n* dui*n*e d*ire* a set f*ein* re nec*h aile*.

Fogab*h*ur in *sét* re aid*h*bri*ud* an*n* sin, ⁊ mana fag*h*bait*er*, l*eth*ene*clann* d'fer na fai[th]ch*e* an*n*, ⁊ c*eth*raim*the* d*ire* ⁊ l*eth*ene*clann* ⁊ l*eth*ai*thgin* d'fer ant seoit.

Cid*h* fo*dera* in bail ata c*eth*raim*e* d*ire*, l*eth*ai*thgin* do be*th* an*n* re t*h*aob*h*? Is e in fa*th* fo*dera*: in bail*e* robai l*eth*d*ire* uad*h* ó c*hi*an*a*ib, robai ai*thgin* co*mlan* re tæb*h* in tan robo cin*n*te narbú les, coir 'no de-sid*he*. An bail*e* ata cet*h*raim*e* d*ire* uad*ha* sun*n*, ce rob*eth* l*eth*ai*thgin* re t*h*æb*h* in ta*n* is les in *séoit*.

Cidh fo*dera* an tan is cundtab*air*t in les no nac*h* les, ⁊ ní fag*h*bur *sét* re aid*h*bri*ud*, l*eth*ene*clann* do be*th* do? Is é in fa*th* fo*dera*: in tan rob*o* cin*n*te ó cianaib*h* cu*r*ub les é, robai l*ethene*cl*ann* uad*h* ina fuat*a*c resi*n* ré; coir 'no de-sid*he* in tan is *cunn*tab*air*t in les no nach les, ⁊ ni fag*h*bur in *sét* ré aid*h*bri*ud*; coir cé rob*eth* l*eth*ene*clann* uad*h*a.

415 I follow the emendation suggested by Binchy, *CIH* 1274, n. d.

If it is from exact property that the thief stole the *sét*s, whether from a precinct or from outside a precinct, and they have a cowherd, full honor-price is owed by the thief then, and half honor-price is owed by the fully unlawful receiver of stolen goods, and half of it [sc., the honor-price] is owed by the half unlawful receiver of stolen goods.

If[416] the *sét* was taken from the neutral third party without permission for it, whether before the time or after the time [either had invoked a surety],[417] and if he is certain that it is not his, full penalty-fine and full honor-price and complete restitution then for the owner of the *sét*, and the equivalent of honor-price there is then for each increase here. It is that equivalent that law adds to the penalty there in addition to the *sét*, and full honor-price for the owner of the green. And if he supposes that it is his, and it is not [found to be] his afterwards, half honor-price for the owner of the green then and half honor-price and half penalty-fine and complete restitution for the owner of the *sét*.

If it is [found to be] his afterwards, half honor-price for the owner of the f. 5va
sét then and half honor-price for the owner of the green, because a person does not pay the penalty-fine of his own *sét* to someone else.

The *sét* is found to be claimed in this case, and if it is not found, half honor-price for the owner of the green then, and quarter penalty-fine and half honor-price and half restitution for the owner of the *sét*.

What brings it about where there is quarter penalty-fine [and] there is half restitution then in addition? This is the reason that causes it: where there was half penalty-fine owed by him just now [i.e., in the recent passage], there was complete restitution in addition when it was certain that it was not his, [is it] just then. Where there is quarter penalty-fine owed by him here, though there might be half restitution as well when the *sét* is his.

What is the reason when he is uncertain whether it is his or not, and the *sét* is not found to be claimed, [for there] to be half honor-price for him? This is the reason that causes it: when it was certain just now [i.e., in the recent passage] that it was his, he owed half honor-price for its carrying off before the time; [it is] just then from that when it is uncertain [whether the *sét*] is his or not, and the *sét* is not found to be claimed, [it is] just though he might owe half honor-price.

416 For the remainder of the commentary from source F, see also sources CC and DD at pp. 182–185 and 192–193. The commentary in source A, §10 preserves the most comprehensive version of the material.

417 See the Introduction, pp. 32–33, for discussion of this material.

col. 606 G [*CIH* 2070.35–2073.9][418] .i. i meod*h*on taid*h*e it*er* an gataig*h*e | día rocen*n*aig, ⁊ ní fit*ir ar*ma gat, ⁊ it*er* in fer aid*h*bris ⁊ in fer rocrec fris.

In fer meod*h*ong*h*ait*e* landlig*h*th*ech*, as [s]í á aithne-sid*he*: ce*n* fis gaite na gat*aig*e aige. ⁊ is sl*an* dó, *acht* co roin*n*ised*h* cia or cen*n*aig ⁊ cia frisi rec*u*-*star*. ⁊ doaisig á in*n*ile do cun*n*rad*h*ac*h* uad*h* .i. do fir bun*aidh*. ⁊ dob*erar* ré n-in*n*saig*h*e dó re iarr*aid* gataig*he*, ⁊ dob*erar* tuin*ide* int seoit i*n*a laim*h*. ⁊ muna in*n*isi inti or cen*n*aig*h*, is fiac*h* cub*hus*brait*h* cin*n*te ł cun*n*tab*artach* uad*h*. Muna in*n*isi into risi rec, is fiach *air*itin no ditin uad*h*.

Deit*h*b*ir* it*er* in fiac*h* airiti*n* ⁊ i*n* fiac*h* ditin .i. an *air*itu doní do fei*n* ⁊ doni do neoc*h* aile. In ditu im*murro*, do neoc*h aile* doni í. In *air*itiu im*murro*, cac*h* u*air* is do fein doni hí, is fiac*h* gaite co n-ait*h*gi*n* in*n*te; ⁊ cach u*air* is do neoc*h* aile, is f*iach gaite* ce*n* ait*h*gi*n*. In ditiu im*murro*, cid*h* dó fei*n* cid*h* do neoc*h aile*, is fiac*h* [gaite][419] co n-ait*h*gi*n* in*n*.

Mas ait*h*gin tarr*us* aig*e*, noc*h*o b*erar* uad*h* í no go tuc*ar* re n-in*n*saig*h*i dó. Mas [s]í an frithcreic t*ar*rus aici, ni*con* b*erar* uad*h* í do gres ł co t*arru*-*star* an ait*h*gi*n* amuig*h*. ⁊ am*ail* t*arrus* in ait*h*gin amuig*h*, cid*h* do n-indud*h* cid*h* cin indud, is am*hlaid* aisict*er* in frit*h*creic uad*h*. No d*an*o c*h*ena, manab cin*n*ti in*n*ud*h* it*ir* do b*e*th agi*n* frit*h*creic, ce rob*e*th in*n*ud*h* i*con* ait*h*gin, *con*a h-aisicea indu laisi*n* frit*h*creic. ⁊ in tan tig g*ataige* re dlig*ed*, icaid*h* ait*h*gin fris-[s]iu*m* co los ⁊ as, ma ta aige, [⁊] dila[id][420] (⁊) ait*h*gi*n* ⁊ enecl*ain*n.

col. 607 Fer meod*h*ongaite landlig*thech*: ci*n* fis g*aite* na gataig*h* sin. ⁊ frit*h*creic t*ar*-*rus* ina lai*mh*, ⁊ in*n*isid*h* inti or cen*n*aig*h* ⁊ inti risi rac. ⁊ dob*eir* a mbi ina laim*h* t*ar*a cen*n* amac*h* do*n* fir frisi rec in s*ét* g*aite*. ⁊ a feg*h*ad*h* a cen*n*ac*h*

418 The commentary to source G appears in two places in the MS. The first commentary is found at *CIH* 2070.35–2073.9. The second commentary is found at *CIH* 2073.34–2075.11.

419 I follow the emendation suggested by Binchy, *CIH* 2071, n. b.

420 Cf. source A, *CIH* 2169.25 *dilaid*.

G i.e., in middle theft between the thief | from whom he bought [it], and he does not know about the theft, and between the plaintiff and the man he sold [it] to.[421] col. 606

The fully lawful receiver of stolen goods, he is characterized thus: he does not have knowledge of the theft or the thief. And he is free from liability, provided that he named the one from whom he bought [it] and the one to whom he sold [it]. And he restores [it] from his own property to the party of the contract, i.e., to the owner. And a period of time for searching is given to him to search for the thief, and possession of the *sét* is given into his hand. And if he does not name the one from whom he bought [it], he owes a fine of certain or uncertain complicity. If he does not name the one to whom he sold [it], he owes a fine for receiving [stolen goods] or sheltering.

The difference between the fine of receiving and the fine of sheltering, i.e., the receiving he does for himself and for someone else. The sheltering, however, he does it for someone else. The receiving, however, every time it is for himself that he does it, [he owes] a fine for theft with restitution for it; and every time is it for someone else, [he owes] a fine for theft without restitution. The sheltering, however, whether for himself or for someone else, [he owes] a fine for theft with restitution then.

If the restitution was found in his possession, it is not taken from him until a period of time for searching is given to him. If it is the counter-purchase that was found in his possession, it is never taken from him until the restitution is found outside [his property]. And as the restitution was found outside [his property], whether with increase or without increase, it is thus that the counter-purchase is restored by him. On the other hand, if it is not certain [whether] the counter-purchase has an increase at all, though the restitution might have an increase, he does not restore the increase along with the counter-purchase. And when the thief submits to judgment, he [sc., the thief] pays restitution to him with increase and growth, if it [sc., the stolen livestock] has it [sc., increase], and he pays restitution and honor-price.

A fully lawful receiver of stolen goods: [he is] without knowledge of the theft or that thief. And the counter-purchase was found in his hand, and he names the one from whom he bought [it] and the one to whom he sold [it]. And he gives away that which may be in his hand for it to the man to whom he sold the stolen *sét*. And it is taken into account [whether] the purchase col. 607

421 The gloss attempts to explain why the receiver of stolen goods is called a 'man of middle theft'; i.e., he is between the thief, on the one hand, and the owner and person he sold it to, on the other.

d'urr*ad* no d'anurr*ad* dó hé; ⁊ mana fag*h*ab*ar* an *sét* re aidb*hred*, ni b*erar in* fri*th*creic uad*ha*-su*m*.

Mas d'ḟir m*edongaite* landlig*thech* rainic in *sét* in ait*hgin* do reir dlig*id* cran*nch*uir, is dublu d'ic fris ca*ch* nei*ch* im*ar* di[g]b*ad*[422] a lam*h* ⁊ enecl*ann*, ɫ coma l*eth*indud*h* ⁊ einecl*ann* beos, ⁊ diabl*ad* ⁊ ait*hgin* d'ic ris on gat*aig*e, ⁊ l*eth*ait*hgin* ⁊ l*eth*diabl*ad* ⁊ l*eth*indud ⁊ l*eth*ceth*ar*da d'ic re fer mbunaig*h* ⁊ enecl*ann*, no coma ceth*ar*da co*mhlan* do. Mas d'fir b*h*unaig*h* rai*n*ic i*n* ait*h*g*in* do reir dlig*id* cran*nch*air, dublu ⁊ enecl*ann* d'ic re ce*chtar* de, no cu*m*a ait*hgin* ⁊ lethdublu[423] ⁊ l*eth*indud d'ic re fer m*edongaite* ⁊ enecl*ann*.

In fer m*edongaite* l*eth*indlig*thech*, isi 'aichne-side: fis gat*aig*i aige ⁊ gan fis gaite, ⁊ cid*h* ait*hgin* cid*h* fri*th*creic t*arrus* aice, noc*h*o tab*arr* re n-in*n*saig*h*e do, *acht* a breit*h* uad*h* fo *cét*oir a n-ait*hgin* co los ⁊ as ⁊ in f*or*b*air*t, ⁊ landire ⁊ l*eth*eineclann.[424]

& in tan tig g*atai*ge re dlig*ed*, ic*aid* ait*hgin* risi*m* co los ⁊ as ⁊ in f*or*b*air*t, ⁊ dubl*ad* ⁊ leit*h*einecl*ainn*. ⁊ isi-sid*he* a laneneclann-*som* u*air* is esbada*ch* a l*eth*eineclann uad*h* um cun*nrad* do de*n*ud*h* risi*n* ngat*aige* dona *sét*aib g*ait*e. ⁊ is an*n* is esb*adac* uad*h* in tan is i cor ɫ a cun*nrad* tug*ad* d*hó* iat, ⁊ ni h-in*n*raic rofocail air.

col. 608 Mas a n-eiric fog*h*la tug*ad* do iat cincub in*n*raic rofoc*ail* air, ɫ cid*h* a cor ɫ a cun*nrad*, mas in*n*raic rofoc*ail air*, noc*h*a de*nann* eisinnr*aic* de.

In fer meod*ongaite* lanin*n*dlig*thech*, as [s]í 'aic*h*ne-sid*he*: co fis g*aite* ⁊ gad*aigi* aige, ɫ co fis g*ait*e nama. Cid ait*hgin* cid*h* fri*th*creic t*arrus* aice, *noch*o fuil re n-in*n*saig*h*e do, *acht* a breit*h* uad*h*a fo *cét*oir i n-ait*hgin* co los ⁊ as ⁊ in f*or*b*air*t, ⁊ landire ⁊ laneneclann. In tan tig gad*aig*e re dlig*ed*, *noch*on ican*n* ní fris man*ar acht*aigh; ⁊ mas ed*h* ro*acht*aig digb*ail* a laim*he* d'ic fris, is a ic.

---

422 I follow the emendation suggested by Binchy, *CIH* 20171, n. k.

423 The ⟨leth⟩ was added above the line with reference marks by the scribe; see also Binchy, *CIH* 2071, n. l.

424 The scribe had originally written a second ⟨n⟩ after ⟨eine⟩, but he expunged it by placing a *punctum* under the letter; see also Binchy, *CIH* 2071, n. m.

of it was from a local freeman or an outsider. And if the *sét* is not found to be claimed, the counter-purchase is not taken from him.

If the fully lawful receiver of stolen goods obtained the *sét* as restitution according to the law of casting lots, double is to be paid to him [by] the person on whose account his hand was emptied and honor-price, or that there should be half increase and honor-price besides, and double [the fine] and restitution to be paid to him by the thief, and half restitution and half doubling and half increase and half four-fold to be paid to the owner and honor-price, or that there should be a complete four-fold for him. If the owner obtained the restitution according to the law of casting lots, doubling and honor-price to be paid to each of them, or that there should be restitution and half doubling and half increase to be paid to the receiver of stolen goods and honor-price.

The half unlawful receiver of stolen goods, he is characterized thus: he has knowledge of the thief and not the theft, and whether the restitution or the counter-purchase was found with him, a period of time for searching is not given to him, but it is taken from him immediately as restitution with increase and growth and the produce, and full penalty-fine and half honor-price.

And when the thief submits to judgment, he [sc., the thief] pays restitution to him with increase and growth and the produce, and doubling and half honor-price. And that is his full honor-price because half his honor-price is lacking from him on account of making a bargain with the thief for the stolen *sét*s. And then it is lacking from him when it is in contract or bargain that they were given to him, and it is not a worthy person who gave [his] word for it.

If it is for a fine for injury that they were given to him, though it is not a col. 608
worthy person who gave [his] word for it, or whether in contract or in bargain, if it is a worthy person who gave [his] word for it, it does not make him an unworthy person.

The fully unlawful receiver of stolen goods, he is characterized thus: he has knowledge of the theft and the thief, or knowledge of the theft only. Whether restitution or counter-purchase was found in his possession, a period of time for searching is not given to him, but it is taken from him immediately as restitution with increase and growth and the produce, and full penalty-fine and full honor-price. When the thief submits to judgment, he does not pay anything to him unless he made a stipulation; and if he stipulated to pay him for lessening his hand, he pays it.

Mas aicn*ed* don ait*hgin* in*n*ud aice, cid aicn*ed* cincob aicn*ed* do*n* f*r*it*h*creic, am*ail* b*erar* in*n*ud lais*in* ait*hgin*, b*erar* laisi*n* f*r*it*h*creic. Mad aicn*ed* don f*r*i[th]creic in*n*ud aice, munab aicn*ed* don ait*hgin*, noc*ho* b*erar* in*n*ud*h* le. Mas t*r*eb*aire* dob*erar* re dilsi, *noch*on ic*ar* ni ris, u*air* noc*h*on fastan*n* treb*aire* na *séotu gaite* do g*r*es.

Masa m*air*bdile rogata an*n*, no beodile acna fuil in f*or*b*air*t, in fuill*em* dob*h*iad*h* leo f*or* treb*aire achtrann* co cen*n* mbliad*h*na corub ed*h* bias leo. Masa beodile 'can(a)[425] aicn*ed* in*n*ud*h* do b*eth*, *acht* ma rucsat in*n*ud*h* amuig*h*, ma m*air*it acu é, is aisic leo. Mana m*air*en*n*, is in*n*ud*h* a m*h*acasam*h*la d'aisic. Mana rucsat in*n*ud amuig*h* it*ir*, is c*étfaid* co mbeit*h* a rog*h*a in*n*ud d'fir b*h*unaid.

Masa t*ar*b*h* rogada and, ⁊ doní d*air* ⁊ *ar*ath*ar*, in*n*ud bo lais ⁊ gnim*h*ra
col. 609 daim*h*. | Mas ina colpt*h*ac*h*aib ɫ ina sam*aisc*ib*h* rogat*ad* iat ⁊ ina mbuaib*h* mora roaidbr*ed*, gabait g*r*eim ait*hgh*ena iat budein, ⁊ dire sa*m*aisce ɫ colp*thaige* leo. Mas ana mbuaib*h* mo*r*a rogat*ad* iat, *acht* ma m*air*it fein, gabait g*r*eim n-ait*hgena*, cid*h* crin cid*h* cæch cid*h* l*eth*colp*ach* iat, ⁊ dire inich leo fo*n* ais a tall*ad*. ⁊ is an*n* si*n* at*a* dire inich ⁊ i*n* ait*hgin* esbad*hach*.

Is an*n* at*a* an ait*hgin* inic*h* ⁊ in dire esbad*ach*: an inb*aid* rob esb*adach* ni don ait*hgin* in tan rogat*ad* í, ⁊ ait*hgin* inic*h* in*n*ti fon ais a tall*ad* í. ⁊ ni m*air*en*n* fe*n* an*n* sin, ⁊[426] dir*e* esb*adach* in*n*ti fo aicn*ed* na h-esbad*h*a robai *ar*in ait*hgin*. Ait*hgin* co los ⁊ as ⁊ in f*or*b*air*t ⁊ landire ⁊ l*ane*n*e*cl*ann* don in*n*raic doní mait*h dá* to[th]c*h*us.

Ait*hgin* co los ⁊ as ⁊ in f*or*b*air*t na colla, ⁊ nochan fuil dire ná einecl*ann* don in*n*r*aic* na dei*n* mait*h* dia to[th]c*h*us. No co mb*eth* lanei*n*ecl*ann*, u*air* at*a* to[th]c*hus* aice, ⁊ noc*h*a fuil dire.

Ait*hgin* cin los ci*n* as cin f*or*b*air*t don eisin*nraic* na dei*n* mait*h* dia to[th]c*hus* ɫ d'in*n*raic in scre*pail*.

425 See also Binchy, *CIH* 2072, n. a.

426 The scribe has placed a *punctum* over the ⟨⁊⟩ in error; see also Binchy, *CIH* 2072, n. c.

If it is known that the restitution has increase, whether it is known or not known regarding the counter-purchase, as the increase is given with the restitution, it is given with the counter-purchase. If it is known that the counter-purchase has increase, unless it is known for the restitution, the increase is not given with it. If a surety is given against forfeiture, nothing is paid to him because a surety never binds the stolen *séts*.

If it is inanimate items that were stolen then, or livestock that have produce, the addition will be with them [sc., with the livestock] in the custody of an external surety until the end of a year so that it [sc., the addition] will be along with them. If it is livestock which are known to have young, provided that they had brought the young away, if they remain [alive] with them, [they] are restored along with them. If it [sc., the young] does not remain [alive], an equivalent young [animal] is restored. If they had not brought the young away at all, it is the opinion [of lawyers] that the owner has his choice of young.

If it was a bull that was taken then, and it bulls and ploughs, the calves [are given] along with him and the labor of an ox. | If they were stolen as two-year- col. 609
old heifers or three-year-old heifers and were claimed as large cows, they themselves are the equivalent of restitution, and the penalty-fine of a three-year-old heifer and a two-year-old heifer [is to be paid] along with them. If they were stolen as large cows, provided they themselves remain [alive], they are the equivalent of restitution, whether they are withered or blind in one eye or half-shanked, and complete penalty-fine with them according to the age in which they had been taken. And in that case the penalty-fine is complete and the restitution is lacking.

It is in the following case that there is complete restitution and the penalty-fine is lacking: whenever anything was lacking from the restitution when it was stolen, and complete restitution for it according to the age when it was stolen. And it itself does not remain [alive] in that case, and penalty-fine is lacking for it according to what was lacking from the restitution. Restitution with increase and growth and the produce, and full penalty-fine and full honor-price for the worthy person who makes good [use] of his property.

Restitution with increase and growth and the produce of the stolen item, and there is neither penalty-fine nor honor-price for the worthy person who does not make good [use] of his property. Or there should be full honor-price because he has property, and there is not a penalty-fine.

Restitution without increase, without growth, without [the] produce for the unworthy person who does not make good [use] of his property, or the value of a scruple for the unworthy person.

Noc*h*an fuil *deith*b*ir* maig*h*ne ł *sechtar*maig*n*e i l*eth* re fer m*edongaite* do g*r*es, ⁊ at*a* re gat*aige*. ⁊ is e an fat*h*-si*n*: am*al* buac*h*aill d'fir bun*aid* gat*aig*e re cois a s*ét*. ⁊ o bias buachaill acna s*ét*aib do g*r*es, noc*h*an fuil *deith*b*ir* maig*h*-
col. 610 ne ł *sechtar*maig*h*ne friu. | ⁊ is as gab*ar* sin: "dia *m*be muicid*he* mbrog*h*fa dib dire, cid f*o* raeda rath rofes as eirit*h* do collna."

Mas a maig*in* tallad*h*[427] gat*aige* na s*éot*a, cid do c*er*tochus cid d'forc*r*aid tothc*us*a, is laneneclann.

Mas a *sechtar*maig*in* t*allad* *gataige* na s*éo*ta, is l*eth*eneclann. ⁊ ni fuil buac*h*aill[428] and, ⁊ ma ta, is lanen*eclann* ann, cid a maig*in* cid a *secht*[ar]maig*in*.

Mas d'for*c*raid t*othchusa* tall*ad* *gataige* na seotu, is lanen*eclann* o fir m*edon*gaite (l*eth*e) lain.[429] Mas do c*er*tochus tall*ad* *gataige* na s*éot*u, is l*etheneclann* ann o fir medongaite l*eth*e.

Is an*n* is cut*r*uma ar fer m*edongaite* leth ⁊ ar *gataige*: in i*n*baid[430] is d'f*or*-c*r*aid t*othchusa* tall*ad* *gataige* na s*éo*ta a *sechtar*maig*in*, ⁊ ni fuil buac*h*aill acu; l*etheneclann* o gat*aig*e, ⁊ lanen*eclann* o fir m*edongaite* lain, ⁊ l*eth*ene-*clann* o fir m*edongaite* let*h*e.

Cid fo*dera* in tan is do c*er*tochus tall*ad* *gataige* na s*éot*u a maig*in* co fuil lanen*eclann* o *gataige* and ⁊ conac fuil *acht* l*etheneclann* o fir m*edongaite* laninndlig*thech*, ⁊[431] in tan is d'for*c*raid t*othchusa* tall gat*aig*i na s*éot*u a *sechtar*maig*in* cona fuil *acht* let[h]en*eclann* o gat*aig*i ⁊ co fuil lanen*eclann* o fir m*edongaite* lain? Is e i*n* fa*th*[432] fo*dera*: in tan is do c*er*toch*us* *tallad* *gataige* na s*éot*u a maig*in*, robi a to[th]ch*us* co*m*lan ac fer bunaid*h* ar cin*n* gat*aig*i, ⁊ coir cia robeth lanen*eclann* uad a n-airb*er*nad*h* in to[th]ch*us*a. Noc*ha* roibe(th)[433] to[th]ch*us* co*m*la*n* in tan dorigne gat*aig*i cundrad*h* re fer m*edongaite* laninndlig*thech*, ⁊ coir gi*n*co b*eth* *acht* l*eth*eneclann uad.

In tan is d'for*c*raid*h* to[th]ch*us*a tall*a* *gataige* na s*éot*u a *sechtarmaigin*, is aml*aid* fuair iat ⁊ ni*con* roibe buachaill acu, ⁊ coir ci*n*co b*eth* *acht* lethene-
col. 611 *clann* uad. A roba buac*h*aill a | leit*h* re fer m*edongaite*, u*air* am*al* b*h*uac*h*aill

427 For the past subjunctive used as a pluperfect after *má*, see *eDIL* s.v. 3 *má*, *ma* I C.

428 The first ⟨a⟩ was added below the line later.

429 The scribe has added the correction *ł lain* above the line; see also Binchy, *CIH* 2072, n. k.

430 The second ⟨i⟩ was written subscript by the scribe; it looks like he originally forgot to write it.

431 The ⟨⁊⟩ was added below the line by the scribe; see also Binchy, *CIH* 2072, n. m.

432 The suprascript ⟨a⟩ was added later, possibly by the scribe.

433 I follow the emendation suggested by Binchy, *CIH* 2073, n. a.

There is never a distinction between the precinct and outside the precinct regarding the receiver of stolen goods, but there is for the thief. And that reason is: a thief beside his *sét*s is like a cowherd for the owner. And when the *sét*s always have a cowherd, there is not a distinction between precinct or outside the precinct for them. | And that is taken from: "if there be a swine- col. 610
herd, penalty-fine is awarded for them, even though [they go] under a great wood of bracken, it is known that [the fine] must be paid for the stolen property."

If it is from a precinct that a thief had stolen the *sét*s, whether from exact property or from excess property, [he owes] full honor-price.

If it is from outside a precinct that a thief has stolen the *sét*s, [he owes] half honor-price. And there is not a cowherd then, and if there is, [he owes] full honor-price then whether in a precinct or outside a precinct.

If it is from excess property that a thief had stolen the *sét*s, full honor-price is owed by the fully [liable] receiver of stolen goods. If it is from exact property that a thief had stolen the *sét*s, half honor-price is owed by the half-liable receiver of stolen goods.

It is here that it is equivalent for the half-liable receiver of stolen goods and for the thief: whenever it is from excess property that a thief had stolen the *sét*s from outside a precinct, and they did not have a cowherd; half honor-price is owed by the thief, and full honor-price is owed by the fully liable receiver of stolen goods, and half honor-price is owed by the half-liable receiver of stolen goods.

What brings it about that when it is from exact property that a thief had stolen the *sét*s from a precinct that there is full honor-price owed by a thief and that there is only half honor-price owed by the fully unlawful receiver of stolen goods, and when it is from excess property that a thief stole the *sét*s from outside a precinct that there is only half honor-price owed by a thief and full honor-price is owed by the fully liable receiver of stolen goods? This is that reason that causes it: when it is from exact property that a thief had stolen the *sét*s from a precinct, the owner had his complete property before a thief [had taken the property], and it is just that full honor-price is owed by him [sc., by the thief] for diminishing the property. He [sc., the owner] did not have his complete property when the thief had made a bargain with the fully unlawful receiver of stolen goods, and it is just though there should be only half honor-price owed by him.

When it is from excess property that a thief steals the *sét*s from outside a precinct, it is as though he found them, and they did not have a cowherd, and it is just though there should only be half-honor-priced owed by him.
And he was as a cowherd as regards | the receiver of stolen goods, because col. 611

d'fir bun*aid* do reir d*ligid*[434] in gat*aig*e do b*heth* re cois a *sét*, ⁊ coir ce rob*eth* lan*e*necl*ann* uad*h*. No d*ano* c*h*ena, rolin*ustar* fer bun*aid* a to[th]*chus* resiu dorig*h*ne g*ataige* cun*nrad* re fer m*edongaite*.[435]

[*CIH* 2073.34–2075.11][436] .i. fer meod*ongaite* lanindlig*thech*, co fis gaite ⁊ g*ataigi* aice .i. noc*ho* tabar*r* re n-in*n*saig*h* do, ⁊ cid*h* frit*h*creic aidbrith*er* aice, b*erar* uad*h* í. ⁊ la*n*dire ⁊ l*an*einecl*ann* uad*h*, ⁊ ait*hgin con*a h-in*n*ud*h* ma ta in*n*ud*h* 'co*n* set. ⁊ muna fuil in*n*ud acon *sét*, no ma *sét* 'gabu aic*en*ta in*n*ud*h* é, da roib*h* in*n*ud*h* bu ferr na 'c*h*eile ac *sét* a comaic*in*ta is tig*h*, gu*r*ub ed*h* dob*erar* leis, ⁊ a rog*h*a in*n*ud*h* don fir amuig*h* .i. læig*h* boinen*n*a laisna buaib*h* ⁊ serr*aig* firin*n*a laisna eachaib*h*, ⁊ in*n*ud*h* bo laisi*n* t*ar*b*h*, ⁊ gnim*hrad* daim*h* ma ta gni*mh*ra daim aice, ⁊ muna fuil is in*n*ud*h* bo namá.

In duine doc*h*uaid*h* i treb*air*e re dilsi int seoit g*aite* fo*r*in gataig*h*e: ma rofit*er* comad re dilse int *séoit gaite* dochuaid*h*, ⁊ muna fiter i*n*ti dia t*ar*dad*h*,
col. 613 curub *sét gaite*, ⁊ rofiter | inti dorat, ait*hgin séoit* inn*r*aic *con*a dubl*ad*, ⁊ eine-cl*ann* do ic do g*ataige* re fer meod*h*ong*aite* ⁊ ait*hgin* ma t*arrus* aice. ⁊ am*al* fer *airiten* in treb*air*e i l*eth* re fer bun*aid* na *séoit*. ⁊ ma robui t*r*eb*air*e ag anfocal na *séoit*, eir*ic* anfocail d'ic do re fer meodong*aite*.

Maine roib*h* in trebire ag anfocal na *séoit*, noc*h*an fuil ní uad*h* *acht*[437] fia*ch* cubus*braith*. Eir*ic* anfoc*ail* ic*us* g*ataige* re fer meod*ongaite*. Muna fiter in t*rebaire* cumad re dil*si* int seoit g*aite* doc*h*uaid*h*, enecl*ann* d'ic do g*ataige* re t*rebairi*, ⁊ eir*ic* anfoc*ail* d'ic do re fer m*edongaite*.

Ma rofit*er* inti dia t*ardad* curba *sét* g*aite*, ⁊ ni fiter an fer [inti dorat] (da t*ardad*),[438] beiri[d] fer bun*aid* a *sét* o fer meod*ongaite* ⁊ noc*h*an ic*ar* ni ris *acht* digb*ail* a laim*h*e nama.

In treb*air*e doc*h*uaid*h* an*n*, *acht* ma rofitir gu*r* *sét* g*aite*, is fia*ch* airitid*h* uait*he* ⁊ noc*h*an ic*ar* ni f*r*ia. ⁊ mas re di[g]b*ail*[439] a laim*h*e doc*h*uaid*h*, icaid*h* in uiletaig*h*. ⁊ mas re dilsi int *séoit*, icaid*h* ait*hgin con*a h-in*n*ud*h*. ⁊ mu*n*a fiter-side, is [s]l*an* di .i. tic fei*n* fo coraib*h*, na h-ican*n* ní, ⁊ ict*ar* fiach anfoc*ail* ria, no co*m*a einecl*ann*.

434 I follow the expansion suggested by Binchy, *CIH* 2073, n. d.

435 The scribe has abbreviated this word as 'm.i.g.'; see also Binchy, *CIH* 2073, n. e.

436 The second commentary from source G begins here.

437 The scribe next wrote ⟨aithg̅⟩, but he expunged it by underlining; see also Binchy, *CIH* 2074, n. c.

438 Cf. Binchy, *CIH* 2074, n. f. The error seems to be in this clause, not the previous one.

439 See also Binchy, *CIH* 2074, n. g.

the thief beside his *sét*s is like a cowherd for the owner according to law, and it is just that there should be full honor-price owed by him [sc., the receiver of stolen goods]. On the other hand, the owner had replenished his property before the thief had made a bargain with the receiver of stolen goods.

i.e., a fully unlawful receiver of stolen goods has knowledge of the theft and thief, i.e., a period of time for searching is not given to him, and whether the counter-purchase is claimed from him, it is taken from him. And full penalty-fine and full honor-price are owed by him, and restitution with the young if the *sét* has young. And if the *sét* does not have young, or if it is unknown if the *sét* has young, if a *sét* of the same kind had a better young [animal] in the house [of the fully unlawful receiver of stolen goods], that is what is given with it. And the plaintiff has his choice of young, i.e., female calves with the cows and male colts with the horses, and calves with the bull, and the labor of an ox if he has the labor of an ox, and if not, there are calves only.

The person who went into suretyship against forfeiture of the stolen *sét* for the thief: if he knew that he went [into suretyship] against the forfeiture of the stolen *sét*, and if the one to whom it was given did not know that it was a stolen *sét*, and the one who gave knew, | restitution of a *sét* fit to be sold with col. 613
the doubling, and honor-price to be paid by the thief to the receiver of stolen goods, and restitution if it was found in his possession. And the surety is like a man who received [stolen goods] with regard to the owner of the *sét*s. And if a surety misrepresented the *sét*s, the fine of misrepresentation is to be paid by him to the receiver of stolen goods.

Unless the surety misrepresented the *sét*, he does not owe anything except a fine for complicity. The fine of misrepresentation that a thief pays to the receiver of stolen goods. If the surety did not know that he went [surety] against forfeiture of the stolen *sét*, honor-price is to be paid by the thief to the surety, and a fine of misrepresentation is paid by him to the receiver of stolen goods.

If the one to whom it was given knew that it was a stolen *sét*, and the one who gave [it] did not know, the owner takes his *sét* from the receiver of stolen goods, and nothing is paid to him except for emptying his hand only.

The surety who went [into suretyship] then, provided that he knew that the *sét* was stolen, a fine of receiving [stolen goods] is owed by him, and nothing is paid to him. And if it is against emptying his hand that he went surety, he pays the total amount. And if it is against forfeiture of the *sét*s, he pays restitution with the increase. And if he did not know, he is free from liability, i.e., he himself impugns the contracts, and he pays nothing, and a fine for misrepresentation is paid to him, or up to honor-price.

In fiad*hu* robi a fiad*naise* int *séoit* 'ca reic: is fiach seill*chechta* no cub*us*braith uai*the* ma rofit*ir*. Mu*n*a fit*ir*, is [s]l*an*.

In fer m*edongaite* le*th*inndlig*thech*, co fis gat*aig*e aice ⁊ gi*n* fis g*aite*, u*air* da mb*eth* fis gaite aige, rob inan*n* do ⁊ fis g*aite* ⁊ gat*aig*e aice m*aræn*. L*eth*dire ⁊ l*eth*enecl*ann* uad ⁊ ait*hgin cona* h-in*nudh*; ⁊ cid*h* fri[th]creic aidbrith*er* aice, b*er*ar uad*h* í, muna fuil indud*h*.

col. 614 In treb*aire* docuaid*h* an*n*, *acht* ma rofit*ir*, is l*eth*fiach *air*it*en* uad*h*. ⁊ mas re digb*ail* a lai*me* do*ch*uaid*h*, ut sup*ra*[440] dixm*us*; ⁊ mu*n*a fit*ir*-side, is [s]l*an* dí, ⁊ ict*ar* fia*ch* anfoc*ail* ria.

In fiad*hu* robai ina fiad*naise*, ut sup*ra* dixm*us*.

In fer meod*ongaite* landlig*thech*, ci*n* fis g*aite* na gat*aig*e aice. Mas colan*n* t*arrus* aici, ait*h*fegth*ar* in cen*nach* d'urr*ad* no in cen*nach* do anurr*ad* do í. Mas cen*nach* do urr*ad* do í, b*erar* ait*hgin cona* h-in*nudh* uad*h*; ⁊ ma cen*nach* do anurr*ad*, is roin*n ar* do. ⁊ noc*h*a roib*h* raith f*r*is ina dilsi an*n* si*n*; ⁊ da mb*eth*, b*erar* uil*e* uad*h* in *sét*, ⁊ ict*ar* fia*ch* anfoc*ail* fris in tan rofin*ntar* é .i. ait*hgin con*a l*eth*gab*ail* diabulta ⁊ enecl*ann*, no [i]s[441] fregra do cen*nach* do urr*ad* si*n*. ⁊ mas f*r*i[th]creic t*arrus* aice, is [s]lan do, *acht* cor in*n*isi inti or cen*naigh* ⁊ inti risi reac.[442] ⁊ m*ana* in*n*is inti risi reac,[443] is fia*ch* dit*en* uad*h*. ⁊ mun*ar* in*n*is inti[444] or cen*naigh*, is fia*ch air*it*en* uad*h*.

Masa fer m*edongaite* co fer m*edongaite*, is roin*n ar* do. Masa fer aidbriuda ⁊ fer m*edongaite* co fer m*edongaite*, is roin*n* a t*r*i; no d*ano*, comad*h* saig*he* aic[d]ech[445] co h-eic[d]ec*h*.

Cuin is mo ⁊ cuin is lug*ha* f*or* fer m*edon*gaite l*an*indlig*thech* na f*or* gat*aig*e? ⁊ cui*n* is cutruma orra?

Is an*n* is mo: in tan tallust*ar* g*ataige* s*éotu* do f*or*c*raid* t*othchusa* a s*echtar*m*aigin* ci*n* ædg*aire*; le*th*d*ire* ⁊ le*th*eanecl*ann*[446] o g*ataige* an*n*, ⁊ land*ire* ⁊ laneneccl*ann* o fir m*edongaite*, u*air* geib*id* g*re*im ædg*aire* gat*aig*e do br*eith* co fer m*edongaite*.

440 One letter has been erased after *supra*.

441 I follow the emendation suggested by Binchy, CIH 2074, n. i.

442 The ⟨a⟩ is written subscript.

443 The ⟨a⟩ is written subscript.

444 This word was added above the line by the scribe; see also Binchy, CIH 2074, n. j.

445 I follow the emendation suggested by Binchy, CIH 2074, n. k.

446 The ⟨a⟩ is written subscript.

The witness who was witness for the *sét* at its sale; he owes a fine [the same as being a] culpable onlooker or complicity if he knew. If he did not know, he is free from liability.

The half-unlawful receiver of stolen goods has knowledge of the thief and not the theft, because if he has knowledge of the theft, it is the same for him as [when] he has knowledge of both the theft and thief. Half penalty-fine and half honor-price is owed by him and restitution with the increase; and though counter-purchase is claimed from him, it is taken from him unless there is increase.

The surety who went [into suretyship] then, provided that he knew, the col. 614 half fine of receiving is owed by him. And if he went [into suretyship] against emptying his hand, *as we said above*; and if he did not know, he is free from liability regarding it, and a fine of misrepresentation is paid to him.

The witness who was witness, *as we said above*.

The fully lawful receiver of stolen goods has no knowledge of the theft or thief. If the stolen item was found in his possession, it is to be considered [whether] the purchase of it was from a local freeman or from an outsider. If it is a purchase from a local freeman, restitution with the increase is taken from him; and if it is a purchase from an outsider, it is divided in two. And there was not a surety for him for its forfeiture in that case; and if there should be, all is taken from him for the *sét*, and a fine of misrepresentation is paid to him when it was known, i.e., restitution with the half-levy of doubling and honor-price, or that refers to a purchase from a local freeman. And if the counter-purchase was found in his possession, he is free from liability, provided that he names the one from whom he bought [it] and the one to whom he sold [it]. And if he does not name the one to whom he sold [it], a fine of sheltering is owed by him. And if he does not name the one from whom he bought it, a fine of receiving [stolen goods] is owed by him.

If it is a receiver of stolen goods with a receiver of stolen goods, it is divided in two. If it is the plaintiff and a receiver of stolen goods with a receiver of stolen goods, it is divided in three; or then, so that it might be one surety who sues another.

When is it [sc., the penalty] greater and when is it less for the fully unlawful receiver of stolen goods than for the thief? And when it is the same for them?

It is here that it is greater: when a thief stole *sét*s from excess property from outside the precinct without a shepherd; half penalty-fine and half honor-price is owed by the thief then, and full penalty-fine and full honor-price is owed by the receiver of stolen goods, because a thief taking [them] to a receiver of stolen goods is equivalent to a shepherd.

col. 615 Is ann is lugha: in tan tallastar gataige séotu do certtochus i maigin; landire ⁊ laneneclann o gataige ann, lethdire ⁊ letheneclann o fer medongaite, uair rohairbernad ar cinn fir medongaite.

Is ann is cutruma: orra in tan tallastar gataige seoit[447] d'forcraid tothchusa a sechtarmaigin; landire ⁊ laneneclann o gataige ann, ⁊ landire ⁊ laneneaclann[448] o fir medongaite.

Ma[449] tuc fer aidbredu a remhad, luighidh intí ocar aidbred nar fitir fein conit gait. Maine thard in luige-sin, beirid in fer [aidbreda][450] amach iarna imdenamh cona fiach gaite fo aicned sellaig lanfiach no lethfiach. ⁊ cincub lais, nombeirenn dia taiscid co festar fer bunaid mas indraic. Manab innraic, tabhrad a laimh innraic é isin crich re h-urnaidh fir bhunaid.

P [*CIH* 713.4–9][451] In fer medongaite lanindligthech, as [s]i a aithnidh-side: fis gaite ⁊ gataighe aige, ɫ fis gaite[452] nama. ⁊ cid aithgin cid frithcreicc tarrthus aige, nochan fuil re n-indsaigthe do, *acht* a breth uad fo cétoir: in aithgin co los ⁊ as ⁊ in forbairt, ⁊ landire ⁊ laneneclann. ⁊ in tan tic cintach re dliged, nochan ictar ni ris, *acht* ma(ine)[453] roachtaigh digbail a laime; ⁊ munar achtaigh, noch[a]n icar ní ris.

CC [*CIH* 171.21–174.6] In set aidhbriudha tuccadh i n-urlaimh choitchind, *acht* ma rauaitghestar[454] nech dib he. Gidh risin re-sin gidh iarsin re, masa cinnte lais guna(a)r[455] lais he, landire ⁊ lan n-eneclainne ⁊ aithghein comhlan d'fir[456] in seoit. ⁊ in cutruma d'enecla[i]nn[e][457] ata ann in cach inut sunn is a cutruma-sin tormaighes cain do smacht ann re tæbh int ṡeoit, [⁊ lán]eneclainne[458] d'ḟir na faichthe.

---

447 The acc. pl. form *séotu* is expected, not the nom. pl., but it could be a case of MI confusion between nom. pl. and acc. pl. case forms. The acc. pl. form is written out in full in the same phrase in source CC below.

448 The ⟨a⟩ is written subscript.

449 For the remainder of this commentary, cf. § 3, sources F and BB.

450 I follow the emendation suggested by Binchy, *CIH* 2075, n. d.

451 See Appendix 4 for the entirety of source P.

452 Approximately two letters have been erased after the ⟨a⟩; see also Binchy, *CIH* 713, n. d.

453 I follow the emendation suggested by Binchy, *CIH* 713, n. e.

454 The verb appears to be a MI 3 sg. pret. of *ad-guid* 'invokes a surety'.

455 I follow the emendation suggested by Binchy, *CIH* 171, n. j.

456 Binchy, *CIH* 170, n. c, states that each of the lenition marks in this commentary were added later; I respectfully disagree in each instance.

457 See also Binchy, *CIH* 170, n. k.

458 I follow the emendation suggested by Binchy, *CIH* 170, n. l.

It is here that it is less: when a thief stole *sét*s from exact property in the precinct; full penalty-fine and full honor-price is owed by the thief then, half penalty-fine and half honor-price is owed by the receiver of stolen goods, because it is prosecuted on behalf of the receiver of stolen goods. col. 615

It is here that it is the same for them: when a thief stole *sét*s from excess property from outside the precinct; full penalty-fine and full honor-price is owed by the thief then, and full penalty-fine and full honor-price is owed by the receiver of stolen goods.[459]

If the plaintiff swears his preliminary oath, the one from whom it was claimed swears that he himself did not know that they are stolen. Unless he swears that oath, the plaintiff takes [them] away after the proof with the fine of theft according to the nature of a culpable onlooker [who owes] half penalty-fine or full penalty-fine. And though it is not his [property], he takes them for keeping until the owner is known, if he is a worthy person. If he is not a worthy person, it is given into the hand of a worthy person in the territory to hold for the owner.

P The fully unlawful receiver of stolen goods, he is characterized thus: he has knowledge of the theft and thief or knowledge of the theft only. And whether restitution or counter-purchase was found in his possession, he does not have a period of time for searching, but it is taken from him immediately: the restitution with increase and growth and the produce, and full penalty-fine and full honor-price. And when the guilty party submits to judgment, nothing is paid to him, except if he made a stipulation for the emptying of his hand; and if he did not stipulate, nothing is paid to him.

CC The disputed *sét* was given to a neutral third party, except if either of them invoked a surety, whether before that time or after the time. If he [sc., the plaintiff] is certain that it [sc., the disputed property] is not his, full penalty-fine and full honor-price and complete restitution for the owner of the *sét*. And the equivalent amount of the honor-price that there is for it in each place here, that is the equivalent amount which law adds to [the] penalty then in addition to the *sét*, and full honor-price for the owner of the green.[460]

---

459 For this last condition to be equal for them both, the thief needs to steal the item from the owner's excess property outside a precinct and with a cowherd present. If the cowherd were not present, the thief would only owe the half-fine.

460 The assumption of the commentary is that the disputed property is livestock and that it is being held on a neutral third party's field until the dispute is settled.

Ma rabai a t*h*uicsi gurba lais, ⁊ is riasin re rauaitg*h*est*ar* he, let*h*dire ⁊ let*h*eneclan*n* [⁊][461] ait*hgh*ei*n* com*h*lan d'ḟir int ṡeoit, ⁊ *leth*enecl*ann* d'ḟir na faic*hth*i. [D](B)agab*ar*[462] in set re aic*h*ne an*n* sin. ⁊ mai*n*e gaitea in set re aidb*r*iud*h*, ceat*r*aim*h*thi[463] dire ⁊ *leth*enecc*lann* ⁊ leathait*hgh*ein d'ḟir int ṡeoit an*n*, ⁊ *leth*enecl*ann* d'ḟir na faic*h*th*e*.

Cid fod*er*a, *in* tan is cu*n*ntab*air*t *in*nosa in leis he, gu fuil let*h*enecl*ann* an*n*, ⁊ *in* tan raba cin(d)[te][464] o c*h*ianaib*h* gun*ar*ba leis he, gu*n*a raib*hi* *acht* let*h*enecl*ann* uaid*h* an*n*? Is e fat*h* fod*era*: ciamad*h* ci*n*nti o c*h*ianaib *conar*ba leis he dobiad*h* let*h*enecc*lann* uaid*h* an*n*; coir 'no d*h*e-sid*h*eicc. I*n* ta*n* is cu*n*ntab*air*t in leis he ge nabeit*h* leit*h*enecc*lann* uaid*h* an*n*.

Cid fo*dera* in baili[465] ata ceat*r*aim*hth*i diri su*n*n, na*ch* ceat*r*aim*hth*i ait*h*ge*n*a fil an*n*? Is e fa*th* fo*dera*: in baili i rraib*h*i let*h*diri an*n* o c*h*ianaib*h*, rab*h*i ait*hgh*ein co*m*hlan an*n*; coir 'no d*h*e-sid*h*eic. In baili ata i*n* ceat*r*aim*hth*i dire su*n*n, gu*m*ad*h* let*h*ait*hgh*ei*n* dabet an*n* re tæb*h* resin re-sin. ⁊ mas *iar*sin re is lan do masa lais. Mainip lais, is aissecc na *h*-ait*hgh*ena.

In fear med*h*ongaitte landlig*h*thec*h*, iss e a aic*h*ni-sid*h*e: cen ḟis[466] gaitte f. 54c na gataig*h*e aicce, | slan do, *acht* gur i*n*aisia intí di*ar* ce*n*naig*h* ⁊ intí ris*ar* recc. Mainir i*n*nis *in*tí di*ar* cen*n*aig*h*, is fiac*h* diten. Mai*n*ir i*n*nis i*n*ti ris*ar* recc, is fiac*h* *air*iten, ł gumad*h* fiac*h* cub*us*brait*h*. Mas ait*h*gei*n* t*ar*r*us* aicci, nucu b*erar* uaid*h* hí no gu tuct*h*ar re n-i*n*dsaig*h*t*h*e do. Masa frit[h]creic t*h*a*r*as aicci, nucu b*erar* uaid*h* hi du g*r*es no cu t*ar*thit*h*er i*nn* ait*hgh*in amuich. ⁊ am*ail* t*ar*thit*h*er in ait*h*gi*n* amuic, gid*h* (g)i(u)*n*nud*h*[467] gid gen

461 I follow the emendation suggested by Binchy, *CIH* 170, n. m.
462 The verb is problematic. It looks like it could be a mistake for *do-gabar*, the 3 sg. pres. pass. of *do-gaib*.
463 The first ⟨a⟩ is written subscript.
464 I follow the emendation suggested by Binchy, *CIH* 170, n. n.
465 The second ⟨i⟩ is written subscript.
466 Binchy, *CIH* 172, n. b, states that the lenition mark was added later.
467 I follow the emendation suggested by Binchy, *CIH* 172, n. d.

If he supposed[468] that it [sc., the disputed property] is his, and it is before the time that he had invoked a surety, half penalty-fine and half honor-price and complete restitution for the owner of the *sét*, and half honor-price for the owner of the green. The *sét* is taken before recognition[469] in that case. And unless the *sét* might have been stolen before claiming [it], a fourth of [the] penalty-fine and half honor-price and half restitution for the owner of the *sét* then, and half honor-price for the owner of the green.

What brings it about, when, just now,[470] he is doubtful that it is his, that there is half honor-price there, and when he is certain, as already mentioned, that it is not his, that there is nothing but half honor-price owed by him there? This is the reason that causes it: although he may be certain, as already mentioned, that it is not his, there should be half honor-price owed by him there; that is proper. When it is doubtful that it is his, there should be half honor-price owed by him there.[471]

What brings it about where there is a fourth of the penalty-fine here, that there is not a fourth of the restitution here? This is the reason that causes it: where there is half penalty-fine, as already mentioned, there was complete restitution there; that is proper. The place where there is a fourth of the penalty-fine here, there is half restitution that should be there in addition before that time. And if it is after the time, he receives the full [amount], if it is his. If it is not his, the restitution is returned.

The fully lawful receiver of stolen goods, he is characterized thus: he has no knowledge of the theft or the thief, | he is free from liability, provided that f. 54c
he names the one from whom he buys [it] and the one to whom he sells [it]. If he does not name the one from whom he buys [it], [he owes] a fine for sheltering. If he does not name the one to whom he sells [it], [he owes] a fine for receiving [stolen goods], or there might be a fine for complicity. If the restitution was found in his possession, it is not taken from him until a period of time for searching is given to him. If it is the counter-purchase that was found in his possession, it is never taken from him until the restitution is found outside [his property]. And as the restitution is found outside

468 The sense of *tuicse* is that he believed the property is his, but he is not completely certain.

469 It is difficult to determine whether *aithne* has the meaning 'hand over' or 'recognize' here.

470 *Innosa* (from *indossa*) refers to the text just mentioned. The word is contrasted later with the phrase *o chíanaib* 'already' to refer to text mentioned previously.

471 The similar commentaries in sources F, CIH 1274.16–35, DD, CIH 800.16–33, and §10, A, CIH 2172.15–2173.26 provide fuller details regarding these fines.

(g)i(u)*n*nud*h*, is amlaid*h* aisceas i*n* frit[h]c*h*rech uaid*h*-siu*mh*. ł da*no* c*h*eana, mainip aiccned inud it*ir* du bit aci*n* frit*h*crecc, ge nabet inud acin ait*hgh*ein, guna ased*h* inud*h* laisi*n* frit*h*c*h*rec. ⁊ in tan tig gataig*h*e re dliged*h*, icad ait*hgh*ein ris gu los ⁊ as, ma ta aicce, ⁊ diablad*h* ait*h*ge(i)n[a] ⁊ enecclaind.

In fe*ar* med*h*ong*h*aite let*h*inddlig*h*theac*h*, is si 'aicc*h*ni-side: fis gataig*h*e aicce ⁊ gan fis gaitte. Gid*h* aithg*h*ein gid*h* frit*h*crec*h* t*arrus* aicci, nucu tab*air* re n-i*n*dsaig*h*the di, ac*h*t a breit*h* uaid*h* fo c*hé*toir, in ait*hgh*ein gu los ⁊ as ⁊ inorbai[r]t, ⁊ landire ⁊ let*h*enecl*ann*. ⁊ i*n* tan tic gataig*h*e re dlig*ed*, icad*h* aithgei*n* gu los ⁊ as ⁊ diablad*h* ⁊ l*et*h*enecl*ann* risiu*m*. ⁊ is e-si*n* a laneneclan*n*-so*mh*, u*air* is esbad*h*ac*h* a let*h*enecl*ann* uaid*h* i*n* cun*n*rad*h* du d*h*enu*mh* resi*n* ngataig*h*e dona setaib*h* gait. Is and is esbad*h*ac*h* a let*h*enecland uaid*h* i*n* tan is [i][472] cor ł cundrad*h* tuccad*h* do iat, ⁊ ni inraicc rafocail air iat.

Mas a n-eraic[473] fog*h*la tuccad*h* do iat, gi*n*gup i*n*nraic rafocail air, ł [i] cor ł cu*n*nrad*h* masa in*n*raic rafocail, nucu de*nann* esindraic de.

In fe*ar* meod*h*ong*h*aitte la*n*inddlig*h*thech, is e a aic*h*ni-sid*h*e: fis gaitte ⁊ gataig*h*e aicci, ł fis gaitte na*m*ma. Gid*h* athge*n* gid*h* (ath)[474] frithcreic t*arrus*
f. 54d ina laim*h*, nucu*n*n [ḟ]uil | re n-i*n*dsaig*h*the do, *acht* a b*r*ith uaid*h* fo c*h*etoir, i*n*n aithg*h*ein uaid*h* gu los ⁊ as ⁊ i*n* [ḟ]orb*airt*, ⁊ landire ⁊ laneneclan*n*. ⁊ in ta*n* ticc gataig*h*e re dlig*ed* nucu*n*n icc*ar* ni ris *acht* mai*n*ir *acht*aig*h*. ⁊ m*a* *r*aac*h*taig*h* dig*h*bail laim*h*i d'ic ris, is a ic ris.[475]

Masa treb*aire* rogab re dilse, nucun ict*ar* ní ris, u*air* nucun asta(r)[476] treab*aire* a seotu gaite do g*res*.

Masa m*ar*bdile ragatad*h* a*nn*, no beod*h*il acna fuil i*n* [ḟ]orb*airt*, i*n* fuilliu*mh* nabiad*h* leo *ar* trebaire ec*h*trand cu cen*n* mbliad*hna* gurub ed*h* beas leo. Masa beodili icga n-aiccenta inud do bith, *acht* m*a* *r*ucu*s*t*ar* i*n*ud*h* amuic*h*, ma m*air*id*h* accu, is a aisiucc leo. Maine m*air*en*n*, is i*n*ud*h* a m*a*csam*h*la d'aisec an*n*. Maini ruccsat i*n*ud*h* a*m*muic*h* it*ir* iat, is cetfaid*h* gu beith a rog*h*u i*n*dud*h*a d'ḟir bu*n*aid*h* an*n*.

---

472 I follow the emendation suggested by Binchy, *CIH* 172, n. i.

473 The ⟨a⟩ is written subscript.

474 See also Binchy, *CIH* 172, n. j.

475 This word is squeezed in above the line to finish the line of text on the same line.

476 I follow the emendation suggestd by Binchy, *CIH* 172, n. k.

[his property], whether with increase or without increase, it is thus that he restores the counter-purchase. Or on the other hand, if it is not known at all [whether] the counter-purchase has increase, or the restitution should not have increase, he does not restore the increase with the counter-purchase. And when the thief submits to judgment, let him pay restitution to him with increase and growth, if it [sc., the stolen livestock] has it [sc., increase and growth], and double restitution and honor-price.

The half unlawful receiver of stolen goods, he is characterized thus: he has knowledge of the thief and not of the theft. Whether restitution or counter-purchase was found in his possession, a period of time for searching is not given to him, but it is taken from him immediately: the restitution with increase and growth and the produce, and full penalty-fine and half honor-price. And when the thief submits to judgment, let him pay restitution with increase and growth, and doubling and half honor-price to him. And that is his full honor-price because half of his honor-price is lacking from him for making the bargain with the thief for the stolen *sét*s. It is then that half his honor-price is lacking from him when they were given to him in contract or bargain, and it is not a worthy person who gave his word for them.

If it is as payment for an injury that they were given to him, though it is not a worthy person who gave his word about it, or in contract or bargain, if it is a worthy person who gave his word, it does not make him an unworthy person.

The fully unlawful receiver of stolen goods, he is characterized thus: he has knowledge of the theft and thief, or knowledge of the theft only. Whether restitution or counter-purchase was found in his hand, he does not have a period of time for searching, | but it is taken from him immediately: the f. 54d
restitution from him with increase and growth and the produce, and full penalty-fine and full honor-price. And when the thief submits to judgment, nothing is paid to him except if he had made a stipulation. And if he had made a stipulation against diminishing of his hand to be paid to him, it is paid to him.

If it is a surety that he took against forfeiture, nothing is paid to him because a surety never binds his stolen *sét*s.

If it is inanimate chattels that were stolen then, or livestock which have growth, that increase will be with them [sc., the livestock] in the custody of an external surety until the end of a year so that is what is with them. If it is livestock that it is known to have young, provided that the young was taken away, if it [sc., the young] remains with them, it is restored with them. If it does not remain [alive], young of the same likeness is restored then. If they had not carried away the young [animals] at all, it is the opinion [of lawyers] that the owner has his choice of young then.

Masa t*harb*h ragatad*h* an*n*, ⁊ dani dair ⁊ b*er*id*h* aratur, indud*h* bo leis ⁊ gni*mh*rad*h* daim*h*. Mas i*na* colpt*hac*haib ł 'na sa*mh*aiscib*h* ragatad*h* iat, ⁊ is na mbuaib*h* mora roaid*h*b*r*it,[477] geibit fein grei*m* n-ait*h*gena, ⁊ dire samaisce no colpt*h*aig*h*e leo.

Mas i*n*na mbuaib mora ragatait iat, ma m*ar*ait iat fein, geibit g*r*eim ait*h*gena, gid*h* crin(ec*h*) [gid caech] gid*h* (lec*h*lob) [lethcholpthach][478] iat, dire inich leo fon æs i tal[l]ad*h*, ⁊ is an*n* sen ata dire inic*h* ⁊ ait*h*gein esbadac*h*. Is an*n* ata ait*hgh*ei*n* inic[h] im*murro* ⁊ in dire esbad*h*ac*h*: in i*n*baid*h* rab esbad*hach* ni don ait*h*gi*n* in inbaid*h* ragatad*h* hi, aithgei*n* inich i*n*nte fon æs i tallad*h*. Ni m*air*et fein and sei*n*, ⁊ dire esbad*h*ach fo aiccnead*h* na h-esbad*h*a rabai *ar*inn ait*hgh*ein.

Ait*hgh*i*n* gu los ⁊ as ⁊ in [ḟ]orb*air*t, ⁊ landire ⁊ let*h*enecc*lann* dun eisi*n*nraic dani mait*h* da t*hoc*h*us*. Ait*h*gei*n* gu los ⁊ as ⁊ in [f]orb*airt*—⁊ nucu*n*n f. 55a [ḟ]uil dire na eneccland—dun i*n*nraicc na de|nand mait*h* da t*h*ot*h*c*us*, ł gu mbeith lan enecla*inne* di, u*air* ata a t*h*ot*h*c*h*us aicce. Ait*h*gein gen los ce*n* as ge*n* in [f]orb*airt* do*nn* eisi*n*nraicc na de*n*and mait*h* da t*h*oc*hus*, no d'i*n*nraicc i*n* scripaill.

Nucu*nn* [ḟ]uil deit*hbir* maigne na *secht*armaigne re fe*ar* meodo*n*gaite do g*res*, ⁊ ata re gataig*h*e. ⁊ is e fath fod*er*a sein: am*al* buac*h*ail d'ḟir bunaid*h* gattaige re cois a set, ⁊ o bias buac*h*ail acna setaib*h* du g*res*, nucu*nn* [ḟ]uil deit*hbir* maigne na *sechtar*maig*h*ne. ⁊ is as gabur-sen: "dia mbe mucaid*h* m[b]rog*h*a dire [díb], gid*h* fo ræda[479] raith."

Mas a maig*h*in tall gataig*h*e na seotu, is lan n-eineclai*n*ne an*n*, gid*h* do certtot*hchus* gid [d']*for*craid*h*[480] tot*h*c*us*a. Mas a *sechtar*maig*h*in, is lethenec*lann*. ⁊ ní [ḟ]uil buac*h*ail acu an*n* sei*n*. ⁊ ma ta, is la*n* n-eneclain*n*e an*n*, gid a maigi*n* gid*h* *sechtar*maig*hin*.

Mas d'[ḟ]orcraid*h* tot*hchus*a tall gataig*h*e na seotu, is lan n-ei*n*eclai*n*ne o ḟir medong*h*aite. Mas du c*h*ertot*hchus* tall gataig*h*e na seotu, let*h*enecc*lann* o fir meodo*n*gaite lai*n* an*n*, ⁊ ceat*r*aim*hth*i enecclain*n*e [o ḟir][481] medo*n*gaite lethe.

---

477 The verb is likely a MI 3 pl. pret. pass. of *ad-fíri* or its later simplex *aidbrid*; see McCone, *A First Old Irish Grammar and Reader*, 208.

478 I follow the emendation suggested by Binchy, *CIH* 173, n. a; cf. *CIH* 2072.10.

479 The word division in *CIH* 173.20 is *foræ da*; cf. the similar passage in sources A, F, and G above.

480 I follow the emendation suggested by Binchy, *CIH* 173, n. c.

481 I follow the emendation suggested by Binchy, *CIH* 173, n. d.

If it is a bull that was stolen then, and it bulls and pulls a plough, calves [are restored] with him and the labor of an ox. If they were stolen as two-year-old heifers or three-year-old heifers, and they were claimed as large cows, they themselves will be equivalent to restitution, and penalty-fine of a three-year-old heifer or a two-year-old heifer with them.

If they were stolen as large cows, if they themselves remain [alive], they will be equivalent to restitution, whether they are withered or blind in one eye or half-shanked, complete penalty-fine with them according to the age when they were stolen, and it is thus that there is complete penalty-fine and deficient restitution. It is here that there is complete restitution, however, and deficient penalty-fine: whenever anything is lacking from the restitution when it was stolen, complete restitution for it according to the age when it was stolen. They themselves do not remain [alive] in that case, and deficient penalty-fine according to the deficiency that the restitution has.

Restitution with increase and growth and the produce, and full penalty-fine and half honor-price for the unworthy person who makes good [use] of his property. Restitution with increase and growth and the produce—there is neither penalty-fine nor honor-price—for the worthy person who does not make good [use] | of his property, or so that there is full honor-price for f. 55a
him because he has property. Restitution without increase, without growth, without the produce for the worthy person who does not make good [use] of his property, or the worth of a scruple for the worthy person.

There is never a distinction of precinct or outside a precinct for the receiver of stolen goods, but there is for a thief. And this is the reason that causes that: a thief beside his *séts* is like a cowherd for the owner, and when the *séts* will always have a cowherd, there is not a distinction of precinct and outside a precinct. And that is taken from: "if there be a swineherd, penalty-fine is awarded for them, even though [they go] under a great wood of bracken."

If it is from a precinct that a thief stole the *séts*, [he owes] full honor-price then, whether from exact property or excess property. If it is from outside a precinct, [he owes] half honor-price, and they do not have a cowherd in that case, and if there is, [he owes] full honor-price then, whether from a precinct or outside a precinct.

If it is from excess property that a thief stole the *séts*, full honor-price is owed by the receiver of stolen goods. If it is from exact property that a thief stole the *séts*, half honor-price is owed by the fully liable receiver of stolen goods then, and a fourth of the honor-price from the half-liable receiver of stolen goods.

Cuin is cutru*m*a *ar* fer medo*n*gaite let*he* ⁊ f*or* gataig*he*? Is and is cut*r*uma orro: i*n*n inbaid*h* is d'[ḟ]orc*r*aid*h* tothc*hu*sa *th*all gataig*he* na seotu *sechtar*maig*h*in ⁊ ni [ḟ]uil buac*h*ail accu; lethe*n*eclan*n* o (gait*he*) [gataige][482] ⁊ let*h*eneccl*ann* o ḟir meodongaite lethe, ⁊ lan enecclai*n*ne o ḟir medongaite lain.

In cen*n*ach d'anurrad*h*, iss e a aic*h*ni-sid*he*: duine risa raib*h*i bescna [i n-]uar[483] cun*n*ar*th*a, ⁊ nucu raibi i *n*n-u*ar* aid*h*briud*ha*. ł da*no*, nucu*n*n [ḟ]itir cuic*h* resa d*er*na cun*n*rad*h*, gurub ed*h* danith*er* roind *ar* do et*ar*ro, ⁊ treab*aire* o cac*h* dib*h* re c*h*eile gibe dib*h* daair a lan *ar* dus do gataig*he* i*m* digbail f. 55b a lam d'ic risin fe*ar* eile. ⁊ c*r*andc*h*ur et*ar*ro i*m*an ait*h*|g*h*in gibe dib*h* da rua i*n*n ait*h*gi*n*.

Mas d'ḟir meodo*n*gaite landlig*h*t*h*ec*h* rai*n*ic i*n*n ait*h*g*h*ei*n* do (ḟer) [reir][484] dligid*h* c*r*andc*h*uir, diablad*h* d'ic ris cac*h* ne[i]ch[485] *immar* dig*h*bad*h* a la*m* ⁊ enecc*l*ann, ł gu*m*mad*h* let*h*inud ⁊ enecc*lain*ni ⁊ diablad*h* n-ait*h*g*h*ena d'ic ris o gataig*he*, ⁊ lea*thaith*g*h*ei*n* ⁊ let*h*diablad*h* ⁊ let*h*inud*h* ⁊ let*h*ceth*ar*d*h*a ⁊ enecl*ann*, ł cumad ceath*ar*da com*h*lan.

Mas d'ḟir bunaid*h* rainicc i*n*n aithg*h*ei*n* do (ḟe*ar*) [reir][486] dlig*h*id*h* c*r*and-c*h*air, diablad*h* ⁊ enecclan*n* d'ic re cec*htar* de, ł gu*m*ad*h* lea*thaith*g*h*ein ⁊ let*h*diablad*h* ⁊ let*h*inud*h* d'ic re fer medo*n*gaite ⁊ enecland. ⁊ is foll*us* as-sein ge rabi in set ac fir bunaid*h* fec*h*t æl[e],[487] gid gait ragata uaid*h* iat, ge*n*mot*h*a

482 I follow the emendation suggested by Binchy, *CIH* 173, n. e.

483 I follow the emendation suggested by Binchy, *CIH* 173, n. f.

484 I follow the emendation suggested by Binchy, *CIH* 173, n. g.

485 See also Binchy, *CIH* 173, n. h.

486 I follow the emendation suggested by Binchy, *CIH* 174, n. b.

487 See also Binchy, *CIH* 174, n. c.

When is it the same [penalty] for a half-liable receiver of stolen goods and for a thief? It is here that it is the same for them: whenever it is from excess property that a thief stole the *sét*s from outside the precinct and they did not have a cowherd; half honor-price is owed by the thief and half honor-price is owed by the half-liable receiver of stolen goods, and full honor-price is owed by the fully liable receiver of stolen goods.

The purchase from an outsider, he is characterized thus: a person for whom there is a treaty at the time of the bargain, and there is not a [treaty] at the time of claiming.[488] Or, on the other hand, each does not know with whom the contract was made, so that it is a division in two that is made between them, and a surety from each of them for the other [to see] which of them would get the complete [amount] first from the thief regarding emptying his hand [in order] to pay [the amount owed] to the other person.[489] And casting of lots between them regarding the restitution | [to see] which f. 55b of them would get the restitution.

If it is the fully lawful receiver of stolen goods who got the restitution according to the law of casting lots, double is paid to him [by] the man on whose account his hand was emptied and honor-price, or it should be half increase and honor-price and double restitution to be paid to him by the thief, and half restitution and half doubling and half increase and half four-fold and honor-price, until there is a complete four-fold.

If it is the owner who got the restitution according to the law of casting lots, doubling and honor-price are paid to each of them, or until there is half restitution and half doubling and half increase to be paid to the receiver of stolen goods and honor-price. And it is clear from that though the owner is wont to have the *sét* on a former occasion, though they were stolen from him

488 The sense is that there was a treaty between the two relevant territories at the time the bargain was made. See also *The MacEgan Legal Treatise* § 5.34–37; and discussion in Kelly, op. cit., 174–175.

489 The sense of the passage is that each of them hires a surety to pursue the thief. Whichever surety receives the entire amount due from the thief not only pays the amount owed to the person for whom he went surety, but he also pays the other party what was owed to him. The logic is that they had to divide the value of the property in half because the receiver of the stolen property acquired the goods in good faith from someone outside the territory, although there had been a treaty between the two territories, presumably, at the time of the purchase. When the original owner claims his stolen property from the receiver of stolen goods, it is divided in half because of this. For each of them to receive the entire amount that each is due from the thief, they each have to take a surety, who then pursues the thief. If either surety secures the entire penalty from the thief, each of the parties receives his half missing from the original division in two.

a rog*h*u i*n* eric*h* uaid*h* as, mainip e rog*h*u fir medo*ngh*aite ni bia (s)c*r*andc*h*ur, u*air* a c*r*andtacc ca*ch* cut*r*uma.

p. 268a DD [*CIH* 800.16–802.5] | In tan is o fir medo*n*gaite fuadaigt*er* in s*ét* iarna aidb*r*iud ɫ riana aidb*r*iud, ⁊ rofit*ir in* fer ronaidbrest*ar* ag fir medo*n*gaite narbo leis in s*ét* rofuaidgest*ar*, lansm*acht* ⁊ laneneclann do*n*tí or fuai[d]gead.

I*n* ta*n* is cun*n*tab*air*t laisin fer ronaidbreast*ar* oc fir m*edongaite in* lais i*n* s*ét* rofuaidgest*ar* ɫ na*ch* leis, l*eth*s*macht* ⁊ l*eth*dire ⁊ l*eth*enecl*ann* do*n*tí or fuaidgead beos.

Mad la fer in aidbreda in s*ét* fuaidgeas o fir m*edongaite*, l*eth*s*macht* ⁊ l*eth*dire ⁊ l*eth*enec*lann* do*n*tí or *fuaitged* beos, ma*n*a fit*ir* armad gaid ⁊ mai*n*ib do gadaigi c*h*eandaigeas.

Gne *aile* d*an*o: in tan chomaitheand in s*ét* i lai*m*, .i. in fer m*edongaite* ⁊ i*n* fer ronaidbreast*ar* i*m*e, ⁊ rofuadaig ne*chtar* de on fir dia raoit*h*nead iar n-aidb*r*iud, ⁊ ro fit*ir* narbo leis in s*ét* rof*uataig*, lans*macht* ⁊ laneneclann do*n* fir asa faic*h*e, ⁊ lans*macht* ⁊ landire ⁊ laneneclann don fir asa s*ét*.

I*n* tan is cundt*h*ab*air*t in laisi*n* fer rofuadaig asa faic*h*e in fir diar ait*h*nead, is l*eth*s*macht* ⁊ l*eth*enecl*ann* o c*echt*ar de do*n*ti asa faic*h*e, ⁊ l*eth*sm*acht* ⁊ l*eth*dire o c*echt*ar de diaraile.

Mad lais fadeisin i*n* s*ét* fuaidges, is l*eth*s*macht* ɫ l*eth*enecl*ann* o ce*ch*tar de d'fir na faic*h*e, ⁊ l*eth*enecl*ann* ⁊ l*eth*dire o ce*cht*ar de diaraile.

Gne *aile* d*an*o: in tan rofit*ir* in fer m*edongaite* is do gadaige rochren, ⁊ ni fit*ir* armad gad, is l*eth*fia*ch* fair, .i. l*eth*sm*acht* ⁊ l*eth*dire dleg*ar* de ara fis is do gadaige.

Mad (rofit*ir*) [rofuaitged][490] o fir m*edongaite* iar ndeidi*n* c*h*irt do, is l*eth*s*macht* ⁊ l*eth*dire ⁊ l*eth*enecl*ann* dligis, uair is comarlecud et*arr*o in tan-si*n*,

490 I follow the emendation suggestd by Binchy, *CIH* 800, n. e.

by theft, in addition he has the choice of penalty from him for it, unless it is the choice of the receiver of stolen goods that there will not be casting of lots because their casting of lots [is] equal [for] each.[491]

DD | When[492] it is from a receiver of stolen goods that the *sét* is stolen after p. 268a
the claiming or before the claiming, and the man who claimed it from the receiver of stolen goods knew that the *sét* that was stolen was not his, full penalty-fine and full honor-price for the one from whom it was stolen.

When the man who had claimed it from the receiver of stolen goods is in doubt that the *sét* that was stolen is his or not, half penalty and half penalty-fine and half honor-price for the one from whom it was stolen nevertheless.

If the plaintiff owns the *sét* that he takes away from the receiver of stolen goods, half penalty and half penalty-fine and half honor-price for the one from whom it was stolen still, unless he knew about the theft and unless it may be from a thief that he buys [it].

A different version then: when he who entrusts the *sét* into [his] hand, i.e., the receiver of stolen goods and the man who had claimed it, and one of them stole it from the man by whom it was recognized after claiming, and he knew that the *sét* that was stolen was not his, full penalty and full honor-price for the owner of the green, and full penalty and full penalty-fine and full honor-price for the owner of the *sét*.

When the man who took it from the green of the man by whom it was recognized is in doubt, half penalty and half honor-price is owed from one of them for the one who owns the green, and half penalty and half penalty-fine is owed by the other.

If he himself owns the *sét* that he takes away, half penalty and half honor-price is owed by one of them for the owner of the green, and half honor-price and half penalty-fine is owed by the other.

A different version then: when the receiver of stolen goods knows that it is from a thief that he bought [it], and he did not know about the theft, he owes half penalty-fine, i.e., half penalty and half penalty-fine is owed by him on account of his knowledge of the thief.

If it was stolen from a receiver of stolen goods after the granting of entitlement to him, it is half penalty and half penalty-fine and half honor-price that he is owed because it is permitted for them in that case because it is the

491 The sense is that each of them has to agree to cast lots in order for it to be valid.

492 For what follows below, cf. also the similar commentaries in sources F and CC at pp. 168–169 and 182–185 and see the commentary in §10, source A.

uair i(d)[s] cutr*um*a a da n-in*n*dlig*ed* .i. creic do gadaig*e* do*n* d*ar*[a] na[e][493] ⁊ fuadach a set fei*n* diaraile. Gid gad*aige* gid fer m*edongaite* f*uaitges*[494] in *sét* a faic*he* in fir in roco*m*aitned, is cutru*m*a a fiac*h* d'fir na faic*he*.

Gne *aile* d*ano*: mad a gadaige f*uaitges* iar ndeidi*n* c*h*irt dó, ⁊ ni la fer i*nn* aidbreada in *sét* rofuadaig*h*, lans*macht* dia fl*aith* in gad*aigi*, ⁊ land*ire* ⁊ laneneecl*ann* do*n* gad*aige* am*ail* adroillith*er* dia ndeine maith dia to[th]*chus*.

I*n* ta*n* is cun*n*tab*air*t in laisin fer ronaidbrest*ar* in *sét* rof*uaitaig*, is l*eth*s*macht* uad di fl*aith* in gad*aigi*, ⁊ l*eth*d*ire* ⁊ l*eth*enecl*ann* do*n* gad*aige* am*ail* adroill*ither*. O*cus* mad la fer in aidbriuda i*n* *sét* fuaidigt*er*, is l*ethsmacht* fagaib la fl*aith*; ⁊ l*eth*d*ire* ⁊ l*eth*enecl*ann* am*ail* adroill*ither*. Iss *ed* fagb*us* lasin ngad*aige*, uair roda*m*ad ceart dó, is co*m*logud et*ar*ru fo*dera* a tabairt a lai*m* in gad*aigi* u*m*ar aidbread i*n*ddlig*iud*. No is fear indraic in rocomaithne lam *for*acaib acu ar tairisi*n* leis. Is cutru*m*a fiac*h* gidbe foxl*us* a lai*m* ar*aile* ł asin lai*m* in rocomait*h*ne i*n* *sét* in fer aidb*r*es, ⁊ in fer uma n-aidbridth*er*.

p. 268b I*n* fer m*edon*gaide landlig*thech*, masa f*rith*creic rohaidbr*ed* aice, is [s]*lan* dó, *acht* co roin*n*isi cia roc*r*eca ⁊ cia f*r*isi ruiri. ⁊ nochan aidb*r*ith*er* frithc*r*eic aice i*m*a br*eith* uad, *acht* ma*n*a fagbait*er* in colan*n* acan fir amuig re h-aidbriud. ⁊ am*ail* digbaith*er* a lam in fir a*m*uig u*m*an aithgi*n* *con*a h-in*n*u ł gan in*n*ad, is a*m*l*aid* digbaith*er* a lam-som umu*n* f*r*ithc*r*eic *con*a h-in*n*ad ł gan in*n*ad. ⁊ mas aicenta ind*ud* agi*n* col*ainn* bun*aid*, cid aici*n*ta ci*n*cub aic*en*ta indud do b*eth* agi*n* f*r*ithc*r*eic, gu*r*ub in*n*ud a co*m*aicenta-sid b*er*ar laisin frithc*r*eic. Mu*n*ab aici*n*ta a b*eth* agin *sét* bun*aid*, ni b*er*ar indad laisi*n* f*r*ithc*r*eic. Masa col*ainn* roh*aidbred* aicce, masa d'anurr*ad* rocendai*g*[495] he, is roin*n* ar do it*er* inad ⁊ aithgi*n*.

Masa urr*ad* rocen*naig* he, is re n-innsaig*the* dob*er*ar dó, ⁊ b*er*ar in *sét* uad iarsan re. ⁊ masa fer m*edongaite* dlig*thech*, ⁊ fer aidb*r*iuda aidb*r*es ag fer m*edongaite* dlig*thech*, is roind a t*r*i, ł saigid aicech co aiccech.

---

493 I follow the emendation suggested by Binchy, *CIH* 800, n. f.

494 I follow the expansion suggestd by Binchy, *CIH* 801, n. b.

495 The scribe put the suspension mark over the ⟨n⟩ in error; see Binchy, *CIH* 801, n. g.

equivalent of two unlawful [people], i.e., buying from a thief by the one and stealing his own *sét* by the other. Whether a thief or receiver of stolen goods takes the *sét* from the green of the man with whom it is entrusted, it is the same fine for the owner of the green.

A different version then: if it is from a thief that he takes it after granting of entitlement to him, and the plaintiff does not own the *sét* that he stole, full penalty [is owed] to the thief's lord, and full penalty-fine and full honor-price for the thief as he is entitled to, if he makes good [use] of his property.

When the man who had claimed the *sét* that was stolen is in doubt, half penalty is owed by him to the thief's lord, and half penalty-fine and half honor-price for the thief as he is entitled to. And if the plaintiff owns the *sét* that is stolen, it is half penalty that the lord gets; and half penalty-fine and half honor-price as he is entitled to. This is what he leaves in the possession of the thief because he had submitted entitlement to him; a mutual concession between them because of his taking from the thief's hand regarding the unlawful claiming. Or it is a worthy person in whose hand he entrusted what he left them for security with him. The fine is the same though he carries away from the hand of another or from the hand into which the *sét* of the plaintiff and the man from whom it is claimed was entrusted.

The fully lawful receiver of stolen goods, if it is the counter-purchase that p. 268b
was claimed from him, he is free from liability, provided that he named the one from whom he had bought and the one to whom he had sold. And the counter-purchase is not claimed from him regarding taking it from him, provided that the stolen item was found by the plaintiff at the time of claiming. And as the plaintiff's hand is lessened regarding the restitution with the increase or without the increase, it is thus his [sc., the receiver of stolen goods'] hand is lessened regarding the counter-purchase with the increase or without the increase. And if it is known that the original principal [sc., the stolen livestock] had increase, whether known or unknown [whether] the counter-purchase has increase, increase of the same nature is taken with the counter-purchase. If it is not known [whether] the original *sét* [had increase], increase is not taken with the counter-purchase. If it is the principal that was claimed from him, if it is from an outsider that he bought it, it is divided in two between increase and restitution.

If it is from a local freeman that he bought it, a period of time for searching is given to him, and the *sét* is taken away from him after the period of time. And if it is a lawful receiver of stolen goods, and the plaintiff claims from a lawful receiver of stolen goods, it is divided in three, or a surety sues another.

I*n* *sét* be*irius* in gat*aige* leis, is and dob*er*ar landire do ait*h*i a in*n*d*eth*b*iruis* fair, ⁊ t*r*ocaire dorined f*r*is can landire uad i*n* ca*ch* *sét* fir-cin*n*tar doib.

D*eth*b*ir*[496] maigne ⁊ *sechtarmaigne* re fer tel*aig* faidc*h*i do g*r*es: lan a maigi*n* ⁊ l*eth* a sec*h*tar*maigin*. Can asi ngaba*r* lan i maig*in* isna *sét*aib ⁊ l*eth* a *sech*tar m*aigin*? Is as gaba*r*: "co direna*r* *ceth*ra. Co h-erena*r* boi*n* asa buail*aid*, ⁊rl."[497] ł d*an*o cena, o robiad buach*aill* i toglen*mai*n a *sét*, laneneclann in*n*tib cid a m*aigin* cid a *sech*tarm*aigin*. Can asa ngabta*r* ón? Is as gabta*r*: "dia *m*be m*uccaide*,[498] ⁊rl."[499]

D*eth*b*ir* *cert*to*chus*a ⁊ f*or*craid to[th]ch*usa* re fer m*edongaite*, ⁊ *no*cho fuil d*eth*b*ir* maigne na *sechtarmaigne*, u*air* am*al* m*aigen* d'fir m*edongaite* cach inat a ndingne a cor ł a cundr*ad*. H-uair [amal][500] buach*aill* d'fer bun*aid* do*na* *sét*aib i*n* gat*aig*i, ⁊ o bias b*uachaill* a toglen*main* na *sét*, [nochon fuil][501] d*eth*b*ir* m*aigne* ł *sech*tar*maigne* riu.

Aithg*ein* ci*n* los ci*n* as cin [in] f*or*bairt don eisindr*aic* na denand m*aith* dia to[th]c*hus*, ł d'in*nraic* in scrip*uil*. Am*ail* ata rig bend; ł d*an*o is a b*eth* am*al* co*m*orba liag i*ma* lan*n*aib lig .i. am*al* co*m*orb*a* cloic*he* bias ar lar maige i*na* luige ci*n* in f*or*bairt aice. Is aml*aid*-si*n* na fuil in*n*ad na i*n* f*or*b*air*t don esi*nn**raic* na denan*n* m*aith* da t*othchus*.

Ait*hgein* co los ⁊ as ⁊ i*n* f*or*b*air*t, [⁊ landire ⁊ laneneclann][502] d'ic d'fir m*edongaite* lani*n*dligthech. Ait*hgein* co los ⁊ as ⁊ i*n* f*or*b*air*t, ⁊ l*eth*dire ⁊ l*etheineclann* d'ic d'fir m*edongaite* l*eth*inndlig*thech*. T*us*ca doacr*ad*[503] fer m*edongaite* and si*n* na gat*aigi*; ⁊ dam*ad* *tus*ca doacarta[504] i*n* gat*aig*i, robo ait*hgein* co los ⁊ as ⁊ i*n* f*or*bairt d'ic do gat*aig*i, ⁊ landire ⁊ *l*anenecl*ann*. Ait*h**gein* co l*os* ⁊ as ⁊ i*n* *forbairt* d'íc do fer m*edongaite* lain.

496 For this part of the commentary, cf. source Z (Appendix 8), *CIH* 673.35–674.25.

497 This source has not been identified, but it also appears in source Z (Appendix 8).

498 See also Binchy, *CIH* 801, n. i.

499 This is the beginning of the same quotation in previous sources, e.g., A and F above, regarding the swineherd and pigs in a forest.

500 I follow the emendation suggested by Binchy, *CIH* 801, n. k; cf. Z, *CIH* 674.2.

501 I follow the emendation suggested by Binchy, *CIH* 801, n. m.

502 See also Binchy, *CIH* 801, n. q; and cf. Z, *CIH* 674.24.

503 The verb is likely a 3 sg, pret. pass. of *acraid*, a simplex derived from *ad-gair* 'sues, prosecutes' with the MI confusion of the preverb *do-* for OI *ro-*; Kim McCone, *The Early Irish Verb*, 2nd ed. (Maynooth: An Sagart, 1997), pp. 196–197.

504 The verb is likely a 3 pl. pret. pass. of *acraid*, a simplex derived from *ad-gair* 'sues, prosecutes' with the MI confusion of the preverb *do-* for OI *ro-*; McCone, *Early Irish Verb*, 196–197.

The *sét* that the thief takes with him, it is then full penalty-fine is given as payment due to absence of reasonable cause for him, and leniency was made for it without full penalty fine [being] owed by him for each *sét* that is 'truly-accused' by them.[505]

[There is] always a distinction of precinct and outside a precinct for the owner of the household green: full [penalty] from a precinct and half from outside a precinct. Whence is taken full [penalty] in a precinct for the *sét*s and half from outside the precinct? It is taken from: "until cattle is paid. Until a cow is paid in respect of a byre, etc." Or on the other hand, when a cowherd will be in possession of his *sét*s, full honor-price for them whether from a precinct or outside a precinct. Whence is that taken? It is taken from: "if there be a swineherd, etc."

[There is] a distinction of exact property and excess property regarding the receiver of stolen goods, and there is not a distinction of precinct nor outside a precinct, because each instance when he could make a contract or bargain is as a precinct for the receiver of stolen goods. Because [he is] as a the owner's cowherd for the thief's *sét*s, and when there will be a cowherd in possession of the *sét*s, there is not a distinction of precinct or outside a precinct for them.

Restitution without increase, without growth, without the produce for the unworthy person who does not make good [use] of his property, or the value of a scruple for the worthy person. As a king of a hill is he; or then he is like an heir of a stone regarding a building of stone, i.e., like an heir of a stone that is on the ground of a plain as he has an oath without the produce.[506] It is thus that there is no increase of the produce for the unworthy person who does not make good [use] of his property.

Restitution with increase and growth and the produce, and full penalty-fine and full honor-price to be paid by the fully unlawful receiver of stolen goods. Restitution with increase and growth and the produce, and half penalty-fine and half honor-price to be paid by the half unlawful receiver of stolen goods. The receiver of stolen goods was prosecuted first [before] the thieves in that case; and if the thieves were prosecuted first, restitution with increase and growth and the produce to be paid by the thief,[507] and full penalty-fine and full honor-price. Restitution with increase and growth and the produce to be paid by the fully [lawful] receiver of stolen goods.

505 Cf. the gloss at the beginning of source F above.

506 The proverbial expressions are obscure to me, but the general sense is that a king of a hill is really a king of nothing, and that an heir of a stone on a plain is an item without profit.

507 The commentary shifts from pl. to sg. with regard to the thief.

§5

Ni teit ait*hgin* tar cen*n* gat*aig*e[508]

G [*CIH* 2075.12–18] .i. ni geib gre*i*m n-ait*h*gen*a* t*ar* cen*n* in gat*ai*g*i*. Cia eirnith*er* *iarum* o fir meod*ongaite* ica n-aidbrith*er* an *sét* no a log*h* .i. cia t*harth*id*h* do lurg no aisneis, ni dilan*n*[509] an colan*n* ce*n* a h-ait*hgin* fein on gat*ai*g*i* manib e fei*n* tidnaices[510] uaid*h* í. ł d*ano* ní dilan*n* ait*hgin* do*n* gat*aig*e cia t*arr*ast*ar* ic fir me*dongaite* let*h*indlig*thech* ł lanindlig*thech*.

Maineb e dotngre[511] .i. tog*h*ranas[512] o fir m*edongaite* dlig*thech*, ł maineb e t*h*oib*h*geas[513] .i. gat*aig*i. Is de isb*eir* .i. o*n* bre*ith*: "ni in*n*ad*h* nec*h*, ⁊rl-"

508 § 5 is found only in source G. As is the case with § 1, it is possible that both extracts from the tract might belong together as a single sentence: *Ni teit aithgin tar cenn gataige, maineb e dotngre* 'Restitution does not apply for a thief, unless it is he who makes a claim for it.'

509 The verb is the 3 sg. pres. ind. of *dílaid* 'satisfies, pays' with a MI conjunct ending.

510 The verb is the 3 sg. pres. ind. rel of *tidnaicid*, a MI simplex form of *do-indnaig*; *eDIL* s.v. *do-indnaig* 'gives, brings, conducts'.

511 This verb is the 3 sg. pres. subj. of *do-greinn* 'overtakes, levies, makes a claim against' with a class C m. object agreement marker; *eDIL* s.v. *do-greinn*.

512 The verb form might be 3 sg. pres. ind. rel. from a MI simplex form of *do-greinn*.

513 The ⟨a⟩ is written subscript.

§5

Restitution does not apply for a thief[514]

G i.e., a thief will not have a claim of restitution. Although it is paid afterwards by the receiver of stolen goods from whom the *sét* or the payment is claimed, i.e., though he [sc., the thief] revealed to him a track[515] or information, he [sc., the receiver of stolen goods] does not pay the principal without its own restitution from the thief, unless it is he himself who brings it from him [sc., the thief]. Or on the other hand, he does not pay restitution to the thief though it was found with the half unlawful or fully unlawful receiver of stolen goods.

Unless it is he [sc., the thief] who makes a claim for it, i.e., he who makes a claim from the lawful receiver of stolen goods, or unless it is he who recovers [it], i.e., a thief. It is from which it is said, i.e., from the judgment: "no one [pays] increase, etc."[516]

514 For a discussion of this section, see the Introduction, pp. 27–28.

515 The reference is to the thief pointing out the track of the stolen livestock; even if he helps in the recovery of the stolen goods, he is not to be compensated for his efforts. Tracking stolen livestock is mentioned in *The MacEgan Legal Treatise* §4; see Kelly, *op. cit*, 158–159, where he suggests that nothing from the early Irish laws on tracking survives in the OI or MI legal material, although there are certainly references to it in later sources. For a discussion and chronological presention of these later sources, see W.N. Osborough, "The Irish Custom of Tracts," *The Irish Jurist*, new series, 32 (1997): 439–458, reprinted in W.N. Osborough, *Studies in Irish Legal History* (Dublin: 1999), pp. 64–80; and also Gearóid Mac Niocaill, "Irish Law and the Armagh Constitutions of 1297," *The Irish Jurist*, new series, 6 (1971): 339–344; and Hiram Morgan, "'Lawes of Irelande': A Tract by Sir John Davies," *The Irish Jurist*, new series, 28/30 (1993/1995): 307–313. There is another reference to tracking stolen cattle in Heptad 64, source J.

516 The commentary is quoting a fragment of tract from *Cáin Ṡóerraith*: *ar ni induth nech diaraile* 'because no one [pays] increase to another'; *CIH* 1771.16–17, also 1542.3; *CCIH* 72; and *AL* 2: 196.9–10.

§6

Ar is faill do neimed cen iarraid a *séoit*, muna feast*ar*[517] bes gad rocria[d], ⁊ munub do gataid[e] rocriad.

A [*CIH* 2171.21–31] .i. cona b*eth* isi*n* tuaith nech na fesed a *sét* do tesb*aid*, ar cia luaige*nd*[518] nech iarna fis, is dire noicfad, ⁊ ni fuicfit*h*ea[519] ni don i*n*dud aigi.

Is ed is cendach d'anurr*ad* and: a ce*n*dach do o fir echt*archóic*id[520] resa raibe besgna i n-uair in ce*n*daig, cia dob*eth* besgna et*ar*ru anosa ce*n*co raib. No da*no* cena, nocharb aithnid do it*ir* he. & mas d'fir *echt*arch*ói*cid,[521] is a roga do [in][522] re n-in*n*saigt*he* rach*us* do [no][523] in roi*n*d ar do fo *cét*oir. ⁊ mad he a roga re n-i*n*dsaigt*hi*, ni fuil l*eth* do asa h-ait*h*li ginco fagbad[524] ni o neoch *aile* .i. onti or cen*n*aig.

Anurr*ad* sin na raib f*or* cur na f*or* faichill ag duine airit*hi* isi*n* crich; ⁊ da mb*eth*, robad i*n*a*n*d cu*n*drad ris ⁊ risin n-urr*ad* fei*n*. Maṣa fer æ*ncóic*id[525] do he, ce tarr*aid* ce*n*co tarr*aid* ni de iar tain, nocha ce*n*dac*h* d'anurr*ad* do he.

---

1 ar] *om.* F. ‖ faill] The scribe of source G wrote the gloss '.i. *ar* treisi' 'i.e., for three days' below *faill.* ‖ do] do*n* F. ‖ neimed] nemed A, neimed*h* F, neim*ed* ⁊rl- EE; source EE does not contain any more of the tract for this section. This citation from source F is found later at *CIH* 1275.2 and ends here. ‖ cen] ci*n* G. The scribe of source G wrote the gloss '.i. in tig re (?)' 'i.e., in a house previously (?)' below *cin.* The last letter of the gloss is obscure. ‖ iarraid] iaraid A, iarr*aid* G. Source A does not contain any more of the tract for this section. ‖ *séoit*] .s. G; source G ends here. 1–2 muna ... rocriad] This part of the tract is found only in source F and pertains to the receiver of stolen goods. There is not enough of the tract remaining to determine in which order the two extracts from the tract should be relative to each other. Source F preserves the extracts from the tract in a different order than source A; the extract of tract which follows this one in the MS belongs with § 2.

---

517 The ⟨a⟩ is written subscript.

518 The ⟨a⟩ is written subscript; see also Binchy, *CIH* 2171, n. l. The sequence ⟨e*nd*⟩ has been added to the end of the line later in a lighter colored ink in the same hand which made the interlinear insertion in the previous section.

519 The verb is a 3 sg. cond. pass. form of *fo-ácaib* 'leaves'.

520 The ⟨id⟩ are written above the line.

521 The ⟨id⟩ are written above the line.

522 I follow the emendation suggested by Binchy, *CIH* 2171, n. m; cf. *CIH* 2075.28.

523 I follow the emendation suggested by Binchy, *CIH* 2171, n. n; cf. *CIH* 2075.28.

524 A ⟨r⟩ has been erased after the first ⟨a⟩; see also Binchy, *CIH* 2171, n. o.

525 The ⟨id⟩ are written above the line.

§ 6

Because it is neglect for a noble not to seek his *sét*, if he does not know that he has bought stolen property, and if he has not bought [it] from a thief.[526]

A i.e., that there should not be anyone in the *túath* who did not know that his *sét* was missing, because someone who buys it after knowing [that it was missing], he will pay a penalty-fine, and nothing from the increase should be left in his possession.

This is buying from an outsider here: he buys it from a man of another province with which there is a protocol at the time of the purchase, whether there might be a protocol between them now or not. Or, on the other hand, he was not known to him at all. And if it was from a man of another province, he [sc., the receiver of stolen goods] has a choice of a period of time for seeking that will be given to him or the division in two immediately. And if he chooses a period of time for seeking, he does not have half afterwards though he might not obtain anything from someone else, i.e., from the one from whom he bought [it].

This is an outsider who is not under contract or in the hire of a particular person in the territory; and if he should be, [making] a bargain with him would be the same as [making a bargain] with the local freeman himself. If he is a man of the same province as himself, whether or not he obtained anything from him afterwards, it is not [considered] a purchase from an outsider regarding it.

---

526 For a discussion of this section, see the Introduction, pp. 28–30. The citation of tract from source F is only preserved in that MS. While the topic of the tract in source F does not follow directly on that in the other sources as it concerns the receiver of stolen goods, the commentary is the same, which is why source F is grouped with the other sources for this section. Furthermore, the beginning of the tract as found in the other sources is quoted in source F below. The last clause of the tract is discussed by Kelly, *The MacEgan Legal Treatise*, 173. Based on the commentaries in § 4, it is crucial that the buyer not know either that the goods were stolen or that the seller is a thief at the time of the sale. Otherwise, he is liable for fines. The commentaries in this section in many ways continue with the subject matter of § 4.

F [CIH 1274.36–1275.40] .i. no *cona* b*eth* isin tuai*th* neach na feisi a *sét* do tesbu uad*ha*, ar cia lauid*he* nea*ch* iarna fis, is dire noicf*ad*, ⁊ ni[527] [ḟ]icfe[528] ni don inda[d][529] aige.

Set sin *test*a o d*h*uine, ⁊ is si faill adeir and a nem*h*iarr*aidh* d'ḟior bun*aidh*, ⁊ fu*air* nech *aile* a n-ecoimde f*rith*i raod*ha* no ṡleib*he*, ⁊ roescc*air* é am*ail* adeir dlig*ed*. Cuide frithe d*ho* do*n* aithg*in* ⁊ leth d*ho* asin indud*h*, u*air* adeir dli*ged*:[530] **feis l*eth* frithgnu[m](d)*ha*.**[531] Iss e in fa*th* fo*dera*: a m*h*uca do b*h*reith do m*h*enn u*air* fer nem*h*besccna in prechan; uair nar essccair lab*hán* iat. **ł is faill do*n* neimed*h*, ⁊rl-**[532] .i. im tiachtai*n* fo coraib*h* *ar ceithre* h-u*aire* *fich*et,[533] ł ce*n* treab*aire* tara c*h*end mad*h* anurr*ad* risi*n* nderna *cunnrad*.

527 This word has been added above the line with reference marks by the scribe; see also Binchy, CIH 1274, n. h.

528 The verb has been emended to a MI 3 sg. fut. form of *fo-ácaib* 'leaves', which is based on the stem *fácb-*. The emendation is based on the corresponding clause in source A above, although a passive verb form would make better sense in English.

529 I follow the emendation suggested by Binchy, CIH 1274, n. i.

530 Cf. Binchy, CIH 1274, n. j, who queries whether the expansion of the final syllable should be *-id*.

531 See also Binchy, CIH 1275, n. a, and cf. § 7, source A, CIH 2171.32.

532 Cf. the tract at p. 200.

533 The ⟨et⟩ are written above the line.

F i.e., or that there should not be anyone in the *túath* who did not know that his *sét* was missing from him, because someone who buys it after knowing [that it was missing], he will pay a penalty-fine, and nothing from the increase will be left in his possession.[534]

That *sét* is missing from someone, and it says that it is neglect then [for] not seeking it by the owner, and someone else found [it] in an unfrequented place [as] something found in a forest or on a mountain, and he gave public notice as law says. He has a share of the find from the restitution and he has half from the increase,[535] because [the] law says: **cattle-trespass of half-labor.**[536] And this is the reason that causes it: his pigs are given to Menn (?), because a raven [is like] a man not governed by protocol; because dirt (?) does not proclaim them.[537] Or **it is neglect for a noble, etc.**, i.e., regarding impugning contracts before 24 hours, or without a surety on his behalf, if it may be an outsider with whom he makes a bargain. This is an outsider who

---

534 The translation of the last clause is tentative because the verb is active here rather than passive as it is in other forms of this clause; cf. source A above.

535 For finding someone else's property and giving public notice about it, see § 8 and Heptad 64.

536 This is a quotation from the tract in § 7; it refers to a form of animal trespass where the animals have laid down and/or grazed in someone else's field; *EIF* 136; and *eDIL* s.v. 2 *feis(s)s*. For finding lost items in out-of-the-way places and the correct procedure for making the find public, see Heptad 64 and § 8 below, and *The MacEgan Legal Treatise* § 5.1–4, which summarizes the commentary from Heptad 64 concerning publicizing anything which has been found.

537 The reason given in the commentary is obscure due to the uncertainty of the translation. In Eugene O'Curry's unpublished translation of Egerton 88 (p. 2143), he renders the explanation as verse: "The reason that caused/Menn to obtain his swine/Because the scald crow is an enemy/For Laban did not proclaim them." The literary or historical reference is not elaborated further in the commentary. While understanding *menn* and *labhán* as personal names solves a variety of philological problems, it might not be the solution. It is possible that the second word is *lápán* 'mire, dirt' and that this is a reference to the crime of intentionally driving someone else's livestock into a mire and causing them to become dirty; see the discussion in *EIF* 164; *CIH* 1181.22 and 26. Perhaps the fact that the livestock were not dirty did not suggest that they had been stolen? An additional problem is the fact that *laban* appears in the tract of § 8, and one could argue that they are different words. It is unusual to find *uair* without the copula or another verb, but the verse interpretation might account for this. Furthermore, the meaning of *menn* here is problematic; the common meanings of 'clear, evident; stammering' do not make much sense. Cf. O'Dav no. 1362: "Rodet, .i. ro dam .i. [leg. *ut est*] "ro det a cron iarsin do mend," .i. ro dam*as*dar iarum asa hathle-sin a *cur* a n-urlaim coitchind. *Rodét*, i.e., he granted, *ut est* 'he granted his possession afterwards to Menn (?)', i.e., so thereafter he allowed it to be put into common patronage."

Anurr*adh* si*n* na fuil ar cur no ar faichill ag duine áirithe isi*n* crich, ⁊ *da* mḃ*eth*,[538] bud*h* inand *cunnradh* do d*h*enam*h* fris ⁊ doneithea risi*n* urr*ad* aga[539] mḃ*eth*.[540]

In cendach d'anurr*adh*, is si 'aithne-sid*he* .i. duine risi raib*he* bescna i n-uair in *cunnurtha* ⁊ ni [ḟ]uil i n-uair in aid*h*bre, is roind *ar* d*ho* et*aru* ⁊ fer bun*aidh*. ł ni h-aithnid*h* d*ho* cuich *dar* c*h*end*aigh*. ⁊ cid*h* ait*hgin* cid*h* fricr*eic* tarr*us* aigi, cid*h* co n-in*n*ud cid*h* ga*n* in*n*ud*h*, ⁊ ní h-ait*h*nid do intí ór cen*n*-aid*h*, is roi*nn* ar do eturr*u*. ⁊ tre*baire* eturr*u* cid*h*be dib*h* tair a lan ar dus do gad*aige* im dig*h*b*ail* a lai*m*e d'ioc reisin fer *aile*.

Mas ait*h*níd do intí or cend*aig*, noch*an* [ḟ]uil a riag*lad* re cen*nach* d'anurr-*ad*, ac*ht* re n-in*n*saig*h* d*ho* mad*h* ferr les, ⁊ cr*ann*cor eaturr*u* uman ait*hgin*. ⁊ anurr*ad* si*n* na raib ar cur na ar faic*h*ill [ag][541] dui*ne* airit*hi* isi*n* cri*ch*. ⁊ *da* mb*eth*, rob inan*n* *cunnrad* res ⁊ resi*n* n-urr*ad* fe*n*, ⁊rl-; ⁊ gac*h* uair iss é a rog*h*a ré n-in*n*saig*hi* do t*h*ab*air*t do, ciamad ail do crec d'anurr*ad* do denam d*he*, noch*an* dingi.

f. 5vd Is *ed* is crec d'anurr*ad* an*n*: a cendach d'fer a*chtarchóic*id*h*, ⁊ noch*an* ait*h*[n]id[542] do intí dar cendaig*h* é. ⁊ gac*h* uair is ó fer a*chtarchóic*id*h* rocen*n*-aig*h* é, is [s]i 'na rog*a* ata an crec d'anurr*ad* dodena d*he* fo *cét*oir, no in re n-*inn*saig*h* rag*hus* do.

Berid*h* cach nem*ed* a set *con*a in*n*ad*h* .i. trian do t*ir* ⁊ *trian* do fric*h*nam ⁊ trian do bunad*h*, ⁊ iss é an bunad*h* t*h*arb ⁊ bo. In inb*aid* is d'urr*ad* cendaig*hus*, ber*i*d*h* ait*hgin* ⁊ *cóic*id*h* [d']in*n*ud*h*.[543] ⁊ in inb*aid* is d'anurr*ad* cendaig*hus*, ber*i*d*h* ait*hgin* ⁊ *in* dar*a* ra*nn* *déc* a indud*h*.

538 The *punctum* over the ⟨b⟩ indicates nasalization.

539 The word *aga* has been written above the erased symbol for *da*; see Binchy, *CIH* 1275, n. b.

540 The *punctum* over the ⟨b⟩ indicates nasalization.

541 See also Binchy, *CIH* 1275, n. c, and cf. *CIH* 1275.5.

542 See also Binchy, *CIH* 1275, n. d.

543 I follow the emendation suggested by Binchy, *CIH* 1275, n. e.

is not under contract or in the hire of a particular person in the territory, and if he should be, making a bargain with him is the same as it would be made with the local freeman regarding that matter.[544]

The purchase from an outsider, he is recognized thus, i.e., a person with whom there is a protocol at the time of the contract and there is not [a protocol] at the time of the claiming, it is divided in two between him [sc., the receiver of stolen goods] and the owner. Or he does not know from whom he bought [it]. And whether restitution or counter-purchase was found in his possession, whether with increase or without increase, and he does not know the one from whom he bought [it], it is divided in two between them. And a surety from each of them [to see] which of them would get the complete [amount] first from the thief regarding emptying his hand [in order] to pay [the amount owed] to the other person

If he knows the one from whom he bought [it], there is not a regulation for the time of buying from an outsider, but a period of time for seeking [is given] to him if he prefers, and the casting of lots between them regarding the restitution. And that is an outsider who is not under contract or in the hire of a particular person in the territory. And if he should be, [making] a bargain with him is the same as [making a bargain] with a local freeman himself, etc.; and each time it is his choice, a period of time for seeking is given to him, though he wishes the purchase from an outsider to be proven regarding it, he does not pay.

This is buying from an outsider then: buying it from a man of another f. 5vd
province, and he does not know the one from whom he bought it. And every time it is from a man of another province that he bought it, it is his choice [whether] he will prove the purchase from the outsider immediately, or the period of time for seeking will be given to him.

Every noble takes his *sét* with the increase, i.e., a third for land and a third for labor and a third for the owner, and he is the owner of bulls and cows. When it is from a local freeman that he buys [it], he takes restitution and a fifth of the increase. And when it is from an outsider that he buys [it], he takes restitution and a twelfth from the increase.

544 Cf. source A above. The translation of the last two words is tentative; it is possible that some of the text is missing.

Mas fer m*edongait*e go fer m*edongait*e, is roin*n* ar do; mas fer aid*h*br*eda* ⁊ fer m*edongait*e go fer m*edongait*e, is roin*n* a t*r*i, no gom*ad* saig*h*i aiged*hach* g*o* h-aig*dech*, ⁊rl- Ma tai*n*ig fer bu*n*ad*h* d'aig*h*br*iud* a *séoit* go fer m*edongait*e d*ligthech*, ⁊ rorec fer m*edongaite* d*ligthech* ré fer m*edongaite* d*ligthech aile*, ⁊ ata tuinid*h* in *séoit* ag fer m*edongaite* d*ligthech*, ⁊ ata re n-in*n*saig*h* dó re h-iarr*aid* fir m*edongaite aile*. Mana fuair sé an *sét* ag fer m*edongaite* resa rac se hé, donit*er* roin*n* ar do it*er* fer m*edongaite* ⁊ fer *aidbreda* im l*eth*innud*h* ⁊ im l*ethaithgin*. Ma docuaid*h* fer *aidbreda* ⁊ fer m*edongaite* go fer m*edongaite aile*, ⁊ go *tarrth*us in *sét* ina laim, is roin*n* a t*r*i an uair-sin eturr*u* .i. a t*r*ian ag(an) [gach][545] fer dib*h*, no d*ano* gom*ad* saig*id* aig*dech* go h-aig*dech*.

Ma t*harr*us an col*ainn* aigi, b*e*rar uaid*h*e hí. Mana tarrus im*murro*, be[r]-ar[546] re do d'iarr*aid* fir in *séoit* resa rac é. Ma fu*air* aigi é, berar uad*h*a é; muna fu*air* im*murro* b*e*rar an fri[th]crec uad*h*-so*m*.

Tria cendairde no t*r*ia cin*n*isli donít*er* ant aid*h*br*iud* anuasana, ⁊ t*r*ia torain*n* leasaid*h* no t*r*ia coschairchid*h* donit*er* sisana.

G [*CIH* 2075.19–34] .i. *cona* beit*h* isi*n* tuait*h* nec*h* na fesad a *sét* do teasb*aid*[547] aire, *ar* cia luaig*h*e nec *iar*na fis, is dire noicf*ad* ⁊ ni faicfid*h*a ní don in*n*ud*h* aige.[548]

col. 616 Is ed*h* is cen*n*ac*h* do anurr*ad* an*n*: a cen*n*ach[549] o fir sec*htar cóic*id risi raib*he* besgna do i n-u*air* in cen*n*aig*h*, ce dob*eth* besgna aturr*u* anois ci*n*co roib, ł ní fuil i *n*-u*air* aidbriuda. No d*ano*, noc*har*b' ait*h*nit do it*ir* é.

Cen*n*ac*h* d'anurr*ad* si*n* ris raibe besc*na* i *n*-u*air* cen*n*aig*h*: cemad*h* isi*n* cric*h* i meod*h*on .i. i cric*h* *cóic*id*h*, ⁊ ni fuil i *n*-u*air* aidbriuda, roin*n* *ar* dó at*ar*u, it*er* in*n*ud*h* ⁊ ait*hgin*.

---

545 I follow the emendation suggested by Binchy, *CIH* 1275, n. j.

546 See also Binchy, *CIH* 1275, n. k.

547 The ⟨a⟩ is written subscript.

548 The scribe gives us his name at the end of the last line of the column: 'Misi Aod*hagan*' 'I am Aodhaghán'.

549 The ⟨h⟩ was added above the line by the scribe.

If it is a receiver of stolen goods with a receiver of stolen goods, it is divided in two. If it is a plaintiff and a receiver of stolen goods with a receiver of stolen goods, it is divided in three, or so that a surety sues another, etc.[550] If the owner came to claim his *sét* from a lawful receiver of stolen goods, and a lawful receiver of stolen goods sold [it] to another lawful receiver of stolen goods, and the *sét* is in the possession of the lawful receiver of stolen goods, and a period of time for seeking [is given] to him for seeking the other receiver of stolen goods. Unless he found the *sét* with the receiver of stolen goods before he sells it, a division is made in two between the receiver of stolen goods and the plaintiff regarding half the increase and half the restitution. If a plaintiff and a receiver of stolen goods went to another receiver of stolen goods and the *sét* was found in his hand, it is divided in three that time between then, i.e., a third for each one of them, or then a surety sues another.

If the principal was found in his possession, it is taken from him. If it had not been found, however, a period of time is given to him for searching for the owner of the *sét* before he sells it. If he found it with him, it is taken from him; if it is not found, however, the counter-purchase is taken from him.

By noble grades or by non-noble grades the claiming is done above, and by its loud noise or by its victoriousness [the claiming] is done below.[551]

G i.e., that there should not be anyone in the *túath* who did not know that his *sét* was missing from him, because someone who buys it after knowing [that it was missing], he will pay a penalty-fine, and nothing from the increase should be left in his possession.

This is buying from an outsider then: buying it from a man outside the col. 616
province with which there is a protocol for it at the time of the purchase, whether there might be a protocol between them now or not, or there is not at the time of the claiming. Or on the other hand, he was not known to him at all.

This is buying from an outsider with whom there is a protocol at the time of the purchase: though he should be in the middle of the territory, i.e., in a territory of the province, and there is not [a protocol] at the time of the claiming, a division in two between them, both increase and restitution.

550 It is possible that the last clause is a quotation from this or another text; the phrase is found again at the end of this paragraph of commentary and in § 4 source DD, CIH 801.25: *saigid aicech co aiccech.*

551 Cf. § 3, source BB, CIH 2096.28.

& mas d'fir *echtarchóic*id*h*, is a rog*h*a dó, i*n* re n-in*n*saig*h*e rac*hus* do no in roin*n* *ar* dó fo *cét*oir. ⁊ mad é a rog*h*a re n-in*n*saig*h*e, ni fuil l*eth* no nac*h* ni do isi[552] h-ait*h*le cinco fag*h*a ní o neoc*h* *aile* .i. onti or cen*n*aig*h*.

Anurr*ad* si*n* na raibe f*or* curu ł f*or* faic*h*ill ac duine airit*h*e isi*n* cric*h*, ⁊ da mb*eth*, robu inan*n* cun*nrad* ris ⁊ risi*n* urr*ad* fein.

Masa fer aon*cóic*id*h* dó é, ce t*art*ha ní de i*ar* tain, *noc*ha cen*nac*h d'anurr*ad* dó é.

EE [*CIH* 842.34–37] .i. *cona* b*eth* isi*n* tuait*h* nec*h* na fesad a s*ét* do tesb*aid*, *ar* cía noluaided*h* nec*h* i*ar*na fis, is dire *noíc*f*ad*, ⁊ ni faiceba ni do*n*n in*n*ad

p. 324 æige .i. im ti*acht*ai*n* fo coraib *ar ceithre* | [h-uairib][553] *fich*it, no ci*n* t*rebaire* t*ar*a cend, ma anurr*ad* risa nderr*n*ad cun*n*rad. Anurr*ad* si*n* na fil *ar* cur na *ar* faic*h*ill.

---

552 Read *asa*; see also Binchy, *CIH* 2075, n. g.

553 I follow the emendation suggested by Binchy, *CIH* 842, n. p.

And if it is from a man of another province, he has a choice [whether] the period of time for seeking will be given to him, or the division in two immediately. And if he chooses a period of time for seeking, there is not half or anything for him afterwards though he does not obtain anything from someone else, i.e., from the one from whom he bought [it].

This is an outsider who is not under contract or in the hire of a particular person in the territory. And if he should be, [making] a bargain with him is the same as [making a bargain] with the local freeman himself.

If he is a man of the same province as himself, though he obtained something from him afterwards, it is not [considered] a purchase from an outsider regarding it.

EE i.e., that there should not be anyone in the *túath* who did not know that his *sét* was missing, because someone who buys it after knowing [that it was missing], he will pay a penalty-fine, and nothing from the increase should be left in his possession, i.e., regarding impugning contracts before 24 | hours, p. 324
or without a surety on his behalf, if it is an outsider with whom he made a bargain. This is an outsider who is not under contract or in hire.

§7

Feis lethfrithgnuma fo bit*h* sguir ⁊ imcoimeta ⁊ uadab*h*ar cinad*ha*.

A [*CIH* 2171.32–36] Cid i*m*a ndeb*airt*-su*m* leth, ⁊ na fuill *acht* t*r*ian frichgna*m*a a*n*d? Coir am a[554] ndeb*airt*-sium, uair[555] *seiss*id[556] tormaiges cull*aig* ⁊ tairb ⁊ retheda; ⁊ in bail i n-abair: "cach *cethram*ad[557] læg (læg) bes aithre*m*ail,"[558] cethr*aimth*e ar *acht*ug*ud* iss [ed ata][559] and. Gach uair is do[560] rer dlig*id* is *seiss*id,[561] ⁊ in *seiss*id risin t*r*ian cu*r*ub l*eth*.

G [*CIH* 2075.35–2076.11] .i. cid*h* 'ma ndeb*hairt*-si*m* l*eth*, ⁊ n*ach* fuil *acht* t*r*ian fri*ch*num*h*a an*n*? Coir am*h* a ndeb*hairt* int uda*r*, u*air seiss*id[562] *th*orm*h*aig*h*it cull*aig* ⁊ reed*h*a ⁊ *tair*b*h*; ⁊ an baile at*a*; "ca*ch* cea*thramha*[563] læg*h* bes ait*h*remail," do fer besa t*air*b*h* cinel in *tar*b*h*-si*n*, cet*h*raim*he ar acht*ug*h* sin an*n*. ⁊ cac*h* u*air* is ce*th*rai*m*he do reir dlig*id*, *ceth*rai*m*he *ar seiss*ed is [s]i [fuil][564] an*n*; ⁊ seis*ed th*uillis in t*r*ian cura l*eth*, ⁊ isi-si*n* l*eth* adeir an*n*.

---

1 lethfrithgnuma] lethfrichgnuma **A**, l*eth* frithgnu[m](d)*h*a **F**, leathfrichnuma **G**, l*eth* fri*ch*nama **EE**. Only source **G** continues after this point. It is uncertain whether what follows belongs to the same clause. The tract is separated by commentary in **G**; the second excerpt starts at *CIH* 2076.8. The citation from **F** is embedded in commentary in §6, *CIH* 1275.1. ‖ sguir] The scribe of **G** wrote the gloss '.i. feoir' 'i.e., of grass' above *fo bith sguir*. ‖ imcoimeta] The scribe of **G** wrote the gloss '.i. i*n* ing*aire*' 'i.e., of the tending' above *imcoimeta*. ‖ cinad*ha*] The scribe of **G** wrote the gloss '.i. o*n* sgur ⁊ on i*m*coi*m*et' 'i.e., from the pasturage and the nurturing' above *uadabhar cinadha*.

---

554 The ⟨a⟩ has been added later at the left edge of the column.

555 The ⟨a⟩ is written subscript.

556 The ⟨id⟩ are written above the line.

557 The ⟨ad⟩ are written above the line.

558 The source of this quotation is unknown.

559 I follow the emendation suggested by Binchy, *CIH* 2171, n. q. The word *and* was added later above the line in a lighter colored ink. The second ⟨s⟩ was added below the line at the time that the rest of the text was being written.

560 The ⟨o⟩ was added below the line by the scribe; see also Binchy, *CIH* 2171, n. r.

561 The ⟨id⟩ are written above the line.

562 The ⟨id⟩ are written above the line.

563 The scribe of G writes a ligatured ⟨ea⟩ which clearly originated as an e caudata, but here the tail has been separated from the ⟨e⟩ and written to the right of it and not far below the baseline. This is his usual method of writing ⟨ea⟩. While at first glance it simply appears as if the first ⟨a⟩ is written subscript, in reality it is part of the scribe's way of writing e caudata.

564 I follow the emendation suggested by Binchy, *CIH* 2075, n. i.

§7

Cattle-trespass of half labor because of unyoking and nurturing and breeding.[565]

A Why did he [sc., the author] say half regarding that, and there is only a third of the labor here? What he said is indeed correct, because stallions and bulls and rams increase by a sixth [concerning labor]; and where it is said: "every fourth calf that is like its sire," a fourth according to stipulation is what there is then. Every time it is according to law, it is a sixth, and the sixth added to the third [of the labor] is a half.

G i.e., why did he say half regarding that, and there is only a third of the labor here? What the author said about it is indeed correct, because stallions and rams and bulls increase by a sixth; and the passage that is: "each fourth calf is like its sire," for a man who has bulls from that bull's stock, a fourth according to that stipulation then. And every time it is a fourth according to law, a fourth added to the sixth, is what there is there; and the third added to a sixth is a half, and that is the half that it says there [in the tract].

565 For a discussion of this section, see the Introduction, p. 30. See *EIF* 50–51, for discussion of the material from source G; the interpretation of *imchoimét* 'nurture, care, guarding' given in *EIF* is followed here. The term *feis* means 'lying-down trespass' and is used of cattle or other livestock which have trespassed on someone else's land to graze, lay down, etc.; *EIF* 135–138. In this section, it is important to keep in mind the fact that the topic concerns what percentage of the increase that the fully lawful receiver of stolen goods receives as a result of the stolen property being in his possession. In other words, he receives a percentage of the labor because of the fact that his own livestock have bred with the stolen livestock (which he had assumed were his by purchase), and for pasturing them on his land and generally caring for them. The tract and commentary both interpret the stolen livestock using the receiver of stolen goods' land and being bred by him as a form of cattle-trepsass due to the fact that the livestock does not actually belong to the receiver of stolen goods. Source EE provides the most succinct breakdown of the profits associated with the increase: the receiver of stolen goods receives the third associated with owning the land, the original owner receives a third because the stolen livestock originates with him, and they both divide the labor third in half because each has supplied half the livestock for breeding and other tasks.

col. 617 An cethr*aimth*e eir *acht*ug*h* sin ł an cethr*amthu* do rer dlig*id*:[566] | ca*ch* u*air* is cethr*aimth*e eir *acht*ug*h* is cet*h*rai*mh*e uirr*e* budei*n*. Ca*ch* u*air* is cet*hrai-mh*e do reir dlig*id*, is cethr*aimth*e eir *seiss*ed*h*, aile d*h*eg an lain eisid*h*e, in *aile déc* ⁊ in *seisse* is cethr*aimth*e.

An[567] inb*aid* is d'urr*ad* c*h*enn*aigh*es, be*ir*id aith*gin* ⁊ *seiss*ed*h* n-inn*ad*h*a*. An i*n*b*h*aid*h* is d'anurr*ad*, be*ir*id*h* aith*gin* ⁊ in d*ar*a rann *déc* .i. l*eth*trian bun*aid* ⁊ cethr*aimth*e tríai*n* tire.

.i.[568] adb*ar* aneich or c*h*inest*ar* .i. cull*aig* ⁊ *tairb*h ⁊ reit*h*ed*h*a. ⁊ ce deir si*n*, ni h-ed*h* fil an*n* *acht* cenna*ch* d'anurr*ad* ⁊ roin*n* *ar* dó an*n*.

EE [*CIH* 842.38–843.2] .i. tria*n* do tir .i. do fir m*edongaite*, ⁊ *t*rian do bunad .i. do fir no mbo, ⁊ *t*rian do fric*hnam*. ⁊ an *t*ria*n* rosoic*h* do fric*h*num de, a l*eth*-sideic d'fir m*edongait*e dlig*thech* a dualg*us* a cullaig ⁊ a tairb ł a reit*he*, ⁊ *in* l*eth aile* do fir bun*aid*, *con*id roin*n* et*ar*u an*n* sein.

566 In the *marg. inf.* of col. 616, the scribe wrote 'A Muire, cin*n*as sin?' 'Mary, how so?'.
567 A paragraph symbol is written *inter. col.* before *ar*; see also Binchy, *CIH* 2076, n. a.
568 The following commentary belongs with the continuation of the tract.

The fourth according to that stipulation or the fourth according to law: | col. 617
every time it is a fourth according to stipulation, it is a fourth for it itself. Every time it is a fourth according to law, it is a fourth added to the sixth, that is a twelfth of the whole, the twelfth and the sixth is a fourth.

Whenever it is from a local freeman that he buys [it], he takes restitution and a sixth of the increase. Whenever it is from an outsider, he takes restitution and a twelfth, i.e., half of a third for origin and a fourth of a third for land.

i.e.,[569] a claim of someone from whom he bought, i.e., stallions and bulls and rams. And though it says that, there is only buying from an outsider and division in two there.[570]

EE i.e., a third for land, i.e., for the receiver of stolen goods, and a third for origin, i.e., for the man who has the cows, and a third for labor. And the third goes to labor from it, half of it for the lawful receiver of stolen goods on account of his stallion and his bull and his ram, and the other half for the owner, so there is a division between them in that manner.

569 The second commentary begins here.

570 See § 6 for buying stolen property from an outsider.

§8

Ni lot los laban

A [*CIH* 2171.37–2172.10] Esc*aire*[571] in frit*hi* tiri cusna *secht* n-*in*adaib ader dli*ged*: co rig, co h-aircin*dech*, co b*r*iug*aid*, co br*eithe*main, co muil*enn* tuait*he*, co p*r*imgabai*nd* t*úaithe*, co fl*aith* ngelfi*ne* in *secht*mad.

Esc*airi* in frithi fairrgi c*us*na *téora* c*r*ic*h*a ata nesam, ⁊ muir in *cethram*ad c*r*ich. ⁊ is c*é*tfaid co*ma* (*read* cusna?) *secht* n-*in*adaib i*n* cach c*r*i*ch* dib-side.

---

1 Ni ... laban] The tract for this section is preserved only in source A.

---

571 Cf. Heptad 64 and *Muirbretha* for making a proclamation with regard to items found on the land or in the sea; see also source F, §6 with regard to giving public notice of found property. The commentary here is close to that found in Heptad 64, source B, *CIH* 1211.25–41. Considering the amount of overlap between the three texts of near-identical commentaries, for example, as seen here, it gives one pause to consider how these collections of texts and commentaries were assembled. Considering the fact that these sections of commentary tend to 'float' from one text to another, is it possible to say with complete confidence that X commentary belongs to Y text if we find the same commentary associated with one or more other texts in sections concerning the same subject matter? The same subject matter also appears in *The MacEgan Legal Treatise* §5.1–4.

§8

... it is not an injury of dirty young cattle[572]

A Proclamation of something found on land throughout the seven places that law says: to a king [e.g., at his court], to an ecclesiastical superior, to a hospitaller, to a judge, at a *túath*'s mill, to a *túath*'s chief smith, to a kindred's lord as the seventh.

Proclamation of something found in the sea throughout the three nearest territories, and the sea [is] the fourth territory. And it is the opinion [of lawyers] that [it should be proclaimed] throughout the seven places in each of the territories.

572 For a discussion of this section, see the Introduction, pp. 30–32. The translation of this fragment of the tract is tentative. In John O'Donovan's unpublished manuscript translation of the text, he does not attempt to translate it, nor does he provide any notes regarding his thoughts on the phrase. The clause is alliterative, so it is possible that it is originally from a line of verse or a legal maxim. Because the clause is out of context, it is difficult to determine whether the first word is *ní* 'any' or *ní*, 3 sg. pres. ind. neg. of the copula *is* 'it is not, no'. *Lot* appears to be the verbal noun of *loittid* 'harm, wound, slay, destroy', and *los* is used in the legal texts for 'young of cattle', especially calves born while the cows are not in the possession of their owner. The word *laban*, however, is more problematic. It is tentatively defined in *eDIL* as a 'legal term in contexts dealing with estrays' and cites O'Donovan's transcript of the text (with no translation); it also cites a passage from British Library MS Egerton 88 (*Aidbred*, source F, §6, *CIH* 1275.2, *uair nar essccair labhán iat*); this passage is not found in source A. See the discussion of this word on p. 203, n. 537, where it is suggested that *laban* is for *lápán* 'mire, dirt' in reference to intentionally dirtying livestock; *EIF* 164. If this is correct, it is used here adjectively; cf. its usage in the phrase *on mbocht labain* 'from the poor man' l. 62, Froinsias Ó Maolmhuaidh, *Lucerna fidelium: seu Fasciculus decerptus ab authoribus magis versatis, qui tractarunt de doctrina christiana*, ed. Pádraig Ó Súilleabháin (Baile Átha Cliath: Institiúid Árd-Léinn Bhaile Átha Cliath, 1962). It is also possible that *laban* is related to words such as the verb *lobaid* 'neglects to comply with' (which is its usual meaning in legal texts), the verbal noun *lobad* 'failure to redeem, negligence in complying with (laws, rules, etc.)', which also has a variant spelling in ⟨a⟩, and *lobthach* 'debtor who has neglected to redeem his pledge'. It is possible that *laban* is an error for *lobad* or *labad* where the final syllable was originally suspended in the MS, i.e., *lob-*. If *laban* is not a mistake, the word most likely has a *fada* over the first and second ⟨a⟩ to form the individuating suffix, which semantically gives the meaning 'a thing which is X', which is derived ultimately from the diminutive in *-án*; see Paul Russell, "Patterns of Hypocorism in Early Irish Hagiography," in *Studies in Irish Hagiography: Saints and scholars*, eds. J. Carey, M. Herbert, and P. Ó Riain (Dublin: Four Courts Press, 2001), 237–249.

p. 21a Ma dorigne a dlig*ed* frit*h*i, ⁊ romair aige co iar ndec*h*maid, is l*an*cuitig fri*th*i do. Mana derna a dlig*ed* frit*h*i, ⁊ rocait*h* ria ndechmaid, is la*n*fia*ch* gaiti uad.

Ma roesc*air* fia lu*cht* ænlis ⁊ æ*n*baili, ⁊ ro*m*air aice co h-iar ndec*hmaid*, is l*eth*cuitig frit*h*e do. Ma roesc*air* fiad lu*cht* ae*n*lis ⁊ ae*n*baili, ⁊ rocait*h* ria ndec*h*maid, is l*eth*fiach gaite uad.

Manar escair, ⁊ ro*m*air aigi co h-iar ndec*hmaid*, ł cia roesc*air* ⁊ rocait*h* ria ndec*hmaid*, is a b*eth* can cuit*ig* frit*h*i do, ⁊ can fia*ch* *gaite* uad.

If he fulfilled the law of finds, and it remained in his possession until after ten days [have passed], he has the full share of what he found. If he does not fulfill the the law of finds, and he used [it] before ten days [have passed], he owes the full fine of theft. p. 21a

If he made a proclamation [that he had found lost property] in the presence of people of [the] same enclosure and of [the same] settlement [where it was found], and it remained in his possession until after ten days [have passed], he has half a share of what he found. If he made a proclamation in the presence of people of [the] same enclosure and of [the] same settlement, and he used [it] before ten days [have passed], he owes half the fine of theft.

If he did not proclaim [the find to anyone], and it remained in his possession until after ten days [have passed], or though he proclaimed [the find at the seven designated locations] and he used [it] before ten days, he does not get a share of what he found, and he does not owe a fine for theft.

§9

Aidbred t*est*a, ⁊rl-

A [*CIH* 2172.11–14] H-æ*n*ur do*n* *test* u*m*un *sét* atces aicce, fer i*n*a deg*h*aid i*m*un *sét* na fac*us* aice .i. bo*air*e medo*n*ach. Fer a n-eg*aid* na h-ant*est*a u*m*un *sét* atces aice, ⁊ dias i*n*a deg*aid* u*m*an *sét* na fac*us* aice .i. *air*e desa no da boaire medo*n*ach. Reama*d* na t*est*a ⁊ na h-a*n*dt*est*a u*m*un *sét* atces aice ⁊ na aices.

G [*CIH* 2076.12–20] .i. a h-æ*nar* do*n* *test* i*m*an *sét* atces aic*e*, fer i*n*a deag*aid*[573] i*m*an *sét* na facas aice .i. bo*air*e meod*h*on*ach*. Fer i *n*deag*aid*[574] na h-ain*n*t*est*a u*m*in *sét* atceas[575] aice, ⁊ dias ina deg*aid* iman set na fac*us* aice .i. *air*e desa no da bo*air*e meod*h*on*ach*a. Rem*h*ad*h* na t*est*a ⁊ na ain*n*t*est*a sin iman *sét* atceas[576] aice ⁊ na h-aices, ⁊rl-.

In eisin*n*r*aic* eith*ech* noc*h*a gab*ar* a fiad*nais*i, ⁊ noc*h*[a]n fast*aid*e a tuar*a*-*stal*,[577] ⁊ *noc*ha gab*ar* a lu*cht* fír*a*, ⁊ *noc*h*o* gab*ar* lu*cht* fíra i*n*a diaig*h*.

In eisin*n*r*aic* n*ach* eith*ech* *immurro*, noc*h*a gab*ar* a fiad*nais*e, ⁊ fast*aid*i a tu*arr*ust*al*, ⁊ noc*h*a gab*ar* a lu*cht* fír*a*, ⁊ gab*ar* lu*cht* fíra ina deag*h*aig*h*.[578]

---

1 Aidbred] Aidbread*h* G. The second ⟨a⟩ is written subscript.

---

573 The ⟨a⟩ is written subscript. Here and below, all the subscript ⟨a⟩s were originally part of digraphs which the scribe has separated into two discrete characters.

574 The ⟨a⟩ is written subscript.

575 The second ⟨a⟩ is written subscript.

576 The second ⟨a⟩ is written subscript.

577 The ⟨a⟩ is written subscript.

578 The first ⟨a⟩ is written subscript.

§ 9

Claiming by a trustworthy witness, etc.[579]

A[580] A trustworthy witness alone [can testify] regarding the *sét* that was seen with him [sc., himself], [with] one person supporting him regarding the *sét* that was not seen with him, i.e., an intermediate *bóaire*. One person supporting the untrustworthy witness regarding the *sét* that was seen with him, and two people supporting him regarding the *sét* that was not seen with him, i.e., an *aire déso* or two intermediate *bóaire*s. The preliminary oath of the trustworthy witness and of the untrustworthy witness regarding the *sét* that was seen with him and that was not seen [with him].

G i.e., a trustworthy witness alone [can testify] regarding the *sét* that was seen with him, [with] one person supporting him regarding the *sét* that was not seen with him, i.e., an intermediate *bóaire*. One person supporting the untrustworthy witness regarding the *sét* that was seen with him, and two people supporting him regarding the *sét* that was not seen with him, i.e., an *aire déso* or two intermediate *bóaire*s. The preliminary oath of the trustworthy witness and of the untrustworthy witness regarding the *sét* that was seen with him and that was not seen [with him], etc.

The unworthy person who swears falsely is not given as a witness, and his evidence does not bind, and he is not given as a compurgator, and he is not given compurgators supporting him.

The unworthy person who does not swear falsely, however, he is not given as a witness, and his evidence is binding, and he is not given as a compurgator, and he is given compurgators supporting him.

---

579 For a discussion of this section, see the Introduction, p. 32.

580 Cf. also *The MacEgan Legal Treatise* § 2.1–12 for similar material on proving by oath. The commentaries here present a system which is consistent with what is found elsewhere, e.g., § 1a, source F above and source JJ (Appendix 3), that a worthy person is able to prove some cases against an unworthy person on the strength of his own oath alone in some circumstances. A similar provision is found in medieval Welsh law where in certain circumstances the oath of a single individual was deemed sufficient evidence, e.g., the oath of a thief before execution, or the oath of a maiden regarding her virginity; Watkin, *The Legal History of Wales*, 73–75; Jenkins, *The Law of Hywel Dda*, 61–62; *Ior.* § 56. See also *GEIL* 203.

§10

⁊ cach aid*h*brid*h* bes neim*id*: ni fuataga*r* ó macha do macha, ac*h*t coruice lias bes nesa*m* dó f*r*i c*r*on ⁊ coi*m*gi. Ni h-indsorgar o crích do crích, a*cht* ait i n-aidbrith*er* is and dleg*h*ar cert ime.

A [*CIH* 2172.15–2173.26] Br*eith*emnus na c*r*ichi ⁊ mi*n*da na c*r*ic*h*i ⁊ mes na c*r*ic*h*i i *n*denta*r* int aidb*r*iud.

Caide defir (read *deithbir*) eta*r*ru-si*n* ⁊ i*n* bail ata: **ni fuataga*r* o mac*h*ad do mac*h*ad, ac*h*t coruice lias bes nesa*m* f*r*i c*r*on ⁊ coi*m*gi**? ⁊[581] rob i a t[h]uicsi a*nd* si*n conach* de*mth*a dlig*ed* do i*n* baili a raibe, ⁊ is [s]*lan* do a fuatac*h* coruice i*n* fo*rus* is nesa do[582] i*n* bail a sailfed dlig*ed* do damt*h*ain do. Oc i*n*draic rohaidbred i*n sét* a*nd* so, ⁊ da*m*aig dlig*ed* n-aidb*r*iuda, ⁊ rofuaitgesta*r*-su*m* he, ⁊ coir cia robe*th* er*aic air* i*n*a fuatach. Mas i*n*draic, ⁊ damai*d* dlig*ed* n-aidb*r*iuda, is a be*th* a*na*[583] lai*m* budein. ⁊ mu*n*a da*m*a*nd* dlig*ed* n-aidb*r*eda, is a tab*air*t a n-u*r*lai*m* coitci*nd*.

Masa esi*n*draic, ⁊ dam*aid* dlig*ed* n-aidb*r*eda, is a br*eth* don i*n*raic le fo *cé*toir. Noc*h*an (u)i*m*(e)[584] i*n sét* fei*n* is esi*n*draic[585] hi, ⁊ da*m*ad ui*m*e. Ce da*m*ad ce*n*co da*m*ad dlig*ed* n-aidb*r*eda, robad, [a] (o) br*eth* don i*n*dr*aic* le

1 ⁊] et **P, FF.** ‖ cach] gac*h* **Q**, cac*h* **FF**, gac **JJ.** ‖ aid*h*brid*h*] aid*h*brig*h* **P**, aib*h*re **AA**, aid*h*bri **JJ.** ‖ neim*id*] nime **P**, nem*id* **Q**, n*eim*i **JJ.** *CIH* expands each of the final syllables in this word as *ed*. The first clause is not found in **A.** 1–2 ni … coi*m*gi] This portion of the tract from **A** is found in the commentary below. A slightly different version from **J** is also found in the commentary at p. 226: 'ni fuatag*har* ac*ht* o macha coruice lias bes nes*am* dó f*r*i cron ⁊ coi*m*ge'. 1 fuataga*r*] fuataga*r* **A**, fuatag*har* **J comm.**, fuadadar **P**, fuadag*har* **Q**, fuada*h*ar **FF**, fuataig*h*-*ter* **JJ.** ‖ ó] o **A, J comm., P, Q, AA** and **FF.** ‖ macha] mac*h*ad **A**, mach*a* **Q, AA**, m*acha* **JJ.** ‖ macha] mach*ad* **A**, mach*a* **Q, AA**, m*acha* **JJ.** Sources **P, Q, AA, FF,** and **JJ** end here. 2 dó] *om.* **A.** ‖ Ni] **J** begins here. The version of the excerpt found in the commentary below from **J** reads 'ni h-in*n*sorg*ar* a c*r*ích do c*r*ích, a*cht* ait'. A slightly different verion of this excerpt is found in the § 11 source **A comm.**: 'ni h-in*n*sorgor o c*r*ich do crich *acht* ait i *n*-aidbrith*er* is a*n*d glether c*er*t ime'; it is taken into account here. ‖ h-indsorgar] h-indsorgor **A**, h-in*n*sorgor **A comm.**, h-in*n*sorg*ar* **J comm.** ‖ o] a **J comm.** ‖ crích] crich **A, J**, c*r*ich **A comm.** ‖ crích] c*r*ich **A**, crich **J, A comm.**; source **A** ends here. ‖ a*cht*] *acht* **A comm.** 3 i n-] a n- **J.** ‖ aid-brith*er*] n-aibhrithar **J.** ‖ and] a*n*d **A comm.** ‖ dleg*h*ar] glether **A comm.** ‖ cert] ceart **J.** ‖ ime] uime **J.**

581 Binchy, *CIH* 2172, n. b, suggests deleting ⟨⁊⟩, but cf. the last paragraph of source J below. With regard to the same clause in source J, Binchy, *CIH* 1973, n. g, queries whether the beginning of the answer to the previous question has been omitted.

582 The ⟨o⟩ was added above the ⟨d⟩ in a lighter ink.

583 The second ⟨a⟩ was added below the line in a lighter ink.

584 I follow the emendation suggested by Binchy, *CIH* 2172, n. e.

585 The ⟨s⟩ was added below the line by the scribe; see also Binchy, *CIH* 2172, n. f.

§10

And each claiming made by a *nemed*:[586] **it is not taken from cattle-enclosure to cattle-enclosure, but as far as the enclosure which is closest to him for possession and protecting. It is not moved from territory to territory, but the place where it is claimed, it is there that justice is required regarding it.**[587]

A Judgment of the territory and oaths of the territory and award[588] of the territory in which the claiming is made.

What is the difference between that and the passage that is: **it is not taken from cattle-enclosure to cattle-enclosure, but as far as the enclosure which is closest for possession and protecting**? And it is his understanding in that case that justice would not be given to him where he was, and he is free from liability to take it as far as the cattle-pound which is closest to him in the place where he would expect justice to be granted to him. The *sét* was claimed from a worthy person in this way, and he submits to the law of claiming, and he [sc., the plaintiff] carried it off, and it is just, though, that there should be a fine [imposed] on him for it being carried off. If he is a worthy person, and he submits to the law of claiming, it remains in his own hand. And if he does not submit to the law of claiming, it is given into the custody of a neutral third party.

If he is an unworthy person, and he submits to the law of claiming, it [sc., the disputed property] is taken by the worthy person with him immediately. It is not regarding the *sét* itself that he is an unworthy person, and he submits [to the law of claiming] regarding it. Whether or not he submits to the law of claiming, it would be taken by the worthy person with him immediately.

586 For a discussion of this section, see the Introduction, pp. 32–33. For a discussion of *nemed* status, see Riita Latvio. "*Neimed*—Exploring Social Distinctions and Sacredness in Early Irish Legal Sources," in *Approaches to Religion and Mythology in Celtic Studies*, eds. Katja Ritari and Alexandra Bergholm, (Newcastle: Cambridge Scholars Publishing, 2008), pp. 220–242; and *EIF* 170–173.

587 This clause is translated in Kelly, *The MacEgan Legal Treatise*, 165, where he identifies this and the excerpt of tract from §11, source J as being from a "fragmentary text on judges." Considering that mulptiple sources from *Aidbred* quote these excerpts as tract and that source J is from a digest, it is likely that the quotations here come from *Aidbred* rather than another text. For general discussion about claiming within and across territories, see ibid., 164–165. The 'he' referred to in the tract is the plaintiff.

588 I take *mess* 'valuation, estimate' to refer here to the payment awarded.

fo c*é*toir. ⁊ mad a[589] h-urlai*m* c*oitchinn*[590] fuitgith*er* in s*ét*, i*n*t ain*m*rai*n*de da enecl*ainn* fei*n* ata d'fir[591] in s*éoit*, cu*r*ab e i*n*t ain*m*rai*n*de[592] da e*n*ecl*ainn* fei*n* bes don u*r*lai*m* coitci*nn*.

Mad on i*n*draic 'c*ar* aidb*r*ed he fuaitgith*er* e, *acht* ma[593] le fei*n* he i*ar* dai*n*, noc*h*an [ḟ]uil ni di *ar*a h-urlam*us acht* a buil[594] di a dualg*us* a s*ét* fo aicn*ed* na re. Mai*n*ib le im*murro* in s*ét* i*ar* dai*n*, a fodlad enecl*ainn*i di am*al* u*r*lai*m* c*oitchinn* com*ith*ig na biad a(c)[595] selb *ar*in s*ét*. ł da*no*, com*ad* fia*ch* indlig*id* .i. *cóic* s*ét*.

Set aidbreda ait*h*fegth*ar* su*n*d it*er* da feche*m*ain a n-u*r*lai*m* coitci*n*d, ⁊ ne*cht*arde do*n* da[596] feche*m*ain rofuaitgest*ar* on u*r*lai*m* ce*n* aire*ch* on, ⁊ is do*n* fir ḟuil[597] aca n-aidb*r*iud rai*n*ic a den*am* do rer a fuid, ⁊ noc*h*a do fei*n* is aichnid e[598] *acht* da blig[r](n)e ł da buach*aill*.

Masa dlig*ed* n-u*r*fuigill rocu*r*set cusi*n* mbr*eith*emai*n* [o]ca re rach*us* do re h-i*n*dsaigid blig*ri* no buach*alla*, [⁊] mass *ed* ader i*n* bre*ith*em cid in*n*raic cid esi*n*draic i*n* blig*re* no in buach*aill*, dlig*id* re n-i*n*dsaig*th*e crich*i* ł *sechtar*cri-c*h*i.

Masa dilg*ed* mbr*eith*emnais rocu*r*set cuice cia re rach*us* do re h-indsaig*id*
p. 21b bl*igri* no buach*alla*, ⁊ iss *ed* ader i*n* br*eith*em, | 'mas i*n*draic in blig*re* no in bu[a]chaill, dlig*id* re n-i*n*dsaig*thi*; ⁊ mas esi*n*draic noc*h*a dleg*ar* re do, uair[599] noc*h*a roic*h* imden*am* in s*éoit* aidb*r*iuda don esi*n*draic [ḟ]uil oca n-aidbriud'.[600]

---

589 The ⟨a⟩ is written subscript; see also Binchy, *CIH* 2172, n. h.
590 See also Binchy, *CIH* 2172, n. i.
591 Two letters have been erased after this word; see also Binchy, *CIH* 2172, n. j.
592 The sequence ⟨i*n*t aim⟩ was written in *marg. sin.* by the scribe directly before ⟨rai*n*de⟩.
593 The ⟨a⟩ is written subscript.
594 This is a nasalized form of *fuil*.
595 I follow the emendation suggested by Binchy, *CIH* 2172, n. k.
596 The ⟨a⟩ was added below the line in a lighter ink; see also Binchy, *CIH* 2172, n. l.
597 This word has been added above the line in a lighter ink with a reference mark; see also Binchy, *CIH* 2172, n. m.
598 This word has been added above the line in a lighter ink; see also Binchy, *CIH* 2172, n. m.
599 The ⟨a⟩ is written subscript; see also Binchy, *CIH* 2173, n. b.
600 The ⟨u⟩ was added below the line by the scribe; see also Binchy, *CIH* 2173, n. c. It is uncertain whether the quotation from the judge ends here or one clause earlier.

And if it is from the custody of a neutral third party that the *sét* is taken, the proportion of his own honor-price that the owner of the *sét* has is the proportion of his own honor-price that the custody of the neutral third party will have.[601]

If it is from the worthy person from whom it was claimed that it is carried off, provided that [the property is proven to be] his own afterwards [sc., the property of the person who carried off the disputed property], he [sc., the worthy person] does not have anything for its [being taken from his] custody except that which he has on account of his *sét* according to the period of time.[602] If the *sét* is not [proven to be] his [sc., the person who carried off the property] afterwards, he [sc., the worthy person] has a share of honor-price [the same] as the suitable neutral third party who would not own the *sét*. Or on the other hand, so that there is a fine for illegality [that will be paid to him], i.e., five *sét*s.[603]

A disputed *sét* is to be considered here between two claimants in the custody of a neutral third party, and neither of the two claimants had carried [it] off from the custody without a noble there [i.e., present], and it is the person making the claim who came to prove it according to his right, and it is not known to him himself, but to his milker or to his cowherd.[604]

If it is the law of arbitration that they submitted to the judge [regarding] what time he will get for a period of time for seeking a milker or a cowherd, and if the judge says whether the milker or cowherd is a worthy person or an unworthy person, he is entitled to a period of time for seeking [in the] territory or outside the territory.

If it is the law of judgment that they submitted to him [regarding] what time he will get for a period of time for seeking a milker or cowherd, and this is what the judge says: | 'if the milker or the cowherd is a worthy person, he is p. 21b
entitled to a period of time for seeking, and, if he is an unworthy person, he is not allowed a period of time [for seeking], because the unworthy person claiming it did not obtain proof of the disputed *sét*'.

601 In other words, whatever proportion of his honor-price that is awarded to the owner as a fine is also awarded to the neutral third party. Versions of this commentary are also found in § 4, sources F, CC, and DD.

602 The translation and interpretation of the last clause is uncertain.

603 It should be noted that five *sét*s is the normal fine for illegal distraint; *EIF* 171.

604 See § 2 tract and commentaries for the periods of delay given to the plaintiff to seek his milker or cowherd when he himself is unable to confidentally identify the disputed livestock as his own.

In set aidbre*da* *tu*cad a n-u*r*lai*m* coitci*n*d, *acht* ma rofuaitgest*ar* cecht*ar*de dib he cid resi*n* re cid iarsi*n* re, masa ci*n*dt(*h*)i lasi*n*ti [r](f)ofuataig[605] he *co*nach leis, landire ⁊ lane*n*ecla*n*d ⁊ aith*gin* coml*an* a*n*d, ⁊ in cutr*uma* d'e*n*ecl*ainn* ata in cach inad su*n*d is e i*n*cutr*uma* tor*m*aiges cai*n* do sm*acht* a*n*d re tæb in s*éoit*, ⁊ lane*n*ecl*ann* d'fir na faic*ht*hi (read *faithche*).[606]

Ma rob i a tuicsi cu*r*ba leis, ⁊ is iarsi*n* re rofuaitgest*ar* he, l*eth*dire a*n*d ⁊ l*eth*enecl*ann* ⁊ ai*thgin* comlan d'fir in s*éoit*, ⁊ l*eth*enecla*n*d d'fir na faic*h*ti (read *faithche*). ⁊ dogab*ar* in s*ét* re aidb*r*iud a*n*d sin, ⁊ mai*n*e fagb*ar*, ceth*ramthu* dire ⁊ l*eth*enecla*n*d ⁊ l*ethaithgin* d'fir in s*éoit* a*n*d, ⁊ l*eth*enecl*ann* d'fir na faic*h*ti (read *faithche*).

Cid fo*dera* in tan is cu*n*dtab*ar*t a*n*d so in leis he, co fuil l*eth*enecl*ann* uad a*n*d? Is e in fa*th*: ciarbo ci*nn*ti cu*r*bo leis o cianaib he, dobiad l*eth*enecl*ann* uad a*n*d, ⁊ coir 'no deiside in tan is cu*n*dtab*air*t in leis no nach leis he cia rob*eth* lethenecla*n*d uad a*n*d.

Cid fo*dera* in bail ata in ceth*ramthu* dire su*n*d nach ceth*ramthu* ait*h*gena [ḟ]uil a*n*d? Is e in fa*th*: in bail roba l*eth*dire and o cianaib, robui aithg*in* comlan a*n*d, ⁊ coir 'no deiside in bail ata ceth*ramthu* dire su*n*d ciamad l*eth*aithg*in* rob*eth* a*n*d ra tæb. Riasi*n* re si*n*, ⁊ ma iarsi*n* re, is [s]l*an* do *acht* ma[607] leis; ⁊ mainib leis, is aisec na h-aith*gena* uad.

Caide adbur na cu*n*dtab*ar*ta-sa inuas?[608] Mas do*n* fir [ḟ]uil aca n-acra rainic a i*m*den*am*, is a i*m*denu*m* do ⁊ a seoit do br*eith* do .i. do*n* fir fuil aca n-aidb*r*iud rai*n*ic a i*m*denu*m* and, ⁊ noc*ha*[609] do budein is aichnid a s*éoit* *acht* da blig*re* no da buach*aill*. ⁊ in tan doriachtat*ar* leis, dofuaitged i*n* s*ét* on u*r*lai*m*, no docuaid a muda he isi*n* u*r*lai*m*, ⁊ cu*n*dtab*air*t leis in di*n*gned ł na di*n*gn*ed* a i*m*den*am*[610] do rer na tu*r*tec*h*t fuair aca blig*re* no aca buach*aill* fori*n* s*ét*.

J [*CIH* 1973.11–40] .i. ní h-in*n*saig*har*, no ni h-in*n*sa i*ar* coir, no noch*an* tab*arr* asin baile a n-ai[d]b*h*rit*h*ar .i. *noch*o tab*arr* occa ni is in*n*sa f*air* o c*r*ích.

605 I follow the emendation suggested by Binchy, *CIH* 2173, n. d.

606 See also Binchy, *CIH* 2173, n. e.

607 The ⟨a⟩ is written subscript.

608 The ⟨u⟩ was added below the line by the scribe; see also Binchy, *CIH* 2173, n. c.

609 This word was inserted below the line by the scribe; see also Binchy, *CIH* 2173, n. g.

610 The ⟨e⟩ was added below the line by the scribe; see also Binchy, *CIH* 2173, n. h.

The disputed *sét* that was given into the custody of a neutral third party, but if it had been carried off by either of them whether before the period of time or after the period of time [assigned to seek the milker or cowherd], if the one who had carried it off is certain that it is not his, full penalty-fine and full honor-price and complete restitution then, and the equivalent from the honor-price that is for each case here, it is the equivalent that law adds to the fine for it in addition to the *sét*, and full honor-price for the owner of the green.

If he believes it is his, and it is after the period of time that he had carried it off, half penalty-fine for it and half honor-price and complete restitution for the owner of the *sét*, and half honor-price for the owner of the green. And the *sét* is found to be claimed in this case, and if it is not found, a fourth of the penalty-fine and half honor-price and half restitution for the owner of the *sét* then, and half honor-price for the owner of the green.

What brings it about when there is doubt in this case that it is his, that he owes half honor-price for it? This is the reason: although it is certain that it is his in the case just now [mentioned], he should owe half honor-price for it, and it is just then from that when it is doubtful that it is his or not that he should owe half honor-price for it.

What brings it about where there is the quarter penalty-fine here, that there is not quarter restitution for it? This is the reason: where there was half penalty-fine for it just now [mentioned], there was complete restitution for it, and it is just then from that where there is quarter penalty-fine here that there should be half restitution for it in addition. That was before the time, and if it is after the time, he is free from liability provided that it is his; and if it is not his, he restores the restitution.

What is the cause of the doubt above? If it is the person suing who came to prove it, it is proved by him and his *sét*s are given to him, i.e., to the person making the claim who came to prove it, and not by him himself is recognition of his *sét*, but by his milker or by his cowherd. And when they came with him the *sét* had been carried away from the pound, or it perished in the pound, and he is doubtful whether he would or would not be [able] to prove it according to the description he got from his milker or from his cowherd for the *sét*.

J i.e., it is not brought, or it is not difficult according to law, or it is not brought from the place in which it is claimed, i.e., anything that is difficult for him is not brought by him from a territory.[611]

611 The translation of the last clause is tentative.

Gach u*air* is ag gat*aig*e no ag fer m*edongait*e lanindlig*thech* no l*eth*indligec rohai[d]b*hred* na s*éotu*, is dul do am*a*c co c*r*ich in fir risi nder*na* in fog*ail* gu*r*ab an*n* b*erar* br*eth* f*air*.

Uair **intí fofich is e teit t*ar* cric*h* co ru*ct*[h]*ar* breath**[612] **f*air* a nem*edh* c*r*ich caic*h* frisi fuich.**[613] No coma isi*n* crich i nderna g*ataig*e cun*n*ra re fer m*edongaite*, co*mad* an*n* si*n* doberta br*eth* f*air*, u*air* is an*n*[614] is i*n*tí fofic*h* é. No d*ano* ch*ena*, g*a*c uair is ag fer m*edongait*e la*n*indlig*thech* no l*eth*indlig*thech* rohai[d]b*hred* na s*éot*u, is a rog*h*a f*ir* bun*aidh* ata in andsa c*r*ich a nderna g*ataige* cun*n*ra re fer m*edongait*e dodena a dlig*ed* umpu, no isi*n* crich *a r*ai[d]b*hrestar* a ts*et*.

In baile ata **ni h-in*n*sorg*ar* a c*r*ích do c*r*ích a*cht* ait**, ag fer m*edongait*e landlig*thech* roai[d]b*hred* in s*ét* an*n* sin, ⁊ is an*n* dleg*har* dlig*ed* uime isin c*r*ich in rohai[d]b*hred*h é. ⁊ in baile ata isin inat *ail*e **intí fofich**, duine eiside col. 483 dorig*h*ne ci*n* | no cur no cun*n*ra no fog*ail* ina c*r*ich budein, ⁊ dochuaid*h* re in*ndeith*b*irus* am*a*c *iar* sin. ⁊ do ait*he* indlig*he* f*air co*nad eig*en* do tia*cht*ain isi*n* crich a nder*na* a cin no cun*nrad* no a fog*ail* gu*r*ab an*n* b*erar* br*eth* f*air*.

---

612 The ⟨a⟩ is written subscript.

613 See also § 11, sources J and GG for this quotation from the tract.

614 *is ann* was written in *marg. dext.* with reference marks by the scribe; see also Binchy, *CIH* 1973, n. e.

Every time it is from a thief or from a fully unlawful or half unlawful receiver of stolen goods that the *sét*s were claimed, he goes out to the territory of the man against whom the trespass is done so that it is there that judgment is given for him.

Because **the one who commits an offense is the one who goes across [the] territory [boundary] so that a judgment may be given on him in [the]** ***nemed*** **territory**[615] **of every person against whom he commits an offense.** Or it is in the territory in which a thief makes a bargain with a receiver of stolen goods, so that it is there that judgment is given on him, because there he is the one who commits an offense. Or, on the other hand, every time it is from a fully unlawful or half unlawful receiver of stolen goods that the *sét*s were claimed, it is the choice of the owner [whether] it is in the same territory in which a thief makes a bargain with a receiver of stolen goods that justice will be done regarding them, or in the territory in which the *sét* was claimed.

The passage that is **it is not moved from territory to territory, but the place**, the *sét* was claimed from a fully lawful receiver of stolen goods in that case, and it is then that he is entitled to law regarding it in the territory in which it was claimed.[616] And the passage that is in the other place **the one who commits an offense**, that person committed an offense | or contract or col. 483
bargain or trespass in his own territory, and he went away without necessity after that.[617] And to punish him for his crime so that violence does not come into the territory where he committs an offense or bargain or his trespass, so that it is there that judgment is given on him.[618] That [is] a stranger,

615 The precise interpretation of '*nemed* territory' is uncertain. The phrase is also found in § 11, sources J and GG. In their discussion of the word *nemed*, Charles-Edwards and Kelly note that *nemed* has a wide semantic range and can be used in the abstract sense of 'sacredness, privilege', but it can also refer to a place, a person, an animal, and even a tree; *Bechbretha*, 107–109; and Latvio, "*Neimed*-Exploring Social Distinctions," 227. The phrase here might refer to the physical location in the territory where judgments are given. I should like to thank Paul Russell for discussion on this phrase.

616 See also the earlier commentary in source J, CIH 1972.29–37 (not edited here), which discusses the plaintiff's right to choose where the judgment should be given. The clause here refers to the territory where the plaintiff wishes the legal proceedings to be conducted.

617 In other words, he did not have a justifiable reason for leaving the territory.

618 The point of part of this seems to be intended to discourage any form of raid, assault, etc., in the other territory in retaliation. On retaliatory raids, see *Anfuigell* § 17.

Ingna si*n*, co tisa dui*n*e asin cric*h* a mbiad*h* a c*r*ich *ail*e do fast*ad* fiac*h* f*air*, *con*id ead*h* is coir an*n* de-sid*h*ein cen a tia*ch*t*ai*n, a*cht* is **intí fofich, ⁊rl-.**

Duine eisid*h*e doroin*n*e cor no cun*nrad* no fog*ail* ina crich budein, ⁊ docuaid*h* aist*e* ré *deith*b*irus* am*ac* i*ar* si*n*, ⁊ rogab*ad* at*h*gab*ail* i*ar* sin amuig*h*, ⁊ noch*ar* deiti*n* dlig*ed* ui*m*pe, ⁊ dochuaid*h* a ndeag*aid* at*h*gab*ala* inun*n* i*ar* si*n* f*or* cula, ⁊ tall rodeiti*n* dlig*h*e uimpe, ⁊ mes na c*r*iche amuig*h* uad*ha* ⁊ br*ei*-*th*em*h*nus na c*r*iche amuich, .i. br*eith*em*h*nus na c*r*iche ⁊ meas na cric*h*e ⁊ min*na* na cric*h*e i ndent*ar* int ai[d]b*h*re.

Caide *deith*bir eat*a*ru-si*n* ⁊ in baile ata: **ni fuatag*har* a*cht* o macha cor-uice lias bes nes*am* dó fri cron ⁊ coi*m*ge?** ⁊[619] rob i a t[h]uicsi*n* an*n* sin *cona* dem*h*tha dlig*h*e do in baile a roib*h*e, ⁊ as [s]l*an* do a br*eth* uad*ha* in baile i sailfead*h* dlig*h*e do dam*h*tain dó.

P[620] [*CIH* 711.25–29] .i. cach aen is ni*med*h oca n-aidbrit*er*.[621]

Ma foth dobera inti laisa fuiricar .i. oca n-aid*h*b*r*itht*er*, is e *im*toing co mui*n*t*ir* a t*h*ig*h*e .i. dogni i*m*dena*m* ⁊ gusi*n* cethrar[622] i ndeagaig*h*, ⁊rl- Mas da indraic ł da eisi*n*raic dorala imin set, is inti aca tarus h*e* a i*m*denam, cidbe fot*h* bus ail lais d'i*m*irt fair.

AA [1930.1–5][623] .i. g*ac* in*n*raic ab*h*res a s*ét* ag eisin*n*raic, ⁊ is fot*h* n-inais imrit a ndis, is laisin inruic i*m*de*n*am co fir t*est*a i*n*a diaig*h*, ach[t] m*ana* t*air*ge ai*n*n*test* oca n-aib*h*rig*h*t*er* fir De. ⁊ dia t*air*ge, ni fuil fir is taire d'i*m*den*am* o neoch 'nas i*n* fir t*air*ges.

O'Dav [*CIH* 1511.28–29][624] In*n*sorgui*n* .i. bid*h* doig*h* comad*h* inan*n* ⁊ gluais-a*cht* no imluag*h*, *ut est* "in*n*sorgui*n* *t*é*ti*;[625] no ní h-in*n*sorga*r* o crich do c*r*ich a*cht* ait i n-aid*h*brit*har*."

619 Binchy, *CIH* 1973, n. g, queries whether the beginning of the answer to the previous question has been omitted. See also the same clause in source A above.

620 For variants from source FF, see Appendix 4; see also § 3.

621 The phrase *et cach aidhbrigh bes nime* in the tract is glossed here. The gloss, however, is not written interlinearly in the MS.

622 The MS reads '*cet*haird'; I follow the emendation suggested by Binchy, *CIH* 711, n. k.

623 See also the similar material in sources Q (Appendix 2) and JJ (Appendix 3). The paragraph also appears in § 3, source F commentary, *CIH* 1270.36–39.

624 O'Dav no. 1140 in Stokes' edition; see 397–398 for readings from his source F and a translation.

625 Breatnach, *CCIH* 142 and 320, identifies the first part of the entry as coming from the text *Uraicecht Cóel.*

a person who comes out of the territory in which he lives into another territory to bind a fine on him, that is what is proper then [i.e., in the section above] regarding that without his coming, except it is **the one who commits an offense, etc.**

That person who made a contract or bargain or trespass in his own territory, and he went out of it out of necessity after that, and distraint was taken after that [while he was] away, and he does not recognize law regarding it, and he went back afterwards to take back the distraint, and there he recognized law regarding it, and he owes the award [sc., payment] of the outside territory and judgement of the outside territory, i.e., judgment of the territory and award of the territory and oaths of the territory in which the claiming is done.

What is the difference between that and the passage that is: **it is not taken except from the cattle-enclosure to the enclosure which is closest to him for possession and protecting**? It is his understanding in that case that justice would not be given to him where he was, and he is free from liability to take it to a place where he would expect justice to be granted to him.

P i.e., every one who is a *nemed* from whom it is claimed.

If the one in whose possession it is found,[626] i.e., from whom it is claimed, brings a claim, it is he who swears with the members[627] of his household, i.e., he proves [it] and with four people supporting him, etc. If it is two worthy or two unworthy people who happened [to quarrel] about the property, it is the one with whom it was found who proves it, whatever claim he wishes to use for it.

AA i.e., each worthy person who claims his property from an unworthy person, and it is a claim of growth that they both bring, it is up to the worthy person to prove [it] with compurgators supporting him, unless the untrustworthy witness, from whom it is claimed, undergoes an ordeal. And if he undergoes [an ordeal], there is not a truth [sc., a proof] which is more wretched to prove by someone than the truth which he offers.

O'Dav *Innsorguin*, i.e., probably it is the same as 'motion' or 'driving', *ut est* "*innsorguin* 'that goes'; or it is not moved from territory to territory but in the place in which it is claimed."

---

626 The form *fuiricar* appears to be the 3 sg. pres. pass. ind. of *fo-ricc* 'comes across, finds'; *eDIL* s.v. *fo-ricc*.

627 While a pl. form of *muinter* is expected, it is possible the word is used in a collective sense here.

§ 11

Decce cia d'ingenum.[628] Intí fofich is e teit *tar* crich co r*u*ct[h]*ar* br*eth* fair a neim*ed* c[h]*ŕ*ich caich f*r*isa fuacha*r*.

A [*CIH* 2173.27–37] Gach uair is ac gataigi no ac fer medo*n*gaite lanindligth*ech* no l*eth*indligth*ech* rohaidbriud na *séoit*, is a dul amach co c*r*ic*h* in fir risi*n* nd*e*rnad in fog*ail* cu*r*ub a*n*d b*e*rth*air* br*eth* fair, u[a]ir[629] **inti fofich is e teit t*ar* crich.** No comad isi*n* crich i nd*e*rnaid gat*aig*i cund*rad* re f*er* medongaiti dob*er*tha br*eth* fair, u*air* is i*n*ti fofich he. No da*no* cena, is ac fer medo*ngaite* lani*n*dligth*ech* no l*eth*indligth*ech* rohaidb*red* na seoit, ⁊ a roga fir bun*aid* ata[630] i*n*d isi*n* crich a raidbrest*ar* a *séot*u dog*en*a dlig*ed* umpu, no is[in][631] c*r*ich a nd*e*rnai gataige cund*rad* re f*er* medo*ngaite*. & in bail ata **ni h-in*n*sorgor o c*r*ich do crich *acht* ait i *n*-aidbrith*er* is a*n*d glether c*er*t ime,**[632] ac fir medo*ngaite* la*n*indligth*ech* rohaidbr*ed* na *séoit* a*n*d sin, ⁊ is a*n*d dleg*air* dlig*ed* u*m*pu isi*n* c*r*ich *ar* h-aidbre*d*i iat.

J [*CIH* 1973.1–10] .i. gad*aig*e no fer m*edongait*e lanindlig[th]ec is é téit *tar*in crich .i. t*ar*a c*r*ic*h* budein amac*h* do c*r*ich in fir risi nderna in fog*ail*.[633]
col. 482 .i. co ruct[h]*ar* br*eth* fair i c*r*ich in fir reis|a nderna in fua*cht*ain fog*la*.[634] U*air* is an*n* si*n* is i*n*tí fofich é. No is duine roel*a* amach re fiac*h*aib*h* an*n*

1 Decce cia d'ingenum] Only source A preserves this excerpt from the tract for this section; source A ends here, although another excerpt of the tract is quoted in the commentary below and taken into account here. ‖ Intí] inti **A comm.**, I*n*ti **GG comm.** The longer excerpt of the tract from J is found in § 10 **comm.**: 'intí fofich is e teit t*ar* cric*h* co ruct[h]*ar* breath f*air* a nem*edh*crich caic*h* f*r*isi fuich'. It is taken into account here. The excerpts from the tract in source **GG** are embedded in the commentary and taken into account here. ‖ teit] t*et* **GG comm.** ‖ crich] cric*h* **J comm.**, c*r*ich **A comm.**, **GG comm.** ‖ co] go **J**, **GG comm.** ‖ r*u*ct[h]*ar*] *rucar* **J.** ‖ br*eth*] breath **J comm.** 2 neim*ed* c[h]*ŕ*ich] nem*edh* crich **J comm.**, ne*m*id *cr*ic*h*i **GG comm.** ‖ caich] caic*h* **J comm.**, **GG comm.** ‖ f*r*isa] f*r*isi **J comm.**, **GG comm.** ‖ fuacha*r*] fuich **A** fuic*h* **J.** The choice between verb forms is arbitrary as both make sense in the context of the tract.

628 Read *imdénum.*

629 Binchy, *CIH* 2171, n. i, states that the subscript ⟨a⟩ that he sees is doubtful.

630 The second ⟨a⟩ is written subscript. The phrase *fir buanid ata* was written *inter col.* with reference marks by the scribe.

631 I follow the emendation suggested by Binchy, *CIH* 2173, n. j.

632 See also § 10 where the wording in the excerpt from source A is slightly different although the meaning is the same.

633 The phrase *Intí fofich is e teit tar crich* is what is glossed. For similar commentary, see also § 10, source J.

634 The phrase *go rucar breth fair a neimed crích caich frisa fuich* is what is glossed.

§11

See who is to prove [their case]. The one who commits an offense is the one who goes across [the] territory [boundary][635] so that a judgment may be given on him in [the] *nemed* territory[636] of every person against whom an offense has been committed.[637]

A Every time it is from a thief or from a fully unlawful or half unlawful receiver of stolen goods that the *sét*s were claimed, he goes out to the territory of the man against whom the trespass had been made so that it is there that a judgment is given on him, because **the one who commits an offense is the one who goes across [the] territory [boundary]**. Or so that it is in the territory where a thief had made a bargain with a receiver of stolen goods that a judgment may be given on him, because he is the one who commits an offense. Or, on the other hand, it is from a fully unlawful or half unlawful receiver of stolen goods that the *sét*s were claimed, and the owner has the choice [whether] it is in the territory in which his *sét*s were claimed that justice will be done regarding them, or it is in the territory in which a thief makes a bargain with a receiver of stolen goods.[638] And the passage that is **it is not moved from territory to territory, but the place in which it is claimed, it is there law is decided regarding it**, in that case the *sét*s were claimed from a fully unlawful receiver of stolen goods, and it is there that he is entitled to justice regarding them in the territory for which they were claimed.

J i.e., a thief or fully unlawful receiver of stolen goods is he who goes beyond the territory, i.e., outside his own territory to the territory of the man against whom he made the offense.

i.e., so that a judgment may be given on him in the territory of the man against | whom he made the offense, because in that case he is the one who col. 482
commits an offense. Or he is the person who evaded penalties [by going] outside [the territory] in that case, and he is entitled to a judgment on him

635 This clause is translated and discussed in Kelly, *The MacEgan Legal Treatise*, 164–165: "he who offends is the one who goes across the boundary."

636 See the discussion on this phrase in §10 at p. 227, n. 615.

637 For a discussion of this section, see the Introduction, p. 33.

638 See also the commentary in source J, *CIH* 1972.29–37 (not edited here), which discusses the plaintiff's right to choose where the judgment should be given.

sin, ⁊ as [s]í br*eth* dlega*r* fair a tab*air*t amuich coruic*e* int in*adh cét*na asa ndech*aid* amac*h*, ⁊ br*eth*em*h*n*us* ⁊ mes na criche ris*ar* fog*ail* uad*h*a. No is at*h*gab*h*ail gab*ar* de, ⁊ a ndeag*aidh* at*h*gab*al*a tic sé amuic*h*, ⁊ cum*adh* cid*h*be a[d]b*har*[639] fa ndeach*aid* se amac*h*. ⁊ manab el*od* dorig*h*ne, is fiac*h* fo aign*ed* an inait a nderna *cunnrad* d'ic do isi*n* c*r*ich a ta a fo*rus*.

GG [*CIH* 865.30–37] Dui*n*e dochuaid re toisce d*eth*bi*r*i ama*ch* an*n* sin, ⁊ is [s]i br*eth* dlig*ther*[640] air: br*eith*emn*us* ⁊ meas[641] na c*r*ichi a t*arr*as he uad. Caite *deith*bir eta*r*ru-si*n* ⁊ *in* baile a n-ab*air* a n-inad *aile*: **i*n*ti fofich is e te*t* *tar* c*r*ich go *r*uc*tar* br*eth* fai*r* a nem*i*d c*r*ic*h*i caic*h* frisi fuacha*r*?** Is *ed* fil an*n*-sidi: dui*n*e roel*ai* ama*ch* re fiach*aib*, ⁊ is [s]i br*eth* dlig*ther air* a tab*airt* amuig*h*, ⁊ br*eith*emn*us* ⁊ mes na c*r*ich*e* i*nar* foghl*aig* uad. I*n*gn*ad* sin, na*ch* he br*eith*emn*us* na c*r*ic*h*i a t*arrus* he ata uada; *con*a ed is coir an*n* de-side. ⁊ athgab*ail* rogab*ad* de an*n*, ⁊ i *n*deg*aid* a a*thgabal*a tic amuig*h*, ⁊ is cu*ma* cidbe adba*r* fo nde*ch*aid se ama*ch*.

639 See also Binchy, *CIH* 1973, n. d.

640 Binchy, *CIH* 865.30 queries the expansion of the final syllable.

641 The ⟨a⟩ is written subscript.

for taking them away as far as the first place from which he departed, and judgment and award of the territory where the offense had been committed by him. Or it is distraint that is taken from him, and after the distraint he comes from outside [sc., he returns], and it is the same although there is a [legitimate] reason he went away. And if he did not evade, the fine to be paid by him is according to the place in which he makes a bargain in the territory in which it is enforced.

GG A person went away on necessary business in that case, and he is entitled to a judgment on him: judgment and award of the territory in which it was taken by him. What is the difference between that and where it says in another place: **the one who commits an offense is the one who goes across [the] territory [boundary] so that a judgment may be given on him in [the]** ***nemed*** **territory of every person against whom an offense has been committed?** This is what there is there: a person who evaded penalties [by going] outside [the territory], and he is entitled to a judgment on him for taking them away, and judgment and award of the territory in which he is injured by him. That [is] a stranger, what he has is judgment of the territory in which it was taken from him; that is what is just regarding it. And distraint was taken from him for it, and after distraint he comes from outside [sc., he returns], and it is the same although there is a reason that he went away.

§ 12

p. 22a |**Duine lasi mbia fod.**[642]

A[643] [*CIH* 2173.38–41] Mas i*n*draic ⁊ esi*n*draic dorala umun s*é*t, cid im i*n*draic aidbres cid aca aidbrith*er*,[644] is le imden*am* cipe foth is ail di de. Mas[645] da indraic no da esi*n*draic dorala umun s*é*t, is leisinti 'ca tarr*us* [imdenam][646] cipe foth bus ail de.

1 Duine lasi mbia fod] This excerpt is found only in A.

642 This is a variant spelling of *foth*.

643 The same commentary is found in *Aidbred* § 3, source F, *CIH* 1271.6–7 and 12–13; and source P (and FF), Appendix 4, *CIH* 711.28–29.

644 *cid im … aidbrither* was written in *marg. sup.* with reference marks by the scribe; see also Binchy, *CIH* 2173, n. k.

645 The ⟨s⟩ was added below the line by the scribe.

646 I follow the emendation suggested by Binchy, *CIH* 2173, n. l.

§12

A person who will have a claim.[647] p. 22a

A If it is a worthy person and an unworthy person who happened [to quarrel] about the *sét*, whether regarding the worthy person who claims or from whom it is claimed, he proves whatever claim that he wishes regarding it. If two worthy people or two unworthy people happened [to quarrel] about the *sét*, it is the one in whose possession it was found who proves whatever claim that he wishes.

647 For a discussion of this section, see the Introduction, p. 33.

Heptad 64

Text, Variants, Commentary, and Translation

What follows is the edited text of Heptad 64 itself, taking into account all five of the MS sources. The quotations from the heptad embedded within the commentaries are not taken into account in the edited heptad presented here, even though they sometimes differ in orthography from what is found in the heptad itself.[1]

Atait *secht* frithe la *Féniu*: frithe treibe, frithe cathrach, frithe fai[th]che, frithe raiti, frith*e* rofeda [nó] frithe sleibe, frithe trachta, frith*e* fairge.

1 Atait] tait **A**, Atat **B**, Atait ... *Féniu om.* **E.** ‖ *secht*] .uii. **A, B, C,** 7 **J.** ‖ frithe] frith*e* **A, B, C,** frit*he* **J.** ‖ la *Féniu*] *om.* C There are no further citations from the heptad in **C.** ‖ frithe] .f. **B**; the word is abbreviated this way for the remainder of the heptad in this source. Frith*e* **E.** ‖ treibe] t*r*ebi **E**, treib*he* **J**; there are no further citations from **J.** ‖ frithe] f*r*ith*e* **E.** ‖ cathrach] ca[th]r*a*ch **B**, *cath*ruc*h* **E.** ‖ frithe] frith*e* **A, B.** ‖ fai[th]che] faich*e* **E.** 1–2 frithe] f*r*ith*e* **E.** 2 rofeda] rofida **A**, rofedha **B**, *om.* **E.** ‖ sleibe] *om.* **E.** The category of items found in a wood or on a mountain is omitted in **E.** ‖ frithe] frith*e* **E.** ‖ trachta] tra*ch*ta **A**, t*r*a*ch*ta **E.** ‖ fairge] In **B**, *frithe fairge* is listed before *frithe trachta.* fairge **E.**

1 See the Introduction, pp. 34–42 for further discussion, and see the section of the Concordance and Manuscript Sources which specifically concern Heptad 64 (p. 74). It should be noted that source J is the same for both *Aidbred* and Heptad 64 as material from each of them is found in Digest D.

There are seven [categories of] finds according to Irish law: something found in a dwelling, something found in an enclosure, something found on a green, something found on rough land, something found in a wood or something found on a mountain, something found on the shore, something found in the sea.

Source A, University of Oxford, Bodleian Library, MS Rawlinson B. 487, ff. 62d–63c, *CIH* 55.18–61.7[2]

f. 62d **[A]tait[3] *secht* frithe la *Féniu*:[a] frithe treibe,[b] frithe cathrach,[c] frith*e* faiche,[d][4] frithe raiti,[e] frith*e* rofida[f][5] [nó][6] frithe sleibe,[g] frithe tra*cht*a,[h] frith*e* fairge.[i]**

[a] .i. atait *secht* frit*h*e dogab*ar*[7] da n-aisneiden*n*[8] in fein*echus*.

[b] .i. dogab*ar* isin t*r*eib.

[c] .i. dogab*ar* isin c*h*at*h*r*aig* t*h*all.

[d] .i. dogab*ar* isin fait*h*c[h]e, .i. isna *cethri* gort*aib* is neasu*m* don baile.

---

2 The Oxford, MS Rawl. B. 487 version of the heptad is arranged in the MS as a series of excerpts of the heptad interspersed with glosses and commentary. In the edited text above, the heptad is given in bold with any glosses and commentary immediately below, although it should be noted that paragraph divisions within the commentaries have been added for ease of reference and the sections of glossed commentary have been grouped together. The text as presented here differs significantly from that which is printed in *CIH*. Some of the shorter commentaries are printed as glosses in *CIH* (e.g., Binchy's gloss 10), and sometimes glosses and commentaries are combined as one long gloss (e.g., Binchy's gloss 11), which have been separated here. It should be noted that some of the glosses do not currently begin with the abbreviation for *ed ón* (e.g., Binchy's gloss 21, which is actually a gloss followed by a commentary). *CIH* prints 30 glosses; only 27 are considered to be glosses here.

3 A space was left for a large initial ⟨a⟩ in the MS, but it was never added in.

4 The spelling *faiche* here and throughout is a late form of *faithche* 'green'.

5 The word *ruud, rúd* 'wood, forest' < *ro-fid* < **rowidu* has a range of variants both in the nom. and gen. sg., including gen. sg. *rofida, raoda*, and *raedha*, all of which are found in this heptad; Rudolf Thurneysen, "Irisches und Gallisches. 4. Der Nominativ zu air. *Roida*," *ZCP* 14 (1923): 5; and *eDIL* s.v. *ruud, rúd*.

6 For this emendation, cf. the material below at p. 244 from *CIH* 57.27.

7 The verb is the sg. pres. pass. ind. of *fo-gaib* 'finds, discovers, obtains'. The preverb *fo-* is frequently replaced by *do-*, especially after the OI period; *eDIL* s.v. *fo-gaib*.

8 The verb is a MI 3 sg. pres. act. ind. prototonic simplex from OI *as-indet* 'declares, tells, mentions'.

There are seven [categories of] finds[9] according to Irish law:[a] something found in a dwelling,[b] something found in an enclosure,[c] something found on a green,[d] something found on rough land,[e] [10] something found in a wood[f] [11] or something found on a mountain,[g] something found on the shore,[h] something found in the sea.[i] [12] f. 62d

[a] i.e., there are seven [categories of] things which are found, which customary law mentions.
[b] i.e., it is found in the dwelling.
[c] i.e., it is found inside the enclosure.
[d] i.e., it is found on the green, i.e., in the four fields which are closest to the settlement.

---

9 The word *fríthe* is a part. of *fo-gaib*, and the form *fríth* would seem to be the vn.; Stefan Schumacher, [with co-authors] Britta Schulze-Thulin, and Caroline aan de Wiel, *Die keltischen Primärverben: ein vergleichendes etymologisches und morphologisches Lexicon* (Innsbruck: Institut für Sprachen und Literaturen der Universität Innsbruck, 2004), pp. 681–682, note (c); and *eDIL* s.v. *fríth*, *fríthe*. The general meaning is 'a find, that which has been found', and it can refer to both animate and inanimate objects. Older translations of the legal material tend to use 'waif' or 'estray', but neither of these words accurately conveys the full sense of the Irish term. The translation, 'lost property found', is proposed in *EIF* 540.

10 Although *raite* can mean 'road', it can also refer to any uncultivated or rough grazing land. For the meaning 'rough land' in this context, see *EIF* 540, and *eDIL* s.v. *raite*. Cf. O'Dav no. 1387, *CIH* 1522.5–6: Raiti, .i. rot, *ut est* "frith*e* raiti," .i. frith*e* dogab*har ar*in rot ł i cu*air*t ingelt*a* ł it*er* fai[th]che ⁊ dirin*n*; o fait*h*i im*a*c[h] is *ed* is raiti an*n*. 'Rough land, i.e., a road, *ut est* "something found on rough land," i.e., lost property found on the road or in a grazing enclosure or between a green and unclaimed land; from a green outwards is what rough land is then'; see Stokes, "O'Davoren's Glossary." For the different categories of roads, see *Róda, cis lir-side?*, ed. and trans. Fergus Kelly, in *EIF* 537–544; and Thomas Owen Clancy, "Spaghetti Junction: OI *rót*, *roüt*, ScG *ròd*, *rathad*, Scots *rod*, *rode*, English *road*, and some other minor by-ways," in *Fil súil nglais: A Festschrift in Honour of Colm Ó Baoill*, ed. Sharon Arbuthnot and Kaarina Hollo (Tigh a' Mhaide, Brig o' Turk, Perthshire: Clann Tuirc, 2007), 17–28. For some of the different categories of land, see "*Tír Cumaile*," ed. and trans. Gearóid Mac Niocaill, *Ériu* 22 (1971): 81–86; *GEIL* 274–275; *EIF* 394–397; and *CCIH* 314.

11 See also O'Dav no. 1388, *CIH* 1522.7: Roed, .i. ro-fid*h* na caill*e*, u*t* est "frithe roed*h* ł sleibe." 'A wood, i.e., the great wood of the forest, *ut est* "something found in a wood or on a mountain;"' see Stokes, "O'Davoren's Glossary."

12 The beginning sections on finding lost property in *The MacEgan Legal Treatise* § 5.1–4 derive from Heptad 64 and its related commentaries; Kelly, op. cit., 161–163.

[e] .i. it*er* fait*h*ce ⁊ dirrain*n*.
[f] .i. dogab*ar* isin rofid*h*.
[g] .i. dogab*ar* isin tsliab*h*.
[h] .i. dogab*ar* isi*n* *tracht*.
[i] .i. dogab*ar* ari*n* fairrge amuig*h*.

Frithe treib*e*: dilis a cuigad do fir fod[n](a)gaib.[13]

Is cut*ruma* ata an c*h*uiti frith*i* cid do fir fine cid do fir anfine, uair is cut*ruma* regait a leas[14] a *sét* do m*ar*t*h*ain doib. ł d*ano* cena cona b*eth* cuiti frit*h*i o fir fine da ceile, uair dl*egar* de *sét* a fine do coim*h*ed in cach inad*h* ana tegemdais[15] cuigi.

Ni ḟuil ni do ḟir geilfine a beod*h*ile a ceth*ar*aird na hi *cu*laird, ar d*le*gar dib coming*h*aire et*ar*ru fein do reir Cor*us*a Fine. C*eth*raime im*morro* do anfine, o sin amach a sleib ł a ndithrub. [Is a][16] tia*cht*ain for cuiti tob*aig* it*er* fine ⁊ anfine, ar ni lug*h*u dl*e*gar cuitig*h*i tob*aig* ḋo fir fine inas do fir anfine.

Marbdili nama indisas[17] sund ⁊ cuit fir anfine, ⁊ beodili ⁊ cuit fir fine, it e na tait*h*met and, a*cht* is friu riagailt*ir*. ⁊ is [s]i riag*ail* fil isna frith*ib*-so: a*n*ni b*eir*is fer anfine a h-eccoimdi[g][18] is *ed* b*eir*is fer fine a coi*m*di[g], ⁊ i*n*ni fuil a coi*m*di[g] an frith*i* romat iss *ed* fuil a h-ecoimde[g] an frith*i* is nesa, cinmot*ha* na frith*e* deid*h*inach*a*—is sain a mb*reith*amna*cht*-said*h*i frisna frith*e* olcena.

13 The emendation is based on the form *fodngaib* which consistently appears below. By the late OI period, there were changes within the system of object agreement markers, and it is possible that the form here reflects those changes; McCone, *Early Irish Verb*, 171, 2.1(d). It is also possible that the ⟨a⟩ is a scribal mistake for ⟨n⟩. I should like to thank the anonymous reader for this suggestion.

14 The ⟨a⟩ is written subscript.

15 The verb appears to be the 3 pl. cond. act. ind. of *do-ecmaing* 'happens, meets'.

16 I follow the emendation suggested by Binchy, *CIH* 55, n. d; cf. also the similar phrase in the version in TCD MS 1336 (source C), *CIH* 1851.31.

17 The ⟨is⟩ are added under the line. The verb is a MI 3 sg. pres. act. ind. rel. form of *indisid*, which comes to replace OI *ad-fét*; *eDIL* s.v. *indisid* 'tells, mentions, recounts'.

18 Throughout the text, a contrast is made between items which are found in a frequented place, *coimtig*, and an unfrequented place, *éccoimtig*, the sense being that frequented places are regularly traversed and unfrequented places are not. The spelling of both words, especially the final syllable, is highly variable in all versions of the heptad due to lenited /d/ and /g/ > /Ø/ in MI. The expansion of these final syllables frequently differs from that printed in *CIH*; no note has been made where this happens.

[e] i.e., between a green and unclaimed land.[19]
[f] i.e., it is found in the wood.
[g] i.e., it is found on the mountain.
[h] i.e., it is found on the shore.
[i] i.e., it is found out on the sea.

Something found in a dwelling: a fifth of it is forfeit [sc., a fifth of its value] to [the] person who finds it.

The share of something found is the same whether for a local or for a stranger,[20] because they will get the same benefit of the property saved by them. Or, on the other hand, so that there might not be a share of something found from a local to another, because he is obligated to guard property from his community in every place in which they would happen across it.

There is nothing for a man of the *gelfine*[21] for animate property [found] in [the] four nearest townlands or in [the] four townlands closest to those, because they are bound by joint grazing between themselves according to *Córus Fine*.[22] One fourth, however, for a stranger, moreover, [from that which is found] on a mountain or uninhabited place. Both a local and a stranger receive a share for recovering, because a local is not entitled to a smaller share for recovering than a stranger is.

Inanimate property only that it [sc., the textual source] discusses here and a stranger's share, and animate property [sc., livestock] and a local's share, those things they do not explain here, but it is regulated regarding them. And this is the law which there is for these things which are found: that which a stranger takes from an unfrequented place is what a local takes from a frequented place [regarding their respective share], and that which is from something found in a frequented place [that we discussed] previously is what is from something found in an unfrequented place [that we discussed] next, except for the things found [which we shall discuss] lastly—their adjudication is different from the other things which are found otherwise.

---

19 The word *dírainn* can refer to any land which is not appropriated; *EIF* 406–408; and *eDIL* s.v. *dírainn*.

20 The phrases *fer fine* 'man of a kindred' and *fer ainfine* 'man of a stranger kindred' are used to make a contrast between those who are local to a community and those who are not.

21 The *gelfine* consists of three generations of kindred; *EIWK* 55–61; and Neil McLeod, "Kinship," *Ériu* 51 (2000): 1–22.

22 *Córus Fine* is a legal text concerning the rights and obligations amongst kinsmen; *CCIH* 235–239.

Dia n-urfog*ra* ⁊ ni rocaith co *dech*m*aid*, is dilis do cuiti frith*i* ⁊ a foimailt. Mana focc*ra* ⁊ rocait*h* ria n*dech*m*aid*, ⁊ corub aisneis dob*er*a fair, is landire fair. Mana fog*ra* co tora a iaraid*h* ⁊ co roic iarr*aid*, ⁊ ni ceil in tan dorig,[23] is dilis a cuitid*h* f*r*ith*i*. Muna fog*r*ad*h* ⁊ rocait*h* ria n*dech*m*aid* ⁊ nir ceil, is l*eth*dire.

Frithi treibe:[j] ma iar teora aid*h*cib tiasar do,[k] mad eccoimded.[l] Mad coim*ded*,[m] a ceathraime do fir fodngaib.[24]

[j] .i. *cói*ced as a eccoimded, ⁊ a c*eth*raime as i coimded*h*.
[k] .i. mad*h* and tias*ar* do fag*hbail* a cin*n* tri[25] n-æid*h*c*h*e.
[l] .i. mad*h* ecomdoig*h* a fag*hbail* do neoch *aili*, is an*n* ata si*n*, .i. in *cói*cid ass.
[m] .i. mad coimdoig*h* a fag*hbail* do neoch aili ⁊ da tig*h*erna fein.

⁊ is and ata sin in tan ata re re teora n-aid*h*ch*i* *ar* iarraig*h*. ⁊ mas aenad*h*aig, is t*r*ian in *cói*cad*h* ł na cet*h*raime. Mas da aid*h*ci, is da t*r*ian in *cói*cid*h* ł na c*eth*raime. ł d*ano* cona b*eth* ni and no co mb*eth* se ar esb*aid* t*r*i n-aid*h*ci.

Frith*e* roead*h* ł sleibe, .i. diaid*h* a ndiaid*h* atait so, is aire is moiti asint sleib*h* ⁊ asin fid*h*. An t*racht* im*morro* ⁊ an fairrgi, is inand iat-said*h*i cid i faich*i* b*h*eit, uair foxlait-sid*h*e an *sét* leo; ni foxland im*morro* in sliab*h* [na in] (ina)[26] fid*h*.

23 The verb appears to be a 3 sg. pres. act. ind. form of *do-roich* 'reaches, arrives'.

24 The 3 sg. pres. act. ind. of *fo-gaib* is combined with a m. class C object agreement marker: 'who finds it'.

25 During the MI period, the forms of the numeral three, m. *trí* and f. *téora*, can be used interchangeably, regardless of the gender of the noun. In the commentary above and in gloss o below, the historically correct form is used. See *eDIL* s.v. *trí*; Liam Breatnach, "An Mheán-Ghaeilge," in *Stair na Gaeilge*, eds. Kim McCone et al. (Maigh Nuad: Roinn na Sean-Ghaeilge, 1994), pp. 221–333, at 261; and McCone, *A First Old Irish Grammar and Reader*, 186.

26 I follow the emendation suggested by Binchy, CIH 56, n. a.

If he makes a proclamation [that he found lost property] and he did not use [it] until [after] ten days [have passed], a share of [the] thing found is forfeit to him and [he can] make use of it. If he does not make a proclamation and he used [it] before ten days [have passed], and [that] information is brought against him, it is [the] full fine [that he owes] for it. If he does not make a proclamation until someone comes seeking it and someone comes [to him] seeking [it], and he does not conceal [it] when he comes, his share of [the] thing found is forfeit to him. If he does not make a proclamation and he used [it] before ten days [have passed] and he did not conceal it, it is half penalty [that he owes].[27]

Something found in a dwelling:[j] if it is found after three nights,[k] if [it is found in] an unfrequented place.[l] If [it is found in] a frequented place,[m] a fourth of it for [the] person who finds it.

[j] i.e., one fifth of it in an unfrequented place, and one fourth of it in a frequented place.
[k] i.e., if it is the case that it is found at the end of three nights.
[l] i.e., if it is unlikley to be found by someone else, it is then that there is, i.e., the fifth from it.
[m] i.e., if it is likely to be found by someone else and by its own master [sc., owner].

And that is the case when it is sought before three nights [have passed]. And if it is one night, it [sc., the share] is a third of the fifth or of the fourth. If it is two nights, it is two thirds of the fifth or of the fourth. Or, on the other hand, there should be nothing [as a share] for it until it might be missing [for] three nights.

Something found in a wood or on a mountain, i.e., these are one after another, therefore there is the greater [share] from the mountain and from the wood. The shore, however, and the sea, those are the same as though they were on a green,[28] because they take away the object with them; nei-

27 See also the commentary in § 8 *Aidbred.*
28 In the explanation found here and in the other versions of the commentary (except for that found in source E), it is difficult to determine why items found on the shore and sea are equated with items found on the green. Perhaps it has to do with the fact that people are as likely to carry away an item as the tide, or it may concern the fact that both the shore and the green are places frequented by people.

Is ed*h* is coimdeg*h* sleibi and: a slig*h*th*i*. Is *ed* is coimded*h* caill*e* and: a cluainti ⁊ a guirtine ⁊ na h-inada a mbi ait*h*ig*h*i caich.

A mairbdili fine ⁊ anfine ata an c*h*uitig-so. Beodili fine im*morro*, ni fuil ni eistib a cuairt comai[th]c[h]esa. Beodili im*morro* o c*h*uairt coimai[th]-c[h]esa amach ic fine ⁊ beodili anfine cid a cu*air*t coimai[th]ch*e*sa, mana dlig*h* coimingaire, is feg*ad* co tab*air* na cota frith*i* am*ail* roraidsim.

Frithe trachta, .i. iss *ed* is coimdig*h* trag*h*a and: ca*ch* ait aithid*h*aid*h* daine ⁊ longa ⁊ ton*n*a co coitcen*n*. Is *ed* is ecoi*m*di[g]: ca*ch* inad*h* ina aithig*h*it *acht* longa a n-æn*ur*.

Cid*h* fodera in frith*e* tra*cht*a co fuil ni as d'fir bunaig*h*? Is e in fat*h* f*odera*: dlig*ed* tab*ar*ta dilsig*h*is in dara de ⁊ dlig*ed* frith*i* dilsidis araili, ⁊ mo dilsidis[29] tab*air*t na frithe.

Cid*h* fodera in frithe dogaba*r* arin muir moir co fuil an t*r*ichadm*adh* rand as do fir bunaig*h*, ⁊ corub tab*air*t dilsid*h*is he ot*h*a sin amach? Is e in fa*th*: fei-med*h* ⁊ airiasa*cht* ⁊ tab*air*t fine dilsidhis in *sét* dogaba*r* ite*r* nai ton*n*a m*ara* ⁊ tir, ⁊ dlig*h*id*h* tab*ar*ta nama dilsig*h*is in *sét* dogab*ar* *ar*in muir moir.

29 Binchy, *CIH* 56, n. c, notes that the scribe originally wrote the sequence ⟨dilsi dis⟩ and then erroneously crossed out the ⟨dis⟩.

ther the mountain nor the wood, however, takes [it] away. This is what is a frequented place of a mountain then: its paths. This is what is a frequented place of a wood then: its glades and its little gardens and the places where everyone frequents.

This share is from [the] inanimate property of a local and a stranger. Animate property of a local, however, there is nothing from them [as a share if they are found] in a neighboring grazing enclosure. Animate property, however, from outside a local neighboring grazing enclosure and animate property of a stranger though in a neighboring grazing enclosure, unless he is entitled to joint grazing, it is considered that he gets the shares of something found as we have said.

Something found on the shore, i.e., this is what is a frequented place of a shore then: each place people and boats and waves frequent in common. This is what is an unfrequented place: each place in which but boats alone frequent.

What is the reason that for something found on a shore there is something from it for the original owner? The reason that causes it is: [it is the] law of taking that gives right in one [case] and [the] law of finds that gives right in the other, and [the law of] taking gives greater right than [the law of] finds.[30]

What is the reason that for something found which is found on the open sea that there is one thirtieth of it for the original owner and that [the law of] taking gives right to it from then onwards? The reason is: refusal and permission and payment of a local make the property which is found between nine waves of the sea and land forfeit, and [the] law of taking only gives right to the property which is found on the open sea.[31]

30 The 'law of finding' refers to finding anything on land or floating on the water between the shore and nine waves of the sea; the 'law of taking' refers to finding anything in the sea beyond the ninth wave or that the finder had to risk life to retrieve. In the law of taking, the percentage of the value the finder receives is significantly higher than in the law of finding.

31 See the discussion on this provision in the Introduction, pp. 39 and 51–55

Cid fod*er*a *con*a mo asin frith*e* tra*cht*a ina asin frithig*h* roeda? Is e in fa*th*: doig*h* muir ⁊ daine do foxail in fri*th*i t*r*a*chta*, ⁊ *no*cho*n* doich a*cht* daine nama do foxal an frith*i* roeda.

.i. Iss *ed* is coi*m*dig*h* t*r*eib*e* and: a l*ar* ⁊ a h-airmed*ha* ⁊ a inada soillsi ⁊ na h-inada a mbi aithig*h*i caich, ł a f*r*aig*h*t*h*i ⁊ a h-urlair ⁊ a sid*hae*. ⁊ iss *ed* is eccoi*m*di do*n* tig*h*: a cuile ⁊ a corrogi, ł a cula ⁊ a lep*tha* ⁊ a h-achlasg*a* ⁊ a inada dorch*a*. ⁊ is and ata sin do: in tan ata re re *téor*a n-aid*h*c*h*i gan fagbail ł ar iaraig*h*.

Mad*h* and tec*htaire*[32] dia fagb*ail* iarna b*heth ar* esb*aid* re re t*r*i n-aid*h*c*h*i, muna raibi se a*cht* aenaid*h*c*h*i ar iaraid*h*, is t*r*ian an *cóic*id*h* ł na c*eth*raime. ⁊ mas da oid*h*c*h*i, is da t*r*ian in *cóic*id*h* ł na c*eth*rai*me*; ł d*an*o cona b*eth* ni and ł co mb*eth* se *ar* esb*aid* tri n-aid*h*c*h*i.

Frith*e* cathrach: dilis a cethruime do fir fodngaib, munub i cuaird lis sluaig.[n]
f. 63a **Mad [e]ad on,[o] is | trian do fir fodngaib.**[p]

[n] .i. munab an*n* dogab*ar* he i*ar* cæ uird baile[33] i mbid*h* in sl[u]ag*h*[34] isin lis.
.i. i*n*a coimde[g].[35]
[o] .i. mad*h* ina coimde[g].
[p] [.i.] a c*eth*raime as i ecoimdig, ⁊ a t*r*ian as i coimdig*h*.

Is and ata sin, munib i cuaird lis sluaig*h*, uair mad eisid*h*i, is t*r*ian do fir fodngaib. C*eth*raime do fir geilfine, mad*h* eccoimdig*h*; mad coimdig*h* is l*eth* ⁊ leat*h* t*r*in do fir g*eil*fine. Iss *ed* is coimdig*h* cathrach an*n*: a h-url*ar* ⁊ a reilgi ⁊

32 Binchy, *CIH* 56, n. d, queries whether his reading 'tech*tair*' is an error for 'tiagair', the 3 sg. pres. pass. ind. of *téit* 'goes'.

33 The sequence from the word *baile* to the end of the gloss is written at the end of the preceding commentary with reference marks.

34 I follow the emendation suggested by Binchy, *CIH* 56, n. e.

35 The second gloss on *sluaig* is written under the word *sluaig* in the MS.

What is the reason that there is a greater [share] from something found on the shore than from something found in the wood? The reason is: it is likely that [both the] sea and people could carry off something found on the shore, and it is likely that only people could carry off something found in the wood.[36]

I.e., this is what is a frequented place of a dwelling then: its floor and its furniture and its bright places and the places where everyone frequents, or its interior walls and its floors and its peaceful places.[37] This is what is an unfrequented place for a house: its pantry and its cistern, or its sides and its beds and its stalls and its dark places. And it is here that he has that: when it is not found or sought before three nights [have passed].

If then someone comes to find it after it had been lost before three nights [have passed], if he was not seeking it but one night, it is a third of the fifth or of the fourth [that the finder gets]. And if it is two nights, it is two thirds of the fifth or of the fourth. Or, on the other hand, there should be nothing then until it might be missing for three nights.

Something found in an enclosure: a fourth of it is forfeit to [the] person who finds it, unless it may be within a host's enclosure.[n] If it be so,[o] it is | a third of it for [the] person who finds it.[p] f. 63a

[n] i.e., unless it is found there along a town's high path when the host is wont to be in the enclosure, i.e., in a frequented place of it.
[o] i.e., if it is in a frequented place of it.
[p] i.e., a fourth of it in an unfrequented place, and a third of it in a frequented place.

That is the case then, unless it may be within a host's enclosure, because if it is that, it is a third for the person who finds it. A fourth for a man of the *gelḟine*, if [it is found in] an unfrequented place; if [it is found in] a frequented place, it is a half and half of a third for the man of the *gelḟine*. This is what is a frequented place of an enclosure then: its marketplace and its

36 The sense is that with something found on the shore, the tide or people could carry it off. With an item found in the woods, it is likely that only a person would carry it off, with the exception of something being carried off by wild animals.

37 The precise interpretation of *sidhae* here is obscure to me. Perhaps the phrase refers to quiet locations where people relax.

a p*r*imsraiti ⁊ ca*ch* inad*h* a mbiad*h* ait*h*ig*h*i caich. Iss *ed* is eccoimdig*h* indti: a cula ⁊ a garrda ⁊ a inada diamra.

Frithe faich*e*:[q] a trian do fir fodngaib, mad eccoimdig*h*. Mad coimdigh, is leath.[r]

[q] .i. frith*e* dogab*ar* isin fait*h*ce.
[r] [.i.] A trian as a[38] h-eccoimdig*h*, ⁊ a l*eth* as a coimdig*h*.

Iss *ed* is coimdig*h*[39] faich*e* and: a tulc*h*ain ⁊ a inada air*echt*ais. ɫ iss *ed* is coimdig*h* faich*e* and: a slig*h*ti ⁊ a inada reid*he* arda ⁊ na h-inada a mbi ait*h*ig*h*i caich.

Iss *ed* is ecoimdig*h* inti: a imli ⁊ a cula. ɫ iss *ed* is eccoimdig*h* f*aithche* and: a cabana ⁊ a h-inada daimr*a* ⁊ in baile nach ait*h*ig*h*ind cach aire.

Iss *ed* is faich*e* and: na ceith*ri*[40] guirt is nesa don baili .i. gort ca*ch* aird ime, ⁊ cid h*e* in sliab bud nesa don bail*i* rob*ad* am*al* faich*i*.

Iss *ed* is se*cht*arfaich*e* an*n*: in air*et* rosoich cuaird ingelt*a* on faiche amach. No is ed*h* is faich*e* and: an rosaig*h* guth an cluig.

Frithe raiti: a l*eth* do fir fodagaib, ma eccoimdi[g]. Ma coimdig*h*, is da trian.[s]

[s] [.i.] A l*eth* as a eccoimdig, ⁊ da t*r*ian as a coimdig*h*.

---

38 Binchy, *CIH* 57, n. b, queries whether here and following *as a* should be read as *asa*. Cf. gloss p above.

39 As noted by Binchy, *CIH* 57, n. c, the first four words of this commentary have been erroneously struck through.

40 As noted by Binchy, *CIH* 57, n. e, the word *ard* originally followed *ceithri* in the MS, but it has been erased.

churchyard and its main streets and each place where everyone could frequent. This is what is an unfrequented place in it: its recesses and its gardens and its secluded places.

Something found on a green:[q] a third of it for [the] person who finds it, if [it is found in] an unfrequented place. If [it is found in] a frequented place, [the finder receives] half of it.[r]

[q] i.e., a lost item which is found on the green.
[r] i.e., a third of it from an unfrequented place, and half of it from a frequented place.

This is what is a frequented place of a green then: its hillocks and its assembly places. Or this is what is a frequented place of a green then: its paths and its high level places and the places where everyone frequents.[41]

This is what is an unfrequented place in it: its borders and its recesses. Or this is what is an unfrequented place of a green then: its hollows and its secluded places and the places every freeman does not frequent.

This is what is a green then: the four fields which are closest to the settlement, i.e., a field on each side around it, and though it may be a mountain which is closest to the settlement, it is [considered] as a green.

This is what is outside the green then: as far as a grazing district reaches beyond the green. Or this is what is a green then: as far as the voice of a bell reaches.[42]

Something found on rough land: half of it for [the] person who finds it, if [it is found in] an unfrequented place. If [it is found in] a frequented place, it is two thirds.[s]

[s] i.e., half of it from an unfrequented place, and two third of it from a frequented place.

---

41 The boundaries of and potential geographic features of the green are discussed in *EIF* 369–370 with particular reference to this passage. Kelly's understanding of the term *faithche* is as "the whole area which surrounds a dwelling;" he suggests translating the term as 'infield' in opposition to *sechtar faithchi* 'outfield', which refers to the area beyond the *faithche*.

42 With regard to distance being measured in terms of how far a sound carries, it should be noted that in medieval Welsh law the chief huntsman's protection extends as far as the sound of his horn can be heard; Jenkins, *The Law of Hywel Dda*, 23; and see also *Llyfr Cyfnerth* in Wade-Evans, *Welsh Medieval Law*, 5.

Iss *ed* is coimd*eth* do: cac*h* baili is mo ait*h*ig*et* daine an ferand. ł iss *ed* is coimd*eth* raiti and: a sl*ig*ti ⁊ a inada reide arda.

Iss *ed* is eccoimd*eth* an*n*: a glentac*ha* ⁊ a claided*ha* ⁊ a inada diamr*a*. ł iss *ed* is eccoimd*eth*: cach bail*e* is lug*h*a ait*h*id*h*it daine in ferann*n*. ⁊ iss *ed* is raiti and: cac*h* inad ot*ha*-si*n* amach, .i. [iter] (in)[43] faich*i* co rud ł dirind. Iss *ed* is rud*h* ł ecm*acht* and: co ria na neithe-sin ⁊ na n*eth*e-sin fein.

Frith*e* rofeda no sleib*e*: dilis a da trian do fir fodngaib, ma eccoim*deg*. Ma coimde[g], is teora ce[t]h(t)ramna do fir fodngaib.[t] Frithe raoda no sleibe: da trian do fir fodngaib ⁊ aentrian do fir isi ae, no do neoch foceirr amach.[u] No confodla eturru i nde[v] a imairiltnig a taisig,[w] muniu broga ne*cht*ar n-aei.[x]

[t] .i. da t*r*ian as a ecoimdi[g] ⁊ teora c*eth*ramna as i coimdi[g].
[u] [.i.] do*n* neoch rocuir*ustar* amac*h* he ar oin.
[v] .i. is cain fodeiligt*er* et*ar*ru *ar* do.
[w] .i. trian amuil eim-airiltnigit[44] a taisic doib.
[x] .i. muna firenaigt*er* ne*cht*arde dib*h* imdenam f*o*ra c*h*eil*e* .i. munob dana[45] re ne*chtar*de dib a sena[46] ł[47] imdenam in tairaista ł na tairaistea.

43 Binchy, *CIH* 57, n. f, notes that *in* is a mistake, although he does not suggest a correction. The emendation here is based on gloss e.

44 The form *airilnigit* is a later 3 pl. pres. ind. of the simplex *áiriltnigid* from earlier *ad-roilli*; *eDIL* s.v. *ad-roilli* 'deserves, is entitled to'.

45 The form *dana* is a MI 3 sg. pres. subj. of *do-gní*; *eDIL* s.v. *do-gní* 'makes, does'.

46 The phrase *a sena* is written by the scribe in *marg. sin.* with reference marks.

47 Binchy, *CIH* 58, n. b, notes that the ⟨ł⟩ was added in later by a different scribe. Although the symbol has a more angular cast than other occurrences of them in this commentary, the ink color is the same and the general shape is the same. The angularity is more likely due to the scribe trying to squeeze it in between two already written letters.

This is what is a frequented place for it: each place that people most frequent the land. This is what is a frequented place of rough land then: its paths and its high, level places.

This is what is an unfrequented place in it: its glens and its ditches and its secluded places. Or this is what is an unfrequented place: each place people frequent the land less. And this is what rough land is then: each place other than those, i.e., between a green up to a wood or unclaimed land. This is what is a wood or inaccessible place in it: up to those things and those things themselves.

Something found in a wood or on a mountain: two thirds of it is forfeit to [the] person who finds it, if [it is found in] an unfrequented place. If [it is found in] a frequented place, it is three fourths for [the] person who finds it.[t] Something found in a wood or on a mountain: two thirds for [the] person who finds it and one third for [the] owner, or for someone who may lose [it].[u] [48] Or it is equally divided between them in two,[v] its restitution [each] mutually deserves,[w] if neither of them establishes [his right to it].[x]

[t] i.e., two thirds of it from an unfrequented place and three fourths of it in a frequented place.
[u] i.e., for the person who lost it on loan.[49]
[v] i.e., it is 'well'[50] they divide between them in two.
[w] i.e., a third as 'promptly'[51] they deserve its restitution for them.
[x] i.e., if neither of them establishes proof over the other, i.e., unless neither of them denies it or proves against the other whether it could be got hold of or not.

48 The commentary here and below brings up the scenario where the person who lost the property is not the actual owner, but someone who had the property on loan.

49 For the different types of loans in Irish law, see McLeod, "*Ón* and *airliciud*," 169–196. *Ón* refers to a private loan.

50 The word *caín* 'fair, beautiful, fine, good' is commonly used in etymological glosses on the element *con-*; Binchy, "The Linguistic and Historical Value of the Irish Law Tracts," 211–212: in *Celtic Law Papers*, 90; and Taylor-Griffiths, *Studies in Medieval Irish Legal Ancillary Material*, 88.

51 The word *éim* 'swift, prompt' is commonly used in etymological glosses on the element *im-*; Binchy, "The Linguistic and Historical Value of the Irish Law Tracts," 211–212: in *Celtic Law Papers*, 90; and Taylor-Griffiths, *Studies in Medieval Irish Legal Ancillary Material*, 44–46.

Taiselb*ad* [i] n-ecnairce dorid*h*ne do*n* *sét* sund,[52] ⁊ cindti cona tarr*us*ta in *sét* ina taiselb*ad* and, ⁊ aithg*in* roic amach an fer doroine an taiselbud*h* .i. inti da tucad ar oin he. ⁊ fuair fer frith*i* in *sét* iar sin a n-eccoimd*eth* raed*ha*[53] no sleib*e*. ⁊ da trian do fer frith*i* as, ⁊ in t*r*ian na b*er*and fer f*r*ith*i* de is a br*eith* do*n* fir doroine in taisealb*ad*. ⁊ damud cin*n*ti co tar*us*ta ina t*h*aiselb*ad* he, in trian nac*h* be*ir*ind fer f*r*it*h*i do*n* *sét*, is e fer bunaig dobera.

Taiselb*ad* [i] n-ecnairci dorinde don *sét* sund, ⁊ contab*air*t in tairista ł na tairistea in *sét* ina taisealb*ad*, ⁊ *leth*aithg*in* roic an fer dorigne an taiselb*ad*. ⁊ f*r*ith an *séoit* iar sin a n-eccimdi[g] sleibe; ⁊ da t*r*ian do fir f*r*ith*i* and, ⁊ in trian ail*e* do roin*n* ara do it*er* fer mbunaid*h* ⁊ in fer dorig*h*ne an taisealb*ad*.

Na *séoit* frith*i* dogeib duine; mad *ru*c leis iat ⁊ rofagaib a n-*i*nad*h* *ailiu*, *acht* munab mesa i*n*t inad*h* ar fagaib iat na int inad*h* a fuair, is sl*an*. ⁊ masa mesa, is fia*ch* fo aicn*ed* a ḟath*a* air. ⁊ duine do*na* dl*eg*ar comur na coming*h*aire sin; ⁊ ma dl*eg*ar, is t*r*ian n-aithg*en*a air ana faicsin ar sechran isin lo it*er* comai[th]ch*iu*, ⁊ aithg*in* isin aid*h*ch*i* isin faicsin ar bru mona ł c*h*uit*h*i.

Da t*r*ian isin f*r*ith*e* raed*ha* ł sleib*e*, ⁊ cethr*aimth*e cach mairt mainig*h*th*er* coland i sleib suidith*er* ara br*eith*, ara fenda[d], *ar*a t*h*aisg*id*, ara comrain*n*. Is ma*cht*n*ad* so ⁊ co na inand inad a fagab*ar* iatt. Is h*e* in fa*th* fo*dera*: in bail*e* ata cethr*aimth*e ca*ch* mairt mainid*h*ther, rob*a* aithne do fer an c*h*ruid*h* and

52 The scribe wrote an incorrect letter after the ⟨u⟩ and attempted to correct part of it to make the following ⟨n⟩.

53 The first ⟨a⟩ is written subscript.

He made an 'assigning possession to one who is absent'[54] regarding the property here, and [it is] certain that the property could not be got hold of when it was assigned, and he paid out restitution to the person who did the assigning, i.e., the one to whom it had been given on loan [pays the restitution]. And a finder [sc., not the person who made the declaration] found the property afterwards in an unfrequented place of a wood or mountain. And two thirds of it to the finder, and the third that the finder does not take from it, it is given to the person who did the assigning. And if it may be certain that it could be got hold of when it was declared, the third that the finder does not take from the property, [the] original owner receives it.

He made an 'assigning possession to one who is absent' regarding the property here, and [it is] doubtful whether the property could be got hold of or not when it was assigned, and the person who did the assigning receives half compensation. And the property is found afterwards in an unfrequented place of a mountain; and two thirds to the finder then, and the other third is divided in two between the original owner and the man who did the assigning.

The property that someone will find; if he takes them [sc., the property] with him and he left [them] in another place, provided that the place he left them is not worse than the place where he found [them], he is exempt from liability. And if it is worse, [he owes] a fine of theft according to the nature of his reason regarding it. And that is a person who is not bound by co-tillage or joint grazing; and if he is bound, he receives a third of the compensation for seeing them astray in the daytime between neighbors, and [full] compensation for seeing [them] in the night on the edge of a bog or pit.

Two thirds for something found in a wood or on a mountain, and a fourth [of its value] for each cow whose flesh is fattened on a mountain, which is proved by carrying it away, by skinning it, by guarding it, by dividing it. This is a surprise seeing that the place where they are found is the same. The reason is: where there is a fourth for each cow which is fattened, he knew the owner of the livestock in that case, and it is proper for him to guard it until

54 *Taiselbad* is the vn. of *do-aissilbi* and has a range of meanings including 'assigning, ascribing, showing, exhibiting'; see *eDIL* s.v. *taiselbad*; Rudolf Thurneysen, "Aus dem irischen Recht II," *ZCP* 15 (1925): 238–276, at 269; and Roland M. Smith, "The Alphabet of Cuigne Mac Emoin," *ZCP* 17 (1928): 45–72, at 51, § 25. The sense here is that someone has found livestock and stated who the owner is; in this case, the owner of the livestock is not present. See also *AL* 5: 329.27; and the Introduction, p. 39.

sin, ⁊ coir do a taisc*id nó* co tisad*h* fer bun*aidh* ⁊ coir cin co b*eth* do a*cht* ceth-
f. 63b *raimthe* | air. *Nochar*b ait*h*ne do fer in cruid*h* isin f*r*ith*e* raed*ha* ł sleibe, ⁊ coir cia dob*eth* da t*r*ian *ar*a fag*h*b*ail*.

Escaire in f*r*it*h*i tiri co *secht* n-i*n*adaib ad*eir* dl*ig*i[d]: fia lu*cht* aenlis ⁊ aenbail*i* an *sechtmad*. Esgaire an f*r*ith*i* fairgi fona t*r*i crichaib is nesa do muir, ł do duine maith an ca*ch* cri*ch* dib*h*, ⁊ a escaire do loingsechaib mara in *ceth*ram*ad* inad*h*. Cosna ceithr*i* inadaib no cosna *secht* n-inadaib ad*eir* dlig*ed* an cach crich dib-sin.

Frithe tra*chta*:[y] dilis do fir fodngaib a*cht cóic*id a loige do fir [bunaid] (odngaib), ma eccoimdi[g]. Mad coimdi[g], is dilis a*cht cóic*ed*h seiss*ed[z] a loige do neoch besa ae riam.

[y] .i. f*r*ith*e* dogab*ar* isin *tracht*.
[z] .i. *ar*in t*r*ic*h*adm*ad* rand.

Cuiged as a ecoimdeg*h* d'fir bun*aid*, ⁊ uil*e* d'fir (buna)[55] frith*i* as a coimdi[g] cinmotha in trich*atmad* rand as d'fir buna[id]. Iss edh is coimdi[g] trag*ha* and: cach inot ait*h*id daine ⁊ longo maraen, ł daine ⁊ tonda co coitcind. Iss ed is eccoimdi[g] trad*ha* and: cach bail*e* na h-aithit *acht* longa a n-oenar no tonda ⁊ is luga ataithit daine.

55 I follow the emendation suggested by Binchy, *CIH* 58, n. c.

[the] original owner should come, and it is right that he should only have but a fourth | for it. He did not know the owner of the livestock regarding something found in a wood or on a mountain, and it is right that he should have two thirds for finding it. f. 63b

Proclamation of something found on land to [the] seven places that [the] law says: in the presence of people of the same dwelling and the same settlement [as] the seventh. Proclamation of something found in the sea throughout the three territories which are closest to the sea, or to a respectable person in each territory of them, and proclaiming it to sailors[56] of [the] sea [is] the fourth place. To the four places or to the seven places, [the] law says, in each territory of these.

Something found on the shore:[y] [it is] forfeit to [the] person who finds it, except a fifth of its value for [the] original owner, if [it is found in] an unfrequented place. If [it is found in] a frequented place, it is forfeit except a fifth of a sixth [i.e., 1/30][z] of its value for [the] previous owner.

[y] i.e., a found item which is found on the shore.
[z] i.e., for the thirtieth part.

A fifth of it in an unfrequented place for [the] original owner, and all of it for [the] finder in a frequented place except the thirtieth part of it for [the] original owner. This is what is a frequented place of the shore then: each place that people and boats both frequent, or people and waves in common. This is what is an unfrequented place of the shore then: each place not frequented but by boats alone or waves and it is least frequented by people.

56 *Loingsech* here can hardly refer to a 'pirate, exile, banished man, or sea-rover'. It is more likely that one of the word's meanings, i.e., 'wanderer', has been tranfered to 'those who wander on the sea', thus 'sailors'. It is very unlikely that the legal commentaries would suggest that the finder should approach bands of pirates on the sea and ask them if they have lost anything lately.

Sruth saile, sal sceo uisci, .i. mas ina*n*d fer f*r*ithe ⁊ fer tire, is 'na rog*h*a ata in cuiti f*r*ith*i* no in cuiti tire bias do; ⁊ is as gabur eiseig: "conte*cht*a gnimea[57] no tire." Masa saine fer f*r*ith*i* ⁊ fer tire, cuitid tire d'fir t*h*ire, ⁊ cuiti f*r*it*h*i do fir frithe.

Mairbdili sin, ł is beodili na coimgend[58] tia*cht*ain as a dualgus a nirt fein, uair da coi*m*gitis, *no*c*h*o bia ni esitib.

O bias fer bunaid*h* a'toig*h*lenm*h*uin a *sét*, ⁊ o doc*h*ifi[59] roim*he* iat in dara fe*cht* cinco faici in fe*cht* aile ł tanaisti, *no*chon fuil cuiti f*r*it*h*i na tob*aig* na tab*ar*ta uad*h*a aistib.

Noch*o*n fuil ni asna beodili do g*r*es i cuairt ingeltad, ⁊ cuiti tob*aig* aistib a *secht*arcuairt ingelt*a*. No cuiti frith*i* aistib a cuaird ingelta ł co mb*et* ar taisc*id* gat*aig*i, ⁊ o b*et* ar taiscid gat*aig*i, is cuiti tob*aig* aistib. Cuiti tobaid aistib a *secht*arcuaird ingeltad, a*cht* munab amlaid*h* robada*r* ⁊ a n-aid*h*id*h* ara tech. ⁊ mas aml*aid*, a*cht* masi cindti co tiucfatais, is [s]l*an* doib ⁊[60] *noch*an [f]uil ni

---

57 There is a *punctum* under the ⟨e⟩. It is difficult to determine whether it is a mistake or meant as a means of deleting the ⟨e⟩. In the line below this word in the MS, the *punctum* would appear between the ⟨u⟩ and ⟨i⟩ of *cuiti*, so it is unlikely that it was intended to be a lenition mark on *cuiti*.

58 The verb *coimgend* is a MI form of the 3 sg. pres. act. ind. of *con-icc* 'can, is able'.

59 The verb is a MI 3 sg. pres. fut. form of *ad-cí* 'sees'; *eDIL* s.v. *ad-cí* 'sees'.

60 From here to the end of the commentary, the ink is rather watery and the letters become rather thicker. In some places the text is difficult to read due to how much the ink from some letters has bled into others.

Stream of saltwater, sea and freshwater,[61] i.e., if the finder and the landowner are the same, it is his choice whether he will have the share of the thing found or the share of the land, and that is taken from: "equally valid are acts or lands."[62] If the finder and the landowner are different, a share of the land for the landowner and a share of the thing found for the finder.

Those [things are] inanimate property, or it is livestock[63] that is not capable of escaping on account of their own strength, because if they were capable,[64] there would not be anything from them.

When the original owner will be pursuing his property, and if he will see them before him at one time though he does not see [them] at another or second time, there will not be a share of the things found, nor of recovering, nor of taking due from him [sc., the original owner] out of them [sc., the property].[65]

There is never anything from the livestock in a grazing enclosure, and a share of recovering from them beyond the grazing enclosure. Or a share of something found from them in a grazing enclosure if[66] they may be in the possession of a thief, and if they may be in the possession of a thief, it is a share of recovering from them. A share of recovering from them beyond the grazing enclosure, unless they had been [found] thus with their face towards their home.[67] And if it is so, provided that it is certain that they would have come [home], he [sc., the finder] is exempt from liability for them and there

---

61 The phrase *sruth sáile sál sceo uisci* is problematic. It is difficult to determine whether the phrase is a list of two, three, or four things: i.e., 'stream of sea saltwater and freshwater', 'stream of saltwater, sea, and freshwater' or 'stream, salt water, sea, and freshwater'. The difficulty is that that gen. sg. of *sál* 'the ocean, seawater', *sáile*, is also a distinct lexical item meaning 'salt water, the sea'; *eDIL* s.v. *sáile*. The editors of *AL* translate the phrase as a list of four items; *AL* 5: 333.5. See also the commentaries on streams in Heptad 64, source J, and *Muirbretha*, sources C and D; the interpretation given here and in Heptad 64, source J, is based on the material in *Muirbretha/Bretha Éitgid*, source C. The commentary here (and the paragraphs immediately following) and in source J seem to be taken from commentary associated with *Muirbretha*.

62 The sense of the quotation seems to be that finding something is equal in terms of a claim to it as that which washes up on someone's own land.

63 *Beodili* 'livestock, animate property' is pl. here.

64 The verb *coimgitis* is a 3 sg. past. subj. of *con-icc* 'able, capable'.

65 The reason that the owner does not owe the finder a share is because he himself is close on the trail of his own property and is likely to find it himself.

66 Although *no co* usually means 'until, unless', the English requires 'if' for the translation to make sense. It is possible that this is an early scribal mistake as the construction appears in other versions of the commentary below.

67 The sense is that the livestock had been found outside the enclosure but facing their homestead and knew their way home.

aistib. Masa cindti na ticfatais, is cuiti tob*aig* coml*an* aistib. Masa m*a*rbdil*i*[68] conic a ngait fein, is cuit tob*aig* aistib do g*r*es.

Trian a cotach frith*i* o daermanach[69] (do g*r*es)[70] ecl*aise* do ecl*ais* no o daerceil*e* fl*ath*a do fl*aith* co rud ł ecmacht ł diraind, ⁊ noma[d] mas and side.[71] C*eth*rami a cota [frithi][72] o saerman*ach* ecl*ais*i d'ecl*ais* co rud*h*, .i. caill,[73] no ecm*acht*, .i. loch,[74] no diraind, .i. sliab*h*,[75] ⁊ ai*le* dec ma[d]h andsid*he*, ⁊ ni [ḟ]uil ni o særceil*e* fl*ath*a do fl*aith* an*n*-side. Can asa ngab*ar* an aile dec, uair nach indisind leb*ar*? Is as gab*air*: "uair is e t*r*ian a cotac*h* ata o daerman*ach* ecl*aise* do ecl*ais* ⁊ o daercail*e* fl*ath*a do fl*aith* co rud*h* ł ecm*acht* no dirind ata uath*aib* a rud*h*;" cub*aid* deiseic com*ad* he t*r*ian na cota ata o saerman*ach* ecl*aise* do ecl*ais* co rud ł ecm*acht* ł dirain*n* dob*eth* uath*aib* a rud*h* fon cum*a* cet*na* .i. aile dec.

Mo isin f*r*ith*e* t*r*ach*t*a na isin f*r*ith*e* raeda. Is e in fat*h* fod*era*: doit*h* muir ⁊ [daine] (tir)[76] do tocsal in frith*i* t*r*ach*t*a, ⁊ ni doit*h* *acht* daine nama do focsal an f*r*ith*i* raed*ha*.

Is aistib ath*a* cuiti f*r*ith*i*: *séoit thes*ta o duine ⁊ ni fit*ir* can a fuil siat, ⁊ cuit f*r*ith*i* donti fuair iat fo aic*ned* coimdi[g] no eccoimdi[g].

Is asta atha cuit tob*aig*: *séoit* toibgis duine do reir dlig*id* ⁊ muna damtar ce*r*t d*h*o, (⁊) [is][77] cuit tob*aig* do fo aic*ned* na crich*e* as*ar* tob[aig] iat.

68 Cf. TCD MS 1336 (source D), *CIH* 2066.37 'beodile'.

69 Binchy, *CIH* 59, n. b, queries whether the suspension mark made over the ⟨h⟩ is an error. It does, indeed, seem to be so.

70 I follow the emendation suggested by Binchy, *CIH* 59, n. c.

71 Binchy, *CIH* 59, n. d, queries whether the reading 'mas and side' is correct. Although the vellum is stained with a substance that has faded the ink and allowed the writing on f. 63c to bleed through the vellum, the reading is correct.

72 I follow the emendation suggested by Binchy, *CIH* 59, n. e.

73 '.i. caill' is an interlinear gloss.

74 '.i. loch' is an interlinear gloss.

75 '.i. sliabh' is an interlinear gloss.

76 Cf. *CIH* 56.24–25 above: *doigh muir ⁊ daine do foxail in frithi trachta, ⁊ nochon doich acht daine nama do foxal an frithi roeda.* It is likely that the commentary ought to read *daine* here instead of *tír*.

77 I follow the emendation suggested by Binchy, *CIH* 58, n. g.

is nothing from them. If it is certain that they would not have come [home], it is a full share of recovering from them. If it is inanimate property which cannot steal themselves,[78] it is always a share of recovering from them.

A third of his share of something found from a base monastic client to his church or from a lord's base client to his lord as far as a wood or inaccessible place or unclaimed land, and a ninth if it is in those [places].[79] A fourth of his share of something found from a monastic free client to his church as far as a wood, i.e., a forest, or inaccessible place, i.e., a lake, or unclaimed place, i.e., a mountain, and a twelfth if it is in those, and there is nothing from a lord's free client to his lord in that case. Whence is the twelfth taken, because [the] book does not say? It is taken from: "because it is a third of his share that is from a base monastic client to his church and from a lord's base client to his lord as far as a wood or inaccessible place or unclaimed land which is due from them in a wood;" it is proper that it may be a third of the share that is from a free monastic client to his church as far as a wood or inaccessible place or unclaimed land which should be due from them in a wood similarly, i.e., a twelfth.

[There is] more for something found on a shore than for something found in a wood. The reason is: it is likely that [both the] sea and people could carry off something found on the shore, and it is likely that only people could carry off something found in the wood.

It is from these that there is a share of something found: property which someone has lost and he does not know where they [sc., the goods] are, and a share of something found for the one who found them according to [whether they are found in] a frequented or unfrequented place.

It is from these that there is a share of recovering: property which a person recovers according to law and unless right is allowed to him, it is a share of recovering for him according to the nature of the land from which he recovered them.[80]

78 This is in contrast to animate property, e.g., slaves, who can run away.

79 According to the commentary, both lay and monastic base clients owe their superior a percentage of the reward they receive for a find. For the same divisions regarding finding a swarm of bees, see *GEIL* 124; *EIF* 407; and *Bechbretha* § 49 and 171(f). See also Brian D. Joseph, "Comparative Perspectives on Bee Law in Indo-European," *Chatreššar* (2018/2): 16–25.

80 This paragraph refers to recovering stolen property which has been found in the possession of a thief.

Is asta ata cuit impi[de]: *séoit* na dlid*h*in*n* do reir dlig*id* ⁊ cin*n*ti ɫ co*n*ndtab*air*t *con*[ad] *ar* impi[de] tuc*ad* iat; ⁊ trian *ar* impi[de] cindti ⁊ seisi *ar* impi[de] *cond*tab*ar*taid. In ta*n* foilis nech in *séotu* ⁊ ni tiubr*atha* d*h*o ma*n*a b*eth* impide, is cuit tob*aig* as fo aic*ned* na crich*e*. Ma ta for tarngaire, ci ar impide tuca, cona b*et* ni aire.

Is asta atait na seoit imluaid*he*: *séoit* robat*ar* ac fir buna[id] a n-ina[d] ail*e*, ⁊ roerb*us*tar do duine airithe dul ara cend, ɫ cincor erb*a*, rob [ḟ]errdi[81] leis a dul ara cend, ⁊ *séoit* imluaid*h* dont*hi* docuaid*h* ara cend fo aic*ned* eled*h*nai[g] ɫ nemhel*adnaig* .i. screp*al* cac*h* eledn*aig* ɫ le*th*screp*al* cac*h* nemeledna[ig]. ⁊ is e air*et* atait na *séoit* imluaid*he* dont*hi* docuaid*h*: co ria cuiti tob*aig* fo aic*ned* na criche, ⁊ ni teit tairis.

[Fr]ithi fairge: dil*es* do neoch fotagaib *acht cóice*d*h seiss*ed*h*[aa] a loid*he* do neoch bes ai riam.

[aa] .i. *ar*in trich*atmad* rand.

A dil*se* uile d'fir *f*rith*i* cinmoth*a* in trich*atmad* rand as a eccoimdi[g] d'fir bun*aid*, ⁊ noch*on* [ḟ]uil coimdi[g] ɫ eccoimdi[g] aice. In duine fuair ɫ fogeb*a* frit*h*i isna h-inotaib-si*n*, is ed dl*eg*ar de. Masa frith*e* tire, a escaire a se*cht*

81 I follow the emendation suggested by Binchy, *CIH* 59, n. i.

It is from these that there is an 'intervention share':[82] property that he is not entitled to according to law, and it is certain or doubtful that it was not by intervention that they were obtained; and [he receives] a third [if it is] certain [that he got the goods] by intervention and a sixth [if it is] doubtful [that he got the goods] by intervention. When someone tracks the property and they [sc., the property] would not be recovered by him [sc., the owner] unless it were [by the] intervention, it is a share of recovering from it according to the nature of the land [where it was found]. If there is a promise for it, though it may be recovered by intervention, there would be nothing for it.

It is from these that there are the *séts* of driving [cattle]: livestock which [the] original owner had in one place, and he had entrusted a certain person to go fetch them, or, though he did not entrust [him], he [sc., the owner] would prefer him [sc., the other person] to go fetch them, and *séts* of driving for the one who went to fetch them according to whether [he is] trained or untrained, i.e., a scruple for each trained [person] or a half scruple for each untrained [person].[83] And this is the amount that the *séts* of driving are due to the one who went [for them]: up to a share of recovering according to the nature of the land, and it [sc., the amount due to the driver] does not go beyond it.[84]

Something found in the sea: [it is] forfeit to [the] person who finds it, except a fifth of a sixth [i.e., 1/30][aa] of its value for [the] previous owner.

[aa] i.e., for the thirtieth part.

Its complete forfeiture to the finder except for a thirtieth part of it for the original owner in an unfrequented place, and it [sc., the sea] does not have a 'frequented' or 'unfrequented' place. The person who found or will find something in these places, this is what he is bound [to do]. If it is something found on land,[85] proclaiming it in the seven places [the] law says: to a

82 The circumstances in this paragraph concern acquiring goods to which one has no clear legal right. The sense is that the goods, while found in someone else's possession, would not have been recovered without the intervention of the person in whose possession the goods are found. Whether the goods were obtained by intervention with all good intentions or as a means of masking theft would depend on the circumstances.

83 The sense here is that the amount that the driver is given depends on how skillfully he does his work.

84 For driving payments, see also Heptad 65, *CIH* 62.26–28.

85 See also *Aidbred* § 8 commentary for the same procedure for proclaiming items found on the land or in the sea.

n-inata ad*eir* dlige[d]: co ri, co h-aircindech, co primgabaind *tuait*he, co briu*gaid*, co breithe*main*, co muilind *tuaithe*, fia lu*cht* aenlis ⁊ oenbail*i*. Masa fr*ith*i fairgi, dl*eg*ar a escaire do duine mait*h* in cach crich dona t*r*i crich*aib* is nesa d*ho*, no coma *secht* n-inata in cach cric*h* dib, ⁊ muir in c*eth*rama[d] cr*ich*. ⁊ da mbe*t*ais daine arin muir, is a n-escaire doib.

Ma roescair fia daine ⁊ dorinde dlige[d] fr*ith*i, ⁊ romair co iar ndechma, is [s]l*an* cuit a fr*ith*e d*h*o. Muna derna a dlige[d][86] *frithi* ⁊ rocait*h* ria ndechm*aid*, is l*an*fiach gaiti uad. Muna derna a dlig*ed* f*rithi* ⁊ romair aice co iar ndechm*aid*, no ma doroine a dlidhe[d] f*rithi* ⁊ rocait*h* ria ndechm*aid*, cin cuite f*rithi* d*ho* ⁊ cin fiach gaiti uaid*h*, *acht* aithgin in frithe.

Cid fo*dera* in *sét* dob*eir* duine leis t*ar* nai tonda m*ar*a co fuil a dil*se* d*ho*, ⁊ in *sét* dogab*ar* arin muir amuich co fuil in trichat rand as d'fir bun*aid*? Is e

f. 63c in fat*h*: in *sét* dob*eir* duine leis tar nai tonda m*ar*a | amuic*h*, ara cend d'aentoisc docuid*h*; coir cema dil*es* d*h*o h*e*. In set dogeib duine arin muir amuich, ni ar cend d'aentoisc docuaid*h* in duine and-seic, coir cia *nobeth* ni as d'fir bun*aid*.

Cid fodeara in frit*h*i trac*h*ta[87] co fuil ni as d'fir bun*aid*, ⁊ in frith*e* dogeib fear fine itir noi tonda mara ⁊[88] [tír] *con*a fuil ni as d'fir bun*aid*? Is e in fa*th*: dlig*ed* tab*ar*ta dilsis in [d]ara[89] de, ⁊ dlig*ed* frith*i* dilsidis arail*e*, ⁊ mo (dil)[90] dilsidis tabairt na frithe.

86 Binchy, *CIH* 60, n. b, notes that this word is followed by ⟨dlid*he*⟩, which the scribe has deleted by underlining.

87 The scribe originally wrote the symbol for *acht/sed*, as he normally does for this word. He then wrote ⟨ct⟩ without trying to cancel the *acht/sed* symbol.

88 Binchy, *CIH* 60, n. d, suggests deleting the '⁊'.

89 I follow the emendation suggested by Binchy, *CIH* 60, n. e.

90 This appears to be an error of dittography.

king [e.g., at his court], to an ecclesiastical superior, to a *túath*'s chief smith, to a hospitaller, to a judge, at a *túath*'s mill, in the presence of people of the same dwelling and same settlement [in which he found it]. If it is something found in the sea, he is bound to proclaim it to a respectable person in each territory from the three territories which are closest to it, or that it may be the seven places in each territory of them, and the sea is the fourth territory. And if there should be people on the sea, they [sc., the found goods] are to be proclaimed to them.

If he made a proclamation [that he found lost property] in the presence of people and he fulfilled the law of finds, and it [sc., the property found] remained [in his possession] until after ten days [had passed], he is free to have a share of what he found. If he does not fulfill the law of finds and he used [it] before ten days [have passed], the full fine of theft is owed from him. If he does not fulfill the law of finds and it remained in his possession until after ten days [have passed], or if he fulfilled the law of finds and he used [it] before ten days [have passed], he is without a share of what he found and the fine of theft is not owed from him, but restitution of what he found.

What is the reason that the property a person brings with him [from] beyond nine waves of the sea is forfeited to him, and for the property that is found [floating] out on the sea there is one thirtieth of it for the original owner? The reason is: the property that a person takes with him [from] beyond nine waves of the open sea |, he purposely went to fetch it, it is right f. 63c
that it should be forfeited to him. The property that a person will find out on the sea, the person did not go purposely to fetch it in that case, it is right that there should be something from it for the original owner.[91]

What is the reason that for something found on the shore there is something from it for the original owner, and for the item that a local will find between nine waves of the sea and land there is nothing from it for the original owner? The reason is: [it is the] law of taking that gives right for one [case] and [the] law of finding that gives right in the other, and [the law of] taking gives greater right than [the law of] finds.

91 The distinction being made here is between someone who goes out beyond the ninth wave of the sea to retrieve an item found floating on the water (presumably the item can be seen from the shore), and someone who happens to be in a boat beyond the ninth wave of the sea who just happens to pick up an item found floating on the water.

Cid fo*dera* in frith*e* dogab*ar* arin muir moir co fuil in t*r*icha rand as d'fir bun*aid*, ⁊ corub tab*air*t dilsidis h*e* o sin amach, ⁊ na *séoit* dob*er*ur as it*er* noi tonda mara ⁊ tir cona dil*es* uile? Is e in fat*h*: feime ⁊ urias*acht*[92] ⁊ fin[e]c[h]aire dilsidis na *séoit* dob*er*ur it*er* noi ton*na* maro ⁊ tir, ⁊ dlige[d] tabarta nama dil*siges* na *séoit* dob*er*ur don muir moir amuich.

Cuiti[93] f*r*it*hi* a beodil*ib* a crich ⁊ marbdil*ib* cid a crit*h* cid sec*ht*ar crich; o gebait beodil*i* indscuch*ud* criche ⁊ o b*eth* ar fuirire*th* gaidi, is cuiti tob*aig* asta.

Cuiti frith*i* a bech*aib* ⁊ a daine doer*aib*; no coma cuit astait*hi*, *acht* m*un*ab e frecr*a* in dair curub[94] ac tia*cht*ain da [tech] (tid) robi se, ⁊ mas e is do rosoich, ⁊ a dul-sum cin ni. Mas aml*aid* frit*h* h*e* ⁊ a cul ri tech, ⁊ nir airb*ert*naid*h* nach ac el*od* robui, is a denam conad ac el*od* robui, ⁊ cuiti tob*aig* as.

Marbdil*i* nama indisis sund ⁊ cuit fir ainbine, ⁊ beodil*i* ⁊ cuit fir fine, it e na tait*h*mit and, *acht* is friu riad*h*ailt*ir*. ⁊ is i riag*ail* fil isna frith*ib*-seo: ani b*erus* fer ainbin*e* a eccoimdi[g], is *ed* ber*is* fer fin*e* a coimdi[g], ⁊ ini [ḟ]uil a coimdi[g] in frit*hi* romut, is *ed* [ḟ]uil a ecoim[dig] in frith*i* is nesa cinmoth*a* na ded*hinc*ha—is [s]ain a mbre*ithe*mn*acht*-saige frisna frith*i* olcena.

A m*ar*bdil*ib* fine ⁊ ainbfi*n*e ath*a* in cuiti frith*i*-seo. Beodil*i* fine im*morro*, ni [ḟ]uil [ní][95] eistib a cuairt comai[th]c*h*esa. Beodil*i* fine im*morro* o cuairt comai[th]ch(c)esa amach, ⁊ beodil*i* ainbine cid a cuairt com[aith]c[h]esa, m*un*ad bid*h* comingaire d*ho*, is fega[d] cota f*r*it*hi* no cota tob*aig* aistib am*ail* roraidsimair.

---

92 Binchy, CIH 60, n. f, queries the correct reading of this word; he is uncertain of the final letter. He queries whether the reading should be 'uriass̄' with the suspension stroke mistakenly put over the first ⟨s⟩. The reading is the MS is 'urias̄'.

93 As Binchy, CIH 60, n. g, notes, this word is followed by an ⟨f⟩ with a suprascript ⟨i⟩ which has been partially erased.

94 The scribe originally wrote 'curbeub' but cancelled the ⟨be⟩ by placing a *punctum* under each letter; see also Binchy, CIH 60, n. h.

95 I follow the emendation suggested by Binchy, CIH 60, n. l.

What is the reason that for the item that is found in the sea there is one thirtieth of it for the original owner, and that [the law of] taking gives right to it from then onwards, and the property which is taken from it between nine waves of the sea and land are completely forfeit? The reason is: refusal and permission and kindred that make the property which is taken between nine waves of the sea and land forfeit, and [the] law of taking only gives right to the property which is taken from the open sea.

A share of something found from livestock in a territory and from inanimate property whether in a territory or beyond a territory; when livestock will depart from a territory and when it might be in consequence of theft, it is a share of recovering from them.

A share of something found from bees[96] and from unfree people;[97] or that it may be a share of detention[98] unless the answer of the unfree person is that he was coming to his home, and if it is so, he can [go], and he [sc., the detainer] goes without anything. If he is found thus and his back [is] to his home, and he does not plead that he is not escaping, and it must be proved that he was escaping, and a share of recovering from it.

Inanimate property only that it [sc., the textual source] discusses here and a stranger's share, and animate property and a local's share, they do not explain them here, but it is regulated regarding them. And this is the law that there is for these things which are found: that which a stranger takes from an unfrequented place is [equivalent to] what a local takes from a frequented place [regarding their respective share], and that which is from something found in a frequented place [that we discussed] previously is [equivalent to] what is from something found in an unfrequented place [that we discussed] next, except for things found [which we shall discuss] lastly—their adjudication is different from the other things which are found otherwise.

From [the] inanimate property of a local or of a stranger there are these shares of something found. A local's livestock, however, there is nothing from them in a neighboring grazing enclosure. A local's livestock, however, outside a neighboring grazing enclosure, and a stranger's livestock although in a neighboring grazing enclosure, unless he is bound by joint grazing, a share of something found or a share of recovering from them is to be considered as we have said.

---

96 On the finder's share of a swarm of bees found on common land, see *EIF* 407, and *Bechbretha* § 49 and 171(f).

97 The commentary mainly concerns detaining anyone considered to be unfree who may or may not be attempting to escape.

98 The share for detention seems to refer to a share for detaining a possible runaway.

Coimdi[g] carut is e eccoimdi[g] escarut isna frith*ib*-seo anuas uil*i*. Is aml*aid*-seo eisid*he*: in tan ata *cóic*ed*h* as a eccoimdi[g] d'fir ainbin*e*, is [s]eisi[d] d'fir fine. C*et*[h]raim*the*[99] as a coi*m*di[g] d'fir ainbine ⁊ *cóic*ed*h* d'fir fine; f*rithe* treibe sin. C*eth*raime as a [ec]*coimdid*[100] d'[ḟ]ir ainfine[101] ⁊ *cóic*ed*h* d'fir fine.[102] T*r*ian as a coimdi[g] d'fir [ainf]ine[103] ⁊ *cet*[h]raim*the* d'fer [ḟ]ine, ⁊ f*rithe* cath*rach* sin. Da t*r*ian mad ecoimdi[g] d'fer anf*ine* ⁊ l*eth* d'fer [ḟ]ine. Mad[104] *coimdig*, is *teor*a *ceth*raime d'fir ainf*ine* ⁊ da t*r*ian d'fer [ḟ]ine; f*rithe* r*ofida* ł s*leibe*. ⁊ *noch*a fed*har coimdig* na ecco*imdig ar*in farce, *acht* diles d'fer f*rithi* cin*m*oth*a* in trich*atmad* rann d'[ḟ]ir bu*n*a[id]. Is aire is mo 'sa coimdi[g] na as ecoi*m*di[g] *ar* docus daine do tecmaisi*n* cuc*a* indtusin. No d*ano* c*ona* b*eth* d*eth*b*ir* fir [ḟ]ine na h-ainbine ca*ch* uair na fil*et cóic* sle*cht*a fith*et* in Cor*us* Fine et*a*ru, ⁊ ma ta, noch*on* [ḟ]uil fia*ch* foimri*me* o cach dib da ceil*e* na cuitit f*rithi*.

Dia n-urfocr*a* ⁊ nir cait*h* co dechm*aid*, is diles do a cuiti f*rithi* ⁊ a fomuilt. Mun[a][105] focr*a* ⁊ rocait*h* ria ndechm*aid*, ⁊ curob aisneis dob*e*rur fair, is landire fair. Mun[a] [f]ocr*a* co tora a iaraid*h* ⁊ co roich iaraid, ⁊ ni ceil in tan doric,[106] is dil*es* a cuit f*r*i*thi*. M*una* focr*a* ⁊ rocait*h* ria ndechm*aid*, is l*eth*dire.

---

99 Binchy, CIH 60, n. m, notes that the scribe originally wrote 'asa coi*m*di', but then crossed it out as it is an error of dittography.

100 I follow the emendation suggested by Binchy, CIH 60, n. n.

101 Binchy, CIH 60, n. o, states that the dot under the ⟨i⟩ is surely not meant as a *punctum delens*. There is also a blotch of ink under the second ⟨i⟩ in this word.

102 Binchy, CIH 60, n. p, notes that three letters have been erased before this word. They appear to be ⟨ain⟩.

103 I follow the emendation suggested by Binchy, CIH 60, n. q.

104 The ⟨a⟩ was added in above the ⟨m⟩.

105 The form here and below are both Mod. Ir. forms of the conj. *má* with the neg. particle; *eDIL* s.v. 3 *má, ma*.

106 Binchy, CIH 61, n. a, queries whether this form is a mistake for *doroich*. The verb form appears to be a 3 sg. pres. act. ind. prototonic form of *do-roich*. In consideration of the fact that this verb form appears above and elsewhere in the other versions of the heptad, it has not been emended as Binchy suggests.

A frequented place of a friend is [equivalent to] an unfrequented place of an enemy for all of these things found above.[107] It is thus: when there is a fifth of it from an unfrequented place for a stranger, it is a sixth for a local. A fourth of it from a frequented place for a stranger and a fifth for a local; that is something found in a dwelling. A fourth of it from an unfrequented place for a stranger and a fifth for a local. A third of it from a frequented place for a stranger and a fourth for a local, and that is something found in an enclosure. Two thirds if it is an unfrequented place for a stranger and half for a local. If it is a frequented place, it is three fourths for a stranger and two thirds for a local; that is something found in a wood or on a mountain. And [neither] a 'frequented' place nor an 'unfrequented' is considered in the sea, but it is forfeit to [the] finder except for one thirtieth for [the] original owner. This is [the] reason that there is more from it in a frequented place than from it in an unfrequented place: because it is probable people [will] happen upon them in these places. Or, on the other hand, that there might not be a difference of local or stranger each time that the 25 divisions in *Córus Fine*[108] are not between them, and if there is, there is not a fine of unauthorized use from each of them to the other of the share of something found.

If he makes a proclamation and he did not use [it] until ten days [have passed], his share of something found and its use are forfeit to him. If he does not make a proclamation and he used [it] before ten days [have passed] and [that] information is brought against him, it is the full fine [that he owes] for it. If he does not make a proclamation until someone comes seeking it and someone comes [to him] seeking [it], and he does not conceal [it] when he comes, his share of the thing found is forfeit [to him]. If he does not make a proclamation and he used [it] before ten days [have passed], it is half penalty [that he owes].

107 The terms *cara* 'friend' and *escarae* 'enemy' are likey being used here as being equivalent to 'local' and 'stranger', respectively.

108 *GEIL* 270; and *CCIH* 235–239.

Source B, RIA MS 23 Q 6 [1243], 40b–41b, *CIH* 1209.16–1212.2

p. 40b **Atat *secht* frithe la *Féniu*: f*rithe* treibe, f*rithe* ca[th]*rach*,[109] f*rithe* faiche,[110] f*rithe* raiti, f*rithe* rofed*ha* [nó][111] f*rithe* sleibe, f*rithe* fairge, f*rithe* tr*ach*ta.**

Is cut*ruma* ata cuiti f*rithi* [cid d]ó fi*ne* (⁊) [cid d]ó[112] anfi*ne*, u*air* is cutrum*a* regait a les a *sét* do mar*thain* doib. No d*ano cona* be*th* cuiti f*rithi* on fir fi*ne da* c*h*eile, uair dlega*r* dé *sét* in fir fi*ne aili* do com*ét* cach uair ata comar ⁊ comingaire aca. ł atait *cóic* s*lechta fich*it[113] in Corusa Fi*ne etar*(u)ra, ⁊ cac*h* uair na filit si*n etar*(u)r*u*, ata cuit f*rithi* ó cac*h* dib *da* ceile, ⁊ ata fiac*h* foimr*ime* ó cac*h* dib *da* ceile.

An scor gi*n* taiselb*ad*: is ai*thgin* in*n*; in scor g*o* taiselb*ad*: is [s]lan. In taiselb*ad* n-ecnairc, masa cin*n*ti g*o* tar*us*ta is [s]l*an*. ⁊ masa con*n*tab*air*t an tar*us*ta, is l*ethaithgin*, ⁊ fiad*nais*e coitcen*n* dogni an*n* sin an tar*usta* no na tar*usta*, ł is ó dui*ne* fei*n* tig.[114] Taiselb*ad* n-ecnairc dorig*hni* don *sét* sun*n*, ⁊ cin*n*ti g*o*na tar*usta* in *sét* i*na* taiselb*ad* an*n*, ⁊ ai*thgin* roíc am*ach* .i. intí da tug*ad* ar oi*n* é.

109 I follow the emendation suggested by Binchy, *CIH* 1209, n. j.
110 The spelling *faiche* here and throughout is a variant of *faithche* 'green'.
111 Cf. source A, *CIH* 55.19, where the same emendation is necessary.
112 Cf. the other versions of this commentary.
113 The ⟨it⟩ are written above the numeral.
114 Cf. the similar commentary in *Findśruth Fíthail*, *CIH* 2137.4–8.

There are seven [categories of] finds according to Irish law: something found in a dwelling, something found in an enclosure, something found on a green, something found on a rough land, something found in a wood or something found on a mountain, something found in the sea, something found on the shore. p. 40b

The share of something found is the same whether for a local or for a stranger, because they will get the same benefit of the property saved by them. Or, on the other hand, so that there might not be a share of something found from a local to another, because he is obligated to guard the property of another local person every time they have joint ploughing and joint grazing. Or the 25 divisions in *Córus Fine* are between them, and every time those are not between them, there is a share of something found from each of them to the other, and there is a fine of unauthorized use from each of them to the other.

The 'unyoking without assigning to the possession [of someone else]':[115] it is restitution for it; the 'unyoking with assigning to the possession [of someone else]': he is exempt from liability. The 'assigning to the possession of one who is absent':[116] if it is certain that it could be got hold of, he is exempt from liability. And if it is doubtful whether it could be got hold of, it is half restitution, and an impartial witness decides in that case whether or not it could be got hold of, or it is stated by the person himself. He made an 'assigning to the possession of one who is absent' regarding the property here, and it is certain that the property could not be got hold of when it was assigned, and he paid out restitution, i.e., the one to whom it had been given on loan [pays

115 *Scor* it has a range of meanings including 'unyoking, unharnessing, ceasing, encampment, band, pasture'; see *EIF* 572, n. 106; and *eDIL* s.v. *scor*. The phrase *scor cen taiselbad* is also found in the source C, *CIH* 1853.17, version of the commentary and in both of the main versions of *Findśruth Fíthail*: *CIH* 787.33 and 2137.3–4. A draft translation of both versions of *Findśruth Fíthail* by Christopher Guy Yocum is available: https://www.academia.edu/4713943/Finn%E1%B9%A1ruith_F%C3%ADthail_Text_A_TCD_H._3._18_and_Text_B_TCD_H_5._15_ Accessed June 13, 2019. Yocum does not provide a discussion of this phrase. See also *GEIL* 285; and *CCIH* 253–257. I follow Thurneysen's interpretation of *taiselbad*; "Aus dem irisichen Recht II," 269; and Heptad 39, *CIH* 37.8; and *AL* 5: 254.8; see also "*The Alphabet of Cuigne mac Emoin*," 51 § 25. It is possible that the phrase refers to animals found grazing on someone's land where the owner of the livestock is not identified; this would be an unlawful grazing. If the owner of the livestock is identified as a local person, no fine is incurred.

116 In this situation, ownership of the livestock is assigned to someone who is not present.

⁊ fuair fer fr*ithi* in *sét* a n-ecoimde[g] red*h*a ł sl*eb*i, ⁊ *in* t*r*ian na b*er*an*n* fer fr*ithi* d*hé*, is a bre*th* don fer dorin*ne* an t*h*aiselb*ad*. ⁊ *damad* cin*n*ti go t*arrusta* i*na* t*aiselbad* é, an t*r*ian na b*er*an*n* fer f*rithi* d*h*e, b*eir*e fer bunad*h*.

Taiselb*ad* a n-ecnairc dorin*ne* do*n* *sét* sun*n*, ⁊ con*n*tab*airt* *in* t*arusta* ł na t*arrusta* *in* *sét* i*na* t*aiselbad*, ⁊ l*ethaithgin* roíc in fer dorig*hni* in t*aiselbad*. ⁊ fri*th* in *séoit* *iar* si*n* a n-ecoimde[g] r*ofeda* ł s*leibe*, ⁊ da t*r*ian d'fer f*rithi* as ⁊ in t*r*ian *aile* do roin*n* ar do it*er* fer mbuna[id] ⁊ *in* fer dorig*hni* *in* t*aiselbad*.

Marbdile nama it é in*nusus* (*read* innises)[117] sun*n* ⁊ cuit fir ainbfi*ne*, ⁊ beodil*e* ⁊ cuit fir fi*ne*, it é na taith*m*it an*n* si*n*, [acht] is friu riag*h*alt*air*. ⁊ is [s]í riagail fil isna frit*h*aib-so: iní b*erus* fer anfi*ne* a h-ecoim*dig* is *ed* b*erus* fer fine a c*h*oim*dig*, ⁊ iní fuil a coim*dig* i*n* fr*ithi* reomat is *ed* fil a h-ecoim*dig* in fr*ithi* is nesa, gi*n*mot*ha* na deig*hin*ach*a*.

A marbdil*ib* fine ⁊ anfi*ne* ata in cuiti fr*ithi*-so. Beodil*e* fi*ne* im*morro*, ni fuil ní eistib i cu*airt* c*omingaire*,[118] ⁊ ata *sech*tair, ⁊ beodil*e* anfi*ne* cid*h* a cu*airt* c*omingaire* …[119]

Coimdig*h* carat is ecoim*dig* ascarat isna frit*h*ib*h*-so anuas uile. ⁊ is aml*aid*-so éisid*he*: i*n* tan ata *cóic*id*h*[120] as ecoim*dig* d'fer ai*n*fi*ne*, is *seiss*id*h*[121] d'fer fi*ne*; *ceth*raime as coim*dig* d'fer ai*n*fine ⁊ *cóic*id*h*[122] d'fer fi*ne*. ⁊ is *ed* is coim*dig* an*n*: a lar ⁊ airmed*ha* ⁊ inadad*h* soillsi ⁊ i*n*t i*n*ad*h* a mbí ait*h*ig*h* caic*h*. ⁊ is *ed* is ecoim*dig* an*n*: gac*h* inad*h* otha si*n* amac*h*; fri*the* treibe so.

Ceth*ramthu* as ecoim*dig* d'fer ai*n*fi*ne* ⁊ *cóic*id*h*[123] d'fer fi*ne*, t*r*ian as coim*dig* d'fer ai*n*fine ⁊ ceth*ramthu* d'fer fi*ne*. ⁊ is *ed* is coim*dig* an*n*: a h-urlair ⁊ a reilg*i*

---

117 I follow the emendation suggested by Binchy, *CIH* 1209, n. r. The MS has two consecutive symbols for ⟨us⟩.

118 See also Binchy, *CIH* 1210, n. a.

119 Part of the commentary seems to be missing; cf. source A, *CIH* 56.11–13.

120 The ⟨id⟩ are written above the numeral.

121 The ⟨id⟩ are written above the numeral.

122 The ⟨id⟩ are written above the numeral.

123 The ⟨id⟩ are written above the numeral.

the restitution]. And someone finds the property in an unfrequented place of a wood or mountain, and the third that the finder does not take from it, it is given to the person who did the assigning. And if it is certain that it could not be got hold of when it was assigned, the third that [the] finder does not take from it, [the] original owner receives it.

He made an 'assigning to the possession of one who is absent' regarding the property here, and it is doubtful whether the property could be got hold of or not when it was assigned, and the person who did the assigning [sc., identification of the owner] receives half restitution. And the property is found afterwards in an unfrequented place of a wood or mountain, and two thirds from it for [the] finder and the other third is divided in two between [the] original owner and the person who did the assigning.

Inanimate property only that it [i.e., the textual source] discusses here and a stranger's share, and animate property [sc., livestock] and a local's share, those things they do not explain here, but it is regulated regarding them. And this is the law which there is for these things which are found: that which a stranger takes from an unfrequented place is what a local takes from a frequented place [regarding their respective share], and that which is from something found in a frequented place [that we discussed] previously is what is from something found in an unfrequented place [that we discussed] next, except for the things found [which we shall discuss] lastly.

From inanimate property of a local and stranger, there are these shares of something found.

Animate property of a local, however, there is nothing from them [as a share if they are found] in a joint grazing enclosure, and [if] they are outside [a local joint grazing enclosure] and animate property of a stranger though in a joint grazing enclosure ...

A frequented place of a friend is an unfrequented place of an enemy for all of these finds above. And it is thus: when there is a fifth of it from an unfrequented place for a stranger, it is a sixth for a local; a fourth of it from a frequented place for a stranger and a fifth for a local. This is what is a frequented place in it: its floor and furniture and bright places and the place where everyone frequents. And this is what is an unfrequented place in it: each place other than those; this is something found in a dwelling.

A fourth of it from an unfrequented place for a stranger and a fifth for a local, a third of it from a frequented place for a stranger and a fourth for a local. And this is a frequented place in it: its marketplace and its churchyard and its

⁊ a p*r*imsraiti ⁊ cac*h* inad*h* a mbi taithi*gud* caic*h*. ⁊ a ecoim*dig*: ot*h*[a] si*n* am*ach*; fri*thi* ca(*r*)t*hrach* so.

p. 41a T*r*ian[124] d'fer ainfine as ecoim*dig* ⁊ *cethr*aime d'fer fi*ne*, ⁊ ma coim*dig*, is l*eth* d'fer ainfi*ne* ⁊ t*r*ian d'fer fine. Is *ed* is coim*dig* an*n*: a tulcain ⁊ a h-inada aire*cht*ais. ł is *ed* is coim*dig* an*n*: a slig*h*t*h*i ⁊ a h-i*n*ada reid*he* arda ⁊ na h-i*n*ada i mbi ait*h*ig*h*i caic*h*. ⁊ is *ed* is ecoim*dig* an*n*: a h-imille ⁊ a cula; frith*i* faith*che* seo.

⁊ is *ed* is fait*h*[ch]i an*n*: na ceith*ri* guirt is nesa do*n* baile .i. g*ort* g*ach*a h-airde ime, ⁊ cid*h* é in sliab*h* is nesa do*n* baile, rob am*al* faith*che*. ⁊ is *ed* is *sechtarfaithche* an*n*: in air*et* rosoit*h* (*read* rosoich) cuaird ingelta on faith*chi* amac*h*. ł is *ed* is f*aithche* an*n*: an rosaig*h* (c)[g]ut*h*[125] in cluig. ⁊ frit*h*i f*aithche* .i.[126] a trian d'fer fodogaib, cet*hramthu* d'fer geilfine, ma écoim*dig*. [Ma coimdig], is l*eth* ⁊ (l*eth*) t*r*ian d'fer g*eilfine*.

Ma ecoim*dig*, is l*eth* d'fer ainfi*ne* ⁊ t*r*ian d'fer fi*ne*. ⁊ ma coim*dig*, is *dá* t*r*ian d'fer ainfi*ne* ⁊ l*eth* d'fer fine. ⁊ is *ed* is coim*dig* an*n*: g*ach* baile is mo ait*h*ig*h*it daine in feran*n* ł a h-i*n*ada reid*he* arda. ⁊ is *ed* is écoim*dig* an*n*: a léntach*a* ⁊ a claid*he* ⁊ a h-i*n*ada diamr*a*; f*rithe* t*i*re si*n*.

Dá trian ma[127] écoim*dig* d'fer ainfi*ne* ⁊ l*eth* d'fer fi*ne*. ⁊ ma coim*dig*, is teor*a* cet*hramthain* d'fer ainfine ⁊ da t*r*ian d'fer fi*ne* .i. da t*r*ian as écoim*dig* ⁊ l*eth* d'fer geilfine.[128] ⁊ ma coim*dig*, is teor*a* ceat*hramthain* d*ho*, ⁊[129] aipgitir a og*h*im benar a h-og*hamh*,[130] *dá* t*r*ian d'fer geilfi*ne*. ⁊ is *ed* is coim*dig* cœille an*n*: a cluai*n*ti ⁊ a guirtini ⁊ g*ac* inad*h* a mbi ait*h*ig*h*i caic*h*; frit*he* rofid*h* no t*h*sleib*he* so.

124 The first nineteen lines in the MS are written in one column due to the irregular size of the vellum. This corresponds to *CIH* 1210.11–32.
125 I follow the emendation suggested by Binchy, *CIH* 1210, n. g.
126 The scribe has written 'not' next to this abbreviation in *marg. dext.*
127 Binchy, *CIH* 1210, n. j, queries whether the reading is 'ma' or 'ina' here.
128 The ⟨f⟩ is inserted above the line by the scribe with reference marks.
129 The scribe has written 'not' next to this in *marg. dext.*
130 The same phrase appears in source D, *CIH* 2065.11. Binchy, *CIH* 1210, n. l, suggests that the phrase is out of place here. That being said, it does appear in two of the four versions of the commentaries.

main streets and each place where everyone frequents. And its unfrequented place: [each place] other than those; this is something found in an enclosure.

A third for a stranger from an unfrequented place and a fourth for a local, p. 41a
and if [it is found in] a frequented place, it is half for a stranger and a third for a local. This is what is a frequented place in it: its hillocks and its assembly places. Or this is what is a frequented place in it: its paths and its high, level places and the places where everyone frequents. This is what is an unfrequented place in it: its borders and its recesses; this is something found on a green.

And this is what a green is then: the four fields which are closest to the settlement, i.e., a field on each side around it, and though it may be a mountain which is closest to the settlement, it is [considered] as a green. This is what is outside the green then: as far as a grazing district reaches beyond the green. Or this is what is a green then: as far as the voice of a bell reaches. And something found on a green, i.e., a third of it for the person who finds it, a fourth for a man of the *gelḟine*, if [it is found in] an unfrequented place. If [it is found in] a frequented place, it is a half [for a stranger] and a third for a man of the *gelḟine*.

If [it is found in] an unfrequented place, it is half for a stranger and a third for a local. And if [it is found in] a frequented place, it is two thirds for a stranger and half for a local. This is what is a frequented place in it: each place that people frequent the land or its high, level places more [often]. And this is what is an unfrequented place in it: its glens and its ditches and its secluded places; that is something found on land.

Two thirds if [it is found in] an unfrequented place for a stranger and half for a local. And if [it is found in] a frequented place, it is three fourths for a stranger and two thirds for a local, i.e., two thirds from an unfrequented place and half for a man of the *gelḟine*. And if [it is found in] a frequented place, it is three fourths for him, and an Ogam alphabet which is carved in Ogam,[131] two thirds for a man of the *gelḟine*. This is what is a frequented place of a forest then: its glades and its little gardens and each place where everyone frequents; this is something found in a wood or on a mountain.

131 The interpretation of this phrase is obscure. It is possible that it is misplaced or something was left out when the text was copied; the phrase also appears in source J.

⁊ *noch*an ait*h*fegar coim[dig][132] na écoim*dig* arin farg*i* a*cht* a dilsi d'fer frit*hi* gi*n*mot*ha* an t*r*ic*h*mada ran*n* as d'fer bunad*h*; f*rithe* f*airrge* sin.

Is *ed* is coim*dig* traga an*n*: gac*h* in*ad* at*h*ait*h*ig*h*it dæine ⁊ longa marœ*n*. ⁊ is *ed* is ecoim*dig* trag*h*a an*n*: gac*h* baile na [a]tait*h*it a*cht* longa 'æonar ł tonn*a* ⁊ is lug*h*a atait*h*it dai*n*e.

Srut*h* saile[133] sal (sal) sceo usg*e*, .i. mas inan*n* fer f*rithi* ⁊ fer tire, is 'na rog*ha* ata an cuiti f*rithi* ł tire bias do, ⁊ is as dogabt*ar* s*i*n: "co*n*tec*ht*a gni*m*a ł tire." Masa sai*n*e fer f*rithi* ⁊ fer tire, cuiti tire d'fer tire, ⁊ cuiti f*rithi* d'fer f*rithi*.

Marbdile si*n*, ł is beodile nac*h* cui*m*gen*n* tia*cht*a*in* as a dualg*us* a nirt fei*n*, uair da cui*n*gidis *noch*a mbiad*h* ní astaib.

⁊ no*ch*an fuil ní asna beodil*ib* do gr*es* a guairt ingelt*a*, ⁊ cuiti tob*aig* astaib a *secht*ar*cuairt* ingelt*a*. ł cuiti f*rithi* astaib a cu*air*t ingelt*a* ł go mb*et* ar taisgi gadaig*h*, ⁊ o b*et* is cuiti tob*aig* astaib. Cuiti tob*aig* astaib a *sechtarcuairt* ing*elta* a*cht* manab am*laid* robadar ⁊ a n-aig*h*i f*or*a tec*h*. ⁊ mas am*laid*,[134] *acht* mas[135] cin*n*ti g*o* tiugfadais, is [s]*lan* doib ⁊ *noch*a fuil ní asta. ⁊ masa cin*n*ti n*ach* tiucf*ai*dis, is cuiti tob*aig* co*mlan* ast*aib*.

T*r*ian a cod*ach* f*rithi* ó dærman*ach* ecl*as*a do ecl*ais* no o dærc*eile* fl*ath*a do fl*aith* go rud*h* ł ecma*cht* ł dirain*n*, ⁊ næm(m̄)ad an*n*-sid*he*. ⁊ cet*hramthu*[136] a cod*ach* f*rithi* ó tsærman*ach* ecl*as*a do ecl*ais* go rud*h* .i. na caille, ł écm*acht* .i. i*n* loch*a*, ł dirain*n* .i. i*n*t sl*e*bi, ⁊ *aile déc* ma an*n*-sid*he*, ⁊ *noch*an fuil ní ó *th*særceile fl*ath*a do fl*aith*.

F*rithe* treibe: dil*us* a *cóic*id[137] d'fer fodogaib, ma iar teor*aib* aid*h*ch*ib* tiasar do, ma ecoim*dig*. Ma coim*dig*, *cethramthu* d'fer fodogaib.

---

132 The usual suspension mark over the ⟨m⟩ has been left out.

133 Two or three letters have been erased after the ⟨l⟩.

134 The scribe had written ⟨as̄ masam̄⟩ after this word but cancelled it by underlining. Originally the scribe had cancelled the previous ⟨masam̄⟩ by underlining, but he partially erased the underline.

135 The ⟨s⟩ was added above the ⟨a⟩ by the scribe.

136 After this word, approximately ten or twelve letters have been erased; see also Binchy, *CIH* 1211, n. e.

137 The ⟨id⟩ are written above the numeral.

And 'frequented' or 'unfrequented' is not considered for the sea, but it is forfeit to [the] finder except for one thirtieth from it for [the] original owner; that is something found in the sea.

This is what is a frequented place of the shore then: each place that people and boats both frequent. And this is what is an unfrequented place of the shore then: each place not frequented but by boats alone or waves and it is least frequented by people.

Stream of saltwater, sea and freshwater, i.e., if [the] finder and [the] landowner are the same, it is his choice whether he will have the share of the thing found or of land, and that is taken from: "equally valid are acts or lands." If [the] finder and [the] landowner are different, a share of [the] land for [the] landowner, and a share of [the] thing found for [the] finder.

Those [things are] inanimate property, or it is livestock that is not capable of escaping on account of their own strength, because if they were capable, there would not be anything from them.

And there is never anything from the livestock in a grazing enclosure, and a share of recovering from them beyond the grazing enclosure. Or a share of something found from them in a grazing enclosure if[138] they may be in the possession of a thief, and if they may be [in the possession of a thief], it is a share of recovering from them. A share of recovering from them beyond the grazing enclosure, unless they had been [found] thus with their face towards their home. And if it is so, provided that it is certain that they would have come [home], he is exempt from liability for them and there is nothing from them. If it is certain that they would not have come [home], it is a full share of recovering from them.

A third of his share of something found from a base monastic client to his church or from a lord's base client to his lord as far as a wood or inaccessible place or unclaimed land, and a ninth in that case. And a fourth of his share of something found from a monastic free client to his church as far as a wood, i.e., the forest, or inaccessible place, i.e., the lake, or unclaimed place, i.e., the mountain, and a twelfth if it is in those [places], and there is nothing from a lord's free client to his lord.

Something found in a dwelling: a fifth of it is forfeit to [the] person who finds it, if it is found after three nights, if [it is found in] an unfrequented place. If [it is found in] a frequented place, a fourth for [the] person who finds it.

---

138 See n. 66 on *no co* in the version of this commentary in source A.

F*rithe* *cath*r*ach*: dil*us* a ceth*ramthu* d'fer dogaib manab a cu*air*t lis tsl*uaig*. Ma ed*h* im*morro*, is t*r*ian d'fer dogaib.

F*rithe* f*ai*thche: a t*r*ian d'fir[139] dogaib, ma ecoim*dig*. Ma coim*dig*, is l*eth*.

p. 41b **F*rithe* raiti**: dil*us* a l*eth* d'fer fodogaib, [ma éccoimdig]. Ma coim*dig*, is *da* t*r*ian.

F*rithe* rofed*ha* ł s*leibe*: d*ilus*[140] a da t*r*ian, ma ecoim*dig*. Ma *coimdig*, it [t]eora ceth*ramthain* do.

F*rithe* rofid*h*: a *da* t*r*ian d'fer dogaib ⁊ æont*r*ian d'fer besa *sét*, ł do neoc*h* foceird amac*h* *ar* oin. No confodlad i nde a imairilltnib taisic, mana b*r*og*h*a nec*ht*ar de f*or* araile.

F*rithe* t*r*a*cht*a: dil*us* d'fer dogaib a*cht* *cóic*id*h*[141] a loig*h*i do fer b*unaid*, ma ecoim*dig*. ⁊ ma coim*dig*, is dil*us* uile a*cht* *cóic*id*h*[142] *seiss*id*h* loig*h*i do fer b*unaid*.

F*rithe* *fair*rge:[143] dil*us* do fer fodogaib a*cht* *cóic*id*h*[144] *seiss*id*h* loig*h*i do neoc*h* besa hé riam*h* ar allob*air* aicsena, .i. a faigsi*n* oga, .i. a rad*h* is leis[145] fei*n* e. ⁊ is aire is mo as c*oimdig* na as écoim*dig* .i. ar com*h*toic*h*[146] iat b*u*d*ein* ⁊ daine *aili da* mb*r*e*ith*.

⁊ as am*laid* atait no cota f*r*i*thi*-so doib .i. a dlig*ed* f*r*ithi do de*n*am*h* friu, ma*r* ader so: eascaire[147] an frith*i* tire g*u*sa *secht* n-i*n*ada-so .i. g*o* rig*h*, g*o* h-

139 'd'fir' was added above the line by the scribe.
140 Cf. the other forms of this word above for this expansion.
141 The ⟨id⟩ are written above the numeral.
142 The ⟨id⟩ are written above the numeral in *cóicidh* and *seissidh*.
143 As Binchy, *CIH* 1211, n. o, notes, the scribe has written ⟨g⟩ with a superscript ⟨r⟩. Based on the textual evidence, the word 'fairrge' (or 'fairge') belongs here, but the scribal abbreviation is puzzling.
144 The ⟨id⟩ are written above the numeral in cóicidh and *seissidh*.
145 The ⟨s⟩ was added above the line by the scribe.
146 The word is a form of *comdóig* 'equally likely'; *eDIL* s.v. *comdóig*.
147 The first ⟨a⟩ is written subscript.

Something found in an enclosure: a fourth of it is forfeit to [the] person who finds [it] unless it may be within an host's enclosure. If it is, however, it is a third for [the] person who finds [it].

Something found on a green: a third of it for [the] person who finds [it], if [it is found in] an unfrequented place. If [it is found in] a frequented place, it is half.

Something found on a rough land: half of it is forfeit to [the] person who finds it, if [it is found in] an unfrequented place. If [it is found in] a frequented place, it is two thirds. p. 41b

Something found in a wood or on a mountain: two thirds of it is forfeit, if it is an unfrequented place. If it is a frequented place, there are three fourths for him.

Something found in a wood: two thirds of it for [the] person who finds [it] and one third for [the] person whose property it is, or for someone who loses it on loan. Or they divide [it] in two, its restitution [each] mutually deserves, if neither of them establishes [his right to it] against the other.

Something found on the shore: [it is] forfeit to [the] person who finds [it] except a fifth of [its] value for [the] original owner, if [it is found in] an unfrequented place. If [it is found in] a frequented place, it is all forfeit except for a fifth of a sixth [i.e., 1/30] of [its] value for [the] original owner.

Something found in the sea: [it is] forfeit to [the] person who finds it except a fifth of a sixth of [its] value for [the] previous owner for reporting seeing [it], i.e., his seeing it, i.e., his saying he himself has it. This is [the] reason that there is more from it in a frequented place than from it in an unfrequented place, i.e., because they themselves are equally likely [to be found by] other people if taken.[148]

And those shares of things found are the same for them: the law of finds gives right to them, as this says: proclamation[149] of something found on land at these seven places, i.e., to a king [e.g., at his court], to an ecclesiastical

148 The translation of the last clause is tentative. It is possible that the text is corrupt or part of it is missing; cf. source A, gloss m, *CIH* 56.29–30.

149 Here and below, see the commentary in *Aidbred* § 8 for the same procedure for proclaiming items found on the land or in the sea. See also the Introduction, pp. 30–32.

aircinnech, go biru*gh* (*read* briugaid),[150] go br*eithemain*, go muilen*n tuaithe*, go[151] primgoband t*uait*he, ⁊ fia lu*cht* ænlis ⁊ ænbaile.

E*scaire* in frith*i fair*rge[152] *gus*na teora *cr*ic*h*a as nesa do muir .i. do dui*ne* mait*h in* gac*h* crich dib,[153] ⁊ mu*ir* fei*n* in ceth*ramad* cric*h*, ł gomo *secht* n-*in*ada a h-esc*aire* i*n* gac cric*h*.

Ma dorin*ne* a d*lig*i[d] f*r*ith*i* ⁊ romair aigi g*o* h-i*ar* n*dechmaid*, is a cuiti f*r*i*thi* do ⁊ a fomailt.[154] ⁊ mana dern*a* a d*liged* f*rithi* ⁊ rocai[t](c)*h*[155] ria n*dech*-*maid*, is lanf*iach*[156] gaide uad*h*a.

Mana derna d*liged* f*rithi* ⁊ romair aigi g*o* h-i*ar* n*dechmaid*, no ma dorin*ne* a d*liged* f*rithi* ⁊ docai[t](c)*h* ria n*dechmaid*, gi*n* cuiti f*r*i*thi* do ⁊ gi*n* fiac*h gaite* uad*ha*, a*cht* ai*thgin* na f*r*i*thi* uad*h*a.

Manar escair a*cht* fia lu*cht* ænlis ⁊ ænbaile, ⁊ romair aigi g*o* h-i*ar* n*dech*-*maid*, is le*th*cuiti f*r*i*thi* do.

Ma*n*ar esc*air* fia lu*cht* ænlis ⁊ ænb*aile*, ⁊ rocait*h iar* n*dech*m*aid*, is le*th*fiach gaide uad*h*a.

Mana fog*r*a g*o* tor*acht* iarr*aid* ⁊ co ric iarr*aid*, ⁊ nir ceil in tan[157] doric, is dil*us* a cuiti f*r*i*thi*. Mana fog*r*a ⁊ (go)[158] roc*aith* ria n*dechmaid*, is le*th*d*ire*.[159]

---

150 See also Binchy, *CIH* 1211, n. q.
151 One letter has been erased after the word *go*.
152 The scribe has written ⟨g⟩ with a superscript ⟨r⟩; cf. n. 143.
153 '.i. … dib' is written as an interlinear gloss by the scribe; see also Binchy, *CIH* 1211, n. u.
154 The phrase '⁊ a fomailt' was added above the line by the scribe with reference marks.
155 I follow the emendation suggested by Binchy, *CIH* 1211, n. x.
156 The ⟨.f.⟩ was written in *marg. dext.* by the scribe.
157 The scribe has written 'not' next to *tan* in *marg. dext.*
158 I follow the emendation suggested by Binchy, *CIH* 1212, n. b.
159 The scribe has written 'not' in *marg. dext.*; see also Binchy, *CIH* 1212, n. a.

superior, to a hospitaller, to a judge, at a *túath*'s mill, to a *túath*'s chief smith, and in the presence of people of the same dwelling and same settlement.

Proclamation of something found in the sea throughout the three territories which are closest to the sea, i.e., to a respectable person in each territory of them, and [the] sea itself [is] the fourth territory, or at the seven places for making a proclamation in each territory.

If he fulfilled the law of finds and it [sc., the item found] remained in his possession until after ten days [have passed], he has a share of what he found and its use. And if he does not fulfill the law of finds and he used [it] before ten days [have passed], he owes the full fine of theft.

If he does not fulfill the law of finds and it remained in his possession until after ten days [have passed], or if he fulfilled the law of finds and he used [it] before ten days [have passed], he is without a share of what he found and he does not owe a fine of theft, but he owes restitution of the found property.

If he only made a proclamation in the presence of people of the same dwelling and same settlement, and it remained in his possession until after ten days [have passed], he has a half share of what he found.

If he did not make a proclamation in the presence of people of the same dwelling and same settlement, and he used [it] after ten days [have passed], he owes half [the] fine of theft.

If he did not make a proclamation until someone comes seeking it and someone comes [to him] seeking [it], and he does not conceal [it] when he comes, his share of the thing found is forfeit [to him]. If he does not make a proclamation and he used [it] before ten days [have passed], it is half penalty [that he owes].

Source C, TCD MS 1336, *olim* H.3.17, cols. 298–302, *CIH* 1851.25–1854.13

Atait[160] *secht* frithe, ⁊rl-

Is *cu*trumu at*a* in cuitig frith*e* cid [d]o[161] f*e*r fine cid [d]o f*e*r ainfine, u*air* is *cu*trum*u* recuit a les a *sét* do marthuin doibh. No dono ch*en*a conach beith cuiti frith*e* o f*e*r fine da ceil*e*, uair dlegar de *sét* a f*ir* fine do c*h*oimet in cach inat[162] a tecemdais c*h*uigi.

Ni fuil ni d'fir geilfine a cethuraird na a culaird, u*air* dlega*r* comingai*r*i eturrud do reir Corusa Fine. Cet*h*ruime imurro d'anfi*n*e[163] i sleib no i ndithreib*h*. A tia*cht*uin for cuiti tob*h*uid*h* it*er* fine ⁊ ainfine, *ar* ni lug*h*a dlegur *cu*iti tob*aig* d'f*e*r fine[164] inas d'fir anfine.

Marbdili nama it e innesas sunn ⁊ *cu*iti fir anfine;[165] ⁊ beodile ⁊ *cu*iti fir fine it e[166] na tait*h*med ann *acht* is friu raig*h*ailt*er*. ⁊ is [s]i riag*ail* fil isna frithib*h*-seo: i*n*ni beirius fer anfine a h-ecoimdig*h* iss ed b*eir*ius [fer][167] fine a coimdig*h*, ⁊ inní fuil a coimdig*h* in frith*i* romut is ed fuil a h-ecoimdig*h* in f*r*ith*i* is
col. 299 neassa cinmot*h*a na frith*e* deid*h*enc*h*a—is [s]ain a mbreithem*h*|nacht-saide f*r*isna f*r*ith*e* olc*h*enæ.

Dia n-urfogr*a*, ⁊ ni rocaith co *dech*muid*h*, is dilus do a cuiti f*r*ith*i* ⁊ a fomuiltt. Munu foc*ra*, ⁊ co rocaith ria n*dech*muid*h*, ⁊ curub aisneis dobera f*air*, is landire f*air*. Munu fog*ra* co tora i*arr*uid*h*, ⁊ co roich iarriud*h*, ⁊ ni roceil in

160 As Binchy, *CIH* 1851, n. f, notes, a space was left for a larger initial ⟨a⟩, but it was never added. Instead, a smaller ⟨a⟩ was added later in lighter ink.
161 I follow the emendation suggested by Binchy, *CIH* 1851, n. g.
162 The word 'inat' is added above the line by the scribe with reference marks.
163 The phrase 'd'anfi*ne*' is added above the line by the scribe.
164 After the ⟨e⟩ it looks as if the scribe has erased one letter.
165 The ⟨an⟩ are added above 'fir' by the scribe.
166 The words 'it e' have been added above the line by the scribe.
167 I follow the emendation suggested by Binchy, *CIH* 1851, n. k.

There are seven [categories of] finds, etc.[168]

The share of something found is the same whether for a local or for a stranger, because they will get the same benefit of the property saved by them. Or, on the other hand, so that there might not be a share of something found from a local to another, because he is obligated to guard property belonging to a local in every place in which they would happen across it.

There is nothing for a man of the *gelfine* [for animate property found] in [the] four nearest townlands or in [the] four townlands closest to those, because they are bound by joint grazing between themselves according to *Córus Fine*. One fourth, however, for a stranger [from that which is found] on a mountain or uninhabited place. Both a local and a stranger receive a share for recovering,[169] because a local is not entitled to a smaller share for recovering than a stranger is.

Inanimate property only that it [sc., the textual source] discusses here and a stranger's share; and animate property [sc., livestock] and a local's share, those things they do not explain here, but it is regulated regarding them. And this is the law which there is for these things which are found: that which a stranger takes from an unfrequented place is [equivalent to] what a local takes from a frequented place [regarding their respective share], and that which is from something found in a frequented place [that we discussed] previously is [equivalent to] what is from something found in an unfrequented place [that we discussed] next, except for the things found [which we shall discuss] lastly—their adjudication | is different from the col. 299
other things which are found otherwise.

If he makes a proclamation [that he found it] and he did not use [it] until [after] ten days [have passed], a share of [the] thing found is forfeit to him and [he can] make use of it. If he does not make a proclamation and he used [it] before ten days [have passed], and [that] information is brought against him, it is [the] full fine [that he owes] for it. If he does not make a proclamation until someone comes seeking [it], and someone comes [to him] seeking [it], and he does not conceal [it] when he comes, his share of [the] thing

168 As with the other versions of the heptad, the commentaries give the reward structure for each type of find in order below.

169 'Recovering' refers, for example, to retrieving stolen property from a thief or detaining someone considered unfree in the act of escaping; see below, pp. 260–263.

tan doric, is dilus a cuit*i* frith*i*. Munu foc*ra*, ⁊ co rocaith ria n*dech*muid*h*, ⁊ ni roceil, is leithdire.

Cuiti frithe isna beodilib i crich ⁊ asna marbdi[lib](re)[170] cid i crich cid a *secht*ar crich; o gebuit beodile innscuch*ud* crich*e* ⁊ o beit mairbdile ar fuiririud*h* gaduig*h*e, is *cu*iti tobuid*h* (*read* tobaig) astud*h*.

Cuiti f*r*ith*i* a bechuib*h* ⁊ a dœinib dœra; ł cu*m*[ad][171] cuiti astaig*h*t*h*i *acht* mu*n*ub é frec*ra* in daoir curup ac tia*cht*ain da tig*h* robui se, ⁊ mas e, is do rosoich, ⁊ a dul-sam can ni. Mas amluid*h* f*r*ith e ⁊ a cul re teach,[172] ⁊ niur airb*e*rtnuid*h* nac*h* ag elog*h* (*read* elodh)[173] robi, is a denum*h* air curub ag elog*h* (*read* elodh) robui, ⁊ *cu*iti tobuid*h* (*read* tobaig) as.

Frith*e* treibe, ⁊rl- .i. is ed is[174] coimdeg*h* treib*e* ann a h-airide ⁊ a h-urrlair oc*us* a h-inut*a* soillsi oc*us* na h-inut*a* a mbid*h* aithide caich. Is ed is ecoimdig*h* ann: cach inut ot*h*a sin amach.

Cuiced*h* as a ecoimdigh, .i. *seiss*ed d'f*e*r geilfine,[175] ⁊ a cet*h*ruime as a coimdig*h* .i. mad comdoig*h* a fag*ail* do neoc*h* eile ⁊ da tig*h*er*na* fein, is ann ata in cethr*uime* as. ⁊ is ann ata sin in tan ata re re t*r*i n-œidc*h*e can fag*ail*. No mas *ar* œnaidh*ch*e, is trian in cuicid*h* na no cethruime. Mas da ag*h*aid*h* (*read* adaig),[176] is da trian in cuicid*h* no na cethruime. ⁊ munu roib*h* acht œenag*h*aid*h* (*read* -adaig), is trian. ł dono *con*ach beit*h* nach ni ann no co roib*e* se ar esb*aid* re re *teor*a n-aid*h*c*h*e .i. iar te*cht* doib as tig*h* ata in feg*ad*-so forna frithib. ⁊ mad*h* 'na tig*h* beid, ni fuil *cu*iti frithe donti fogaib ni ann. Coimdig*h* carud is ecoimdig*h* escarut isna frithib-so uile.

Frithe cathr*ac*, ⁊rl-a .i. trian as a coimdig*h*, .i. cethruime d'fir g*elfine*,[177] ⁊ cethruime as a ecoimdig*h*. [Is ed] as(a)[178] ecoimdi[g] .i. lar na cill*e* no in

170 I follow the emendation suggested by Binchy, *CIH* 1852, n. a.

171 I follow the emendation suggested by Binchy, *CIH* 1852, n. b.

172 The ⟨a⟩ is written subscript.

173 See Binchy, *CIH* 1852, n. c.

174 The scribe wrote 'frithe' after *is*. It was cancelled by putting a *punctum* under each letter.

175 This phrase '.i. *seiss*ed d'fer geilfine' was written in *marg. sin.* by the scribe. Based on other versions of the commentary, it looks as though the scribe initially skipped this phrase in his exemplar and added it in the margin.

176 See Binchy, *CIH* 1852, n. f.

177 The phrase '.i. cethruime d'fir *gelḟine*' was written above the line by the scribe. It looks as though the scribe initially skipped the phrase in his exemplar and added it in later.

178 I follow the emendation suggested by Binchy, *CIH* 1852, n. i.

found is forfeit [to him]. If he does not make a proclamation and he used [it] before ten days [have passed], and he did not conceal it, it is half penalty [that he owes].

A share of something found from the livestock in a territory and from inanimate property whether in a territory or beyond a territory; when livestock will depart from a territory and when it might be in consequence of theft, it is a share of recovering from them.

A share of something found from bees and from unfree people; or that it may be a share of detention unless the answer of the unfree person is that he was coming to his home, and if it is so, he can [go], and he [sc., the detainer] goes without anything. If he is found thus and his back to his home, and he does not plead that he is not escaping, and it must be proved that he was escaping, and a share of recovering from it.

Something found in a dwelling, etc., i.e., this is what is a frequented place of a dwelling then: its furniture and its floor and its bright places and the places where everyone frequents. This is what is an unfrequented place then: each place other than those.

A fifth of it from an unfrequented place, i.e., a sixth for a man of the *gelfine*, and a fourth of it from a frequented place, i.e., if it is likely to be found by someone else and by its own master [sc., owner],[179] it is then that there is the fourth from it. And that is the case when it is not found before three nights [have passed]. Or if it is for one night, it is a third of the fifth or the fourth. If it is two nights, it is two thirds of the fifth or of the fourth. And if it was there only one night, it is a third. Or, on the other hand, there should be nothing [as a share] for it until it was missing [for] three nights, i.e., this looking at the things found is after their coming out of a house,[180] and if they may be in a house, there is not a share of something found for the one who finds anything there. A frequented place of a friend is an unfrequented place of an enemy for all of these things found.

Something found in an enclosure, etc., i.e., a third from it in a frequented place, i.e., a fourth for a man of the *gelfine*, and a fourth from it in an unfrequented place. This is what is an unfrequented place, i.e., interior of the

179 Cf. source A, gloss m.

180 In other words, the lost items are found outside of a house.

col. 300 duine ł ani timcillitt |[181] na tig*h*i. Iss ed*h* is comdig*h* cathruch and: a h-urrlair ⁊ a h-inut*a* reide, a reilgi ⁊ a p*r*im*h*sraited*h* ⁊ cac*h* inad a *m*bid aithid*he* caich. Is ed*h* is ecoimdig*h* ann: cac*h* inad ot*h*a si*n* amach.

Frith*e* faith[ch]*e*: a trian do fir fodngaib mad ecoimdig*h*. Mad coimdig*h*, is leth .i. a da trian do fir fodgaib, ceathruime do fir geilfine. Mad coimdig*h*, is leth d'fir anfine ⁊ *tr*ian do fir geilfine. Iss ed is coimdig*h* faith[ch]e and: a slig*h*t*h*i ⁊ a h-inata reide arda ⁊ na h-inuitt a mbid*h* aithide caich. Is ed is ecoimdig*h* ann: cach inut ot*h*a sin amach.

Frithe raite: a leth do fir fotngaib mad ecoimdig*h*. Ma coimdig*h*, is da trian ann .i. cuairtt ingeltta .i. it*er* fai[th]che ⁊ diroinn. Is [ed is] coimdig*h* rait*e* ann: a slig*h*t*h*i ⁊ a h-inut*a* reide *ar*da.

Is aire is mor cuiti fag*h*bal*a* astud*h*-so: fo bith connega*r* a ndichleth .i. a leth ma ecoi*m*dig*h*. Ma coimdig*h*, is da trian ⁊ leth do fer g*elfine*.

Frithe roeda ł sleib*e*: diles a da trian do f*e*r fodogaib ma ecoimdig*h*. Mad coimdig*h*, it teora cethruime .i. fogaba*r* i rofid*h* na caill*e* .i. o chu*air*t ingeltt*a* amach.

Diaig i ndiaig*h* (it) atait[182] so, is aire is moiti asi*nt* sleib ⁊ isin fid. In tra*cht* im*morro* ⁊ in fairrgi, is inunn iat-saide cid a faithce beid, uair foxluid-sid*he* an *sét* leo; ni foxluit imurro in sliab nach i*n* fid*h*. Is ed is coimdig*h* sleib*e* ann: a slig*h*t*h*i. Is *ed* is coimdig*h* caill*e* ann: a cluainti ⁊ a guirti*ne* ⁊ na h-inut*a* a mbid*h*[183] aithide caich.

A m*air*bdilib fine ⁊ anfine ata in cuiti-so. Beodile fine imurro, ni fuil [ní][184] eistib i cu*air*t comaithc*h*esa. Beodile fine imurro o cuairt comach[th]chesa

---

181 A large tear runs diagonally across the top of the column. The tear had been stitched together before the scribe wrote the text.

182 See Binchy, *CIH* 1852, n. j, who suggests this is an error of dittography.

183 After *mbidh* the scribe had written ⟨ambid⟩, then cancelled it by both underlining and overlining it.

184 I follow the emendation suggested by Binchy, *CIH* 1853, n. a.

church or the people or that which is surrounding | the house. This is what is a frequented place of an enclosure then: its marketplace and its level places and its churchyard and each place where everyone frequents. This is what is an unfrequented place in it: each place other than those. col. 300

Something found on a green: a third of it for [the] person who finds it if [it is found in] an unfrequented place. If [it is found in] a frequented place, it is half, i.e., two thirds of it for the person who finds it, a fourth for a man of the *gelfine*. If [it is found in] a frequented place, it is half for a stranger and a third for a man of the *gelfine*. This is what is a frequented place of a green then: its paths and its high level places and the places where everyone frequents. This is what is an unfrequented place in it: each place other than those.

Something found on rough land: half of it for [the] person who finds it if [it is found in] an unfrequented place. If [it is found in] a frequented place, it is two thirds then, i.e., a grazing enclosure, i.e., between a green and unclaimed land. This is a frequented place of rough land then: its paths and high, level places.

This is the reason that there is a larger share from them for finding [them]: because their concealment is possible, i.e., half of it if [it is found in] an unfrequented place. If [it is found in] a frequented place, it is two thirds and half for a man of the *gelfine*.

Something found in a wood or on a mountain: two thirds of it is forfeit to [the] person who finds it, if [it is found in] an unfrequented place. If [it is found in] a frequented place, there are three fourths, i.e., it is found in the great wood of the forest, i.e., outside a grazing enclosure.

These are one after another, this is the reason there is a greater [share] from the mountain and from the wood. The shore, however, and the sea, those are the same as though they are on a green, because they take away the object with them; neither the mountain nor the wood, however, takes [it] away. This is what is a frequented place of a mountain then: its paths. This is what is a frequented place of a wood then: its glades and its little gardens and the places where everyone frequents.

This share is from [the] inanimate property of a local and a stranger. Animate property of a local, however, there is nothing from them [as a share if they are found] in a neighboring grazing enclosure. Animate property, how-

[amach],[185] munur dlig*h* coming*aire*, is feg*ad* cot*a* tobuid (*read* tobaig) no coda frith*e* am*ail* roraidsi*m*.

Frithe trachta: dilius do fer fodagaib *acht* cuice[d] a loig*h*i do fer[186] bunuid*h* mad ecoimd*ig*. Ma coimdig*h*[187] imurro, is dilus *acht cóic*ed *seiss*ed*h* a loig*h*i col. 301 do neoch besa h-æ riam*h* .i. is ann | rofacb*ad* he an*n* sin, uair damad*h*[188] ann rocuired*h* in muir, rob*ad* dilius uile .i. munu t*h*i[189] coimdi[g] tonn tairis, is *ed* a ecoimdig*h*. Is ed is coimdig*h* trag*h*a ann: cac*h* inad i n-ait*h*id*h*it dæine ⁊ longa maræ*n* ⁊ tonna m*a*ru co coitcenn. Iss ed is ecoimdi[g] ann: cac*h* inad*h* na tathuig*h*it *acht* longa a n-æonu*r* .i. is dilus do ḟir geilfine *acht cóice*d*h* a loig*h*i uad*h*u d'fir bun*aid*.

Frith*e* ræd*h*a: a da trian do fer (f)[d]odongaib*h*,[190] æontria*n* do fer besa *sét* ł do neoc*h* foceird amac*h ar* oi*n*. ł canfodlut (*read* confodlat)[191] eturru in nde [.i.] [c]æemdeilig*h*it eta*r*u ar do, a h-imairilltib taisicc, munu mbrog*h*a nechtarde dib*h* imdenum*h* for *araili* .i. munu fire*n*uig*h*e nec*h*tar*de* dib*h* indenum f*or* araili .i. scor cen taisselb*ad* dorinned*h*, ⁊ cinnte na tarr*us*tea. O roícc fer h-ona in aithg*in* ber*id* a oenu*r* in trian-sin .i. in t(*r*i)an[192] is cunntobuirt in tarrustea [n](f)o na tarrusta.

Frith*e* fairrgi: diles do neoch fodongaib*h acht cóiced seiss*id a loig*h*i do neoc*h* besa æ riam*h* .i. d'fir bunuig*h*,[193] ar allabui*r* aicse*n* .i. arin folab*h*radh doni aca faicsi*n*, a rad*h* is leis fein he.

185 I follow the emendation suggested by Binchy, *CIH* 1853, n. b.
186 After *fer* the scribe had written 'fodagaib', but it was canceled by placing a *punctum* under each letter.
187 One letter has been erased after *coimdigh*.
188 The ⟨d⟩ is written above the second ⟨a⟩.
189 Although the form is the same as the 3 sg. pres. subj. of *téit* 'goes', the meaning is obscure to me here. The text could possibly require an emendation.
190 I follow the emendation suggested by Binchy, *CIH* 1853, n. e.
191 The form is the 3 pl. pres. act. ind. of *con-fodlai* 'divides, shares jointly'.
192 I follow the emendation suggested by Binchy, *CIH* 1853, n. g.
193 The phrase 'i. d'fir bunuig*h*' was written above the line by the scribe. It is hard to determine whether it is a gloss or part of the commentary that was skipped in the exemplar as the two previous interlinear phrases were.

ever, from outside a local neighboring grazing enclosure, unless he is entitled to joint grazing, it is considered that he gets a share of recovering or a share of something found as we have said.

Something found on the shore: [it is] forfeit to [the] person who finds it except a fifth of its value for [the] original owner, if [it is found in] an unfrequented place. If [it is found in] a frequented place, however, it is forfeit except for a fifth of a sixth of its value for [the] previous owner,[194] i.e., and it is there | that he could find it in that case, because if it may be there that col. 301
[the] sea put it, all [of it] may be forfeited to him, i.e., unless it is likely that a wave brings [it] (?), this is what is an unfrequented place. This is what is a frequented place of the shore then: each place where people and boats both frequent and waves of the sea in common. This is what is an unfrequented place then: each place that only boats alone frequent, i.e., it is forfeit to a man of the *gelḟine* except for a fifth of their value from them for the original owner.

Something found in a wood: two thirds of it for [the] person who finds it, one third for [the] person whose property it is, or for [the] person who lost it on loan. Or they divide [it] between them in two, i.e., they separate [it] between them in two, its restitution [each] mutually deserves, if neither of them establishes proof over the other, i.e., an 'unyoking without assigning to the possession [of someone else]'[195] was done, and it is certain that it could not be got hold of.[196] When [the] lender receives the restitution he himself takes that third, i.e., the third which is [for] whether it could be got hold of or not.

Something found in the sea: it is forfeit to anyone who finds it except for a fifth of a sixth of its value for [the] previous owner, i.e., for [the] original owner, for information of seeing [it], i.e., for the talking that he does seeing it, his saying he himself has it.

194 Cf. source A, *CIH* 58.25–27.

195 See also source B, *CIH* 1209.23, for the same phrase and discussion.

196 The last clause appears to be out of place, and it is possible that the commentator was linking one of the meanings of *scor* 'unyoking' with the verb of separating in the previous line. It is also possible that something is missing; cf. the similar material in source B above and discussion in note 115.

Cid*h* fo*dera* in *sét* dobeir tar næe tonnuib mar*a* co fuil a dilsi do, ⁊ in *sét* dogaba*r* arin muir moir amaic*h* co fuil in *tr*ichutmud*h* rann as d'fer bunuid*h*? Is e in fat*h* fod*e*ra: in *sét* dob*eir* duine tar næe to*nn*uibh m*aru*, aru cenn d'ac*en*toisg doc*h*uaid*h*, ⁊ coir cema diles do é. In *sét* dobeir duine arin mui*r* moi*r*, noc*h*an aru ce*nn* d'ac*en*toisg teit in duine an*n*-se*de*, ⁊ coir ciad *no*be*th* ni as do f*ir* bunud*h*.

Cid fo*dera* in frithe trachta co fuil ni as do fir bunad*h*, ⁊ na seoit dogeib fer fine it*er* naoi ton*n*ad*h* mar*a* ⁊ tír *con*a fuil ni as d'fir bunud*h*? Is *e* in fath: dlig*ed* tabarta dilsigas in dara de, ⁊ f*r*ith*e* dilsig*h*as araile, ⁊ mo dilsi[g]us[197] tabairt na frithe.

Cid fo*dera* in frit*h*e dogabur arin muir co fuil (co fuil)[198] in trichadmud*h* ran*n* as d'fir bunud*h*, ⁊ gurub tabairt dilsi[g]us ot*h*a sin amach, ⁊ na seoit

col. 302 dob*e*rar as it*er* | næ tonnuib maru ⁊ tír *con*id dilus uile? Is *e* in fat*h*: feimed ⁊ airias*acht* ⁊ finechai*re* dilsig*hus* na seoit dob*e*rur as itir noe tonna mara ⁊ tir, ⁊ dlig*ed* taburta nama dilsig*h*us na seoit dob*e*rur don muir moir amaich.

Cid fodera *con*id mo isin frithe [trachta][199] na isin frithe rofed*h*a? Is e in fath: comdoig*h* muire oc*us* dæeine do toxul in frithe *tr*acht*a*, ⁊ noc*h*a doig*h* *acht* dæine nama do tox*ul* in frithe ræd*h*u.

A trian n-aill do fer foc*eir*d amach[200]

.i. taiselb*ad* n-ecnuirce dorinne ann, ⁊ cinnte na tairrestea in *sét* ina *th*aisel-b*ad*, ⁊ aithg*in* roic amach i*na* taiselb*ad* in f*e*r dorinned in taiselb*ad*. ⁊ fuair fer f*r*ithe i*ar* s*in* é i n-ecoi*m*dig*h* sleibe. ⁊ da trian do fer frithe as, ⁊ in trian nach berunn fer frith*i* de, is a breith don fer dorin*ne* in taiselb*ad*. ⁊ dama cinnti na tairristea ina taiselb*ad* e, in trian nach b*e*runn f*e*r frithe, is e (b)f*e*r bunuid roberud*h*. ł confog*h*lat etar*r*u in de .i. taiselb*ad* n-ecnuircc fos, ⁊ *cunn*tabuirt in tairrestea no na tairristea in *sét* ina taiselb*ad*, ⁊ leth roic in f*e*r dorin*ne*

197 I follow the emendation suggested by Binchy, *CIH* 1853, n. i.
198 The scribe made an error of dittography; see also Binchy, *CIH* 1853, n. j.
199 I follow the emendation suggested by Binchy, *CIH* 1853, n. k.
200 Although this clause is written in larger letters than the following commentary, it is not part of the heptad itself. The same reward structure is found in commentary to source A, *CIH* 57.29–30.

What is the reason that the property that a person brings [from] beyond nine waves of the sea is forfeited to him, and for the property that is found out on the open sea there is one thirtieth of it for [the] original owner? The reason is: the property that a person takes [from] beyond nine waves of the sea, he purposely went to fetch it, it is right that it should be forfeited to him. The property that a person takes on the open sea, the person does not go purposely to fetch it in that case, it is right that there should be something from it for [the] original owner.

What is the reason that for something found on the shore there is something from it for [the] original owner, and the property that a local will find between nine waves of the sea there is nothing from it for [the] original owner? The reason is: [it is the] law of taking that gives right in one [case] and [the] law of finds that gives right in the other, and [the law of] taking gives greater right than [the law of] finds.

What is the reason that for the property that is found in the sea there is one thirtieth of it for [the] original owner, and that [the law of] taking gives right to it from then onwards, and the property which is taken from
it between | nine waves of the sea and land are completely forfeit? The rea- col. 302
son is: refusal and permission and kindred that make the property which is taken from it between nine waves of the sea and land forfeit, and [the] law of taking only gives right to the property which is taken from the open sea.

What is the reason that there is a greater [share] from something found on the shore than from something found in the wood? The reason is: it is likely that [both the] sea and people could carry off something found on the shore, and it is likely that only people could carry off something found in the wood.

The other third of it for [the] person who loses it

i.e., he made an 'assigning possession to one who is absent' here, and [it is] certain that the property could not be got hold of when it was assigned, and he paid out compensation for assigning it to the person who the assigning. And a finder [sc., not the person who identified the owner of the livestock] found the property afterwards in an unfrequented place of a mountain. And two thirds of it to [the] finder, and the third that [the] finder does not take from it, it is given to the person who did the assigning. And if it may be certain that it could be got hold of when it was assigned, the third that [the] finder does not take, [the] original owner should take [it]. Or they divide [it] between them in two, i.e., an 'assigning possession to one who is absent' still, and [it is] uncertain whether the property could be got hold of or not when

in taiselb*ad*. ⁊ frith i*ar* sin i n-ecomdig*h* sleib*e*, ⁊ a da trian d'fer f*rithi*, ⁊ in trian na ruc f*er* frithe de is roin*n* ar do it*er* f*er* in bunuid ⁊ in fer dorinde in taiselb*ad*.

Na s*éoit* frith*i* dogeib duine; ma ruc leis as iad ⁊ rofacuib a n-inad*h aile* iad, *acht* munub mesa int inud ar facuib[201] ina int inut a fuair, is [s]l*an* do. ⁊ masa mesa, is fiach fo aicned a f*atha*[202] fair. ⁊ duine dona dleg*ar* comu*r* ⁊ co*m*ing*h*uire sin; ⁊ ma dlegar, is trian aith*gen*a air (i*ar* sin)[203] ina faicsin i*ar* sin *ar* sechrán isin lo itir comaichib, no aithg*in* isin*n* aid*hch*e i*n*a faicsi*n* ar
col. 303 bru ḟeith*e*[204] no c*h*uith*i*. |

201 The scribe had written ⟨na⟩, then cancelled it by both underlining and overlining.

202 The phrase 'a f*atha*' was written in *marg. dext.* by the scribe.

203 I follow the emendation suggested by Binchy, *CIH* 1854, n. g.

204 Assuming that this is not a mistake for *móin* 'bog, waste' (cf. source B, *CIH* 1211.17), it appears to be from *féith* 'twining plant, woodbine'; *eDIL* s.v. 2 *féith*. Perhaps the sense is that the livestock is on the edge of uncultivated land where the livestock could get tangled and caught in the undergrowth.

it was assigned, the person who did the assigning gets half. And finding afterwards in an unfrequented place of a mountain, and two thirds of it for [the] finder, and the third [that the] finder does not take from it is divided in two between the original owner and the person who did the assigning.

The property that someone will find; if he takes them [sc., the property] with him and he left [them] in another place, provided that the place he left [them] is not worse than the place where he found [them], he is exempt from liability. And if it is worse, [he owes] a fine according to the nature of his reason regarding it. And that is a person who is not bound by co-tillage or joint grazing; and if he is bound, he receives a third of the compensation for seeing them astray in the daytime between neighbors, and [full] compensation for seeing [them] in the night on the edge of a wooded area (?) or a pit. | col. 303

Source D, TCD MS 1337, *olim* H.3.18, p. 383b, *CIH* 906.30–35[205]

Frith*e* t*r*ebi: dil*es* a *cóic*id*h* do fer fodngaib, mad i*ar trí* aidchib tiasair.

F*r*ith*e* *cath*ruc*h*:[206] dil*es* a ceth*raimth*i do fer fodngaib, m*an*ap cuairt lis sloig*h*; ma e-side, ailed a l*eth* do fer fodngaib.

Frithe faich*e*: a t*r*ian do fer fodngaip*h*, a t*r*ian n-aill do fer besa ae.

F*r*ith*e* raiti: a l*eth* do fer fodngaib.

Frith*e* t*r*ac*h*ta: dil*es* *acht cóic*ed a loig*h*i do fer besa he.

Frith*e* fairge: dil*es* do fer fodngaib *acht cóice*d*h* *seiss*id*h* a loig*h*i do fer besa he ar alla[b]*air*[207] n-aicsen.

---

205 TCD MS 1337, pp. 382b–383b, *CIH* 905.10–906.38 consists of excerpts from the heptads with Old Irish glosses. Within the MS, this forms part of a larger section (pp. 358a–383b, *CIH* 874.35–906.38) containing glosses on fragments of texts from the first and middle thirds of the *Senchas Már* legal collection; *CCIH* 40 and 291. None of the actual heptad itself is contained amongst the rest of the glossed heptad extracts. The text here corresponds to some of the material in source A, which follows the heptad proper and is written in larger letters. See also the discussion in source A for the MS layout and editing rationale. It should be noted, however, that there are minor differences between the two sources and that source D includes only six locations rather than seven; items found in a wood or on a mountain are not included. Furthermore, the text here is written as a block in the MS at the end of all the glossed extracts from the heptad collection. In effect, the text which follows each excerpt functions as a gloss; cf. the same glossing technique in the other sources for the heptad where the glossed excerpts are interspersed with commentary. It should be noted that in this MS, the excerpts from Heptad 64 are followed by a block quotation from Heptad 65. Of interest is that the quotation from Heptad 65 is from the commentary, not the heptad itself, and which, in Oxford, Rawl. B. 487, is also written in the larger letters normally used by the scribe for writing tract.

206 It looks like the scribe might have originally written a different letter before turning it into ⟨.k.⟩ for *cath*-.

207 I follow the emendation suggested by Binchy, *CIH* 906, n. i.

Something found in a dwelling: a fifth of it is forfeit to [the] person who finds it, if it is found after three nights.

Something found in an enclosure: a fourth of it is forfeit to [the] person who finds it, unless it may be [in] a host's enclosure; if it is, half of it is entitled to [the] person who finds it.

Something found on a green: a third of it to [the] person who finds it, [the] other thirds of it [are] for [the] owner.

Something found on rough land: half of it for [the] person who finds it.

Something found on the shore: [it is] forfeit [to the person who finds it], except for a fifth of its value for [the] owner.

Something found in the sea: [it is] forfeit to [the] person who finds it, except for a fifth of a sixth [i.e., 1/30] of its value for [the] owner for reporting seeing [it].[208]

208 Cf. the similar clause in sources B and C, *CIH* 1211.22 and 1853.21, respectively. The last clause pertains to the finder, not the owner, i.e., the finder receives 29/30 for spotting the lost property.

Source J, TCD MS 1336 [*olim* H.3.17], cols. 595–602 *CIH* 2062.27–2067.26[209]

"[D]iam[210] frithe fog*h*ba, .⁊rl-."[211]

In[212] frit*he*, at e an*n*so a gnethe: ria n*dech*maid*h* ⁊ i*ar* n*dech*m*aid*. Ma roescair ria n*dech*m*aid*, ⁊ ni rocait*h*, lancuite frit*he* do. Masa gat ⁊ b*r*at imrub*air*t f*air*, is landire f*air* am*ail* bid gat. Mana roesc*air* co *dech*m*aid*, ⁊ ni rocait*h*, ⁊ ni roceil[213] *ar* lu*cht* in baile, b*erar* in s*ét* uad ci*n* cuite f*r*ithe dó. Mana roescair, ⁊ rocait*h* ria n*dech*m*aid*, ⁊ ni roceil in ta*n* teg*ar* día i*arriaidh* cuige, is dubl*ad*
col. 596 uad*h*. Ma roescair fia lu*cht* œnlis ⁊ œnbaile, ⁊ rocait*h* ria n*dech*m*aid*, | gen cuite[214] frit*he* do ⁊ l*eth*fiach g*ait*e uad*h*.

Sain—In ni fil in el*od* co *dech*m*aidh* is *ed* fil iar n*dech*m*aidh* gi*n* el*od*.[215]

Mas i*ar* ndechm*aid*, is [s]lan do a cait*hem* *acht* cuit fir bun*aid* uad*ha* ma ronesc*air*. Mana ronesc*air*, ⁊ rocait*h* i*ar* n*dech*m*aid*, is l*eth*dubl*ad* int s*éoit* uada.

Mana rocait*h*, ⁊ ni roesc*air*, in s*ét* do breit*h* uad*ha* gen cuit do and.

Masa gat roimir f*air*, ⁊ tuc eig*en* failsigte uad, is landire g*ait*e f*air* ind.

---

209 This material is from Digest D (46); *CCIH* 83.

210 A space was left for a large initial ⟨d⟩ in the MS, but it was never added in. Although the scribe has written this clause in larger letters than the surrounding commentary, it is not part of the heptad itself, but it rather belongs to another text. The following commentary, however, directly relates to and largely repeats (with some important differences) the material on the same topic in the commentaries in sources A, B, and C. See also the Introduction, pp. 30–32 and 39–41.

211 Cf. O'Dav no. 488, *CIH* 1484.10–11, which is printed at the end of this version of the heptad.

212 There is an oblong hole in the vellum towards the bottom right side of the column. The scribe has written the text around it.

213 The ⟨i⟩ is written subscript. It is common for this scribe to write ⟨i⟩s subscript when they follow ⟨e⟩. No further note will be made of this feature.

214 The scribe wrote the word *cuite* twice by mistake, but he cancelled the second one by underlining; see also Binchy, *CIH* 2062, n. i.

215 The sentence 'Sain—In ni fil in el*od* co *dech*m*aidh* is *ed* fil iar n*dech*m*aidh* gi*n* el*od*.' is written *marg. sup.* above col. 596. The sentence is noted in the Brehon law transcripts, but it is omitted in *CIH*. The word 'sain' 'different' is not mentioned in the Brehon law transcripts. It is written by the scribe in the far upper left corner of the page. The first letter (or perhaps letters) is difficult to read, so the reading presented here is tentative.

"If you may find lost property, etc."

The things found: their types are below: before ten days [have passed] and
after ten days [have passed]. If he made a proclamation [that he found it]
before ten days [have passed], and he did not use [it], he has [the] full share
of what he found. If [charges of] theft and plundering are brought against
him, it is [the] full fine for it as there would be for theft. If he did not make a
proclamation [that he had found it] until ten days [have passed], and he did
not use [it], and he did not conceal [it] from people in the settlement, the
property is taken from him [and] he does not get a share of what he found. If
he made a proclamation [that he found it], and he used [it] before ten days
[have passed], and he did not conceal [it] when someone comes to him look-
ing for it, he owes double. If he made a proclamation [that he found it] in the
presence of people of the same dwelling and the same settlement [in which
he found it], and he used [it] before ten days [have passed], | he does not get col. 596
a share of what he found and he owes half [the] fine of theft.

Different [material]—That which is the [case of] evasion until ten days [have passed] is what is not evasion after ten days [have passed].

If it is after ten days [have passed], he is free to use it except that he owes the original owner's share if he made a proclamation. If he did not make a proclamation, and he used it after ten days [have passed], he owes half doubling of the [value of the] property.[216]

If he did not use [it], and he did not make a proclamation, the property is to be taken from him and he does not get a share for it.

If it is theft that was inflicted on him, and it was revealed by him that violence took [it], he receives [the] full fine of theft for it.

216 'Half doubling' refers to the fine being 1 ½ times the value of the property.

Mana caithe co *dech*maid*h* ⁊ doni urfog*r*a, is diles do a cuite f*rithe* ⁊ a fomailt. Mana fogra, ⁊ rocait*h* ria n*dech*m*aid*, gu*r*ab faisneis dob*erar*[217] fair, is landire fair.

Mana fogra co torad*h* iarr*aid*, ⁊ ni ceil in tan dorig*h*ne, is dil*es* cuit f*rithe*. Man*ar* fog*air*, ⁊ rocait*h* ria n*dech*m*aid*, ⁊ nir ceil, is l*eth*dire fair.

Escaire in frit*he* tire isna *secht* n-inadaib*h* adeir dlig*ed* .i. co rig*h*, co aircin*n*ech, co briug*aid*, co br*eithe*m*ain*, co p*r*im*h*gab*h*ain*n* *tuait*he, co muilen*n* *tuaith*e, fia lu*cht* æonlis ⁊ æonbaile in *secht*mad.

E*scaire* in frit*he* fairrge fone *tr*i crichaib is nesa do muir, ⁊ a escaire do loingsec*ha* in m*ar*a in ceat*h*ram[ad],[218] ⁊ *g*usna c*eth*ra h-inadaib (i*n*) [adeir][219] dlig*ed* i ng*a*c crich dib-sin.

Atait 7 frit*he* la F*éniu*: frit*he* treib*he*, ⁊rl-.

Dil*es* a c*ói*ce[d] mad iar teora aid*h*ce, .i. i*ar* te*cht* doib as a tig*h* ata in feg*ad*-sa fo*r*na f*r*it*h*ib*h*, .i. mad a tig*h* beit, ni fuil cuite f*r*ithe do*n*ti dogeib*h* ni an*n*.

Mairbdile nama it e in*n*ises sund; ⁊ cuit fir ainfine, ⁊ beodile, ⁊ *cu*it fir fine it e na tait*h*met and, *acht* as f*r*iu riag*h*ail*ter*. ⁊ is [s]i riag*ail* fil *for*sna f*r*ithib*h*-seo: aní beires fer ainfine a h-ecoimde[g] is *ed* beres fer fine a coimde[g], ⁊ ani fil a coi*m*de[g] asna[220] frit*h*ib*h* rem*h*at as *ed* fil a h-ecoi*m*de[g] na f*rithe*

---

217 Binchy, *CIH* 2062.39, queries whether the expansion is correct for 'dob*err*'. Similar material in source A, *CIH* 61.5, has the verb form 'dob*e*rur'. Both *doberr* and *doberar* are 3 sg. pres. pass. ind. forms of *do-beir* 'gives, brings'. The suspension mark in the MS here is ambiguous and would allow for either expansion.

218 I follow the emendation suggested by Binchy, *CIH* 2063, n. c. The first ⟨a⟩ is written subscript.

219 I follow the emendation suggested by Binchy, *CIH* 2063, n. d.

220 The scribe originally wrote 'isna' but corrected it to 'asna' by adding the correction 'ɫ a' above the ⟨i⟩. See also Binchy, *CIH* 2063, n. f.

If he did not use [it] until ten days [have passed] and he makes a proclamation, his share of what he found and its use are forfeit to him. If he does not make a proclamation, and he used [it] before ten days [have passed], and information is brought against him, it is [the] full fine for it [that he owes].

If he does not make a proclamation until someone arrives seeking [it], and he does not conceal [it] when he reached[221] [him], [his] share of what he found is forfeit.

If he did not make a proclamation, and he used [it] before ten days [have passed], and he did not conceal [it], it is a half fine for it.

Proclamation of something found on land in the seven places that [the] law says, i.e., to a king [e.g., at his court], to an ecclesiastical superior, to a hospitaller, to a judge, to a *túath*'s chief smith, at a *túath*'s mill, in the presence of people of [the] same dwelling and same settlement [in which he found it] as the seventh.

Proclamation of something found in the sea throughout the three territories which are closest to [the] sea, and proclaiming it to sailors of the sea as the fourth [territory], and at the four places[222] that [the] law says in each territory of these.

There are seven [categories of] finds according to Irish law: something found in a dwelling, etc.

A fifth of it is forfeit if it may be after three nights, i.e., this looking at the things found is after their coming out of his house, i.e., if they may be in a house, there is not a share of something found for the one who will find anything there.

It [sc., the textual source] only discusses inanimate property[223] here; and a stranger's share, and animate property [sc., livestock], and a local's share, they do not explain [those things] here, but it is regulated regarding them. And this is the law which is for these things which are found: that which a stranger takes from an unfrequented place is [equivalent to] what a local takes from a frequented place [regarding their respective share], and that which is from the things found in a frequented place [that we discussed] previously is [equivalent to] what is from the things found in an unfrequented

221 The precise meaning of *dorighne*, 3 sg. perf. ind. of *do-gní* 'makes, does', in this context is obscure to me.

222 Cf. the source A version of similar material at CIH 58.24, which adds seven places in each territory as an alternative to just the four.

223 *Mairbdile* is pl. here.

as nesam do, cenmot*ha* na frit*he* deig*h*ana*c*a—is sain a mbr*eithemhnacht*-side f*r*isna f*r*it*he*[224] olcena. Co n-urfogra ⁊ cin a cait*h*em*h* co *dechmaid* …[225]

Is cutruma ata in cuite frithe-so cid [d]o fir fi*n*e cid*h* [d]o fir ainfine, u*air* is cutrama recait a les a s*ét* do m*ar*t*h*ain doib*h*. ł d*ano* *co*n*a* b*eth* cuit a[226] fri-the o*n* fir fine *dá* ceil*e* it*ir*, u*air* dleg*ar* de s*ét* in fir fine *aile* do coi*mét* i ngac ina*d* a tice*m*dais c*h*uice.

Ma [a]tait a s*éoit* a n-ecmais fir bun*aid ar* tri aid*h*ce, is an*n* ata cuit[e] f*r*i-
col. 597 t*he* uad*h* .i. a t*r*ian *ar* œnaid*h*ce ⁊ a da t*r*ian *ar* da aid*h*|ce; ⁊ ni fil ni d'fir frithe coruice si*n*, u*air* ade*ir*: "mad i*ar* teora aidce, tiasair do."[227]

Coimde[g] carat, ⁊ is é ecoi*m*de[g] esc*ar*at isna frit*he*-so anuas uile; is am*hlaid*-so eisid*he* in tan ata *cóice*d*h* as a ecoimde[g] d'fir ainfi*ne* is *seisse*d*h* d'fir fine. C*eth*raim*he* as a coi*m*de[d] d'fir ainfine ⁊ *cóice*[d] do fir fine;[228] *fri-the* treib*he* si*n*. T*r*ian as a coimde[g] d'fer ainfin[e] ⁊ ceth*raimth*e d'fer fine, ⁊ frit*he* cat*h*rach si*n*. ⁊ ceth*raimthe* as a ecoi*m*de [d'fir ainfine][229] ⁊ *cóice*[d] d'fer fine, ⁊ *frithe* cat*h*rac si*n*.

Frit*he* fait*h*ce: t*r*ian do fir ainfine as a ecoi*m*de[g] ⁊ *ceth*raime d'fir fi*ne*. Mad coi*m*de[g], is l*eth* d'fir ainfine ⁊ t*r*ian d'fir fi*ne*.

F*rithe* fait*h*ce: a trian do fer fogeib, cethr*aimthe* d'fir ge*il*fine,[230] mad ecoi*m*-de[g]. Mad coi*m*de[g] is l*eth*, ⁊ (l*eth*)t*r*ian[231] d'fir geilfine.

Mad ecoi*m*de[g], is l*eth* d'fir ainfi*ne* ⁊ t*r*ian d'fir fine. Mad coi*m*de[g], is da trian d'fir ainfi*ne* ⁊ l*eth* d'fir fi*ne*, ⁊ frit*he* raite si*n* .i. it*er* fait*h*ce ⁊ dirain*n*. Da t*r*ian mad ecoi*m*de[g] d'fir ainfine ⁊ l*eth* d'fir fi*ne*. Mad coi*m*de[g], is teora ceth*raimth*e d'fir ainfi*ne* ⁊ da t*r*ian d'fir fine, ⁊ *frithe* raod*h*a ł sleib*h*e si*n*.

---

224 The phrase 'is sain a mbr*eithemhnacht* side f*r*isna f*r*it*he*' has been omitted from *CIH* 2063.13. It should also be noted that the same phrase has been omitted from the O'Curry and O'Donovan Brehon law transcripts.

225 It appears as though the scribe has left out some of the text; cf. the similar material in source A, *CIH* 55.37, and source C, *CIH* 1851.39.

226 The ⟨a⟩ has been added below the line by the scribe.

227 It is uncertain whether the commentary is directly quoting another text here.

228 The scribe originally wrote 'ainfine', but cancelled the ⟨ain⟩ by underling; see also Binchy, *CIH* 2063, n. i.

229 I follow the emendation suggested by Binchy, *CIH* 2063, n. l.

230 The scribe added '.g.' in *marg. dext.* with reference marks.

231 Binchy, *CIH* 2063, n. n, notes that the scribe has written 'not' 'note' in *marg. dext.*, possibly to indicate that 'l*eth*t*r*ian' is a mistake for 't*r*ian'.

place [that we discussed] next, except for the things found [which we shall discuss] lastly—their adjudication is different from the other things which are found otherwise. With proclamation and without using them up to ten days ...

The share of this thing [which is] found is the same whether for a local or for a stranger, because they will get the same benefit of the property saved by them. Or, on the other hand, so that there might not be a share of something found by the local to another at all, because he is obligated to guard property belonging to another local person in every place in which they would happen across it.

If the property is absent from [its] original owner for three nights, it is in that case that he owes a share of something found, i.e., a third of it for one night and two thirds of it for two nights; | and there is nothing from [the] col. 597
finder beyond that, because it says: "if it is after three nights, it belongs to him."

A frequented place of a friend, and it is an unfrequented place of an enemy for all of these things found above; and it is like that when there is a fifth from it in an unfrequented place for a stranger which is a sixth for a local. A fourth from it in a frequented place for a stranger and a fifth for a local; that is something found in a dwelling. A third from it in a frequented place for a stranger and a fourth for a local, and that is something found in an enclosure. And a fourth from it in an unfrequented place for a stranger and a fifth for a local, and that is something found in an enclosure.

Something found on a green: a third of it for a stranger in an unfrequented place and a fourth for a local. If [it is found in] a frequented place, it is half for a stranger and a third for a local.

Something found on a green: a third of it for [the] person who finds [it], a fourth for a man of [the] *gelḟine*, if [it is found in] an unfrequented place. If [it is found in] a frequented place, it is half, and a third for a man of [the] *gelḟine*.

If [it is found in] an unfrequented place, it is half for a stranger and a third for a local. If [it is found in] a frequented place, it is two thirds for a stranger and half for a local, and that is something found on rough land, i.e., between a green and unclaimed land. Two thirds if [it is found in] an unfrequented place for a stranger and half for a local. If [it is found in] a frequented place, it is three fourths for a stranger and two thirds for a local, and that is something found in a forest or on a mountain.

Ni fil ni d'fir geilfi*n*e a beodile i cet*har*aird nac*h* a culaird, *ar* dleg*air* dib*h* comi*n*gaire atarr*u* do reir in Cor*us*a Fine; ⁊ atait in *cu*it-se tuas a m*airb*h*d*ile fine ⁊ ai*n*fine.[232]

Ceth*raimthe immorro* do ainfine o si*n* amach i sleib*h* ł i *n*dithraib. A tiac*ht*ain f*or* cuite tob*aig* it*er* fine ⁊ ainfine, *ar* ni lug*h*a dleg*ar* cuite tob*aig* d'fir fine inas d'fir ainfine. Mana dlig*h* co*m*ingaire de, is feg*h*a[d] cota tob*aig* eistib*h* ł cota frit*he* am*ail* roraidsem.

Noch*an* ait*h*feg*htar* coimde[g] na ecoi*m*de[g] *ar*in f*airrgi acht* a dilse d'fir frit*he* genmot*ha* an t*r*ic*h*adma ran*n* as d'fer bun*aid*. ⁊ is aire is mo asa coi*m*-de[g] na asa ecoi*m*de[g] *ar* doch*us* daine do tecmaisi*n* c*h*uca and si*n*. ł d*ano* co*n*a be*th deith*bir fir fine na fir ai*n*fine ríu-sin g*a*c uair na fuilit *cóic* slec*ht*a .20. an Corasa Fi*n*e et*a*rru, ⁊ mad [a]ta, noch*an* fuil fiac*h* foi*m*rime o cac*h* dib dia ceil*e* na cuite f*r*ithe.

Is *ed* is coi*m*de[g] treib*he* an*n*: a airit*he* ł a sraid ⁊ a url*ar* ⁊ a h-inada soillsi.
col. 598 Is *ed* is ecoi*m*dig*h*: a cula ⁊ a cuiled*h*a ⁊ a lepta ⁊ a h-inada | dorch*ai*.

Is *ed* is coi*m*de[g] cat*h*rach and: a sraite ⁊ a urlair ⁊ a reilge ⁊ a p*r*imraite ⁊ g*ách* inad a mbí ait*h*ig*he* c*h*áic*h*. Is *ed* is ecoi*m*de[g] cat*h*rach an*n*: a culsraite ⁊ a culg*arr*ada ł g*arr*ad*a*[233] ⁊ a h-inada diamra.[234]

Is *ed* is coimde[g] fai[th]ce an*n*: a slig*h*te ⁊ a h-inada reid*h*i arda ⁊ in baile a tait*h*id cach. Is *ed* is ecoi*m*de[g] an*n*: a cab*h*ana ⁊ a h-inada diamra ⁊ in baile na ait*h*igen*n* cach.

Is *ed* is faith[ch]e an*n*: na *ceithri* guirt is nesa do*n* baile, .i. gort cac*h*a *air*de ime. ł is sí in faith[che]: in rosaig gut*h* cluic. ⁊ cid*h* e in sliab*h* ba nesa do*n* baile, roba am*al* fait*h*[ch]e.

---

232 The scribe has written *gné n-aill* in *marg. dext.*

233 Although the scribe has written 'ł *garrada*' as part of the commentary, Binchy, *CIH* 2064, n. a, queries whether it is a correction for 'culg*arr*ada'.

234 Binchy, *CIH* 2064, n. b, notes that the following text, which appears after 'diamra', is out of place here: la*cht* no gnim*hrad* na s*éoit* frit*he*, t*r*ian tire d'fer in ferain*n*, ⁊ t*r*ian bun*aid* d'fer in cruid*h*, ⁊ t*r*ian fric*h*nam*ha* do*n*ti dorig*h*ne in f*r*ichnam*h*. 'the found property's milk or labor, a third of land for the owner of the land, and third of origin for the owner of the livestock, and a third of labor for the one who did the labor'.

There is nothing for a man of [the] *gelfine* from animate property [found] in [the] four nearest townlands or in [the] four townlands closest [to those], because they are bound by joint grazing between them according to *Córus Fine*; and these are the shares above from inanimate property of a local or a stranger.

A fourth, however, for a stranger, moreover, [from that which is found] on a mountain or in uninhabited places. Both a local and a stranger receive a share for recovering, because a local is not entitled to a smaller share for recovering than a stranger is. Unless he is bound by joint grazing, a share of recovering from them or a share of something found is to be considered as we have said.

'Frequented' or 'unfrequented' is not taken into account for the sea, but it is forfeited to [the] finder except for a thirtieth part from it for [the] original owner. And the reason there is more from it in a frequented place than from it in an unfrequented place is because it is probable people [will] happen upon them in that case. Or, on the other hand, that there might not be a difference of local or stranger regarding those each time the 25 divisions in *Córus Fine* are not between them, and if there is, there is not a fine of unauthorized use from each of them to the other of the share of something found.

This is what is a frequented place of a dwelling then: its furniture or its path and its floor and its bright places. This is what is an unfrequented place: its corners and its store rooms and its beds and its dark | places. col. 598

This is what is a frequented place of an enclosure then: its streets and its marketplace and its churchyard and its main streets and each place where everyone frequents. This is what is an unfrequented place of an enclosure then: its back streets and its back gardens or gardens and its secluded places.

This is what is a frequented place of a green then: its paths and its high level places and where everyone joins [together].[235] This is what is an unfrequented place in it: its hollows and its secluded places and the place that each [person] does not frequent.

This is what is a green then: the four fields which are closest to the settlement, i.e., a field on each side around it. Or this is what a green is: as far as the voice of a bell reaches. And though it may be a mountain which is closest to the settlement, it is [considered] as a green.

235 The last clause refers to places where people often meet up.

Is *ed* is coimde[g] raite and: a slig*h*te ⁊ a h-inada reid*he* arda. Is *ed* is ecoi*m*de[g] an*n*: a [g]lé*n*ta*cha* ⁊ a claide[236] ⁊ a h-inata diamra.

Is *ed* is raite an*n*: in airet rosoi[c](t)*h* cu*air*t ingelta, ɫ o*n* faiche amac*h*, .i. it*er* faic*he* ⁊ dirain*n*.

Is *ed* is coimde[g] ræda and: a slig*h*te ⁊ a guirtinig*h*. Is *ed* is [e]coimde[g] an*n*: g*a*c inad ot*ha* si*n* amach.

Is *ed* is coim*de*[g] sleib*he* an*n*: a slig*h*te ⁊ a h-i*n*ada reide *ar*de. Is *ed* is ecoi*m*de[g] and: g*a*c inad ot*ha* sin amac*h*.

F*r*ithe ræda ⁊ rofeda:[237] is aire is mor cuit a fagbala eistib*h*: fo bit*h* co*necar* a ndicle*th*.

Frithe tra*ch*ta: cuiced as a ecoi*m*de[g] d'fer bun*aid* o*n* fer frit*he*, ⁊ a dilsi uile ota si*n* amac*h* d'fer frit*he*. ⁊ is [aire] (an*n*)[238] rofagad e an*n* sin, *uair* damad an*n* rocuired*h* muir é, rob*ad* dil*es* do uile.

Is *ed* is coi*m*de[g] traga an*n*: g*a*c baile is no i *n*-at*h*aig*h*it dai*ne* co coitcen*n* ⁊ longa. ⁊ is *ed* is ecoi*m*de[g] ot*ha* si*n* amach.

Is aire[239] is mo isi*n* frithe *tracht*a na isin frithe r*aoda*: doig*h* muir ⁊ daine d'foxal i*n* frithe *tracht*a, ⁊ noc*ha* doig*h* ach[t] daine nama d'foxal in fri*th*[e][240] ræda.

Frit*he* f*airr*ge, .i. noch*a*n fuil coimde[g] na ecoi*m*de[g] aice-side *acht* a dilsi d'fir f*r*ithe cenmot[h]a in t*r*ichadma[d] ran*n* as d'fer bunaig*h*.

Cid fo*dera* i*n* s*ét* dobe*ir* dui*ne* leis t*ar* næ ton*na* m*ara*, a dilsi do, ⁊ *in sét* dogeib dui*ne ar*in muir moir amuig*h* co fuil ni as d'fer bun*aid*? Is e in fa*th*: in s*ét* dobeir d*uine* leis *tar noí tonna* m*ara*, ara cen*n* d'ae*n*toisc doc*h*uaid*h*, ⁊ coir cia*ma* dil*es* do é. In s*ét* dogeib*h* dui*ne ar*i*n* muir moir amuig*h* *immorro*,

236 Cf. the acc. pl. 'claided*ha*' in source A, *CIH* 57.22.

237 It is unclear why two spellings of the same word for a wood are being used here. It is possible that one was orginally a gloss which has crept into the text.

238 I follow the emendation suggested by Binchy, *CIH* 2064, n. d.

239 The word 'aire' is added by the scribe in *marg. sin.* with reference marks; see also Binchy, *CIH* 2064, n. e.

240 The scribe wrote an extra ⟨t⟩ at the end of the word, but cancelled it with a *punctum*; see also Binchy, *CIH* 2064, n. g.

This is what is a frequented place of rough land then: its paths and its high, level places. This is what is an unfrequented place in it: its glens and its ditches and its secluded places.

This is what is rough land then: as far as a grazing district reaches, or from the green outwards, i.e., between a green and unclaimed land.

This is what is a frequented place of a wood then: its paths and its little gardens. This is what is an unfrequented place in it: each place other than those.

This is what is a frequented place of a mountain then: its paths and its high, level places. This is what is an unfrequented place: each place other than those.

Something found in a wood or great wood: this is the reason that there is a larger share from them for finding it: because their concealment is possible.

Something found on the shore: a fifth of it in an unfrequented place for the original owner from the finder,[241] and its entire forfeiture from that onwards to the finder. And the reason that he could find it then, because if it may be there that [the] sea put it, all [of it] may be forfeited to him.

This is what is a frequented place of the shore then: each place in which people and boats often frequent in common. This is what is an unfrequented place: [any place] other than those.

This is the reason that there is more for something found on the shore than for something found in the wood: it is likely that [both the] sea and people could carry off something found on the shore, and it is likely that only people could carry off something found in the wood.

Something found in the sea, i.e., it does not have a 'frequented' or 'unfrequented' place but its forfeiture to [the] finder except for the thirtieth from it for [the] original owner.

What is the reason that the property that a person brings with him [from] beyond nine waves of the sea, it is forfeited to him, and the property which a person will find out on the open sea, that there is something from it for the original owner? The reason is: the property that a person takes with him [from] beyond nine waves of the sea, he went purposely to fetch it, and it is right that it is forfeit to him. The property that a person will find out on the

241 In other words, the finder receives the total value of the found property except for a fifth of its value, which the original owner gets.

col. 599 *no*ch*on* *ara*[242] | cen*n* d'æntoisc doc*h*uaid*h* in dui*ne* an*n* sin, ⁊ có*ir* cé robe*th* ni as d'fer bun*aid*.

Cid fo*dera* in frithe tr*ach*ta co fuil ni as d'fer b*unaid*, ⁊ in frithe dogeib duine, .i. fer fi*ne*,[243] it*er* *noí* ton*n*a m*ar*a ⁊ tir *con*a fuil ni as d'fer b*unaid*? Is e in fa*th*: dlige*d* tab*ar*ta dilsig*h*es in d*ar*a de ⁊ dlige*d* frit*h*e dilsiges *araile*, ⁊ mo dilsig*h*es tab*air*t na frithe.

Cid fo*dera* deiseic in frithe dogab*ar* *ar*in muir moir co fuil an trichatmad*h* r*ann* as d'fer b*unaid*, ⁊ gurab tab*air*t dilsig*h*es é o si*n* ama*ch*? Is e in fa*th*: fei-me*d* ⁊ airiasa*cht* ⁊ tab*air*t fine dilsig*h*es in *sét* dogab*ar* it*er* *noí* ton*n*a m*ar*a ⁊ tir, ⁊ dlig*ed* tab*ar*tais nama dilsig*h*es in *sét* dogab*ar* *ar*in muir moir amuigh.

F*rithe* roed*h*a: a da t*r*ian do fer dodgaib*h*, æntrian do fer besa *sét* ł do nec*h* focerr am*a*c[h]. F*rithe* ræd*ha* ł sleib*he*: da t*r*ian as ecoi*m*de[g], l*eth* d'fer[244] ge*il*fine. Ma coimde[g], is teora ceth*raimth*e do; ⁊ aipgiti*r* og*h*aim ben*ar* aip-giti*r* og*h*im; da t*r*ian d'fir ge*il*fine.

Taiselb*ad* n-ecn*air*ce dorin*n*ead an*n*, ⁊ cin*n*te na tarraistea in *sét* i*n*a tai-selb*ad*, ⁊ ait*hgin* roíc am*ach* ina taiselb*ad*; inti dá *tuc* *ar* oin é in fer dorin*n*e a taiselb*ad*. ⁊ fu*air* fer fine i*ar* si*n* é i *n*-ecoi*m*de[g] sleib*he*, ⁊ da t*r*ian d'fer frit*h*e as; ⁊ an t*r*ian nad beiren*n* fer frithe de, is a bre*th* do*n* fer dorin*ne* in taiselb*ad*. ⁊ dama cin*n*te *con*a tarraiste i*n*a taiselb*ad* é, in t*r*ian na beiren*n* fer frithe de, is a fer b*unaid* robérad*h*. ł *con*fod*h*lat et*ar*ru i *n*dé, .i. taiselb*ad* n-ecn*air*c[e] fos, ⁊ cun*n*tab*air*t i*n* tarraistea ł na tarraistea i*n* *sét* i*n*a taiselb*ad*, ⁊ l*eth* roíc in fer dorin*ne* i*n* taiselb*ad*. ⁊ frith in *séoit* i*ar* sin i n-ecoi*m*de[g] sleib*he*; ⁊ a

242 The following material, *CIH* 2065.27–29, is written by the scribe at the bottom of col. 598: Caite foc*h*raic t*r*ian ł (the scribe wrote 't*r*ian' a second time and cancelled it by underlining) ceth*raimth*e, .i. *seissedh* i cu*m*ain na mbeodile dubla[d], ⁊ oc*ht*ma[d] i cu*m*ain na m*airbh*dile u*air* is belingai*re* te*t* forra; *ar* dia mbe treb*aire* *echt*rann isi*n* fuilliug, ⁊ ni aiscid 'What is [the] reward? A third or a fourth, i.e., a sixth in return for livestock doubled, and an eighth in return for inanimate chattels because it is a loan guaranteed by a promise for which he goes surety, because if there may be an external surety adding to it, and he does not seek after [it]'. The citation begins with a paragraph symbol, and there are no reference marks to place it anywhere within the text in either coloumn. Binchy, *CIH* 2065, n. g, notes that the text is out of place here, although he prints it at the end of the text from col. 599. It should be noted that the Brehon law tran-scripts place this citation in the same relative location as Binchy. For the translation of *bélingaire* as 'loan guaranteed by a promise', see McLeod, "*Ón* and *airliciud*," 181.

243 The phrase '.i. fer fi*ne*' is added above 'dogeib' by the scribe; see also Binchy, *CIH* 2065, n. b.

244 Opposite this in *marg. dext.* the scribe wrote 'tab*air* foder[a]' 'notice!'; Binchy, *CIH* 2065, n. c, queries whether it is in reference to the clause regarding Ogam which follows.

open sea, however, the person did not go purposely to fetch it |, and it is right that there should be something from it for [the] original owner. col. 599

What is the reason that for something found on the shore there is something from it for the original owner, and that which a person will find, i.e., a local, between nine waves of the sea and land that there is nothing from it for the original owner? The reason is: [it is the] law of taking that gives right in one [case] and [the] law of finds that gives right in the other, and [the law of] taking gives greater right than [the law of] finds.

What is the reason that for the item that is found on the open sea there is one thirtieth of it for the original owner, and that [the law of] taking gives right to it from then onwards? The reason is: refusal and permission and giving of kindred[245] make the property which is found between nine waves of the sea and land forfeit, and [the] law of taking only gives right to the property which is found out on the open sea.

Something found in a wood: two thirds of it for [the] person who finds it, one third to [the] person whose property it is, or for someone who may lose [it]. Something found in a wood or on a mountain: two thirds from it [in] an unfrequented place, half for a man of [the] *gelḟine*. If [it is found in] a frequented place, it is three fourths for him; and an Ogam alphabet which is carved in Ogam;[246] two thirds for a man of [the] *gelḟine*.

It was an 'assigning possession to one who is absent' that was done then, and [it is] certain that the property could not be got hold of when it was assigned, and he paid out compensation for assigning it; the one to whom it had been given on loan [pays] the person who assigned it. And a local found it afterwards in an unfrequented place on a mountain, and two thirds to the finder from it; and the third that the finder does not take from it, it is given to the person who did the assigning. And if it is certain that it could not be got hold of when it was assigned, the third that the finder does not take from it, the original owner should get it. Or they divide [it] in two between them, i.e., still an 'assigning possession to one who is absent', and [it is] uncertain whether the property could be got hold of or not when it was assigned, and the person who did the assigning gets half. And the property that is found afterwards in an unfrequented place of a mountain, and two thirds of it for

245 The precise interpretation of *tabairt fine* 'giving of kindred' is obscure to me.

246 The sense of this clause is obscure to me. It seems to be out of place. Cf. the similar clause in source B, CIH 1210.26–27.

da t*r*ian d'fer frit*he*, ⁊ in t*r*ian nad r*uc* fer frit*he* de, is a roin*n ar* dó it*er* fer mbun*aid* ⁊ *in* fer dorin*ne* i*n* taiselb*ad*.

Na s*éoit* frithe dogeib*h* dui*ne*, mad r*uc* leis iat ⁊ roḟagaib*h* a n-in*ad aile* iat, *acht* manab mesa int i*nad ar* fagaib*h* iat i*na* [in]t[247] inad*h* a fu*air*, is sl*an* dó. ⁊ masa mesa, is fiac*h* fo aigne fa*tha* air. ⁊ dui*ne* do*na* dleg*har* coma*r* na co*mingaire* si*n*; ⁊ ma dleg*har*, is t*r*ian na ait*hgena* air i*na* faicsin *ar* sechran is isi*n* lo it*er* comaithc*hiu*,[248] ł ait*hgin* isan aid*h*ce i*na* faicsin *ar* brú m*h*ona no c*h*uithe.

col. 600 Da t*r*ian isi*n* frithe ræda ł sl*eib*i, ⁊ cethr*aimth*e g*ach* m*air*t mainig*h*ter a sleib*h* suidig*hter*; ⁊ is mac*h*mad (read *machtnad*])[249] so*n* ⁊ *cona* inan*n* inad a fag*h*baith*er* iad. Is é in fa*th* so*n*: in b*h*ail*e* ata *cethraimthe* cac*h* m*air*t mainig*hter*, rob ait*h*nit do fer in c*r*uid*h* an*n* si*n*, ⁊ coir do a taisce no co tis*ad* fer bun*aid*, ⁊ coir cenco be*th* ac*ht* cethr*aimth*e *air*. ⁊ noc*har*b ait*h*nid do fer in c*r*uid*h* isi*n* frit*he* r*aoda*, ⁊ coir ce nobe*th* da t*r*ian *ar* fag*h*b*h*ail. Cuide frithe asna beodile[250] ⁊ asna m*airbh*dile, cid*h* a crich cid*h* a *secht*arcrich; ⁊ o g*h*eb*h*ait beodile in*n*scuch*ad* c*r*iche, ⁊ o be*t* m*airbh*dile *ar* fuiririug*h* gaite, is cuite tob*aig* astu.

Cuite f*r*ithe a bec*h*aib*h* ⁊ a daine dæ*raib*; ł co*m*a cuiti fastaig*the acht* manab e f*r*ec*r*a an dair gu*r*ab ag tia*cht*ain da tig*h* dobui se, ⁊ mad se, is do rosoich ⁊ a dul-sam gan ni. Mad saml*aid* frith é ⁊ a cul re tech, ⁊ nir *air*bertnaig*h* nach ag elo[d] robai, is a de*n*am *air* gu*r*ab ag elo[d], ⁊ cuite tob*h*aig*h* as.

Is eistib ata cuite f*r*ithe: s*éoit* test*a* o duine, ⁊ noch*a*n fit*ir* c'ait i*na* fuilit siad, ⁊ cuite f*rithe* do*n*ti fu*air* iad fo aigne coi*m*de[g] ł ecoi*m*de[g].

Is eistib ata cuite tob*aig*: s*éoit* dlig*h*es dui*ne* do rer dligi*d* ⁊ imna da*mhtar* dlig*ed* do, ⁊ cuite tob*aig* do*n*tí rotoibgest*ar* iat fo aigne na c*r*iche as*ar* tob*aig* iat.

247 I follow the emendation suggested by Binchy, *CIH* 2065, n. e.

248 Binchy, *CIH* 2065, n. f, queries whether 'it*er* comaith*chu*' (his reading) should be read as 'i tir comaith*ig*'. For the reading given here, cf. the source A version at *CIH* 58.13.

249 I follow the emendation suggested by Binchy, *CIH* 2065, n. h.

250 The ⟨o⟩ is written above the line by the scribe with reference marks.

the finder, and the third [the] finder does not take from it, it is divided in two between [the] original owner and the person who did the assigning.

The property[251] that a person will find, if he took them with him and he left them in another place, provided that the place where he left them is not worse than the place where he found [them], he is exempt from liability. And if it is worse, [he owes] a fine according to the nature of [his] reason regarding it. And that is a person who is not bound by co-tillage or joint grazing; and if he is bound, he receives a third of the compensation for seeing them astray in the daytime between neighbors, or [full] compensation for seeing them in the night on the edge of a bog or pit.

Two thirds for something found in the wood or on a mountain, and a col. 600
fourth of each cow fattened on a mountain which is proved; and that is surprising seeing that the place where they are found is the same. This is the reason for that: where there is a fourth for each fattened cow, he knew the owner of the livestock in that case, and it is proper for him to guard it until [the] original owner should come, and it is right that he should have only a fourth for it. And he did not know the owner of the livestock regarding what was found in the wood, and it is right that he should have two thirds for finding [it]. A share of something found from the livestock and from the inanimate property, whether in a territory or outside a territory; and when livestock will depart from a territory, and when it might be in consequence of theft, it is a share of recovering from them.

A share of something found from bees and from unfree people; or that it may be a share of detention unless the answer of the unfree person is that he was coming to his home, and if it is so, he can [go], and he [sc., the detainer] goes without anything. If he is found thus and his back to [his] home, and he does not plead that he is not escaping, it must be proved that he was escaping, and a share of recovering from it.

It is from these that there is a share of something found: property which someone has lost and he does not know where they [sc., the goods] are, and a share of something found for the one who found them according to [whether they are found in] a frequented or unfrequented place.

It is from these that there is a share of recovering: property which a person is entitled to according to law and regarding which right is allowed to him, and a share of recovering for the one who recovered them according to the nature of the land from which he recovered them.

251 The 'property' is pl. here.

Is eistib*h* ata cuit[e] impide: s*éoit* na dlig*enn* dui*ne* do rer dlig*id*, ⁊ cin*n*te ł cun*n*tab*airt con*ad *ar* impide t*uc*a iat. ⁊ t*r*ian *ar* impid*he* cin*n*te ⁊ *seiss*ed *ar* impide cun*n*tab*artaigh*. In tan *immorro* dlig*h*es nec*h* in s*éotu*, ⁊ ni tib*har*tai dó m*ana* b*eth* an i*m*pide, is cuite tob*aig aire* fo aig*ned* na cric*he*. Ma [a]ta *immorro* for t*airr*gire, cid *ar* impide t*uc*a[d], *co*n*a* b*eth* ni *aire*.

Is eistib*h* atait s*éoit* imluaid*h*: s*éoit* robata*r* a n-i*n*ad *aile*, ⁊ roerbast*ar* do dui*ne* airit*he* dul *ara* cen*n*, ł gi*n*gu*r* erb*ustar* rob f*err*de leis a dul, ⁊ s*éoit*
col. 601 i*m*luaid | do*n*ti docuaid*h ar*a cen*n* fo aig*ne*[d] eladhn*a*ig ł nemeladh*naig*, .i. sc*r*ep*al* no l*eth*sc*r*ep*al*. ⁊ is e *air*et atait na s*éoit* imluaid: co ria cuite tob*aig* [fo aic*n*ed] na c*r*ic*he*, ⁊ noch*an* teit t*ar*is.

Mana dub*air*t re dui*ne* dul *ara* cen*n* iti*r*, ł ce dub*hair*t, m*an*a f*err*de leis, no*ch*an fuil ni do*n*ti docuaid*h ar*a cen*n*, ⁊ noch*an* fuil ní uad*ha acht* na rodit*h*le. ⁊ mada ndit*h*le, is a n-aisec co lanfia*ch*aib g*ait*e. ⁊ is fo aigne[d] inti docuaid*h ara* cen*n* bid na s*éoit* imluaid*h in* inb*aid* is e fer bun*aid* adub*air*t ris dul *ara* cen*n*, ł fo aigne[d] intí docuirfed fer bun*aid ar*a cen*n* ma*n*ab e adub*air*t ris dul *ara* cen*n*.

Mas inan*n* fer f*r*it*he* ⁊ fer tire, is i*n*a rog*h*a ata i*n* cuite f*rithe* bias do ł i*n* cuite tire. Is as gab*ar* sin: "*con*techta gnim*ha* [ł] (la)[252] tir." Ma sain fer f*r*it*he* ⁊ fer tire, cuite t*obaig* d'fer tire ⁊ cuite f*rithe* d'fer f*rithe*.

Srut*h* saile, sal, sceo uisce:[253] m*air*bdile si*n*, no is beodile na cui*m*ge*nn* te*ch*tain as a dualg*us* a neirt fei*n*, u*air* da cuimgitis, noch*an* biad*h* ni aistib*h*.

252 Cf. source A, *CIH* 58.35, 'no'.
253 See the note on this phrase in source A.

It is from these that there is an 'intervention share': property that he is not entitled to according to law, and it is certain or doubtful that it was not by intervention that he obtained them. And [he receives] a third [if it is] certain that [he got the goods] by intervention and a sixth [if it is] doubtful that [he got the goods] by intervention. When someone, however, is entitled to the property, and they would not be recovered by him unless there was the intervention, it is a share of recovering from it according to the nature of the land [where it was found]. If there is, however, a promise for it, though it may be recovered by intervention, there would be nothing for it.

It is from these that there are the *sét*s of driving [cattle]: property which was in another place, and he had entrusted a certain person to go fetch them, or though he did not entrust [him], he would prefer him to go fetch
them, and *sét*s of driving | for the one who went to fetch them according to col. 601
[whether he is] trained or untrained, i.e., a scruple or a half scruple. And this is as much as the *sét*s of driving are: up to a share of recovering according to the nature of the land, and it [sc., the amount due to the driver] does not go beyond it.

If he did not ask someone to go fetch them at all, or though he asked, unless he preferred it, there is nothing for the one who went to fetch them, and he does not owe anything except that which he took away. And if it is [a case of] theft, they are restored with [the] full fines of theft.[254] And it is according to the nature of the one who went to fetch them [what] the *sét*s of driving will be whenever it is [the] original owner who told him to go fetch them, or according to the nature of the one whom [the] original owner would send to fetch them if he did not tell him to go fetch them.

If [the] finder and landowner are the same, it is his choice whether he will have the share of the thing found or the share of land. That is taken from: "equally valid are acts or land." If [the] finder and landowner are different, a share of recovering for [the] landowner and a share of the thing found for [the] finder.

Stream of saltwater, sea and freshwater:[255] that [is] inanimate property, or it is livestock that is not capable of escaping on account of its own strength, because if it were capable, there would not be anything from them.

---

254 This appears to be a reference to tracking stolen livestock; see *The MacEgan Legal Treatise* §4; Kelly, op. cit., 158–159; Osborough, "The Irish Custom of Tracts;" Mac Niocaill, "Irish Law and the Armagh Constitutions of 1297;" and Morgan, "'Lawes of Irelande': A Tract by Sir John Davies." There is another reference to tracking stolen livestock in the commentary in *Aidbred* §5. See also the discussion on this topic in the Introduction, p. 28.

255 Cf. the similar commentary in Heptad 64, source A, and *Muirbretha*, source C.

O bias fer bun*aid* a' toig*h*lenmai*n* a seoit, ⁊ o doc[h]ifi[256] roi*me* iat i*n* d*ar*a fe*cht* ci*n*go fac*a* an fe*cht aile*, *noch*an fuil cuite tob*aig* na fri*th*e na tob*ar*ta uad*h*a eistib*h* o b*hus* crich bescna i*n* cr*í*ch i*n*a gab*h*ait roi*me*.

No*ch*an fuil ni asna beodile do gres i cu*air*t i*n*gelta, ⁊ cuite tob*aig* aistib a *sechtar*cu*air*t i*n*gelta. No cuite frithe aistib*h* i cu*air*t i*n*gelta nó co mbeit *ar* taisce gat*aig*e, ⁊ o be*t*, is cuite tob*aig* aistib. Cuite tob*aig* aistib a *sechtar*cu*air*t i*n*gelta *acht* manab am*hlaid* robat*ar* ⁊ a n-aig*h*aig*h* *ar*a tech. ⁊ mas am*hlaid*, *acht* masa cin*n*te co tiucfaitis, is[257] sl*an* doib*h* ⁊ noch*an* fuil ni aistib*h*. Masa cin*n*te na tiucfaitis, is cuite tob*aig* aistib*h*. Masa cun*n*tab*air*t, is l*eth*cuite tob*aig* aistib*h*. Masa beodile conic a ngait fei*n* iat, is cuite tob*aig* aistib*h*.

T*r*ian a cot*a*c frithe o daorman*a*c ecl*ai*si do ecl*ais* ⁊ o dærceile fl*ath*a do fl*aith* co rud no ecma*cht* ł dirai*n*d, ⁊ nomad*h* an*n*-side. C*eth*raime a cod*ach* o særman*a*c ecl*ai*si do ecl*ais*(i) co rud .i. na caill*e*,[258] ł ecma*cht*, .i. i*n* loc*h*a,
col. 602 ł dirain*n*, .i. i*nt* sleib*h*e, | ⁊ *aile déc* mad an*n*-side, ⁊ noch*an* fuil ni o særceile fl*ath*a do flait*h*. Can asa ngab*ar* an *aile déc*, i*n* u*air* na in*n*isen*n* leb*har*? Is as gab*ar*: "am*ail* as e t*r*ian a cotach ata o dærman*a*c ecl*aise* do ecl*ais* ⁊ o dærceile fl*ath*a do fl*aith* co rud ł dirai*n*n no ecma*cht* ata uat*h*aib*h* a rud;" cub*aid* de-side cemad t*r*ia*n* a cotach o særman*a*c ecl*ai*si do ecl*ais* co rud ł ecm*acht* ł dirai*n*n do b*eth* uat*h*aib*h* a rud*h* fo*n* cu*m*a c*é*tna, i*n* aile *déc*.

---

256 The verb is a MI 3 sg. pres. fut. form of *ad-cí* 'sees'; *eDIL* s.v. *ad-cí* 'sees'.

257 The ⟨s⟩ is added above the line by the scribe.

258 This explanation and the two which follow the other two items listed are written as interlinear glosses in the source A version of the heptad.

When [the] original owner will be pursuing his property, and if he will see them before him at one time though he does not see [them] at another time, there will not be a share of recovering the item nor of taking due from him out of them when the territory in which they are previously is a territory covered by protocol.

There is never anything from the livestock in a grazing enclosure, and a share of recovering from them beyond the grazing enclosure. Or a share of something found from them in a grazing enclosure if[259] they may be in the possession of a thief, and when they may be, it is a share of recovering from them. A share of recovering from them beyond the grazing enclosure, unless thus they had been with their face towards their home. And if it is so, provided that it is certain that they would have come [home], he is exempt from liability for them and there is nothing from them. If it is certain that they would not have come [home], it is a share of recovering from them. If it is doubtful, it is half a share of recovering from them. If it is livestock which themselves can be stolen, it is a share of recovering from them.

A third of his share of something found from a base monastic client to his church and from a lord's base client to his lord as far as a wood or inaccessible place or unclaimed land, and a ninth if it is in those [places]. A fourth of his share from a monastic free client to his church as far as a wood, i.e., the forest, or inaccessible place, i.e., the lake, or unclaimed land, i.e., the mountain, | and a twelfth if it is in those, and there is nothing from a lord's free col. 602
client to his lord in that case. Whence is the twelfth taken, because [the] book does not say? It is taken from: "as it is a third of his share that is from a base monastic client to his church and from a lord's base client to his lord as far as a wood or unclaimed land or inaccessible place which is due from them in a wood;" it is proper that it may be a third of the share from a free monastic client to his church as far as a wood or inaccessible place or unclaimed land which should be due from them in a wood similarly, i.e., a twelfth.

259 The use of *no co* 'unless, until' does not make sense here as the reward for livestock in a grazing enclosure is given only when a thief has been caught in the grazing enclosure with the livestock.

Sruth uaisce an*n*sa at*air*betaig ca*ch* rec*h*ti.[260] Mad sruth[261] firuisce, a ceth*raimth*e co f*or*cend nai crich, a t*r*ian co forcend da crich *déc*, a l*eth* o dib cric*h*aib *déc* coruice tir besa nesa do muir, ⁊ a da t*r*ian a tir besa nesa do muir. Dia roa muir, is diles *ar*a tabh*air*t d*ar noí* ton*n*a.

Mad tabairt ant sro*th*a, is a t*r*ian *ar* tri h-orb*aib* ⁊ a da t*r*ian *ar* se h-orb*aib*, ⁊ uile *ar* nai n-orb*aib*. Mad i*ar* n-airiasa*cht* ⁊ femed, ł mana be in fer [be](i)sa *sét ar* aird ci*n*co be airiasa*cht*, dia feme[d] cach ...[262]

Ma toch*ar* sro*th*a sail sceo uisce, is a l*eth* co f*or*cen*n noí* crich,[263] ⁊ a da t*r*ian ó *noí* crichaib co f*or*cen*n* da c*r*ich *déc* coruice tir bes nesa*m* do muir. Ma fo cosmailes toch*air* sro*th*a uisce cosmailigt*er* toch*ar* ant srotha-so ...[264] Oc*us* is a cosmailes br*eith*e tab*ar*ta b*erair* in br*eth*-so, uair an i*nbaid* bei*r*is dil*es* a t*r*ian *ar*a tab*air*t a sru*th* uisc*i*, is a l*eth* is dil*es ar*a tob*air*t (s)a[265] sru*th* saile ⁊ us*ci* imale.

Mad f*r*i toch*ar* sro*th*a mu*r*gabl*a* riagailt*er* toc*har* in sro*th*a-so, is a ceth*raimth*e is dil*es* a f*or*cen*n trí crich*, ⁊ a l*eth ar* se crich*aib*, ⁊ a t*r*i ceth*raimth*e *ar noí* crich*aib*, ⁊ uile *ar* dib c*r*icha *déc*; uair is ceth*raimth*e fil it*er* a da tab*air*t, gurab ceth*raimth*e d*ano* it*er* a da tochar.[266]

---

260 The last three words of the sentence are problematic, and it is possible that the scribe has left something out or made a copying mistake. The form 'at*air*betaig', assuming that it should not be interpreted as 'a t*air*betaig', is obscure to me. It is potentially a form of *ad-tairbir* 'returns, delivers back'; cf. its vn. *atairbert* and *tairbert*, the vn. of *do-airbir* 'subdues, yields, gives, hands over'. It is possible that the form *atairbetaig* should be *atairbertaig*, a form from a simplex possibly arising from a conflation of *ad-tairbir* and *do-airbir*. The form *rechti* appears to be the pl. part. of *rigid* 'stretches, extends, rules'; if so, its meaning is not entirely clear.

261 The scribe added the ⟨s⟩ above the ⟨d⟩ in 'mad'.

262 Binchy, *CIH* 2067, n. b, notes that the sentence is incomplete.

263 The phrase '*noí* crich' is added above 'co f*or*cen*n*' by the scribe.

264 Binchy, *CIH* 2067, n. b, notes that this sentence is incomplete.

265 I follow the emendation suggested by Binchy, *CIH* 2067, n. e.

266 The scribe originally wrote ⟨tab̄t⟩, but cancelled it by underlining. He wrote 'tochar' above it with reference marks.

A[267] stream of water then that delivers each [item which is] regulated.[268] If it is a stream of freshwater, a fourth of it up to the end of nine territories, a third of it up to the end of twelve territories, half of it from twelve territories up to the land which is closest to the sea, and two thirds of it from the land which is next to the sea. If it reaches the sea, it is forfeit on account of its being carried beyond nine waves.

If the stream has brought it, it is a third of it for three territories and two thirds of it for six territories, and all of it for nine territories. If it is after refusal and permission, or if the person whose property it is is not present, though there is not permission, if each refusal …

If a stream of salt and freshwater casts it ashore, it is half of it up to the end of nine territories, and two thirds of it from nine territories up to the end of twelve territories, up to the land which is closest to the sea. If it is similar to being cast ashore by streams of water, they are likened to being cast ashore by this stream … And it is from a similarity of the judgment of bringing that this judgment is given, because whenever it brings [a judgment of] forfeiture of a third of it on account of its being carried by a stream of water, it is half of it which is forfeit on account of its being carried by a stream of salt and freshwater together.

If the casting ashore by those streams is regulated as the casting ashore by a stream which is an inlet of the sea, it is a fourth of it which is forfeit from the end of three territories, and half of it for six territories, and three fourths of it for nine territories, and all of it for twelve territories; because it is a fourth which is amongst the two carryings [to shore], so there is a fourth then amongst the two castings ashore.[269]

---

267 From here to the end of this commentary, cf. the commentaries from *Muirbretha*, source D, *CIH* 959.7–9, and the fullest version in *Muirbretha/Bretha Éitgid*, source C, *CIH* 315.30–316.8. See also the discussion in the Introduction, pp. 51–54. The commentary presents a system of reward percentages for items which have either been cast ashore by a stream, or which have been carried out of a stream's current by the finder. If the item has been rescued from the current itself, the finder receives a greater percentage than for items which have been cast ashore. The farther the item has traveled, the larger the percentage for the finder. Unfortunately, parts of this material are missing from this commentary; a fuller version is found in the commentary from *Muirbretha*, source C. Based on how skewed the reward percentges are and the degree of repetition of scenarios and contradictory reward percentages, it appears as though a variety of copying mistakes happened rather than simply omitting some of the material in the exemplar.

268 The translation of this sentence is tentative.

269 The precise meaning of *itir* in the last two clauses is uncertain.

Mad tab*air*t a sruth sail sceo uis*ci*, is a l*eth* *ar* t*r*i cricha, ⁊ uile *ar* se crich*aib*. Ma toch*ar* srot*h*a murgabhl*a*, is a t*r*ian *ar* t*r*i c*r*ich*aib*, ⁊ a da t*r*ian *ar* se crich*aib*, ⁊ uile *ar noí* crich*aib*.

Ma toch*ar* srot*h*a mu*r*gabl*a*, is a t*r*ian *ar* t*r*i crich*aib*, ⁊ a da trian *ar* se crich*aib*, ⁊ uile *ar ceithri* crich*aib*[270] co l*eth*, ⁊ is l*eth* do c*r*ichaib*h* tormaig f*r*i dilsiug toch*ar* ce*chtar*de in da srut*h*-sa sech a tab*air*t an tan is f*r*i sru*th* mu*r*gab*hla* riagailt*er* srut*h* sail sceo usce. Finit.

O'Dav no. 488 [*CIH* 1484.10–11] Com*air*ser, .i. fiag*h*fraig*hi*,[271] *ut est* "diam frit*h*i fo[g]b*a*,[272] fo th*uathaib*[273] co*mair*ser," .i. dena at*h*com*ar*c fona tuatha.

270 Opposite this word in *marg. dext.*, the scribe has written '*fech*' 'look!'. Binchy, *CIH* 2067, n. g, queries whether this is to bring attention to the fact that the compensation structure here contradicts that found in the paragraph above, *CIH* 2067.22.

271 The verb appears to be a 2 sg. pres. ind. form of *fíafraigid*, a MI simplex from *íarmi-foich* 'seeks, inquires, makes an inquiry'; I owe this suggestion to Paul Russell.

272 Binchy, *CIH* 1484, n. e, quoting Bergin, "On the Syntax of the Verb in Old Irish," 200, n. 1, suggests the emendation 'frithe fogbae'.

273 Binchy, *CIH* 1484, n. f, notes that the MS reads ⟨th̄⟩, but he prints 'tuath*aib*' at *CIH* 1484.10.

If a stream of salt and freshwater has brought it, it is half of it for three territories, and all [of it] for six territories. If a stream of an inlet of the sea cast it ashore, it is a third of it for three territories, and two thirds of it for six territories, and all [of it] for nine territories.

If a stream of an inlet of the sea casts it ashore, it is a third of it for three territories, and two thirds of it for six territories, and all [of it] for four up to half; and half of it for territories in addition to forfeiture of what has been cast ashore by both of those two streams beyond what it has brought when it is by a stream of an inlet of the sea that a stream of salt and freshwaters is regulated. *It finishes.*

O'Dav[274] *Comairser* 'you should inquire', i.e., you inquire, *ut est* "if you may find lost property, you inquire throughout [the] *túath*s," i.e., you should make an inquiry throughout the *túath*s.

274 Stokes, "O'Davoren's Glossary;" no. 488; and *GEIL* 124, n. 164.

Muirbretha

Text, Variants, Commentary, and Translation

Source A, Oxford, Bodleian Library MS Rawl. B. 506, ff. 40d–41a, *CIH* 139.32–140.8[1]

In rodercaid*h*: Ma darig*h*ni a dliged*h*, rodercaid*h*,[2] set foraca (⁊)[3] di uinge do (ł)[4] masa or ł *air*get ł allm*h*aire set ⁊ set f*or*aicce se scripla do masa i*ar*and ł sec*h*ed*h*a ⁊ escub[5] meala[6] ł fina ma ta mil ł fin indte.

Maine d*er*na a dlig*h*ed*h* im*morro* masa ci*n*nti gu t*ar*raistea ⁊ ci*n*nti i raib*h*i inti, aithg*h*in a codach gu cetraimt*h*i diri a codac*h* ⁊ gu ceatraim*h*t*h*i eneclainde d'ic do re ca*ch* fe*ar*.

Masa ci*n*nti gu tarrista ⁊ cu*n*ntab*hairt* i rraib*h*i indti, *secht* cum*al*a d'ic do ⁊ ait*h*g*h*in a c*h*oda gu ceatraimt*h*i dire a c*h*oda gu cetraimt*h*i enecclai*n*ne d'ic re cac*h* fe*ar* do*na* *secht* cum*al*a-sei*n*.

f. 41a Masa | cu*n*ntab*air*t in tarraistea ⁊ cindti i rab*h*i inti, let*h* *secht* cum*al* on rig*h* an*n* ⁊ let*h*ait*h*g*h*ein a codac*h* gu n-oc*h*tmad*h* dire a codac*h* ⁊ gu n-oc*h*tmad*h* enecl*ainne* d'ic re cac*h* fe*ar* di let i rraibi indte.

Masa cu*n*ntab*air*t i t*ar*raista ⁊ cu*n*tab*air*t i rraib*h*i inti, leat*h* *secht* cum*al* on rig*h* an*n* ⁊ leat*h*aithg*h*ei*n* a c*h*oda gu n-oc*h*tmad*h* dire a coda ⁊ gu n-oc*h*tmad*h* eneclai*n*ne d'ic do ra cac*h* fe*ar* an*n* leat*h* na *secht* cum*al*.

Masa ci*n*nti guna tarraista, gid*h* ci*n*nti gid*h* cu*n*ntabairt i rraib*h*i in*n*te, is slan do-sum*h* ⁊ iccad in ri *secht* cum*al*a an*n*; ⁊ damad*h* eisiu*mh* daneit*h* a aisneis-sen, gu *m*beit*h* a trian do-s*omh* *ar* aisneis.

---

1 The scribe of this commentary is the same scribe who copied the *Muirbretha* commentary later in the same MS, (Source B), edited below at pp. 322–325. See also *CCIH* 18; cf. *Anfuigell* § 29 (*CIH* 2155.16–34) where the commentary also concerns the watchman's share; and Charlene M. Eska, "Early Irish Trade: *Cnóe Gnáe* 'Beautiful Nuts' Revisited," *Cambrian Medieval Celtic Studies* 78 (2019): 101–109, at 102. The watchman's reward here is the same as it is given in the commentary in *Anfuigell* § 29, however, the system of various fines he could owe differs in some details, e.g. the king is not mentioned in *Anfuigell*.

2 It is possible that *rodercaidh* should be interpreted here as the noun for 'watchman' instead of the 3 sg. perf. of *dercaid* 'looks (at)'.

3 I follow the emendation suggested by Binchy, *CIH* 139, n. b.

4 I follow the emendation suggested by Binchy, *CIH* 139, n. b.

5 For *escop* as a measure for honey or wine, see *EIF* 581.

6 The first ⟨a⟩ is written subscript.

The watchman:[7] If he has done his duty, he has watched, he gets a *sét* worth two ounces if it is gold or silver or imported goods, and he gets a *sét* worth six scruples[8] if it is iron or hides, and a vessel of honey or wine if her cargo[9] is honey or wine.[10]

If he does not do [his duty] properly, however, if it is certain that she could have been seized and it is certain what her cargo was, restitution of his [sc., the watchman's] share with a fourth of [the] compensation of his share and with a fourth of [the] honor-price to be paid by him to each person [who would have lawfully had a share in the boat's value].

If it is certain that she could have been seized and there was doubt about what her cargo was, seven *cumal*s are to be paid by him and restitution of his share with a fourth of [the] compensation [and] with a fourth of [the] honor-price to be paid to each person from those seven *cumal*s.

If it is | doubtful whether she could have been seized and certainty about f. 41a
what her cargo was, half of the seven *cumal*s [is due] from the king in that case and half restitution of his share with an eighth of [the] compensation of his share and with an eighth of [the] honor-price to be paid to each person from the half that was in it [sc., from half of the seven *cumal*s].

If it is doubtful whether she could have been seized and doubt about what her cargo was, half of the seven *cumal*s [is due] from the king in that case and half restitution of his share with an eighth of [the] compensation of his share and with an eighth of [the] honor-price to be paid by him to each person there, half of the seven *cumal*s.

If it is certain that she could not have been seized, whether there was certainty or doubt regarding what her cargo was, he is exempt from liability, and let the king pay seven *cumal*s in that case;[11] and if it might be he [himself, sc., the watchman] who informed [about] it, there should be a third of it for him [sc., the watchman] for informing.

---

7 See the Introduction, pp. 45–46 for discussion; and Wooding, *Communication and Commerce*, 33 and 68–71.

8 For the relative value of currency terms, see the Introduction, p. XIX and *EIF* 589–595.

9 Although the commentary does not use one of the terms for cargo, such as *lucht*, *indte* 'in her' is here used in reference to the ship's cargo.

10 This paragraph is translated and discussed in Wooding, *Communication and Commerce*, 69.

11 See also *Muirbretha*, source B.

Source B, Oxford, Bodleian Library MS Rawl. B. 506, ff. 56d–57a, *CIH* 177.34–178.26[12]

Masa ri benas fe*ar*and ri muir, ⁊ itat caillte ina [ḟ]earund,[13] is ceit*h*ri *secht* cum*al*(ad*h*)[14] i *n-i*notach*t*[15] cac*h*a bliad*na* da eccl*ais* bu*n*aid*h* fei*n*: *secht* cum*ala* ar it*h* ⁊ *secht* cum*ala ar* blic*h*t ⁊ *secht* cum*ala*[16] *ar* meas ⁊ *secht* cum*ala ar* tiac*h*tain long ⁊ b*ar*c. A c*h*eat*r*aim*h*t*h*i-sid*h*e o rig*h* *cóic*id ⁊ cet*r*aim*h*t*h*i na ceat*r*amthana o rig*h* Er*end*, ⁊ nucu*nn* [ḟ]uil ni o rig*h* *cóic*id*h* ł (n)o[17] rig*h* Erend[18] do*na* t*r*i *secht* cum*al* ele, *acht* a n-ic do rig*h* tuait*h*e a ænur.

Occ*us* o dab*er*a ri tuait*h*e na ceitri *secht* cum*ala*-sain a*m*ac*h* da ecclais bu*n*aid*h* cac*h*a bliad*na*, nucu*nn* [ḟ]uil ni uad*h* i*n*na nem*h*thoc*h*ur (read *tochur* ?),[19] *acht* mana millt*er* mess ł ith i*ar*na thaidhb*h*siu, ł da n-i*m*paider longa o thir. Atat *secht* cum*ala* o rig*h* d*ar* eise cac*h* neic*h* dib*h*; in da *secht*
f. 57a co*mal* [ḟ]uil o rig*h* d*ar*a eise etha ⁊ blec*h*ta, a comroind gu coitc*h*end | fon tuait*h* uile .i. a cuit do t*h*ab*air*t do cac*h* duine dib conic fub*ha* ⁊ rub*ha* ⁊ biathad*h*. Na *secht* cum*ala* [ḟ]uil i *m*milliud*h* in meassa, a breit*h* do luc*h*t na coilli a n-ænur.

Na *secht* cum*ala* [ḟ]uil i *n*n-impud*h* long ⁊ b*ar*c, ma rofes in port *air*ithe, is a leat*h* na *secht* cum*al* do. Mai*n*e feas, leat*h* *secht* cum*al* do luc*h*t na port uili ⁊ co*mh*rannait et*ar*ro he; ⁊ in leat*h* eile do tuait*h*, ⁊ comra*n*nait fo c*h*ut*r*uma,

12 The scribe of this commentary is the same scribe who copied the *Muirbretha* commentary earlier in the same MS (source A).

13 The ⟨a⟩ is written subscript.

14 I follow the emendation suggested by Binchy, *CIH* 177, n. i.

15 The MS reads 'i*m*notac*h*t'. The scribe's suspension mark for ⟨m⟩ seems to be a misinterpretation of a series of minims in his exemplar; see also Binchy, *CIH* 177, n. j.

16 The second ⟨a⟩ is written subscript and was added later by the scribe; see also Binchy, *CIH* 177, n. k.

17 Binchy, *CIH* 177, n. l, queries whether this word should be omitted as it seems to be an error of dittography.

18 The MS reads 'Erig*h*'; see also Binchy, *CIH* 177, n. m.

19 The MS reading is likely a mistake as the king, according to the rest of the commentary, does not pay the church anything from the profits that he makes from items washed up on shore unless other sources of revenue should fail.

If[20] it is a king [who has] territory which borders [the] sea, and there are harbors[21] in his territory, [the value of] 28 *cumals* at the beginning of every year [is due] to his own original church: seven *cumals* worth of grain and seven *cumals* worth of milk and seven *cumals* worth of mast and seven *cumals* for the arrival of boats and ships; a fourth of that from [the] king of the province and a fourth of the fourth from [the] king of Ireland,[22] and there is nothing from [the] king of the province or [the] king of Ireland from the other 21 *cumals*, but they are paid by [the] king of [the] *túath* alone.

And when [the] king of [the] *túath* brings those 28 *cumals* away to his original church each year, there is nothing [due] from him of anything which is cast ashore,[23] unless [the] mast or grain are ruined after their appearance,[24] or if ships are turned away from land. There are seven *cumals* from [the] king instead of each one of them. The fourteen *cumals* which are from [the] king instead of grain and milk, they are to be divided commonly | f. 57a
throughout the entire *túath*, i.e., a share to be given to each person who is capable of *fuba* and *ruba* and feeding.[25] The seven *cumals* which are for the destruction of the mast, they are given only to the people of the wood.

The seven *cumals* which are for boats and ships being turned away, if the particular landing place was known, half of the seven *cumals* [are due] to him.[26] If it was not known, half of the seven *cumals* [are due] to the people of all the landing places, and they divide it between them; and the other half is for the *túath*, and they divide [it] equally, i.e., for each one who is capable of

20 For discussion of this source, see the Introduction, pp. 46–47

21 Kelly, *EIF* 408, takes *caillte* as the pl. of *calad* 'shore, port'. Although the expected nom. pl. for a m. *o*-stem is *calaid*, the pl. here seems to be formed from a f. *iā*-stem; cf. f. *iā*-stem *cailte* 'meanness', which is derived from 2 *calad* 'hard, stingy', the substantive of which gives rise to 1 *calad* 'port, shore', where the semantic extension of a place which is hard becomes the firm place to land a ship; *eDIL* s.vv. *cailte*, 1 *calad*, and 2 *calad*.

22 According to the second commentary in source C, the provincial king and king of Ireland both receive a percentage of the profits from any shipwrecks in the local king's territory. The historical reality (or not) of these designations will not be discussed here. For an overview of the general debate, see Bart Jaski, *Early Irish Kingship and Succession* (Dublin: Four Courts Press, 2000).

23 According to some legal sources, the king is entitled to a percentage of any valuables found on the road, unclaimed land, or in the sea (including what has been washed up on shore); *EIF* 407–408; and *Bechbretha*, 171(g).

24 The translation of this clause is tentative.

25 These are some of the regular duties clients owe their lord; *GEIL* 29–36.

26 Presumably this is in reference to the king.

.i. da ca*ch* æn gunicc fub*ha* ⁊ rub*ha* ⁊ biathad*h*. ł da*no* gia dab*er*ad ri *secht cumala ar*a *th*oc*h*ur, maini t*ar*la iat, atat *secht* cum*al*a uad*h* d*ar* eis ca*ch* nei*ch* dib*h*, ⁊ *in* com*h*raind c*h*eana atrubr*am*ar rom*h*aind orru.

Gid bratan gid ron gid mucc m*ara* t*h*i doc*hum* tiri, ma ruccad *im*mach *ar*issi he, ⁊ nugud*h* a du[a]l[g]us[27] a nirt fein dac*h*uaid*h*, *secht* cum*ala* o rig*h* d*ar* eis ca*ch* nei*ch* dib*h*, ⁊ leat*h* na *secht* cum*al* d'ḟir[28] p*h*uirt ⁊ a leat*h* do t*h*uait*h*; mas a dual[g]*us* a neirt doc*h*uat*ar* *im*mac*h* nuccu*nn* [ḟ]uil ni o rig*h* d*ar*a eise.

Cid fo*dera* gid*h* a dualg*hus* a *n*neirt dechsat na daini[29] *im*mach co fuilet *secht* cum*ala* o rig*h* d*ar*a n-eisi, ⁊ na fuil d*ar*a n-eisi-sium*h*?

Is e fat*ha*: Iss e a n-ait*h*reib*h* gnat*h*ach-so bith fo*n* muir, ⁊ is e atreab*h* gna*th*ach na ndoini[30] bit*h* f*or* tir.

Bairc conscara fri tir,[31] .i. b*ar*c so c*h*omb*r*ister f*r*isin tir; ca*ch* ni tucc*us*tar duini da setaib*h* d*ar* nai ton*n*aib m*ar*a amuig*h* is a dilsi do, ⁊ ca*ch* ni thuccad it*er* næ to*nn*a m*ara* ⁊ tir, feimed*h* ⁊ uiriasac*h*t ⁊ finec[h]aire loc*h*ta na tuait*he* uile do riag*h*ail riu. Ca*ch* ni tainic i tir da setaib*h*, maine mo na log*h* *cóic sét* [ḟ]uil an*n*, a b*r*ith d'ḟir puirt a ænur. Ma ta *im*macraid*h* air, a leat*h* do luc*h*t na tuait*he* ⁊ a leat*h* d'ḟir p*h*uirt. ⁊ ge t*arrus* seoit na b*air*ce-sea uile, atat *secht* cum*al*a o rig*h* d*ar*a n-eise, u*air* is meiste iat a fliuchad*h*.

---

27 I follow the emendation suggested by Binchy, *CIH* 178, n. c.

28 Binchy, *CIH* 178, n. d, states that the lenition mark was added later. Here and throughout this section of the MS, I respectfully disagree with Binchy's assessment.

29 The MS reads 'daim'; I follow the emendation suggested by Binchy, *CIH* 178, n. e.

30 The MS reads 'no*n*mi'; I follow the emendation suggested by Binchy, *CIH* 178, n. e.

31 Cf. O'Dav no. 477 below at pp. 346 and 347.

fuba and *ruba* and feeding. Or, then, although a king might give seven *cumal*s on account of his [receiving] items which have been cast ashore, unless he produces them, there are seven *cumal*s [due] from him instead for each one of them, and the division of booty as we have said before for them.

Whether salmon or seal or porpoise come towards shore, if it was taken out [of the sea] subsequently and it was not on account of its own strength that it went [out of the sea],[32] seven *cumal*s from [the] king instead of each one of them, and half of the seven *cumal*s for the owner of the shore and half of it for [the] *túath*. If it is on account of their own strength that they had gone out [of the sea], there is nothing [due] from [the] king instead of it.[33]

What causes [the situation] that [when] it is by their own strength that the people had gone out [to get the sea animals] that there are seven *cumal*s [due] from [the] king instead of them [sc., the sea animals themselves], and there is nothing instead of them [when the sea animals come out of the water on their own]?

The reason is: their [sc., the sea animals'] usual dwelling is to be under the sea, and the usual dwelling of the people is to be on land.

A boat which breaks against land, i.e., a boat that is broken against the land; each thing that a person brought from its valuables from beyond nine waves of [the] sea is forfeit to him, and each thing that was carried [by the water to] between nine waves of the sea and land, refusal and permission and the local people of the entire *túath*[34] to rule regarding them.[35] Each thing which came to land from its valuables, unless its value is greater than the amount of five *sét*s, it is given only to the owner of the shore. If it is more than that [in terms of it value], half of it [is given] to the people of the *túath* and half of it to the owner of the shore. And though all [the] valuables of that boat were seized, there are seven *cumal*s from [the] king instead of them because they are the worse for their getting wet.[36]

---

32 The reference here is to catching the salmon, seals, etc. versus their coming to shore themselves whether being carried by the tide or of their own volition.

33 According to the commentary, the king is entitled to a certain amount of the marine animals which are caught; *EIF* 282–285. The legal principle here is similar to that surrounding royal fish in England; Moore and Moore, *The History and Law of Fisheries*, 191; Baker, *English Legal History*, 406; Kowaleski, *The Havener's Accounts of the Earldom and Duchy of Cornwall*, 6, 15, 17, 18, and 26–27.

34 The phrase *finec*[h]*aire lochta na tuaithe uile* is difficult to interpret. The sense seems to be that the local residents of the entire *túath* decide how to divide any of these items.

35 For these conditions, see sources C, D, and E below and Heptad 64, sources A, C, and J.

36 The sense of the last clause is that the king does not give any of the rescued cargo itself because the cargo is damaged as a result of getting wet. Instead, the king gives other items valued at seven *cumals*.

Muirbretha/Bretha Éitgid

Source C, *Bretha Éitgid*, TCD MS 1433 [*olim* E.3.5], pp. 49b–50b, *CIH* 314.17–316.36[37]

Diles i muirbreth*aib* airi ruanada dar nae tondaib,[38] .i. cid seoit fir fi*ne* cid seoit fir anfi*ne*, cid seoit fir bescna cid seoit fir nei*m*bescna, o dob*ertar* tar[39] nae ton*na* m*ar*a amuig iat, ⁊ dula d'ae*nt*oisg d*ar*a cen*n*, is a ndilsi uili do*n*ti tucas iat. Mas et*ar* nae ton*na* m*ar*a ⁊ tir *t*ucast*ar* iat, is femed*h* ⁊ uriasac*ht* fir fi*ne* do riagail riu, u*air* is riu ata feimed ⁊ uriasa*cht* ⁊ fine*chaire* do riagail riu. Set dob*er*ar a aicenaib, ⁊ a armaigib, ⁊ a coirib cuairdill, ⁊ a saebcoirib, ⁊

37 See also *Anfuigell* § 22 (*CIH* 2153.17–40, especially source O, *CIH* 315.5–28, which is printed below at pp. 330–335) and § 29, *CIH* 2155.16–34, and cf. the version of this material in source E, below at pp. 342 and 343 *CIH* 1212.3–34. See also *AL* 3: 422.1–433.17; and Wooding, *Communication and Commerce*, 68–71, and 95.

38 Although the dat. pl. of *tonn* 'wave' is unexpected here, in MI the prep. *tar* is occasionally found governing the dat. case instead of the acc.; *eDIL* s.v. *tar, dar*.

39 Binchy, *CIH* 314, n. c, notes that the material from *tar* (314.19) through *riu* (314.22) is 'written in smaller and more closely pressed script' than the other material in this col. and queries whether it might have been written by a different scribe. While the script is, indeed, more compact for these lines, I would suggest that the lines in question were written by the same scribe of this section of the MS (pp. 21–60); the letter ⟨f⟩ and the Tironian note are distinctive.

Muirbretha/Bretha Éitgid[40]

Free from claim in sea-judgments [is the] load of a strong man [taken from] beyond nine waves,[41] i.e., whether valuables belonging to a local person [lit. man of the kindred] or valuables belonging to a stranger [lit. man of a stranger kindred],[42] whether valuables belonging to a man [from a territory governed by a] protocol, or valuables belonging to a man from a territory not governed by a protocol, because they are brought from beyond nine waves of [the] sea, and he went purposely to get them, they are forfeited entirely to the one who brought them. If he brought them [from] between nine waves of the sea and land, it is [the] refusal and permission of a local person which regulate them because there is refusal and permission and a group of locals[43] which regulate them. Property which is brought from waters, and from

40 For a discussion of the following material, see the Introduction, pp. 47–51 *GEIL* 277 has the following to say about the three commentaries here: 'The first ... deals with ownership of flotsam, the second with ownership of jetsam, and the third with ownership of goods carried off by a stream and either deposited downstream or washed out to sea'. Unfortunately, the definitions of 'flotsam' and 'jetsam' used by Kelly and *eDIL* do not conform to the standard defintions of these terms used in international maritime law. 'Flotsam' is anything which has not been deliberately thrown overboard; this is usually as a result of accident or shipwreck. 'Jetsam' is anything which has been deliberately thrown overboard; this is usually in an attempt to lighten a ship in distress. Depending on the nature of the item, both flotsam and jetsam can float, both can sink, and both can be carried to the shore. With regard to the Irish commentaries, the first concerns items floating on the water, the second concerns items which have washed up on shore, and the third concerns items which have been carried by the current of salt or freshwater streams.

41 Cf. source E below and Heptad 54 for similar material. Based on the third commentary below, Kelly, *EIF* 569–570, estimates that the distance between the shore and the ninth wave of the sea as 200 cubits = 300 feet. Regardless of the precise distance, the concept is that any item beyond the ninth wave is far enough out to sea that there is no guarantee that it will be washed ashore. If someone spots an item in the water from shore and goes out beyond the ninth wave to retrieve it, he has rights to the item due to the potential risk involved in retrieving it from that distance out from shore. The word used for 'strong man', *rúanaid*, can also refer to a champion; *eDIL* s.v. 2 *rúanaid*.

42 The contrast here may not be so much between kinsmen and non-kinsmen, but as between locals and non-locals.

43 The term *finechaire* is difficult to render here. Although the term formally refers to a family group, here it is being equated with *fer fine* 'man of kindred, local person'. Thus the sense seems to be similar to what is seen in source B above; it refers to a group of local residents.

a tig teined, ⁊ it*er* nae tondaib mara ⁊ tire; ⁊ ma robi d'aicbeile na h-oidida ni risna tairnic a n-airiasa*cht* d'fir bunaid, is i*n*and do ⁊ dobeit*h* feimead an*n* no uiriasa*cht*[44] nama.

Masa femed ⁊ uiriasac*h*t fir fi*n*e, is a ndilsi uile donti tuc as iat.

Masa femed no uiriasac*h*t fir fi*n*e, is dil*es* a da t*r*ian donti tuc as iat.

Masa urias*acht* ar ai*n*e fir fi*n*e, is dil*es* a t*r*in[45] donti tuc as iat.

Masa femed ⁊ uirias*acht* fir anfi*n*e, is dil*es* a da t*r*ian don dui*n*e tuc as iat.

[Mas f*emed* ł airr*acht* fir ainfine, is dilsi a t*r*ia*n*.][46]

Masa uirias*acht* ar ai*n*e fir anfi*n*e, is da t*r*ian i*n* t*r*in no a l*eth* in t*r*in, no a beit*h* can ni.

Can asa ngabar da t*r*ian i*n* t*r*in ata d'fir anfi*n*e 'na airias*acht* ar ai*n*e, uair na*ch* i*n*disen*n* lebar? Is as gabair: "o fir fi*n*e, uair i bail ata a ndil*se* a da t*r*i[n] d'fir fi*n*e ina femed*h* no 'na n-urias*acht* is dilsi a t*r*in ata d'fir anfi*n*e ina femed no 'na uirias*acht*."[47] Coir 'no deiside, uair is t*r*ian ata d'fir fi*n*e 'na urias*acht* ar ai*n*e, cemad [d]a[48] t*r*ian i*n* t*r*in dobeit*h* d'fir anfi*n*e 'na airias*acht* ar aine uair[49] na i*n*disen*n* lebar. Is as gabair: "o fir fi*n*e, uair a bail ata dilsi a da t*r*ian

44 The scribe initially wrote 'uiriac', but corrected his mistake by adding a bottom open bow to the ⟨c⟩, effectively turning the ⟨c⟩ into a roman script ⟨s⟩.

45 Binchy, *CIH* 314, n. d, states that there is an error here, but he does not say whether the error is linguistic or legal. The same formula is repeated in a version of this commentary found in source E, *CIH* 1212.10.

46 Supplied from source E, *CIH* 1213.12. The scribe of TCD MS 1433 either skipped a line of text, or his exemplar was defective.

47 The source of this and the other quotations in the commentary is unknown, although it is likely to be a either another commentary on the same subject, or a version of the tract no longer extant.

48 I follow the emendation suggested by Binchy, *CIH* 314, n. e.

49 Binchy, *CIH* 314, n. f, queries whether *uair* (*CIH* 314.35) through the first *airiasacht* (*CIH* 314.39) might be an instance of dittography or whether some words have been skipped by the scribe. The text has been edited and translated as it appears in the MS, although it does not make much sense as it stands. A coherent version of this material is found in source E below.

battlefields, and from whirlpools, and from maelstroms, and from a burning house, and between nine waves of [the] sea and land; and if there is wont to be the danger of violent death regarding anything which he got by permission from the owner, he gets the same [amount] as there should be for refusal in that case or permission only.

If it is [with] a local's refusal and permission, they are forfeit entirely to the one who brought them out [of the water].

If it is [with] a local's refusal or permission,[50] two thirds of it is forfeit to the one who brought them out.

If it is [with] a locals's permission for amusement,[51] a third of it is forfeit to the one who brought them out.

If it is [with] a stranger's refusal and permission, two thirds of it is forfeit to the person who brought them out.

[If it is with a stranger's refusal or permission, a third of it is forfeit.]

If it is [with] a stranger's permission for amusement, it is two thirds of the third or half of the third, or he does not get anything.

Whence is the two thirds of the third taken [sc., what is the source] for a stranger's permission for amusement, because [the] book does not say? It is taken from: "from a local, because wherever there is forfeiture of two thirds of it from a local for their refusal or for their permission, there is forfeiture of a third of it from a stranger for their refusal or for their permission." That is proper, when there is a third [forfeit] from a local for his permission for amusement, even though there should be the third of the third that there should be from a stranger for his permission for amusement, because[52] [the] book does not say. It is taken from: "from a local, because wherever there is

50 Exactly how this set of conditions would work in reality is unclear because of the sense of 'or'. If the condition is that the owner does not refuse to retrieve his own goods and also gives someone else permission to help with the salvaging, then it makes sense. If the owner does not refuse to retrieve his own goods and does not give permission to someone else to help, then the third for the salvager does not make sense. Further explanation on this point is provided in source D, but, though it is also not entirely satisfactory in terms of reality, it makes perfect sense in terms of a set of proportional divisions for the salvager.

51 Although the translation of *áine* as 'amusement, sport, pleasure' sounds a bit awkward in the English, the concept is that the salvager is trying to retrieve the goods of his own accord and for his own sense of sport. The use of 'permission' in the phrase is also in need of explanation as the commentaries say further on that the salvager in this scenario does not have the owner's permission to retrieve the goods. Perhaps the sense of the phrase is more along the lines of the owner not expressly telling the salvager not to retieve the goods.

52 See the note for the Irish regarding the corrupt text here.

d'fir fi*ne* ina femed no 'na airias*acht* is dilsi a t*r*ian ata d'fir anfi*ne* i*n*a femed no 'na airias*acht*." Coir ł deiside, uair ata t*r*ian d'fine 'na airias*acht* ar aine, cemad l*eth* *in* t*r*in dobeit*h* d'fir anfine 'na airias*acht* [ar aine]. Is as gabair a beit*h* can ni: "mad airiasac*h*t ar aine fir anfi*ne* acna bi uirias*acht* fir cota, ni aile cuit it*ir* la nec*h* dob*eir* as."

Is ed is femed ⁊ is uirias*acht* an*n*: femed a set ac fir bunaid, ⁊ *in* fer aile da uirias*acht* de dul ara cen*n*. Is ed is fem*ed* an*n* no uiriasac*h*t: nec*htar*de dib*h*. Is ed is airias*acht* as ai*ne*: dul do neoch ar' aineches fein.

Diles tochur[53] do fir puirt, .i. is dil*es* d'fir puirt a tarla c*h*uici coruici *cóic séotu*; ⁊ o rac*h*as tarrsu, is comrai*nn* bairci dlig*thige* air. I*n* tan tainic fo tom*us* p. 50a tuait*he* airit*h*i hi. ⁊ ni h-i*n*dti dorala hi, *acht* doseit gæt*h* | hi a c*r*ich aile dar ai*n*deoin, (⁊) [is][54] comrai*n*d bairce dlig*thige* uirre isi*n* c*r*ich i tarla.

⁊ is aml*aid* donit*er*-si*n*: In set is ferr i*n*dti do rig na tuait*h*i, ⁊ fuill*ed* ris co roib t*r*ian na bairci an*n*, ⁊ a t*r*ian do t*h*uait*h* ⁊ a t*r*ian d'fir puirt. ⁊ t*r*ian *in*

53 *Tochur* refers to any valuable washed up on shore, whether technically flotsam, jetsam, or wrack.

54 I follow the emendation suggested by Binchy, *CIH* 315, n. a.

forfeiture of two thirds of it from a local for his refusal or for his permission, there is forfeiture of a third of it from a stranger for his refusal or for his permission." That is proper, because there is a third [forfeit] from a local for his permission for amusement, there should be the half of a third that there should be from a stranger for his permission [for amusement]. It is from [this] that it is taken that he should have nothing: "if it is [with the] permission for amusement of a stranger who does not have the permission of the owner of the property, there is no other share at all for someone who carries it out."

This is what refusal is and [what] permission is in the following case: an owner refuses [to go after] his *sét*s, and the other person has his [sc., the owner's] permission to go fetch them. This is what refusal is or permission in the following case: either of them. This is what permission for amusement is in the following case: someone goes [to get them] for his own amusement.

Items cast ashore belong to the owner of the shore, i.e., the owner of the shore where she [sc., the ship] landed owns up to [the amount of] five *sét*s; and whenever it will go beyond them [sc., anything worth above and beyond the five *sét*s], it is a division of a lawful ship [that is made] of her. When she [sc., the ship] came seeking a specific *túath*, and she did not land in it, but the wind | blew her into another territory by force, and it is a division of a p. 50a
lawful ship of her in the territory in which she landed.

And it is thus that that is done: the best item of value in her is [given] to the king of the *túath*, and it is added to until there is a third of the [value] of the ship then, and third of it [sc., of the value of the ship] to the *túath*, and a third of it to the owner of the shore. And a third [of the value] of the best

s*éoit* is ferr rainic do rig tuait*h*i uad do rig *cóic*id, fuill*ed* ris co roib *cethraimth*i cota*ch* tuait*h*i and, ⁊ cethr*aimth*i na cethr*amth*an o rig *cóic*id[55] do rig Eiren*n*.

In t*r*ian rosoic*h* do t*h*uait*h*, a comroi*n*d doib et*ar*u a coitci*n*di do ca*ch* oen dib conic fuba ⁊ ruba ⁊ biath*ad* ⁊ congbail ⁊ coi*m*et loc*h*ta na bairci. In t*r*ian rosoic*h* d'fir [puirt],[56] nocon [ḟ]uil ni uad do neoc*h*, *acht* mana fuil flait*h* daerait*h* air, *acht* in cut*r*uma b*e*res a ecl*ais* bunaid a dualg*us* cota*ch* frit*h*i a manaig*h*.

Is and ata l*eth* a set uait*h*i ar cen*naig*e*cht* do denum ria don leit*h* aili: *in* tan tainic fo tomus tuait*h*i airit*h*i hi, ⁊ is *in*ti dorala hi; l*eth* a set uait*h*i don tuait*h* ar cen*naig*e*cht* do denu*m* ria don l*eth* aile. ⁊ *no*con urailend dlig*ed* uirri-si l*eth* a set uait*h*i doib-sium no co ndernat cen*naig*e*cht* ria. ⁊ *no*cun urailen*n* dlig*ed* ari*n* tuait*h* cen*naig*e*cht* do denu*m* ria *no* co tuca si l*eth* a s*ét* doib a n-aiscid, ⁊ o dob*era* is dlig*ed* cenda*cht*a do denu*m* ria. Cid fo*dera* l*eth* a set uait*h*i ar cen*naig*e*cht* it*ir*? Is e fa*th* fo*dera*: is ris doc*h*uaid men*m*a in udair co mb*e*rdais-[s]ium d'i*m*arc*r*aid isin l*eth* recait ni is mo ina l*eth* dob*e*rait i n-aiscid.

---

55 The ⟨id⟩ were written above the line by the scribe.

56 I follow the emendation suggested by Binchy, *CIH* 315, n. b.

valuable item that the king of the *túath* received [is given] by him to the king of the province, it is added to until it is a fourth of the *túath*'s share then, and the fourth of the fourth from the king of the province [is given] to the king of Ireland.[57]

The third that the *túath* received, it is divided by them amongst them equally for each one of them who is capable of attack and defense and feeding and maintaining and guarding the ship's cargo.[58] The third that the owner of the shore received, he does not give anything to anyone, unless there is a lord of base clientship over him, but [it is] the equivalent that his family's church gets in respect to a share of its monastic client.[59]

The case in which half of her valuables [sc., cargo for trade] is [given] by her to conduct commerce with her with the other half: when she came seeking a specific *túath*, and she landed in it [sc., the territory the ship was seeking]; half of her valubles [is given] by her to the *túath* to conduct commerce with her with the other half. And law does not require her [to give] half of her valuables to them until they conduct commerce with her, and law does not require the *túath* to conduct commerce with her until she gives half her valuables to them gratis, and when she gives [them], it is lawful to conduct commerce with her. What is the reason that half of her valuables is [given] by her for commerce at all? The reason is: the idea of the author was that they [sc., the shipowners] would receive in addition more for the half that they sell than for the half that they give gratis.

---

57 This hierachical list of tributes is reminiscent of the idealized lists found in *Lebor na Cert*; *Lebor na Cert: The Book of Rights*, ed. and trans. Myles Dillon. Irish Texts Society 46 (Dublin: Irish Texts Society, 1962). As noted by Kelly, a similar division of goods into thirds is found in *Frithfolaid Ríg Caisil fri Túatha Muman*, edited as part of *Dál Caladbuig* § 9.10–11: *dlegait Muscraige trian cach thurchairthe dia duirend tond hi tir nErenn acht rand ríg Temrach*. 'the Múscraige are entitled to a third of everything which is cast up by a wave on the land of Ireland, except for the share of the king of Tara'; "*Dál Caladbuig* and Recipricol Services between the Kings of Cashel and Various Munster States," ed. J.G. O'Keeffe in *Irish Texts* i, eds. J. Fraser, P. Grosjean, S.J., and J.G. O'Keeffe (London: Sheed and Ward, 1931), §§ 1–7 of O'Keeffe's edition from *Dál Caladbuig*; translation by Kelly in *EIF* 408, n. 61. See also the discussion of this text in Jaski, *Early Irish Kingship and Succession*, 205–207.

58 *Lochta* is the gen. sg. of *lucht*, which can refer to the contents of the ship, i.e., its cargo, but also to its crew. The passage here suggests that we understand *lochta* to refer to both the ship's crew and its cargo; see *eDIL* s.v. *lucht*.

59 This sentence refers to the share of something found which a lord's client or a monastic client is obligated to give to their superior.

Is[60] an*n* ata *sét sé* screp*al* uait*h*i no *sét* foraici uingi: i*n* tan tainic fo t*h*om*us* dui*n*e airit*h*i hi, ⁊ ni 'na [ḟ]lesc lama-sin fei*n* dorala iat *acht* a feran*n* dui*n*e aile 'na comoc*us*, ⁊ *sét sé* screp*al* do ar con*n*ad ⁊ uisci do lecad di masa seic*h*ida ⁊ iaran*n* ⁊ saland ata i*n*dti, no *sét* foraici ui*n*gi masa cno gnae ⁊ cuirnd [buabaill],[61] ⁊ escup fi*n*a no mela ma ta fi*n* ł mil indti.[62]

Log saethair mad o srot*h*aib, .i. log seat*h*air do mad o srot*h*aib i*n* mara amuich dob*er*a he. Masa toc*h*ur srot*h*a firuisci, a cethr*aim*t*h*i dar nae n-orba, a t*r*ian ar da orba dec, l*eth* ot*h*a si*n* coria; i*n* tir-si*n* is nesu do *muir*; a da t*r*ian mad an*n*-side.

I*n* t*r*ian ail*e* is f*or* cai*n* mara rosuidig*h*ed*h* *cethair coícat* cubat re h-or tire a toc*h*ur, no dar noe ton*n*a mara anall cid a toc*h*ur cid a tabairt. Masa toc*h*ur, i*n* t*r*ian-si*n*, a cethr*aim*t*h*i ar aen *coícait*, a let*h* ara do, a t*r*i cethr*aim*t*h*i ara t*r*i, uile ara cethair. Masa tabairt it*er* noe ton*n*aib mara ⁊ tir, femed ⁊ uirias-

60 Cf. *Anfuigell* § 29, *CIH* 2155.21–26, and O'Dav no. 105 below in the collection of citations from *O'Davoren's Glossary* pertaining to *Muirbretha*.

61 Cf. *Anfuigell* § 29, *CIH* 2155.22; and see Binchy, *CIH* 315, n. c.

62 The word *indti* is added above the line with reference marks by the scribe.

The case in which there is an item worth six scruples[63] [given] from her [sc., the ship] or an item worth an ounce: when she came seeking a specific person, and they did not land in his own domain but in the land of another person close to him, and an item worth six scruples [is given] to him for allowing her firewood and freshwater, if there are hides and iron and salt in her, or an item worth an ounce if there are fine woolens[64] and drinking horns,[65] and a jar[66] of wine or honey, if there is wine or honey in her.

Reward of labor if it may be from streams,[67] i.e., [the] reward of labor he gets if it may be from the sea's streams that he takes [it] out. If a freshwater stream casts it ashore, [he gets] a fourth of it [sc., its value] [if the item is carried] across nine territories, a third of it [if the item is carried] twelve territories, half [of it] from that [distance] onwards, until it reaches that land which is closest to the sea; two thirds of it if that is the case.

The other third is according to the law of [the] sea, which has established four fifties of cubits before the boundary of land for items which have been cast ashore, or beyond nine waves of [the] sea,[68] whether it has been cast ashore or carried by the water. If it has been cast ashore, [he gets] that third, a fourth of it for 50 cubits, half of it for two [fifties of cubits], three-fourths for three [fifties of cubits], all [of it] for four [fifties of cubits]. If it has been carried between nine waves of [the] sea and land, refusal and permission

63 A scruple is worth 1/24 of an ounce; see *EIF* 593. For a discussion of this passage, see Rudolf Thurneysen, "Nachträgliches," *ZCP* 16 (1927): 409–410.

64 For the identification of *cnóe gnáe* as 'fine woolens' and not 'beautiful nuts'; see Eska, "Early Irish Trade," 101–109. The interpretation presented here supersedes that given in § 22 of the edition of *Anfuigell* where this commentary is edited and translated. For previous scholarship on this phrase; see Kelly, "Drifting on the Ocean," 211–218; *GEIL* 165; and Wooding, *Communication and Commerce*, 70.

65 For drinking horns, see Proinsias Mac Cana, "Ir. *Buaball*, W *Bual* 'Drinking Horn'," *Ériu* 44 (1993): 81–86. The amount due to the landowner increases with the value of the ship's cargo; similarly, the watchman's reward for spotting a shipwreck increases with the value of the cargo.

66 For *escop* as a jar used as a standard measure of wine and honey, see *EIF* 581.

67 Cf. Heptad 64, source J, for a similar version of this material. The word *saethar* 'work, labor, effort' is used here in the sense that the finder gets a percentage of the item's value due to his efforts retrieving it from the water itself; *sruth* can refer to a stream or a current. See the Introduction, pp. 52–54, Table 7, which lists the reward percentages given below.

68 See *EIF* 569–570. 1 cubit = 1.5 feet; *EIF* 565. The 200 cubits referred to here is the distance reckoned as being beyond the ninth wave; cf. the first paragraph in this source above.

acht ⁊ fi*n*ec*h*aire do riagail risi*n* t*r*ian. Masa tabairt in srot*h*a-si*n* fei*n*, a t*r*ian ara t*r*i, ⁊ a da t*r*ian ara *sé*, uile ara *noí*.

Masa toc*h*ur srotha saile sceo uisce, a ceth*raim*t*h*i ar t*r*i orbaib, a let*h* ara *sé*, a t*r*i *cethraim*t*h*i ara noe, uile ara do dec; a tochor sain. Masa tabairt i*n*t srot*h*a-si*n* fei*n*, a t*r*ian ara do, a let*h* ara t*r*i, a da t*r*ian ara ceth*air*, uile ara *sé*.

Masa toc*h*ur srot*h*a murgabail, i*n*and ⁊ tabairt srot*h*a glain: a t*r*ian ar t*r*i orba, a da t*r*ian ara *sé*, uile ara nae; a toc*h*ur sin. Masa tabairt int srot*h*a-si*n* fei*n*, a l*eth* ara da, a da t*r*ian ara t*r*i, uile ara ceth*air* co l*eth*; l*eth* ca*ch* toc*h*air i*n*a tabairt cen*m*ot*h*a i*n* tabairt srot*h*a glai*n*. ⁊ i*n*t ain*m*rai*n*di ata i*n*a toc*h*ur ł i*n*a tabairt do srot*h*aib, corub e i*n*t ain*m*rai*n*di-si*n* bes i*n*a toc*h*ur ł ina t*h*a-
p. 50b bairt a faball i*n*t ṡrot*h*a-si*n*. ⁊ ni faball ma focoisli, .i. ni faball | it*ir* he madia foxla srut*h* ni as, uair foxlait srot*h*a ⁊ ni foxlait fabaill.

Masa i*n*and fer frit*h*i ⁊ fer tire, is ’na rog*h*a ata i*n* cuitig frit*h*i bias do no i*n* cuitig tire; is as gabar: “contechta gni*m*a no tire.” Masa sai*n* fer frit*h*i ⁊ fer tire, cuitig frit*h*i ⁊ cuitig tire do fir frit*h*i.

Marbdile si*n*, no is beodil*e* nach cui*m*gen*n* tia*cht*ain as a dualg*us* a nirt fei*n*, uair da cui*m*gidis na beodil*i* tia*cht*ain as a dualg*us* nirt fei*n*, *no*co bia ni astu.

Uair cid fata bes fer bun*aid* a toiglen*main* a set, ⁊ o ’tcit*h*fer roi*m*e iat i*n* dara fe*cht* cenco faicea in fe*cht* aile, nocon [ḟ]uil cuitig frit*h*i na toc*h*air na tabarta uad eistib mana ric a les tabairt, ⁊ ma ric a les tabairt is a riagailt re tabairt fi*n*e no anfine.

and a group of locals regulate [it] regarding the third. If that stream itself has carried it,[69] a third of it [if it was carried across] three [territories], and two thirds of it for six [territories], all [of it] for nine.

If a salt and fresh stream casts it ashore,[70] a fourth of it for [being carried across] three territories, half of it for six, a three-fourths of it for nine, all [of it] for twelve; that is an item which has washed up on shore. If that stream itself has carried it, a third of it for two [territories], half of it for three, two thirds of it for four, all [of it] for six.

If a stream which is an inlet of the sea casts it ashore, it is the same as being carried by a freshwater stream: a third of it for three territories, two thirds of it for six, all [of it] for nine; that is an item washed up on shore. If that stream itself has carried it, half of it for two, two thirds of it for three, all [of it] for four up to half; half of each cast ashore item which has been carried [by a stream] except that which a freshwater stream has carried. And the proportion which is for its being cast ashore or its being carried by streams, that is the proportion which is for its being cast ashore or for its being carried by the conveyance of that stream. And it is not [considered] 'conveyance' if it removes, i.e., it is not [considered] conveyance | at all if a stream removes p. 50b
anything from it, because streams remove and conveyances do not remove.

If the finder and the landowner are the same, it is his choice whether he will have the share of the thing found or the share of the land; that is taken from: "equally valid are acts or lands." If the finder and the landowner are different, a share of the thing found and a share of the land for the finder.[71]

Those [things are] inanimate property, or it is animate property[72] that is not capable of escaping on account of its own strength, because if they are animate property capable of escaping on account of their own strength, there would not be anything from them.

Because however long the owner may be pursuing his property, and if he will see them before him at one time though he does not see [them] at another or second time, there will not be a share of the things found, nor of recovering, nor of taking due from him from them, unless he wishes [to give a share for] taking.[73] And if he wishes [to give a share for] taking, it is regulated by [the rule of] taking for a local or non-local.

---

69 This likely refers to the item carried by a river.

70 This likely refers to an item found on the banks of an estuary.

71 Heptad 64, source A, has a different version where the owner of the land receives the share for the land, and the finder receives the share for the find.

72 Animate property includes livestock and slaves.

73 The reason that the owner does not owe the finder a share is because he himself is close on the trail of his own property and is likely to find it himself.

Cuitig frit*h*i isna marbdil*ib* do gres, cid a crich cid a *secht*arcrich, cid a cuairt ingelta cid a *secht*arcuaird i*n*gel*ta*, no [co m]beit*h*[74] ar taiscid gataid*he*, ⁊ o beit is cuitig tobaig*h* eistib.

Cuitig frit*h*i a bec*h*aib ⁊ a dainib daera do gres, no comad cuitig*h* astaid*he*, *acht* manab e a frec*ra* in dair coned ac tia*chtain* da tig dobi he. ⁊ mas e a frec*ra*, a imdenu*m* do *con*ad ac tia*chtain* da t*h*ig*h* robi he. Mas amlaid frit*h*[i] he, ⁊ a aigid doc*h*um a t*h*ig*h*i, is a imdenu*m* do conac*h* ac elod robi, ⁊ cen nac*h* ni do as. Mas amlaid frit*h*i he, ⁊ a cul re t*h*ec*h*, ⁊ nir airb*er*tnaig*h* nach ac el*od* robi, is a i*m*denu*m* donti fuair he *con*[id](ac*h*)[75] ac elod robi, ⁊ cuitig tobaig*h* astu.

Nocon fuil ni dona beod*ilib* i cuaird i*n*gelta,[76] ⁊ cuitig tob*aig* estib *secht*air cuaird i*n*gelta. No d*ano* *ch*ena, is cuitig tob*aig* eistib a cuaird i*n*gelta *acht* co mbeit ar taiscid gataid*e*, ⁊ o beit [ar taiscid gataidi],[77] is cuitig tob*aig* eistib *secht*ar cuaird i*n*gelta, *acht* narab aml*aid* beit ⁊ a n-aigaid ara tec*h*. ⁊ mas amlaid*h*, *acht* masa ci*n*dti co ticfaitis, *no*con [ḟ]uil ni esitib. Ma cun*n*tabairt i*n* ticfaitis no na ticfaitis, is l*eth*cuitig tob*aig* eistib. Masa ci*n*dti na ticfaidis, is cuitig tob*aig* comlan eistib.

Masa beod*ile* conic a gait budei*n*, is cuitig tob*aig* eistib do gres. I*n* dui*ne* daer, is a ci*n* d'ic da tigerna ł co ngaba nec*h* aile 'na seilb he ar daig*h*in achtaig*h*t*h*i, ⁊ o geb*us*, is a ci*n* d'ic do.

74 Binchy, *CIH* 316, n. a, queries emending the text to 's̄ co m-', but cf. Heptad 64, source A, *CIH* 58.41 'ł co mb*et*'.

75 I follow the emendation suggested by Binchy, *CIH* 316, n. b; cf. Heptad 64, source A, *CIH* 60.22 'conad'.

76 The scribe inserted the ⟨l⟩ above the line with a caret mark; see also Binchy, *CIH* 316, n. c.

77 Binchy, *CIH* 316, n. d, queries whether some of the text is missing; the text has been supplied by comparison with Heptad 64, source A, *CIH* 58.42 'o b*et* ar taiscid gat*aigi*'.

A share of something from inanimate property always, whether in a territory or beyond a territory, whether in a grazing enclosure or beyond a grazing enclosure, or until they may be in the possession of a thief, and if they may be [in the possession of a thief], it is a share of recovering from them.

A share of something found from bees and from unfree people always;[78] or that it may be a share of detention unless the answer of the unfree person is that he was coming to his home. And if it is his answer, he proves that he was coming towards his home. If he is found thus, and his face to his home, and he proves that he was not escaping, and he [sc., the detainer] goes without anything from it. If he is found thus, and his back to the house, and he does not plead that he is not escaping, and it must be proved that he was escaping by the one who found [him], and a share of recovering from it.

There is not anything from the livestock in a grazing enclosure, and a share of recovering from them beyond the grazing enclosure. Or, instead, a share of recovering from them in a grazing enclosure, if[79] they are in possession of a thief, and when they are in possession of a thief, a share of recovering from them. [A share of recovering from them] beyond a grazing enclosure, unless they had been thus with their face towards their home. And if it is so, provided that it is certain that they would have come [home], there is nothing from them. If it is uncertain whether they would or would not have come home, it is half the share of recovering from them. If it is certain that they would not have come [home], it is a full share of recovering from them.

If it is animate property which can steal themselves,[80] it is always a share of recovering from them. The unfree person, his crime is paid by his lord,[81] until someone else takes him as his possession on account of an agreement, and when he will take [him], his crime is paid by him [sc., his new master].

78 The commentary mainly concerns detaining anyone considered to be unfree who may or may not be attempting to escape.

79 The use of *no co* 'unless, until' does not make sense here as the reward for livestock in a grazing enclosure is given only when a thief has been caught in the grazing enclosure with the livestock.

80 This is in reference to slaves who can run away.

81 The legal liabilities of the unfree are paid by their lord; *GEIL* 33–35.

Source D, TCD MS 1337 [*olim* H.3.18], p. 425a, *CIH* 959.7–16[82]

Ni[83] baiter[84] a srothaib:[85] mana t*h*oc*h*aithe[d] *in dechmad* c*r*ich, is ceth*rai*-*mth*e coa f*or*cend ⁊ t*r*ian o *noí* c*r*ich co f*or*cen*d* na da c*r*ich decc, ⁊ leth a f*or*cen*n*-sidhe corige tír bes nesam do muir; da t*r*ian mad i sodain.

Mad*h* airiasacht[86] *ar* ai*ne*,[87] .i. dia *m*be feimed ⁊ uiriasachd, is uile do anfine. Mad*h* feimed ce*n* airias*acht*, is da t*r*ian. Mad*h air*is*acht* cen feimed*h*, is t*r*ian *ar* t*r*ian f*r*i h-[air]ias*acht* ⁊ da t*r*ian f*r*i feimed. Ma[d] cen feimed cen *air*ias*acht*, is da t*r*ian t*r*in; ⁊ is do anfi*ne* i*n* sli*cht*-so.

Mad*h* fi*ne* im*morro*, dia *m*be feimed cengo be [air]ias*acht*,[88] is uile doib-side. ⁊ mad [air]ias*acht* ce*n* feimed, is da t*r*ian. Mad*h* cen feimed cen [air]ias-*acht*, is t*r*ian; do fi*ne* i*n* sli*cht*-so.

---

82 Breatnach, *CCIH* 305 identifies *CIH* 959.7–13 as likely belonging to *Muirbretha* and notes the correspondace of *CIH* 959.10–13 with O'Dav no. 108. Cf. similar material in source C, *CIH* 314.26–30, source E, *CIH* 1212.27–31, and Heptad 64 sources A, C, and J, but note that this material also overlaps with some of the commentary to Heptad 54, *CIH* 49.20–23.

83 There is a paragraph symbol next to this word in *marg. sin.*

84 There is a very faint *punctum* over the ⟨t⟩ which might not be a *punctum* at all, but ink bleeding through from the other side of the vellum.

85 Although the first clause is not written in larger letters than the surrounding commentary, it appears to be an extract from the tract itself.

86 The MS reads 'airrecht'; see also Binchy, *CIH* 959, n. b.

87 Cf. O'Dav no. 108 below.

88 For the use of *íasacht* for *airiasacht*, see *eDIL* s.v. *íasacht* 'loan, temporary possession'.

It[89] is not destroyed in streams:[90] if it was not used up[91] in the tenth territory, it is a fourth up to its end [sc., up to the end of nine territories], and a third from nine territories to the end of the twelve territories, and half from that end [sc., twelve territories] to [the] land which is closest to the sea; two thirds if that is the case.

If it is [with] permission for amusement, i.e., if there may be refusal and permission, it is entirely [forfeit] by a stranger. If it is [with] refusal [and] without permission, it is two thirds. If it is [with] permission [and] without refusal, it is a third of the third for permission and two thirds for refusal. If it is without refusal [and] without permission, it is two thirds of a third; and this division is for a stranger [sc., a stranger's goods].

If it is a local, however, if there may be refusal though there may not be permission, it is entirely [forfeit] by them [sc., the locals]. And it if it [with] permission [and] without refusal, it is two thirds. If it is without refusal [and] without permission, it is a third; this division [is] for a local.

---

89 For a discussion of this material, see the Introduction, p. 51. The material here is divided into three sections. The first concerns the percentage of an item's value that the finder is permitted regarding items which have been carried by a freshwater stream across a number of territories. These are items which, for example, might be found along the bank of a river. The next two sections concern items which are salvaged between the shore and the ninth wave of the sea. The reward percentages given here correspond to those given in source C for items cast ashore by a freshwater stream.

90 The translation is tentative as the phrase is out of any linguistic context. This is particularly problematic as *srothaib* could be translated as 'currents'.

91 The verb *do-caithi*, later *tochaithid* 'spends, consumes', refers here to the item still being of use, despite having been carried some distance in the water.

Muirbretha/Bretha Éitgid

Source E, RIA MS 23 Q 6 [1243], 42a, *CIH* 1212.3–34[92]

p. 42b **Dil*us* a muirbreath*aib* aire ruanad*h* tar næ ton*na*,**[93] .i. cid*h* *séoit* fir[94] fine cid*h* *séoit* fir ai*n*fine, cid*h* *séoit* fir bescna cid*h* *séoit* fir nemhbesc*na*, is a ndilsi uile ob*us* t*ar* næ ton*n*a mara amuig*h* dob*er*a iat.

Mas it*er* nai ton*n*a mara ⁊ tir tucust*ar* iat, is fei*me*[d] ⁊ airias*acht* ⁊ fi*n*e-*ch*aire do riag*h*ail i l*eth* riu.

Mas fem*ed* ⁊ airiasa*cht* fir fine, is a ndilsi uile.

Mas fé*med* ɫ arias*acht* fir fi*n*e, is dil*us* a *da* t*r*ian.

Mas airr[ias]*acht*[95] ar aine fir fi*n*e, is dilsi a trín.

Mas fé*med* ⁊ *airiasacht* fir ai*n*fi*n*e, is dilsi a *da* trian.

Mas fé*med* ɫ a*iriasacht* fir ainfine, is dilsi a[96] *trian*.

Mas arr[ias]*acht* ar aine f*i*r anfi*n*e, is *da* t*r*ian i*n* t*r*in ɫ l*eth* an trin, ɫ b*eth* gan ní.

Can asa ngabt*ar* *da* t*r*ian in t*r*in ata d'fer ainf*ine* a n- *arr*[ias]*acht ar* ai*n*e? Is as gabt*air* i*n* *da* t*r*ian: "g*a*c baile is uile d'fi*n*e, is *da* t*r*ian d'anfi*n*e."[97]

Can asa ngabt*ar* l*eth* i*n* t*r*in? Is as gabt*air*: "g*a*c bail*e* is *da* t*r*ian d'fi*n*e a fem*ed* ɫ a n-airias*acht*, is t*r*ian d'fer ai*n*fi*n*e, ⁊ an cut*r*um*a* ata d'fer fine an*n* si*n* is a l*eth* d'fer ai*n*fine." ⁊ coir in tan ata t*r*ian d'fer f*ine* a n-arr*iasacht* [ar] (fir)[98] ai*ne* gorab e l*eth* an t*r*in-si*n* dob*eth* d'fer ainf*ine*.

92 Cf. similar material in source C, *CIH* 314.17–315.3. The commentary here directly follows Heptad 64 (source B) in the MS. The way the two texts are arranged in the MS, there is not a clear break between them even though the heptad commentary ends at p. 41b and this commentary starts on p. 42a. Thematically the commentary here follows on the commentary in Heptad 64 because they both concern finding and retrieving lost property. In source C the opposite was true; commentary associated with Heptad 64 follows after the material related to *Muirbretha*.

93 Although the citation is not written in larger letters than the surrounding text as scribes often do to distinguish tract from commentary, this clause is clearly a quotation from the tract itself; cf. source C, *CIH* 314.17.

94 The scribe wrote 'fir' twice and cancelled the second by underlining.

95 I follow the expansion suggested by Binchy, *CIH* 1212, n. f.

96 One letter has been erased after *a*; see also Binchy, *CIH* 1212, n. h.

97 Neither this nor the other textual quotations in the commentary have been securely identified.

98 I follow the emendation suggested by Binchy, *CIH* 1212, n. j; cf. the same phrase above.

Muirbretha/Bretha Éitgid

Free[99] from claim in sea-judgments [is the] load of a strongman[100] [taken from] beyond nine waves, i.e., whether valuables belonging to a local freeman [lit. man of the kindred] or valuables belonging to a stranger [lit. man of a stranger kindred],[101] whether valuables belonging to a man [from a territory governed by a] protocol, or valuables belonging to a man from a territory not governed by a protocol, they are forfeit entirely here to the one who brought them [from] beyond nine waves of the open sea. p. 42b

If he brought them [from] between nine waves of the sea and land, it is refusal and permission and a group of locals which regulate regarding them.

If it is [with] a local's refusal and permission, they are forfeit entirely [to the one who brought them out of the water.]

If it is [with] a local's refusal or permission, two thirds of it is forfeit.

If it is [with] a local's permission for amusement, a third of it is forfeit.

If it is [with] a stranger's refusal and permission, two thirds of it is forfeit.

If it is [with] a stranger's refusal or permission, a third of it is forfeit.

If it is [with] a stranger's permission for amusement, it is two thirds of the third or half of the third, or he does not get anything.

Whence[102] is the two thirds of the third taken [sc., what does the source text say] for a non-kinsman's permission for amusement? The two thirds is taken from: "wherever there is forfeiture of all [of it] by a local, it is two thirds for a stranger."

Whence is the half of the third taken? It is taken from: "wherever it is two thirds for a local for refusal or permission, it is a third for a stranger, and the amount a local has in that case, it is half of it for a stranger." And [it is] right that when a local has a third for permission for amusement that there should be half of that third for a stranger.

---

99 For a discussion of this material, see the Introduction, pp. 51–55.

100 Literally 'a champion's burden'.

101 The contrast here is not really between kinsmen and non-kinsmen, but between locals and non-locals.

102 This and the following two paragraphs are an attempt to explain the three different reward amounts given in the text regarding when someone fetches a stranger's property for amusement. The text states that the salvager receives two thirds of the third (i.e., 2/9), half of a third (i.e., 1/6), or nothing; the commentaries explain the logic behind each of these three conflicting amounts.

Can asa ngabt*ar* a b*eth* gi*n* ní? Is as g*abthair*: "mad*h* arr[ias]*acht ar* ain*e* fir ai*n*fi*ne* ogna bí airiasa*cht* fir cota,[103] ní aile cuit it*ir* la *Féniu* a*cht* ni durtast*ar* do," .i. d*úlchinne*[104] *ar* dleistin*us* sin, ł is d*úlchinne ar* ben*nacht*ain, ł g*omad* (?) d*úlchinne ar* be*nnachdain*.[105]

Is *ed* is f*émed* an*n*: fer bun*ad*a d'f*émed* dul *ar*a cen*n*.

Is *ed* is uirias*acht* an*n*: a cetu d'fer b*unaid*[106] a m*ar*bl*och* (?) ⁊ a m*ar*blin*n*ti ⁊ it*ir noí* ton*na* m*ara* ⁊ *tír* ata i*n* riag*ail*-si*n*.

Ma[s][107] *uriasacht* ⁊ fem*ed*, is uile d'anf*ine*.[108]

Ma[s][109] f*émed* gi*n* urias*acht*, is *da* t*r*ian, ⁊ ma[s] [air]ias*acht* gi*n* f*émed*, is trian; ⁊ is d'anf*ine* i*n* sli*cht*-sin.

Ma[s] f*émed* gi*n* [air]ias*acht*, is uile, ⁊ ma[s] [air]ias*acht* gi*n* f*émed*, is *da* t*r*ian, ⁊ ma[s] gi*n* [air]ias*acht* gi*n* f*émed*, is t*r*ian; ⁊ is fi*n*e si*n*.

Atait[110] *secht* n-*airi* ruan*ada* ada comdil*us* do cac*h* ric*ht* .i. t*abairt*[111] a rodom*un*, t*abairt* a h-uat*h*bas, a t*abairt* a tret*h*an, t*abairt* a tine, t*abairt* a h-*armaig*, t*abairt* fuidb[112] fir dotuit a ræ, [tabairt] t*ar* clo[113] a suai*n*emnaib, seol form*na*.

---

103 Cf. O'Dav no. 108, below at pp. 346 and 347 and the version of this commentary in source D, *CIH* 959.10–16.

104 Binchy, *CIH* 1212, n. l, suggests expanding MS .d. as *duthracht* 'wish, desire'. While the translations 'desire to be of service' and 'wish for a blessing' are grammatical, it is likely that .d. stands for *dúlchinne* 'remuneration, recompense, reward' and refers to a payment made to the salvager for helping retrieve the property from the water; Pierre-Yves Lambert, *"Pretium benedictionis,"* in *Early Medieval Ireland and Europe: chonology, Contacts, Scholarship A Festschrift for Dáibhí Ó Cróinín*, eds. Pádraic Moran and Immo Warntjes (Turnhout: Brepols, 2015), pp. 215–223.

105 Binchy, *CIH* 1212, n. m, does not attempt to expand MS ⟨b̄d⟩. Approximately two letters are erased after this abbreviation.

106 One or two letters have been erased after *bunaid*.

107 The scribe has written ⟨.s.cus⟩ in *marg. sin.*, which Binchy, *CIH* 1212, n. q, would tentatively expand as 'sencus'.

108 The material here and in the next two paragraphs is also found as part of the commentary to Heptad 54, which immediately follows in the MS; cf. the text in Oxford, Rawl. B. 487, *CIH* 49.20–23. The question, then, is whether the commentary associated with Heptad 54 actually belongs to Heptad 54, or whether it originally derives from *Muirbretha*. Cf. also the similar commentary and content in source C, from *Muirbretha/Bretha Éitgid*, printed above at pp. 326–331.

109 The scribe has written 'not' 'note!' in *marg. sin.*

110 This is a version of Heptad 54; see Appendix 9 for the relevant parts of the Oxford, Rawl. B. 487, version of the heptad. The heptad and relevant glosses are too long to print here as a footnote.

111 I follow the expansion suggested by Binchy, *CIH* 1212, n. u.

112 The MS reads 'fuibd'; I follow the emendation suggested by Binchy, *CIH* 1212, n. w.

113 Cf. *CIH* 49.31 'turchlu'; the meaning of *turchlu* is uncertain; *eDIL* s.v. ? *turchlu*.

Whence is it taken that he should get nothing? It is taken from: "if it is permission for amusement of a stranger who does not have the permission of [the] owner, there is not another share at all according to Irish law except that which is carried by him," i.e., that is a price for service, or it is a price for a blessing, or there may be a price for a blessing.

This is what is refusal then: [the] original owner refuses to go fetch them.

This is what is permission then: when they are [the] original owner's in a standing pond or standing pool and that rule is [the same as when they are] between nine waves of the sea and land.[114]

If it is permission and refusal, it is [forfeiture of] all [of it] by a stranger.

If it is refusal without permission, it is two thirds, and if it is permission without refusal, it is a third; and that division is for a stranger [sc., for a stranger's property].

If it is refusal without permission, it is [forfeiture of] all [of it], and if it is permission without refusal, it is two thirds, and if it is without permission [and] without refusal, it is a third; and this is [for] a local [sc., for a local's property].

There are seven [categories of] champion's burdens which are equally forfeit[115] according to each authority, i.e., taking from a great depth,[116] taking from terror, taking from a stormy sea, taking from a fire, taking from a battlefield, taking spoils of a man who falls in combat, taking by a hook in ropes,[117] a moving sail.[118]

---

114 The translation here is tentative.

115 The sense of this heptad mirrors the tract quoted above where anything taken away under dangerous circumstances becomes the property of the person who takes it. Here, the inherent danger in each situation is the legal justification for the item becoming the rightful property of the one who takes it.

116 Kelly, *GEIL* 277, citing *CIH* 2103.13, *treorach … i murbreathaib 7 i rodomnaib*, a judge should be 'versed in sea-judgements and in great depths', interprets the last phrase as referring to the rights 'to ownerhip of property taken or recovered from a great depth'; see also Rudolf Thurneysen, "Aus dem irischen Recht V," *ZCP* 18 (1930): 353–408, at 363, §§ 27–28; and *CCIH* 85.

117 The sense deals with taking valuable items by means of using a rope to lower oneself or to get an object by means of a hook attached to a rope. Perhaps this refers to those who retrieve bird eggs from the sides of cliffs; *AL* 5: 301.21–22. See also Thurneysen, "Aus dem irischen Recht II," 259.

118 The last item yields a total of eight situations instead of seven. It is difficult to determine whether this last item is in any way related to the seventh. It is possible that it started out as a gloss which later crept into the text. If it is originally a gloss, it might refer to a situation where someone has climbed the rigging of a wrecked ship, possibly to take away the sail, vel sim.

Citations in *O'Davoren's Glossary*:[119] nos. 105–106, 108, 273, 477–479, 682, 790–791, 1180–1181, 1253, and 1370–1371

No. 105:[120] Aice, .i. bid*h* doig*h* co*m*a inun*n* ⁊ fíu, u*t est* "*sét* foraice uinge," .i. is fiu uinge re fir dechsai*n*.

No. 106:[121] Arabí, .i. is ferr, u*t* est (.i.) "[*sét*][122] arabí *sét*uib,"[123] .i. *sét* is ferr fir-bís do*na* *sét*uib*h*.

No. 108:[124] Ai*ne*, .i. aibnes, u*t est* "mad*h* *air*iasacht *ar* ai*ne* ocna bí *air*ias*acht* fir cota," .i. aire*chtaighe* *ar* æibnes ɫ aire*cht*aig*he* done in fer anfine *ar* aine-ch*us* dó fei*n* im dul *ar* cend na *sét* cin escail do on fir besa aí.[125]

No. 273:[126] Bl*eth*, .i. mil mor, ut *est* "dlegur do gach bairc ⁊ do g*a*c bleit*h* *sét* rod*h*airc."

No. 477:[127] Conscara, .i. comsgail*ed*, *ut est* "barc t*ar* buait*h* *con*scara fri tir," .i. rocomscail*ustar* ɫ bris*ustar* re h-aig*h*i i*n* ferin*n*.

---

119 See *CCIH* 305 for these identifications and 100–159 for further discussion. Whitley Stokes, ed. and trans., "O'Davoren's Glossary," in *Archiv für celtische Lexikographie*, eds. Whitley Stokes and Kuno Meyer, 2 (Halle: Niemeyer, 1904), pp. 197–504. All of the citations above are found in BL, MS Egerton 88, which is Stokes' source E. While some of these citations can be associated with a particular part of the text, this is not true of all of them. Those which can be so identified are cross-referenced in the footnotes. It is likely that all of the clauses which follow *ut est* are taken from the tract, glosses, or commentaries associated with *Muirbretha*; they have been put in quotaion marks.

120 *CIH* 1469.39–40. There is similar material in *Muirbretha/Bretha Éitgid*, source C, *CIH* 315.24, and *Anfuigell* § 22, *CIH* 2153.32, but none of these sources contains the head-word; see also *CCIH* 111, n. 20; and Thurneysen, "Nachträgliches," 409–410.

121 *CIH* 1469.41.

122 I follow the emendation suggested by Binchy, *CIH* 1469, n. f.

123 This clause is also found in commentary to *Cethairṡlicht Athgabálae*, *CIH* 411.15; see also *CCIH* 111, n. 21.

124 *CIH* 1470.1–3. *CCIH* 305, notes the correspondence between this entry and source D, *CIH* 959.10–13, which Breatnach identifies as potentially being from *Muirbretha*. The commentary in *CIH* 959.7–16 is considered here as being from *Muirbretha* and is edited separately; cf. also the version of the *Muirbretha* commentary in source E, *CIH* 1212.21–22, and *Muirbretha/Bretha Éitgid*, source C, *CIH* 314.39; see also *CCIH* 111, n. 22.

125 The scribe wrote 'aí' twice; also noted by Binchy, *CIH* 1470, n. a.

126 *CIH* 1476.24.

127 *CIH* 1483.28–29.

No. 105:[128] *Aice*,[129] i.e., it is likely the same as *fíu* 'worth', *ut est* "an item worth an ounce [of silver]," i.e., it is worth an ounce for the person seeing [it].[130]

No. 106: *Arabí* 'which surpasses', i.e., it is best,[131] *ut est* "a *sét* which surpasses *séts*," i.e., a *sét* which truly is the best of the *séts*.

No. 108: *Aine* 'amusement', i.e., delight, *ut est* "if it is permission for amusement by the one who does not have the permission of the owner," .i.e., consent for delight or consent which the stranger does for his own amusement regarding going to fetch the valuables without having permission from the person whose property it is.

No. 273:[132] *Bleth* 'whale', i.e., a whale, *ut est* "a *sét* for sighting [it] is due for every ship and every whale."

No. 477:[133] *Conscara* 'breaks', i.e., tearing apart,[134] *ut est* "a ship with valuables[135] breaks against land," i.e., it tore apart or it broke against the land.

128 All translations of these entries are my own.

129 The meaning of this word is obscure to me, but it probably refers to the second element in the verb *for-aicci* 'overlooks' < **for-ad-cí*, although the meaning 'equivalent value' is intended in the entry here.

130 The context of the last two clauses, as they are found in *Bretha Éitigd* and *Anfuigell*, concerns the payment that a landowner receives when a ship which has been blown off course comes to ground on his land.

131 This is a later use of *ferr* as the superl. of *maith* 'good'; *eDIL* s.v. *maith*.

132 The translation here is based on that given in *CCIH* 116, n. 39; see also *GEIL* 107–108; *EIF* 284; and *Cethairślicht Athgabálae*, 11(b), *CIH* 888.10–14, in Appendix 10.

133 Cf. *Muirbretha*, source B, *CIH* 178.20; see also *CCIH* 122, n. 72.

134 The form *comsgailed* could also be the 3 sg. pret. pass. of *comscaílid* 'lets loose, dissolves, tears apart' which would give 'it has been torn apart'.

135 The phrase *tar buaith* is obscure. The interpretation given here understands the prep. *tar* with an adjectival function or perhaps with a meaning of 'excelling, abounding in', and *buaith* as being a form of *búaid* 'victory, profit, advantage'. The sense of the phrase is that the ship is carrying valuable goods which are worth salvaging when it wrecks; Cf. O'Dav no. 682 below.

No. 478:[136] Coblu*th*, .i. curach no long beg f*or*a mbi imr*am*, *ut est* “coblat[137] f*or* rot ramat,” .i. ani f*or*a comimluait*er* na ramad, .i. *cóic*sesach no *secht*ses*ach*, no cur*ach*.

No. 479:[138] Cuire, .i. [i]umad, *ut est* “cobodail *nóe*c[h]uire[139] bait*er*,” .i. coibdeil*iugud*-so arin [i]u*m*ad bait*er* isi*n* noí.

No. 682:[140] Duis, .i. uas*al*, *ut est* “b*a*rc *co n*duisib inga*n*taib,” .i. co *sét*uib uaisl*ib*.

No. 790:[141] Eascop fina, .i. esc*r*a, .i. æs a g*h*ob, asint sesra.

No. 791:[142] Érd*r*at, .i. impod, u*t est* “do g*a*c eth*ar* dodaertrat,” .i. do g*a*c eth*ar* nos*ar*tron*n*,[143] .i. *no*simpan*n*[144] f*or* cula, ł dodanarrat.[145]

No. 1180:[146] Luc*h* no loch, .i. imad, *ut est* “a luchtair dofet*h* gæt*h* í tir,” .i. as in imad toirit*h*nec*h* dofairgen*n* gæt*h* a tír.

---

136 *CIH* 1483.30–31.

137 Stokes, “O Davoren's Glossary,” 272, emends the reading to *coblach*.

138 *CIH* 1483.32–33.

139 I follow the expansion suggested by Binchy, *CIH*, 1483, n. k; see also *CCIH* 122, n. 74, which suggests reading *nóechuiri*.

140 *CIH* 1491.21.

141 *CIH* 1496.13.

142 *CIH* 1496.13–15.

143 The verb form is obscure, but it might be a later 3 sg. pres. act. ind. simplex form from *do-ertrat* ‘turns back (?)’, with a MI conjunct ending and 3 sg. m. class A object agreement marker.

144 The verb might be a later 3. sg pres. act. ind. conjunct form of *imm-sói* ‘turns around’ with a 3 sg. m. class A object agreement marker used reflexively. For the later simplex form *impáid*, see *eDIL* s.v. *imm-sói*.

145 The verb *do-arrat* is obscure to me.

146 *CIH* 1513.11–12.

No. 478: *Cobluth* 'a rowing boat',[147] i.e., a coracle or small boat which is for rowing, *ut est* "a boat on a road of oars," i.e., that in which the oars are plied together, i.e., five-benched or seven-benched, or a coracle.

No. 479:[148] *Cuire* 'troop', i.e., many, *ut est* "a division of a boat crew who are drowned," i.e., this division of the many who are drowned in the boat.

No. 682:[149] *Duis* 'treasure', i.e., fine, *ut est* "a ship with wonderful treasures," i.e., with fine goods.

No. 790:[150] *Eascop fina* 'a jar of wine', i.e., a vessel, i.e., *æs a ghob*[151] 'out of its mouth', out of the *sesra*.[152]

No. 791:[153] *Érdrat* 'turning', i.e., turning around, *ut est* "for each boat which turns itself back", i.e., for each boat which turns itself back, i.e., it turns itself back around, or turns itself around.[154]

No. 1180:[155] *Luch* or *loch* 'abundance',[156] i.e., abundance, *ut est* "from a skiff[157] which a wind brings to shore," i.e., it is the helpful abundance which a wind delivers to land.

147 For this definition of *cobluth*, see *CCIH* 122, n. 73.

148 A partial translation of this entry is found in *CCIH* 122, n. 74.

149 A partial translation of this entry is found in *CCIH* 128, n. 101.

150 Kelly, *EIF* 581, and Breatnach *CCIH* 131, n. 115, note a similar entry in *Sanas Cormaic* (Y.539), which explicitly names *Muirbretha* as the source: *Epscop fina isna Muirbrethaib .i. escra tomais fina la ceandaighaib Gall ⁊ Franc.* 'A jar of wine in the 'Sea-Judgements', i.e., a vessel for measuring wine amongst the merchants of the Gauls and Franks'; the text is taken from the Early Irish Glossaries Database https://www.asnc.cam.ac.uk/irishglossaries/ Accessed June 18, 2019.

151 The phrase is an etymological gloss on *eascop*.

152 A *sesra* holds approximately six fluid ounces; for discussion of this term, see *EIF* 577.

153 See also *CCIH* 131, n. 116. The translation of this entry is tentative.

154 The translation of the last clause is tentative based on the other verbs in the entry.

155 The translation here is based on that found in *CCIH* 143, n. 171.

156 The meaning of the headword is obscure, but can be inferred from the explanation.

157 For *luchtair*, cf. *O'Mulconry's Glossary* 807: *Luchtar .i. coiti bís for usque.* 'Luchtar, i.e., a boat found on water'; *De Origine Scoticae Linguae* (*O'Mulconry's Glossary*), ed. and trans. Pádraic Moran, Corpus Christianorum 7 (Turnhout: Brepols Publishers, 2019), p. 233.

No. 1181:[158] Luaig*h*ne, .i. log*h*mar, *ut est* "a*cht* luaig*h*ne long," .i. a*cht* na h-íi log*h*ma*r*a dob*er*ar isna longaib.

No. 1253:[159] Murcran*n*, .i. seolcran*n*, no cran*n* giu*is*, *ut est* "mad*h* tascur æn-*séoit* i tír ł mad*h* mu*r*cran*n* ad*h*amra."

No. 1370:[160] Raa,[161] .i. imrum, u*t est* "cach re*cht* nad*h* rat*har* nad snáter," .i. nach*a*n dent*ar* a imram co direch ⁊ nochan [f]et*ar* a snamh.

No. 1371:[162] Rot, .i. d*ar* liu*m* is inond ⁊ imrom, u*t est* "coblath for rot rama," .i. na fir doniat comluth for imrum na rama.

---

158 *CIH* 1513.13–14.

159 *CIH* 1516.24–25.

160 *CIH* 1521.9–10.

161 As Binchy, *CIH* 1521, n. a, notes, the initial ⟨r⟩ was cut off with part of the vellum margin. The ⟨r⟩ was added in later on the paper guard on which the vellum is currently mounted.

162 *CIH* 1521.11–12.

No. 1181:[163] *Luaighne* 'valuables',[164] i.e., precious, *ut est* "except the valuables of boats," i.e., except the precious items which are brought in the boats.

No. 1253:[165] *Murcrann*[166] 'mast', i.e., mast, or tree of pine, *ut est* "if it is a casting of one valuable item on land or if it is a very wonderful mast."

No. 1370: *Raa* 'voyaging', i.e., rowing, *ut est* "each law that is not rowed, that is not swum," i.e., its rowing is not done straightly and it does not know how to swim.[167]

No. 1371: *Rot* 'road', i.e., I think it is the same as *imrom* 'rowing', *ut est* "a boat on a road of oars," i.e., the men who display *comluth*[168] 'equal vigor' for rowing the oars.

---

163 A partial translation of this entry is found in *CCIH* 143, n. 172.
164 The meaning of the headword is obscure.
165 See also *CCIH* 145, n. 183.
166 *Murchrann* literally means 'sea-tree'.
167 The entry might concern laws which are applied inconsistently; see *eDIL* s.v. *ráïd* 'rows, voyages, proceeds'.
168 *Comluth* is an etymological gloss on *coblath*.

APPENDIX 1

Transcriptions of the Canonical Tract of *Aidbred*

What follows is a collection of all of the transcriptions of the canonical tract of *Aidbred.* The fragments are presented here in their unedited form so as to make editorial decisions in the main edition more transparent. The fragments are organized by source and section number. Not every fragment can be securely attached to a particular section, and not every fragment may belong to *Aidbred.* The notes within the edition provide further discussion on those citations. Citations from *O'Davoren's Glossary* are not listed here because they were not used to create the edited text.

Source A

§ 1 Aidbriud ardnemed fola di maigin nad narliu uad rath na cundrad na hoin na haithne na hairliugud na haititiu ⁊rl- ⁊ imtongar and sin o g*r*adaib ecal*sa* f*or* g*r*adaib tuait*h*e ar dilat .uii. ngraid ecl*as*a f*or* .uii. ng*r*adaib.t.

§ 2 Doberar dal .iii. ł .u. no .x.

§ 3 Cach aidbriud docuisin

§ 4 Nach fer medongaite docuisin

§ 6 Ar is faill do nemed cen iaraid

§ 7 Feis lethfrichgnuma

§ 8 Ni lot los laban

§ 9 Aidbred t*es*ta ⁊rl-

§ 10 Ni hindsorgor o crich do c*r*ich

Ni hin*n*sorgor o c*r*ich do crich *acht* i *n*aidbrith*er* is a*n*d glether ce*r*t ime

Ni fuatag*ar* o mac*h*ad do mach*ad*, ac*h*t coruice lias bes nesa*m* f*r*i c*r*on ⁊ coi*m*gi

§ 11 DEcce cia dingenum

Inti fofich is e teit t*ar* c*r*ich

§ 12 Duine lasi mbia fod

Source F

§ 1 Aidbriud ardneimid

Folu do maigin

§ 2 Doberar dail treisid ⁊rl-

§ 3 Cach aidbriud docuisin cach laisi naidbrith*er*. Is la tuinide co tartur a fol*od* f*r*is amail rogab cia fothu disli fosuidi tarraig. Foreith dilis nindlis

Inti na daim a rer f*or*is, ⁊rl-

⁊ intí d*h*aim*us*, ⁊rl-

Ni suit*er* f*r*i remdilsi cia b*eth* it*er* taitib

 | DOI:10.1163/9789004520721_010

Ní suiter fri remdilsi, ⁊rl-
§ 4 Nach fear m*edongaite* docuisi*n*
§ 6 is faill do*n* neiemd*h*, muna feast*er* bes gad rocria ⁊ munub do gataid rocriad
§ 7 feis l*eth* f*r*ithgnud*h*a

Source G
§ 1 & imtongar o g*r*ad*h*aib*h* ecalsa
Ar dolaat .uii. g. e. f*or* .uii. g.t.
§ 2 Co tuca cach a saidbre
§ 3 Cach aidbriud docuisin
§ 4 Nach fer meodong*h*aite
Nach fer meodongaite dochuisin
§ 5 Ni teit ai*thgin* tar cen*n* gat*aig*e
Maineb e dotngre
§ 6 Ar is faill do neimed ci*n* iarr*aid* a .s.
§ 7 Feis leathfrichnuma fo bit*h* sguir ⁊ imcoimeta ⁊ uadab*h*ar cinad*h*a
§ 9 Aidbread*h* t*est*a ⁊rl-

Source J
§ 3 Oc*us* cach aib*h*re dochuisi*n*, ca*ch* laisi naib*h*rig*hter* is lais a tuin*id*e
§ 10 Ni hindsorgar o crich do crich a*cht* ait a naib*h*rit*h*ar is and dleg*h*ar ceart uime
Ni hin*n*sorg*ar* a crích do crích a*cht* ait
Ni fuatag*har* a*cht* o macha coruice lias bes nes*am* dó f*r*i cron ⁊ coi*m*ge
§ 11 INtí fofich is e teit t*ar* crich
Intí fofich is e teit t*ar* cric*h* co r*u*ctar breath f*air* a nem*ed*h c*r*ich cai*ch* f*r*isi fuich
Intí fofich
Intí fofich, ⁊rl-

Source P
§ 3 Cach aidb*r*iud*h* docuisi*n*, cac*h* laisia naid*h*b*r*itht*er* is lais a tuinide
Inti da*m*as a reir forais as oca bis tuinide
Ni suit*er* fri reimdilsi cia b*eth* itir t*h*aitib. Ni tabair re na tuinig*h*e fri cura na reimd*h*ilsi, cia focertat tatahat ilar cor fair eturru imanetar, is di t*h*aitib diren
Ni suit*er* fri rei*md*h*i*lsi cia b*eth* iter t*h*aitib, ⁊rl-
Ni suit*er* fri re*m*dilse, ⁊rl-
§ 4 Nach fer medongaite docuisi*n*, ⁊rl-
§ 10 ET cach aid*h*b*r*ig*h* bes nime
Ni fuadadar o macha do macha

Source Q

§ 1 id*h*br*iud* ardnei*m*e fol*ad* do magi*n*

§ 2 ⁊ Dob*erar* dail t*r*esi no *cóic*the no *dech*m*aid*i ł miss

§ 10 ⁊ Ga*ch* aid*h*br*i*d*h* bes nem*id*; ni fuadag*har* o mach*a* do mach*a*

Source AA

§ 1 Aidb*r*iud*h* ardneim*id* fol*ad* do maig*in*

§ 2 ⁊ dob*erar* dal t*r*eisi ł .U.te ł .10.m*aidi* ł mis

§ 3 Ni suit*er* f*r*i reimdilsi cia b*eth* it*er* taitib, .⁊rl-
ni suit*er* f*r*i reimdilsi

§ 10 ⁊ Gach aib*h*re bes neim*id* ni fuataga*r* o mach*a* do mach*a*

Source BB

§ 3 IS lais a tuinide

Source EE

§ 6 *Ar* is faill do neim*ed* ⁊rl-

§ 7 Feis l*eth* f*r*i*ch*na*m*a

Source FF

§ 3 Cach aidb*r*iud docuisi*n*, cach laisa naid*h*b*r*ith*er*, is lais a tuinide.
Inti damas a re......ca bis tui*n*ide

§ 4 Na*ch* fer medongaite docuisin, ⁊rl-

§ 10 Et ca*ch* aid*h*bri.......im..
Ni fuadad*har* o macha do macha

Source GG

§ 11 I*n*ti fofich is e t*et* t*ar* c*r*ich go r*uct*a*r* b*r*e*th* f*air* a ne*m*id c*r*i*ch*i cai*ch* f*r*isi fuacha*r*

Source JJ

§ 1 aid*h*b*r*i airdnei*m*e fol*ad* do maig*in*

§ 2 dob*erar* t*r*eisi no *cóicth*i no *dech*m*aide* no mios

§ 10 ⁊ g*ac* aid*h*b*r*i bes n*eim*i; ni fuataig*hter* ó m*ach*a do m*ac*ha

APPENDIX 2

Source Q [*CIH* 1144.36–1145.11], RIA 23 Q 6 [1243], p. 4a–b, Digest A (8)

Doni[1] dlig*us* nec fort*ac* f*or* nec ó dobera min*d*a, m*ana* t*u*ca in lit*ach* a cosm*ailecht*[2]

[A]id*h*bri*ud*[3] ardneim*e*[d] fol*ad* do magi*n*,[4] .i. (n)[m]á *tuc* fer aidb*reda* reamo*d*, luig*id* intí ag*ar* h-aid*h*bre*d*h na fid*ir* gu*r*ab gad. ⁊ m*ana* luig*i*, ber*igh* in fe*ar* [aidbreda][5] amac*h* iarna[6] imdenu*m* *con*a fiac*h* gaide, fo aigne seall*aig* lai*n*feich no l*eth*feich. ⁊ gi*n*gurub leis, *nos*beir*e* dia taisg*he* go fest*ar* fe*ar* bunaid*h*.[7]

⁊ **Gac*h* aid*h*brid*h* bes nem*id*; ni fuadag*har* o mach*a* do mach*a*,** .i. g*ac* in*nraic* aidb*ris* a *sét* ag eisindr*aic*, ⁊ is fot*h* n-infais imrit a ndis, is laisin indr*aic* imde*nam*h go fior *testa* ina diaig, ac*h*[t] m*ana* t*airg*e in ant*est* oga n-aid*h*brid*h*th*er* fior Dé; ⁊ dia t*airg*e, ni bfuil fir is t*aire* d'*im*denum*h* o neoch 'nas in fior t*airgus*.[8]

⁊ **Dob*erar* dail tresi no *cóic*the no *dech*m*aidi* ł miss.** ⁊ Is aire isb*erar* na rée-seo, *ar* m*ana* fagb*a* fer aidbr*eda* in*nracus* imdenm*ha* f*risin* re-sin, is don fer oga mbé

---

1 *CCIH* 48. The digest entry continues until *CIH* 1145.26 and largely repeats material given in source JJ, Digest B (27) edited in Appendix 3 below.

2 The same heading is also found in source AA, Digest C (19), *CIH* 1929.37–38.

3 A space has been left in the MS for an initial ⟨a⟩; see also Binchy, *CIH* 1144, n. j.

4 The material from Digest A (8) corresponds to material in source AA, Digest C (19), *CIH* 1929.37–1930.26 and source JJ, Digest B (27), and *CIH* 1314.5–35. The *CIH* citations are for the entire Digest entries for both; specific correspondences are given below where relevant. Fragments of the text from *Aidbred* are quoted in the commentary. Although the quotations from the text are not indicated in the commentary itself by the standard scribal practice of using larger letters for text and smaller letters for commentary, the quotations from the text are given in bold here and in the translation for ease of reference. It is possible that there are quotations from the text in this commentary which are not attested in the other surviving copies of the material. This clause is part of the beginning of the tract; see *Aidbred* § 1.

5 For this emendation, see source BB, *Aidbred* § 3.

6 Binchy, CIH 1144, n. l, states that there is a gap after *iarna* where three letters would fit. Due to staining on the page, it is difficult to determine whether the scribe left a gap or erased some letters. Based on the material from source AA, *CIH* 1929.41, and source JJ, *CIH* 1314.9, nothing seems to be missing from source Q.

7 The first half of the paragraph belongs with *Aidbred* § 1a.

8 The second paragraph belongs with *Aidbred* § 10. In the MS, the first two paragraphs are written as one block of text.

 | DOI:10.1163/9789004520721_011

That a person is entitled to assign liability to another if he swears oaths, unless the accused person does the same.[9]

A high noble claims [his] property immediately, i.e., if the man claiming swore [his] preliminary oath, the one from whom it was claimed swears that he did not know that it was stolen. And unless he swears [thus], the man claiming takes away [the property] after proving it along with the fine of theft, the same as that of a culpable onlooker [guilty to the extent of] full fine or half fine. And though it is not his, he takes it to guard it until [the] original owner is known.

And each claiming made by a *nemed*: it is not taken from cattle enclosure to cattle enclosure, i.e., each worthy person who claims his property from an unworthy person, and it is a claim of growth that they both bring, it is up to the worthy person to prove [it] with compurgators supporting him, unless the untrustworthy witness, from whom it is claimed, undergoes an ordeal. And if he undergoes [an ordeal], there is not a truth [sc., a proof] which is more wretched to prove by someone than the truth which he offers.[10]

And a delay of three days or five days or ten days or a month is given. And it is from that that those times are mentioned, because unless a worthy person claiming

9 The translation is that given in *CCIH* 48.

10 If the religious proof involves a physical ordeal, such as the ordeal of the cauldron, rather than swearing on relics, it is possible that the verb should be translated as 'than it produces', referring to the physical evidence of the person's truth produced by the ordeal; *GEIL* 209–211; and Christophe Archan, "Ordeal by Fire in Medieval Ireland," *Peritia* 24–25 (2013–2014): 197–212. For a discussion of ordeals, see the Introduction, p. 21.

leic*ter* imdenu*m*. ⁊ ma*r* ad*er*: "no ma tru*ma* t*arrus*tar tan*us*[t]i do tiug[laithiu][11] taidbsi teor*a* tond,"[12] .i. doni tri*ar* la h-*indraic* a fuil for in*nraic*, no la eisindr*aic* f*or* esin*nraic*. ⁊ dia t*air*ge in ciontach dul do fir Dé, is do leg*thear*, *ar* ni fuil fior is t*aire* d'*im*den*am*h 'nas in fior t*airges*.[13]

11 I follow the emendation suggested by Binchy, *CIH* 1145, n. a. Cf. source AA, *CIH* 1930.8 'tuighl*aithi*'.

12 I have not been able to find the source of this alliterative clause. It is possible that it does not belong with *Aidbred*.

13 See Binchy, *CIH* 1145, n. c, for this expansion. The last paragraph belongs with *Aidbred* §2.

may find proof against that matter, the person who has it is allowed to prove [it]. And as it says: "or if conclusive evidence is obtained by the tanist at the last day of life shown by three waves,"[14] i.e., three people prove with a worthy person who is against a worthy person or with an unworthy person against an unworthy person. And if the first undergoes a successful ordeal, it is permitted for him, because there is not a truth [sc., a proof] which is more wretched to prove than the truth which he offers.

14 The translation of this clause is tentative.

APPENDIX 3

Source JJ [*CIH* 1314.5–35], BL Egerton 88, f. 22vb, Digest B (27)

f. 22vb Gibé[1,2] min*n*a dob*e*r-sa, gu*r*ab hí-si*n* an firin*n*e: tuga(c)[d]*h*[3] an biub*a* na min*n*na-si*n*, ⁊ mana tuga is dam*h*-sa t*é*t a sena no imd*h*enam, ma*r* aderid na dlith*i*-so sis.

Aid*h*bri[d] airdnei*me*[d] fol*ad* do maig*in*,[4] .i. mad*h* t*h*ug fer aid*h*bri a remo*d*,[5] luig*h*i anti og*ar* aid*h*bri[d] na fit*ir* gu*r*ab gad. ⁊ m*a*na luig*h*, berid*h* in fer [aidbreda][6] am*a*c iarna imd*h*en*a*m *con*a fiach gaide fo aic*ned* sell*aig* lainḟeic*h* no le*th*feth (*read* lethfeich). ⁊ gi*n*gorab leis, *no*sbeir*enn* dia t*h*aisce go *f*est*ar* fer buna[d].

⁊ **g*a*c aid*h*bri[d] bes n*eimi*[d];**[7] **ni fuataig*h*t*er* ó m*a*c*h*a do m*a*cha**, .i. g*a*c in*n*r*aic* aid*h*bris a s*é*t ag eisi*n*nraic, ⁊ is fot*h* n-i*n*ais imrid a nḋís, is laisin in*nraic* imd*h*enam go fior t*esta* ina diag*h*, ac*h*[t] mu*n*a tairg*e* an ai*nntest* oga n-aid*h*brit*er* fíor Dé. ⁊ dia tairg*e* ni ḟuil fior is t*aire*, .i. d'imdenam[8] [o neoch] 'nas in fior tairges.[9]

---

1 The older foliation given in *CIH* is 21d. All of this commentary is written in Domhnall's hand; O'Sullivan, "The Book of Domhnall Ó Duibhdábhoireann," 291.

2 The material from Digest B (27) corresponds to material in source Q, Digest A (8), *CIH* 1144.36–1145.26 and source AA, Digest C (19), and *CIH* 1929.37–1930.26. The *CIH* citations are for the entire Digest entries for both; specific correspondences are given below where relevant. See *CCIH* 57. Fragments of the text from *Aidbred* are quoted in the commentary. Although the quotations from the text are not indicated in the commentary by the standard scribal practice of using larger letters for text and smaller letters for commentary, the quotations from the text are given in bold here and in the translation for ease of reference. It is possible that there are quotations from the text in this commentary which are not attested in the other surviving copies of the material.

3 I follow the emendation suggested by Binchy, *CIH* 1314, n. b.

4 This clause is part of the beginning of the tract; see *Aidbred* § 1.

5 Binchy, *CIH* 1314.8, queries his expansion of the final syllable, but cf. § 1, sources Q and AA, both of which have *-ad* as the expanded final syllable in the same line of text as above.

6 For this emendation, see source BB, *Aidbred* § 3.

7 The scribe has written 'ni' with the suspension mark mistakenly placed through the center of the ⟨n⟩.

8 The phrase '.i. d'imdenam' is written as an interlinear gloss in Domhnall's hand; it appears to be some of the actual commentary which was left out. Sources Q, *CIH* 1145.5 and AA, *CIH* 1930.5 have *o neoch* following this.

9 This paragraph belongs with *Aidbred* § 10.

 | DOI:10.1163/9789004520721_012

Whatever oaths I may give, that it may be the truth: let the defendant give those oaths, and if he does not give [those oaths], I succeed in disproving him or proving [against him], as the laws below say.[10] f. 22vb

A high noble claims [his] property immediately, i.e., if the man claiming swore his preliminary oath, the one from whom it was claimed swears that he did not know that it was stolen. And if he does not swear [thus], the man claiming takes away [the property] after proving it along with the fine of theft the same as that of a culpable onlooker [guilty to the extent of] full fine or half fine. And though it is not his, he takes it to guard it until [the] original owner is known.

And each claiming made by a *nemed*: it is not taken from cattle enclosure to cattle enclosure, i.e., each worthy person who claims his property from an unworthy person, and it is a claim of growth that they both bring, it is up to the worthy person to prove [it] with compurgators supporting him, unless the untrustworthy witness, from whom it is claimed, undergoes an ordeal. And if he undergoes [an ordeal], there is not a truth [sc., a proof] which is more wretched,[11] i.e., to prove by someone than the truth which he offers.[12]

10 See *CCIH* 57 for the designation and a translation of the first sentence. The text here is concerned with some of the ways evidence can be provided; it specifically concerns oaths and ordeals.

11 The precise meaning of *táire*, the superl. of *táir* 'mean, base, valueless', is obscure to me; *eDIL* s.v. 1 *táir*.

12 For a discussion of ordeals, see the Introduction, p. 21.

⁊ ma*r* ade*r*: **dobe*rar* [dal][13] treisi no *cóict*hi no *dech*maide no mios.** ⁊ is aire isberar na ree-so, *ar* man fag*h*ba fer aid*h*bri[da] in*nracus* imd*hen*ma frisi*n* ré-sin, is do*n* fer aga mbé leict*ir* imd*hen*am. ⁊ ma*r* ader: "no ma t*ruma* tar*ustar* tai*n*aisti do tiog*h*l[aith]i[14] taid*h*b*h*si teora ton,"[15] .i. doní triar la h-in*nraic* a fuil f*or* in*nraic* no la eisin*nraic* f*or* eisin*nraic*, ⁊ dia tairg*e* in cointa*c* d*u*l d'fior Dé is do leict*er*, *ar* ni fil fior is t*air*i (ís .t.)[16] 'nas i*n* f*ir* t*airges*.[17]

⁊[18] ma*r* ader: "f*or*toing comarb*ae* ré a t*h*ire," .i. teora h-*air*naili imd*hen*ma ón fer nodonaid*h*brit*er*,[19] .i. nec[h] dia*ma*[d] log*h* en*ech* ina diag*h* in i*n*b*aid* [no]feim*enn*[20] *intí* uma nd-aid*h*brit*er* i*m*d*hen*am. ⁊ dia*m* let*har*d a n-uaisl*etaid*i, ⁊[21] dila bes in*n*-*raic* cid*h* uath*ad*, .i. mu*n* fag*h*bait i*n* lio*n* is coir d'i*m*dhe*n*am n*eich*, dotoi*ng* i*n*ti f*or*sa lit*er*.[22] ⁊ ce fag*h*b*a* in eisin*nraic* o*ch*tar, man fag*h*b*a* i[n][23] noma*d* fer, isí in in*nraic* dod*hen*a g*o* t*ri*ur; ł mu*n* fag*h*b*a* in ain*ntest* i[n] nonba*r*, is do*n* t*est* leg*ar* fo*n* lion fogeib*h*. ⁊ ni g*ach* fuil ail*us* airdf*or*g*ell*, .i. *mana* fag*h*b*a* intí arar fora in fuil lu*cht* fiora, is dontí f*or*a lit*er* leict*ir* a se*na*(na)[24] fo aic*ned* in*nraca* no eisin*nraca*. ⁊ dia t*airge* fior dé intí doleig i*n* fuil, ni dent*ar* f*air* g*an* f*ir* ndai*ne*,[25] a*cht* *mana* t*airg*[e][26] *intí* arar fera f*ir* dé. ⁊ dia t*airge* is é rag*hus* do, *ar* ní fuil f*ir* [is tairi].[27]

---

13 I follow the emendation suggested by Binchy, CIH 1314, n. e; cf. also source Q, CIH 1145.6 *dail* and source AA, CIH 1930.5 *dal*.

14 Cf. source AA, CIH 1930.8 'tuighl*aithi*'. A suspension mark is missing here.

15 The alliteration of this clause suggests that it is verse.

16 I follow the emendation suggested by Binchy, CIH 1314, n. f.

17 See the end of the previous paragraph and Binchy, CIH 1314, n. g, for this expansion. This paragraph belongs with *Aidbred* § 2.

18 The remainder of the digest does not seem to contain any material from *Aidbred*, although the subject matter is relevant; CCIH 48.

19 The verb is a 3 sg. pres. pass. ind. of *ad-fíri* 'sues, claims' with the conjunct verbal particle *no* and a class C m. object agreement marker.

20 For the emendation, cf. sources Q, CIH 1145.13 *nofeiminn* and AA, CIH 1930.12 *nodfeimenn*. The verb is a MI pres. ind. 3 sg. conjunct form of *éimdid* 'refuses, rejects; fails'.

21 The following material is also found in *Cóic Conara Fugill*; CIH 1032.9–15; CCIH 233–234; GEIL 280; Rudolf Thurneysen, *Cóic Conara Fugill: Die fünf Wege zum Urteil*. Abhandlungen der preussischen Akademie der Wissenschaften. Phil.-hist. Klasse; Nr. 7. (Berlin, 1925), p. 37. See also, idem, "Eine neue Handschrift von *Cōic Conara Fugill*," ZCP 19 (1933): 165–173.

22 The verb is a 3 sg. pres. pass. ind. of *lüd* 'charges, accuses'; *eDIL* s.v. *lüd*.

23 I follow the emendation suggested by Binchy, CIH 1314, n. h.

24 I follow the expansion suggested by Binchy, CIH 1314, n. i. Cf. also source Q, Digest A (8), CIH 1145.19 *ṡena*.

25 I follow the expansion suggested by Binchy, CIH 1314, n. j. Cf. also source Q, Digest A (8), CIH 1145.21 *fir ndaine*.

26 I follow the emendation suggested by Binchy, CIH 1314, n. k.

27 I follow the emendation suggested by Binchy, CIH 1314, n. m.

And as it says: **a delay of three days or five days or ten days or a month is given.** And it is from that that those times are mentioned, because unless a worthy person claiming may find proof against that matter, the person who has it is allowed to prove [it]. And it says: "or if conclusive evidence is obtained by the tanist at the last day of life shown by three waves,"[28] i.e., three people prove with a worthy person who is against a worthy person or with an unworthy person against an unworthy person, and if the first undergoes a successful ordeal, it is permitted for him, because there is not a truth which is more wretched than the truth which he offers.

And as it says: "an heir proves by oath regarding his land," i.e., three kinds of proof from the one from whom it is claimed, i.e., anyone who has an honor-price supporting him whenever the one from whom it is claimed rejects [the] proof. And if their nobility [sc., their social status] may be unequal, and a worthy person may be [considered] equal although [he has] a small number [of compurgators], i.e., unless they obtain the full number [sufficient to perform the legal action], it is legal to prove against someone, the one who is accused denies by oath. And though the unworthy person may find eight people, unless he finds the ninth man, it is the worthy person who will succeed with three people, or unless the one not qualified to give evidence finds the nine people, the one qualified to give evidence is permitted with the full number [of necessary people] which he will obtain. And every place where a noble witness entreats, i.e., unless the one who is accused obtains [the noble witness] along with compurgators, it is permitted for the one who is accused to disprove him according to worthiness or unworthiness [to perform a legal action]. And if the one who is rejected there undertakes an ordeal, it is not proved against him without compurgators, unless the one who is accused undertakes an ordeal. And if he undertakes [the ordeal], he will succeed because there is not a truth which is more wretched.

28 The translation of this clause is tentative.

⁊ m*ac* sanaisi, .i. mac i*n* fir graid*h*; is airé ata fir dé on mnai d'fast*ad* a meic *for*-san g*r*aid*h* n-ecl*as*a sun*n* uair ni fuil aititiud*h* co*mraic* aigi. ⁊ is aire dogni sí *go* fior nd*he* u*air* ni t*air*gan*n*-so*m* a*cht* fir dai*ne*. ⁊ dia tairg*e*-sim fir de, rob*a* leis, u*air* na fuil aititiug*h* co*mraic* uad*h*a-som.

⁊ tuar*asndal* na cana-so g*a*c fol*ad*[29] f*or*t*ac*,[30] ⁊ tu*aras*d*a*l d*r*oc*h*duin*e* f*or* d*r*oc*h*-d*uine*, ⁊ fec*h* na brait*h*reca[31] d*h*oib*h*-so dogebair air, ⁊rl-

29 The expansion of the final syllable of this word is in doubt across all three versions of the commentary; cf. source Q, CIH 1145.26 'fol*oing*' and source AA, 1930.25 'fol*ad*'. Binchy, CIH 1145, n. l, queries whether the reading should be 'fol*ad* fol*oing*'.

30 For a translation of this clause, see CCIH 195.

31 Source AA, CIH 1930.26 has 'dl*igi*' following this word. Source Q does not have this line of text. The word *bráithreca* is the nom. pl. form of the adj. *bráithrech*, which *eDIL* equates with *bráithremail* 'brotherly, consisting of brothers or members of the same kin-group'.

And a child of secrecy, i.e., a child of a man of the [lay] grades: it is regarding him that there is an ordeal by the woman to bind her child on the ecclesiastical grade here because there is not an acknowledgement of sexual relations with him. And it is regarding him that she performs an ordeal because she does not undertake [an ordeal] provided that [there are] compurgators. And if she undertakes [an ordeal], [the child] will be his because there is not acknowledgement of sexual relations by him.[32]

And this is the law of evidence [for] each possession [which is liable to] proving by oath, and evidence of a low status person against a low status person, and the fines of the members of the same kin-group for them will be taken from him, etc.

32 Ordeals were also used in paternity cases; see Bartlett, *Trial by Fire and Water*, 19; and *Immathchor nAilella 7 Airt* § 7 and the discussion in Johan Corthals, "Affiliation of Children: *Immathchor nAilella 7 Airt*," *Peritia* 9 (1995): 92–124, at 123.

APPENDIX 4

Source P [*CIH* 711.24–713.26], TCD MS 1337, *olim* H.3.18, pp. 185a–188a

p. 185a **Cach[1] aidb*r*iud*h* docuisi*n*, cac*h* laisia[a] n-aid*h*b*r*ith*ter*, is lais a tuinide.**[b] [2]

[a] .i. oca

[b] .i. a airisam[3]

Et cach aid*h*brig*h* bes nime[d], .i. cach aen is ni*m*ed*h* oca n-aidb*r*it*er*, **ni fuadadar o macha do macha.**[4] Ma foth dobera inti laisa fuiricar, .i. oca n-aid*h*b*r*ith*ter*, is e

---

1 The material edited here corresponds to that in source FF, *CIH* 859.34–861.14. It contains both fragments of the tract and commentary. As with source FF, not all of the fragments identified as tract belong with *Aidbred*. One of the difficulties of working with a fragmentary corpus is dealing with multiple fragmentary texts, many of which have not been confidently (or at all) identified. Fragments of tract, even those which cannot confidently be said to come from *Aidbred*, are printed in quotation marks as per the editorial method followed throughout the book. Without other sources associated with *Aidbred* also quoting the same material, it is difficult to make a case that the quotations come from *Aidbred*. Where there are any relevant orthographic differences between sources FF and P, they are given in the footnotes. See also *CCIH* 31 and 39.

2 This fragment is from *Aidbred* § 3. *CIH* 859.34 does not print any more material from p. 341 of the MS. Binchy, *CIH* 859, n. n, states that the last seven lines of the MS page are illegible and that the material is not in the O'Curry transcript. The transcription following is based on what is visible on the image posted on the Irish Script on Screen website https://www.isos.dias.ie/.

Cach aidb*r*iud docuisi*n*, cach laisa n-aid*h*b*r*ith*er*, is lais a tuinide. Et cac*h* aid*h*bri.....
..im..i. Cac*h* aen is ni*m*eid oca n-aidb*r*it*her*, **ni fuadad*h*ar o macha do macha.**
Ma fot*h* dobera i*n*ti laisa fuiricar .i. [?] oca n-ai[d?b*r*]it*her* is e i*m*toing c.......
a t?ig[he?] .i. i*m*de*m*am ⁊ gusi*n* *ceth*aird i ndea.ai.. ⁊rl- ... ..
i*n*draic ł da eisi*n*raic dorala i... set, is i*n*ti oca tarus .. a ....
be fot*h* bus ail lais d'i*m*irt f*air*. **Inti damas a re......**
ca bis tui*n*ide .i. cid i*n*draic cid eisindraic ...as dlig*ed* is coir .....
..coro
⁊ Co t*ar*da ......

Although not much can be read, there is enough of the text to feel confident that it is largely the same as that found in source P. Note 'aid*h*b*r*ith*er*' against *CIH* 859.34 'aidb*r*ith*er*', and that the final ⟨e⟩ of 'tuinide' is not visible on the online image of the MS page.

3 Neither of these glosses is in FF. The glosses in P are written in the scribe's hand.

4 These two fragments of tract seem to belong with *Aidbred* § 10; see also sources FF, Q, AA,

 DOI:10.1163/9789004520721_013

Every claiming that there is, everyone from whom[a] **it is claimed, it is in his possession.**[b] p. 185a

[a] i.e., from whom
[b] i.e., its remaining

And each claiming made by a ***nemed***, i.e., every one who is a *nemed* from whom it is claimed, **it is not carried off**[5] **from cattle-enclosure to cattle enclosure.** If the one

and JJ. These sources suggest that there is a different version of this section of the tract than that found in sources A and J.

5 The form *fuadadar* appears to be the 3 sg. pres. pass. ind. of *fúataigid* 'snatches away, carries off forcibly, takes away illegally'; *eDIL* s.v. *fúataigid*.

*im*toing co muint*ir* a t*h*ig*h*e, .i. dogni i*m*denam ⁊ gusi*n* cethrar[6] i ndeagaig*h* ⁊rl- Mas da indraic ł da eisi*n*raic dorala imin set, is inti aca tarus h*e* a i*m*denam, cidbe fot*h* bus ail lais d'i*m*irt fair.

Inti da*m*as a reir forais,[c] **as oca bis tuinide,**[7] .i. cid indr*ai*(d)[c][8] cid eisi*n*r*ai*(d)[c] da*m*us dlig*ed*, is coir tui*n*id*h*e i*n*t*h*seoit oca *acht* co roda*m*a dlig*ed* ⁊ co tarda t*r*eb*ai*re aire.

[c] .i. dlig*ed*

Cid fodeara, in tan is etairise i*n* tuata, *con*[id i n-]urlai*m*[9] coitcind dobe*r*ar in g*eall*,
p. 185b ⁊ i*n* dui*n*e aca n-aid*h*b*r*it*er* i*n* set aidb*r*iug[a], cid | etairisi h*e*, ma da*m*a dlig*ed* n-aid*h*briug*a*, *con*ad e[10] dleg*a*r a b*eth* ina laim? Is e i*n* fat*h* fod*era* i*n* gell do tabairt i n-urlai*m* coitcind in tan[11] is etairisi i*n* tuata: fui*r*ired*h* tid*h*naice o neoch *aile* bis forin gill, ⁊ noch[a]n urail*inn* dlig*ed* ar dui*n*e a geall do tabairt *acht* a lai*m* is tairise leis.[12] In set aid*h*briug*a* im*morro*, *noch*an ar fui*r*irug*ud* tidnaice bid*h* se. ⁊ cid etairisi*m*[13] in dui*n*e aca n-aid*h*b*r*it*er* h*e*, ma da*m*a dlig*ed* n-aid*h*b*r*ig*a*, is ed*h* dleg*a*r a b*eth* a lai*m* na eisindr*a*ca.

"Comfer tire tuinide;[d] air*m*[14] ina tartaig*h*,[15] is and a tuinig*h*[e].[e] [16] Cacha toraic a[17] tuinig*h*[e]," .i. is ed*h* is leisin cach airgid*h*ar a tai forin ferand tui*n*id*h*e in ferai*n*d

---

6 The MS reads 'ce*th*aird'; I follow the emendation suggested by Binchy, *CIH* 711, n. k. Note that source FF has the same reading as source P.

7 This fragment likely belongs with *Aidbred* § 3; cf. sources F, *CIH* 1270.24, and FF.

8 The emendation here and two words later follow Binchy, *CIH* 712, n. b. The scribe has written what could be read as a ⟨d⟩ above the ⟨r⟩, but I am not entirely convinced that the letter is a ⟨d⟩.

9 See also Binchy, *CIH* 712, n. c and 859, n. o.

10 The ⟨e⟩ is written suprascript.

11 Binchy, *CIH* 859, n. r, states that the phrase *in tan* is written in *marg. sin.* with reference marks. The reference marks are visible on the image, but the phrase is not. Source P, *CIH* 712.7, contains the phrase.

12 In source FF, it is possible that one word has been written between *tairisi* and *leis*; there is a space at the beginning of the line in the MS. The MS page also has a stain in the upper left corner of the page, which makes some of the readings in *CIH* difficult to confirm. There are no extra words in the same passage of text in source P, *CIH* 712.9.

13 The adj. is superl. where one would expect the comp.

14 Source FF reads 'airi*m*'; see See Binchy, *CIH* 860, n. a.

15 Source FF reads 't*h*araid', *CIH* 860.4.

16 Source FF reads 'tui*n*ide', *CIH* 860.4.

17 Source FF reads 'o'; see Binchy, *CIH* 860, n. a.

in whose possession it is found,[18] i.e., from whom it is claimed, brings a claim, it is he who swears with the members[19] of his household, i.e., he proves [it] and with four people supporting him, etc. If it is two worthy or two unworthy people who happened [to quarrel] about the property, it is the one with whom it was found who proves it, whatever claim he wishes to use for it.

The one who submits according to law,[c] **it is he who has possession**, i.e., whether it is a worthy or an unworthy person who submits to judgment, it is proper that he has possession of the property provided that he submitted to judgment and that he gives a surety for it.

[c] i.e., law

What brings it about, when the layman[20] is untrustworthy, that the pledge is given to a neutral third party, and the person from whom the disputed *sét* is claimed, although | he is untrustworthy, if he submits to the law of claiming, that it is right p. 185b
that it should be in his hand [i.e., in his possession]? This is the reason that causes the pledge to be given to a neutral third party when the layman is untrustworthy: expectation of handing it back[21] by someone else who has the pledge, and law does not command a person to give his pledge except into a hand that is trustworthy in this opinion. The disputed *sét*, however, there is not an expectation that it would be returned. And though the person from whom it is claimed is more untrustworthy, if he submits to the law of claiming, it is right that it should be in the hand of the unworthy person.

"An occupier of the land has possession;[d] the place where he found[22] [him], it is there that [he establishes] his possession.[e] [23] Each person found[24] in possession," i.e., this is what is bound on each who may be on the land that he should have

18 The form *fuiricar* appears to be the 3 sg. pres. pass. ind. of *fo-ricc* 'comes across, finds'; *eDIL* s.v. *fo-ricc*.

19 While a pl. form of *muinter* is expected, it is possible the word is used in a collective sense here.

20 For the translation of *túata* as 'layman', cf. *The MacEgan Legal Treatise* § 2.7.

21 The phrase *fuiriredh tidhnaice* seems to suggest that there is every likelyhood that the pledge will be returned to the one who gives it.

22 The form *tartaigh* and variants, such as *tarraid*, are all 3 sg. pret. forms of *do-airret*, although *eDIL* notes that forms like *tarthaid*, *tarthaigh* may be later pres. forms of a simplex verb.

23 The translation presented here differs slightly from that in *Anfuigell* § 26.

24 The form *tóraic* is understood here to be the vn. of *do-fuiric* 'comes upon, finds'; *eDIL* s.v. *do-fuiric*.

do b*eth* aice. "Et bid f*er* tecair tuinid[e] i *n*-air*m* nae," .i. bid leisi*n* f*er* acart*ar*[25] an*n* p. 186a tuinide in f*erainn* | do b*eth* aice.[26] "Air*m* ina[27] tartaig*h*[28] is and a tui*n*ide," .i. air*m*, baile no inad*h*, i *m*bith*er*[29] imun nae, i*m*in caingin; ł air*m*, baile no in*eth*,[30] a tarus e is an*n* a tuinid*h*[e].[31]

[d] .i. a tairise*m*

[e] .i. i*m*dena*m*

"Rosoillsith*er* se*n*chi nad sic*h*[32] saml*aid*; ni se(d)[g]a*r*[33] di*m*in tar inddi*m*in," .i. no*ch*an i*n*saidar a di*min* o fer in tuinig*h*e tar in*n*eimin f*er* in fuait*r*ia. "Ni h-i*m*pait talam tar tare*cht*ain to*m*ailt*ha*," .i. no*ch*an impuit*er* in tir co f*er* i*n* fuaitirtha onti oca *tar*aiter oca to*m*ailt.[34] "Atsuit*er* saire a tarus," .i. art*ai*he[35] fon saire ł fo n[d]aire[36] a tarus he.

---

25 Source FF reads 'acart*h*tar'; Binchy, CIH 860, n. b, queries whether the *punctum* over the first ⟨t⟩ is meant to indicate deletion.

26 In source FF, the scribe wrote ⟨aiece⟩, but partially erased the first ⟨e⟩; see also Binchy, CIH 860, n. c.

27 The ⟨a⟩ is written subscript.

28 Source FF reads 'tart*h*aid'.

29 Following this form the scribe wrote ⟨imbit*her*⟩; as noted by Binchy, CIH 712, n. f, this appears to be an error of dittography.

30 Source FF reads 'i*n*ad'.

31 The first fragment of tract in this paragraph is from *Anfuigell* § 26. In the edition, not all of the fragments of tract from sources P or FF were confidently identified as such. Fragments of this section of *Anfuigell* are also found in Digest D (12) (source J), CIH 1961.17–20 (CIH 1961.20–23 belongs with *Aidbred* § 3), part of 1961.20 is repeated at 1921.26; see CCIH 78; and *Anfuigell* § 26, n. 499. The relevant material from Digest D (12) is as follows: "⁊ comfér tire tuinide; *airm* i*n*a tar*raid*, is an*n* a tuinide," .i. in tan is in*n*raic ⁊ dam*haid* dlig*ed* n-ai[d]b*h*reda, is tuinid[e] in feoir ⁊ in f*er*ain*n* ina laim*h* co nderntar dlig*ed* uime. "Oc*us* cach tor*aic* a tui*n*ide," .i. is laisin f*er* foreca*r* f*or*san tir *tuinide* in tire. "Oc*us* bid fir teca*r* *tuinide*." '"And an occupier of the land has possession, the place where he found [him], it is there that he [establishes] his possession," i.e., when he is worthy and he submits to the law of claiming, possession of grass and land is in his hand until a judgment is made regarding it. "And each person found in possession," i.e., it is the person who is found on the land who has possession of the land. "And a person withholding possession will be."' The translation of the last clause is tentative.

32 Source FF reads 'sic*h*tar'.

33 I follow the emendation suggested by Binchy, CIH 712, n. g. Source FF has the same reading as P; cf. also source J, Digest D (12), CIH 1961.3 'segar'.

34 The same material with minor differences is also found in source J, Digest D (12), CIH 1961.3–6.

35 Source FF reads 'ast*aither*', CIH 860.13. In source P, read *astar*, following Binchy, CIH 712, n. h.

36 See Binchy, CIH 860, n. e, and source P, CIH 712, n. i.

possession of the land.[37] "And a person withholding possession will be where the litigation is," i.e., the person who is sued there should have possession | of the land. p. 186a
"A place where he found [him], it is there [that he establishes] his possession," i.e., *airm* 'place', *baile* 'where', or *inad* 'place', in which it will be regarding the litigation, regarding the case; or *airm* 'place', *baile* 'where', or *ineth*[38] 'place', in which he was found, it is there [that he establishes] his possession.

[d] i.e., his remaining
[e] i.e., proof

"An historian made known that he did not assert the same; certainty is not sought against uncertainty," i.e., its proof is not sought from the possessor against the uncertainty of the opposing party. "He does not return[39] the territory [sc., land claimed] beyond receiving compensation for use," i.e., the land is not returned to the opposing party from the one who is found using it. "A period of immunity is established when he was found," i.e., it is established according to the nobility or baseness [of the person] who had found him.

37 The translation of this fragment of tract and gloss is tentative.
38 This is an earlier nom. sg. form of *inad*; *eDIL* s.v. *inad*.
39 The form *impait* is a later 3 sg. pres. ind. from *imm-sói*; *eDIL* s.v. *imm-sói*.

"Ana cach tuinide donescarth*ar*.[f] Nac*h* cobdail sruit*he* suire[40] soco*m*et sern*ar*."[g]

[f] .i. fir liu*m* i*n* fer*ann* do*n*ti esct*ar*th*ar*[41] i*na* t*uinide*.[42]

[g] .i. *noch*a coibdeilid*h*thi na h-uasail aurrain*n* risi*n*ti sret*hnaigther* 'ga ded-comed.[43,44]

p. 186b "Is[45] an*n* dleg*ar* abad*h*[46] do tab*airt*:" i*n* tan is cuntab*airt* in cin no na f|eic*h*, ⁊ masa cindti, nocha dleg*ar* a tab*airt*.

"Inti[47] da tucud*h* amac*h* in fer*ann* ar foc*h*raic, ma ta(t)[48] toc*hus* graid co co*mlan* d'fer*ann* focrecca aige, is enecl*ann* co*mlan* do, ⁊rl-"

"Ni[49] h-acl*aid* indlig*ed*[50] fri h-in*n*dlig*ed*,"[51] .i. noc*h*a tabair acl*aide* fiac*h* ar feiche*main toicheda*[52] ce done*th* ni bud*h* indlig*thech* risi*n* n-i*n*bleog*h*an, risi*n* n-i*n*dlig*h*th*ech*, risi*n* ci*n*tach.

"In[53] at*hgabail* gaba*r* gu h-i*n*dlig*thech*, sla*n* a fuatac*h* gu h-i*n*dlig*thech*."

"Comraite[54] cen dire cen ait*hgin*: s*é*t nim*e*[d] ł s*é*t carat do gait[55] a n-ainbfis,[56] ⁊ a tabairt uada fo c*é*toir cen a cuin*d*c*he*, ⁊rl-"

---

40 Source J, Digest D (12), *CIH* 1960.33 reads 'suirn'.
41 Source FF reads 'escerth*ar*'.
42 The gloss was written above the line by the scribe in both sources.
43 The gloss was written above the line by the scribe in both sources. In source FF, the gloss was written by the scribe starting above the line and ending under the line in the right gutter. In source P, the gloss continues under the main text.
44 It is possible that the penultimate letter is an ⟨o⟩. The same material with minor orthographic differences is also found in source J, Digest D (12), *CIH* 1960.32–34.
45 There is a small paragraph symbol in *marg. sin.*
46 The first four words are written in a larger script size than the rest of the surrounding text.
47 There is a small paragraph symbol *inter col.*
48 Cf. source FF 'ta', *CIH* 860.20.
49 There is a small paragraph symbol *inter col.*
50 Binchy, *CIH* 712, n. l, queries whether the final syllable of *indliged* (both times) should be expanded as *-thech*.
51 See also *CIH* 866.37, which is a collection of citation on various topics; *CCIH* 39.
52 See also Binchy, *CIH* 712, n. m, for this expansion.
53 There is a small paragraph symbol *inter col.*
54 There is a small symbol *inter col.* to the left of the ⟨c⟩ which I cannot identify.
55 The phrase *do gait* is omitted in source FF.
56 The first ⟨i⟩ and the ⟨b⟩ were inserted above the line with reference marks by the scribe.

"Thus every ownership that is proclaimed.[f] Any equal division of privileged nobles [for its] good-guarding is ordered."[g] [57]

[f] i.e., it is true in my opinion that the land [should be] in the possession of the one who is expelled.[58]
[g] i.e., the nobles do not apportion a share from that which is settled for its good-guarding.

"It is here that he is entitled to give notice:" when there is uncertainty of the crime or of the | fine, and if it is certain, he is not entitled to give it. p. 186b

"The one to whom he gave away the land for rent, if he has [his] rank's property qualification along with [the] complete rent payment of the land, complete honor-price [is owed] to him, etc."

"An unlawful person does not inculpate an unlawful person," i.e., liability of fines is not imposed on the plaintiff though he had done something that would be unlawful against the kinsman surety, against the unlawful person, against the guilty party.

"The distraint which is taken illegally, exempt is carrying it off illegally."[59]

"Intention without penalty, without restitution: a noble's property or a friend's property [taken] by theft in ignorance, and it is given [back] by him immediately without requesting it, etc."[60]

57 The second fragment of text does not seem to follow directly on the first.

58 The glossator attempted a etymological gloss on *donescarthar* from *do-escair* 'proclaim, give warning', but the phrase *donti esctarthar*, where the verb is from *escartaid* 'expell, drive out', does not quite match the sense of the tract.

59 The sense seems to be that illegally carrying off property which itself had been illegally distrained is not subject to legal action.

60 This fragment deals with a situation where someone has accidentally taken someone else's property. The obligation is on the accidental thief to return the property to its rightful owner immediately upon realizing the mistake.

"Gataig*he*[61] forecar og gait,"[62] .i. i*n* tan is iar sluin*neth* ⁊ aithne, la*n*fiach i*n*d, ⁊ lanfiach na gaite do ic o fi*ne* dia t[ar]*rustar*[63] gait 'na laim. Mana tar*rustar gait* ina lai*m*, is fir de o fi*ne* d'i*m*de*nam* na gaite risi *n*dec*h*aid. Mad*h con*ainces a fast*ad*, is la*n*fiac*h* i*n*d-sid*he*.[64]

p. 187a "Atait[65] *tr*iar i tuait*h* nad aile othr*us* na fiac*h*ud[h] [66] maine *th*abra cai*n* no cairde: fer astoing cac*h* richt, fer fell*us* f*or*a ine*ch*, fer gat*us* indile caich."[67]

[h] .i. enecl*ann*

Nach fer medongaite docuisi*n*, ⁊rl-[68] In f*er* medongaite lan*i*ndlig*thech*, (a)[i]s [s]i[69] a aithnid*h*-side:[70] fis gaite ⁊ gataig*he* aige, ł fis gaite[71] nama. ⁊ cid aithgin cid frit*h*creicc tarrt*hus* aige, nochan fuil re n-i*n*dsaig*the* do *acht* a br*eth* uad fo c*é*toir: in ait*h*gi*n* co los ⁊ as ⁊ in forbairt, ⁊ landire ⁊ lan*e*necl*ann*. ⁊ *in* tan tic cinta*ch* re dlig*ed*, nochan ict*ar* ni ris, *acht* mai*ne*[72] ro*acht*aig*h* digb*h*ail a lai*me*; ⁊ munar[73] *acht*aigh, noc*h*[a]n[74] icar ni ris.

---

61 There is a small paragraph symbol *inter col.*

62 See also *CIH* 1042.9, which is part of a collection of citations from various topics; *CCIH* 44.

63 I follow the emendation suggested by BInchy, *CIH* 712, n. o.

64 The last four words are written below the end of the column.

65 There is a small paragraph symbol in *marg. sin.*

66 The ⟨i⟩ was added below the line by the scribe with reference marks; see also Binchy, *CIH* 713, n. a.

67 This fragment of text is from *Bretha Crólige* § 43; "*Bretha Crólige*," ed. and trans. D.A. Binchy, *Ériu* 12 (1938): 1–77, at 34–35; *CIH* 2298.1–3; and *CCIH* 31.

68 The tract here is from *Aidbred* § 4. There is a small paragraph symbol in *marg. sin.*

69 Binchy, *CIH* 713, n. c, suggests reading 'as s-'; the emendation suggested by Binchy, *CIH* 860, n. j, source FF, is '(a)is [s]i'.

70 Source FF reads 'aithne'.

71 One or two letters have been erased after the ⟨a⟩; see also Binchy, *CIH* 713, n. d.

72 Source FF reads 'ma'.

73 In source FF, the scribe originally wrote 'marn*ar*' but expunged the first ⟨r⟩ by placing a *punctum* under it; see also Binchy, *CIH* 860, n. m.

74 This same error is in source FF, *CIH* 860.39.

"A thief was found robbing," i.e., when it is after confessing and handing over [the property], [he owes the] full fine for it, and the full fine of the theft is to be paid by the kin-group if the stolen property is caught in his hand. Unless the stolen property is caught in his hand, an ordeal by the kin-group is [needed] to prove the theft against he who examines.[75] If proving it is an equally difficult case, [he owes the] full fine for it.

"There are three people in a *túath* who are not entitled to sick-maintenance[76] nor fines[h] unless law or treaty give it [to him]: a man who refuses [hospitality to] every class of person,[77] a man who proves false to his honor, a man who steals everyone's property." p. 187a

[h] i.e., honor-price

Any receiver of stolen goods that there is, etc. The fully unlawful receiver of stolen goods, he is characterized thus: he has knowledge of the theft and thief, or knowledge of the theft only. And whether restitution or counter-purchase was found in his possession, he does not have a period of time for searching, but it is taken from him immediately: the restitution with increase and growth and the produce, and full penalty-fine and full honor-price. And when the guilty party submits to judgment, he does not pay anything to him, except if he made a stipulation for the emptying of his hand; and unless he made a stipulation, nothing is paid to him.

75 The sentence seems to mean that if the kin-group wants to contest the theft (even though the thief was caught with the item in his/her hand), an ordeal is necessary. The verb *déchaid* probably refers to the person responsible for examining the thief's wound vel sim. after the ordeal.

76 Sick-maintence was the social institution whereby if an injured party's wounds had not healed by the end of nine days, the assailant was liable to pay for all the medical, food, accommodation, and associated expenses until the injured party was completely cured; D.A. Binchy, "Sick-maintenance in Irish Law," *Ériu* 12 (1938): 78–134; and GEIL 130–131.

77 For this interpretation, see *Bretha Crólige* § 43.

Ni[78] suit*er* fri reimdilsi cia b*eth* itir t*h*aitib.[i][79] **Ni tabair re na[80] tuinig*h*e fri cura na reimd*h*ilsi,**[j][81] **cia focertat tat(a)ha[i]t[82] ilar cor fair eturru imanetar, is di[83] t*h*aitib diren[ar].**[k][84]

p. 187b [i] .i. nochan astaid*h*ther *'na* laim he ge rob*eth* dilsi rei*mi* ite*r* n|a gataig*h*ib re fer i*n* aid*h*briug*ha*[85]
[j] .i. fri h-indsaig*id* na cor tucud dó re dilsi rei*mhe*
[k] .i. is dona gatai[gi]b[86] eirnith*er* ima b*hreth* uaithib*h*; no is uait*h*ib icth*ar* sm*acht*

Cid fo*dera* urlai*m* c*h*oitc*hind* do damail[87] don eisi*nn*raic isi*nn* inad*h* eile ⁊ se 'ga rad*ha*:[88] **ni suit*er* fri rei*md*h*ilsi cia b*eth* ite*r* t*h*aitib,** ⁊rl-? Is e in fat*h* fo*dera*: eisindrucus rei*mthechta*ch[89] i*n* n-ernailib rei*mthechta*cha eile dorinde in dui*ne* 'san i*nn*ad ele,[90] [⁊][91] ama*l* fer medongaite landlig*h*t*hech* i*m*on s*ét*-si*n* he, ⁊ coir cia rod*h*-

78 There is a small paragraph symbol in *marg. sin.* It is likely that this is a quotation from *Aidbred.* See below at l. 9.
79 From this point to the end of the material printed here, all of the fragments of tract are written in a larger script size than the surrounding commentary and glosses, except for the fragments of tract embedded within the commentaries themselves. This is not the case in source FF, where all of the material is written in the same script size. See also *Aidbred* § 3, source AA, Digest C (38), *CIH* 1940.39–1941.4; *CCIH* 77. Part of the material is also found in Digest B (16), beginning at *CIH* 1306.34.
80 The ⟨a⟩ is written subscript.
81 Along with source P, *CIH* 713.11–12, this fragment of tract is also found in Digest B (32), *CIH* 1318.23–24; *CCIH* 58; and *AL* 4: 268.26 under the erroneously named textual heading *Téd an Fearann a Cintaib.*
82 Source FF reads 'tat*h*at'. The scribe of source P originally wrote 'teatahat' but expunged the ⟨e⟩ by placing a *punctum* under it.
83 Source FF reads 'do'.
84 *AL* 4: 268.27–28. Source FF reads 'diranar'.
85 Binchy, *CIH* 713, n. b, notes that the gloss is interlinear; half of the gloss is interlinear, the other half is written at the top of p. 187b. Unlike the previous glosses in this source, the remainder in this paragraph are written around the tract. It is clear that the scribe has left room for the glosses and commentary in the page layout.
86 I follow the emendation suggested by Binchy, *CIH* 861, n. a. In source P, both the ⟨a⟩s are written subscript.
87 For source FF, Binchy, *CIH* 861, n. b, notes that the scribe originally wrote ⟨ḋamā*i* ḍạịḷ⟩, where the *puncta* indicate deletion, and he suggests that we should read ⟨damthain⟩. The word *damáil*, however, is a later form of the vn. of *daimid*; *eDIL* s.v. *damáil* 'submits to'.
88 In source FF, '⁊ … radha' is written after 'eile' with transposition marks showing its correct placement; see also Binchy, *CIH* 861, n. c.
89 *in n-ernailib reimthechtacha om.* source FF.
90 Source FF reads 'aile'.
91 I follow the emendation suggested by Binchy, *CIH* 713, n. i; see also source AA, Digest C (38), *CIH* 1941.1.

It is not established by prior right though it may be amongst thieves.[i] **Neither time nor possession is given against contracts or prior right,**[j] **though thieves place an abundance of contracts on it amongst themselves in turn, it is by thieves that it is paid.**[k]

[i] i.e., it is not seized in his hand though there should be previous possession amongst the | thieves before the person claiming.[92] p. 187b
[j] i.e., against suing or contract that it was given to him before previous possession.
[k] i.e., it is by the thieves that it is paid regarding its judgment by them, or it is from them that [the] fine is paid.

What causes submission to a neutral third party by the unworthy person in the other place and its saying: **it is not established by prior right though it may be amongst thieves, etc.**? This is the reason that causes it: previous unworthiness regarding other previous things that the man had done in the other place, and he is as a fully lawful receiver of stolen goods regarding that *sét*, and [it is] proper that it was submitted

92 In other words, the fact that the thieves had the item in their possession before the claim was made against it by the owner does not entitle the thieves to a claim of prior right.

amtha urlai*m* *ch*oit*ch*enn do. ⁊[93] in baile ata sund im*morro*, **ni suit*er* fri re*m*dilse,**
p. 188a **⁊rl-**; i*m*un s*é*t-sa | fein rofes essindruc*us* in duine-se, ⁊ f*er* medongaite indlig*h*th*e*ch[94] imon s*é*t-so hé, ⁊ coir ci*n*co damtha urlai*m* *ch*oit*h*chend dó.

"Fortha[95] nad cria nech di[96] dernand dondaig;[l 97] dian c*r*ia,[98] is dire thadait aridmbia[99] iaram."[m 100]

[l] .i. na rocen*n*aig*h*e do lai*m* in gataig*h*e

[m] .i. is athg*ein* ⁊ dire ⁊ sm*acht*, is ed*h* bias de fair iara*m*, ⁊ f*er* medongaite laninddlig*h*thech hé.

---

93 From here to the end of the paragraph, see also *Aidbred* § 3, source F, *CIH* 1270.28–30.

94 In source FF, the scribe originally wrote a second ⟨l⟩ after the ⟨g⟩ and partially erased it.

95 There is a small paragraph symbol in *marg. sin.* I have not been able to find this fragment of tract elsewhere other than in sources P and FF; it may or may not belong with *Aidbred.*

96 Source FF reads 'do'.

97 The form *dondaig* is the 3 sg. pres. ind. of *do-aig* with a class C m. object agreement marker.

98 The verbal phrase *dian cria* is the 3 sg. pres. subj. of *crenaid* and a class C m. object agreement marker attached to the conj. *día n-*.

99 Source FF reads 'f*or*sa mbia'. The form here should probably be read as *foridmbia,* the 3 sg. fut. of *for-tá* with a class C m. object agreement marker.

100 The scribe left room for both of the glosses in the MS layout.

to a neutral third party by him. And the place here, however, there is **it is not established by prior right, etc.**; regarding that *sét* | itself, he knew the unworthiness of p. 188a
that man, and he [is as] an unlawful receiver of stolen goods regarding that *sét*, and it is proper that it was not submitted to a neutral third party by him.

"Furthermore that no one should buy from a hand that seizes it;[l] if he should buy it, a theft penalty will be imposed upon him afterwards."[m]

[l] i.e., that he should not buy from the thief's hand

[m] i.e., restitution and penalty and fine, this is what will be from him for it afterwards, and he [is as] a fully unlawful receiver of stolen goods

APPENDIX 5

Commentary associated with *Cáin Aicillne* (SM 6) [*CIH* 1786.26–29 and 1788.10–25], TCD MS 1336, *olim* H.3.17, cols. 210 and 213

See also *CCIH* 72 and *AL* 2: 264.20–23 and 270.6–26. The material here is partially quoted in § 1b, source A.

"Ogdilsi in rat*h*a ar *secht* mbiad*h*uib co ngab*ail* trebuire, co tabuirt[1] *sét* turcl*uid*i, co teacmuisi*n* ega na fl*ath*a. A l*eth*dilsi *ar trí* biaduib*h* co l*eth* mbid*h*, a *t*riandilsi ar da mb(l)*iad*(*n*)a[2] co triun mbid." [*CIH* 1786.26–29]

col. 213 "Dilsi in rath*a* ar *t*ri biaduib*h*, co ngab*ail* tre*buir*e, cin tabuirt s*éo*tu turcl*uid*e, co teacmuisi*n* eca na flath*a*, .i. *t*rian gan biad et*ir*, ⁊ *seissed*h cech*t*arde in da *cét*biad*h*, ⁊ *t*rian arin tres mbiad*h*.

Dilsi in rath*a* ar *secht* mbiaduib*h*, co ngab*ail* treb*air*e, co tabuirt[3] s*éo*tu turcluide, co teacmuisin eca na fl*ath*a. A l*eth*dilsi ar *t*ri biaduib*h* co let[h] mbid*h*, a *t*riaindilsi ar da mbiaduib*h* co triu*n* mbid*h*.

Cid fo*dera* cu bfuil dilsi *t*riain in rath*a* sunn cin biad it*ir*, ⁊ dilsi a da *t*rian ar da mbiad*aib*, ⁊ *co n*-abuir tall i Ḟut[4] Ḟeineachuis: 'na*ch* dilius dag*h*rat*h* destina fl*ath*a, ⁊rl-', uair cid dorata in da biad*h* tall, muna tarda in tres biad*h*, ni bfuil ni ar*a* sgat*h*? At*a* biad*h* acin c*hele th*all ⁊ ni h-ail do a tabuirt, ⁊ is ail le comorbu na fl*ath*a in biad do tobuirt doib*h*.

Sunn im*murro* ni fuil in biad acun c*hele*, ł ce ta, is com*h*d*h*eoin doniat eturrud*h*. ⁊ in fl*aith* is m*a*rb an*n* s*in*. ⁊ mas e in cele is marb ann, cid mor do biud*h* dorat don fl*aith*, munu gab*a* trebuire re dilsi in rath*a*, ni dilis in rat*h* dona com*ar*b*aib*, ⁊ is *ed* dleg*ar* cele ar mís,[5] ł comruinn dibuid*h* don fl*aith*. Mas é in fl*aith* is marb ann, sícc."[6] [*CIH* 1788.10–25]

---

1 The second ⟨t⟩ was added above the ⟨r⟩ by the scribe.

2 I follow the emendation suggested by Binchy, *CIH* 1786, n. m.

3 The scribe wrote the final ⟨t⟩ over an ⟨e⟩; see also Binchy, *CIH* 1788, n. d.

4 The *punctum* over the ⟨f⟩ is used here to indicate nasalization.

5 It is difficult to determine whether the mark over the ⟨i⟩ is meant to be a length mark or to indicate the ⟨i⟩ in a row of minims.

6 The word *sícc* might be for Latin *sic* 'thus'. Perhaps the scribe used it to indicate a correction, i.e., he has already copied the material where the lord is dead and accidently started the same section again; this is purely conjecture. I should like to thank Paul Russell for discussion of this word. Any mistakes are my own.

 | DOI:10.1163/9789004520721_014

"The fief is completely forfeit after [paying] seven food rents with taking a surety, with giving *sét*s of submission, until the lord's death occurs. Half of it is forfeit after [paying] three and a half food rents, a third of it is forfeit after [paying] two and a third food rents."

"The fief is forfeit after [paying] three food rents, with taking a surety, without giving *sét*s of submission, until the lord's death occurs, i.e., a third with [paying] food rent at all, and a sixth for each of the two first food rents, and a third after the third food rent. col. 213

The fief is forfeit after [paying] seven food rents, with taking a surety, with giving *sét*s of submission, until the lord's death occurs. Half of it is forfeit after [paying] three and a half food rents, a third of it is forfeit after [paying] two and a third food rents.

What is the reason that a third of the fief is forfeit here without [paying] food rent at all, and two thirds of it is forfeit after [paying] two food rents, and that it says there in *Fot Féinechais*: 'nor is a good fief forfeit to the remnants of a lord, etc.', when[7] the two food rents were given there, unless he gives the third food rent, [what is the reason that] there is nothing in compensation for it? The client there has the food rent and he does not want to give it, and the lord's heirs want the food rent to be given to them.

Here, however, the client does not have the food rent, or though he does, they make a mutual agreement. And the lord is dead in that case. And if it is the client who is dead then, though it may be for a long time that he gave [food rent] to the lord, unless he [sc., the lord] takes a surety against forfeiture of the fief, the fief is not forfeit to the heirs, and he [sc., the lord] is entitled to a client [from the heirs of the client] for a month, or a portion of the property [to be given] to the lord. If it is the lord who is dead then, thus."

7 The passage seems to be corrupt; cf. the similar passage in § 1b, source A above.

APPENDIX 6

Source U [*CIH* 2110.10–19], TCD MS 1336, *olim* H.3.17, col. 659b *marg. inf.* and *dext.*

The following commentary is found appended to the end of the fragmentary text on deposits, *Córus Aithni*, and corresponds to some of the commentary found in *Aidbred* §1e, sources A and Y. The commentary is written in a different hand from the main text hand and has been added in the lower margin of col. 659b and continued in the right margin of the page. The last paragraph of the text on col. b is written in a very compressed hand by the scribe as he is clearly trying to get the last of the material he has in front of him to fit on the page. This page of the MS is full of interlinear glosses and marginal notes in various hands. The fact that the commentary printed below was added by a later scribe in the margin suggests that it was not part of the material that the scribe had in front of him and casts doubt on whether the commentary actually belongs with *Córus Aithni* or it was copied onto the page from elsewhere because it concerns deposits. Thus, it is uncertain whether the scribe who copied this commentary got it from sources A and/or Y or some other source. It is also entirely possible that all three attestations of the commentary come from the same source. See *CCIH* 85 and 308, and *GEIL* 278.

Dia[1] ngaba t*r*eb*ai*ri i*n* f*er* di*ar* ait*h*n*eth* i*n* ait*h*ni, is sla*n* do cidb*eth* dona*ir*b,[2] ⁊ mai*ne* be faill taisc*eth*a f*air* *acht* am*al* a crod fe*n* ⁊ ci*n* faill f*air*-sid*h*e. Sla*n* do da*no*, cia gabaid*h* treb*ai*ri ci*n*co gaba, dia fes*ar*a fer i*n*n ait*h*ni faill taisc*eth*a f*or* crud*h* i*n* fir di*ar* ait*h*n*eth*.

Sl*an* do da*no*, dia ngaba t*r*eb*air*e cia b*eth* faill taisc*eth*a uad*h* mad*h* deit*h*b*ir* do[3] i*n* faill.

---

1 There is a paragrapgh symbol at the start of the commentary.

2 The verb appears to be a 3 sg. pres. ind. of *do-airb* with a class A m. object agreement marker. This verb is poorly attested; sources A and Y have 3 sg. pres. ind. forms of *do-airret* 'seize, get' in the same part of the text. See *eDIL* s.v. ? *do-airb*.

3 'do … mai*ne*' is written under col. a.

 | DOI:10.1163/9789004520721_015

If the man to whom the deposit was entrusted takes a surety, he is free from liability whatever misfortune befalls it, and there is not neglect guarding it, but like [he guards] his own cattle, and it is not neglected.[4]

He is free from liability, whether he takes a surety or not, if the owner of the deposit knows of neglect of guarding the cattle of the one to whom it is entrusted. He is free from liability then if he takes a surety, though there may be neglect of guarding by him, if he has a reason for the neglect.

4 The property referred to in the last clause is the property of the person to whom the plaintiff's property is entrusted.

Ait*h*gi*n* f*air* i*mmurro*, mai*n*e gaba tre*bairi* dia*m* be faill taisc*eth*a uad*h*. O*cus* ait*h*-gi*n* f*air* da*no*,[5] cia[6] b*eth* treb*air*e mai*n*e be faill taisc*eth*a[7] co fis do*n*n ḟir oca facab*ar* ⁊ *co n*-a*n*ḟis do*n* fir roait*hin*. Let*h*ait*h*gi*n* f*air* dia[8] *n*gaba t*rebairi*[9] i*m* slan do dia*m* be faill, ⁊ ni do gres f*air acht* tecmaisi*n* æ*nuair*i. L*eth*ait*h*ci*n* f*air* da*no*, dia*m*[10] be co*met* coitte*cht*a ⁊ ni gab treb*air*i i*m* slan do.

5 Binchy, *CIH* 2110.14 reads 'im̄' but questions the reading.
6 The commentary continues in *marg. dext.*
7 The second ⟨a⟩ is written subscript.
8 The ⟨a⟩ is written subscript.
9 I follow the expansion suggested by Binchy, *CIH* 2110, n. i.
10 The ⟨a⟩ is written subscript.

Restitution for it,[11] however, unless he takes a surety, if there is neglect of guarding by him. And restitution for it then, though there may be a surety, if there is neglect of guarding with knowledge [of it] by the man with whom it has been left and with ignorance of the owner of the deposit. Half restitution for it if he takes a surety regarding being free from liability, if there is neglect of guarding, and never continually for it, but occurring once. Half restitution for it then if there is proper guarding and he does not take a surety regarding being free from liability.

11 It is difficult to determine whether *fair* in the Irish refers to the deposited property itself or the owner of the deposited property, i.e., 'restitution for it' or 'restitution for him', respectively.

Source W [*CIH* 684.17–21], TCD MS 1337 [H.3.18], p. 151 (x); *CCIH* 30

The commentary here corresponds to material in the commentaries to *Aidbred* § 4.

In fear meodong*aite* la*n*dlig*thech*: ga*n* fis g*aite* na g*aitaig*e aige. Ma tharus cholan*n* aige, aithfeght*ar* in cen*n*ach d'urraidh ł *in* cen*n*ach d'anurr*ad*. Masa cendach d'urr*ad*, be*r*ar aithgi*n* co*n*a h-*in*dudh uagha. ⁊ masa cen*nach* d'*an*urraigh, is roi*nn* ar do etarugh. ⁊ mu*n*a tharrus colan*n* it*ir* aige, sl*an acht* gu*r* in*n*ise inti or cen*n*aigh ⁊ *in*ti frisa rac.

 | DOI:10.1163/9789004520721_016

The fully lawful receiver of stolen goods: he has no knowledge of the theft nor of the thief. If the [stolen] item was found in his possession, the purchase from a local freeman or the purchase from an outsider is to be considered. If [the] purchase is from a local freeman, restitution is given by him along with the increase. If [the] purchase is from an outsider, it is divided in two between them [sc., between the receiver of stolen goods and the owner]. If the [stolen] item was not found in his possession at all, he is free from legal liability, provided that he names the one from whom he bought [it] and the one to whom he sold [it].[1]

1 This commentary is discussed and partially translated in Kelly, *The MacEgan Legal Treatise*, 174; see § 5 of the *The MacEgan Legal Treatise* for a summary of the legal principles presented in this and the other commentaries which concern the person who receives stolen goods.

APPENDIX 8

Source Z [*CIH* 673.35–674.25], TCD MS 1337 [H.3.18], pp. 144–145a, citations on various topics with commentary

The material repeats a lot of material found in *Aidbred* § 4, source DD [*CIH* 801.28–802.5].

p. 144 D*eth*b*ir*[1] maigni ⁊ sec*htar*maigni re fer teall*aig* faichi do g*res*: lan a maigin ⁊ l*eth* a *sechtarmai*(*r*)gin.[2] Can asa gaba*r* lan a maig*in* isna *sét*aib ⁊ l*eth* a sec*htar*maigi*n*? (⁊)[3] Is ass gabur: "co direna*r cethrae*.[4] Co h-erana*r* boin asa buailaid, ⁊rl-."[5] No d*ano* ceana, o robia buac*h*aill a togleanm*ain* a sét, lanene*clann* in*n*tib, cid a maigi*n* [cid i sechtarmaigin].[6] Can asa gaba*r* (o)[i]n[7] sin? Is as gabur: "dia mbe muici, ⁊rl-"

De*t*[h]b*ir* cert*tochusa* ⁊ *for*craid tochusa[8] re fer medongaite, ⁊ nochon fuil d*eth*b*ir* maig*ni* na seac*htar*maig*ni*, oir am*al* maigi*n* d'fir medongaiti g*ac* i*nadh* i *n*digned*h* a cor ł *conn*(*in*)*rad*, oir am*al* buacuill d'fir bun*aidh* gatt*aig*i re cois na *sét*, ⁊ o bias buac*h*uill a toiglenm*ain* na *sét*, is ris ata de*t*[h]b*ir* maigni ⁊ sec*htar*maig*h*ne.

Ait*h*gi*n* co los ⁊ ás ⁊ *in* [ḟ]orb*airt*, ⁊ noc*h*an fuil dire na ene*clann* do*n* in*nraic* na dénan*n* mai*th* do to[th]c*hus*. Ait*hgin* co los ⁊ as ⁊ *in*[ḟ]orboirt, ⁊ landire ⁊ lanene*clann* do*n* in*nraic* doni mai*th* da toc[th]*hus*.

Ait*h*gi*n* co los ⁊ as ⁊ in [ḟ]orb*airt*, ⁊ landire ⁊ l*eth*ene*clann* don eisindr*aic* doni mai*th* da to[th]ch*usa*, no co*m*ad l*eth*dire. Aithgin cin los cin as ci*n* in [ḟ]orb*airt* don ei(n)sinr*aic*[9] na*ch* dena[nn](c*h*)[10] mai*th* da to[th]ch*us*, no d'in*nraic* in scrip*uil*.

---

1 *CCIH* 35.

2 I follow the emendation suggested by Binchy, *CIH* 673, n. k.

3 I follow the emendation suggested by Binchy, *CIH* 673, n. l; and cf. source DD, *CIH* 801.30.

4 The MS has '.iiii.', but cf. source DD, *CIH* 801.30 *cethra* above; Binchy, *CIH* 673, n. m.

5 This source has not been identified.

6 I follow the emendation suggested by Binchy, *CIH* 673, n. n.; cf. source DD, *CIH* 801.31.

7 See Binchy, *CIH* 673, n. o; and cf. source DD, *CIH* 801.32 *ón*. Either *on* is edited to *in* here, or *sin* is deleted.

8 Binchy, *CIH* 673, n. p, notes that 'tochusa' is written in *marg. sin.* with reference marks. Only ⟨a⟩ and the reference mark are visible on the image available on the Irish Script on Screen website. Accessed July 10, 2020.

9 See also Binchy, *CIH* 674, n. a.

10 I follow the emendation suggested by Binchy, *CIH* 674, n. b; cf. source DD, *CIH* 801.37.

 | DOI:10.1163/9789004520721_017

[There is] always a distinction of precinct and outside the precinct for the owner of p. 144
the household green: full [penalty] from a precinct and half [penalty] from outside a precinct. Whence is taken full [penalty] from a precinct for the *sét*s and half from outside a precinct? It is taken from: "until cattle is paid. Until a cow is paid in respect of a byre, etc." Or on the other hand, when a cowherd will be in possession of his *sét*s, full honor-price for them, whether from a precinct or outside a precinct. Whence is that taken? It is taken from: "if there be a swineherd, etc."

[There is] a distinction of exact property and excess property for the man who receives stolen goods, and there is not a distinction of precinct or outside a precinct, because each instance when he could make a contract or bargain is a precinct for the receiver of stolen goods, because a thief beside his *sét*s is as a cowherd for the owner, and when there will be a cowherd in possession of his *sét*s, it is for him [sc., the thief] that there is a distinction of precinct and outside a precinct.

Restitution with increase and growth and the produce, and there is neither penalty-fine nor honor-price for the worthy person who does not make good use of his property. Restitution with increase and growth and the produce, full penalty-fine and full honor-price for the worthy person who makes good use of his property.

Restitution with increase and growth and the produce, and full penalty-fine and full honor-price for the unworthy person who makes good use of his property, or up to half penalty-fine. Restitution without increase, without growth, without the produce for the unworthy person who does not make good use of his property, or

Am*ail* ata (ata)[11] rig b*enn*; no d*ano* *acht* a mb*eth* am*al* com*o*rbo liacc ima lan*n* licc .i. am*al* comorba cloic*h*i bis *ar* lar muigi ina luigi cin in[ḟ]orp*airt* aice. Is aml*aid*-si*n* na fil in*n*ad na in [ḟ]orb*air*t don eisin*n*r*aic* nac*h* deini maith da to[th]ch*us*.

Masa ar maigi*n* tall*ad*[12] *gataige* na *séot*u, is laneneclann o fir meodongaite lain, ⁊ *letheneclann* o fir m*edongaite* leth*i*. Masa a maigi*n* tall*ad* *gataige* na *séot*u, cid do c*er*ttoc*hus* cid [d']f*orcr*aid[13] to[th]c*hus*a, is laneneclann uada.

Mas a se*cht*armaigi*n* tall*ad* *gataige* na *séot*u, is l*eth*eneclann. ⁊ ni fil b*úachaill* *acu* an*n* sin, ⁊ ma ta, is (l*eth*)[lán]en*eclann* and, cid a m*aigin* cid a sea*chtar*maigin.

p. 145a Masa d'forcraid[14] tall*ad* *gataige* na *séot*u, is laneneclann (d) [o][15] fir meodongaite lain, ⁊ l*eth*enecland o fir meodongaite leithi. Masa do c*er*t to[th]chusa tall*ad* *gataige* na *séot*u amach, cid be b*úachaill* *acu* cingo be, *aithgin* co los ⁊ ás ⁊ in[ḟ]orbort, ⁊ laneneclann ⁊ landíri d'ic do gataidi and.

Aithgi*n* co l*os* ⁊ a*s* ⁊ in [ḟ]orb*air*t, ⁊ landiri ⁊ (l*eth*)[lán]en*eclann*[16] (d) [o] fir meodongaite lanindlig*thech*. A*ithgin* co los ⁊ ás ⁊ in [ḟ]orb*air*t, ⁊ l*eth*d*íre* ⁊ leithen*eclann* d'ic o fir meodongaite leithindlig*thech*.

---

11 As suggested by Binchy, *CIH* 674, n. c, this appers to be an error of dittography.

12 Here and below, 'tall*ad*' against *CIH* 'talla'.

13 I follow the emendation suggested by Binchy, *CIH* 674, n. f.

14 The first ⟨d⟩ was written above the ⟨f⟩ by the scribe.

15 I follow the emendation suggested by Binchy, *CIH* 674, n. j.

16 I follow the emendation suggested by Binchy, *CIH* 674, n. n.

the value of a scruple for the worthy person. He is as a king of a hill; or on the other hand, he is like an heir of a stone that is on the ground of a plain as he has an oath without the produce. It is like that that there is not an increase of the produce for the unworthy person who does not make good use of his property.

If[17] it is from a precinct that a thief had stolen the *séts*, the fully [unlawful] receiver of stolen goods owes full honor-price, and half honor-price is owed by the half unlawful receiver of stolen goods. If it is from a precinct that a thief had stolen the *séts*, whether from exact property or excess property, he [sc., the thief] owes full honor-price.

If it is from outside a precinct that a thief had stolen the *séts*, [he owes] half honor-price. And there is not a cowherd with them in that case, and if there is, [the thief owes] full honor-price then, whether from a precinct or outside a precinct.

If[18] it is from excess property that a thief had stolen the *séts*, the fully [unlawful] p. 145a
receiver of stolen goods owes full honor-price, and half honor-price is owed by the half unlawful receiver of stolen goods. If it is from exact property that a thief had stolen away the *séts*, whether there may be a cowherd with them or not, restitution with increase and growth and the produce, and full honor-price and full penalty-fine is paid by a thief then.

Restitution with increase and growth and the produce, and full penalty-fine and full honor-price is owed by the fully unlawful receiver of stolen goods. Restitution with increase and growth and the produce, and half penalty-fine and half honor-price is to be paid by the half unlawful receiver of stolen goods.

17 The penalties here for the receiver of stolen goods contradict the penalties as laid out in the second paragraph of this commentary.

18 The penalties here for the receiver of stolen goods contradict the penalties as laid out in other commentaries from § 4.

APPENDIX 9

Heptad 54 [*CIH* 49.8–35], Oxford, Rawl. B. 487, f. 61c–d

What follows is the heptad itself and the glosses relevant to the version of the heptad given at the end of *Muirbretha*, source E. The material printed here does not take into account other versions of the heptad. The numbering of the glosses follows that given in *CIH*. See also *AL* 5: 298.8–300.20

[A]tait *secht* n-aire ruanada la *Féniu* ata comdilsi do cach ric*ht*: tab*air*t foidb fir
f. 61vb dotuit a re; tabuirt a ro | domain;[3] tabuirt a uathbas; (a) tabuirt tar trethan;[5,6] tabuirt
a teine; tabuirt a h-armaig; turchlu a suainemnad,[9] seol formna.[10]

[3] .i. caire cuairtbill .i. a h-aic(d)e*n*aib ⁊ a murlo*ch*aib.

[5] .i. do lar na fairgi.

[6] .i. iar feim*ed* ⁊ uriasa*cht* do anfine ł iar feim*ed* nama do fine .i. Mad airiasa*cht* tar nai tondaib, is dilis do *acht cóic*id *seiss*id loig*h*i; a tret*h*an (*read* trían) mad airiasacht fir fine ⁊ is snam, *ce*t*h*raim*he* mad a n-eath*ar*. Mana fuil an*n* itir in fer is a *sét*, is da t*r*ian do mas a h-eth*ar* dosfuc. Mad f*or* snam dob*er*a, is dilis do *acht cóic*ed *seiss*id loig*h*i do fir b*unaid*. Mad airiasa*cht* ⁊ feim*ed*, is uil*e* do anfine. Mad feim*ed* cin airiasa*cht*, is da trian. Mad iasa*cht* ci*n* feim*ed*, is t*r*ian; ⁊ is do anfine in sli*cht*-so. Mad fine im*morro*, ma feim*ed* cin iasa*cht*, is uili. Mad iasa*cht* cin feim*ed*, is da t*r*ian. Mad cin iasa*cht* cin feim*ed*, is trian.

[9] .i. ini dob*eir ar* clo is tar inti saig*h*es risin suainem*ain*, int allaide ł in rodaige.

[10] .i. ini dob*e*rar donti atci in lunig (*read* luing) fo seol ina foru*m* .i. in *sét* rodercad*h*.

 | DOI:10.1163/9789004520721_018

There are seven [categories of] champion's burdens which are equally forfeit according to each authority: taking spoils of a man who falls in combat; taking from a great | f. 61vb
depth;[3] taking from terror; taking it across a stormy sea;[5,6] taking from a fire; taking from a battlefield; taking (?) in ropes,[9] a moving sail.[10]

[3] i.e., a whirpool, i.e., from deep waters and from lagoons.

[5] i.e., from the bottom of the sea.

[6] i.e., after refusal and permission by a stranger or after refusal only by a local, i.e., if it is permission beyond nine waves, it is forfeit to him except for a fifth of a sixth of its value [for the owner]; a third of it, if it is [with] a local's permission, and it is [retrieved by] swimming, a fourth if it is [retrieved] in a boat. If the owner of the *sét* is not there at all, two thirds [is forfeit] to him if it is by a boat that he got it. If he gets it by swimming, it is forfeit to him except for a fifth of a sixth of its value for the original owner. If it is permission and refusal, it is [forfeiture of] all [of it] by a stranger. If it is refusal without permission, it is two thirds. If it is permission without refusal, it is a third; and this division is for a stranger. If it is a local, however, if it is refusal without permission, it is [forfeiture of] all [of it]. If it is permission without refusal, it is two thirds. If it is without permission and without refusal, it is a third.

[9] i.e., that which he gets by a hook which is beyond the one who advances by the ropes, the cliff climber or the builder.[1]

[10] i.e., that which is given to the one who sees the ship moving under sail, i.e., the watchman's *sét*.[2]

---

1 The translation of *rodaige* is tentative; *eDIL* suggests a builder or some other craftman. It is also possible that the word glosses *allaide* and, thus, is simply another term for a cliff climber or someone who uses ropes or rods in the same way as part of their profession.

2 Cf. O'Dav no. 273.

APPENDIX 10

Citations from a Variety of Texts which Refer to the *muirchuirthe*

1.[1] *Tecosca Cormaic*[2] §1, ll. 25–27

Bárca do thochor i port,
Allmaire sét,
Murchuirthe dílse.

2. Heptad 17, University of Oxford, Bodleian Library MS, Rawl.B. 487, f. 56c, *CIH* 17.17–18[3]

Eiric tar cend murcuirt*hi*[7] cin apu[d] do rig*h*[8] no do nech bes ai[9]

[7] .i. (s)[d']ic, no frecra dia nemt*arracht*ain no do tia*cht*ain fo coraib,[4] .i. cia roelai[5] in mu*r*churt*hi*, .i. saermurchure.[6]

[8] .i. gin urfocra dul don rig*h* t*ar*a cen*n*.

[9] .i. g*r*ad*h* flatha, .i. aile, .i. ica mbi se, cid*h* isle na rig*h*, .i. fear grin.[7]

1 On the *muirchuirthe* in general, see the Introduction, pp. 49–50, and Charles-Edwards, "The Social Background of Irish *Peregrinatio*," 46–50; and Neil McLeod, "*Di Ércib Fola*," *Ériu* 52 (2002): 123–216, at 167, n. 149.

2 The text is from *Tecosca Cormaic*, ed. and trans. Kuno Meyer, in *The Instructions of King Cormac Mac Airt*. Todd Lecture Series 15. (Dublin: Hodges, Figgis, & Co., 1909); see also Maxim Fomin, *Instructions for Kings: Secular and Clerical Images of Kingship in Early Ireland and Ancient India* (Heidelberg: Carl Winter Universitätsverlag, 2013), pp. 150–151. This part of the text is not in *CIH*; see also *GEIL* 284–285.

3 *AL* 5: 182.9–10. All of the readings in *CIH* have been checked against the relevant MSS. The numbers assigned to the glosses follow those given in *CIH*.

4 The phrase 'no do tia*cht*ain fo coraib' *om.* *CIH* 17.25.

5 The verb is a 3 sg. pres. subj. form of *fo-ceird.*

6 The last two parts of the gloss are written above the first part.

7 This gloss is squeezed into the space above 'no do nech' and below the first part of the gloss.

1. *Tecosca Cormaic* § 1, ll. 25–27[8]

Ships coming to port,
Imported goods,
Ownership of property which has been cast ashore.

2. **Heptad** 17, University of Oxford, Bodleian Library MS, Rawl.B. 487, f. 56c, *CIH* 17.17–18[9]

***Wergeld* on behalf of a foreigner[7] without giving notice to a king[8] or to the person whose [responsibility] he is[9]**

[7] i.e., to pay or answer for his non-appearance or impugning contracts, i.e., although the foreigner absconds, i.e., a free foreigner.

[8] i.e., without proclamation going to the king on his behalf.

[9] i.e., [one of the] noble grades, i.e., another, i.e., with someone whose [responsibility] he is, though he is lower than a king, i.e., a land owner.

8 The translation is based on that of Meyer. See also *GEIL* 7. The lines are from a list of signs of a successful king.

9 The heptad concerns seven *wergeld*s which should not be paid.

3. ***Díre-tract***, TCD MS 1336 (*olim* H.3.17), col. 426, *CIH* 1913.10–18[10]

Trian loige eneach caich dia murchuru.

Trian n-ene*clainne* do daer tairisi na n-isel,ceth*ramtha* do daer Erendach, *secht*mad enecl*ainne* do daer tair*is* na n-uasal, *ocht*mad do daer Erindach. Dogab*ar* in tria*n* ⁊ in ce*th*raime ⁊ in *secht*mad i liub*har*, ⁊ nochan [ḟ]agb*har* int ochtm*ad*, *acht* am*ail* tiagar isin roin*n* is neasa dona h-islib a tri*un* a ceth*ramthaid*. Coir 'no deiside ce rodeachdais issin roin*n* is neasu don*a* h-uaislib a *secht*mad i n-o*cht*mad. Cid fo*dera con*id mo do ina[11] dær tairis na 'na dær Erendach? Is e fa*th* fo*dera*: luga ata freisc[si]u[12] imscair acan dær tairis na acan dær Erendach. Cid fo*dera con*ad mo do dær tairis? Am*ail* ad*eir* a n-Uircept Bec …[13]

Col. 428, *CIH* 1915.26–27

Trian loge [e]neach[14] caich dia murcora *acht* rig*h* *con*a comg*rad*h*aib, is *secht*mad loige a eineac*h*-sen …

4. ***Bretha Comaithchesa***, TCD MS 1433 (*olim* E.3.5), p. 6a, *CIH* 204.1–5[15]

.i. da scr*epal* o murcort*h*i ina lu lai, dairt *cethair* scr*epal* ina *cóic*, .i. lu lai in deoraid ⁊ medontai lai muir*chuirthi*. Colp[th]*ach ocht* screp*al* a medontai lai in deor*aid*, ⁊ bo indlaeg o urr*ad*, ⁊ lu lai in urr*aid*; u*air ocht* scr*epail* o urr*ad* ina lu lai ⁊ bo indlaeg*h* se scr*epal deec* i*n*a medo*n*tai lai, ⁊ bo indlaeg o deor*ad* ina cleit*h*i lai, *cóic séoit* da tecaid da ba o urr*ad* ina cleit*h*i lai.

---

10 Rudolf Thurneysen, *Irische Recht: I. Díre. Ein altirischer Rechtstext, II. Zu den unteren Ständen in Irland.* Abhandlungen der preussischen Akademie der Wissenschaften. Phil.-hist. Klasse; Nr. 2. (Berlin, 1931), p. 39. This and the following citation are discussed in *GEIL* 6, n. 38; and Charles-Edwards, "The Social Background of Irish *Peregrinatio*," 48–50.

11 *ina* has been added above the line by the scribe.

12 I follow the emendation suggested by Binchy, *CIH* 1913, n. f.

13 The commentary breaks off here.

14 I follow the emendation suggested by Binchy, *CIH* 1915, n. m.

15 *AL* 4: 152.19. See also the version at *CIH* 1858.3–8; *CCIH* 292. A critical edition and translation of this text is currently in preparation by Thomas Charles-Edwards.

3. *Díre-tract*, TCD MS 1336 (*olim* H.3.17), col. 426, *CIH* 1913.10–18

A third of each person's honor-price for his foreigner.

A third of the honor-price for the lowest unfree foreigner, a fourth for an unfree Irishman, a seventh of the honor-price for the unfree foreigner, an eighth for an unfree Irishman. The third and the fourth and the seventh are found in a book, and the eighth is not found, but as it is found in the part which is next to the lowest from a third of a fourth of it, it is right moreover that it should go in the part which is next to the nobles from a seventh of an eighth of it. What is the reason that there is more for him for the unfree foreigner than for the unfree Irishman? The reason is: there the unfree foreigner has less hope of departing than the unfree Irish man has. What is the reason that it is greater for the unfree foreigner? As it says in *Uraicecht Bec* ...

Col. 428, *CIH* 1915.26–27

A third of each person's honor-price for his foreigner, except for a king along with those of equal rank [to the king], it is a seventh of his honor-price ...

4. ***Bretha Comaithchesa***, TCD MS 1433 (*olim* E.3.5), p. 6a, *CIH* 204.1–5[16]

i.e., two scruples from a foreigner for his small offense, a yearling heifer [worth] four scruples for five [stakes], i.e., the stranger's small offense is the same as a foreigner's middle offense. A two-year-old heifer [worth] eight scruples for the stranger's middle offense, and an in-calf cow from a local freeman, and it is the local freeman's small offense, because [it is] eight scruples from a local freeman for his small offense, and an in-calf cow [worth] sixteen scruples for his middle offense is the same as an in-calf cow from a stranger for his highest offense, five *sét*s which amount to two cows are due from a local freeman for his highest offense.

16 The commentary concerns damage to fences ranging from minor to serious offenses.

5. ***Córus Íubaile***, TCD MS 1363 (*olim* H.4.22), p. 54a, *CIH* 1556.1–24[17]

p. 54a **Coirpdire caich t*ra***

.i. is si-so i*n* coirp*dire* dobe*r*ar in cach nduin*e* ite*r* isil ⁊ uasal.

Mad urr*ad* marbus deor*ad*, it t*r*i cum*al*a dire i*nd* ⁊ cum*al* aithg*en*a. Mad urr*ad* marb*us* mur*coirthe*, it *cethair* bai ⁊ sam*aisc* a coirp*dire* ⁊ c(o)um*al* aithg*en*a. Mad urr*ad* marbus dær, cum*al* ind, ⁊ in cut*r*uma ata uaith-si*m* i*nd*-sim is a b*eth* uad-su*m* isi*n* urr*ad*.

Ma[d] deor*ad* marbus a cele, it *cethair* bai ⁊ sam*aisc* a coirp*dire* ⁊ cum*al* aithg*en*a; is *ed*-si*n* on urr*ad* do*n* mur*choirthe* ⁊ on mur*choirthe* do urr*ad*. ⁊ is and si*n* is comor coirp*dire* do*n* deor*ad* ⁊ do mur*choirthe*[18] ⁊ don (m)urr*ad*.[19]

Masa deor*ad* marbus mur*choirthe*, is l*eth* a fuil o*n* deor*ad* diaraile ata o cac*h* dib da ceili, on deor*ad* do mur*choirthe* ⁊ o*n* mur*choirthe* do*n* deor*ad*, .i. da ba ⁊ colp*thach* *trí* screp*al* do coi[r]p*dire* ⁊ cum*al* aithg*en*a.

Mad mur*choirthe* marbus mur*choirthe*, is bo ⁊ *tri* scrip*uil* in coirp*dire* ata o cach dib da ceile ⁊ cum*al* aithg*en*a re' tæb-si*n*. Ma[d] deor*ad* marbus dær, it *ceith*ri *secht*-

17 *CCIH* 68 and 239–241. See also *CIH* 865.15–29.

18 The last three words are added in *marg. inf.* by the scribe with reference marks. *CIH* prints these words at the end of the paragraph, but the reference marks appear after 'deor*ad*'.

19 I follow the emendation suggested by Binchy, *CIH* 1556, n. b.

5. *Córus Íubaile*, TCD MS 1363 (*olim* H.4.22), p. 54a, *CIH* 1556.1–24[20]

This is the body-fine[21] of each p. 54a

i.e., this is the body-fine which is given for each person both humble and noble.

If it is a local freeman [sc., a local in a community] who kills a stranger, there are three *cumals* for a fine and a *cumal* for restitution. If it is a local freeman who kills a foreigner, there are four cows and a three-year-old heifer[22] for his body-fine and a *cumal* for restitution. If it is a local freeman who kills someone unfree, a *cumal* for it, and the amount which is owed by him for that is that which is owed from him for the local freeman.[23]

If it is a stranger who kills another [stranger], there are four cows and a three-year-old heifer for his body-fine and a *cumal* for restitution; this is what is owed by the local freeman for the foreigner and by the foreigner for a local freeman. And this is the case where body-fine is as much for the stranger as for a foreigner and for the local freeman.

If it is a stranger who kills a foreigner, it is a half which is owed by the stranger for another [stranger] which is owed by each of them for the other, from the stranger for a foreigner and from the foreigner for the stranger, i.e., two cows and a two-year-old heifer[24] worth three scruples for body-fine and a *cumal* for restitution.

If it is a foreigner who kills a foreigner, it is a cow and three scruples for the body-fine which is from each of them for the other and a *cumal* for restitution in addition to that. If it is a stranger who kills someone unfree, there are four sevenths of the

---

20 For material relating to raids and retaliatory raids, see *Anfuigell* §§16–17.

21 The term *coirpdíre* 'body-fine' is one of the fines associated with injury. Fines for injury and homicide consist of two parts. The first part consists of the victim's honor-price, or a portion thereof, and is based on the victim's social status. The second part is the *éric* '*wergeld*', which consists of the *coirpdíre* (worth up to six *cumals*) and *aithgein* 'restitution' (worth up to one *cumal*). The *éric* fine depended on the severity of the injury inflicted on the victim. The maximum was seven *cumals* for homicide. For a discussion of these terms and the fines associated with injury and homicide, see Neil McLeod, "Assault and Attempted Murder in Brehon Law," *The Irish Jurist* new series 33 (1998): 351–391, at 351. See also *Di Ércib Fola* §1.9–12 and the section on injury in *CIH* 1266.16–1267.17 discussed by McLeod, "*Di Ércib Fola*," 167, n. 149. The approximate values of the items listed are as follows: 1 milch cow = 1 ounce (of silver) = 24 scruples = 2 *séts* = 1/3 *cumal*; *GEIL* 115–116; and *EIF* 587. In the legal texts we find a mixture of both livestock and metal (and other items, such as garments) being used to make payments; see *EIF* 593–599; and Liam Breatnach, "Forms of Payment in the Early Irish Law Tracts," *Cambrian Medieval Celtic Studies* 68 (2014): 1–20.

22 Usually a *samaisc* = 12 scruples; *EIF* 588.

23 In other words, what the unfree person would owe for injury to the local freeman.

24 Usually a *colpthach* = 8 scruples; *EIF* 588.

m*ad* na cu*maile* ata o urr*ad* do dær is *ed* ata o deor*ad* do daer[25] ⁊ [on daer][26] don
p. 54b deor*ad*; da *secht*mad | ⁊ in *cethramad* ran*n* *déc* o murc*hoirthe* do*n* dær ⁊ on daer don murc*hoirthe*, *secht*mad on d(a)eor*ad*[27] diaraile.

Daine si*n* tangadar re fogail n-i*n*dlis isi*n* crich ɫ re forlosc*ud*, ⁊ rucsad *séo*t*u*[28] na crithi (*read* crichi) leo. ⁊ is [s]*lan* a marb*ad* cin slainded, cin ait*h*ne, cin cae*m*achtain a fast*aide* i n-u*air* denma na fogla fo *cét*oir. ⁊ is [s]*lan* cach duine muirbfit*er* *ina* ri*cht*; ⁊ *ind*et*h*em fastaig*h*i rucad *cucu* an*n* ⁊ ni raibi[29] cæ*macht*ain a fast*aide*.

.i. Daine si*n* tancadar re fog*ail* n-i*n*dlis isi*n* crich, ⁊ na h-uile daine risna fog*ail* a nd*er*sat,[30] ⁊ dligis fodail enecl*ainne* asi*n* fog*ail*-si*n*. ⁊ is [s]*lan* co t*r*ian doib cach fog*ail* dodenait riu cu cæ*macht*ain a fast*aide* chena; ⁊ mu*n*a raib, is [s]*lan* uile.

6. *A late tract dealing with wounding*, TCD MS 1337 (*olim* H.3.18), p. 172, *CIH* 702.6–9[31]

D'urraid ata smacht med (*read* metha)[32] cinaidh comlan, ⁊ a leith do deoraid, ⁊ a cethruime do muircoirthe; ⁊ nocon fuil ni do doer, ⁊ noca fuil uad acht munab daor aga da in cuicraith cedach e. Mas eadh, is beith amal muircoirthe um cethruime do ...[33]

7. *Ántéchtae* (*Breth*), TCD MS 1387 (*olim* H.5.15), p. 30a,[34] *CIH* 2186.10–11

O urr*ad* [sin][35] ⁊ a l*eth* o deor*ad* ⁊ a *cethramthu* o muirc*huirthe*, ⁊ nochan [ḟ]uil ni o dær u*air* is *ar* so*n* s*machta* ita.[36]

25 The ⟨e⟩ is written above the ⟨a⟩.
26 I follow the emendation suggested by Binchy, *CIH* 1556, n. e.
27 The ⟨o⟩ is added subscript by the scribe.
28 The ⟨u⟩ is written above the ⟨s⟩.
29 The first ⟨i⟩ is written subscript.
30 Binchy, *CIH* 1556, n. h, states that the reading from 'risna' to 'nd*er*sat' is corrupt and suggests potentially reading "risa (*or* risna) foglatar."
31 For the identification of this tract, see *CCIH* 30.
32 I follow the emendation suggested by Binchy, *CIH* 702, n. c.
33 In *CIH*, Binchy follows O'Curry's reading from the transcripts; *CIH*, 702, n. d. Most of the page is illegible due to the use of reagent. I cannot confirm the reading given here.
34 The page is given as 29a in *CIH*, but the second half of the MS has been repaginated since *CIH* was published; see also *CCIH* 166–169.
35 I follow the emendation suggested by Binchy, *CIH* 2186, n. i.
36 The last word is squeezed in below the line by the scribe.

cumal which is owed by a local freeman for someone unfree [which] is what there is from a stanger for someone unfree and from the unfree person for the stranger; two sevenths | and the fourteenth part from a foreigner for the unfree person and from the unfree person for the foreigner, a seventh from the stranger for another. p. 54b

Those people who came into the territory to [conduct] an unlawful attack or for arson, and they took the territory's *séts* with them. And there is no liability for killing them without [knowing their] name, without recognition, without being able to apprehend them at the time that the attack was made. And there is no liability for each person whom they will have killed in this way;[37] and they had intended on apprehending [them] then and they could not apprehend them.

i.e., those people who came into the territory to [conduct] an unlawful attack, and all the people who opposed their attack which they made, and it merits a distribution of honor-price from that attack. And there is no liability up to a third for them for each injury they [sc., the locals] will inflict against them [sc., the raiders] [if they] could apprehend them besides; and if not, it is completely free from liability.

6. *A late tract dealing with wounding*, TCD MS 1337 (*olim* H.3.18), p. 172, *CIH* 702.6–9

For a local freeman a fine for omission of a crime is full, and half of it for a stranger, and a fourth of it for a foreigner; and there is nothing for the unfree, and there is nothing owed by him except if he is a subject of one who owns an estate consisting of five *raths*. If it is so, it would be the same as a foreigner regarding a fourth for …

7. *Ántéchtae (Breth)*, TCD MS 1387 (*olim* H.5.15), p. 29a, *CIH* 2186.10–11

That is a local freeman and half of it from a stranger and a fourth of it from a foreigner, and there is nothing from the unfree when it is on account of those fines.

37 The translation of the last clause is tentative; it is possible that it should be 'in mistake for them', referring to accidently killing someone in mistake for an outlaw or raider.

8. ***Bretha Déin Chécht***, NLI MS G11, p. 452, *CIH* 2308.20–27; *CCIH* 90

⁊ *in* sam*aisc* ad*eir* an*n* don air*ig* ech*t*a, is o muir*chuirthe* codn*a*c at*a* i fuil *in*gni. ⁊ *in* colp[th]*ac*[h] *ocht* scre*pal* ad*eir* an*n*, is o mur*chuirthe* codn*ach* a fuil *in*gni, ⁊ frith*aigid* [ḟ]uil an*n*. *In* d*air*t ar colp[th]ac*h* [ḟ]uil an*n ar sé* scre*plaib*, is o mur*chuirthe* *leth*cuin*n* ⁊ *leth*ceilli at*a* a fuil *in*gni. *In* dairt *cethair* scre*pal* ad*eir* don ocair*ig*, is o mur*chuirthe* leth*cuinn* ⁊ *leth*ceilli at*a* a fuil *in*gni, ⁊ frith*aig*i [ḟ]uil an*n*. Na *trí* screpail[38] ad*eir* don (bidb*aid*) [fiur midbad],[39] is o *murchuirthe* leth*cuinn* ⁊ *leth*ceille ata do deor*ad* i fuil *in*gni. *In* da scre*pal* ad*eir* do bruigfeoir (*read* bruider),[40] is o mur*chuirthe* leth*cuinn* ⁊ *leth*ceille at*a* do deoraid a fuil ingni, ⁊ frith*aig*i [ḟ]uil and.

9. Citations from various sources with commentary, BL MS Egerton 88, f. 53va, *CIH* 1426.23–25

T*r*ian coll*a ar* fais*neis*, no l*eth* coll*a ar* [ḟ]ais*neis* d*i*re ⁊ coll*a*; t*r*ian ⁊ *seissed* o gat*aige* urr*aid* d'fer fais*nesen*, t*r*ian ⁊ *leth* in *seissid* o gat*aige* deor*aid*, t*r*ian ⁊ *cethraim*e in *seisse*[d] o gat*aige* murcu*r*ta, t*r*ian n-aith*gena ar* gat*aige* dæir.

f. 53ra, *CIH* 1424.41–1425.2

T*r*ian n-ai*thgena* gac *séoit* ⁊ *aile deec* ai*thgena* a fais*neis* gac seoit, ⁊ in c*eth*raim*ed* r*ann fich*it na h-ai*thgena* a fais*neis* gac *séoit* uil*i ar* muir*chuirthe*, ⁊ t*r*ian a*ithgena* a fais*neis* gac *séoit* uil*i ar* dær.

38 *Screpail* has been added in above the line.
39 I follow the emendation suggested by Binchy, *CIH* 2308, n. h.
40 I follow the emendation suggested by Binchy, *CIH* 2308, n. i.

8. *Bretha Déin Chécht*, NLI MS G11, p. 452, *CIH* 2308.20–27

And the three-year-old dry heifer it mentions here for the *aire échta*, it is owed by a legally competent foreigner[41] for a wound of a nail [sc., scratching].[42] And the two-year-old heifer [worth] eight scruples it mentions here, it is owed by a legally competent foreigner for a wound of scratching, and there is a counterclaim for it. The yearling heifer worth a two-year-old heifer that is here [which is] worth six scruples, it is owed by a half legally competent and half-sensed foreigner for a wound of scratching. The yearling heifer [worth] four scruples it mentions for the *ócaire*, it is owed by a half legally competent and half-sensed foreigner for a wound of scratching, and there is a counterclaim for it. The three scruples it mentions for the *fer midboth*, it is owed by a half legally competent and half-sensed foreigner to a stranger for a wound of scratching. The two scruples it mentions for a *bruider*, it is owed by a half legally competent and half-sensed foreigner to a stranger for a wound of scratching, and there is a counterclaim for it.

9. Citations from various sources with commentary,[43] BL MS Egerton 88, f. 53va, *CIH* 1426.23–25

A third of the principal[44] for information, or half of the principal for information of penalty and principal; a third and a sixth [is owed] from a local thief to an informer, a third and half of the sixth from a non-local thief, a third and a fourth of the sixth from a foreign thief, a third of the restitution for an unfree thief.

f. 53ra, *CIH* 1424.41–1425.2

A third of the restitution of each *sét* and a twelfth of the restitution for information of each *sét*, and the twenty-fourth part of the restitution for information of each *sét* entirely for a foreigner, and a third of the restitution for information of each *sét* entirely for the unfree.

---

41 Binchy, *Bretha Déin Chécht* § 12, translates *muirchuirthe* as 'stranded person'. *GEIL* 252, follows Binchy's interpretation. While it is difficult to determine whether the interpretation is 'foreigner' or 'castaway' in this commentary, the fact that the text makes a distinction between individuals of differing social status suggests that the text is referring to foreigners.

42 For this interpretation of *ingen*, see Binchy's translation in *Bretha Déin Chécht* § 12.

43 See *CCIH* 64.

44 *Colainn* can refer to a pledged item or any substance of a contract.

10. **Citations from various sources with commentary**, Copenhagen, Det Kongelige Bibliotek, NKS 261b, f. 3vb, *CIH* 2244.6–7[45]

Nonbur dona h-aithnith*er* a tuait*h*

.i. na deoraig*hi* ⁊ na mur*chuirthi* ⁊ na dꜵi*r* ⁊ na fꜵ́ndleg*h*a ⁊ na h-u*r*foc*r*a ⁊ na meic[46] go*r* ⁊ na meic[47] ingo*r*.

11. ***Cethairṡlicht Athgabálae***, BL MS Harley 432, f. 7vc,[48] *CIH* 369.1–8[49]

a) im dingbail tascuir lir[1,2]

[1] .i. biath*ad* na loingsech, .i. ł are in puirt na tora tascur don lir, ł a comaire iar tia*cht*ain. .i. biath*ad* na murchuirt*hi* .i. tauscair.

[2] .i. fer puirt gab*us* im tuid*echt* do co*m*rai*n*n na bairci ł 'ma comet; ł fer puirt biad*tus* lu*cht* na bairci, uair is la tir f*r*isa suidigt*er* dleg*air* a to*dech*aide, a n-idnaide, a mbiadh*ad*, a taire*cht*aib; ł fer fine robiat*hustar*[50] dar cend,[51] a ceili an*n* sin, ⁊ aith*gin* a bid ar aine do. Tar muir tancat*ar* na daine-so, ⁊ ni h-ed tancat*ar* na daine tiss.

b) TCD MS 1337 (*olim* H.3.18), pp. 368b–369a, *CIH* 888.10–14

Dingbail tascu*r* lir .i. siche raet docuiredar h-i t*r*acht maru co tuaith, im luchtlag do
p. 369a doi*n*ib no | mil mar, dleg*air* do tuait*h* h-uil*i* a dingbail din purt, .i. tet aige fine asa

45 This citation is discussed and translated in Whitley Stokes, "On the Copenhagen Fragments of the Brehon Laws," *ZCP* 4 (1903): 221–233, at 231.

46 In the MS, this form is written as '.i.' with a suprascript ⟨c⟩; I follow the expansion given at *CIH* 2244.7.

47 In the MS, this form is written as '.i.' with a suprascript ⟨c⟩; I follow the expansion given at *CIH* 2244.7.

48 A quarter of the way down col. b, the scribe shifts from his usual two-column format to a three-column format.

49 *AL* 1: 128.12–24; *CCIH* 286–287.

50 The ⟨ro⟩ was added below the line by the scribe.

51 The MS has ⟨dā ar⟩; I follow the emendation suggested by Binchy, *CIH* 369, n. b.

10. **Citations from various sources with commentary,**[52] Copenhagen, Det Kongelige Bibliotek, NKS 261b, f. 3vb, *CIH* 2244.6–7

Nine people to whom a deposit is not made [sc., with whom nothing is deposited][53] **in a *túath***

i.e., the strangers and the foreigners and the unfree and the vagrants and the proclaimed and the dutiful sons and the undutiful sons.

11. ***Cethairṡlicht Athgabálae***, BL MS Harley 432, f. 7vc, *CIH* 369.1–8

a) regarding warding off a band of sea raiders[1,2]

[1] i.e., feeding the sailors, i.e., or watching the landing place[54] so that a band of raiders may not come from the sea, or keeping a watch on them after [they have] arrived, i.e., feeding the foreigners,[55] i.e., of a company.

[2] i.e., the owner of the landing place who proceeds on arriving to divide the ship or preserve it; or the owner of the landing place feeds the crew, because the territory in which it has landed is bound to protect[56] them, detain[57] them, feed them, supply[58] them; or a local person feeds [them] on behalf of another in that case, and he gets restitution of their food before fasting. These people came from across the sea, and it is not the case regarding those people who came [who are mentioned] below.

b) TCD MS 1337 (*olim* H.3.18), pp. 368b–369a, *CIH* 888.10–14

Warding off a band of sea raiders, i.e., whatever[59] thing which is cast on the sea shore in a *túath*, whether a shipwrecked crew or | a large whale,[60] the entire *túath* p. 369a
is bound to remove it from the landing place, i.e., the head of the kindred from the

52 See *CCIH* 89–90.
53 For legal deposit, see *GEIL* 120.
54 Irish *port* can refer to both the shore and a landing place. In some of the glosses and commentary, it is not always clear which is meant.
55 The sailors in this citation may or may not be castaways.
56 The translation of *todechaide* is based on that given in *AL* 1: 129.22.
57 The translation of *idnaide* is tentative.
58 The translation of *tairechtaib* is tentative.
59 The translation of *siche* is based on that given in *AL* 1: 129.26.
60 Cf. O'Dav no. 273 above; *EIF* 284–285; and *GEIL* 107 citing *CIH* 371.30, *AL* 1: 124.7–8 in reference to the bones of a beached whale being divided amongst the members of the community.

tir i mbi co rig[61] tuath*e* ⁊ *tr*osccaid *aire*; ascong*air*-side don tuait*h*, no gaibaid a n-ath*gabail*, ⁊ dingaib li*n* uile iarum.

c) BL MS Harley 432, f. 10vb, *CIH* 382.18[62]

do murchurti[17]

[17] .i. tairis,[63] .i. dair.[64]

d) f. 11vb, *CIH* 388.18[65]

Muirbretha[5]

[5] .i. im cait*h*im tasc*air* do tuinde, .i. na muirc*h*oirt*h*e.[66]

e) TCD MS 1336 (*olim* H.3.17), col. 44, *CIH* 1677.22–26

Mas ium cinuid*h* deor*aid*, is let *cóic séoit*. Mas ium cinuid muircurthu, is *ceth*ruime *cóic séoit*.

In doer, mas ium cinuid*h* na n-urruid*h* rogab*ad* i n-at*hgabail* e, is *cóic séoit* do dul i llob*ad* de ar g*a*c lait*h*e naicunta, ⁊ let*h cóic séoit* mas ium cinuid*h* deoruid*h*, ⁊ *ceth*ruime *cóic séoit* mas [fognama] (i)[67] murcurt*h*u.

---

61 *rig* is followed by ⟨na⟩, but the letters have been expunged by a *punctum* under each.
62 *AL* 1: 156.30.
63 Note that here we find *tairis* being equated with *muirchuirthe*; the two terms are also equated with each other in the commentary from the *Díre-tract* quoted above.
64 The glosses are written in the MS as two separate glosses on *do murchurti*.
65 *AL* 1: 182.1.
66 The second gloss is written above the first one.
67 I follow the emendation suggested by Binchy, *CIH* 1677, n. i.

land in which it is goes to the king of the *túath* and fasts against him; he [sc., the king] proclaims [it] for the *túath*, or he takes [it] in distraint, and he takes away all of it afterwards.

c) BL MS Harley 432, f. 10vb, *CIH* 382.18

for a foreigner[17]

[17] i.e., a foreigner, i.e., unfree.

d) f. 11vb, *CIH* 388.18

Muirbretha **'Sea-judgments'**[5]

[5] i.e., regarding using items cast ashore by the sea, i.e., the property cast up by the sea.

e) TCD MS 1336 (*olim* H.3.17), col. 44, *CIH* 1677.22–26

If it is regarding a stranger's crime, it is half of five *séts*. If it is regarding a foreigner's crime, it is a fourth of five *séts*.

The unfree, if it is regarding [his] crime that the local freeman took it in distraint, it is five *séts* going into forfeiture for it for each natural day, and half of five *séts* if it is regarding a stranger's crime, and a fourth of five *séts* if it is paying for a foreigner.

APPENDIX 11

Fishing Rights: *Cethairślicht Athgabálae*, BL Harley 432, f. 9ra, *CIH* 369.9, 12–16

im[1] corus lin,[2] [2] im chain n-inbir[3]

[2] .i. a cuit do lin coitcen*n* na fine, .i. nesam he i n-aimsir gnimr*aid*, .i. in brath*air* roleic a cuit ara ceile de, .i. uisci ł eisc it*er* co*m*orb*u*.

[3] .i. ini cuirth*er* a h-in*n* in uisci, ar in*n* in b*er*a, int iasc, ł is [i]ma den*am* gab*air*, ł in cora coitcend na fine, ⁊ is nesam int iasc, ⁊ in brath*air* roleic a cuit ara ceile de.[3]

---

1 See also *AL* 1: 122.16.

2 The tract and glosses are taken from a section of *Cethairślicht Athgabálae*; *CCIH* 286–287. This section of the text lists situations where there is a stay of distress for one day. The selections above concern fishing, both with nets and within a weir. In both selections, a stay of distress is granted to provide necessary labor for the kindred's fishing nets or weir when one member of the kindred has absconded from his duties, thus making it necessary for another family member to step in and perform his labor. For fishing methods in medieval Ireland, see *EIF* 285–298, especially 286–290. For material of a similar nature, see *Coibnes Uisci Thairidne* § 9 and gloss 4 (*CIH* 460.9–10, 18–19), and *Anfuigell* § 55 (Source A, *CIH* 2163.6–9) which refer to damming a third of the breadth of a river or a sixth, depending on whether the owner owns one or both sides of the river (this corrects the summary in Eska, *A Raven's Battle-Cry*, 45). Kelly, *GEIL* 277 suggests that the material above on fishing rights might be part of *Muirbretha*. It should be noted that the citations from *Cethairślicht Athgabálae* also appear in the collection of Old Irish Glosses on the *Senchas Már*, TCD MS 1337, p. 369a, *CIH* 888.15–17: Im cor*us* lin .i. piscium .i. ait coitcend bis do*n* tuaith i n-uisce. Im tairecc (*CIH* 888.15 reads *tairec*) lin uadaib uil*ib* ar cend i*n*t snam*h*a isin aitsin. I*m* cain n-inbir .i. im coraid coitcin*n*. 'Regarding [the] regulation of nets, i.e., *piscium* 'of fish', i.e., a common place which the *túath* has in water. Regarding providing nets from all of them to fetch that which swims in that place [i.e., fish]. Regarding [the] law of [the] estuary, i.e., regarding a common fishing weir;' see also *CCIH* 40 and 338–353. The word *piscium* was added above the line by the scribe as a gloss on *im corus lin*. For general discussion on fishing rights, see Stuart Archibald Moore and Hubert Stuart Moore, *The History and Law of Fisheries* (London: Stevens and Haynes, 1908).

3 *a....de* was written in *marg. sin.* with reference marks; see also Binchy, *CIH* 369, n. e.

 | DOI:10.1163/9789004520721_020

regarding [the] regulation of nets,[2] regarding [the] law of [the] estuary[3]

[2] i.e., his share [of work] for the kindred's common fishing-net, i.e., it is necessary in time of work, i.e., one kinsman abandoned his share [of the work] to the other, i.e., water or fish amongst heirs.

[3] i.e., that which is brought from the surface of the water, on the end of the stake [of the fishing weir], the fish, or it is for doing it [sc., the fishing] that [distraint] is taken, or the kindred's common fishing weir, and the fish is necessary, and one kinsman abandoned his share [of the work] to the other.

APPENDIX 12

List of Variant MS Readings against *CIH*

Below is a list of variant MS readings against those given in *CIH*. The list is divided by text, page, and line number for each edited text. For variant readings in *Aidbred*, the section number is also supplied. Further divisions are made within the list of variants for Heptad 64 and *Muirbretha* for ease of finding variants associated with each textual source.

Aidbred

§1 84.4 'fola[d]' against *CIH* 2164.4 'folad'.
84.6 'do' *om. CIH* 2164.6.
84.13 'inr*aic*' against *CIH* 2164.12 'i*n*raic'.
88.3 'a t*r*i' *om. CIH* 2164.33.
88.10 'co h-adha' *om. CIH* 1269.22. The scribe mistakenly wrote the phrase twice, but *CIH* does not mention this mistake.
88.12 'cid*h*' against *CIH* 1269.25 'cid'.
90.3 'aidb*hred*' against *CIH* 1269.27 'aidhbre*d*'. The scribe has place the *spiritus asper* over the ⟨b⟩ in error.
92.1 'an*n*[t]*est*a' against *CIH* 1269.39 'an*n*testa'.
92.2 'dober' against *CIH* 1269.40 'dobeir'.
92.9 'aid*h*bris' against *CIH* 1270.6 'aidhbriud'.
92.12 'trí' against *CIH* 1270.10 'tri'.
92.13 'fot*ha*' against *CIH* 1270.10 'fol*ad*'.
92.15 'esmancha' against *CIH* 1270.12 'esmanchu'.
92.15 'ní' against *CIH* 1270.13 'ni'.
96.11 '.i.' *om. CIH* 2165.11.
100.4 'ł' *om. CIH* 2165.34.
102.4 'mbeath*aid*' against *CIH* 2166.7 'mbeth*aid*'. The ⟨a⟩ is written subscript.
104.10 'inbaid*h*' against *CIH* 85.10 'inbaid'.
104.11 'nea*chtar*' against *CIH* 85.11 'nechtar'.
104.12 'i*n*biad*h*' against *CIH* 85.12 'i*n*biad'.
104.13 'd'athc*h*ur' against *CIH* 85.13 'd'athcur'.
104.23 'roc*h*uir' against *CIH* 2166.28 'rocuir'.
106.18 'dilsitar' against *CIH* 2167.1 'dilsiter'.
108.1 'd'fir' against *CIH* 2167.2 'o fir'.

 | DOI:10.1163/9789004520721_021

110.13 'uad' against *CIH* 2167.29 'uada'.
112.1 'urrnaid*m*' against *CIH* 847.37 'urnaidm'.
112.3 '.i.' *om. CIH* 847.38.
112.6 'don*airet*' against *CIH* 848.1–2 'donair, ⁊'.
114.1 'Ɣ' against *CIH* 2167.40 '⁊'.

§ 2 **118.6** 'i[a]rraid]' against *CIH* 2168.21 'iarraid'.
118.10 'fen' *om. CIH* 2168.25.
118.14 'f*h*uit*h*' against *CIH* 1275.42 'fuith'.
118.16 'mí' against *CIH* 1276.2 'mi'.
118.16 'ní' against *CIH* 1276.2 'ni'.
118.18 'fe*n*' *om. CIH* 1276.4.
120.7 't*r*í' against *CIH* 1276.10 't*r*i'.
120.10 'ó' against *CIH* 1276.13 'o'.
120.14 'ló' against *CIH* 1276.17 'lo'.
122.26 'e' against *CIH* 2070.30 'é'.

§ 3 **126.2** 'fol*ud*' against *CIH* 1270.17 'fol*od*'.
126.5 'fil' against *CIH* 2168.29 'fuil'.
126.10 'esi*n*draic' against *CIH* 2168.34 'esi*n*dric'.
128.13 'cr*eca*' against *CIH* 2169.6 'cr*eicce*'.
128.14 'cr*eca*' against *CIH* 2169.7. 'cr*eicce*'.
128.17 'c*ét*oi[r]' against *CIH* 1270.21 '.c.oir'.
130.7 'ní' against *CIH* 1270.28 'ni'.
134.1 'mem*h*ur' against *CIH* 1271.16 'memur'.
136.15 'cr*eca*' against *CIH* 2073.29 'chr*eca*'.
136.19 'é' against *CIH* 2073.32 'e'.
136.19 'ní' against *CIH* 2073.33 'ni'.
140.6 'i*m*un' against *CIH* 713.20 'i*mi*n'.
140.16 'ṡet' against *CIH* 2096.25 'set'.
142.2 'i*m*mach' against *CIH* 2096.30 'amach'.

§ 4 **152.10** 'i*n*dti' against *CIH* 2170.26 '⁊ dti (?)'; cf. *CIH* 2072.13.
156.6 'tall*ad*' against *CIH* 2171.1 'tall'.
158.10 'meod*h*angaid*he*' against *CIH* 1271.36 'meodhangaide'.
160.18 't*h*arb*h*' against *CIH* 1272.24 'tharb'.
164.5 'tall*tha*' against *CIH* 1273.16 'tall*ad*'.
166.1 'nach*ar*' against *CIH* 1273.34 'nach̄'. Binchy, *CIH* 1273, n. j, states that the suspension mark is an error, but cf. *CIH* 1273.38 'nochar̄', where, although the suspension mark is an error, the form itself is correct.

168.8 '*cu*(tu)trum*a*' against *CIH* 1274.19 'cutrum*a*'.

168.23 'cianaib*h*' agaist *CIH* 1274.33 'cianaib'.

168.23 'resi*n* ré' *om. CIH* 1274.33.

168.25 'cé' against *CIH* 1274.34 'ce'.

170.16 't*arr*us*tar*' against *CIH* 2071.5 'tarrt*ar*ar'. Binchy, *CIH* 2071, n. d, notes that the form as he has printed it is an error of dittography. The reading printed above expands the suspension mark over the ⟨t⟩ differently than Binchy.

170.16 'ait*h*gin' against *CIH* 2071.6 'aitgin'.

170.20 'f*r*is-[s]iu*m*' against *CIH* 2071.9 'fris-sium'.

172.7 'no' against *CIH* 2071.19 'ł'.

172.15 'leit*h*einecl*ainn*' against *CIH* 2071.27 'lethenecl*ainn*'.

174.8 'in*n*ud*h*' *om. CIH* 2072.3.

174.14 'ait*hgh*ena' against *CIH* 2072.8 'aithgena'.

174.22 '*dá*' against *CIH* 2072.16 'á'. Binchy, *CIH* 2072, n. d, missed the compendium for *da* and suggests emending 'á' to 'dá'.

176.5 'f*o*' against *CIH* 2072.26 'f*or*'.

176.8 Here and below 'tall*ad*' for *CIH* 2072.31 ff. 'tall*ais*'.

176.15 'lain' against *CIH* 2072. 36 'láin'. The stroke is above the ⟨i⟩ to differentiate minums.

176.23 'airb*er*nad*h*' against *CIH* 2073.1 'airb*er*nad'.

178.1 'b*heth*' against *CIH* 2073.7 'beth'.

178.1 '⁊' against *CIH* 2073.7 '7'.

182.1 'tall*astar*' against *CIH* 2074.43 'tall*ais*'.

182.4 'tall*astar*' against *CIH* 2075.3 'tall*ais*'.

182.18 'c*h*oitc*h*ind' against *CIH* 171.21 'choitcind'.

184.16 'fear' against *CIH* 172.6 'fer'; the ⟨a⟩ is written subscript.

184.17 'intí' against *CIH* 172. 7 'inti' and further below.

184.21 'th*a*ras' against *CIH* 172.10 'tharras'.

184.22 'amuic' against *CIH* 172.12 'amuic*h*'.

186.4 'ait*hgh*ein' against *CIH* 172.15 'aith*h*ein'.

186.8 'inorbai[r]t' against *CIH* 172.20 'inorba it*ir*'. Binchy, *CIH* 172, n. h, suggests that 'it*ir*' should be omitted. The scribe has forgotten to write the ⟨r⟩ and made a suspension mark over the ⟨t⟩ by mistake.

186.26 'm*air*id*h*' against *CIH* 172.37 'marid*h*'.

188.22 'm[b]rog*h*a' against *CIH* 173.19 'ni rog*h*a'.

196.6 'buail*aid*' against *CIH* 801.30 'buail*e*'; cf. *CIH* 673.37 buailaid.

196.19 'ait*hgein*' against *CIH* 801.40 'ait*hgin*.'

196.20 'ait*hgein*' against *CIH* 802.1 'ait*gin*'.

196.23 'ait*hgein*' against *CIH* 802.3 'ait*hgin*'.

196.24 'ait*hgein*' against *CIH* 802.4 'ait*hgin*'.

§ 5 198.5 'do*n*' against *CIH* 2075.16 'do'.
198.8 'de' against *CIH* 2075.18 'do'.

§ 6 200.9 'in*n*saigt*h*e' against *CIH* 2171.26 'in*n*saigte'.
202.2 'noicf*ad*' against *CIH* 1274.38 'noicf*a*'.
202.4 'd'ḟior' against *CIH* 1274.39 'd'fior'.
202.9 'neimed*h*' against *CIH* 1275.2 'neiemdh'.
204.2 'mḃ*eth*' against *CIH* 1275.5 'mbeth'.
204.3 'mḃ*eth*' against *CIH* 1275.6 'mbeth'.
204.7 'ór' against *CIH* 1275.10 'or'.
204.13 'iss' against *CIH* 1275.16 'is'.
206.17 'luaig*h*e' against *CIH* 2075.20 'luaigen*n*'.
206.17 'ní' against *CIH* 2075.21 'ni'.
208.9 'cía' against *CIH* 842.35 'cia'.
208.9 'noluaided*h*' against *CIH* 842.35 'noluaided'.
208.9 '*no*ícf*ad*' against *CIH* 842.35 'ŀícf*a*'.

§ 10 226.12 'roai[d]b*h*r*ed*' against *CIH* 1973.24 'roabhr*ed*'.
228.14 'aid*h*b*r*itht*er*' against *CIH* 711.27 'aidhbhritht*er*'.
230.1 'Intí' against *CIH* 1973.1 'inti'.

§ 11 230.5 'risi*n*' against *CIH* 2173.29 'riri'.
230.12 'la*n*indligth*ech*' against *CIH* 2173.36 'laindligth*ech*'.

Heptad 64

Source A

240.7 'fait*h*c[h]e' against *CIH* 55.22 'faithche'.
242.11 'beod*h*ile' against *CIH* 55.28 'beodile'.
242.14 'lug*h*u' against *CIH* 55.31 'lugu'.
244.14 'mb*eth*' against *CIH* 56.5 'mbet'.
246.10 .f. =fo*dera* against *CIH* 56.16 .fo. = fo*dera*.
246.13 'Cid*h*' against *CIH* 56.19 'Cid'.
246.13 't*r*ichadm*adh*' against *CIH* 56.19 't*r*ichatm*ad*h'.
248.9 'Mad*h*' against *CH* 56.34 'Mad'.
248.9 'tec*htaire*' against *CIH* 56.34 'techt*air*'.
250.5 'fait*h*ce' against *CIH* 57.9 'faithche'.
254.15 'comai[th]ch*iu*' against *CIH* 58.13 'comaich*i*'.
254.17 'I' against *CIH* 58.15 'in'.

256.1 'tisad*h*' against *CIH* 58.18 'tisad'.
256.1 'bun*aidh*' against *CIH* 58.18 'bun*aid*'.
256.7 'ad*eir*' against *CIH* 58.24 'ader'.
256.10 '*cóic*ed*h*' against *CIH* 58.26 '.u.ed'.
258.3 't*h*ire' against *CIH* 58.36 'tire'.
258.3 'fir' against *CIH* 58.36 'fer'.
258.8 '*no*ch*o*n' against *CIH* 58.39 'tch*o*n'.
262.3 'd*ho*' against *CIH* 59.21 'do'.
262.10 'dont*hi*' against *CIH* 59.27 'donti'.
264.5 'mb*et*ais' against *CIH* 59.38 'mbetis'.
268.3 'C*et*[h]raim*the*' against *CIH* 60.33 'Cethraim*the*'.
268.4 'd'[ḟ]ir' against *CIH* 60.34 'd'fir'.
268.5 'c*et*[h]raim*the*' against *CIH* 60.35 'cethraim*the*'.
268.12 'Cor*us*' against *CIH* 61.2 'cor*uis*'.

Source B

272.6 'r*ofeda*' against *CIH* 1209, n. p, 'roida'.
272.20 'fri*the*' against *CIH* 1210.7 'frithi'.
274.10 'rosoit*h*' against *CIH* 1210.17 'rosoich'.
274.13 'ge*ilfine*' against *CIH* 1210, n. i, 'gelfine'.
274.17 'f*rithe*' against *CIH* 1210, n. f, 'frithi'.
274.21 'd'fer' against *CIH* 1210.27 'dh'fer'.
276.2 'as' *om. CIH* 1210.30.
276.2 'f*rithe*' against *CIH* 1210, n. m, 'frithi'.
276.23 'd'fer' against *CIH* 1211. 10 'do fer'.
278.4 '*da*' against *CIH* 1211.13 'a'.
280.11 'frit*hi*' against *CIH* 1211.37 'fri*the*'.

Source C

282.1 'frithe' against *CIH* 1851.25 'frith*i*'.
282.11 'riag*ail*' against *CIH* 1851.35 'riagh*ail*'.
284.8 'ni' against *CIH* 'ní'.
284.11 'frithe' against *CIH* 1852.10 'frith*i*'.
284.16 'cethr*uime*' against *CIH* 1852.15 'cethr*amthu*'.
284.23 'coimdig*h*' against *CIH* 1852.22 'coimdig'.
288.11 '(f)[d]odongaib*h*' against *CIH* 1853.13 'dodongaib'; Binchy, *CIH* 1853, n. e, suggests the emendation of the preverb.
288.18 'fodongaib*h*' against *CIH* 1853.20 'fodongaib'.

Source D

294.3 'sloig*h*' against *CIH* 906.31 'sloig'.

Source J

296.9 'Sain—In ni fil in el*od* co *dech*m*aidh* is *ed* fil iar n*dech*m*aidh* gi*n* el*od*' *om* CIH 2062.33.
298.2 'dob*erar*' against *CIH* 2062.39 'dob*err* (?)'.
298.16 'as' against *CIH* 2063.10 'is'.
300.2 'is sain a mbr*eith*em*h*n*acht* side frisna frit*he*' *om. CIH* 2063.13.
300.9 'ad*eir*' against *CIH* 2063.21 'ader'.
300.18 'g*eil*fine' against *CIH* 2063.29 'g*el*fine'.
300.23 'raod*ha*' against *CIH* 2063.34 'rædha'.
302.2 'm*air*b*h*dile' against *CIH* 2063.37 'marbhdile'.
306.13 'g*eil*fi*ne*' against *CIH* 2065.10 'g*el*fi*ne*'.
306.14 'g*eil*fine' against *CIH* 2065.12 'g*el*fine'.
308.7 'comaith*chiu*' against *CIH* 2065.25 'comaith*chu*'.
308.16 'g*h*eb*h*ait' against *CIH* 2065.36 'gebhait'.
308.19 'dobui' against *CIH* 2065.39 'dobuí'.
310.2 '*con*ad' against *CIH* 2066.7 'conadh'.
310.8 'aig*n*e[d]' against *CIH* 2066.13 'aig*ned*'.
312.5 'nó' against *CIH* 2066.31 'no'.

Muirbretha

Source A

320.14 'coda' against *CIH* 140.4 'choda'.

Source C

336.11 'si*n*' *om. CIH* 316.7.
338.11 'beo*dilib*' against *CIH* 316.27 'beodil*ib*'.
338.18 'beod*ile*' against *CIH* 316.34 'beod*il*'.

Source D

342.2 'cid*h*' against *CIH* 1212.3 'cid'. The *punctum* is partially obscured by the descender of the ⟨f⟩ on the line above it.
342.7 '*da*' *om. CIH* 1212.9.
342.11 'arr[ias]*acht*' against *CIH* 1212.13 'airracht'.

Appendix 2

356.5 'taisg*he*' against *CIH* 1145.1 'taisge'.
358.3 'fior' against *CIH* 1145.10 'ni'. Binchy, *CIH* 1145, n. b, notes that the reading ought to be 'fi(o)r' and that the reading given by O'Curry, 'ni', is a mistake.

Appendix 3

360.8 'nd̓ís' against *CIH* 1314.12 'ndís'.
362.12 'fo*n*' against *CIH* 1314.26 'fo'.

Appendix 4

366.3 'airisam' against *CIH* 711.25 'airiseam'.
366.5 'aid*h*b*r*ithte*r*' against *CIH* 711.27 'aidhbhrithte*r*'.
368.12 Source FF 'g*ill*' against *CIH* 859.39 '.s.'. The scribe's ⟨g⟩s and ⟨s⟩s can look similar.
368.12 'noch[a]n' against *CIH* 712.8 'nochun'.
370.1 Source FF 'f*er*' against *CIH* 860.6 'f*ir*'.
370.8 Source FF 'dimi*n*' against *CIH* 860.11 'di*min*'.
370.8 Source FF 'h-impait' against *CIH* 860.12 'himpaite*r*'.
370.10 'art*ai*he' against *CIH* 712.22 'art*ar*'.
372.3 ''ga' against *CIH* 712.25 'ta'. It should be noted that Binchy queries his reading. The lower part of the ⟨g⟩ has been partially erased.
372.13 Source FF 'n-anfis' against *CIH* 860.26 'nancis'.
378.2 'i*m*un' against *CIH* 713.20 'i*min*'.

Appendix 5

380.8 'l*et*[h]' against *CIH* 1788.14 'leth'.
380.8 't*r*iaindilsi' against *CIH* 1788.15 't*r*iandilsi'.
380.9 'mbid*h*' against *CIH* 1788.15 'mbídh'.
380.11 'destina' against *CIH* 1788.17 'deistína'.

Appendix 6

384.2 'da*no*' against *CIH* 2110.14 'im̄ (?)'.
384.3 '*co n-*' *om. CIH* 2110.16.
384.4 'f*air*' *om. CIH* 2110.17.
384.5 'coitte*chta*' against *CIH* 2110.18 'coitechta'.

Appendix 8

388.6 'D*et*[h]b*ir*' against *CIH* 673.40 'dethb*ir*'.
388.8 '*con*n(*in*)*rad*' against *CIH* 674.2 'con*nrad*'.
390.4 'Masa' against *CIH* 674.13 'Mas'.
390.4 'tall*ad*' against *CIH* 674.14 'tall*a*'.

Appendix 10

394.8 'dia' against *CIH* 17.25 'da'.
394.8 'no do tia*cht*ain fo coraib' *om. CIH* 17.25.
396.12 'comg*r*ad*h*ab' against *CIH* 1915.27 'comg*r*adhaibh'.
396.17 'indlaeg*h*' against *CIH* 204.4 'indlaeg' (first occurrence in the line).
398.5 'bai' against *CIH* 1556.4 'ba'.
398.12 'do' against *CIH* 1556.8 'don'.
400.4 'forlosc*ud*' against *CIH* 1556.18 'forlosc*ad*'.
400.4 'rucsad' against *CIH* 1556.18 'ruicsad'.
400.5 'crithi' against *CIH* 1556.19 'crichi'.
402.6 'l*eth*cuin*n*' against *CIH* 2308.24 'lethcum̄'.
402.9 'deoraid' against *CIH* 2308.27 'deor*ad*'.

Glossary

Due to the fragmentary nature of the Old Irish texts *Aidbred* and *Muirbretha*, it is not always possible to determine a word's part of speech with certainty. The headwords (and most definitions) are given as they appear in *eDIL*, when present. Otherwise, they are given in the nom. sg. for nouns and 3 sg. pres. act. ind. for verbs. The nom. sg. is not given when it is identical to the headword; the 3 sg. pres. act. ind. is not given for verbs when it is identical to the headword. For each noun, the Old Irish gender is given, when known. The words themselves are listed as found in the text and/or commentary. The numbers refer to the sections of text in *Aidbred*. The glossary contains all of the words found in the canonical Old Irish texts along with words of legal or linguistic interest; the glossary is not comprehensive for the commentaries. When a word is found in the Old Irish tract of *Aidbred*, the section number and subsection letter, where relevant, are given in **bold**; when it is found in the commentary, the section number is followed by the MS *siglum* and printed in roman; the same system also operates for the material from Heptad 64 and *Muirbretha*. Each citation within the glossary is prefixed by an abbreviation for the source text, e.g., *Aid* = *Aidbred*, *Hep* = *Heptad 64*, and *Muir* = *Muirbretha*. Fragments of the tract which are found in the commentary are listed with the section number, MS *siglum* and the designator 'Comm.' in **bold**, e.g., *Aid***3F Comm.** refers to a fragment of the canonical tract of *Aidbred* § 3 found in the commentary from source F.

ɫ *nó* 'or': *passim*

⁊ *ocus* 'and': *passim*

1 a m./n. poss. pron., leniting 'his, its': *Aid***2**, *Aid***3**, *Aid***6**

2 a n. def. art. 'the': nom. sg. *Aid***3**

acht conj. 'but, save, except': *Aid***10**

acraid (simplex from *ad-gair*) 'sues, prosecutes': pret. pass. 3 sg. *doacrad Aid* 4DD; pret. pass. 3 pl. *doacarta Aid*4DD

ad-cí 'sees': pres. ind. fut. 3 sg. *dochifi* A, *doc[h]ifi Hep*J

ad-fíri (simplex *aidbrid*) 'claims, sues, identifies': pres. ind. pass. 3 sg. *-aidbrither Aid***3**, **10**; pres. ind. rel. 3 sg. *aidbres Aid*3A, *abhres Aid*10AA; impv. 3 sg. *aidbriud Aid***1a**; pret. pass. 3 sg. *aidbred Aid*3A; pret. pass. 3 pl. *roaidhbrit Aid*4CC

ad-guid 'invokes a surety': pret. ind. 3 sg. *rauaitghestar Aid*4CC

ad-noí 'entrusts, commends to, deposits': subj. pres. 3 sg. *adrona Aid*1eA, *atrona Aid*1eY

ad-roilli 'deserves, is entitled to' (simplex *áiriltnigid*): pres. ind. 3 pl. *airiltnigit Hep*A

aidbred m. vn. of *ad-fíri* 'claiming, suing; publicizing': nom. sg. *aidbriud Aid***3**, *aidbred Aid***9**, *aidhbridh Aid***10**; gen. sg. *aidbredu Aid*4G, *aidhbriudha Aid*4CC, *aidbreda Aid*4DD, *aidhbreda Aid*6F, *aidbriuda Aid*10A

áine f. 'amusement, sport, play': acc. (or dat.) sg. *aine MuirC*, *MuirD*, *MuirE*

ainteist 'a person who is not capable of being a witness, an untrustworthy witness': nom. sg. *anntest Aid3F*, *Aid10AA*; gen. sg. *andtesta Aid9A*, *aintesta Aid9G*

aire m. 'load, burden': nom. sg. *MuirE*, *airi MuirC*

airíasacht 'leave, permission': nom. sg. *uiriasacht MuirC*, *MuirE*, *airisacht MuirD*, *uiriasachd MuirD*

airitiu f. vn. of *ar-eim* 'receiving': nom. sg. *Aid4A*; gen. sg. *airitin Aid4A*

airlicud m. vn. of *ar-léici* 'lending, commercial loan': acc. sg. *airliugud Aid1f*

airlúaidid 'gives': pret. ind. 3 sg. *erluaidestar Aid1bA*

áitt f. 'place, position, dwelling': *áitt i n-* conj. 'where': *ait a n- Aid10*

aithgein f. vn. of *ad-gainethar* 'restitution, compensation': nom. sg. *aithgin Aid4A*, *Aid5*

1 **aithne** n./f. vn. of *ad-noí* 'depositing, entrusting': *aithne* acc. sg. *Aid1e*

2 **aithne** n./f. 'recognizing, knowing, recognition, characteristic': nom. sg. *aicinta Aid4F*, *aichni Aid4CC*

aititiu f. vn. of *ad-daim* 'acknowledgement, recognition': *aititiu* acc. sg. *Aid1g*

amal conj. 'like, as, how, in what state, manner, why': *amail Aid3*

anurrad 'stranger, non-local': nom. sg. 6F; dat. sg. *anurrad Aid3A*, *Aid7A*, *Aid7G*

ar conj. 'for, because': *Aid1i*, *Aid6*

ardne(i)med m. 'high noble, person possessing high legal status or privileges': nom. sg. *ardnemed Aid1a*

as-indet 'declares, tells, mentions': pres. ind. 3 sg. *-aisneidenn HepA*

as-luí 'departs, absconds, evades': pret. ind. 3 sg. *-arlui Aid1b*; pret. 3 sg. *-arla Aid1aF* **Comm.**

at-tá subst. vb. 'there is': pres. ind. 3 pl. *[a]tait HepA*, *atat HepB*, *atait HepC*, *HepJ*; pres. cons. rel. 3 sg. *bis AidP* **(App. 4)**; fut. 3 sg. *-bia Aid12*; subj. past 3 sg. *beth Aid3F* **Comm.**, *Aid3AA* **Comm.**, *AidP* **(App. 4)**

aurrae, aurrad m. 'surety': acc. sg. *urrad Aid2F*; 'local': dat. sg. *urrad Aid3A*, *Aid7A*

báidid 'drowns, wrecks, sinks, is destroyed': pres. ind. pass. 3 sg. *baiter MuirD*

baránta 'guarantor, surety': acc. sg. *baranta Aid2F*

bárc f. 'ship': nom. sg. *MuirB*

bech m. 'bee': dat. pl. *bechaib HepA*, *bechuibh HepC*, *bechaibh HepJ*

beirid 'carries, passes judgment': pres. subj. pass. 3 sg. *-ruct[h]ar Aid11*

bélingaire 'loan guaranteed by a promise': nom. sg. *HepJ*

bíth vn. of *benaid*: as prep. *fo bith* 'for the purpose of, on account of, because' *Aid7*

breth f. vn. of *beirid* 'judgment, judging': nom. sg. *Aid11*, *Aid11J*

cach pronominal adj. 'each, every': nom. sg. *Aid2*, *Aid3*, *Aid10*

cách pron. 'the one, each, everyone, all': gen. sg. *caich Aid11*

calad m. 'shore, port': nom. pl. *caillte MuirB*

cathair f. 'enclosure, fortress, monastic settlement, city, settlement': gen. sg. *cathrach Hep*A, *ca[th]rach Hep*B, *cathruch Hep*E

cen prep. with acc. 'without, not having': *Aid*6

cenn n./m. 'head': acc. sg. *cenn Aid*5

cert m. 'justice, right, claim, entitlement': nom. sg. *Aid*10, *Aid*11A **Comm.**

certtochus 'exact property': dat. sg. *certtochus Aid*4a, *certtothchus Aid*4F

1 **cía** conj. 'even though, although, as to, as regards, in the case that,': *Aid*3F **Comm.**, *Aid*3AA **Comm.**, *Aid*P **(App. 4)**

2 **cía** interr. and indef. pron. 'why, what is, how': *cia Aid*3, *Aid*11

ciniud m. 'offspring': gen. sg. *cinadha Aid*7

co conj., nasalizing 'so that, until, in order that': *Aid*2, *Aid*3, *Aid*11

cóicthe f. 'period of five days': gen. sg. *cóicthe Aid*2

coimge f. 'protecting, guarding': acc. sg. *coimgi Aid*10

coimtig adj. 'frequented': nom. sg. *coimdig Hep*B, *coimdegh Hep*C, *coimde[g] Hep*J; dat. sg. *coimdi[g] Hep*A

colpthach f. 'two-year-old heifer': dat. pl. *colpthachaib Aid*4A

comdóig adj. 'equally likely': nom. pl. *comhtoich Hep*B

con-icc 'can, is able': pres. ind. 3 sg. *coimgend Hep*A; past. subj. 3 sg. *coimgitis Hep*A

coricci prep. with acc., derived from pres. ind. 2 sg. of *ro-icc* 'until, up to, as far as': *coruice Aid*10

cor m. 'contract': acc. pl. *cura Aid*P **(App. 4)**; gen. pl. *cor Aid*P **(App. 4)**

coscraige f. 'victoriousness': acc. sg. *cascacraige Aid*3BB, *coschairchidh Aid*6F

crannchor 'casting lots': nom. sg. *cranncor Aid*6F; gen. sg. *crandcair Aid*4A, *crandchair Aid*4CC

crenaid 'buys': pres. subj. 3 sg. *rocria Aid*6; past subj. 3 sg. *rocriad Aid*6

crích f. 'territory, district': acc. sg. *crich Aid*11; dat. sg. *crích Aid*10

cron m. 'possession, property, claim': acc. sg. *cron Aid*10

cullach m. 'boar': gen. sg. *cullaig Aid*7EE; nom. pl. *cullaig Aid*7A

cundrad m. 'contract, commerce': acc. sg. *cundrad Aid*1c

daimid 'subjects to a judgment, accepts law': pres. ind. 3 sg. *daim Aid*3F **Comm.**, *damaid Aid*10A, *damaig Aid*10A; pres. ind. rel. 3 sg. *dhaimus Aid*3F **Comm.**, *damas Aid*P **(App. 4)**

dál f. 'delay, respite'; nom. sg. *Aid*2

dechmad f. 'period of ten days': gen. sg. *dechmaidi Aid*2

di prep. with dat., leniting, 'of, from': *Aid*1a, *Aid*P **(App. 4)**; *do Aid*6

día conj. 'if' (with subj.), nasalizing: with cop. pres. subj. 3 sg. *diam Hep*J

dígbál f. vn. of *do-gaib* 'taking away, lessening, diminishing': acc. sg. *digbail Aid*4A

dílaid 'satisfies, pays': pres. ind. 3 sg. *dilann Aid*5G

díles adj. 'possession, property, forfeited to (*do*), forfeited by (*ó*), not subject to claim, immune from legal consequences, appropriate, proper, lawful': nom. sg. *dilis Aid*3, m. nom. sg. *Muir*C, *dilus Muir*E; gen. sg. *disli Aid*3

dírann 'undivided land': acc. sg. *dirrainn Hep*A

dítiu f. vn. of 1 *do-eim* 'sheltering': nom. sg. *Aid*4A; gen. sg. *ditin Aid*4A

dligid 'deserves, merits': in pass. 'is required, is due from': pres. ind. pass. 3 sg. *dleghar Aid*10

do prep. with dat., leniting, 'to, for, by': *Aid*6, *Aid*10, *Muir*C; *d' Aid*11; with 3 sg. m./n. affixed object agreement marker *dó Aid*10

do-airret, do-áirret 'overtakes, seizes, finds, obtains': pres. ind. 3 sg. *tarthend Aid*1aA; pret. ind. 3 sg. *-tarraig Aid*3; pret. pass. 3 sg. *tarrus Aid*4A

do-aisicc 'makes restitution, restores': pres. subj. 3 pl. *doaiscebat Aid*1bA

do-alla 'takes away, steals': pres. ind. 3 sg. *talla Aid*4G; pret. ind. 3 sg. *tall Aid*4A, *Aid*4CC; pret. ind. 3 sg. *tallustar Aid*4F, *tallastar Aid*4G; pret. pass. 3 pl. *tallthа Aid*4F; past subj. 3 sg. *tallad Aid*4A, *talladh Aid*4G

do-beir 'gives, places, brings, gets, takes outs, passes judgment': pres. ind. 3 sg. *dober Aid*1b; pres. ind. pass. sg. *doberar Aid*2, *tabair Aid*P (App. 4), *-tartur Aid*3; pres. subj. 3 sg. *-tuca Aid*2

do-caithi (simplex *tochaithid*) 'spends, consumes': pret. pass. 3 sg. *thochaithe Muir*D

do-coissin 'there is, there are': pres. ind. 3 sg. *docuisin Aid*3, *Aid*4

do-éccai 'sees, beholds, looks at': impv. 2 sg. *decce Aid*11

do-ecmaing 'happens, meets': pres. ind. cond. 3 pl. *tegemdais Hep*A

do-fairget 'offers, attempts': pres. ind. 3 sg. *tairge Aid*3F; pres. ind. rel. 3 sg. *tairges Aid*2AA, *Aid*10AA, *Aid*Q (App. 2), *Aid*JJ (App. 3), *thairgus Aid*3F, *tairgus Aid*Q (App. 2)

do-gaib 'takes away, lessens, diminishes': pret. pass. 3 sg. *digbad Aid*4A

do-gní 'makes, does': pres. subj. 3 sg. *dana Hep*A; perf. ind. 3 sg. *dorighne Hep*J

do-greinn 'overtakes, levies, makes a claim against': pres. ind. 3 sg. with a class C m. object agreement marker *dotngre Aid*5; (?) pres. ind. rel. 3 sg. *toghranas Aid*5G

do-icc 'comes, approaches': past subj. pass. 3 3g. *rotista Aid*1eA

do-indnaig (simplex *tidnaicid*) 'gives, brings, conducts': pres. ind. rel. 3 sg. *tidnaices Aid*5G

do-lá 'prevails over, rejects, expels': pres. ind. 3 pl. *dilaat Aid*1i

do-ren 'pays': pres. ind. pass. 3 sg. *diren[ar] Aid*P (App. 4)

do-roich 'reaches, arrives, happens': pres. ind. 3 sg. *dorig Hep*A, *doric Hep*A

duine m. 'person, man': nom. sg. *Aid*12

é pron. 3 sg. m. 'he, it': *Aid*1b, *Aid*5, *e Aid*11

éccoimtig adj. 'unfrequented': nom. sg. *écoimdig Hep*B, *ecoimdigh Hep*C, *ecoimde[g] Hep*J; dat. sg. *eccoimde[g] Hep*A

eclais f. 'church': gen. sg. *ecalsa Aid*1h, *Aid*1i

eclastacda adj. 'ecclesiastic': nom. sg. *eclasdacda Aid*3A

eisinnraic adj. 'not in good legal standing, unworthy, untrustworthy': nom. sg. m. *Aid*9G, *esinraic Aid*3A, *eisindraic Aid*12A; acc. sg. *esindraic Aid*4A; dat. sg. m. *esindraic*

*Aid*3A; nom. du. m. *eisinraic Aid*10P, *Aideisindraic* 12A

escaire, esngaire n. later f. (?) vn. of *as-congair* 'public notice, proclamation, proclaiming': nom. sg. *Aid*8A, *Hep*A, *Hep*B, *Hep*J, *escairi Aid*8A

eter, etir prep. with acc. (sometimes with dat.) 'between, amongst': *iter Aid*3F **Comm.**, *Aid*3AA **Comm.**, *itir Aid*P **(App. 4)**; with 3 pl. affixed object agreement marker *eturru Aid*P **(App. 4)**

faill f. 'neglect, negligence': nom. sg. *Aid*6

fairrge, fairge f. 'the open sea, the ocean': gen. sg. *fairge Hep*A, *Hep*B, *Hep*E

faithche, faidche f. 'green, lawn, open space in front of a residence or church, green meadow': nom. sg. *Hep*B; acc. sg. *faithce Hep*A; gen. sg. *faithche Aid*4F, *faiche Hep*A, *Hep*B, *Hep*E; dat. sg. *faithce Hep*A

feis f. 'cattle-trespass,': nom. sg. *Aid*7

féith f. 'twining plant, woodbine': gen. sg. *feithe Hep*C

fém(m)ed m. vn. of *fo-émid* 'refusing, refusal': nom. sg. *Muir*E, *femed Muir*C, *feimid Muir*D, acc. sg. *feimed Muir*D

Féni nom. pl. 'freemen of full legal capacity, the Irish':[1] acc. pl. *Féniu Hep*A, *Hep*B, *Hep*J

fer m. 'man, person': nom. sg. *Aid*4; dat. sg. *fir Muir*C

fíada m. 'witness, one who gives testimony': nom. sg. *fiadhu Aid*4G

fír n./m. 'truth, proof': *fír Dé* lit. 'proof of God', 'ordeal' acc. sg. *fior Dé Aid*3F

fo prep. with acc. or dat., leniting, 'under, beneath, subject to': *Aid*3, *Aid*7

fo-ceird 'puts, places': pres. ind. 3 pl. *focertat Aid*P **(App. 4)**

fo-fich 'commits an offense, does injury': *Aid*11; *-fuich Aid*11

fo-gaib 'finds': pres. ind. 3 sg. with 3 sg. m. class C object agreement marker *fodngaib Hep*A, *fotngaib Hep*C, *Hep*B; pres. ind. pass. 3 sg. *dogabar Hep*A; pres. subj. 2 sg. *foghba Hep*J

folud n./m. 'substance, wealth, property; reason, consideration, cause': nom. sg. *Aid*3; acc. sg. *fola[d] Aid*1a

for prep. with acc. or dat., 'on, over, in regard to': *Aid*1h, *Aid*1i; with 3 sg. m./n. affixed object agreement marker *fair Aid*11, *Aid*P **(App. 4)**

forbart f. vn. of *for-beir* 'growth, increase, maturity': acc. sg. *[ḟ]orbairt Aid*4A; dat. sg. *forbairt Aid*4G

forus n. 'law': gen. sg. *foris Aid*3F **Comm.**, *forais Aid*P **(App. 4)**

fo-reith 'is equivalent to, takes the place of': pres. ind. 3 sg. *Aid*3

fo-ricc 'comes across, finds': pres. ind. pass. 3 sg. *fuiricar Aid*10P

foth m./n. 'claim, title, right': nom. sg. *Aid*12A, *fod Aid*12

fotha m. 'cause, reason, basis': nom. sg. *fothu Aid*3

fri prep. with acc. 'against, to, towards, on account of': *Aid*10, *Aid*3F **Comm.**, *Aid*3AA **Comm.**, *Aid*P **(App. 4)**; with

---

1 For this definition, see *GEIL* Index of Irish Terms, s.v. *Féni*.

3 sg. m./n. affixed object agreement marker *fris Aid*3; with rel. pron. *frisa Aid*11

fríth, fríthe m. 'something found, a find': nom. sg. *frithe Hep*A, *Hep*B, *Hep*J, *Hep*E; gen. sg. *frithi Aid*8A; nom. pl. *frithe Hep*A, *Hep*B, *Hep*C, *Hep*J; dat. pl. *frithaib Hep*B, *frithibh Hep*C

frithchrec f. 'counter-purchase, goods acquired in exchange': nom. sg. *[ḟ]rithcreic Aid*4A; acc. sg. *frithcrec Aid*4A

fúataigid 'takes away illegally, carries off forcibly': pres. ind. pass. 3 sg. *-fuatagar Aid*10; pret. ind. 3 sg. *rofuaitgester Aid*10A

fuba(e) n./m. vn. of *fo-ben* 'attacking, attack': acc. sg. *fubha Muir*B

fuillem m. vn. of *fo-slí* 'addition, increase, interest, earnings': nom. sg. *fuilleam Aid*4A

gaibid 'takes, derives, declares': pret. 3 sg. *rogab Aid*3

gait f. 'theft, stolen property': nom. sg. *gad Aid*6; gen. sg. *gaite Aid*4A

gataige m. 'thief': nom. sg. *Aid*4A, *Aid*4G, *Aid*10J, *Aid*11J, *gataigi Aid*4A; gen. sg. *gataigi Aid*4A, *gataige Aid*5; dat. sg. *gataige Aid*5G, *gataid[e] Aid*6, *gataigi Aid*11A

gléid 'decides, concludes, makes clear': pres. ind. pass. 3 sg. *glether Aid*11A **Comm.**

grád n. 'grade, rank, order': nom. pl. *graid Aid*1i; dat. pl. *gradaib Aid*1h, *Aid*1i

i prep. with acc. or dat., nasalizing, 'into, in, for, regarding, as, by': *Muir*C, *a Muir*D, *Muir*E; with dat. i *Aid*1b, *a n- Aid*3, *Aid*3F **Comm.**, *Aid*11, *Aid*P **(App. 4)**; with 3 sg. m./n. affixed object agreement marker *and Aid*1h; *and* 'then, there' *Aid*10; rel. *i n- Aid*10

í indecl. pronom. demon. particle: with def. art. nom. sg. m. *intí Aid*11, *Aid*3F **Comm.**; *inti Aid*3F **Comm.**, *Aid*P **(App. 4)**

íarraid f. vn. of *íarraid* 'seeking, searching': acc. sg. *iarraid Aid*6

íarmi-foich (simplex *fíafraigid*) 'seeks, inquires, makes an inquiry': pres. ind. 2 sg. *fiaghfraighi Hep*J (O'Dav no. 488)

ilar n./m. 'abundance, multitude': acc. sg. *ilar Aid*P **(App. 4)**

imchomét m. 'guarding, nurturing': gen. sg. *imcoimeta Aid*7

imdénam m. vn. of *imm-déni* 'proving, proof': dat. sg. *ingenum* (read *imdénam*) *Aid*11

imm prep. with acc. 'about, around, regarding, concerning': with 3 sg. m./n. affixed object agreement marker *ime Aid*10, *Aid*11A **Comm.**

immaig adv. 'outside, away, afar': *amuig Aid*4A

immanetar, immenetar adv. 'mutually, in turn': *imanetar Aid*P **(App. 4)**

imm-beir 'puts, places': pres. ind. rel. 3 sg. *imres Aid*3A, *imris Aid*3F; pres. ind. 3 pl. *imrit Aid*3F; pret. 3 sg. *roimir Aid*2AFG

impide f. 'intercession, intervention, entreaty': gen. sg. *impi[de] Hep*A

imm-toing 'swears': pres. ind. pass. sg. *imtongar Aid*1h

in def. art. 'the': nom. sg. n. *a Aid*3

indad, indoth m. 'young animals, calves, increase, produce': acc. sg. *indud Aid*4A; dat. sg. *innud Aid*6F

indisid 'says, tells, names, recounts, mentions': pres. ind. 3 sg. *indisi Aid*4A; pres. ind. rel. 3 sg. *indisas Hep*A, *innesas Hep*C, in*n*ises *Hep*J

indles adj. 'not forfeit, not due, not one's absolute property': acc. sg. *indlis Aid*3

indraic adj. 'in good legal standing, worthy, trustworthy': nom. sg. m. *Aid*3A, *Aid*4A, *Aid*10A, *Aid*12A; dat. sg. m. *indraic Aid*3A; nom. du. m. *indraic Aid*10P, *Aid*12A

-indsoirg 'drives out, sets in motion, moves': pres. ind. pass. 3 sg. *-indsorgar Aid*10

is copula 'is': pres. ind. 3 sg. *Aid*3, *Aid*6, *Aid*10, *Aid*11, *Aid*P **(App. 4)**, *iss Aid*1b, *is, as Aid*P **(App. 4)**; neg. *ni Aid*8; pres. subj. rel. 3 sg. *bes Aid*6, *Aid*10

la prep. with acc. 'with, at, by, belongs to, according to': *Hep*A, *Hep*B, *Hep* J; with 3 sg. m. affixed object agreement marker *lais Aid*3; with rel. *laisi* (*n*-) *Aid*3, *lasi* (*n*-) *Aid*12

lápán adj. 'dirty, filthy': nom. sg. *labhán Aid*6F; gen. pl. *laban Aid*8

lethfrithgnam m. 'half labor, half service': gen. sg. *lethfrithgnuma Aid*7

lías m. 'pen, fold, enclosure': acc. sg. *lias Aid*10

lóg n. 'value, equivalent, reward, payment, price': nom. sg. *log Muir*C

loingsech 'exile, wanderer, pirate, sailor': dat. pl. *loingsechaib Hep*A

los m. 'young of cattle': gen. pl. *los Aid*8

lott m. vn. of *loittid* 'injury, damage, wound': nom. or acc. sg. *lot Aid*8

lucht m. 'cargo, people': gen. sg. *lochta Muir*C

luige n. vn of *tongaid* 'oath, swearing': acc. sg. *luighi Aid*1b

má, ma conj. 'if': with neg. *muna Aid*6; with cop. pres. subj. 3 sg. *mad Muir*C; with neg and pres. subj. 3 sg. cop. *maineb Aid*5, *munub Aid*6

macha 'cattle-enclosure': dat. sg. *macha Aid*10, *machad Aid*10A **Comm.**

maigen f. 'place, precinct': dat. sg. *maigin Aid*1a, *Aid*4A

medóngait 'middle theft, receiving stolen goods': gen. sg. *medongaite Aid*4; in phrase *fer medóngaite* 'receiver of stolen goods', literally 'man of middle theft' *Aid*4

mes(s) m. 'valuation, judgment': nom. sg. *Aid*10A

mí m. 'month': gen. sg. *mis Aid*2

muirbreth f. 'sea-judgment' in pl. 'sea-judgments, maritime law': dat. pl. *muirbrethaib Muir*C, *muirbreathaib Muir*E

1 ná conj. 'nor': *na Aid*1c, *Aid*1d, *Aid*1e, *Aid*1f, *Aid*1g, *Aid*P **(App. 4)**

2 ná rel. neg. 'who/which not': *na Aid*3F **Comm.**

nach indef. pron. adj. 'any, whatever': m. nom. sg. *Aid*4

nád conj. neg. in subordinate clauses 'that … not': *nad Aid*1b

ne(i)med m. 'person possessing legal status or privileges': nom. sg. *Aid*6F; gen. sg. *neimid Aid*10; dat. sg. *neimed Aid*6

ne(i)medcrích '*nemed* territory': dat. sg. *neimedcrích Aid*11

ní neg. 'not': *Aid*5, *Aid*10, *Aid*3F **Comm.**, *Aid*3AA **Comm.**, *Aid*P **(App. 4)**, *Aid*10A **Comm.**, *Muir*D

nó conj. 'or': *Hep*A, *Hep*B

noí num. 'nine': *nae Muir*C, *Muir*E

ó prep. with dat., leniting, 'of, from, by': *Aid*1**h**, *Aid*10; *o Aid* 10, *Muir*C; with 3 sg. m. affixed object agreement marker *uaghaAid* **1a F Comm.**, *uad Aid*1**b**

oc prep. with dat. 'at, by, with': with 3 sg. m. affixed object agreement marker *oca Aid*P **(App. 4)**

ocus adj. 'near': superl. *nesam Aid*10

ón, óin f. vn of *oidid* 'private loan, lending': acc. sg. *oin Aid*1**d**, acc. (or dat.) sg. *oin Hep*A

port m. 'place, spot, bank, shore, landing-place': gen. sg. *puirt Muir*C

raite f. and m. 'rough land, uncultivated land, rough grazing': gen. sg. *raiti Hep***A**, *Hep***B**, *Hep*E

rath m. 'fief of stock': dat. sg. *rath Aid*1**b**, *Aid*1**F Comm.**

ré n./f. 'time, period of time': nom. sg. *re Aid*P **(App. 4)**

reithe m. 'ram': gen. sg. *reithe Aid*7EE; nom. pl. *retheda Aid*7A, *reedha Aid*7G

remdílse f. 'pre-ownership, prior right': acc. sg. *reimdhilsi Aid*P **(App. 4)**, *remdilsi Aid*3**F Comm.**, *reimdilsi Aid*P **(App. 4)**, *Aid*3**AA Comm.**

remi-tét 'goes before, precedes': pres. ind. 3 sg. *remuteit Aid*1aA

ríar f. 'will, decision': dat. sg. *rer Aid*3F **Comm.**, *reir Aid*P **(App. 4)**

rodercaidh m. 'watchman': nom. sg. *Muir*A

ro-finnadar 'finds out, discovers': pres. subj. 3 sg. *-feastar Aid*6

rúanaid m. 'a strong man, champion': gen. sg. *ruanada Muir*C, *ruanadh Muir*E

ruba(e) n./m. vn. formation from *ro-ben-* 'wounding, defense': acc. sg. *rubha Muir*B

ruud m. 'a wood or forest': gen. sg. *rofida Hep***A**, *rofedha Hep***B**; dat. sg. *rofidh Hep*A

saethar n. 'work, labor, reward': gen. sg. *saethair Muir*C

saidbre f. 'property, possession, wealth': acc. sg. *saidbre Aid*2

samaisc f. 'three-year-old heifer': dat. pl. *samascaib Aid*4A

scor m. vn. of *sciurid* 'unyoking, pasture, paddock, enclosure': nom. sg. *Hep*B, *Hep*C gen. sg. *sguir Aid*7

secht num. 'seven': *Aid*1**i**, *Hep***A**, *Hep***B**, *Hep*C, *Hep*J

sechtarmaigen 'outside a precinct': dat. sg. *sechtarmaigin Aid*4A

sellach m. 'culpable onlooker': gen. sg. *seallaig Aid*3F, *sellaig Aid*4G

sénaid 'denies': pres. ind. 3 sg. *sena Aid*4F; pret. ind. 3 sg. *rosena Aid*4F

sét m. 'item of value, property': gen. sg. *séoit Aid*6

sin demon. pron. 'that': *Aid*1**h**

slíab n./m. 'mountain, moorland': gen. sg. *sleibe Hep***A**, *Hep*B

sruth m. 'stream, river, current': nom. sg. *Hep*A, *Hep*J; gen. sg. *srotha Muir*C; dat. pl. *srothaib Muir*C, *Muir*E

suide anaphoric pron.: dat. sg. *fo suidi* 'according to, under which' *Aid*3

suidid 'establishes': pres. ind. pass. 3 sg. *suitir Aid*3**F Comm.**, *suiter Aid*3**F Comm.**, *Aid*3**AA comm.**, *Aid*P **(App. 4)**

táid m. 'thief': nom. pl. *tat(a)ha[i]t Aid*P **(App. 4)**; dat. pl. *taitib Aid*3F

Comm., *Aid*3AA **comm.**, *thaitib Aid*P **(App. 4)**

táir adj. 'mean, base, valueless': superl. *taire Aid*2AA, *Aid*3F, *Aid*10AA, *Aid*Q (App. 2), *Aid*JJ (App. 3)

taiselbad m. vn. of *do-aissilbi* 'assigning, ascribing, showing, exhibiting': nom. sg. *Hep*A, *Hep*C; acc. sg. *taiselbad Hep*B

tar, dar prep. with acc. 'across, over, beyond': *Aid*11, *Muir*E *dar Muir*C; *tar cenn* 'on behalf of' *Aid*5

tarb m. 'bull': nom. sg. *Aid*4A, *tharbh Aid*4CC; gen. sg. *tairb Aid*7EE; nom. pl. *tairb Aid*7A

tarraing, tairring f. vn. of *do-srenga* 'pulling, dragging, pulling out, tearing away': acc. sg. tarrai[n]g *Aid*3

teist f. 'witness, legally capable witness, trustworthy witness': gen. sg. *testa Aid*3F, *Aid*9; dat. sg. *test Aid*9A, *Aid*9G

téit 'goes': *teit Aid*11, *teit tar cenn* 'gives' *Aid*5

tochor m. vn. of *do-cuirethar* 'putting, sending, what is thrown on shore': nom. sg. *tochur Muir*C

toísech adj. 'first, prior': comp. *taisce Aid*1aA

tongaid 'swears': pres. ind. rel. 3 sg. *tangas Aid*1eA

tonn f. 'wave': acc. pl. *tonna Muir*E; dat. pl. *tondaib Muir*C

torannchless 'loud noise, explosion': acc. sg. *torand*[*ch*]*lesaige Aid*3BB

trácht n./m. 'shore': gen. sg. *trachta Hep*A, *Hep*B, *Hep*E

treb f. 'dwelling, farm, holding': gen. sg. *treibe Hep*A, *Hep*B, *treibhe Hep*J

trebaire f. 'surety, security, guarantee': nom. sg. *Aid*4G; acc. sg. *trebaire Aid*6EE

treise f. 'period of three days': gen. sg. *treisi Aid*2

túath f. 'territory, community, people, lay people': gen. sg. *tuaithe Aid*1h, *túaithe Aid*1i; acc. pl. *tuata Aid*3A

tuicse f. MI vn. of *do-ucci* 'understanding, supposing, believing': nom. sg. *tuicsi Aid*4CC

tuinide f. 'possession, ownership': nom. sg. *Aid*P **(App. 4)**, *tuinighe Aid*P **(App. 4)**; dat. sg. *tuinide Aid*3

turracht 'support': *turracht* acc. sg. *Aid*2F

turtacht (?) 'description': nom. sg. *Aid*3F

úadadbar 'material': gen. sg. *uadabhar cinadha* 'heredity, breeding' *Aid*7

Bibliography

Manuscripts

Copenhagen, Det Kongelige Bibliotek, NKS 261b
Digital Bodleian https://digital.bodleian.ox.ac.uk/
Dublin, Royal Irish Academy MS 23 Q 6 [1243]
Dublin, Trinity College MS 1316 [H.2.15B]
Dublin, Trinity College MS 1336 [H.3.17]
Dublin, Trinity College MS 1337 [H.3.18]
Dublin, Trinity College MS 1363 [H.4.22]
Dublin, Trinity College MS 1387 [H.5.15]
Dublin, Trinity College MS 1433 [E.3.5]
London, British Library MS Cotton Nero A7
London, British Library MS Egerton 88
O'Donovan, John. Brehon law transcripts O'D 1630–1653 and translation 1917–1955, Royal Irish Academy, Dublin
Oxford, Bodleian Library MS Rawl. B. 506
Oxford, Bodleian Library MS Rawl. B. 487

Printed and Digital Sources

Aided Echach maic Maireda, ed. and trans. Ranke de Vries. In *Two Texts on Loch nEchach*, 142–256. Irish Texts Society 65. Dublin: The Irish Texts Society, 2012.

"The Alphabet of Cuigne Mac Emoin," ed. and trans. Roland M. Smith. *Zeitschrift für celtische Philologie* 17 (1928): 45–72.

Ancient Laws and Institutes of Ireland, eds. and trans. W.N. Hancock et al., 6 vols. Dublin: His Majesty's Stationery Office, 1865–1901.

Anfuigell, ed. and trans. Charlene M. Eska. In *A Raven's Battle-Cry: The Limits of Judgment in the Medieval Irish Legal Tract Anfuigell*. Medieval Law and Its Practice 27. Leiden: Brill, 2019.

Bechbretha, eds. and trans. Thomas Charles-Edwards and Fergus Kelly. Early Irish Law Series 1. Dublin: Dublin Institute for Advanced Studies, 1983.

The Black Book of St. David's, ed. and trans. J.W. Willis-Bund. London: The Honourable Society of Cymmrodorion, 1902.

"*Bretha Crólige*," ed. and trans. D.A. Binchy. *Ériu* 12 (1938): 1–77.

"*Bretha Déin Chécht*," ed. and trans. D.A. Binchy. *Ériu* 20 (1966): 1–66.

"*Bretha im Gatta*," ed. and trans. Vernam Hull. *Zeitschrift für celtische Philologie* 25 (1956): 211–225.

Cáin Aicillne, ed. and trans. [into German] Rudolf Thurneysen, "Aus dem irischen Recht I [1. Das Unfrei-Lehen]." *Zeitschrift für celtische Philologie* 14 (1923): 335–394.

Cáin Fhuithirbe, ed. and trans. Liam Breatnach. In "The Ecclesiastical Element in the Old-Irish Legal Tract *Cáin Fhuithirbe*." *Peritia* 5 (1986): 36–52.

Cáin Lánamna: An Old Irish Tract on Marriage and Divorce Law, ed. and trans. Charlene M. Eska. Medieval Law and Its Practice 5. Leiden: Brill, 2010.

"*Cáin Ónae*: An Old Irish Law Text on Lending," ed. and trans. Liam Breatnach. In *Mír Cúrad: Studies in Honor of Calvert Watkins*, edited by Jay Jasanoff, H. Craig Melchert, and Lisi Oliver, 29–46. Innsbruck: Institut für Sprachwissenschaft der Universität, 1998.

Cáin Ṡóerraith, ed. and trans. [into German] Rudolf Thurneysen, "Aus dem irischen Recht II [2. Das Frei-Lehen]." *Zeitschrift für celtische Philologie* 15 (1925): 238–260.

Calendar of the State Papers, Relating to Ireland, of the Reign of James I, 1615–1625, Preserved in Her Majesty's Public Record Office, and Elsewhere, ed. Charles W. Russell and John P. Prendergast. London: Longman & Co., 1880.

"*Coibnes Uisci Thairidne*," ed. and trans. D.A. Binchy. *Ériu* 17 (1955): 52–85.

Cóic Conara Fugill: Die fünf Wege zum Urteil, ed. and trans. [into German] Rudolf Thurneysen. Abhandlungen der preussischen Akademie der Wissenschaften. Phil.-hist. Klasse; Nr. 7. Berlin: Verlag der Akademie der Wissenschaften, 1925.

Corpus Iuris Hibernici, ed. D.A. Binchy. 6 vols. paginated consecutively. Baile Átha Cliath: Institiúid Árd-Léinn Bhaile Átha Cliath, 1978.

Córus Bésgnai: An Old Irish Tract on the Church and Society, ed. and trans. Liam Breatnach. Early Irish Law Series 7. Dublin: Dublin Institute for Advanced Studies, 2017.

Damweiniau Colan, ed. Dafydd Jenkins. In *Damweiniau Colan: Llyfr y Damweiniau yn ôl Llawysgrif Peniarth 30*. Aberystwyth: Cymdeithas Lyfrau Ceredigion, 1973.

de Bracton, Henry. *De Legibus et Consuetudinibus Angliæ*, 4 vols., ed. George Woodbine, trans. Samuel E. Thorne. London: Publications of the Selden Society, 1968–1977. http://amesfoundation.law.harvard.edu/Bracton/Common/index.htm

De causis torchi Corc' Óche, ed. and trans. Ranke de Vries. In *Two Texts on Loch nEchach*, 53–141. Irish Texts Society 65. London: The Irish Texts Society, 2012.

Di Astud Chor, ed. and trans. Neil McLeod. In *Early Irish Contract Law*. Sydney Series in Celtic Studies 1. Sydney: University of Sydney, 1992.

"*Di Ércib Fola*," ed. and trans. Neil McLeod. *Ériu* 52 (2002): 123–216.

Early Irish Glossaries Database, eds. Paul Russell, Sharon Arbuthnot, and Pádraic Moran. 2nd ed. Cambridge: Department of Anglo-Saxon, Norse and Celtic, 2009. http://www.asnc.cam.ac.uk/irishglossaries.

eDIL 2019: An Electronic Dictionary of the Irish Language, based on the Contributions to a Dictionary of the Irish Language. Dublin: Royal Irish Academy, 1913–1976. https://dil.ie

"A Fragmentary Old Irish Text on Oaths," ed. and trans. Liam Breatnach. In *Fír Fesso*:

A Festschrift for Neil McLeod, edited by Anders Ahlqvist and Pamela O'Neill, 53–64. Sydney Series in Celtic Studies 17. Sydney: The University of Sydney, 2018.

Frithfolaid Ríg Caisil fri Túatha Muman, ed. J.G. O'Keeffe, in "*Dál Caladbuig* and Reciprical Services between the Kings of Cashel and Various Munster States." In *Irish Texts* i, edited by J. Fraser, P. Grosjean, S.J., and J.G. O'Keeffe, 19–21. London: Sheed and Ward, 1931.

Gerald of Wales. *Topographia Hibernica*, ed. James F. Dimok. In *Giraldi Cambrensis Opera*, vol. 5. London: Longman, Green, Reader, and Dyer, 1867.

Gerald of Wales. *Instruction for a Ruler* (*De Principis Instructione*), ed. and trans. Robert Bartlett. Oxford: Clarendon Press, 2018.

Die Gesetze der Angelsachsen, ed. and trans. [into German] Felix Liebermann. 3 vols. Halle: M. Niemeyer, 1903–1916.

Giolla na Naomh Mac Aodhagáin. *The MacEgan Legal Treatise*, ed. and trans. Fergus Kelly. In *The MacEgan Legal Treatise: An Early Modern Irish Law-Text by Giolla na Naomh Mac Aodhagáin (†1309)*. Early Irish Law Series 8. Dublin: Dublin Institute for Advanced Studies, 2020.

Immathchor nAilella 7 Airt, ed. and trans. Johan Corthals, in "Affiliation of Children: *Immathchor nAilella 7 Airt*." *Peritia* 9 (1995): 92–124.

"The Irish Ordeals, Cormac's Adventure in the Land of Promise, and the Decision as to Cormac's Sword," ed. and trans. Whitley Stokes. In *Irische Texte mit Wörterbuch*, edited by Ernst Windisch and Whitley Stokes, 4 vols., vol. 3:1, 183–229, and 283. Leipzig: S. Hirzel, 1891.

Irish Script on Screen https://www.isos.dias.ie/

Latin A, ed. Hywel D. Emanuel. In *The Latin Texts of the Welsh Laws*, 97–171. Cardiff: University of Wales Press, 1967.

Latin B, ed. Hywel D. Emanuel. In *The Latin Texts of the Welsh Laws*, 172–268. Cardiff: University of Wales Press, 1967.

Latin D, ed. Hywel D. Emanuel. In *The Latin Texts of the Welsh Laws*, 294–407. Cardiff: University of Wales Press, 1967.

Laxdœla Saga, trans. Magnus Magnusson and Hermann Pálsson. New York: Penguin Classics, 1969.

Laxdœla Saga: Halldórs Þættir Snorrasonar Stúfs Þáttr, ed. Einar Ól. Sveinsson. Íslenzk Fornrit 5. Reykjavík: Hið Íslenzka Fornritafélag, 1934.

Lebor na Cert: The Book of Rights, ed. and trans. Myles Dillon. Irish Texts Society 46. Dublin: Irish Texts Society, 1962.

"The Lecan Glossary," ed. Whitley Stokes. In *Archiv für celtische Lexikographie*, eds. Whitley Stokes and Kuno Meyer, 1, 50–100. Halle: Niemeyer, 1898.

The Legal Triads of Medieval Wales, ed. and trans. Sara Elin Roberts. Cardiff: University of Wales Press, 2007.

Llyfr Blegywryd, ed. Melville Richards. In *Cyfreithiau Hywel Dda yn ôl Llawysgrif Coleg yr Iesu LVII Rhydychen*. 2nd ed. Caerdydd: Gwasg Prifysgol Cymru, 1990; and eds. Stephen J. Williams & J. Enoch Powell. In *Llyfr Blegywryd*, 2nd ed. Caerdydd: Gwasg Prifysgol Cymru, 1961.

Llyfr Colan, ed. Dafydd Jenkins. In *Llyfr Colan: Y Gyfraith Gymreig yn ôl Hanner Cyntaf Llawysgrif Peniarth 30*. Caerdydd: Gwasg Prifysgol Cymru, 1963.

Llyfr Cyfnerth, ed. and trans, Arthur W. Wade-Evans. In *Welsh Medieval Law Being a Text of the Laws of Howel the Good, Namely the British Museum Harleian MS. 4353 of the 13th Century, with Translation, Introduction, Appendix, Glossary, Index, and Map*. Oxford: Clarendon Press, 1909.

Llyfr Iorwerth, ed. Aled Rhys Wiliam. Cardiff: University of Wales Press, 1960.

Marriage Disputes: A Fragmentary Old Irish Law-Text, ed. and trans. Fergus Kelly. Early Irish Law Series 6. Dublin: Dublin Institute for Advanced Studies, 2014.

Nomos Rhodon Nautikos: The Rhodian Sea-Law, ed. and trans. Walter Ashburner. Oxford: The Clarendon Press, 1909.

"O'Davoren's Glossary," ed. and trans. Whitley Stokes. In *Archiv für celtische Lexikographie*, eds. Whitley Stokes and Kuno Meyer, 2, 197–504. Halle: Niemeyer, 1904.

"An Old-Irish Text on Court Procedure," ed. and trans. Fergus Kelly. *Peritia* 5 (1986): 74–106.

Ó Maolmhuaidh, Froinsias. *Lucerna fidelium: seu Fasciculus decerptus ab authoribus magis versatis, qui tractarunt de doctrina christiana*, ed. Pádraig Ó Súilleabháin. Baile Átha Cliath: Institiúid Árd-Léinn Bhaile Átha Cliath, 1962.

O'Mulconry's Glossary, ed. and trans. Pádraic Moran. In *De Origine Scoticae Linguae* (*O' Mulconry's Glossary*). Corpus Christianorum 7. Turnhout: Brepols Publishers, 2019.

Róda, cis lir-side?, ed. and trans. Fergus Kelly. In *Early Irish Farming*, Early Irish Law Series 4, 537–544. Dublin: Dublin Institute for Advanced Studies, 1997.

"*Sanas Cormaic: An Old Irish Glossary*," ed. Kuno Meyer. In *Anecdota from Irish Manuscripts*, eds. O.J. Bergin, R.I. Best, K. Meyer, and J.G. O'Keefe, 4, 1–128. Halle: M. Niemeyer, 1912.

Tecosca Cormaic, ed. and trans. Kuno Meyer. In *The Instructions of King Cormac Mac Airt*. Todd Lecture Series 15. Dublin: Hodges, Figgis, & Co., 1909.

"*Tír Cumaile*," ed. and trans. Gearóid Mac Niocaill. *Ériu* 22 (1971): 81–86.

Vita Griffini filii Conani: The Medieval Latin Life of Gruffudd ap Cynan, ed. and trans. Paul Russell. Cardiff: University of Wales Press, 2005.

Welsh Medieval Law Being a Text of the Laws of Howel the Good, Namely the British Museum Harleian MS. 4353 of the 13th Century, with Translation, Introduction, Appendix, Glossary, Index, and Map, ed. and trans. Arthur W. Wade-Evans. Oxford: Clarendon Press, 1909.

Secondary Sources

Abbott, T.K., and E.J. Gwynn. *Catalogue of the Irish Manuscripts in the Library of Trinity College, Dublin*. Dublin: Hodges, Figgis, & Co., 1921.

Archan, Christophe. "Ordeal by Fire in Medieval Ireland." *Peritia* 24–25 (2013–2014): 197–212.

Baker, John. *An Introduction to English Legal History*. 5th ed. Oxford: Oxford University Press, 2019.

Bartlett, Robert. *Trial by Fire and Water: The Medieval Judicial Ordeal*. Oxford: Oxford University Press, 1986.

Bemmer, Jacqueline. "The Early Irish Hostage Surety and Inter-Territorial Alliances." *Historical Review* 89 (May 2016): 191–207.

Bergin, Osborn. "On the Syntax of the Verb in Old Irish." *Ériu* 12 (1938): 197–214.

Binchy, D.A. "Sick-maintenance in Irish Law." *Ériu* 12 (1938): 78–134.

Binchy, D.A. "The Linguistic and Historical Value of the Irish Law Tracts." *Proceedings of the British Academy* 29 (1943): 195–227, also separately paginated 3–35.

Breatnach, Liam. "Addenda and Corrigenda to 'The Cauldron of Poesy' (*Ériu* 32, 45–93)." *Ériu* 35 (1984): 189–191.

Breatnach, Liam. "An Mheán-Ghaeilge." In *Stair na Gaeilge*, edited by Kim McCone et al., 221–333. Maigh Nuad: Roinn na Sean-Ghaeilge, 1994.

Breatnach, Liam. "On the Original Extent of the *Senchas Már*." *Ériu*, 47 (1996): 1–43.

Breatnach, Liam. *A Companion to the Corpus Iuris Hibernici*. Early Irish Law Series 5. Dublin: Dublin Institute for Advanced Studies, 2005.

Breatnach, Liam. *The Early Irish Law Text Senchas Már and the Question of its Date*. E.C. Quiggin Memorial Lecture 13. Cambridge: Department of Anglo-Saxon, Norse and Celtic, 2011.

Breatnach, Liam. "Forms of Payment in the Early Irish Law Tracts." *Cambrian Medieval Celtic Studies* 68 (2014): 1–20.

Byrne, Mary E. "On the Punishment of Sending Adrift." *Ériu* 11 (1932): 97–102.

Charles-Edwards, T.M. "The Social Background of Irish *Peregrinatio*." *Celtica* 11 (1976): 43–59.

Charles-Edwards, T.M. "Review Article: The *Corpus Iuris Hibernici*." *Studia Hibernica* 20 (1980): 141–162.

Charles-Edwards, T.M. *Early Irish and Welsh Kinship*. Oxford: Clarendon Press, 1993.

Charles-Edwards, T.M. "The Three Columns: A Comparative Perspective." In *Tair Colofn Cyfraith: The Three Columns of Law in Medieval Wales: Homicide, Theft and Fire*, edited by T.M. Charles-Edwards and Paul Russell, 26–59. The Welsh Legal History Society v. Bangor: The Welsh Legal History Society, 2007.

Charles-Edwards, T.M. "The Welsh Laws of Theft: Iorwerth *v* the Rest." In *Tair Colofn Cyraith. The Three Columns of Law in Medieval Wales: Homicide, Theft and Fire*, edited by T.M. Charles-Edwards and Paul Russell, 108–130. The Welsh Legal History Society v. Bangor: The Welsh Legal History Society, 2007.

Charles-Edwards, T.M. "Whitley Stokes and Early Irish Law." In *The Tripartite Life of Whitley Stokes (1830–1909)*, edited by Elizabeth Boyle and Paul Russell, 161–174. Dublin: Four Courts Press, 2011.

Charles-Edwards, T.M. "The Manuscript Transmission of *Bretha Comaithchesa*." In *Authorities and Adaptations: The Reworking and Transmission of Textual Sources in Medieval Ireland*, edited by Elizabeth Boyle and Deborah Hayden, 95–120. Dublin: Dublin Institute for Advanced Studies, 2014.

Clancy, Thomas Owen. "Spaghetti Junction: OI *rót, roüt*, ScG *ròd, rathad*, Scots *rod, rode*, English *road*, and some other minor by-ways." In *Fil súil nglais: A Festschrift in Honour of Colm Ó Baoill*, edited by Sharon Arbuthnot and Kaarina Hollo, 17–28. Tigh a' Mhaide, Brig o' Turk, Perthshire: Clann Tuirc, 2007.

Davies, Wendy. *Small Worlds: The Village Community in Early Medieval Brittany*. London: Duckworth, 1988.

Doolan, Riona. "Marginalia, Incorporated Commentaries or Reference Commentaries: The Terminology of Later Legal Sources." In *Fír Fesso: A Festschrift for Neil McLeod*, edited by Anders Ahlqvist and Pamela O'Neill, 87–96. Sydney Series in Celtic Studies 17. Sydney: The University of Sydney, 2018.

Eska, Charlene M. "Varieties of Early Irish Legal Literature and the *Cáin Lánamna* Fragments." *Viator* 40 (2009): 1–16.

Eska, Charlene M. "Women and Slavery in the Early Irish Laws." *Studia Celtica Fennica* 8 (2011): 29–39.

Eska, Charlene M. "Early Irish Trade: *Cnóe Gnáe* 'Beautiful Nuts' Revisited." *Cambrian Medieval Celtic Studies* 78 (2019): 101–109.

Eska, Charlene M. "The Transmission of Glosses: Script Size and Irish Legal Commentary." *North American Journal of Celtic Studies* 6 (2022): 78–101.

Eska, Joseph F. "Where Have All the Object Pronouns Gone? The Growth of Object Agreement in Earlier Celtic." *Zeitschrift für celtische Philologie* 57 (2009–2010): 25–47.

Finnane, Rowena. *Late Medieval Irish Law Manuscripts: A Reappraisal of Methodology and Context*. Sydney Series in Celtic Studies 13. Sydney: The University of Sydney, 2013.

Fomin, Maxim. *Instructions for Kings: Secular and Clerical Images of Kingship in Early Ireland and Ancient India*. Heidelberg: Carl Winter Universitätsverlag, 2013.

Frankot, Edda. "Medieval Maritime Law from Oléron to Wisby: Jurisdictions of the Law of the Sea." In *Communities in European History: Representations, Jurisdictions, Conflicts*, edited by Juan Pan-Montojo, and Frederik Pedersen, 151–172. Pisa: Pisa University Press, 2007.

Frankot, Edda. *'Of Laws of Ships and Shipman': Medieval Maritime Law and its Practice in Urban Northern Europe*. Edinburgh: Edinburgh University Press, 2012.

Griffith, Aaron. "Old Irish Pronouns: Agreement Affixes vs. Clitic Arguments." In *Formal Approaches to Celtic Linguistics*, ed. Andrew Carnie, 65–93. Cambridge: Cambridge Scholars Publishing, 2011.

Hudson, Benjamin. *Irish Sea Studies 900–1200*. Dublin: Four Courts Press, 2006.

Hull, Vernam. "Miscellanea Hibernica." *Zeitschrift für celtische Philologie* 30 (1967): 7–11.

Hunnisett, R.F. *The Medieval Coroner*. Cambridge: Cambridge University Press, 1961.

Jaski, Bart. *Early Irish Kingship and Succession*. Dublin: Four Courts Press, 2000.

Jenkins, Dafydd, ed. and trans., *The Law of Hywel Dda: Law Texts from Medieval Wales*. Llandysul, Dyfed: Gomer Press, 1986.

Jenkins, Dafydd. "Crime and Tort and the Three Columns of Law." In *Tair Colofn Cyfraith: The Three Columns of Law in Medieval Wales: Homicide, Theft and Fire*. The Welsh Legal History Society v, edited by T.M. Charles-Edwards and Paul Russell, 1–25. Bangor: The Welsh Legal History Society, 2007.

Johnson, Tom. "Medieval Law and Materiality: Shipwrecks, Finders, and Property on the Suffolk Coast, ca. 1380–1410." *American Historical Review* 120 (2015): 407–432.

Joseph, Brian D. "Comparative Perspectives on Bee Law in Indo-European." *Chatreššar* (2018/2): 16–25.

Kelly, Fergus. *A Guide to Early Irish Law*. Early Irish Law Series 3. Dublin: Dublin Institute for Advanced Studies, 1988 (2009 reprint with updated bibliography).

Kelly, Fergus. *Early Irish Farming*. Early Irish Law Series 4. Dublin: Dublin Institute for Advanced Studies, 2000.

Kelly, Fergus. "Drifting on the Ocean: Are Old Irish *Cnoe Gnáe* 'Beautiful Nuts' to be Identified as Sea Beans?." In *Bile ós Chrannaibh: A Festschrift for William Gillies*. Ed. Wilson McLeod et al., 211–218. Ceann Drochaid, Perthshire: Clann Tuirc, 2010.

Kelly, Fergus. "Whodunnit? Indirect Evidence in Early Irish Law." *Proceedings of the Harvard Celtic Colloquium* 35 (2015): 1–17

Kelly, Matthew, trans. *Cambrensis Eversus*. 3 vols. Dublin: The Celtic Society, 1848–1854.

Kim, Keechang. *Aliens in Medieval Law: The Origins of Modern Citizenship*. Cambridge: Cambridge University Press, 2000.

Kowaleski, Maryanne. *The Havener's Accounts of the Earldom and Duchy of Cornwall, 1287–1356*. Exeter: Devon and Cornwall Record Society, 2001.

Laing, Lionel H. "Origins of the Admiralty Jurisdiction in England." *Michigan Law Review* 45 (1946): 163–182.

Lambert, Pierre-Yves. "*Pretium benedictionis*." In *Early Medieval Ireland and Europe: chonology, Contacts, Scholarship A Festschrift for Dáibhí Ó Cróinín*, eds. Pádraic Moran and Immo Warntjes, 215–223. Turnhout: Brepols, 2015.

Latvio, Riita. "*Neimed*—Exploring Social Distinctions and Sacredness in Early Irish Legal Sources." In *Approaches to Religion and Mythology in Celtic Studies*, eds. Katja Ritari and Alexandra Bergholm, 220–242. Newcastle: Cambridge Scholars Publishing, 2008.

Loveluck, Christopher, and Aidan O'Sullivan. "Travel, Transport and Communication to and from Ireland, *c.* 400–1100: An Archaeological Perspective." In *The Irish in Early Medieval Europe: Identity, Culture and Religion*, edited by Roy Flechner and Sven Meeder, 19–37. London: Palgrave, 2016.

Lynch, John. *Cambrensis Eversus*. Saint Malo, 1662.

Mac Cana, Proinsias. "Ir. *Buaball*, W *Bual* 'Drinking Horn'." *Ériu* 44 (1993): 81–93.

Mac Niocaill, Gearóid. "Jetsam, Treasure Trove, and the Lord's Share in Medieval Ireland." *The Irish Jurist*, new series, 6 (1971): 103–110.

Mac Niocaill, Gearóid. "Irish Law and the Armagh Constitutions of 1297." *The Irish Jurist*, new series, 6 (1971): 339–344.

Mac Niocaill, Gearóid. "Aspects of Irish Law in the Late Thirteenth Century." In *Historical Studies 10: Papers Read before the Eleventh Irish Conference of Historians, 1973*, edited by G.A. Hayes-McCoy, 25–42. Indreabhán, Co. na Gaillimhe: Cló Chois Fharraige, 1976.

Mac Niocaill, Gearóid. "The Interaction of Laws." In *The English in Medieval Ireland: Proceedings of the First Joint Meeting of the Royal Irish Academy and the British Academy, Dublin, 1982*, edited by J. Lydon, 105–117. Dublin: Royal Irish Academy, 1984.

McCone, Kim R. *The Early Irish Verb*, 2nd ed. Maynooth: An Sagart, 1997.

McCone, Kim R. *A First Old Irish Grammar and Reader Including an Introduction to Middle Irish*. Maynooth: Department of Old and Middle Irish, National University of Ireland, Maynooth, 2005.

McCormick, Michael. *Origins of the European Economy: Communications and Commerce AD 300–900*. Cambridge: Cambridge University Press, 2001.

McLeod, Neil. *Early Irish Contract Law*. Sydney Series in Celtic Studies 1. Sydney: University of Sydney, 1992.

McLeod, Neil. "Property and Honour-Price in the Brehon Law Glosses and Commentaries." *The Irish Jurist*, new series 31 (1996): 280–295.

McLeod, Neil. "Assault and Attempted Murder in Brehon Law." *The Irish Jurist* new series 33 (1998): 351–391.

McLeod, Neil. *Bloodshed and Compensation in Ancient Ireland*. Perth: Centre for Irish Studies, Murdoch University, 1999.

McLeod, Neil. "Kinship." *Ériu* 51 (2000): 1–22.

McLeod, Neil. "Review Article: A True Companion to the *Corpus Iuris Hibernici*." *Peritia* 19 (2005): 136–163.

McLeod, Neil. "*Ón* and *airliciud*: Loans in Medieval Irish Law." In *Celts and their Cultures at Home and Abroad: A Festschrift for Malcolm Broun*. Sydney Series in Celtic Studies 15. Edited by. Anders Ahlqvist and Pamela O'Neill, 169–196. Sydney: University of Sydney, 2013.

Melikan, Rose. "Shippers, Salvors, and Sovereigns: Competing Interests in the Medieval Law of Shipwreck." *The Journal of Legal History* 163 (1990): 163–182.

Mitchell, W. *An Essay on the Early History of the Law Merchant*. Cambridge: Cambridge University Press, 1904.

Moore, Stuart A. *A History of the Foreshore and the Law Relating thereto. With a hitherto Unpublished Treatise by Lord Hale, Lord Hale's "De jure maris," and Hall's Essay on the Rights of the Crown in the Sea-shore*, 3rd ed. London: Stevens & Haynes, 1888.

Moore, Stuart Archibald, and Hubert Stuart Moore, *The History and Law of Fisheries*. London: Stevens and Haynes, 1908.

Morgan, Hiram. "'Lawes of Irelande': A Tract by Sir John Davies." *The Irish Jurist*, new series, 28/30 (1993/1995): 307–313.

Ó Cuív, Brian. *Catalogue of Irish Language Manuscripts in the Bodleian Library at Oxford and Oxford College Libraries*. Dublin: Dublin Institute for Advanced Studies, 2001.

Ó Corráin, Donnchadh. *Clavis Litterarum Hibernensium: Medieval Irish Books & Texts (c. 400–c. 1600)*, 3 vols. Turnhout: Brepols, 2017.

Ó Donnghaile, Andrew. "An Overview of Inter-Territorial Law in Early Medieval Ireland." *Peritia* 30 (2019): 197–214.

O'Grady, Standish Hayes. *Catalogue of Irish Manuscripts in the British Museum*, vol. 1. London: The British Museum, 1926.

Ó Muraíle, Nollaig. *The Celebrated Antiquary: Dubhaltach Mac Fhirbhisigh (c. 1600–1671), his Lineage, Life and Learning*. Maynooth Monograph 6. Maynooth: An Sagart, 1996.

O'Neill, Pamela. "Old Irish *Muirchrech* 'Sea Boundary'," *Ériu* 67 (2018): 1–10.

O'Neill, Timothy. *Merchants and Mariners in Medieval Ireland*. Dublin: Irish Academic Press, 1987.

Osborough, W.N. "The Irish Custom of Tracts." *The Irish Jurist*, new series, 32 (1997): 439–458. Reprinted in W.N. Osborough, *Studies in Irish Legal History*, 64–80. Dublin: Four Courts Press, 1999.

O'Sullivan, William. "The Book of Domhnall Ó Duibhdábhoireann, Provenance and Codicology." *Celtica* 23 (1999): 276–299.

O'Sullivan, William. "The Manuscript Collection of Dubhaltach Mac Fhirbhisigh." In *Seanchas: Studies in Early and Medieval Irish Archaeology, History and Literature in Honour of Francis J. Byrne*, edited by Alfred P. Smyth, 439–447. Dublin: Four Courts Press, 2000.

Pryce, Huw. *Native Law and the Church in Medieval Wales*. Oxford: Clarendon Press, 1993.

Pryce, Huw, and Gwilym Owen. "Medieval Welsh Law and the Mid-Victorian Foreshore." *The Journal of Legal History* 35 (2014): 172–199.

Rio, Alice. "'Half-Free' Categories in the Early Middle Ages: Fine Status Distinctions before Professional Lawyers." In *Legalism: Rules and Categories*, edited by Paul Dresch and Judith Scheele, 129–152. Oxford: Oxford University Press, 2015.

Robinson, O.F., T.D. Fergus, and W.M. Gordon. *European Legal History: Sources and Institutions*. 3rd ed. Oxford: Oxford University Press, 2000.

Rose, Susan. *The Medieval Sea*. London: Continuum, 2007.

Russell, Paul. "The Sounds of a Silence: The Growth of Cormac's Glossary." *Cambridge Medieval Celtic Studies* 15 (1988): 1–30.

Russell, Paul. "Laws, Glossaries and Legal Glossaries." *Zeitschrift für celtische Philologie* 51 (1998): 85–115.

Russell, Paul. "Patterns of Hypocorism in Early Irish Hagiography," in *Studies in Irish Hagiography: Saints and Scholars*, edited by J. Carey, M. Herbert, and P. Ó Riain, 237–249. Dublin: Four Courts Press, 2001.

Russell, Paul. "Arrangement and Development of the Three Columns Tractate." In *Tair Colofn Cyfraith: The Three Columns of Law in Medieval Wales: Homicide, Theft and Fire*, The Welsh Legal History Society v, edited by T.M. Charles-Edwards and Paul Russell, 60–91. Bangor: The Welsh Legal History Society, 2007.

Russell, Paul. "*Y Naw Affaith*: Aiding and Abetting in Welsh Law." In *Tair Colofn Cyfraith: The Three Columns of Law in Medieval Wales: Homicide, Theft and Fire*, The Welsh Legal History Society v, edited by T.M. Charles-Edwards and Paul Russell, 146–170. Bangor: The Welsh Legal History Society, 2007.

Russell, Paul. *'Read it in a glossary': Glossaries and Learned Discourse in Medieval Ireland*. Kathleen Hughes Memorial Lectures 6. Cambridge: Department of Anglo-Saxon, Norse, and Celtic, 2008.

Russell, Paul. "Bilingualisms and Multilingualisms in Medieval Wales: Evidence and Inference." *Transactions of the Honourable Society of Cymmrodorion* (2019): 7–22.

Schumacher, Stefan, [with contributions by] Britta Schulze-Thulin and Caroline aan de Wiel. *Die keltischen Primärverben: ein vergleichendes etymologisches und morphologisches Lexicon*. Innsbruck: Institut für Sprachen und Literaturen der Universität Innsbruck, 2004.

Scowcroft, R. Mark. "*Leabhar Gabhála*, Part I: The Growth of the Text." *Ériu* 38 (1987): 81–142.

Sharpe, Richard. "Dispute Settlement in Medieval Ireland: A Preliminary Inquiry." In *The Settlement of Disputes in Early Medieval Europe*, edited by Wendy Davies and Paul Fouracre, 169–189. Cambridge: Cambridge University Press, 1986.

Simms, Katharine. "The Brehons of Later Medieval Ireland." In *Brehons, Serjeants and Attorneys: Studies in the History of the Irish Legal Profession*, edited by Daire Hogan and W.N. Osborough, 51–76. Blackrock, Co. Dublin: Irish Academic Press, 1990.

Simms, Katharine. "The Contents of Later Commentaries on the Brehon Law Tracts." *Ériu* 49 (1998): 23–40.

Smith, Llinos Beverly. "The *Gravamina* of the Community of Gwynedd Against Llywelyn ap Gruffudd." *Bulletin of the Board of Celtic Studies* 31 (1984): 158–176.

Stacey, Robin Chapman. "Law and Order in the *Very* Old West: England and Ireland in the Early Middles Ages." In *Crossed Paths: Methodological Approaches to the Celtic Aspect of the European Middles Ages*, edited by Benjamin T. Hudson and Vickie.

Stacey, Robin Chapman. *The Road to Judgment: From Custom to Court in Medieval Ireland and Wales.* Philadelphia: University of Pennsylvania Press, 1994.

Stokes, Whitley. "On the Copenhagen Fragments of the Brehon Laws." *Zeitschrift für celtische Philologie* 4 (1903): 221–233.

Taylor-Griffiths, Alice Rebecca. *Studies in Medieval Irish Legal Ancillary Material.* Unpublished Ph.D. dissertation: Department of Anglo-Saxon, Norse and Celtic, University of Cambridge, 2020.

Thurneysen, Rudolf. "Irisches und Gallisches. 4. Der Nominativ zu air. *Roida.*" *Zeitschrift für celtische Philologie* 14 (1923): 5.

Thurneysen, Rudolf. "Aus dem irischen Recht I [1. Das Unfrei-Lehen]." *Zeitschrift für celtische Philologie* 14 (1923): 335–394.

Thurneysen, Rudolf. "Aus dem irischen Recht II [2. Das Frei-Lehen; 3. Das Fasten beim Pfändungsverfahren]." *Zeitschrift für celtische Philologie* 15 (1925): 238–276.

Thurneysen, Rudolf. "Aus dem irischen Recht III [4. Die falschen Urteilssprüche Caratnia's; 5. Zur Überlieferung und zur Ausgabe der Texte über das Unfrei-Lehen und das Frei-Lehen]." *Zeitschrift für celtische Philologie* 15 (1925): 302–376.

Thurneysen, Rudolf. *Cóic Conara Fugill: Die fünf Wege zum Urteil.* Abhandlungen der preussischen Akademie der Wissenschaften. Preussische Akademie der Wissenschaften zu Berlin. Jahrgang 1925. Phil.-hist. Klasse; Nr. 7. Berlin, 1926.

Thurneysen, Rudolf. "Aus dem irischen Recht IV [6. Zu den bisherigen Ausgaben der irischen Rechtstexte]." *Zeitschrift für celtische Philologie* 16 (1927): 167–230.

Thurneysen, Rudolf. "Nachträgliches." *Zeitschrift für celtische Philologie* 16 (1927): 406–410.

Thurneysen, Rudolf. "Aus dem irischen Recht V [7. Zu Gúbretha Caradniad; 8. Zum ursprünglichen Umfang des Senchas Már; 9. Zu der Etymologie von irisch *ráth* 'Bürgschaft' und zu der irischen Kanonensammlung und den Triaden; 10. Nachträge zur Bürgschaft." *Zeitschrift für celtische Philologie* 18 (1930): 353–408.

Thurneysen, Rudolf. *Irische Recht: I. Díre. Ein altirischer Rechtstext, II. Zu den unteren Ständen in Irland.* Abhandlungen der preussischen Akademie der Wissenschaften. Preussische Akademie der Wissenschaften zu Berlin. Jahrgang 1931. Phil.-hist. Klasse; Nr. 2. Berlin, 1931.

Thurneysen, Rudolf. "Eine neue Handschrift von *Cōic Conara Fugill.*" *Zeitschrift für celtische Philologie* 19 (1933): 165–173.

Thurneysen, Rudolf. "Das keltische Recht." *Zeitschrift der Savigny-Stiftung für Rechtsgeschichte. Germanisch Abteilung* 55 (1934): 81–104. [Translated into English in "Celtic Law."] In *Celtic Law Papers: Introductory to Welsh Medieval Law and Government.* Edited by Dafydd Jenkins, 51–70. Studies Presented to the International Commission for the History of Representation and Parliamentary Institutions 42. Bruxelles: Les Editions de la Librairie Encyclopédique, 1973.

Thurneysen, Rudolf. *A Grammar of Old Irish*, eds. and trans. D.A. Binchy and Osborn Bergin. Dublin: Dublin Institute for Advanced Studies, revised edition, 1946.

Valante, Mary A. "Taxation, Tolls and Tribute: The Language of Economics and Trade in Viking-Age Ireland." *Proceedings of the Harvard Celtic Colloquium* 18 (1998): 242–258.

Ward, Robin. *The World of the Medieval Shipmaster: Law, Business and the Sea, c. 1350–1450*. Woodbridge, Suffolk: The Boydell Press, 2009.

Watkin, Thomas Glyn. *The Legal History of Wales*. 2nd ed. Cardiff: University of Wales Press, 2012.

Whitelock, Dorothy, trans. *English Historical Documents: Vol. 1, c. 500–1042*, 2nd ed. London: Eyre & Spottiswoode, 1979.

Wooding, Jonathan. *Communication and Commerce along the Western Sealanes AD 400–800*. Oxford: Tempus Reparatum, 1996.

Wycherley, Niamh. *The Cult of Relics in Early Medieval Ireland*. Turnhout: Brepols, 2015.

Index